GLENN'S NEW COMPLETE
BICYCLE MANUAL

GLENN'S *NEW* COMPLETE BICYCLE MANUAL

SELECTION · MAINTENANCE · REPAIR

by CLARENCE W. COLES and HAROLD T. GLENN
Enlarged and Updated by JOHN S. ALLEN

CROWN PUBLISHERS, INC.
NEW YORK

*Published by Crown Publishers, Inc.,
201 East 50th Street, New York, New York 10022. Member of the Crown Publishing Group.*

Random House, Inc. New York, Toronto, London, Sydney, Auckland

CROWN is a trademark of Crown Publishers, Inc.

Manufactured in the United States of America

*Library of Congress Cataloging in Publication Data
Coles, Clarence W.
Glenn's <u>new</u> complete bicycle manual.
Previously published as: Glenn's complete bicycle manual. 1973.
Includes index.
1. Bicycles—Maintenance and repair. I. Glenn,
Harold, T. II. Allen, John Stewart, 1946-
III. Coles, Clarence W. Glenn's complete bicycle
manual. IV. Title. V. Title: New complete bicycle manual.
TL430.C65 1987   629.28'772   86-16658
ISBN 0-517-54313-3 (pbk.)
10 9 8 7 6*

CONTENTS

ACKNOWLEDGMENTS   viii
PREFACE   ix
INTRODUCTION   xi

PART ONE · GETTING STARTED

---

1 · SELECTING A BICYCLE AND ACCESSORIES   1

Types of Bicycles   1
How to Shop for a Bike   7
Judging Quality   8
Accessories   10
Installing Accessories   15

2 · FITTING THE BICYCLE TO YOU   17

Basic Measurements   17
Adjustments   20
Experimentation   25

3 · RIDER PERFORMANCE   26

Getting Started   26
Traffic Sense   28

Avoiding Hazards—Steering, Braking, Jumping   37
Riding with Other Bicyclists   41
A Review   43
Bicycling Horizons   43
Bicycle Magazines   48
Books   48

4 · TOOLS AND SUPPLIES   50

Basic On-the-road Tool Kit   50
On-the-road Repair Materials   52
Equipping the Workshop   53
Cleaning Parts   57
Setting Up the Home Workshop   59
Organizing and Planning Your Work   59

PART TWO · BASIC REPAIRS

---

5 · MAINTENANCE BASICS   61

Avoiding Creeping Decay   61
Periodic Maintenance   62
Some Basic Mechanical Theory   62
Lubricants and Lubrication   66

6 · BASIC REPAIR PROCEDURES   69

Removing Wheels   69
Installing Wheels   72
Tire Maintenance   78
Cable and Lever Maintenance   88

PART THREE · THE DERAILLEUR DRIVETRAIN

7 · THE MULTI-SPROCKET DRIVETRAIN   98

Drivetrain Problems   98
Inspecting the Drivetrain   101
Chain Maintenance and Repair   105

8 · SERVICING SIMPLE FRONT AND REAR HUBS   108

Types of Hubs   108
Service Note   110
Overhauling a Nutted Front Cup-and-cone Hub   113
Overhauling a Quick-release Front Hub   120
Overhauling a Freewheel or Fixed Rear-wheel Hub   124
Sealed-cartridge-bearing Hubs   126
Overhauling a Cartridge-bearing Hub with Sleeve Nuts   127
Overhauling a Cartridge-bearing Hub without Sleeve Nuts   130

9 · GEARING IMPROVEMENTS   135

Planning the Derailleur Gearing System   136
Recommended Gearing Progressions   139

10 · SERVICING FREEWHEELS   142

Service Procedures   142
Sprocket Removal and Installation   142
Servicing Sprockets on a Lugged Freewheel   143
Servicing Sprockets on a Fully Threaded Freewheel   148
Freewheel Removal and Installation   151
Shimano Freehub Body Removal and Installation   154
Overhauling a Freewheel Body   155

11 · SERVICING REAR DERAILLEURS   161

Service Procedures   161
Removing, Installing, and Adjusting the Derailleur   164
Servicing Shimano Rear Derailleurs   168
Servicing SunTour Rear Derailleurs   176
Servicing Campagnolo or Simplex Rear Derailleurs   182
Servicing Sachs-Huret Rear Derailleurs   190

12 · SERVICING FRONT DERAILLEURS   194

Service Procedures   194
Overhauling a Parallelogram-type Front Derailleur   195

PART FOUR · THE NON-DERAILLEUR DRIVETRAIN

13 · THE SINGLE-SPROCKET DRIVETRAIN   205

Problems with Single-sprocket Drivetrains   205
Lugged Sprockets   206
Threaded Sprockets   207
Gear Ratios   207
Single-sprocket Chain   208

14 · GEARED AND COASTER-BRAKE HUBS   209

Service Notes   210
Servicing Coaster Brakes   214
Overhauling a Shoe-type Single-speed Coaster Hub   217
Overhauling a Disk-type Single-speed Coaster Hub   229
Overhauling a Sturmey-Archer AW or Similar Three-speed Hub   240
Overhauling a Shimano Three-speed Hub   256
Overhauling a Sturmey-Archer Four- or Five-speed Hub   275
Overhauling a Sturmey-Archer Three-speed Coaster Hub   286
Overhauling a Shimano Three-speed Coaster Hub   302

PART FIVE · CRANK, BRAKE, WHEEL, AND FRAME WORK

15 · CRANK HANGERS AND PEDALS   313

Hanger Sets   313
Pedals   314
Parts Interchangeability   315
Overhauling a Cottered Crankset   316
Overhauling a Cotterless Crankset   318
Overhauling a One-piece Crank   325
Overhauling Rubber-block Pedals   330
Overhauling Metal Pedals   331
Sealed-bearing Bottom-bracket Units   335
Cartridge-bearing Pedals   337

16 · BRAKES   338

Types of Brakes   338
The Braking System   340
Servicing Rim Brakes   342

Overhauling Sidepull Caliper Brakes   343
Overhauling Centerpull and Cantilever Brakes   351
Overhauling a Hub with Expander-type Brake
   or Disk Brake   360

17 · WHEELBUILDING AND WHEEL REPAIR   366

How Spoked Wheels Work   366
Building a Wheel   367
Wheel Repair   382

18 · FRAME AND STEERING   390

Checking for Damage   390
The Bicycle Steering Mechanism   390
Frame Repair   394
Parts Compatibility   396
Overhauling a Headset   397

ACKNOWLEDGMENTS

My work in revising *Glenn's* would not have been possible without the assistance of many people.

I especially thank my father, Gordon W. Allen, for encouraging my early interest in working with tools; Fred DeLong, John Forester, and the authors of the first edition of *Glenn's*, Harold T. Glenn and Clarence Coles, for reference works which steered my interest; Rodale Press for many opportunities to practice my craft as a writer; John Schubert, editor of *Bicycle Guide* magazine, for his consideration in releasing me from editorial responsibilities; Sheldon Brown, who has taught me innumerable mechanical and photographic techniques; the Broadway Bicycle School of Cambridge, Massachusetts, for many opportunities to try out repair techniques; Yarmouth Bicycle Shop, Cove Cycle and Enterprise Bicycle Shop of Cape Cod, the Bicycle Exchange of Cambridge, Massachusetts, John Temple of Sturmey Archer, John Uhte of Shimano Sales Corporation, and Sandy Chapman of SunTour USA for loan of equipment; and Howard Sutherland for the valuable knowledge gained while working with him.

Also, Phil Wood & Co. for information about its products; Cannondale, Univega USA, Hon Bicycle Corporation, Alex Moulton, Terry Bicycles, New England Cycling Academy, and New England Handcycles for supplying photographs; Elisse Ghitelman, Louise Kipping, Osman Isvan, Mike Koch, Jacek Rudowski, the Charles River Wheelmen, and the Cambridge Visiting Nurse's Association for helping with photographs; the Hy-Land Youth Hostel in Hyannis, Massachusetts, for the use of studio space; and Bob Howell for cheerfully developing over thirty rolls of film and hundreds of prints.

JOHN S. ALLEN

ACKNOWLEDGMENTS
FOR THE FIRST EDITION

The authors wish to express their grateful appreciation and indebtedness to the Schwinn Bicycle Company, and to Mr. Ray Burch, Vice-President, Marketing, and Mr. Peter Kaszonyi, Service Promotion Manager, Schwinn Bicycle Company, for their assistance and permission to use certain illustrations. The use of these illustrations in no way relieves the copyright privileges held by the Schwinn Company.

A very special thanks is extended to Mr. Mel Pavlisin of Circle Cycle in Torrance, California, for the use of his shop facilities to photograph the disassembly and assembly sequences used throughout the book. Without the assistance of Mr. Pat Hirz, bicycle mechanic at Circle Cycle, the detailed and special instructions included in the text would not have been possible.

A sincere expression of gratitude is due Anna Glenn, for her patience and understanding and for her assistance in proofreading the manuscript.

To Mark Tsunawaki for his contribution with the artwork and to Brian Coles for his help during the paste-up, we are indeed grateful.

We would also like to express our appreciation to the League of American Wheelmen for their inspiration during the writing of this book.

CLARENCE W. COLES and HAROLD T. GLENN

PREFACE

The new edition of *Glenn's* attempts to build upon the strengths of the old. To the detailed, step-by-step repair procedures, unique in any book for public consumption, I have added a new section on setting up the home workshop. The new edition covers many components introduced since the first edition was published, particularly sealed-bearing components. Diagnostic aids such as problem charts have been greatly expanded. Where unavailable parts may require substitutions, I attempt to give practical solutions for the home mechanic. The section on wheelbuilding and wheel repair is much more detailed. There is an entirely new section on frame repair.

I hope that the new edition serves its readers well. Any suggestions for improvements are welcome and may be forwarded to the publisher.

JOHN S. ALLEN

PREFACE
TO THE FIRST EDITION

This is a comprehensive repair and adjustment manual for virtually all makes of bicycles. The first section provides invaluable information in the following areas: (1) making a sensible selection of a bicycle and accessories; (2) adjusting the bicycle to your physique so that you will maintain optimum efficiency and comfort; (3) riding efficiently and safely; (4) equipping your workshop; (5) performing the necessary periodic maintenance; and (6) basic repairs which every bicyclist needs to know.

The remaining chapters are devoted to work on the principal parts of the bicycle. Detailed illustrated step-by-step instructions are provided to tell you exactly how to make complete repairs and adjustments using a minimum number of tools.

Procedures were written by actually performing the job and photographing each step as the work progressed. This method of developing and presenting the material gives the reader a sensitive "feeling" for what is to be done, how, and why. We suggest that you read through the complete section before starting any task to become familiar with the particular parts, or with the special techniques employed in making repairs, such as counting the number of loose ball bearings, placement of shims and spacers, the use of right- or left-hand threads, and how some parts are removed, overhauled, installed, and adjusted.

Procedural illustrations accompanying the text are identified by a circled number in the lower right-hand corner. These numbers are keyed and are correlated so closely with the steps, which are also sequenced with circled numbers, that legends are not required. Exploded views for many makes of each assembly are included together with specific directions advising you which parts are interchangeable with similar manufactured items.

Each section in each chapter is a complete unit, except for steps which are the same for many procedures, such as removing and replacing the wheel. These are referenced for easy access.

The illustrations supporting the text have been specially treated to drop out the backgrounds.

CLARENCE W. COLES and HAROLD T. GLENN

INTRODUCTION

The first edition of *Glenn's* was published in 1973, at the height of a "bicycle boom." Many factors led to an explosion in bicycle sales that year: interest in physical fitness, increasing availability of the mass-produced multispeed bicycle, awareness of environmental issues, and above all a fuel shortage. In 1973 and 1974, the public was grabbing up the first great wave of ten-speed bicycles from the bike shops as fast as they could be produced.

Now, in 1986, bicycling's popularity continues to increase. Many of the people who bought bicycles back in 1973 had only vague, idealistic notions about how they might use them—but they learned with time. The early wave of enthusiasm, the idea that America would abandon its cars and take to the bicycle, died out within a year or two—but higher-performance bicycles brought higher expectations and achievements nonetheless. Bicycle sales have slowly climbed back up to the 1973 level. Trips for exercise, sightseeing, and commuting have become much more common. Long-distance bicycle touring has increased manyfold. Bicycle clubs that had 50 members in 1973 now have 500.

In 1984, Americans carried away the largest share of bicycling medals at the Olympics. Bicycle racing now attracts frequent television coverage, while only a few short years ago it played to a few spectators lining the racecourse. Entirely new sports such as bicycle motocross, all-terrain bicycling, and triathlons have developed in America.

Through these years of bicycling's growth, *Glenn's* has been a standard reference on bicycle maintenance and repair. It has sold over 300,000 copies. Most purchasers of the book have been home mechanics—people who wanted to learn to maintain their own bikes. This is a healthy situation, both for bicyclists and for the bicycle industry.

WHY MAINTAIN YOUR OWN BICYCLE?

Why should an average bicycle user learn to do maintenance work which could be left to professional mechanics?

Or, asking the question another way, why do many bicycle shops conduct repair classes which might seem to take work away from their mechanics?

The answer? If you ride a bicycle, you are in the best position to maintain that bicycle.

Since you have to propel it with your own strength, a bicycle is built light. A bicycle's peak performance depends on frequent fine-tuning, not just an occasional overhaul such as a washing machine or power lawnmower needs. Bicycle maintenance is not very difficult or time-consuming, but your involvement is part of the prescription for keeping your bicycle running well.

The moving parts of the bicycle are mostly on the outside, where you can see and hear them. You feel them through your hands, your feet, and your rear end. You, the rider, get to know your bicycle better than anyone else; you are with it every moment that it is running.

In the peak riding season, you may have to leave your bicycle at a bike shop for a week to wait its turn for a repair which takes a few minutes with simple tools. You'd probably rather be riding your bike.

Working on your bicycle makes it more useful, and has additional rewards as well.

There is probably no better focus for learning basic mechanical skills than a bicycle. To work on bikes, you need only a small collection of moderately priced tools. A bike is small; you don't need a big workspace. Without an engine, it is relatively clean; the dirt of bike work can be easily managed. Bicycle maintenance rarely requires brute strength; more often, it requires skilled hands and a fine touch.

When you're out on the road on your bike, your mechanical skills can keep you rolling. Getting to your destination is rewarding enough, but the sense of accomplishment is an even greater reward.

The common repairs, like fixing a flat tire, are simple; yet there is no limit to the skill you can apply to mechanical work on bicycles. With time and patience, you build from one accomplishment to another. Given a bit of patience, almost anyone can learn to maintain his or her own bike; for those who wish to go farther, designing and building bicycles can be a lifework for a talented artisan.

And you don't have to worry about putting the bike shop out of business. People who maintain their bikes *use* their bikes, and are valued customers.

However far you wish to go, the road begins here.

Getting Started

1 · SELECTING A BICYCLE AND ACCESSORIES

There's good news for bicycle purchasers: A constantly growing market and vigorous competition have kept prices low. Dollar prices for good-quality bicycles have hardly risen since the first edition of this book was published in 1973, even though the dollar was worth twice as much back then.

Also, the variety of bicycles and accessory equipment available has increased enormously. Here's a list of products which were unknown, or high-priced rarities only a few years ago: all-terrain bicycles, sturdy BMX bikes for children, helmets, high-performance nylon-cord tires, lightweight aluminum cranksets, wide-range hill-climbing sprockets, rechargeable-battery lights, reflectorized clothing, Gore-Tex rainwear, and specialized bicycle clothing and shoes. Today you can buy these products at any bicycle shop. This trend can be expected to continue.

This chapter will get you started with the information you need to buy the right bicycle and the accessories necessary to use it well.

TYPES OF BICYCLES

Six principal types of bicycles are sold for adult use:

• The one-speed "tank" or cruiser bicycle, heavy, with wide tires, flat handlebars, and usually a coaster brake. (For safety in traffic, it should have a front handbrake as well.) Cost: $60–$200.

• The utility bicycle, such as the English three-speed, with moderately wide tires, handbrakes, and fenders for wet-weather riding. Some utility bikes, with wider tires, are upgraded "cruiser" bicycles with five or six speeds. Cost: $80–$300.

• The lightweight multispeed bicycle, with dropped (ram's-horn-shaped) handlebars and narrow tires. This category subdivides into "sport" bicycles, with a short wheelbase for quick maneuvering, and "touring" bicycles, with a longer wheelbase and lower gears for comfort. Cost: $100–$1500.

• The multispeed all-terrain bicycle or "mountain bike," which combines the durability and surefootedness of the "tank" bicycle with sporty performance and the ability to climb steep grades easily. Cost: $250–$1500.

• The small-wheeled folding bicycle, which falls somewhat short in performance, but is the best if you wish to travel with your bicycle or if storage space is limited— for example, in a city apartment. Cost: $150–$400.

• Specialty machines. This category includes tandems, track-racing bicycles, recumbents, arm-powered vehicles, and more—machines with special features or for special uses.

One- and Three-speed Bicycles

It is easy to think the more gears, the better. In the last thirty years, popular bikes have gone from one gear to three, then to ten, now to twelve, fifteen, and eighteen. But more gears do not necessarily make a bicycle right for you.

One- and three-speed bicycles offer mechanical simplicity, durability, and low cost. They are adequate for short trips in moderate terrain, and less prone to theft if you need to lock your bike outdoors where you shop, work, or go to school.

The typical one-speed bike is designed to withstand the heavy punishment that a youngster or anyone using it for constant delivery or patrol work may give it. The frame is constructed of heavy-gauge steel, the tires are heavy-duty balloon type, and the braking system is contained within the rear hub or possibly in the front hub, as with the internal-expanding brake-shoe type. For the most part, these bicycles require no external levers or cables. The standard version resembles the conventional bicycles commonly seen until the early 1950s.

Three-Speed Bikes

If you plan to travel short distances or use your bike only occasionally, a three-speed bicycle with internally geared rear hub and caliper brakes, costing less than $100, may be the answer. People living in the Midwest, or any other relatively flat area, will find that the three-speed bicycle meets their requirements. It can move along at a reasonable speed, with sufficient shift range for climbing moderate grades. Those who commute short distances may not need the more complicated equipment of the derailleur-equipped bike. Three-speed hubs are available with a built-in coaster brake or drum brake, useful in wet weather when rim brakes don't work as well.

A five-speed internally geared hub is available. It has a wider gear range and closer spacing. For in-town utility riding and commuting, this offers all of the advantages of derailleur gearing without the disadvantages.

Internally geared hubs are rugged and weather-resistant. They shift instantly, even when the bike is stopped. For this reason, they are the ultimate for stop-and-go city riding. Also, the internal gear mechanism requires much less frequent maintenance than a derailleur gearing system.

Multispeed Bicycles

Multispeed bicycles allow you the full enjoyment of bicycling as a sport and recreation. With their larger number of gears and wider range, they can climb steep

hills easily. After a couple of months' practice, almost anyone can easily travel 50 to 100 miles per day on a road bike with dropped handlebars. An off-road bike, with its wide tires, is about 10 percent slower on good roads, but is surefooted on dirt roads, trails, and potholed streets, and more resistant to abuse—a plus for beginners.

A ten- or twelve-speed bike is suitable for most uses. Bicycle racers rarely use more than a twelve-speed bike.

A fifteen- or eighteen-speed bike gives you the widest possible gear range. It has real advantages for touring in hilly country and for off-road riding.

Narrow-tired road bicycles are sold in a wide range of prices. Generally, expect to spend $200 or more for a bicycle of good quality. At this price level, the bicycle will be equipped with aluminum rims and crankarms, the most effective way to save weight. A higher price will bring added refinements: more precise construction of components and a frame of somewhat lighter, stronger material. High-grade frames use light, thin-

A typical multispeed derailleur-geared bicycle with dropped handlebars offers high performance for longer trips.

A typical heavy-duty bicycle with a three-speed internally geared hub is suitable for short trips. It is equipped with fenders for use in wet weather. By turning its handlebars upside down and lowering the gear range, its performance can be improved considerably.

A racing bicycle has a short wheelbase—note how close the rear wheel is to the seat tube—and no low gears.

walled alloy steel tubing brazed into lugs, or welded. Butted tubing means the ends of the tube inside the lugs have a double thickness for added strength. As the price of the bike increases, the number of butted tubes in the frame increases; top-quality machines have butted tubes throughout. A decal affixed to the frame will proudly show that the tubing is Reynolds 531, Columbus, Ishiwata, Tange, or another high-grade brand. Increasing numbers of high-grade frames are made of even lighter aluminum, graphite fiber, or titanium.

In the higher-quality ranges, road bicycles divide into two major categories, as mentioned above.

Sport bicycles are designed for high performance: quick maneuvering and acceleration, but at some expense in comfort, utility, and durability—like a sports car. The seat tube and head tube of the frame are more nearly upright to shorten the wheelbase. Usually, a sport bicycle has a narrow gear range, appropriate for racing and for riding without baggage. The tires are especially narrow, for low rolling resistance. There may be no mounting points for fenders or a baggage rack. Some sport bicycles make compromises to be more useful for all-around riding; at the other end of the scale are the out-and-out racing bicycles.

Touring bicycles are designed for long-distance travel with or without baggage. The seat tube and head tube are less upright than those of a sport bike, for a smoother, more comfortable ride. The wide gear range makes it easier to climb long grades, even while carrying full camping gear. Fifteen- and eighteen-gear systems are common on touring bicycles. Tires are of moderate width, and the wheels are sturdy enough to carry the rider plus baggage.

The wide tires of the *all-terrain bicycle* are not the only way it is different from a road bike. The top tube of the frame is lower, for easier mounting and dismount-

The all-terrain bicycle is light in weight and has ultra-wide-range gears. The wide handlebars and fat tires are ideal for rough ground.

ing. The crank spindle is higher, for more ground clearance. The long wheelbase and wide handlebars give sure, steady handling. The gearing is lower; the best all-terrain bicycles, like the best touring bicycles, have fifteen or eighteen gears. The inner chainwheel is extra-small for ease in climbing steep slopes.

A *folding bicycle* is practical transportation for the person on the go. Smaller folding bicycles can be packed as baggage and carried onto public transportation, making it possible to use the bicycle to make connections at both ends of a commuting trip. A folding bicycle is ideal for use along with a car, boat, or airplane. As an example, when you leave a car off to be repaired, you can ride the folding bike home.

Folding-bike designs and prices vary widely. Two examples are illustrated here. The Hon is compact enough to fit under an airplane seat. The Moulton is less compact, but its performance rivals that of any all-around touring bicycle.

The touring bicycle has a long wheelbase, an ultralow gear, shallower head-tube and seat-tube angles, and racks and fenders. This and the preceding photograph are of bicycles with large-diameter, lightweight aluminum frame tubes.

With its spring suspension, triangulated frame, derailleur gears, and bolt-on baggage racks, the Moulton offers unusual comfort and touring-bike performance, yet it comes apart for easy storage.

When folded, this Hon Convertible bicycle will fit under an airplane seat. The folding bicycle sacrifices some riding performance, but is by far the most practical to use in combination with a car or public transportation.

Many bicyclists own more than one bicycle—typically, a multispeed bicycle for pleasure rides and a rugged, simple bicycle for short utility trips.

Specialty Bicycles

A good *tandem* is a fine experience for two people who like to ride together. On a tandem, two people of differing skill or strength can ride without becoming separated—a couple, or a parent and child. If you don't have a regular partner for a tandem, owning one is a great way to meet people. Tandems are somewhat faster on level ground than solo bicycles, because the rear rider contributes little wind resistance.

It is important to shop carefully for a tandem. It's a big investment—$1,000 or more for a good one. Before buying a tandem, try one out to be sure that both riders will enjoy it. High quality is especially important in a tandem, because all moving parts must bear twice the load. A wide-range gearing system is necessary, because tandems go downhill fast and uphill slowly. Rider fit is also very important. Modern tandems tend to have a stiffer frame and more room for the rear rider, so they are the best choice unless the rear rider is small and light.

The *track racing bicycle* is designed for only one purpose, racing on a surface specially constructed for bike races. These machines are the ultimate in light weight.

Track bikes have a direct-drive system from the chainwheel to the fixed rear sprocket, thereby eliminating the front and rear derailleurs, and their friction. This means that as long as the rear wheel is turning, the crank is also rotating; thus the rider's legs are always in motion. The track bike does not have any braking system; the rider slows it by pushing back against the turning pedals.

Often, people get very excited about *recumbent bicycles,* because some of them have set speed records of up to 65 miles per hour. In order to do this, they must be equipped with a streamlined windshell which is very sensitive to sidewinds. A shell is impractical for everyday use, except on a three-wheeled vehicle. In fact, streamlined adult tricycles have been built, but they are not yet widely available. The most practical tricycle designs are not as fast as the record-setting machines, but they are much smaller and more maneuverable.

Recumbent bicycles without a windshell are widely available now. They are longer and so less maneuverable than a conventional bicycle; they are a little faster on level ground, but slower on hills. A recumbent's most important selling point is comfort rather than speed. It does not put strain on the back and arms.

The tandem bicycle is an unusually good way for two people to ride together, or for introducing beginners to bicycling. A good tandem has heavy-duty components throughout, and ultra-wide-range gears.

The main advantage of the recumbent bicycle is comfort; its performance is about equal to that of a conventional bicycle.

This hand-powered tricycle offers outdoor exercise and travel at bicycle speeds to a person who cannot use the legs for pedaling.

Many people prefer a recumbent for these reasons. For other people, a recumbent is the only choice; a person who has a bad back or has lost the use of one arm has no problems at all in riding a recumbent.

Some manufacturers also maintain that a recumbent is safer. Surely, a fall is less likely to be serious; but a safety flag, as shown in the illustration, is important for visibility over a hillcrest or behind a car.

Even greater degrees of specialization are possible—for example, the hand-powered tricycle illustrated. This allows mobility at bicycle speeds for a person who cannot use the legs for pedaling.

Children's Bicycles

Children's bicycles have special requirements. Small children who ride tricycles are safer on the laid-back "Big Wheel" design; the traditional upright tricycle is topheavy and unsteady.

As the name implies, sidewalk bikes, many of which are classified as toys, are intended for use only on the sidewalk and are built for tiny tots aged three to five. The least expensive models are rather dangerous because they do not have brakes.

The more expensive sidewalk bike contains some solid material and better workmanship. A coaster-type brake is standard equipment, giving the child some control of stopping by applying pressure in a reverse direction.

Trainer wheels, which attach to the axle on both sides of the rear wheel, are available. However, considerable controversy exists as to whether they should be used or not. Many argue that the child will develop his balance and coordination more quickly if he is assisted by a parent or older brother when first learning to ride. A child can learn to balance without assistance on a scooter, or on a bicycle that has had its pedals

The true BMX (bicycle motocross) bicycle is rugged, to withstand a child's abuse and off-road riding. With its low saddle position and single gear, it is made to maneuver easily with the rider in a standing position. It is not suitable for travel beyond a mile or so.

The "high-riser" child's bicycle looks sporty, like a motorcycle, but high handlebars and rearward rider position decrease its stability.

removed and seat lowered so that both feet can touch the ground.

For a child eight to twelve years old, the rugged BMX (bicycle motocross) bike is appropriate and is widely available. Usually it is a single-speed bike with a coaster brake and perhaps a handbrake. It is well designed for short distances and off-road riding. The BMX bike has straight frame tubes and a small saddle. Curved frame tubes, high handlebars, and a long "banana" saddle are characteristic of the earlier "high-riser" design, less durable, less sporty, and less safe to ride.

The BMX bike is very popular with children, but it is designed for rough use, not for traveling any great

A typical sidewalk bicycle for a small child has 16-inch wheels and a coaster brake.

distance. This is due not only to its single speed but also to the saddle position—ideal for jumping over obstacles on a dirt track, but too low for efficient pedaling while seated.

For older children, small three-speed and multispeed bikes are better for longer distances and to keep up with adults on family trips. The type of bicycle for a particular child depends on the type of riding to be done. One important rule, however: Never buy a bicycle which is too big for a child; an oversize bicycle is difficult to control.

HOW TO SHOP FOR A BIKE

If you are buying a new bike, go to a full-service bike shop. A department store or discount outlet is a fine place to buy a stereo set or vacuum cleaner, but not a bicycle. The usual department-store marketing approach is to offer the lowest-priced, lowest-quality bicycles, built to sell, not to ride. Such bikes are sold in the carton for the customer to assemble. Until you are familiar with most of this book, you cannot count on being able to assemble a bicycle correctly.

Warranty service is a serious problem at department stores. Unlike most other consumer products, bicycles are serviced where they are sold, not by regional warranty centers. Repairs at a department store may be overpriced, because the absence of a trained mechanic makes it necessary to replace an entire module—such as a wheel—rather than to make small repairs and adjustments. Much time may be lost waiting for a replacement part from a distant distributor or the factory. In the meantime your bike sits idly in the garage, your feet itch, and your heart demands that you get the pedals in motion.

Bike Shop Service

A good bike shop, on the other hand, has trained mechanics and a complete stock of spare parts. A good bike shop will not sell inferior bicycles; they're too much trouble to service, and can damage a shop's

The full-service bike shop backs up its products with a well-equipped workshop, a full stock of spare parts, and trained mechanics. This is the place to buy a bicycle.

reputation. The people who work in a good bike shop will help advise you on your purchase, set the bike up for you, and inspect it. Prices at bike shops are higher, but the price difference is more than justified.

Some bike shops offer better service than others. Talk with other bicyclists and visit three or four shops before you make your final decision. Typically, the differences among shops are more important than the differences among the brands of bicycles they sell. Bike shops, like car dealerships, are highly competitive. Bicycles and accessories can be heavily discounted, especially in the off-season; comparison shopping may turn up some unusually good deals.

Custom-made Bicycles

It is possible to have a bicycle made to order like a suit of clothes. Needless to say, the price is high—typically $600 and up—but it is often justified, whether for a racer or a tourist. Ready-made bikes are proportioned for average customers, and there are many people who need a custom bike simply for comfort.

Custom bikes are built by *framebuilding shops.* Try to find one close enough to visit. You are more likely to get the exact bike you need if the framebuilder can measure you and talk about your needs with you.

Used Bikes and Used Parts

If you are looking for a bargain in a bike, the best approach is to buy a used bike. A bike shop is a good place to buy one. A rebuilt and guaranteed used bike will probably be as trouble-free as a new bike: Bike shop overhauls are often better than factory assembly.

If, on the other hand, you buy a used bike from a private party, you usually cannot count on its being well maintained or in good adjustment. Add the cost of an overhaul to the purchase price. Sometimes you can assemble a complete bicycle from parts of two or more damaged or incomplete bicycles. Used bicycles can be found at yard sales and through classified ads, and many are real bargains even counting the overhaul. Others are not worth fixing up, so have an experienced bicyclist pass judgment before you put down your money.

Scavenging parts is a valuable way to put together useful types of bikes which you would have trouble finding in a store. For example, you could install a fixed-gear track hub on a road bike. This combination gives great sensitivity to the road surface, and so is excellent for winter riding.

Another useful combination is a three- or five-speed internal hub on a lightweight bike for fast riding in the city. Internally geared hubs are usually sold on bikes with heavy steel wheels, but there is no reason that you

can't mix and match to suit yourself. In this way you can assemble a custom bike yourself—once you have mastered the assembly procedures described in this book.

JUDGING QUALITY

Two bicycles with $200 difference in price might appear to have the same type of equipment at first glance and, therefore, present a puzzling question: Why such a great difference in price? The answer is in quality of the construction, the finishing techniques, and the components attached to the frame. Close inspection and attention to workmanship, along with a knowledge of name-brand derailleurs, pedals, hanger sets, and brakes, is necessary to determine how well the figure on the price tag reflects the true value of the bicycle.

When judging a bicycle, look first at the frame. Better frames have reinforced joints: Either the line of one frame tube should flow into another with a rounded, smooth contour, or there should be a reinforcing sleeve (called a *lug*) over the joint. Cheap frames have one tube crudely welded to the other, and often break apart in a minor accident or heavy use. Good frames do not.

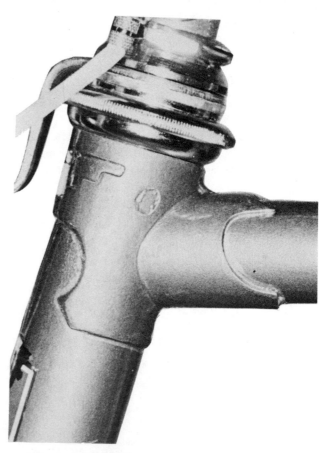

This good-quality bicycle frame has its tubes fitted into reinforcing sleeves, called *lugs,* then brazed.

The frame tubes that hold the rear wheel are under the most stress at their forward ends, near the saddle and cranks. In better frames, these tubes are tapered—larger near the saddle and cranks and smaller where they meet at the hub of the rear wheel. On cheaper frames, these tubes will be untapered and

may be squashed flat against the sides of the *dropouts*—the metal plates which hold the ends of the hub axle. On better frames, the tubes will have rounded ends at the dropouts.

Better frames are lighter, yet stronger, because of better materials and construction. You will rarely find a bike shop selling a bike with a poor frame, because the frame is the most difficult part of the bike to replace.

Be especially sure that the frame fits you. There is much more to correct fit than being able to stand over the bicycle. To inform yourself, read Chapter 2 before you go shopping.

Women have to shop carefully for a bicycle that fits; most frames are still proportioned for men, whose arms are relatively longer and legs shorter. Ironically, "mixte" or "ladies' " bicycle frames are likely to have a longer reach to the handlebars than diamond ("men's") frames; demand for diamond frames is greater, increasing design flexibility. Most women who tour or race on bicycles use diamond frames anyway; "ladies' " frames offer few important advantages.

The frame is the only part usually made by the company whose brand name is on the bike—Univega, Raleigh, Lotus, Fuji, Schwinn, etc. Components such as hubs, rims, crank, chain, and saddle are made by outside suppliers. Bicycles are unlike other consumer products in that different manufacturers may have models equipped with the same components. The best buy may depend on which shop has better service.

The largely interchangeable, "generic" character of bicycle parts works to your advantage in another way as well: Unlike most other consumer products, bicycles usually do not become obsolete because of unavailability of spare parts. Many different brands of parts will fit your bike, so any good bike shop can

Another method of high-quality construction reinforces the brazed or welded joints of the frame by building them up into rounded contours.

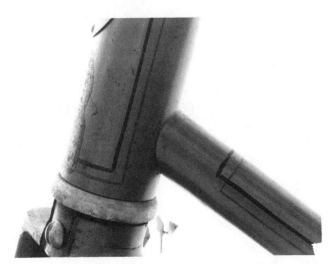

A frame with sharp contours at the joints and no lugs will generally be both heavier and weaker than a reinforced frame.

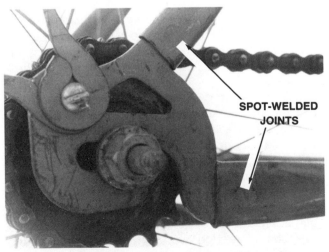

SPOT-WELDED JOINTS

Stays (rear frame tubes) flattened against the forkends and spot-welded in place are another sign of a low-quality frame.

Steel vs. aluminum. Note the pearly gloss and bulkier contours of the derailleur on the right, and the high gloss and "bent and folded" appearance of the one on the left. Their performance is almost identical, but the all-steel one weighs nearly twice as much.

service it—not just a dealer who sells the same brand. A knowledgeable bicyclist may even scavenge usable parts from worn-out or damaged bikes to save on repair bills.

Also, it is simple to replace parts which do not suit you. Many bike shops will make substitutions on new bikes at a low cost. For example, if your new bike does not have low enough gears or if the saddle is uncomfortable for you, the shop can easily correct these problems.

Make sure that the components on your bike are of known name brands and can be serviced easily. If ever there was a time when you needed to put your trust in a name-brand item, it is now. The manufacturers of quality items installed on the finest machines, both domestic and imported, have built their business and reputation on quality and performance. Winners of the Grand Prix races held throughout Europe and at the Olympic games have relied on those components which have given them the edge over competition. The tried-and-true bicycle components of reputable brand names like SunTour, Sugino, TA, Weinmann, Dia-Compe, Strong-

light, Campagnolo, and Shimano can be repaired easily; bike shops carry spare parts for major brands. Off-brand components, most commonly seen on cheaper bikes, come and go from year to year, and spare parts are not available.

Components of fine quality may be made of either steel or aluminum (called "alloy" by bicyclists). Identify steel components by their mirrorlike chrome-plated finish; aluminum components, by their softer, pearly-gray or colored finish and their bulkier contours. To achieve the same strength, aluminum components must be bulkier, but they are nonetheless lighter. Light weight makes a bike more fun to ride, so most good-quality components for multispeed bikes use a lot of aluminum.

The choice is not so clear on three-speed and one-speed bikes, which are not intended for long-distance riding. As long as you stick with brands sold through bike shops, good steel components are common.

Aluminum offers the greatest advantage in the wheel rims, where its light weight increases maneuverability and acceleration. Brakes work much better in wet weather on aluminum rims. Generally, bikes with aluminum rims cost $225 or more new, but if you are buying a bicycle for more than occasional use, you should be shopping in this quality range anyway.

While light weight is an advantage, it can be taken to extremes. The lightest bikes, with 1-inch-wide tires and thin-walled frame tubing, are fine for racers, but they are too delicate for general use. For touring or utility riding, a multispeed road bike should have 1¼-inch-wide tires; and as mentioned earlier, the 2-inch-wide tires of the mountain bike are best for riding on poor surfaces.

Maintaining Your Bicycle

No matter what kind of bicycle you buy, it will need regular attention to maintain its safety and performance. Tires need pumping once a week, and there are a number of other minor adjustments that need regular attention. Every bicyclist is wise to learn how to fix a flat tire and perform other minor on-the-road repairs. This book can teach you not only how to perform this minor maintenance, but how to overhaul every part of your bicycle.

ACCESSORIES

It is a very common mistake to buy only a bicycle without the accessories which are needed to use it well. Plan on spending at least $100 on accessories. Every bicyclist needs the first few accessories in the following list; you may or may not need the remaining ones, depending on the conditions under which you will ride.

Helmet

Seventy-five percent of fatal and permanent injuries in bicycle accidents are head injuries. A hard-shell helmet, as now used by the majority of regular bicycle users and required by national bicycle racing organizations, will prevent most head injuries. Several brands are available. Make sure that the helmet you buy conforms to the ANSI (American National Standards Institute) standards for protection.

A small rear-view mirror which clips to the helmet is the most effective type for bicycling. No mirror, whether on a car or a bicycle, substitutes for a look over the shoulder; but with a bit of practice in its use, the mirror can be helpful in many situations.

Tool Kit

Expect to spend about $20 for a small tool kit as described in Chapter 4. The kit should include an adjustable wrench, screwdriver, spoke wrench, air-pressure gauge, tire-patch kit, tire irons, and carrying pouch. These tools will be adequate to fix a flat tire and perform most other on-the-road repairs.

Pump

You'll need this to inflate a tire you've patched, and to top up tire pressure, a weekly chore. Buy a small pump which clips to the bicycle frame. The best type has a locking head to secure it to the tire valve. A pump

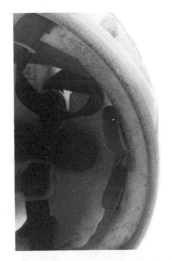

The helmet on the right saved a life. When a stick jammed his front wheel, the owner landed full-force on the front of the helmet. Note the crushed-down foam liner of the helmet, and the deep scratches on the outside. The owner went back to work the next day.

which connects to the tire with a small hose is more difficult to use.

Gloves

In cold weather, you'll wear ordinary winter gloves. In warm weather, fingerless bicyclist's gloves cushion your hands while you ride and prevent skinned palms when you take a fall. Gloves typically cost $10 to $25.

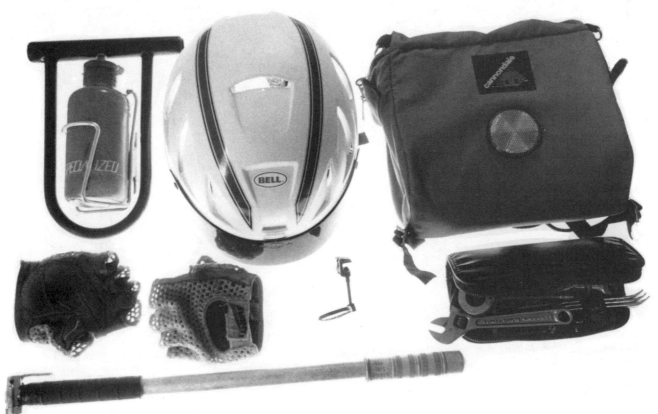

Accessories every bicyclist should have: U-lock, water bottle, helmet (with optional mirror), handlebar bag, tool kit, pump, gloves.

Lock

A bicycle is a prime target for theft, since it is its own getaway vehicle. Buy one of the large U-shaped locks sold at bike shops. Use it correctly to secure the rear wheel and frame; with a front quick-release hub, it can secure the front wheel as well.

Accessories such as the rack and fender here may be attached at the brake bolt. Make sure that the bolt is properly secured, and that the accessories do not interfere with the operation of the brake.

ing on your bike, you will need a baggage rack. Better racks clamp to the brake bolt or use eyelets which grip the frame tubes above the rear wheel; avoid the type that clamps the frame tubes between two flat plates of metal. *Pannier bags* that attach to a front or rear rack are available to carry large loads. Buy a couple of bungee cords (rubber stretch straps) to secure loose objects to the top of the rack.

Used as shown, the U-lock secures the frame, rear wheel, and quick-release front wheel. The lock may optionally pass around the seat tube if it reaches. The most common error is to secure only the frame, or one wheel.

Water Bottle

On a trip of ten or more miles, you need to drink water to replenish moisture lost through perspiration. A bicycle water bottle in its frame-mounted cage lets you do this conveniently without stopping.

Bags and Racks

For comfort and safety, attach baggage to the bicycle, not to yourself. For casual riding, you could use a small backpack; more convenient is a small *handlebar bag* with a top map case. If you go shopping or camp-

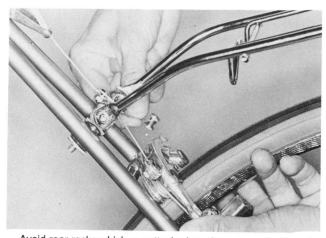

Avoid rear racks which are attached as shown here, by clamping two plates against the seatstays. These racks tend to be unstable.

Lights and Reflective Equipment

Most bicycles are sold with reflectors, but these only make you visible to drivers whose headlights happen to be pointed at you—not to pedestrians, other bicyclists, or drivers approaching in side streets ahead of you. A white headlight and red rear reflector or taillight are required by law for night riding, and even when riding under streetlights you need them to be seen.

Generator lights are the most practical for all-around use. They are the only kind that make sense for tours of several days in areas where batteries may not be available. The better generator headlamps are bright enough for riding on unlighted roads.

Small battery-powered lamps are suitable for city riding under streetlights—not bright enough to light your way, yet bright enough so you can be seen. Aim both the front and rear lamps level if they are of this type. If you use these lights often, you will save money by equipping them with nickel-cadmium rechargeable batteries, available at any hardware store.

High-powered battery lighting systems are available at a higher cost. These are by far the best type of lights for commuting where there are no streetlights.

Since a taillight bulb can burn out without your knowledge, you should always use rear-facing reflectors too. Those in a typical new-bike set are not as bright as they ought to be. A larger rear reflector is a good idea, as well as a reflective vest, pedal reflectors, tape on the frame and helmet, and ankle bands.

Fenders

Fenders are necessary to protect you and the bike from tire splash in wet weather. Some bikes come equipped with fenders, and they can be added to any bike except an all-out racing bike. To keep your feet dry, the front fender should have a mudflap which extends nearly to the ground. You can make one easily by cutting out one corner of a plastic milk carton and bolting it onto the rear of the fender. Cloth toeclip covers also help keep your feet dry.

Rainwear

In anything short of a downpour, appropriate rainwear will keep you dry and comfortable. Bicyclists use a *rain cape,* like a poncho but tailored to fit you in riding position; it has loops which you place over your thumbs or the brake levers to extend the front. A conventional camper's poncho is *not* suitable: It will flap in the wind or catch in the spokes.

A Gore-Tex rainsuit is usable for bicycling, though steamy in warm weather and expensive—about $120. A rainsuit of coated nylon or rubber will soak you in condensed perspiration; you will get as wet as if you had let the rain fall on you.

Unless you wear glasses, goggles are a good idea to keep stinging raindrops out of your eyes.

Clothing and Shoes

You can ride a bicycle in ordinary clothing—tuck your trouser cuffs into your socks to keep the chain from soiling them—but special clothing has real advantages if you ride much.

A bicycle jersey is cut long so you won't get a patch of sunburn on your lower back from leaning over the handlebars. It fits snugly so the wind can't blow it around. The pockets are in the back, where their contents are held steady against your body. Bicycle jerseys typically are dyed in bright colors, which increase your visibility and safety.

Lights and reflectors are required for safe and legal night riding. Streaks in this time exposure are from a steady taillight and the up-and-down motion of a leg light. Reflectors on the rear fender, pedals, vest, and helmet are revealed by the camera's flash.

Comfortable riding in wet weather requires a rain cape and fenders, as shown.

As this recumbent rider demonstrates, cold-weather riding is practical with the correct clothing: heavy gloves, wool cap under the helmet, and layers of clothing like a cross-country skier's. The face mask and windshield further aid comfort in cold weather.

The upper shoe is cleated; the lower shoe, for touring, has a stiff sole with a rubber traction surface for the pedals.

Bicycle shorts are cut long, and fit snugly around the legs so they won't ride up. Seams are carefully stitched so they won't chafe you. The shorts are black, to hide marks from the chain and the saddle. Inside the shorts is a soft chamois or terry-cloth liner to ease the pressure of the saddle. For maximum comfort, the shorts are worn without underwear.

For cooler weather, a long-sleeved jacket and tights (like shorts, but with long legs) keep you warm. For very cold weather, you should dress like a cross-country skier, with windproof, lined mittens, shoe covers—or two pairs of socks—an insulated face mask, and several light layers of clothing which you can add or remove as necessary. With proper clothing, there's no problem with riding in temperatures well below freezing.

Wool, wool blends, and polypropylene are preferred materials for jerseys, shorts, and tights. Because of their water-resistant properties, they keep you cool in hot weather and warm in cool weather.

Bicycle shoes are lightweight, with stiff soles to spread the load from the pedals; the uppers are reinforced to resist wear from toestraps. Some shoes are intended to be used with slotted cleats, others without.

With toeclips and straps, cleats fasten your feet more securely to the pedals and improve efficiency, especially in climbing, though they are an annoyance if you must get off the bike frequently. Fortunately, many designs of bicycle touring shoes without cleats are now available, and serve their purpose well. As this is written, new, cleatless locking shoe-pedal systems are just beginning to reach the market.

INSTALLING ACCESSORIES

Fenders, racks, and generator lights must be bolted to the frame of the bicycle. There are too many different kinds to describe the installation of all of them here. Have the bike shop install accessories on a new bike, or follow the instructions supplied with them. Be careful to tighten nuts and bolts carefully, especially those which also hold the brakes in place. If you are not yet experienced in mechanical work, it is a good idea to have a mechanic install accessories for you.

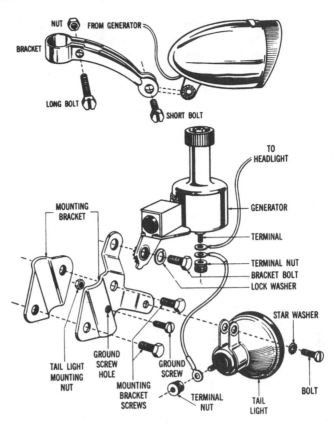

Where the fender and rack braces attach to the frame at the eyelets of the forkend, they must be tightly secured.

Exploded view of a typical tire-sidewall generator lighting system. The front and rear lamps are wired to the generator, but the electrical return path is through the frame, requiring the ground screw to establish electrical contact. Running a second, ground wire between the generator and lamp brackets increases reliability.

Fender braces should be passed through the eyebolt and cut short, not bent over.

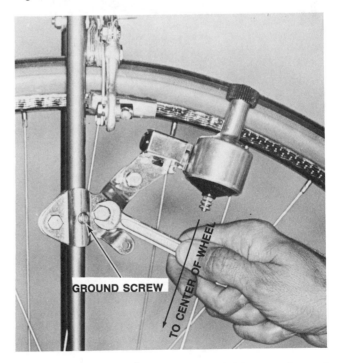

To prevent excess tire wear, the centerline of the generator must intersect with that of the wheel axle.

Fender braces usually feed through eyebolts at their outer end. Trim the braces so they can't catch on your clothing, but leave them straight—don't bend them over. This way, if a fender jams against the wheel, it will disengage rather than stopping the wheel from turning. Avoid fenders with U-shaped braces: They don't have this safety-release feature.

A tire-sidewall generator must bear on a surface of the tire which is coated with rubber. Sidewalls of light-weight tires are too thin, so tilt the generator up to run on the side of the tread. The center of the roller surface should contact the tire, and the generator's axis should point exactly toward a line extended from the end of the wheel's axle, or the generator roller will wear the tire. A front-wheel generator must always be ahead of the fork, to lessen the chance of its tangling in the spokes.

2 • FITTING THE BICYCLE TO YOU

Careful attention to fitting your bike can bring about a tremendous improvement in your riding style, comfort, and control. And, to your advantage, most of the dimensions that affect fit are easily changed—not set forever when you buy a bicycle. Some parts may have to be exchanged, but many bicycle shops offer parts exchange on new bicycles free or at a reduced cost. The following sequence of tests and adjustments is given in the order you'd carry them out when choosing and setting up a bike. Run through this list before buying a bike or when checking one over.

BASIC MEASUREMENTS

Consider having yourself measured using a system such as the Fit Kit, available at bicycle shops. This will help zero in on the correct adjustments and will provide a written record helpful in setting up another bicycle in the future.

Frame Height

You should be able to stand over the bicycle's top tube with about an inch of clearance. An oversize frame is unacceptable; a frame an inch or two undersize is no serious problem.

Next, run a preliminary test of top-tube length. Place the back of your elbow at the front of the saddle. Your fingers should reach the handlebars, give or take an inch. This crude measurement will indicate whether the top-tube length is wildly incorrect.

To avoid difficulty reaching the handlebars, short people—particularly short women—need to be especially careful about top-tube length, maybe even buying a bike with smaller-than-usual wheels.

Crank Length

Check crank length when purchasing a bicycle. The length is usually marked on the inside face of the crank

You must be able to stand over the frame with an inch of clearance.

For a rough test of handlebar distance, place your elbow on the front of the saddle. Your fingertips should reach the handlebars. This frame is too long for the rider.

arms. Common lengths on new bikes are 165mm and 170mm. If you're much over 6 feet tall, 170mm may not be enough. If you're short, 165mm is long for you, but this is not as much of a problem. More detail on crank length later.

Handlebars

Handlebars are available in a variety of widths, and should be about as wide as your shoulders. Dropped handlebars, offering the widest variety of hand positions, are best for long-distance riding. People who are used to them will likely prefer them for urban riding too. The straight, flat handlebars on all-terrain bikes are well-suited to their purpose. These need to be extra-wide for leverage in tough off-road riding.

The upward-and-backward-curved handlebars used on British three-speeds are too close and too high for

An average woman has more of her height in the legs than a man. Ideal for a woman under 5 feet 3 inches, this bicycle has a smaller front wheel that decreases distance to the handlebars.

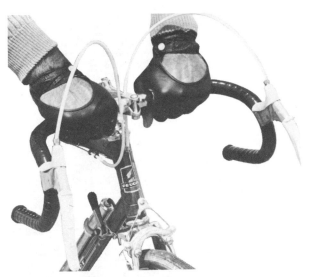

Switch handlebar positions so one set of arm and back muscles can rest while another takes the load. The top position is best to stretch your back, or for leisurely riding.

The position with hands on the tops of the brake levers is ideal for pedaling while standing off the saddle. Moderate braking is possible over the hoods of the levers.

This position is comfortable and places the hands within easy reach of the brake levers.

With the hands below the brake-lever hoods, the rider is prepared for rapid or prolonged braking. This position is best for fast downhill runs or when approaching an intersection in traffic.

efficient riding, unless turned upside down. Sitting completely upright wastes much of the power of the leg-straightening gluteus muscles, since your legs are already close to straight at the hip joints. The increase in available power when leaning 45 degrees forward is dramatic. In addition, lower handlebars put more of your weight over the bicycle's front wheel, giving better road-holding and steering control.

Leaning forward does involve some compromise in comfort. The head no longer balances on the neck; the muscles at the back of the neck have to hold it up. These muscles will strengthen after a couple weeks of riding. However, if you ride too little to condition your neck muscles, you may never be comfortable in the deeply crouched position and will want a higher position and flat handlebars.

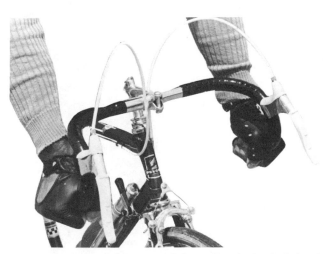

The lowest position on the handlebars offers the least wind resistance and is best for speed runs or when bucking a strong headwind.

The Saddle

If the saddle on your bike doesn't agree with you, replace it as you would replace shoes that don't fit. Women have wider-spaced pelvic bones than men and often find a narrow saddle uncomfortable. Fortunately, well-designed "anatomic" saddles have become widely available in recent years. You may have to try a few different saddles before you find your favorite.

Having chosen and installed a saddle, check the saddle tilt. This adjusts with the bolts at the seat clamp directly under the saddle. Start with the saddle level so that your weight will not slide you forward or backward off the saddle. You may wish to make corrections after you have ridden the bicycle.

ADJUSTMENTS

You must mount the bicycle to test further adjustments. By leaning one hip against a wall or post and holding the handbrakes, you can sit up on the bike and backpedal. A mirror against an opposite wall will let you check the adjustments. Or use an assistant to hold the bike and observe your position.

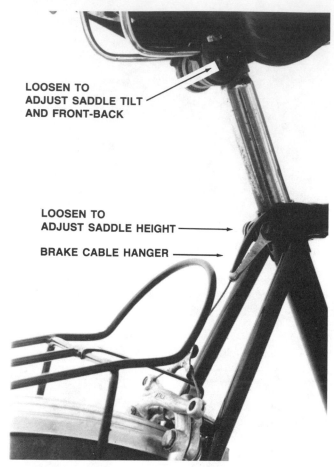

LOOSEN TO ADJUST SADDLE TILT AND FRONT-BACK

LOOSEN TO ADJUST SADDLE HEIGHT

BRAKE CABLE HANGER

Saddle front-back position and tilt adjust at the seat clamp, under the saddle. A brake-cable hanger must point directly toward the brake after adjusting saddle height at the seatpost clamp on the frame.

Saddle Adjustment

First adjust the height. In the normal pedaling position with the ball of the foot on the pedal, the leg should be slightly bent when relaxed at the bottom of the stroke. The knee should rest perhaps 10cm forward of its locked position. Many riders place the saddle too low because they try to climb onto the saddle first, instead of using the pedal as a step.

Before raising the saddle, pull the seatpost all the way out of the bike. Make sure that at least 2 inches will be inside the bike. If less, get a longer seatpost.

Set the saddle's forward-back position. This is adjusted at the seat clamp along with saddle tilt. Typically, the tibial tuberosity (the bump in the bone just below the knee) should be over the pedal spindle when the crank is facing directly forward.

Seat clamps allow a considerable range of front-to-back adjustment. Inexpensive steel clamps allow the greatest adjustment of all; they can be flipped over to allow the saddle to move forward another inch, often necessary with a short rider. If you raise or lower your

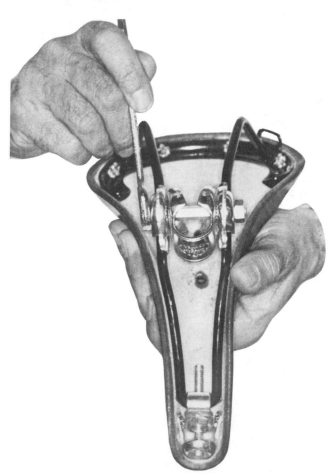

This least expensive type of seat clamp can be flipped completely over to position the saddle farther forward.

How to get onto a bicycle. Stand *ahead* of the saddle and push down on one pedal. As the push starts you moving, it raises you to the saddle.

With the saddle at its proper height, you cannot reach the ground with both feet. People often position the saddle too low, having become accustomed as children to sitting on a tricycle with both feet on the ground.

saddle very far or change crank length, you will have to readjust saddle front-back position too.

Handlebar Adjustment

First adjust the forward-back position. We've already checked that the frame's top tube length will allow this adjustment to be correct.

For an accurate test of handlebar distance, sit on the bicycle. With dropped handlebars, place your hands on the drops. A plumb line from the end of your nose should fall about 2cm behind the centerline of the handlebars at the top. If the handlebars are too close, you will feel cramped, and if they're too far away, your shoulders and arms will get sore.

With flat handlebars, crouch down as if you were in dropped-handlebar position. The center of the handlebars should be in approximately the same position or perhaps 2cm farther forward.

The handlebar distance is corrected by choosing a different handlebar stem—the L-shaped part which grips the center of the handlebars. Stems are available with a forward extension of from 4cm to 14cm. If a

bicycle frame is too long with dropped handlebars, it may still be usable with flat handlebars.

Now adjust the height of the handlebars. The height range depends on the type of handlebars, but the stem allows a few centimeters of adjustment. Typically, the handlebar center is as high as the top of the saddle, or a few centimeters lower.

If you are out of shape, you may want your handlebars higher. Like the seatpost, the handlebar stem should be pulled completely out of the bike so you are sure there will be at least 2 inches inside after you have positioned it.

To free the stem for height adjustment, loosen the bolt at the top rear of the handlebar stem a couple of turns, then tap on this bolt head with a wooden mallet (or hammer and wood block).

Now set the handlebar angle. Choose this so your wrists are straight and the wrist muscles will not have to strain to support your weight. Generally, the lower part of dropped handlebars should point to the rear dropouts. With flat handlebars, too, the grips should always tilt down toward you. The final adjustment is measured by comfort.

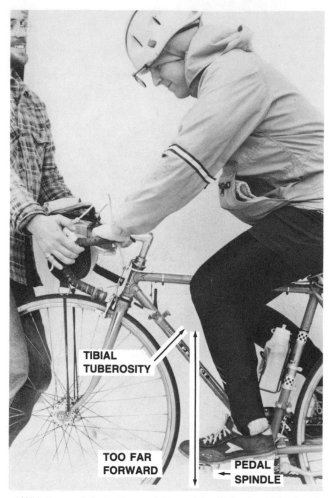

TIBIAL TUBEROSITY

TOO FAR FORWARD

PEDAL SPINDLE

With the crank facing forward, the pedal spindle should be directly under the tibial tuberosity (bump below the knee). The saddle on this bike places the rider too far forward.

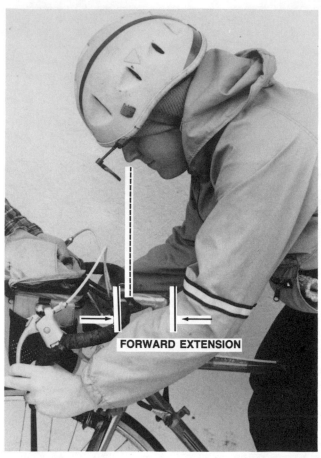

FORWARD EXTENSION

With the hands below the brake levers, the tip of the nose should be about an inch behind the handlebars. Handlebar distance is changed by using a stem with a different forward extension.

Handlebar angle is adjusted after loosening the bolt under the front of the stem.

To adjust handlebar height, loosen the stem bolt two or three → turns and tap it down with a mallet to release the clamp inside, then reposition the stem.

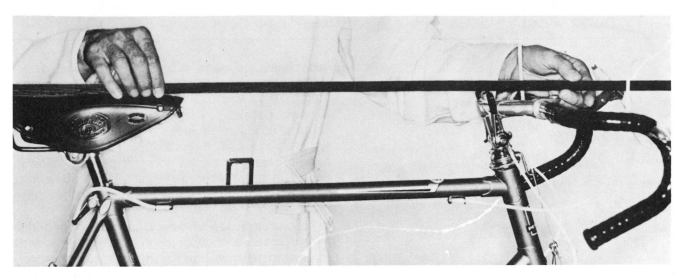

The handlebar stem should be approximately level with the saddle; it can be an inch or two lower once you become comfortable with the dropped position.

The handlebar drops should angle more or less toward the rear hub, so the hands are comfortable. Brake levers on dropped bars should tilt upward somewhat, allowing you to brake over the tops.

Positioning Control Levers

Brake levers should fall comfortably under your fingers. The tops of brake levers on dropped handlebars should tilt up about 35 degrees. It is then possible to use them as handrests, and to brake lightly from the tops, even without extension levers. Rubber brake hoods increase comfort.

Extension levers ("safety levers") at the tops of dropped handlebars prevent you from installing rubber hoods, and they are poor for emergency stops—they are too flexible, and the hand position reduces steering control while braking. If you feel that you must use extension levers, you may need a shorter handlebar stem, or the brake levers may be too big. Small brake levers are available for small hands as a special-order item.

Brake levers for flat handlebars should not face directly downward, but should be splayed outward so they fall under the fingers.

On flat handlebars, the trigger control for a three-speed hub can be placed just inboard of the brake lever so you can operate both at once. Place a trigger control at the end of dropped bars.

The most convenient derailleur shifters for flat bars are the handlebar-mounted "thumb shifters" commonly used on all-terrain bikes. For dropped bars, handlebar-

This "thumb shifter" is very convenient with flat handlebars, as are handlebar-end shifters with dropped bars. Downtube-mounted shifters are acceptable. Shifters at the center of the handlebars look convenient but are actually clumsy to use.

end shifters are the most convenient, but downtube shifters work well—the reach to the levers is a clean, single stroke, and both levers can be operated at once with one hand.

Handlebar-stem shifters, at the center of the handlebars, look convenient, but you have to fold up your arm, with nothing to brace it against, and every little jolt from the road interferes with your attempt to shift. Stem shifters can also be hazardous in an accident.

Crank Choices

With more leverage per stroke, long cranks give the same power output at lower rpm—advantageous for the standup style of pedaling needed on rough ground. Short crank arms allow the feet to spin faster and give more cornering clearance: They are preferred by track racers.

If you are of average height, the crank that came with your bike will probably work fine for you. If you are short, the crank arms may be too long in proportion to your legs and you will be apt to pedal slower; short cranks may suit you better. Lengths from 150mm to 180mm (5.9 to 7.1 inches) are available on special order.

If you are tall, longer cranks will probably give you more power—at a cost in cornering clearance. (The expensive way around this problem is to buy a custom frame; the cheap way is to use 27-inch wheels on a frame made for 26-inch wheels.)

Pedal and Toeclip Choices

Pedals are sold in two basic types: one-sided and two-sided. If you won't be using toeclips, make sure

your pedals are made to be used either side up.

Extra-wide pedals will drag in corners, and if you use toeclips, they won't position your feet as positively as narrower pedals.

But be sure that the pedals are wide enough to allow your feet to rest at their natural angle. Most feet toe outward slightly. If narrow pedals force them to toe in, knee damage will eventually result. This is true with or without toeclips or cleats. Pedals are available in a great variety of widths.

Toeclips increase efficiency and are a good idea except for very slippery or rough conditions. At speeds too low to balance, toeclips may cause a relatively harmless fall for an inexperienced rider who hasn't yet learned to pull the foot back to release it.

At higher speeds, toeclips prevent serious falls by keeping the feet from slipping off the pedals. Unfortunately, many riders overemphasize the minor early risk of toeclips and are unaware of the benefits.

Two pedals of very similar design, one narrow, the other wide. The nonstandard off-center toeclip position on the wide pedal was needed to match a normal outward rotation of the rider's feet.

Do *not* put the end of the toestrap through the lower slot in the buckle. If the end hangs loose, the strap can be tightened and loosened easily without looking down.

Be sure toeclips are the right length. Those supplied with your bicycle may not fit you any more than a randomly chosen pair of shoes would. It helps to get toeclips a bit on the large side, so you can pull the straps behind the widest part of the shoes to hold them more securely.

Proper threading of toestraps makes them easy to adjust. Thread them from outside to inside of the pedal. Twist the strap under the pedal so it won't slip. Do not tuck the end of the strap into the little slot at the bottom of the buckle. Then you can pull on the strap end to tighten it, and push on the buckle with your thumb to loosen it.

If you use cleated shoes, as racers and many tourists do, you must be especially careful about cleat angle to avoid leg strain. The Rotational Adjustment Device included in the Fit Kit will allow the dealer to set the angle on your shoes.

EXPERIMENTATION

With pedals and toeclips, we come to the end of the main adjustments and equipment choices which determine rider position and comfort.

If you go through the sequence given here, you'll get the adjustments nearly right; but be prepared to readjust your saddle position and handlebar height. By continued experimentation you will find the adjustments which suit you best, and equally valuably, you'll learn how a bike feels when the adjustments are slightly incorrect. Then adjustments will go faster next time and you'll be better able to help other people adjust their bikes, too.

3 • RIDER PERFORMANCE

This is mostly a book about bicycle maintenance. But proper care of the machine is far from the entire story of making bicycling enjoyable, safe, and useful.

Good bicycling involves the rider, not just the machine. The bicyclist is not only the driver but also the engine, and weighs four to ten times as much as the bicycle. A bicycle steers quickly but is smaller and usually slower than other vehicles on the road. Clearly, bicycling requires some special skills.

Yet these skills are infrequently taught; most people haven't been exposed to them. Rather, people have been exposed to a long tradition of poor information.

From 1900 to 1950, as automobiles gained popularity, bicycling became almost entirely a children's pastime in the United States. As a result, bicycling was "taught" to children by parents and teachers who had not ridden for many years.

This type of teaching is folklore—beginners' advice, less and less accurate as it is passed down from one generation to the next and anchored in parents' fear for the safety of their children.

It is right for beginners' advice to consist mostly of cautions. We advise a child not to go into water over his head, but this would be useless and insulting advice for a Red Cross–trained swimmer or certified scuba diver.

Though much information is available about the athletic and mechanical sides of bicycling, even experienced bicyclists often have little knowledge of maneuvering skills or traffic tactics. It is the purpose of this chapter to improve performance beginning with the rider.

The advice given here in condensed form is drawn from the tested and proven *Effective Cycling* program of instruction—the bicyclist's equivalent of a Red Cross water safety course.

The Effective Cycling program equips its graduates to use the bicycle safely and confidently under almost any condition of terrain or traffic. Graduates have a proven accident rate *one-fifth* or less that of the average American adult bicyclist. For more details about the program, see the list of bicycling organizations later in this chapter.

GETTING STARTED

If you need to teach a child to balance and steer a bicycle, lower the saddle and remove the pedals. Have the child "scooter" down a slight grade. If the bike has handbrakes, the child can use them *gently* to slow and stop; otherwise he can drag his feet. Or you can teach the child to balance on a platform-type scooter. Scootering is easier than learning by falling off or with training wheels.

Once the child has learned to balance and steer, he can work on developing the most power for the least effort.

Efficient Riding Position

An efficient position on the bicycle, described in Chapter 2, divides the body's weight evenly among the feet, hands, and rear end and positions the weight of the upper body to help the legs in pedaling.

At first you may wish to raise the handlebar stem slightly, but within a few weeks, the neck strengthens to hold the head up even on longer rides. The bolt-upright "bulldozer operator" position favored by beginners sends road impact straight up the spine and makes you work twice as hard; you have to pull on the handlebars to push with your legs.

Efficient Pedaling

To many beginners, pedaling a bicycle feels like climbing stairs. Beginners often think they are getting good exercise by pushing hard—like weightlifting. They think that other bicyclists who pass them, feet spinning, are pushing even harder—super-athletes. This misconception prevents many beginners from developing as bicyclists.

Shift to a lower gear; pedal *lightly* and fast. The people with spinning feet are *not* working harder. They are working *less*.

When you walk, your legs swing like pendulums, at a marching beat of about 60 per minute. When you ride your bicycle, your legs are like the connecting rods in an engine, and can turn at any speed. By turning faster in a lower gear, your legs put out more power, without straining. You will go faster, while getting much better exercise for your lungs and heart. This will feel so good that you will want to ride farther. Work at 50 or 75 percent of maximum power output so you don't overheat or tire out.

Save heavy pedal pressure for the few short bursts of acceleration you need during a ride. After all, you can lift a heavy barbell only a few times before you tire out; but you will turn the crank about 2,000 times in a 5-mile ride!

Having learned to pedal fast, anybody in normal good health can build up over a couple of months to ride 100 miles in a day and enjoy it.

Toeclips

Use toeclips and straps, or a locking shoe-pedal system, to make fast pedaling easier by keeping your feet mated to the pedals. These also reduce the chance of an accident by preventing your feet from slipping off the pedals.

You must practice a few times to learn to get your feet into toeclips. Strap one foot in *before* you start, then step up to the saddle as described in Chapter 2. When your other foot is in position, flip the other pedal up with your toe to insert your foot. If it doesn't flip up on the first try, ride along with the pedal upside down until you build up enough speed to coast and try again.

Even a long, steep hill is much easier if you shift down, sit down, and spin, rather than straining your legs.

Beginners are afraid that they won't be able to re-move their feet from toeclips if they have to stop or dismount quickly. You must simply learn to pull your foot back instead of to the side. If your foot gets stuck, you will fall sideways—but this is rare and happens only at a very low speed. It's more funny than painful. With locking shoe-pedal systems which substitute for toeclips and straps, inserting and removing your feet is even easier.

Shifting Gears

Practice shifting gears until your feet always spin at the same speed with the same effort. Shift down *before* you come to a hill and *before* you stop for a traffic light. If your bicycle doesn't have gears low enough to master the hills where you ride, this book has information on how to improve them (see Chapter 9).

Refueling

With correct pedaling technique, bicycling is very easy on the muscles. A marathon runner is sore and exhausted after two hours, but with proper attention to food and water intake, a bicyclist can keep going until he must stop for sleep.

To ride more than an hour or two, you must refuel. If you do not drink, you will become parched. If you do not eat, you will suddenly become very hungry or else run out of energy and have to stop. But you must "meter" your supply of food and drink. If you eat a big meal or hard-to-digest, greasy foods during a ride, your legs will fight with your digestive system over the blood supply, and you will get a bad stomachache.

Eat plenty the night before a long ride, but have a moderate breakfast. During the ride, eat before you are hungry and drink before you are thirsty. Sip from your frame-mounted water bottle and nibble small snacks of easy-to-digest unsalted sweet or starchy food; pastries, Fig Newtons, fruit. Drink plain water—not soft drinks, milk, or other beverages which actually absorb water out of your system. Proper "in-flight refueling" will keep you going all day.

TRAFFIC SENSE

To ride a bicycle safely and enjoyably, you need to know how to maneuver on the road.

A bicycle on the road moves most smoothly and safely according to rules of traffic flow which are the same for all vehicles. But because a bicycle is narrow and comparatively slow, the details of applying these rules are different sometimes.

Where to Ride on the Road

Traffic on the road divides up according to its speed. Slow vehicles keep to the right, and faster ones pass on their left. A bicycle usually keeps more or less near the right side of the road, but your correct lane position also depends on whether the right lane is *wide or narrow.*

These words have a special, exact meaning for bicyclists. In a *wide* lane, a car can pass the bicyclist without swerving. In a *narrow* lane, a car must merge partway into the next lane to pass the bicyclist. The distinction between a wide and narrow lane depends to some degree on conditions such as the speed of traffic and the smoothness of the road surface.

In a wide lane, ride 3 or 4 feet to the right of where the cars go. Then they can pass you safely without having to merge into the next lane. A typical two-lane highway without shoulders is just wide enough for this.

If the lane becomes extra-wide, keep the *same* position just to the right of the cars. Do *not* move all the way over to the curb just because there is extra room. A very common type of car-bike collision happens when a car overtakes a bicyclist from behind, then turns right. If you are way over at the curb, you will not see the car until it is broadside in front of you. If you are closer to the car, you will see it begin to turn. You can turn with it and avoid the accident.

Gauge your lane position on the *left* side of the lane, not the right side. The common "folklore" instruction is to ride as far to the right as possible. This is dangerous advice. A bicyclist who follows this advice wanders left and right with every pothole. It is much safer to ride in a predictable straight line.

Be especially careful not to weave in and out between parked cars. As you duck in past a parked car, it hides you from drivers behind you. Then you pop out again. Surprise! Instead, keep a straight line 3 feet from parked cars, out of the reach of opening car doors. At normal bicycle speeds, you could *not* stop in time if someone opened a door—you would be forced to swerve out in front of a moving car or else hit the door.

Riding in a straight line also helps keep you clear of road-edge hazards such as potholes and trash. These can cause accidents and at the very least can give you lots of flat tires. The "gutter" style of riding is unsafe, even though the people who do it *think* they are doing the safe thing.

What if a lane is too narrow for a car to pass you? Then you must *control the situation.* Usually, this means that you must ride in the *middle* of the lane. Drivers of cars will then have to merge into the next lane to pass you safely, or else slow down and wait until there is room to pass.

This may seem like daring advice, but think about

In an extra-wide lane, ride at the right side of the through traffic—not all the way over at the curb. Car 1 noses out from a driveway so the driver can see; but this car does not block the bicyclist. Car 2 passes safely to the bicyclist's right, instead of cutting him off. Car 3's driver can see the bicyclist and yields to him, since the bicyclist is in the normal flow of traffic.

Do not ride too close to parked cars, or your only choice may be to swerve left into the path of an overtaking car.

the opposite choice: You could ride all the way over at the right side, as many bicyclists do, inviting drivers to pass you even though it isn't safe. This is how bicyclists get squeezed off the road, when motorists try to pass and then find that there isn't room.

You have a legal right to the road space you need for your safety. If cars have to wait behind you for a long time, courtesy and the law require that you pull aside when safe and let them pass—but you need to do this rarely, since your bicycle is narrow. Farm tractors and slow-climbing trucks have to pull aside more often, since they block the road more than a bicycle.

In traffic at normal city speeds, you will have to stay in the middle of a narrow right lane all of the time to hold your position in traffic. This isn't as difficult or daring as it seems, because the motor traffic is only going 10 or 15 miles per hour faster than you.

On a multilane road, it is especially important to claim a narrow right lane, since motorists are less careful about squeezing past you when they are not risking a head-on collision. If your position makes it clear that they must merge into the passing lane, they will treat you the same as a slow car in the right lane.

On a narrow two-lane rural road with lighter, faster traffic, there's no need to ride in the middle of the right lane all of the time. By keeping farther to the right, you extend a courtesy, letting cars overtake you without

having to swerve as far. But if cars are approaching from the front and rear at the same time, you must claim the lane, moving farther toward its center to prevent drivers behind you from overtaking you unsafely.

Curves and Hilltops

On a curve to the right which is blocked by a wall or bushes, you need to adjust your lane position so motorists can avoid you. If the lane is wide, keep well to the right so motorists will have plenty of room.

If the right lane at the blind curve is narrow, ride at its center or left, so motorists from behind can see you in time to slow and follow you. At a curve in a narrow lane, motorists behind you *must* slow and follow, in case another car is coming from the front. Keeping all the way to the right is the worst thing you could do, because it would guarantee that motorists behind you would see you too late to avoid you.

Even when the curve in a narrow road is to the left, you may need to claim the lane or make a slow signal (arm down, palm facing back) to a driver behind you, in case a car might be coming from the front. When you can see that the road is clear around the curve, you may wave the driver past you.

Climbing slowly up a hill, you need less room to stop or swerve. Pull farther to the right, to let cars pass you. As you go over the hilltop, you will be hidden from drivers behind you. Keep to the right until you have gained speed and enough distance so that drivers behind you will see you in time to avoid you.

As Fast as the Cars

As you continue down the hill, you may soon be going as fast or nearly as fast as the cars. Now move to the middle of the right lane. At high speeds, you need more maneuvering room, and you have to be farther from the edge of the road to see and be seen in time.

It is especially dangerous to ride along on the right side of a car which is traveling just as fast as you. You are in the driver's right-side blindspot. The driver could easily drift a few inches to the right, forcing you off the road at high speed. It is much safer to take your position in the line of traffic. After all, you aren't delaying the motorists. You are traveling as fast as a motorcycle, so ride the same way as a motorcyclist.

The same rule applies when cars are moving slowly—for example, on a crowded city street. Ride in the middle of the lane as long as you are keeping up with the car ahead of you. If it speeds up, return to your normal lane position. If it slows down, then you will pass it on the *left* as any other driver would.

The idea behind the lane positioning rules is to be as

predictable and visible as possible, and to place yourself out of range of hazards hidden in road-edge blindspots. Especially where the road is "walled in" by parked cars, bushes, or other objects, stay out of the road-edge strip where a pedestrian, car door, or car nosing out of a driveway could suddenly appear in front of you.

On rural roads, put yourself in the place of a driver a few hundred feet behind you; do what you must so this driver can see you and avoid you. This is especially important at hillcrests, on curves, and where lanes get narrower. The rules given above are a good starting point, but use your own good judgment in applying them.

Changing Lane Position

When conditions require you to move farther into the lane, you must prepare in advance so that you can make the move safely.

Don't wait until the last moment and then try to move over. Look ahead a few hundred feet for situations which require you to move farther into the lane—for example, a double-parked car. When you see one, glance back for traffic. If there's no car in the lane, make your change in lane position. If a car is close and gaining on you fast, wait until it has gone by.

When there's a car far enough back for the driver to react, *communicate* with the driver. Put out your hand for a turn signal. Give the driver a couple of seconds to

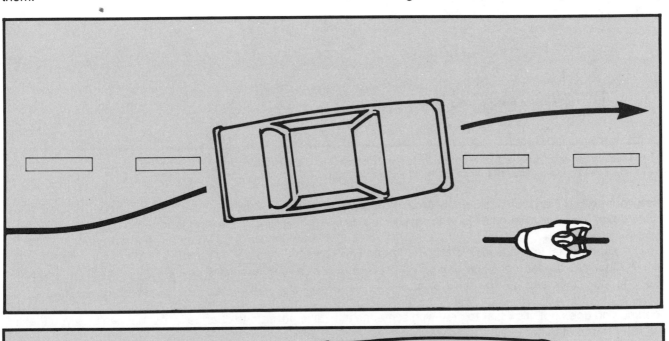

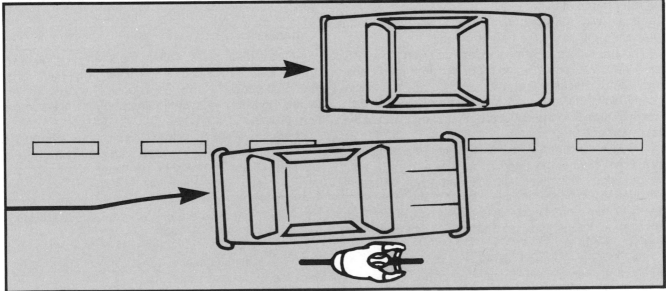

Ride in the middle of a narrow lane. As shown in the top drawing, motorists will then overtake you in the next lane. Riding at the right side of a narrow lane invites the "squeeze-out," as shown in the lower drawing.

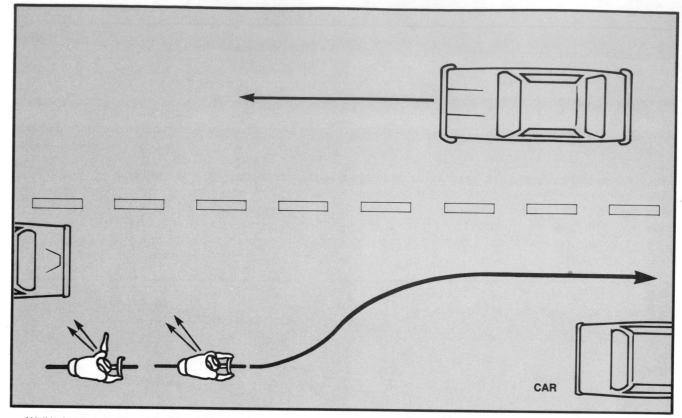

Well before you reach a parked car or other narrow spot in the road, look back and signal to a motorist behind you. Move left only after you have checked that the motorist has made room for you.

see your signal, then look back again. Most drivers will slow down or move to another lane to make room for you.

The hand signal is a *question:* "Will you let me into line?" Change your lane position only after you take a second look back and get the driver's *answer.*

Most drivers will cooperate with you. If the driver behind you does not, it's wiser to deal with someone in a better frame of mind. Wait till the car has passed and try again with the next driver. That's why you started preparing the lane change extra-early.

This procedure for changing lane position is the only safe way. You *establish* your position in a predictable way, after checking that it is safe. Compare the way many bicyclists approach a narrow spot in the road: staying "glued" to the right curb, then darting out at the last moment.

If you are not used to looking over your shoulder, practice it in an empty parking lot. Ride along a straight painted line while glancing back. Since your organs of balance are inside your ears, it takes a little practice to learn to turn your head without swerving. It helps to think about keeping the handlebars straight while turning your head.

Swiveling your head in an upright position is something of a neck stretch. Ducking your head sideways from a low handlebar position is easier, though it takes a little while to get used to the sideways view of the road behind you. Dropping your left arm from the han-

dlebar makes it easier to turn around. Some riders glance *under* the arm when in dropped position.

Just make sure you look all the way behind you; the exact style doesn't matter. Don't rely on your hearing, or a rearview mirror. Wind noise can drown out a car, not to speak of a silent bicycle behind you, and any mirror has blindspots. The mirror can often tell you that it is *not* safe to change lanes, but can't tell you that it *is* safe.

Intersections

Where streets cross, traffic on one street must have *right of way* over traffic on the other, to prevent false starts, confusion, and accidents. Where heavily traveled streets cross, traffic signs or signals determine right of way.

Where there are no signs or signals, the traffic on the larger, more important street has the right of way. Yield when entering a road from a driveway, or a main road from a side street. When two vehicles reach an un-signaled intersection or four-way stop sign at the same time, the law makes the one on the left yield, since it has an extra half road-width to stop.

So far, these rules are the same for bicycles as for cars. The remaining instructions are a little bit different, because bicycles are narrower.

The key to smooth, safe travel through an intersection is to approach it in the correct lane position, depending on which street you will take out of the intersection—right, left, or straight. To arrive at the correct position for the direction you want to go, you use your lane-changing technique. No matter which street you will take out of the intersection, you want to position yourself *with the flow of traffic headed for that street.*

A right turn is easy: Just stay at the right side of the street and go around the corner. Before you reach the intersection, look for pedestrians and for cross traffic. You must *yield* to them—they have the right of way, unless a traffic light or sign commands them to wait for you.

When you are going straight through an intersection, you usually should *not* keep all the way to the right of the road. Position yourself to the left of a right-turn lane. On a two-lane street, glance back, then pull slightly away from the right side so right-turning drivers will pass on your right.

A very common mistake is to ride along the right curb, then head straight out across the intersection into the path of a right-turning car. Bicyclists who make this mistake give themselves away by complaining that cars cut *them* off as they try to ride across intersections.

Left turns take the most preparation, because you must cross the most lanes. Make your left turn from the right side of a special left-turn lane, or the left side of a left-and-through lane. If there is no special left-turn lane, make your turn from near the center of the street.

To reach the left-turn position, cross each lane in two steps. One step gets you across the lane in which you are riding, so you are at its left side. The next step gets you just across the lane line, to the right side of the new lane. Waiting to move across the lane line gives you a chance to look back into the new lane before entering it. At each step, look back, signal, and look back again to make sure that the driver behind you has made room for you.

This procedure works in city or suburban traffic, where cars travel up to 15 miles an hour faster than you. On high-speed highways, you may have to wait for a gap in the traffic and move across all of the lanes at once.

The secret of a left turn is all in the preparation. Once you have changed lanes to reach the correct starting point, the rest is easy. You move to the center of the street to deal with all of the traffic behind you *before* you reach the intersection. From the left-turn-lane position, you can then concentrate on traffic ahead and to the sides.

If you are not sure of your lane changing, it is fine to walk a left turn. But be sure to come to a complete stop at the far right corner of the intersection. If you try to follow the right-hand crosswalks to make a left turn without stopping, you are asking for trouble. At the far right corner, you have to check for traffic in every direction at once. You don't have 360-degree vision like a rabbit, so it's not very safe. Besides, the left turn from the center of the street is easier and faster—you have to cross only half as many lanes of traffic.

The principles for making a left turn apply to other situations in which you must change lanes. Think them

As you approach an intersection, keep to the left of a right-turn lane to avoid conflicts with right-turning traffic.

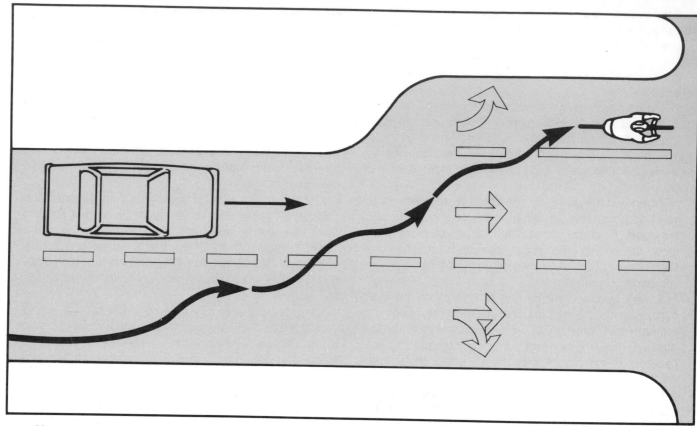

Move across each lane in two steps: one to cross the lane and another to enter the new lane. As shown, turn left from the right side of a special left-turn lane.

through as you approach each one. An example: A traffic circle is a two-lane, one-way road that swallowed its tail. It has several streets going off to the right and none to the left, so the right lane is a continuous right-turn lane. Ride around in the inner lane if you are going past the first exit, then change lanes back to the outside before you leave. You can handle other odd intersections by planning your lane changes in advance, this same way.

How to Pass Cars, Trucks, and Buses

Bicycles are sometimes faster than cars. Where a row of cars is waiting to make a right turn, or where a bus or truck pulls to the curb, you may have to pass.

Pass on the left, like other vehicles. This can be done safely and easily. Look back, and make your lane change well in advance, just as when you prepare for a left turn. Give yourself plenty of room.

Once you have passed, you may need to make a right-turn signal to indicate that you want to return to your normal lane position. Use your right hand—the left-hand-over-head right-turn signal makes sense only for people cooped up in cars.

A common mistake in passing a bus is to sneak along close to its left side, with the idea that it provides

some sort of shelter—as if the serious danger is from cars coming from behind. It isn't. As you pass the front end of a bus, a pedestrian could walk out into your path. Also, you are too close to the bus to be seen in the bus driver's rearview mirror; and if the bus starts moving, it could begin to merge to the left, into you.

The solution is to pass in the next lane, at least five feet to the left of a long truck, bus, or any moving vehicle. At this distance, you are far enough away to avoid a pedestrian crossing in front of the truck or bus. You are where a passing car would be—where the driver of the truck or bus will look for you when preparing a merge left. If the truck or bus does start to move, you have time to slow down and fall back.

In a traffic jam in which cars are completely stopped, you may move up cautiously on the right or between lanes—but go very slowly. Remember, a car door could open at any time, or a pedestrian could appear in front of you without warning. If there is an open lane, use it; and if the traffic starts moving, pull into line between cars even if this means that you must slow down.

It is *very* foolish to pass a bus or long truck on the right, next to the curb. A passenger getting off the bus could land on your handlebars, or the bus could make a right turn and roll over you.

Make a left turn from near the center of the road. Then, as shown, you avoid conflicts with through traffic. The bicyclist in the background of the upper photo is weaving between cars in a way only too common.

For the same reason, never pass the first car waiting in line at an intersection. Wait *behind* that car, so that it cannot turn toward you as it starts up. If you are farther back in line, also wait *between* cars; then the car in front of you is no threat, and the driver behind you can see you. Never wait beside a car, in the driver's blind-spot.

Anticipating Accident Situations

The best way to avoid an accident is to prevent it—by correct maneuvering, and by testing that drivers have seen you. For example, as you approach an intersection where the cross street has a stop sign, look into the driver's window of the first car in the cross

Even "difficult" traffic patterns like a rotary intersection sort themselves out when you take the correct lane positions. The bicyclist is going around in the inner lane to avoid conflicts with entering and exiting traffic such as the cars just behind him.

street. A driver who is looking at you has almost certainly seen you. Also look to see that the car is slowing or stopping to let you by.

At night, wigwag your handlebars a little to flash your headlight at the driver, and watch for the car to stop. Don't go through the intersection until you have attracted that driver's attention. Call out, look for the face in the window to turn toward you, watch for the car to stop.

Sometimes an aggressive motorist will try to outbluff you by inching forward at a stop sign. Keep moving and keep pedaling—and 999 times out of 1,000, the motorist will stop and grant you your legal right of way. The 1,000th time, you can easily get out of the way of an accident. The necessary quick-stop and turn techniques are described a little later in this chapter.

The Basic Approach

By now, the basic approach of the advice here should be clear: Be as courteous as you can, but give yourself room and space you need. Recognize that you have rights as well as responsibilities under the traffic law—you have the right to use the road, and the responsibility to be predictable and obey the law. Rights and responsibilities go together.

Most untrained bicyclists know the traffic law, but they have not learned the special bicycle maneuvers needed to ride correctly. They sneak along, weaving right and left at the edge of the road to stay in "shelter" from the cars behind them as much as possible. It is exactly this behavior which *makes* overtaking traffic dangerous. To avoid this danger, wear bright-colored clothing, use lights and reflectors at night, ride in a visible, predictable straight line, and check with the drivers behind you before changing lane position. This way, you also avoid the hazards of turning and crossing traffic ahead of you.

Sidewalks, Bike Paths, and Bike Lanes

It may sometimes seem safer to ride on a sidewalk, to avoid traffic. But watch out! Sidewalks are too narrow for safe bicycle travel. Pedestrians can walk out in front of you from behind walls and bushes; there is too little room to avoid them.

Car-bike collisions are actually *more* common for a bicyclist on a sidewalk; a car driver in a side street or driveway will look only for slow pedestrian traffic, then cross the sidewalk. For bicyclists traveling on the left sidewalk, accidents are about *ten times* as common as when riding properly on the road. Most of these accidents happen when cars pull out of side streets.

If you must ride on a sidewalk—and sometimes you

must—go slowly. Pedestrians can suddenly change direction, so get the attention of every pedestrian before you pass. Be aware of all blindspots from which a car, pedestrian, or other bicyclist could enter your path.

A bike path can be pleasant if it takes you away from roads, into a quiet, scenic area where you could not otherwise ride. But many bike paths are no wider than sidewalks, and pedestrians use them—so they present the same problems as sidewalks. Also, untrained, unpredictable bicyclists ride more often on bike paths.

A bike path which parallels a street like a sidewalk is dangerous no matter how wide, because it creates the same conflicts with crossing and turning traffic as a sidewalk. Every accident study shows that this type of bike path is more dangerous than riding on the road.

Bike lanes painted on the street have been shown to have little overall effect on bicyclists' safety—however, they do encourage bicyclists and motorists to make incorrect turns. Untrained bicyclists tend to make left turns from a bike lane without merging left, and motorists often make a right turn across a bike lane. If the correct maneuver requires you to change lanes out of the bike lane, then leave it. Painted stripes do not change what you have to do for safety.

The reason for these problems is that very few highway engineers are bicyclists. Many highway engineers still think of the bicycle as a sidewalk toy. A meaningful program to improve bicycling would spend much less money on bike lanes and bike paths and much more on law enforcement and on bicyclist and motorist education.

AVOIDING HAZARDS—STEERING, BRAKING, JUMPING

Even with the best traffic tactics, people make mistakes sometimes—and you might find yourself headed for an accident. To be ready to avoid an accident, you must learn some basics about how your bicycle steers and brakes, and then practice until the maneuvers are second nature. Accident-avoidance maneuvers are not hard to learn—though most bicyclists have never heard of them!

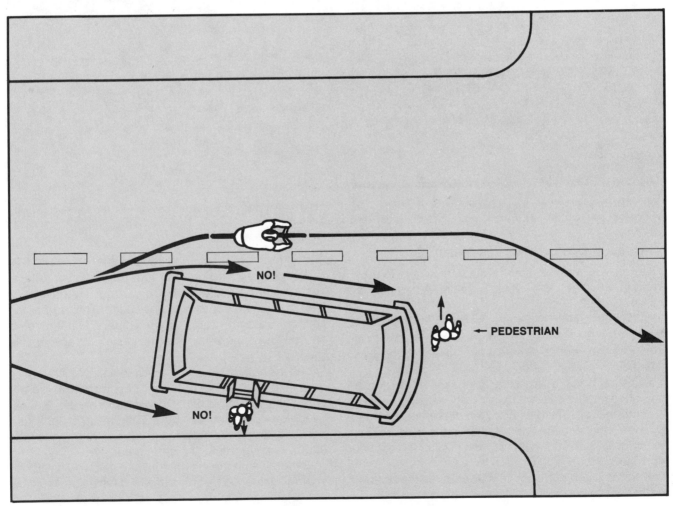

Give a bus lots of clearance, moving far enough away that the driver can see you in the rearview mirror and that you will see a pedestrian coming around the front of the bus. Never sneak along either side of a bus or any vehicle.

Blind intersections on a sidewalk require that you ride very slowly. A small child or animal could step out unseen from the stairs at the right. The young man would be safer riding properly in the street—and wearing a helmet.

Avoiding Bad Drivers: The Instant Turn

When you want to make a quick right turn in a car, you turn the steering wheel to the right. A bicycle is the same, isn't it?

It isn't. If you turn the handlebars quickly to the right, the bicycle will steer to the right and you will fall to the left. The car would also fall over if it had only two wheels.

But then how do you steer a bicycle at all? Maybe you guessed. If you want to turn right, you momentarily steer to the *left*. The bike goes left under you, and then you are leaning to the right. You whip the handlebars to the right to keep your balance, and presto, there is your right turn.

Normally, you don't notice this; you use the bicycle's normal slight weave to start a normal gentle turn. But in an emergency, you may need to force a turn.

Practice the instant turn, yanking the handlebars to one side, then recovering to turn the other way. At higher speeds, you need to turn the handlebars less, so practice carefully until you can quickly develop a lean of 35 to 40 degrees at any speed. This is near the limit of traction on clean, dry pavement. Remember to lift the inside pedal so that it doesn't scrape on the road.

The instant turn is useful to avoid a car which makes an unexpected move. If a car coming toward you begins a left turn, turn right to pass in front of it. If a car overtakes you from behind and then turns right, turn right with it. If a car pulls out in front of you from a side street, turn right into the side street.

A variation on the instant turn can help you if you find yourself going too fast on a downhill turn. Your instincts are to steer straight, to keep your balance. You must do exactly the opposite: Turn your front wheel slightly toward the *outside* of the turn, then back to deepen

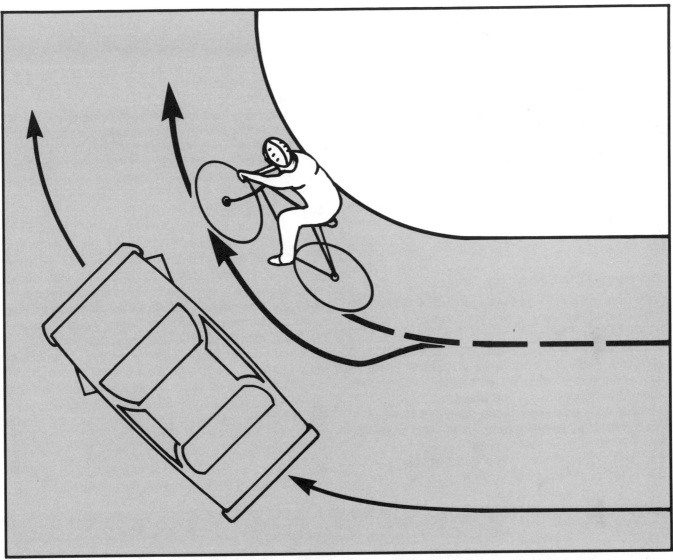

To make an instant turn, you must first turn *toward* the hazard you want to avoid. The bicyclist yanks the handlebars to the left to avoid the right-turning car.

your lean and turn more sharply. Usually, your tires have enough traction to get you around the turn. If they let go, you will slide out on your side. That hurts, but it is much better than going off the road headfirst.

Avoiding Road-surface Hazards: The Rock Dodge

Small bumps in the road are no serious problem. The bicycle's air-filled tires will "swallow" bumps which are too small to crush the tires flat against the rims. Hold the pedals level, rise off the saddle, and flex your arms and legs to cushion the ride.

You must scan the road surface for hazards which could cause a fall or damage your bicycle. If a bump is high enough to reach the rim, you must avoid it by dodging, jumping, or in an extreme case, getting off and carrying the bike.

Suppose that you see a rock on the pavement just in front of you—but you can't change direction to avoid it: You would go off the road or in front of a car. Then you must use the *rock dodge,* a maneuver related to the instant turn.

You start the rock dodge just as you do the instant turn, by yanking the handlebars to one side. The bicycle steers around the rock, but it is off balance. You then quickly *oversteer* in the opposite direction, farther than with the instant turn, so that you recover balance and direction. In a well-done rock dodge, your bicycle weaves quickly to one side and then to the other, but your body continues to travel in a straight line. With the rock dodge, like the instant turn, practice makes perfect.

Railroad Tracks and Storm Grates

A crack or step in the pavement nearly parallel to

your line of travel is more serious than a bump. For example, diagonal railroad tracks can steer your front wheel out from under you and drop you to the pavement. Look behind for traffic, then turn to cross at a right angle.

Even worse than railroad tracks is a parallel-bar sewer grate or bridge expansion joint. Your wheel can fall right in. A steel-grating bridge is very treacherous; when wet it can steer you as if you were on tracks, preventing you from balancing. Wet leaves, a wet manhole cover, or a patch of oil can drop you; as you approach such a hazard, slow down, ride straight without braking or pedaling, and be prepared to put a foot to the pavement.

Braking—The Emergency Stop

To understand bicycle brakes, try a little experiment. Walk next to your bicycle with your hands on the brake levers, rolling it forward.

Then apply the rear brake. The rear wheel will lock and skid. Apply the front brake. The front wheel will lock and the rear wheel will lift off the pavement. The same can happen while you are riding.

When you apply either brake, weight transfers to the front wheel, making the rear wheel skid easily but keeping the front wheel from skidding. For this reason, the front brake is much more effective than the rear brake. But because of a bicycle's high center of gravity,

applying the front brake too hard could pitch you over the handlebars.

For an emergency stop on a bicycle, you must apply the front brake as hard as possible without pitchover. There's a trick to this.

Squeeze the front brake lever *three times as hard as the rear brake lever.* Increase braking force until the rear wheel just begins to skid. The skidding is your signal that there isn't much weight on the rear wheel, so reduce front brake force slightly. Continue to adjust front brake force up and down to keep the rear wheel just on the edge of skidding.

This braking technique eliminates the risk of pitchover, and will stop you in two-thirds the distance you would need using both brake levers equally. Because the usual, incorrect advice leads to a lot of skidding, *and* fear of the front brake, most bicyclists never learn a proper emergency stop. The most common braking error is overuse of the *rear* brake, causing excess skidding, loss of control, and tire wear.

When you ride on a slippery or bumpy surface or when turning, your traction is reduced, so you cannot use the brakes as hard. Then, use mostly the rear brake—and use it lightly. Keep your speed down so you won't need to brake hard. Slow down *before* you come to a curve.

Practice braking techniques, so you will know them when you need them. In an empty parking lot, practice the emergency stop until you have mastered it.

This time exposure shows a rock dodge. The up-and-down curve is from a leg light, and the flatter S-curve is from a steady taillight. The camera's flash catches the bicyclist at the moment of turning his front wheel to the right to correct his balance. Note that his body has hardly changed its line of travel, while his wheels are well to the left to avoid the rock.

A grating or railroad tracks can steer the bicycle out from under the rider, while an expansion joint or storm grate like this can swallow a wheel. On this street, the bicyclist should ride out of range of this hazard, just inside the traffic lane.

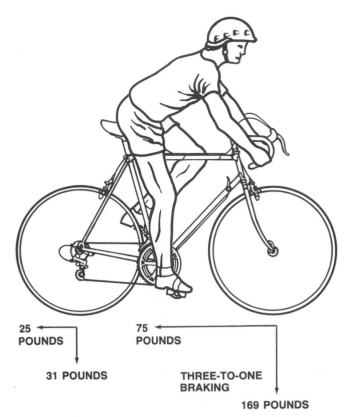

25 POUNDS

75 POUNDS

31 POUNDS

THREE-TO-ONE BRAKING

169 POUNDS

An emergency stop uses the front brake three times as hard as the rear brake, and achieves 100 pounds of drag for this 200-pound bike and rider. When the rear wheel skids, it is a signal to release the front brake slightly. A rear brake alone achieves only 60 pounds of drag.

Many bicyclists panic and grab the brakes harder as soon as the bicycle begins to go out of control. If the rear wheel leaves the pavement, you must make it second nature to *release* the brakes so you regain control. At a very low speed, practice by applying the front brake so hard that the rear wheel actually lifts off the pavement. As soon as it lifts, instantly release the brakes. Also release them whenever your bike begins to skid out of control.

For an emergency maneuver to avoid an accident, brake *or* turn, or else brake *then* turn. If you do both at once you will lay the bicycle down on its side—actually the best way to keep from going headfirst into a wall or a ditch.

Jumping

Suppose you see a big pothole ahead of you: too wide to dodge, too late to stop. If you ride into it, you'll dent your rims. With practice, you can *jump over* it.

First crouch down, with the crank horizontal. Then, as you reach the bump, yank up on the handlebars. This gets the front wheel over. As the rear wheel reaches the bump, jump up straight and draw your legs up under you. With toeclips and straps, this will lift the rear wheel over. If you do not have toeclips and straps, lifting the wheel is a bit more difficult—but BMX riders do it anyway; they call it the "bunny hop." They rotate the handlebars away to lift the rear of the bike.

Jumping is easiest on an unloaded bike. It can't be done with heavy baggage, on a recumbent, or—except with superb teamwork—on a tandem.

This cyclocross rider is poised for shock absorption or for a jump: pedals level, arms and legs flexed, slightly up off the saddle.

RIDING WITH OTHER BICYCLISTS

Bicyclists often ride together, for companionship or in competition. Riding in a group makes it possible for bicyclists to look out for each other; in this way it can be safer than riding alone. Riding in a group also makes it more likely that bicyclists will collide with each other, so there are some special cautions to observe.

The Informal Group

Normally, ride single-file. In an extra-wide lane, every second bicyclist may ride slightly farther to the right. Then each bicyclist can see farther ahead. In an informal group, keep your distance behind the rider in front of you; if you run your front wheel up against the side of another rider's rear wheel, you will not be able to balance, and your bike will be thrown out from under you.

Pass other bicyclists in an informal group only on the left. Passing is *your* responsibility. Don't sneak by on the right and force another member of your group farther into the road. Just as when passing a car, check behind for traffic before you move left to pass. Warn the bicyclist you are passing, by saying, "On your left." Give three feet of clearance—don't pass elbow-to-elbow. Bicycles are not as wide as cars, but they can turn to the side just as fast, so they need as much passing clearance.

When riding in a group, do not swerve even slightly unless you have looked back first. When you hear someone say "On your left," don't turn to see who's there—you might swerve. Ride predictably, in a straight line.

Riding side by side is necessary in order to talk with another bicyclist while riding. Side-by-side riding is legal in all but a few states. It is OK on a straight, flat road, but don't ride double-file on a crowded street or on a winding, hilly road where drivers behind you couldn't see you in time.

Don't pull up on the left of another rider unless you are sure that you can check for overtaking cars. A rearview mirror makes this easier. Courtesy requires that you pull back into a single line *before* an overtaking driver would have to slow and wait.

In a group, *every rider is on his or her own lookout.* Don't "follow the leader." It is not safe for you to change lane position or cross an intersection just because it is safe for the rider ahead of you.

When changing lanes, a line of bicyclists should "snake" across, each in turn, each looking back for traffic. This always gives an overtaking motorist a safe course of travel through the group. Stay in a neat single line or double file as you wait at an intersection—don't pile up. It is discourteous, dangerous, and illegal to swarm around cars and block their path.

The lead rider in a group should call attention to hazards ahead, calling out—for example—"Dog left," "Car up," "Glass." The first rider also points to glass and other road-surface hazards, and signals turns for the following members of the group.

The last, or "sweep," rider should be alert to overtaking traffic, and warns the group with calls of "Car back." The sweep also signals to overtaking motorists: slow signal, turn signal, or wave-by, as necessary.

An informal, unstructured group requires special attention from every member, because anyone may drift into position as lead or sweep.

Pacelines

Racers and fast tourists often *draft* one another in a structured group called a *paceline.* This is a single or double file in which each rider follows very closely behind the one in front. The following riders are sheltered from air drag by the leader, and do not have to work as hard. Every few hundred feet, the leader drops back along the side of the group, and the next rider "takes a pull."

Pacelines are fast, but there is always the risk of tangling wheels with the rider in front of you and being thrown to the ground. Draft or let yourself be drafted only if you can pay close attention and ride at a steady speed. Let the rider in front of you know when you want to draft. This rider has the right to refuse permission. If someone is drafting you, avoid using the brakes. Be especially careful to call out road hazards and to announce maneuvers—for example, saying "Slowing."

A REVIEW

Now that you have read the material on riding techniques, here is a list of common "folklore" sayings about bicycling. **CAUTION: The following statements are completely or partly incorrect. If they seem to make sense to you, go back and read this chapter!**

The "racing" riding position is an uncomfortable contortion.
Always give the right of way to cars.
Ride as if you were invisible.
Push the pedals hard for good exercise.
Do not use the front brake harder than the rear brake.
Signal all stops and turns.
Toeclips make you more likely to fall and have an accident.
Always ride as far right as possible.
Always ride single-file.

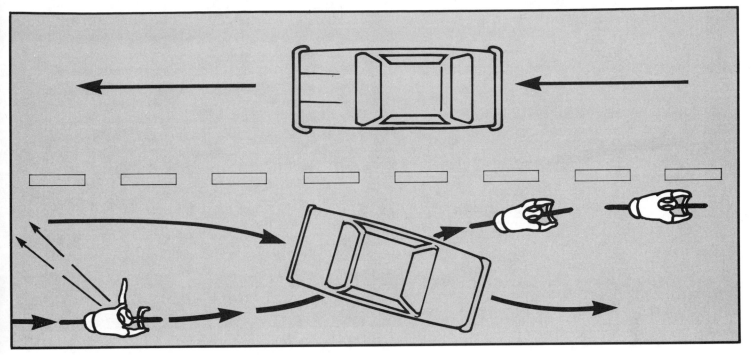

A string of bicyclists should change lanes in turn, so as to leave a car a safe path.

Watch out for the doors of parked cars and be ready to stop.

Walk across intersections.

Ride on the left so you can see what is coming.

It is impossible to ride safely on a four-lane road.

It is crazy to ride in city traffic.

Bicycling is very dangerous.

If we build bike paths and bike lanes, bicycling will be much safer.

After reading this chapter, you should be able to see the mistakes in advice of this type. If you practice and use the techniques described in this chapter, you should be able to get started in any type of bicycling. The usefulness and enjoyment of bicycling will develop rapidly for you, and your accident rate should be low—with correct riding techniques and a helmet, the lifetime risk exposure is about the same as for driving in a car.

BICYCLING HORIZONS

There are many ways to use a bicycle—for touring, racing, or commuting or just for fun and exercise. Your enjoyment of bicycling, and your progress in the sport, can be greatly increased by joining in group rides and other activities. Most urban areas of any size will have a bicyclists' organization, and in many places there are several clubs from which to choose. Different clubs emphasize recreational riding, commuting, touring, racing, and off-road riding.

To find out about local bicycle clubs, check the bulletin boards of bicycle shops. If you have already done a lot of riding on your own, you probably have a good idea what type of club might interest you. If the first club you try isn't to your liking, try another. Most will be more than happy to allow nonmembers to participate in their rides, except for sanctioned races.

If you are a beginner, take care to find a club which is interested in working with you at your level. Some clubs, even nonracing clubs, are made up almost entirely of people who like to ride fast. You will be frustrated on their rides, struggling to keep up with the group. Other clubs have a training program, or a selection of rides to suit all abilities.

Many bicycle clubs are affiliated with national organizations, which organize regional and national bicycling events and provide a framework for activities in each type of bicycling. Here's a list of national bicycling organizations:

BICYCLE USA (LEAGUE OF AMERICAN WHEELMEN)

During the early years of the bicycle, riders of the high-wheeled "ordinaries" were dubbed "wheelmen." It was only natural, therefore, that when a small band of about 120 hardy wheelmen gathered at Newport, Rhode Island, in the spring of 1880 to unite as an effective working organization, they simply called themselves the League of American Wheelmen.

The chosen name identified their membership as bicycle riders and gave an indication of their purpose.

At the pre-ride announcements of a bike club outing, the leaders describe the route and welcome newcomers.

Webster defines "league" to mean "an association of persons, parties, or countries formed to help one another" and that was exactly why the L.A.W. formed and was able to function continuously to the present. This fact enables it now to claim the distinction of being the oldest cycling club in America.

In its own words, the original purpose of the League was to "promote the general interests of bicycling; ascertain, defend and protect the rights of wheelmen; and encourage and facilitate touring."

In the early 1880s, the League established a touring bureau to furnish information relative to routes, maps, accommodations, etc. Each state division gathered information and many divisions published road books covering conditions in their area. Hotels granting reduced rates to League members were listed, in addition to railroads which permitted bicycles to be carried as luggage.

The Wheelmen's growth kept abreast of the expanding bicycle boom and by 1889 the League boasted a phenomenal membership of 102,636 cyclists. A host of famous Americans whose names have become a part of our nation's history were members of the League, including Orville and Wilbur Wright, Commodore Vanderbilt, and Diamond Jim Brady.

The League's powerful legislative efforts were responsible for the paving of streets and roads throughout the United States, before the introduction of the automobile.

Following the introduction of the mass-produced "horseless carriage," the roster of the Wheelmen dwindled to about 9,000 in 1902 and to less than 1,000 after World War II. Still this stalwart organization continued to function. In 1955, what was thought to be its last convention was held in St. Charles, Illinois, and during the following nine years the L.A.W. existed almost in name only.

A new birth through reorganization in October 1964 caused the League of American Wheelmen to spring back to life with renewed vigor and determination. Monthly, its numbers increased, and by 1985, more than 20,000 modern cyclists had rallied to its call. Members now hail from all fifty states. Many local bicycle clubs are affiliated with the League.

In the early days, the case of the individual cyclist or affiliated club was defended by the League in court and at lawmaking sessions. Today, as then, the L.A.W. continues to champion the cause of the cyclist by encouraging favorable legislation at all levels of government; acquainting bicyclists with their neighbors who share similar interests in the joys of cycling; distributing information of interest to individuals and organizations; assisting in planning and conducting cycling programs; informing the cyclist in correct riding techniques to enhance his riding enjoyment; and aiding in establishing modern bicycle facilities.

In 1984, the League adopted the trade name Bicycle USA, by vote of its directors, who felt that the original name had become confusing. Along with the name change came a shift in emphasis toward promoting bicycling rather than taking a strong stand on bicyclists' legal rights. Every year, Bicycle USA conducts three or more major rallies in various parts of the country. Here, 1,000 or more bicyclists will spend a long weekend at a college campus or other convenient accommodation, riding every day over a selection of routes ranging from a few miles to over 100, and participating in other activities which include workshops on all aspects of bicycling as well as social gatherings.

The League trains Effective Cycling instructors, has an excellent illustrated monthly publication, *Bicycle USA,* distributes detailed information on cycling events and activities, and provides special embroidered patches which may be sewn onto the cyclist's clothing to commemorate participation in particular rides or rallies.

For information, write Bicycle USA, 6707 Whitestone Road, Baltimore, MD 21207; telephone 301-944-3399.

AMERICAN YOUTH HOSTELS

Today, thousands of cyclists crisscross many countries around the world each year traveling individually, in pairs, as a family, or in groups large and small, safely and comfortably. Some join organized groups, such as the International Youth Hostel Federation, founded in Germany by Richard Schirrmann. From the single hostel he established in 1909, the number in the network has increased into the thousands. Hostels provide dormitory-style sleeping quarters, as well as cooking facilities, making it possible to travel by bicycle on a low budget, but without carrying camping gear. Facilities are located in dozens of countries in Europe, North and South America, Asia, and Africa. Total membership of all participating segments of the federation has now passed the 2 million mark.

American Youth Hostels (AYH) is the U.S. affiliate of the International Youth Hostel Federation. Membership and use of the facilities are open to people of all ages. Besides its hostels, AYH organizes group bicycle and hiking tours ranging from day trips to summer-long excursions in the United States and many foreign countries.

AYH serves individuals and organizations, such as Scouts, churches, colleges, high schools, recreation departments, Ys, and outing clubs. It's a unique world of travel, taking advantage of low-cost hostels, camps, lodges, huts, and camping areas.

In the U.S.A. and Canada, a hostel may be a school, camp, church, student house, mountain lodge, community center, farmhouse, or specially built facility for overnight accommodations. Some overseas hostels

A youth hostel such as this one on Martha's Vineyard Island in Massachusetts provides low-cost accommodations for individual bicyclists and touring groups.

are found in picturesque old castles, villas, or even retired sailing ships.

Some hostels are sponsored by local organizations or committees of townspeople. They are chartered by the national headquarters of AYH. They meet standards set by AYH and are inspected by field staff members. At these hostels, "house parents," usually retired couples, receive the traveler when he arrives. They have dorms and washrooms, a common kitchen where hostelers may cook their meals, and, usually, a recreation room. Bunks, blankets, cooking utensils, and cleaning equipment are provided, but all services are on a do-it-yourself basis.

There are hostels in the New England, Middle Atlantic, Great Lakes, and West Coast states, usually in scenic, historic, and recreational areas, with some located in cities. Often they are within a day's bike ride of each other. Smoking is not permitted in bunkrooms; alcoholic beverages and illegal drugs are not permitted.

If your budget requires careful accounting of dimes and dollars, then the hosteling program may be for you. It is nonprofit, nonsectarian, nonpolitical—a corporation organized "exclusively for charitable and educational purposes."

For information about American Youth Hostels, contact a hostel, a regional office, or the national office at P.O. Box 37613, Washington, DC 20013-7613; telephone 202-783-6161.

BIKECENTENNIAL

Bikecentennial is a nonprofit organization founded in the mid-1970s to plan a coast-to-coast bicycle tour celebrating the bicentennial of the American Revolution. It has continued since then, developing a coast-to-coast route, the Transamerica Trail, as well as several other long-distance touring routes which use scenic back roads wherever possible. Bikecentennial publishes a magazine, *BikeReport,* as well as providing maps of its routes, selling touring equipment and books, and organizing frequent group tours. For information about membership, contact Bikecentennial, P.O. Box 8308, Missoula, MT 59807; telephone 406-721-1776.

EFFECTIVE CYCLING LEAGUE

Following the Bicycle USA name change, the ECL was formed by cyclists who felt that another organization was needed to maintain a stronger position on bicyclist education and legal rights. The Effective Cycling League champions Effective Cycling instruction, and is especially willing to help advise bicyclists who feel that governmental actions—such as unreasonable bans on bicycle use on certain roads—need to be challenged to improve conditions for bicycling.

For information, contact the Effective Cycling League, 726 Madrone Avenue, Sunnyvale, CA 94086; telephone 408-734-9426.

BICYCLE FEDERATION OF AMERICA

The Bicycle Federation is an organization mainly of bicycle specialists and planners working in government at the local, state, and federal level. It publishes a newsletter, *Pro-Bike News,* is developing bicycle-education materials, and organizes conferences which bring together planners, researchers, journalists, and representatives of many bicyclists' organizations. For information, contact the Bicycle Federation of America, 1818 R Street N.W., Washington, DC 20009; telephone 202-332-6986.

NATIONAL ASSOCIATION OF BICYCLE COMMUTERS

The purpose is clear from the name. NABC publishes a newsletter full of ideas on commuting equipment and tactics. The address is 2904 Westmoreland Drive, Nashville, TN 37212.

TANDEM CLUB OF AMERICA

The Tandem Club publishes a newsletter and holds yearly rallies at which tandemists gather, ride together, and compare notes. For information, contact Peter Hutchinson, Route 1, Box 276, Esperance, NY 12066.

THE WHEELMEN

An organization of antique bicycle collectors and riders, the Wheelmen split off from the League of

Up the gangplank! These bicycle tourists rode from Boston to the end of Cape Cod, and are now taking the boat back home. Most ferryboat services provide roll-on bicycle service. Airlines, railroads, and buses often require bikes to be boxed—phone for information.

American Wheelmen many years ago when interests began to diverge. Not only do Wheelmen restore old bicycles, they also hold colorful rallies and participate in parades, where they ride in costume to demonstrate the bicycles of earlier times. For information, contact Marge Fuehrer, 1708 School House Lane, Ambler, PA 19002; telephone 215-699-3187.

Commercial Bicycle Touring Organizations

In recent years, large numbers of commercial bicycle touring companies have sprung up, serving the needs of people who want a preplanned trip. The first, Vermont Bicycle Touring, was founded in 1973. It is typical of many others. Bicyclists finish each day of a tour at a country inn. Meals and rooms are provided at the inn; ride leaders and a following van with a good stock of spare parts help take care of any difficulty on the road.

Some touring companies specialize in off-road tours and others in overseas tours; some plan routes for experienced bicyclists who want to travel without a leader, while others make bicycle touring as easy as possible for the beginner. Bicycle touring companies serve a very useful purpose for the bicyclist who must plan a vacation tightly, and who is willing to spend somewhat more money than the independent bicycle camper or hosteler. Listings of bicycle touring companies may be found in the classified advertisement pages of bicycle magazines.

Racing Organizations

Several national organizations sanction competition in each of the major areas of bicycle racing.

UNITED STATES CYCLING FEDERATION

The USCF coordinates the activities of local clubs which organize traditional road races and velodrome (oval-track) races, ranging from local competitions up to national championship races, and United States participation in yearly world championships and the Olympics. Every person who wishes to participate in regional and nationwide competition of this type must be a USCF member.

The USCF maintains a national office and publishes a monthly magazine, *Cycling USA*. For more information, contact USCF, 1750 East Boulder St. #4, Colorado Springs, CO 80909.

NATIONAL OFF-ROAD BICYCLE ORGANIZATION

If you are interested in all-terrain bike competition and rallies, this is the organization for you. NORBA sanctions races, holds regional and national rallies, and works to defend the rights of off-road bicyclists to travel on trails in publicly and privately owned lands.

A "pack" of racers speeds by spectators in a USCF-sanctioned road race. Average speed in such a race is usually over 25 miles per hour. The road is closed to normal traffic to allow the racers to maneuver freely.

For information, contact NORBA, P.O. Box 1901, Chandler, AZ 85244; telephone 714-681-1135.

TRIATHLON FEDERATION USA

Triathlons—races involving more than one sport, usually swim-bike-run—are popular with athletes who want more well-rounded training and competition than they can get from a single sport. The Triathlon Federation is the sanctioning organization. It is affiliated with numerous local triathlon clubs.

For information, contact Triathlon Federation USA, 646 Elmwood Drive, Davis, CA 95616; telephone 916-753-2831.

INTERNATIONAL HUMAN-POWERED VEHICLE ASSOCIATION

The IHPVA organizes races for new and different types of bicycles, as well as human-powered airplanes and boats. Streamlined human-powered vehicles have beaten every type of bicycle speed record, and the thinking behind them is having an increasing effect on other types of bicycling. For example, IHPVA members' research led to the spokeless wheels and streamlined helmets used by United States Olympic track racers.

If you might be interested in building or racing an HPV or attending a race, contact IHPVA, P.O. Box 2068, Seal Beach, CA 90740; telephone 714-987-8003

BICYCLE MOTOCROSS

Two organizations, the American Bicycle Association and the National Bicycle League, sanction compe-

A racer changes from swimming to bicycling clothes at the transition area of a sanctioned triathlon. In the background, another racer leaves on his bicycle.

tition in bicycle motocross (short races on dirt tracks)—mostly a teenagers' sport.

For information, contact the American Bicycle Association, P.O. Box 718, Chandler, AZ 85224; telephone 602-961-1903; or the National Bicycle League, 84 Park Avenue, Flemington, NJ 08822; telephone 201-788-3800.

BICYCLE MAGAZINES

Besides the magazines mentioned above published by bicyclists' organizations, there are many independent magazines that serve bicyclists' needs. Magazines keep you up to date with bicycling news and new products. They provide useful "how-to" articles on many aspects of bicycling. Find magazines at a bike shop or a newsstand or by inquiring at the addresses given below.

General-interest Magazines

Bicycle Guide. P.O. Box 2325, Boulder, CO 80322.
Bicycling. Rodale Press, 33 East Minor St., Emmaus, PA 18049.
Cyclist. 20916 Higgins Court, Torrance, CA 90501.

Specialty Magazines

Bicycle Forum. Magazine relating to governmental planning, bicyclist education, and law enforcement. P.O. Box 8311, Missoula, MT 59307.
Bicycle Rider. Touring emphasis. TL Enterprises, 29901 Agoura Road, Agoura, CA 91301.
Bike Tech. Publishes articles on scientific research related to bicycling. Rodale Press, 33 East Minor St., Emmaus, PA 18049.
Fat Tire Flyer. All-terrain bike magazine. P.O. Box 757, Fairfax, CA 90501.
Tri-Athlete. 6660 Banning Drive, Oakland, CA 94611.
Triathlon. 8641 Warner Drive, Culver City, CA 90230.
Velo-News. Bicycle-racing newspaper, giving race results and articles of interest to racers. P.O. Box 1257, Brattleboro, VT 05301.
Winning: Bicycle Racing Illustrated. Monthly magazine on bicycle racing, with extensive coverage of European races. 1127 Hamilton St., Allentown, PA 18102.

BOOKS

There are many books about bicycling. Here is a list of a few important ones containing information outside the scope of the book you are reading now.

How-to Books

The Bicycling Book, edited by John and Vera Kraus (New York: Dial Press, 1982). A big smorgasbord of articles about all types of bicycling—informative and fun.
Effective Cycling, by John Forester (Cambridge, MA: MIT Press, 1984). This book contains a very thorough description of traffic riding techniques, besides extensive how-to information on other bicycling subjects.
The Mountain Bike Book, by Rob van der Plas (New York: Velo Press, 1984). A how-to book for all-terrain bike riders.
Beginning Bicycle Racing, by Fred Matheny (Brattleboro, VT: Velo-News, 1983). A guide for the person interested in road or track racing.
The Bicycle Touring Book, by Tim and Glenda Wilhelm (Emmaus, PA: Rodale Press, 1980). How-to for long-distance bicycle travel including bicycle camping.
Multi-Fitness, by John Howard, Albert Gross, and Christian Paul (New York: Macmillan, 1985). A book which applies fitness goals to any type of exercise; Howard is the inventor of the triathlon.
Designing and Building Your Own Frameset, by Richard P. Talbot (Babson Park, MA: Manet Guild, 1984). Besides showing how to make a bicycle

frame for yourself, this book has invaluable background material on frame fitting, maintenance, and design and construction principles.

Background Reading

Bicycle Transportation, by John Forester (Cambridge, MA: MIT Press, 1983). The essential text on transportation planning for bicycling; no government program related to bicycling should be undertaken without reference to this book.

Sutherland's Handbook for Bicycle Mechanics, by Howard Sutherland et al., fourth edition (Sutherland's, P.O. Box 9061, Berkeley, CA 94709). The bible of parts interchangeability, a must item for every professional mechanic or bike shop.

Guide for the Development of New Bicycle Facilities—1981. $3.75 from the American Association of State Highway and Transportation Officials (AASHTO), 444 N. Capitol St., N.W., Suite 225, Washington, DC 20001. A federally sanctioned handbook on bicycle facilities and programs, largely based on suggestions from bicyclists.

Bicycle Facilities Planning and Design Manual, 1982. $6.65 from the Florida Department of Transportation, 605 Suwanee St., Tallahassee, FL 32301. The information is based on the AASHTO guide, above, but also includes a description of the bicycle planning process.

Bicycle Parking. $4.95 from Ellen Fletcher, 777-108 San Antonio Road, Palo Alto, CA 94303.

Bicycling Science, by Frank Rowland Whitt and David Gordon Wilson, second edition (Cambridge, MA: MIT Press, 1981). The essential source book on the scientific principles of bicycle design, construction, propulsion, and maneuvering. Very readable—not an engineering text!

4 • TOOLS AND SUPPLIES

You don't need many tools and supplies to work on your bicycle, but you need the right ones. You can buy some of your tools at any hardware store; others are special items available only at bike shops. The first tools you buy should prepare you to handle common on-the-road repairs such as a flat tire.

A full maintenance program in a home workshop requires more tools, and some thought to organizing your work area. You can save yourself time and money by maintaining a stock of spare parts. This chapter is intended to give the guidance you might need to set up an efficient bicycle workshop.

BASIC ON-THE-ROAD TOOL KIT

Buy the following tools and carry them with you whenever you ride your bicycle. They will get you through most on-the-road repairs. Except for the tire pump, which clips to the frame, all of these tools fit in a small pouch. Sometimes you can buy a neatly packaged kit which includes most of these tools, but every bicycle has a few special tool requirements, so you may have to make a few additions to a prepackaged kit.

Buy good-quality tools. Cheap tools wear out fast and can damage your bike, so they cost more in the long run. Some major brands of fine tools carry a lifetime guarantee.

Framefit Tire Pump

Buy a pump which clips to your bicycle's frame and fits your tire valves. There are two common types of tire valves in use on bicycles: Schraeder (automotive-type) and the smaller Presta.

The cheapest framefit (carry-along) bicycle pumps have a hose that attaches to the tire valve. Inflating a tire fully can be difficult with a cheap pump, especially if you do not have strong arms. Better pumps have a locking head which clamps around the valve stem and prevents air from escaping. A pump with a thin barrel is preferable; it may take a few more strokes to reach full pressure, but it is much easier to push.

Tire-pressure Gauge

Most tire-pressure gauges sold at auto parts stores register only up to 50 pounds per square inch. Buy yours at a bicycle shop; it must read to 100 pounds or more. Schraeder and Presta valves require different tire-pressure gauges. Buy the gauge which fits your valves. A few framefit bicycle pumps have a built-in gauge, making a separate gauge unnecessary.

Tire-patch Kit

Buy a small patch kit at a bicycle shop. It should have thin, tapered patches, a small tube of patch cement, and a scrap of sandpaper. Large patches in kits intended for automobile inner tubes are not only bulky but work poorly. Their thick patches overstress a thin bicycle inner tube, and the coarse metal grater included in these kits can cut right through one.

Tire Irons

Usually sold in a set of three, tire irons aid in levering a tire off the rim to get at the inner tube. If you lose one of your tire irons, don't despair; two will do the job. Your screwdriver is no substitute, though; too often, it will make a new hole in the inner tube.

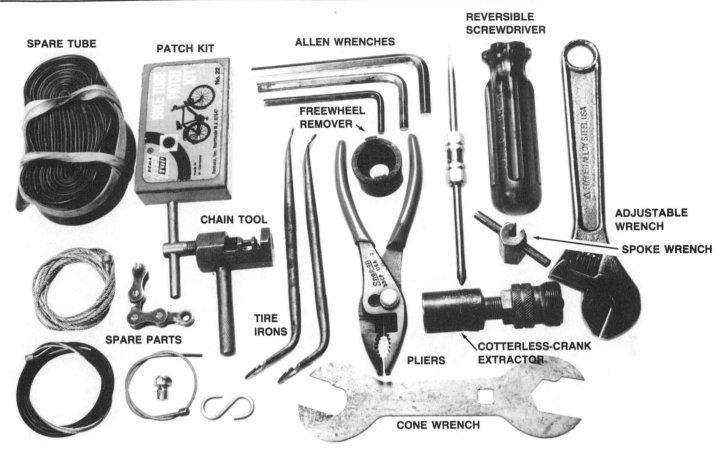

The basic on-the-road tool kit includes tire-repair supplies, adjustable wrench, cone wrenches, Allen wrenches, reversible screwdriver, spoke wrench, freewheel remover, cotterless-crank extractor, and chain-rivet tool.

Adjustable Wrench

The adjustable wrench is important because there are so many different sizes of nuts and bolts on bicycles. There are two systems of English dimensions, besides metric. Often, all will be represented on the same bicycle. While a bicycle shop will have a full set of fixed wrenches of each type, these would be heavy baggage in a traveling tool kit.

Buy a 6-inch adjustable wrench for general use. If you have weak hands, buy an 8-inch one instead, for more leverage. It is best to buy a high-quality American-made wrench, which will weigh less and last longer. Usually, the best deals on wrenches are in the tool department of a hardware store or department store.

Open-end and Box-end Wrenches

In addition to the adjustable wrench, it is helpful to carry a few small open-end and box-end wrenches in the more common sizes, especially for work on brakes. Save weight by buying double-ended wrenches. Common useful sizes are 7, 8, 9 and 10 mm. Check your bike to see what it needs. Bike shops carry these wrenches.

Hub-cone Wrenches

These are thin open-end wrenches used to adjust hub bearings. Cone-wrench sizes differ from one bicycle to another, so either buy a full set or take your bicycle with you to the bike shop when you buy one.

Allen Wrenches

Many modern bicycle components have recessed-head bolts with the hexagonal holes for these wrenches. Allen wrenches are simple and lightweight. On bicycles, 5mm and 6mm Allen fittings are common; 3mm, 4mm, and 7mm fittings are less common. Buy these wrenches at the bike shop or at a well-stocked hardware store; take your bicycle so you can find out what you need.

Spoke Wrench

This small, slotted wrench is needed to replace broken spokes and to repair a damaged wheel. Spoke nipple dimensions are not all the same; check the fit before buying your spoke wrench.

A frame-mounted tire pump is essential for on-road repairs. The type at the right, with a locking head, is easier to use.

Cotterless-crank Extractor

Most bicycles are sold with cotterless cranks these days; each arm of the crank has a square hole which fits over a square axle end. The cotterless-crank extractor is two tools in one: a wrench to turn the bolt that holds the crank to the axle, and a small gear-puller to pull the crank off the axle. Buy this at a bicycle shop. Different models of crank require different extractors, so take the bike with you.

Chain-rivet Extractor

This tool is necessary to replace a chain on a derailleur-equipped bicycle, and is helpful to clean a chain. On-the-road trouble with a chain is rare, but this tool is small, light, and convenient. Sometimes it is easier to take a chain apart to remove it from the derailleurs than to take them apart. Some types of chain, particularly the Shimano Uniglide chain, require a special extractor; check before you buy yours.

ON-THE-ROAD REPAIR MATERIALS

There are a few spare parts which it makes sense to carry in your on-the-road tool kit.

Spare Cables

Brake and shift cables can break without warning, so carry a spare for the *rear* brake or derailleur: Coil up the excess length if it is the front cable that needs replacement.

A cable has a molded-on metal fitting at one end to secure it to the brake lever or shift lever. "Universal" cables are sold with a different type of fitting on each end. Have the bike shop cut off the end you don't need, or cut it off yourself—or else you won't be able to install the cable. A drop of instant glue on the cut end will prevent the cable from unraveling.

Spare Bulbs and Batteries

If you ride at night, carry spares for your lights. Some lights have a clip for a spare bulb inside the housing; otherwise, you can carry bulbs in a 35mm film can cushioned with tissue.

Spare Spokes

Especially on a longer trip, you may need to replace a broken spoke. Spare spokes must be of the same length as those on your bicycle; sometimes lengths are different on the front and rear wheels. You can carry your spokes taped to the bicycle frame.

Screwdriver

Small bolts on your bicycle may have plain slotted or Phillips (cross-slotted) heads. The most convenient screwdriver has a reversible shaft to fit both. This may not even be necessary on your bicycle, as most Phillips screws used on bicycles have one slot widened so they will also work with a plain screwdriver. Check to see.

Freewheel Remover

You'll need this special splined or slotted tool to fit the brand and model of freewheel (rear-wheel sprocket assembly) on a derailleur-equipped bike. This will let you take off the freewheel to install a new one, or to get at a broken spoke on the right side of the rear hub.

Lubricants

A small can of lightweight spray lubricant is helpful to quiet a squeaky chain and is worth carrying on a lengthy tour, especially if there might be bad weather. During a longer ride, a small bottle or can of medium-weight oil also comes in useful for cables, brake pivots, and threaded parts. Buy a good bicycle oil. **CAUTION: So-called "household" oil, such as 3-in-1, has a vegetable base and contains acids. It will harden and gum up mechanical parts.**

You'll rarely need grease for an on-road repair, but it has many uses in the home shop; you might as well buy it with the other lubricants. Buy a good multipurpose bicycle grease.

Spare Inner Tube and Tire

If your bicycle has quick-release hubs, it is much faster to replace an inner tube than to patch one—especially helpful in bad weather or if you are commuting to work. Also, a tire or tube sometimes becomes damaged beyond repair, so it's worth carrying spares on a long tour. Special foldable tires are available, but you can also roll a conventional tire into *three* loops and fit it into a small bicycle bag. Tape it together so it

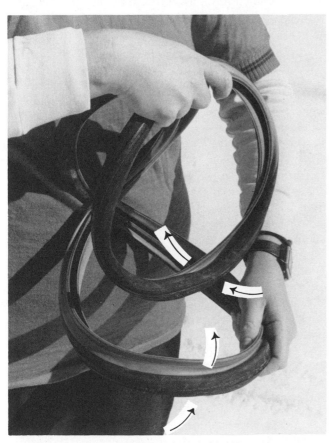

It is easy to roll a tire into a triple loop as shown, so it will fit into a bicycle bag.

won't pop open unexpectedly. Don't try to roll it into two loops—you'll just end up with a large, clumsy figure-eight.

EQUIPPING THE WORKSHOP

Beyond the on-the-road tool kit, additional tools are required for overhauls.

Many of the tools listed here are common and inexpensive; others are rare or expensive. In many cases, you could make a substitute tool cheaply, or use a somewhat more time-consuming technique that does without the tool. Such possibilities are covered in the following section and in the chapters on overhaul of the different parts of the bike. If you doubt whether you need a tool, you can afford to wait until you are learning the particular repair in which the tool is used.

Tools are listed here in approximate order of importance.

Work Stand

A work stand raises the bicycle to a convenient height and allows both wheels to turn. Many commercial work stands are available. Some are floor-standing; others attach to a wall and double as bicycle storage racks. Many have a clamp which secures the bicycle by one of its frame tubes.

CAUTION: Always position the frame-tube clamp of a work stand over a bare section of the frame. A fitting or cable under the work stand's clamp can dent the frame.

A compact, improvised work stand for the home shop can be made of a couple of loops of rope hung from hooks in the ceiling, about 3 feet apart. One loop goes under the saddle, the other under the handlebars. You could even hang the front of the saddle over an overhead pipe or a tree branch—especially useful in on-the-road repairs. If you happen to have a car-trunk rack for your bicycle, this can also serve as an outdoor work stand.

CAUTION: Do not rest a bicycle with dropped handlebars upside down. The weight will fall on the brake cables and kink them. Even on a bicycle with wide, upturned handlebars, it's inconvenient to work on parts which rest on or near the floor. It's better to prop the bike against a wall or lay it on its side for many jobs.

Bottom-bracket Tool Set

It is possible to rebuild a bottom bracket (crank axle assembly) using a hammer and punch or large lock-joint pliers, but they will leave a visible mark. A set of tools made especially for your brand of bottom bracket

An inexpensive and effective work stand may be made from loops of rope strung from hooks in the ceiling.

Do not turn a bicycle with dropped handlebars upside down, or you will damage the brake cables.

will include all of the necessary wrench sizes. You may be able to use substitutes for some of these tools or make them yourself; see Chapter 15 for more details.

12-inch or 15-inch Adjustable Wrench

A 12-inch adjustable wrench fits most headsets (steering assemblies). The 15-inch size also fits bottom-bracket cups with wrench flats. Either a 12-inch or a 15-inch adjustable wrench will turn a freewheel remover. Buy one at a hardware store.

Cable Cutters

These are special wire cutters with four-sided jaws, sold at a bike shop. Cable cutters will clip a multistrand bicycle control cable neatly; regular wire cutters will fray a cable.

Files

A flat file is needed to shape crank cotters and neaten cable-housing ends, and is useful for many small jobs of smoothing and fitting. Buy a relatively small file, with medium-fine teeth. A small half-round file and rattail (round) file are also useful for a few jobs where you have to cut an inside curve.

Adjustable Pin Spanner

This special wrench turns headset parts, bottom-bracket cups, freewheel lockrings, and other parts which have two small drilled holes opposite each other.

Chain Whips

You must have two chain whips (lengths of bicycle chain attached to metal handles) to remove sprockets from a multi-sprocket freewheel. Chain whips are inexpensive, and they are also easy to make out of scraps of metal and some old chain.

Punches

A set of small drift punches (punches with flat ends) in several sizes is needed to install and remove some parts of multispeed hubs.

A center punch (pointed-end punch) will establish the position of holes for drilling and also stake (lock) parts together.

Buy these at a hardware store or department store.

Hammers and Mallets

You'll need a hammer with a steel head to drive

punches and to loosen some reluctant parts. A normal-weight (approximately 16-ounce) carpenter's claw hammer will do, if you already have one for woodwork, though a ball-peen hammer (with a flat face like a carpenter's hammer and a ball-shaped face which replaces the claw) is more traditional for metalwork—it allows you to reshape sheet-metal parts and flatten rivets.

A well-equipped shop will have a rubber mallet for frame-straightening work and a plastic mallet to loosen handlebar-stem bolts. If you do such work only rarely, use your regular hammer cushioned with a wooden block.

Tweezers

Ordinary tweezers from a drugstore are ideal for installing bearing balls without getting dirt on them and for handling other small parts.

Slip-joint Pliers

A small pair of slip-joint pliers will help you pull cables tight and will perform a large number of grabbing and holding tasks. **CAUTION: Pliers do not substitute for wrenches: They will round off nuts and bolts.**

Measuring Tools

An accurate metal ruler with etched divisions lets you check for wear in a bicycle chain and measure spokes. Accuracy is important; don't use a wooden or plastic ruler, which can change size with the weather, or a ruler with painted-on divisions, which may never have been accurate. A foot-long ruler with inch and metric divisions is enough.

A ¼-inch-wide flat self-retracting tape measure 3 meters or 8 feet long, preferably with metric divisions, is useful to measure rims for spokes, and to measure bicycle frame sizes.

A vernier caliper can help you measure the diameter of parts very accurately and keep you from assembling parts which don't really fit each other. An adjustable wrench can be used to substitute for this tool much of the time.

A thread gauge, inch and metric, will help you avoid threading together parts which do not fit properly. It is possible to compare threads directly in many cases and get by without this tool.

Bench Vise

A *large* metalworker's bench vise makes freewheel

removal easier than with an adjustable wrench; even a small vise is very useful to hold small assemblies while working on them. A large vise can be expensive unless you buy it used or on sale. The vise must bolt to a workbench for full effectiveness.

Socket Wrenches

The wrenches listed up to this point will turn all of the fasteners on your bicycle. However, it is more convenient to have wrenches of different types for some uses. Work goes faster if you have a ¼-inch-drive metric socket wrench set with a ratchet, spinner, 4-inch extension, universal joint, and Allen, Phillips, and slotted-screwdriver fittings. A well-equipped shop will also have full sets of metric and inch-size open and box-end wrenches.

Universal Cotterless-crank Extractor

This special bike tool is larger and heavier than the one which fits only one type of crank, but it is worth having if you work on several bicycles. Note that it does *not* fit older Stronglight cranks correctly; you will need the correct Stronglight tool.

Pedal Wrench

It is possible to remove and install most pedals with your adjustable wrench, but some pedals need this special narrow wrench. It is extra-long, providing the leverage needed to remove rusted-in pedals.

Floor Pump

This inflates tires much faster than your framefit pump. It is a real convenience if you do much work on wheels or if you have lightweight tires which must be reinflated frequently. Better floor pumps have a built-in air reservoir and pressure gauge.

Vise-grip Pliers

These special pliers with a double-leverage system are especially useful for gripping rounded or frozen nuts and bolts. They will loosen parts which it is no longer possible to turn with a wrench. A 10-inch Vise-Grip works for large jobs; a 4-inch is worth carrying in your on-the-road tool kit. Buy these at a hardware store.

Hacksaw

A hacksaw will help you build brackets and fittings. You may also occasionally need it to cut apart a component that has rusted or bent and cannot be removed normally.

Rim Jack

This special bike tool pulls out flat spots in a damaged wheel—a real help if you do much wheel work.

Dishing Gauge

This tool is used when building a spoked wheel, to determine that the rim is properly centered on the hub axle.

Drill and Drill Bits

A small electric or hand drill with a set of drill bits is very useful in fashioning brackets and fittings for accessories on your bicycle.

Soldering Iron and Electrical Solder

These hardware-store items will help you make se-

cure connections in bicycle lighting systems and tin the ends of control cables so they can't unravel.

Bench Grinder

An electrically powered grinding wheel is useful to sharpen other tools and to resurface and shape some small bicycle parts, especially ones of very hard steel which a file will not cut.

Specialty Tools

The tools listed above will assemble and disassemble conventional bicycle components. Unusual components—for example, sealed-bearing components—may require special tools.

This may be obvious from the appearance of the component, but always read the manufacturer's instructions before working on an unusual component. Sometimes a special tool is necessary to avoid damaging a component on which the conventional tool would appear to work properly. This is especially true of sealed-bearing components.

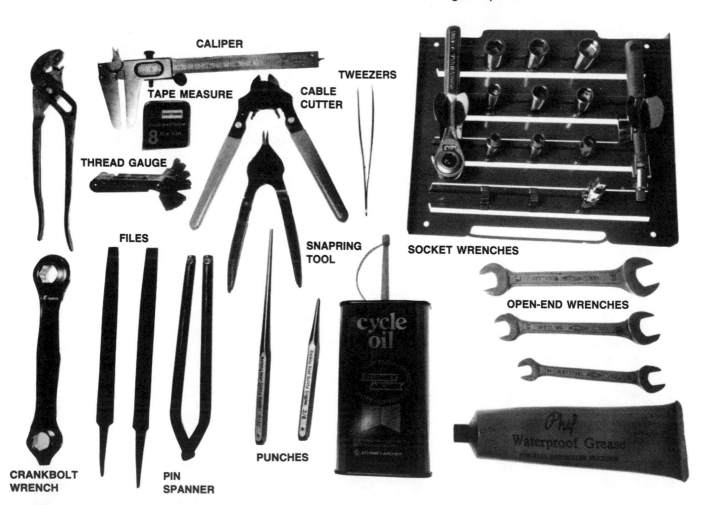

A selection of small tools for the workshop.

CLEANING PARTS

When rebuilding the bearings and other mechanical parts of a bicycle, it is very important to get them perfectly clean. During a ride, sand and grit can enter through the crack between the moving and stationary parts of a bearing. Also, normal wear releases tiny flakes of metal. If these are allowed to accumulate in the lubricant, wear will speed up and the bearings will fail prematurely. Regular rebuilding with thorough cleaning of parts is important to replace old, contaminated grease *before* serious wear begins.

Solvents

To clean mechanical parts, you must use a solvent which dissolves and washes away the old grease or oil along with the dirt. Some good solvents for bicycle work are kerosene, paint thinner, automotive-parts cleaner, and isopropyl alcohol.

You can buy kerosene at hardware stores and at some gasoline stations. Paint thinner is sold at hardware stores. These will cut grease faster if you add in a commercial auto-parts cleaning compound, sold at auto-parts stores. Follow the mixing instructions on the can. Some types of parts cleaner can damage paint. Keep them away from the painted parts of your bicycle and other painted or plastic surfaces.

Solvents smell unpleasant, and getting them on your hands and breathing the vapors is not good for you. Automotive-parts cleaning fluid is unhealthier than kerosene alone. Read the cautions on the label. Use solvents in a well-ventilated place, outdoors if possible, and if you will be handling parts wet with solvent very much, wear rubber gloves.

Isopropyl alcohol is an effective solvent. It costs more than kerosene or paint thinner, but it is much less smelly and unhealthful. If you must work where there is poor ventilation, it's the best choice. You can buy it at a drugstore.

CAUTION: Do not use gasoline! It is very dangerous. It evaporates quickly, and the vapor flows along the floor, where any tiny spark or flame is enough to set off a big explosion and fire.

Lacquer thinner is not the same as paint thinner. Like gasoline, it evaporates very rapidly and can make you sick.

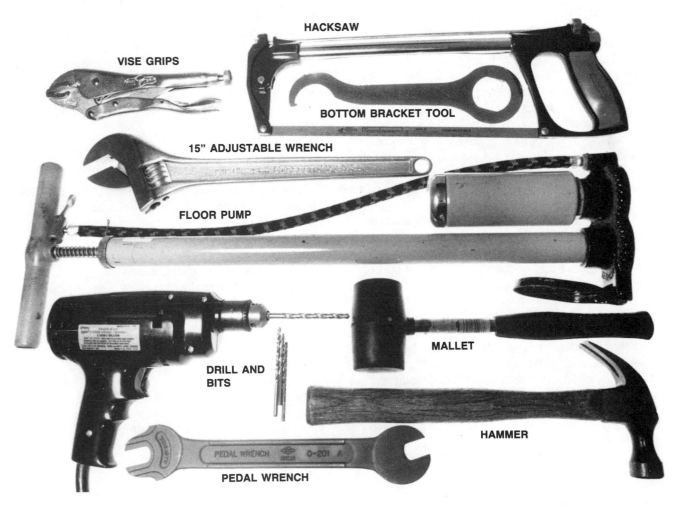

Larger workshop tools.

Cleaning supplies: solvent, parts cleaner, scrub brush, old toothbrush, "invisible glove," and hand cleaner.

The Parts Washer

You could just slosh parts around in a pan with your solvent, but especially with small parts, a well-designed parts washer makes the job neater and makes the solvent last much longer.

You can buy a commercial parts washer or make one. Use an old gallon paint can and a small-mesh food strainer. Fill the can with solvent. Drop small parts into the strainer to soak. The strainer lets you retrieve parts easily, while dirt particles sink to the bottom. Every once in a while, pour off the solvent in the top of the can and dispose of the grit in the bottom. When the solvent becomes too oily to cut grease, dispose of it in a service station's oil-recycling barrel.

CAUTION: Do not run solvent down a sewer. It can damage septic-tank systems and can contaminate water supplies.

Often, scrubbing is necessary to remove hardened grease from mechanical parts. Make sure you remove it all, so you can see bare metal. A screwdriver will scrape dirt from between chainwheels. An old toothbrush is ideal for scrubbing out small nooks and crannies. Rags and a small scrub brush will take care of larger parts. For parts too large to fit into the parts cleaner, lay out old newspapers or a cookie tin and use a scrub brush dipped in solvent.

After the solvent bath, a final washing with dishwashing detergent and rinsing with water are good to get parts completely clean. Commercial parts-cleaning fluids in fact require a water rinse. Water is cheap, so you can run a lot of water over a part to get rid of those few last particles of grit. Don't worry about rusting; just dry the parts thoroughly before reassembling them.

Cleaning the Outside of the Bicycle

Clean the outside of a mechanical assembly as well as the inside; when you put it back together, grit might fall into the new clean grease and spoil it right away. When you rebuild a hub or pedal, clean the shell; when you rebuild a headset or bottom bracket, clean the surrounding area of the frame inside and outside. If you rebuild the entire bike at once, you have a good opportunity to clean the entire frame.

CAUTION: Some commercial parts-cleaning compounds dissolve paint, so don't use them to clean the frame. Kerosene, paint thinner, and isopropyl alcohol are safe on paint. These are useful where greasy dirt has accumulated.

Hosing the frame off with detergent and water is effective for road dirt and mud on the frame and rims. Try to keep too much water from seeping inside the frame tubes where the components attach. A coat of automobile wax or furniture wax will help preserve the paint and make it easier to clean next time.

CAUTION: Keep wax, solvent, and lubricants away from rubber parts and rim braking surfaces. They can damage rubber and can make the brakes slip or grab.

If you ride your bike much in muddy or slushy conditions, you may be tempted to clean the frame frequently. However, excessive cleaning can wash dirt and water into the bearings. Unless the bearings have been converted for oil lubrication or forced grease lubrication (page 67), it is better to leave the bike dirty until rebuild time.

Keeping Yourself Clean While Working

Fortunately, you are unlikely to get dirt all over yourself when working on a bicycle, but you can get your hands dirty.

Chain marks are the main hazard to your clothing. A shop apron helps prevent them. For an on-the-road repair, use your rain cape, inside out.

The chain is the part which most often leaves lasting dirt on your hands. Avoid handling it if you can. Keep a thin pair of work gloves for chain work. If the chain comes off the sprockets during a ride, hold it with a screwdriver, a piece of paper, or a leaf as you lift it back into place.

For a long repair session, auto-supply stores sell a compound which forms an "invisible glove." Be sure to get a lot of it under your fingernails. Cooking oil rubbed into your hands is also fairly effective.

Mechanics' waterless hand cleaner is best to clean greasy hands. Rub it in until it lifts the dirt, then wash with soap and water.

A small fingernail brush helps remove the last traces of dirt.

SETTING UP THE HOME WORKSHOP

Bicycle work can be much more pleasant if your work area is organized to make it easy to find tools and keep projects in order.

The Work Area

Your work area needs to be large enough so you can walk around your bicycle on its work stand. The work area should be well lighted, dry, and well ventilated, with a hard floor surface which can be mopped clean.

It is convenient to keep your shop set up permanently; it's easier to leave a project and come back to it if you can leave parts spread out on a bench. However, the tools and supplies you need for bicycle work will fit in a couple of cardboard boxes in a closet. Then you can carry them to where you will use them. If you have to work on bikes on your living-room floor, roll back the carpet so you won't lose small parts in it or stain it. In good weather, you can work outdoors—maybe the only option if you live in a cramped apartment or dormitory.

A traditional workbench with a metalworker's vise is best, but any sturdy table will do. Bike parts can be oily and dirty, so cover your workbench with newspapers or other protection if you also use it for woodwork or for dining. Especially if your work-area floor might become damp, it helps if the workbench has a shelf underneath to store boxes of tools and parts.

Tool Storage

A mechanic's tool box will keep together your collection of hand tools, or you may hang them on the wall either with a pegboard or by driving nails into a sheet of plywood. Outlines of the tools drawn with a felt-tip marker will show you instantly which ones have strayed at the end of a work session. A freestanding chest with drawers makes sense if you have a lot of tools and spare parts.

Parts Storage

If you don't buy a parts chest, you can organize spare parts quite well using salvaged containers. Plastic gallon milk jugs with the top cut down diagonally, leaving the handle, are convenient for storing medium-sized parts such as pedals and freewheels. Several milk jugs will fit in a cardboard box, making it easy to haul them up from under the workbench. Then you can lift each jug out by its handle. Keep extra cardboard boxes for larger parts.

For small parts like nuts, bolts, and bearing balls, a set of miniature shelves with drawers is most convenient; hardware stores sell these. Plastic 35mm film cans also work well for small parts. Any photo processing shop will give these away. Take a couple of dozen.

Label containers for your parts and tools, especially if the storage container hides them. Keep a roll of masking tape and a felt-tip marker in the shop. Then you won't have to open all of your film cans to know which one has the ¼-inch bearing balls.

ORGANIZING AND PLANNING YOUR WORK

Plan your bicycle maintenance projects for the long term, and maintain a stock of spare parts to save time and money.

Planning a Project

Before you begin any maintenance project, first try to obtain all supplies you may need. This way, you can ride to the bike shop before you have disassembled your bicycle. A reputable bike shop will take back parts that you don't need, so keep your receipt.

Make telephone calls to bike shops to locate the parts you need. Unless you're sure what you need, take the bike, or the part which you are going to rebuild, with you when shopping. Do not throw away any old parts until you have made sure that your new parts match them. Take notes as you rebuild a part so that you'll know the parts needed for your next rebuild.

Stocking Up on Spare Parts

There are a few spare parts used so often that it always makes sense to buy them in advance: bearing balls, inner tubes and tires, handlebar tape, small nuts

A well-equipped home workshop, with storage area *(left),* tool board, and work stand.

and bolts, and similar items which you need repeatedly but which are not worth a trip to the bike shop.

CAUTION: Never mix bearing balls from different sources, or new and worn balls. Balls from different production runs may be different enough in size that the larger balls will carry all of the load.

Beyond keeping regularly needed supplies, you can save money on rebuilds by stocking up on parts for your make and model of bicycle. Bike shop sales, used-part bins, mail-order offerings in the bicycle magazines, bicycle club bulletins, flea markets, and classified advertisements are sources for new and used parts at bargain prices.

You may accumulate parts toward the next rebuild of your current bike, or you may try to scrape together most of the parts to build up a complete "new" bike. As you come to know what is marketable, you may also buy parts to trade with other bicyclists. If you're not in a hurry, you can cut your component costs way down. Fortunately, bicycle parts are compact. A couple of cardboard boxes will hold a stock of parts which will last for years.

Make a special effort to look for spare parts if your bike has any unusual or old components. Many parts have gone in and out of production over the years. Especially, stock up on chainwheels and on parts for geared hubs; it is annoying to have to replace an entire hub or crankset for the lack of one crucial part. Many models which are no longer in production were once very common, and there are still many of them available for salvage.

Upgrading Your Bicycle

Every time a part wears out, you have an opportunity to replace it with one which fits your needs better. If you have to replace a worn-out component anyway, you might as well replace it with something more to your liking.

You could buy a component which will last longer, makes the bike fit you better, or suits it better to your particular use. For example, it makes good sense to replace an uncomfortable saddle, even if it's in good condition; and it makes good sense to equip your bike with lower gears if you live in hilly country.

One useful trick, especially if you ride in a city, is to put together a bicycle out of high-grade parts which look beat-up. This rides like a new bike but is unattractive to thieves. There are a couple of pitfalls to avoid in an upgrading project, though.

It doesn't make sense to put high-grade components on a poor-quality or damaged frame. It won't be good to ride or worth much to sell. The positive side of this is that a bargain frame is an especially nice find, the starting point for a bike-building project.

You can't save money by assembling all-new components. Thanks to manufacturers' buying power, a complete, assembled bike costs less than the parts to build one. Nonetheless, some people choose to assemble new components into a bike, simply so they can choose the exact parts they want.

Basic Repairs

5 • MAINTENANCE BASICS

This chapter outlines a regular maintenance program for your bicycle. It also includes some basic information on tool use, mechanical construction of the bicycle, and lubrication.

For the cyclist active in racing, touring, or merely riding for pleasure or health, the results of maintenance work are immediately evident in less effort for the distance traveled, or in more speed for the amount of energy expended, not to mention the dollar savings in parts and labor.

A national study, including all types of bicyclists, classed 17 percent of bicycle accidents as being due to mechanical failure. Another study, limited to adult bike club members, found only 3 percent of accidents due to mechanical failures. Why the difference?

Mostly, it's that the bike club members kept mechanical performance high, catching problems before they led to abrupt failures. The good riding skills of these cyclists also contributed to their accident rate, one-fifth of the national average.

AVOIDING CREEPING DECAY

It is easy to let a bicycle's performance deteriorate when changes happen slowly. Brakes wear out, bearings loosen up, cables dry out and stick, but there are no dramatic changes from one day to the next.

If you let your bike deteriorate, you tend to ride within its limitations. You can't ride fast because you know that it wouldn't be safe. The brakes are weak, the steering is shaky, the tires are about to blow out.

Don't let it happen. Your bike could fail you when you can't afford to lose control.

If your bicycle does not seem to work right, read through the problem charts in the chapters about the different parts of the bicycle. These will help you find the cause of the problem; then perform the necessary maintenance. If you follow the instructions in this book and rebuild your bike regularly, you will not only put it into peak condition, you will know how to fix common problems as they crop up.

Inspect Before Riding

Before getting on a bicycle, give it a quick inspection for tire pressure, wheel rotation, gear and brake operation, and rattles. Pinch the tires, spin the wheels, squeeze the brake levers, and shift through all of the gears. Bounce the bike off the ground a couple of times and listen for rattles. See whether anything falls off. **CAUTION: Be especially sure that nothing could fall into the spokes.**

A pre-ride inspection is especially important if you were not the last person to ride the bicycle, if you are carrying baggage, or if the bicycle has been through any unusual treatment—a fall, a trip in an airline baggage compartment, a long period of storage. Many accidents and breakdowns can be avoided by a simple checkover.

Inspection and maintenance don't stop when you get onto the bicycle. The mechanical parts of a bicycle are on the outside, so most problems give clear warning signs. If anything sounds, looks, or feels unusual, stop for a safety check.

Tracing Problems

Trace a noise or vibration according to where you hear and feel it, and how often it repeats.

Does a noise repeat once every time the wheels turn around? Then it almost certainly is in a wheel—a bent rim rubbing a brake pad, a loose spoke sawing against its neighbor, a lump in the tire.

Does it repeat once every time the pedals turn around? Look for a bent chainwheel or a loose crank or pedal. Or it could be a creak or squeak in the saddle or handlebars as your weight shifts with pedaling.

The chain comes around once for every three or four turns of the pedals. A bent chain link will catch that often; a dry link will squeak that often.

Little experiments can help you trace noises and vibrations. For example, for a squeak once every time the pedals come around, try standing up to see whether it is the saddle; then try pedaling with one foot at a time to see if it is in a pedal. Shift the front derailleur to see whether the squeak changes—it might be in the chainwheels.

A well-maintained bicycle does not rattle. A rattle deserves your serious attention. Most things that rattle will eventually shift position or fall off.

For example, a loose generator could eventually fall into the spokes. Then you will come to a very quick unplanned stop. This is a fairly common type of accident—yet the generator was rattling for miles before it got loose enough to slip.

If you hear a rattle, stop to identify it. Lift each wheel off the ground a couple of inches and drop it. Find the rattle and tighten up the loose part.

PERIODIC MAINTENANCE

The accompanying illustration and listings point out specific areas requiring periodic attention and the type of lubrication to be used. The tasks are keyed to the illustration.

If you ride your bicycle through the winter, a good time to perform annual maintenance tasks is in the spring, when the sloppy weather is over.

Maintenance intervals are flexible. If you ride in foul weather or on dirt, service your bicycle more frequently. If a bicycle is out of use, maintenance can be postponed; but after two or three years, lubricants and rubber parts may dry out, so a bicycle should be inspected and overhauled as necessary before returning it to service.

Weekly Maintenance Tasks

W1 Inflate the tires to the correct pressure. Bicycle tires lose pressure much faster than car tires. Some tubulars, with latex inner tubes, need *daily* reinflation.

W2 Spray the chain with a lightweight lubricant.

W3 Pry out glass splinters and other small penetrating objects from the tire treads. Check the tires for wear and damage.

W4 Test hub and crank bearings for looseness or binding.

W5 Check the adjustment of a derailleur or internally geared hub.

W6 Check all bolted-on parts for looseness, and tighten as necessary.

Monthly Maintenance Tasks

M1 Lubricate front hub. Use a few drops of light oil if an oil fitting is provided. Use grease if equipped with a fitting.

M2 Lubricate the rear hub. Use a few drops of light oil or grease depending on the type of fitting.

M3 Clean the chain and relubricate it. Clean the sprockets.

M4 Apply a few drops of lightweight oil to the ends of the brake and shift cables where they enter the housings.

M5 Apply lightweight oil to all pivot points of the caliper brakes.

M6 Apply lightweight oil to the moving parts and pivot points of the rear derailleur.

M7 Apply lightweight oil to the pivot points of the front derailleur.

M8 Pedals—apply medium-weight oil at the oil hole in the dustcap, if any.

M9 Apply lightweight oil to the freewheel mechanism.

M10 Clean the saddle with warm soap and water. For a leather saddle, use saddle soap.

Annual Maintenance Tasks

A1 Overhaul the front-wheel hub. See Chapter 8.

A2 Overhaul the pedals. See Chapter 15.

A3 Overhaul the headset. See Chapter 18.

A4 Overhaul the rear derailleur. See Chapter 11.

A5 Overhaul the front derailleur. See Chapter 12.

A6 Overhaul the rear hub. This task applies to single-speed and multispeed rear hubs. See Chapter 14.

A7 Overhaul the hanger set. See Chapter 15.

A8 Overhaul the freewheel cluster body. See Chapter 10.

A9 Remove, inspect, and relubricate all control cables. Replace as necessary. See Chapter 6.

SOME BASIC MECHANICAL THEORY

Working on your bicycle is easier if you think of it as a collection of basic mechanical elements—bearings, screw threads, friction surfaces, and a few others. Each part of your bike is a system of these basic mechanical elements.

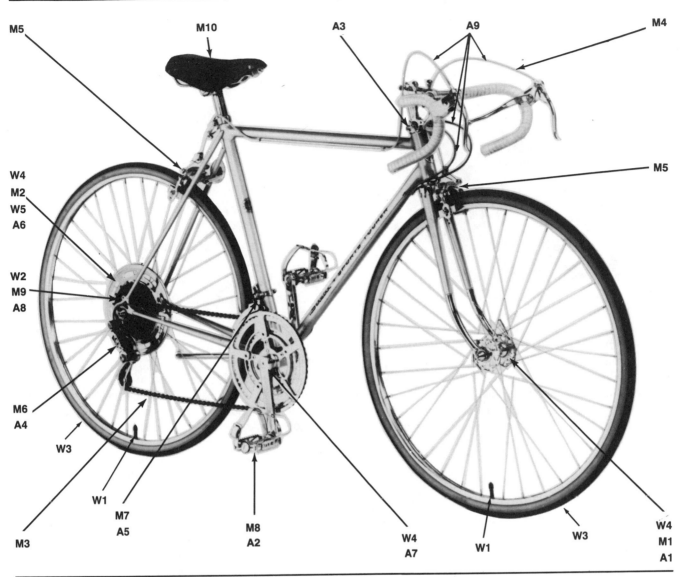

Periodic maintenance of a typical derailleur-equipped bicycle. The letter prefixes indicate W for weekly, M for monthly, and A for annual tasks, as outlined in the text.

For example, a wobbly wheel and a chattering brake arm may seem very different, but each of them rotates around a bearing, and the bearing is too loose. You will learn to adjust both bearings in very much the same way. If you think about similarities like this, you will progress quickly as a mechanic.

About Bearings

A bearing is the connection between two parts in relative motion—for example, the brake arm and the brake bolt on which it pivots, or the turning wheel and the stationary axle. A bearing shouldn't be loose, but it shouldn't be so tight the parts jam together.

A non-turning axle passing through a hole in the turning wheel is an example of a *sleeve bearing*. This is the simplest kind of bearing, used in a primitive donkey cart. The sliding motion between the axle and the wheel generates friction, making more work for the donkey.

Bicycle brakes still use sleeve bearings—the brake bolt passes through a hole drilled in each brake arm. The hole is just a little larger than the bolt, so the brake arm can swivel and press the brake shoe against the rim.

There needs to be something to keep the brake arm from sliding lengthwise off the bolt, so behind the brake arm there is a widened part of the bolt to keep the brake arm from sliding back. In front of the brake arm a couple of nuts are screwed onto the threaded end of the bolt, one behind the other. These nuts keep the brake arm from slipping forward off the bolt.

DOUBLE NUTS

Two nuts tightened against each other are used to set the adjustment of bearings in the brake, the hub, and other moving parts.

These nuts also let you adjust the bearing. When you use the brake, the brake arm and nuts slowly wear each other down, so the brake will slowly get looser. Every once in a while, you need to adjust the nuts so there is just a tiny bit of space between the inner nut and the front brake arm. Then the brake arm can swivel freely, but it can't wobble or chatter.

Ball Bearings

Like the brake or the donkey cart, the first bicycle wheels had sleeve bearings. Since bicyclists complain about overwork better than donkeys, ball bearings were invented for bicycle use, toward the end of the nineteenth century.

Each end of a bicycle's hub shell has a cup-shaped recess. A ring of steel *bearing balls* rolls around inside. The axle passes through a hole in the bottom of the cup.

The axle is threaded, and a *cone* is screwed onto each end. The inner, angled surface of the cone contacts the balls in the cup. The balls rolling between the cup and cone eliminate the sliding contact of the sleeve bearing, greatly reducing friction. Ball bearings are used in the hubs, pedals, bottom bracket (crank bearings), and headset (steering bearings)—wherever low friction is important.

As you screw the cone down tighter, you are reducing the clearance inside the bearing, just as you did with your brake. This stops the wheel from wobbling.

Once you have the cone in its correct position, you have to keep it from unscrewing. A *locknut* holds the cone in position once it has been adjusted. The same principle is used on the hub, the brake, and wherever else a bearing's clearance is adjusted.

This is slightly different from using a nut and bolt to clamp a fender bracket or handlebar in place. We simply want to tighten these down; but we don't want to tighten down the hub cones or brake arms. We want them just loose enough to turn freely. For this reason, we use two nuts and tighten them *against each other.* The *double-nut* system of hub cone and locknut, or the two nuts on the brake bolt, allows free motion in the bearing while securing the adjustment.

You check the hub cone or brake arm for tightness or wobble, and turn the nuts bit by bit until the bearing is adjusted perfectly—just short of binding.

Tightening Threaded Parts

Threads on a bolt, hub axle, or other part work like a wedge wrapped diagonally around the bolt. Turning a nut on a bolt moves it slowly along the bolt. This multiplies the force you apply with your wrench. The nut and the bolt head can be made to squeeze other parts tightly together between them, securing these parts.

If you do not tighten a nut or bolt enough, it might loosen. If you overtighten it, you could strip the threads or break it off. How do you tell that you have tightened it enough?

There is a tool, called a *torque wrench,* for measuring the tightness of nuts and bolts, but you should not need to use one on a bicycle. With a little experience, you can tighten nuts and bolts by feel.

As a nut or bolt tightens, it becomes harder and harder to turn, for maybe a sixth of a turn. At this point, it begins to get harder much more quickly. Turning it backward, in the loosening direction, becomes almost as hard as turning it forward. Tighten the nut or bolt into this zone, but not too far. Test by trying to turn it both ways, to make sure that it will not unscrew easily. The exact amount of tightening will depend on the size of the nut or bolt. Smaller-diameter threads and thinner nuts must be tightened with less force.

A screwdriver does not apply enough force to tighten a bolt securely. Use the screwdriver to start the bolt, and to hold the bolt from turning while you tighten the nut onto it with a wrench. As the nut tightens, friction will help keep the bolt from turning.

If a nut or bolt gets harder to turn and then easier, you have overtightened it and stripped the threads; the part should be replaced. Usually, axles are made of harder metal than axle nuts, so you have to replace only the nut. First, clean out any pieces of the nut still wrapped around the axle threads.

Every nut or bolt head should press evenly against a flat surface. A *washer* is used to provide such a surface where it does not already exist. The fork ends of a bicycle are a good example. Because of the axle slot,

When tightening, hold the bolt steady and turn the nut. Friction between the bolt and the parts being assembled will help keep the bolt from turning.

the nut does not bear down all the way around. If it is tightened directly against the fork end, without a washer, it will grab harder on one side of the slot or the other, and "walk" along the slot. The wheel will move out of position. With a washer, the nut will tighten securely.

Washers also prevent damage to the parts, by keeping them from scraping over each other as they are tightened. In some applications, special lockwashers or non-turn washers are used. Don't leave out the washers when you reassemble parts!

Lubricate Before Tightening

To aid in tightening a threaded part, oil or grease the threads and the surface against which the part tightens. **CAUTION: Failure to oil threads can result in stripped nuts, especially axle nuts.** Lubrication also

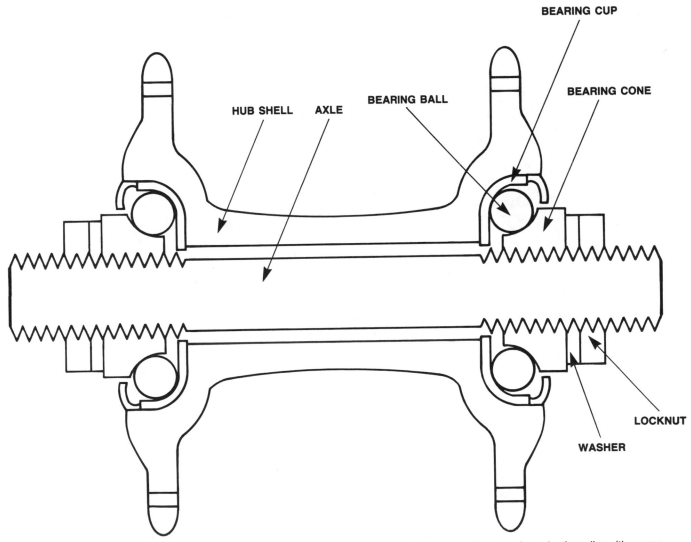

A cross-section drawing of the bearings of a conventional cup-and-cone front hub. The bearing adjustment is set by threading either cone along the axle. Then the cone is secured with the locknut. Compare this drawing with the front hub on your bicycle.

prevents the parts from rusting together. A very few threaded parts should *not* be lubricated; these exceptions are given in the rebuilding instructions in later chapters.

Using Tools

A good feel for tools is basic to bicycle work, as to any other type of mechanical work. Special techniques are described in the rebuilding instructions, but for the basics of how to hold and apply tools, it is best to spend a few hours working alongside an experienced mechanic. There's nothing mysterious about tools, but they serve you much better when you are using the right one for the job and applying it effectively.

You must use a wrench of exactly the correct size to prevent damage to parts. Unless the wrench fits snugly, do not use it. You must *make* an adjustable wrench the right size. Every time you turn it to a new position, rock it lightly into place while tightening the adjusting screw with your thumb.

Each time you turn an adjustable wrench to a new face of a bolt or nut, rock the wrench and tighten the adjusting screw to fit the wrench to the nut.

LUBRICANTS AND LUBRICATION

For bicycle work, you use grease, which is thick and sticky, like butter; medium-weight oil, about the consistency of salad oil; and lightweight spray lubricant, thin as turpentine.

Lubricants spread into a slippery layer between moving parts. Lubricants make the parts move easily, smoothly, and quietly over each other. Lubricants also repel water and keep parts from rusting.

Each lubricant has its proper use in bicycle maintenance.

Multipurpose grease is appropriate where you need a lubricant that will stay put, as for the bicycle's headset (steering) bearings and other major bearing assemblies, and also to coat brake cables, seatposts, and handlebar stems to prevent corrosion.

Medium-weight cycle oil is sold in squirter cans at bike shops. It is appropriate where you must run lubricant into a part, between overhauls. It is also the right lubricant for three-speed hubs and is acceptable for non-derailleur chains.

CAUTION: Do not use "household" oil on a bicycle. Good cycle oil has a light, sweet smell. Acid "household" oil feels watery between the fingers and smells sour.

Lightweight spray lubricant such as LPS-3® or Tri-Flow® is appropriate for derailleur chains; a heavier lubricant would attract excessive dirt. A lightweight spray lubricant also penetrates cracks, to help you disassemble parts which are stuck.

The lighter a lubricant, the faster it will run off or evaporate. You must spray your chain regularly, or else it will squeak and waste your energy pedaling. Do not use spray lubricant where you would normally use oil or grease, unless you want your bike to wear out quickly.

Grease eventually becomes contaminated with metal wear particles and road dirt. To avoid rapid wear:

Rebuild or relubricate your bicycle's moving assemblies regularly. Clean parts very carefully to remove old, dirty grease and oil. Replace worn-out

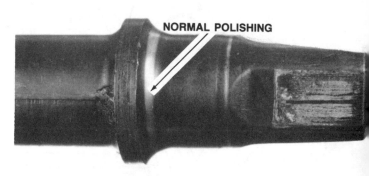

NORMAL POLISHING

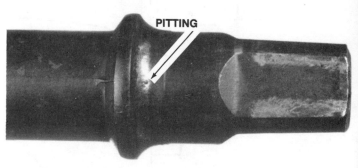

PITTING

The upper axle can be reused; its bearing track is polished smooth with normal wear. The bearing track of the lower axle has begun to flake off, leaving tiny pits. This axle must be replaced.

parts—they're where metal chips come from. Adjust bearings carefully to prevent excess wear.

Keep your stock of lubricants clean. Grease, especially, picks up dust and dirt easily. If you bought grease in a can, scoop it out only with a *clean* tool. Take out as much as you need for a work session, pack it in a clean paper cup, and then put the lid back on the can. If you bought grease in a tube like toothpaste, keep the cap on the tube except when you're squeezing the grease out. Don't touch the end of the tube to anything dirty. Plastic tubes can suck dirty grease back inside when you release pressure on them.

An ordinary pipe cleaner wrapped around the gap between dustcap and cone can serve as an effective dust shield.

Sealing Bearings

You can prolong the life of lubricants and reduce wear by sealing bearing assemblies to prevent dirt from getting into them.

Most bicycle bearings, as sold, are *shielded* with dustcaps which cover most of the opening through which grit could enter, but they are *unsealed*—between the turning and stationary parts there is an open crack which can let grit in, especially in dusty or wet riding conditions.

Some very simple tricks will help keep the grit out. Fenders go a long way to keep dirt off the bike. They also keep it off you! A ring of inner-tube rubber around the headset bearings will seal them. Ordinary pipe cleaners wrapped around hub cones, crank axle ends, and pedal spindles seal them quite well.

A bike store can sell you a plastic sleeve that fits between the bottom bracket cups. It protects the bearings from dirt inside the frame. If your bike has an open-topped seatpost, plug its top. This will keep dust and sand from falling down the seat tube.

Adding Oil or Grease Fittings

Consider adding oil or grease fittings to the hubs, pedals, and crank housing. With these fittings, you can add lubricant from *inside* the bearings and flush dirt out.

You can drill oil holes in pedal dustcaps, hub barrels, and bottom-bracket shell—install the bottom bracket without a plastic sleeve, or puncture the sleeve with a heated spoke.

Drill the oil holes during a rebuild, so that you can clean out the metal chips from drilling. Grease the bearings lightly—you'll need the grease to hold the bearing balls in place during assembly. Plug pedal oil holes with toothpicks or leave them uncovered; install hub barrel clips from another model of hub; plug a bottom-bracket oil hole with a self-tapping screw.

Another tactic: If you've carefully cleaned out your bike's frame and capped the seatpost, you can remove the cap and squirt oil down the seat tube into the bottom bracket.

Heavy (SAE 90) gear lubricant from an auto-parts store stays put longer, so it's better than cycle oil for ball bearings, except in three-speed and coaster hubs. An on-the-road oiling kit is available from Custom Cycle Fitments, 726 Madrone Avenue, Sunnyvale, CA 94086.

Oil once a week, and after riding in wet weather. Oil when you bring the bike home; don't wait until you're going for a ride. After oiling, lay the bike on its side on a bed of old newspaper. Then wait a while, oil again, and lay the bike on its other side so oil will get to both sides

The spring clip at the center of the hub barrel covers an oil hole. Frequent oiling will flush dirt from bearings and increase their life.

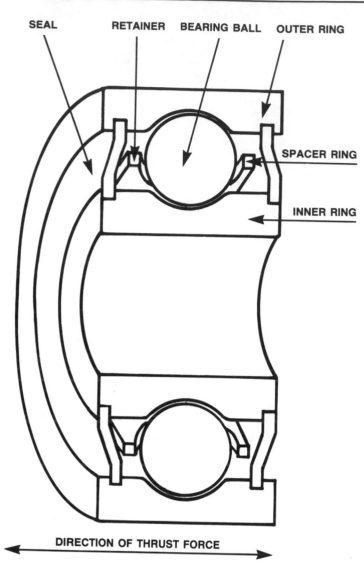

SEAL   RETAINER   BEARING BALL   OUTER RING

SPACER RING

INNER RING

DIRECTION OF THRUST FORCE

Sealed-bearing components use radial-contact bearing cartridges. A spacer ring positions the balls into a full circle. Thrust (lengthwise) forces must be kept low to avoid damage; special procedures are detailed in Chapters 8 and 14 on hubs and Chapter 15 on crank hangers and pedals.

of the bearings. Oil hubs sparingly and wipe off the excess afterward, or oil will run down the spokes to the rims. Then your brakes will slip or grab.

Grease fittings avoid the runoff problem, and are especially recommended for hubs. A grease fitting must be installed in a threaded hole. You can buy the fittings and a grease gun at an auto-parts store. A good hardware store will carry the tap (threading tool) and special-sized drill required to install grease fittings. A bike shop may be able to sell you a replacement axle for a nutted hub with a grease fitting on the end.

If you can't be bothered with oil or grease fittings, do what is more common but less effective: Rebuild and regrease your bottom bracket, hubs, and pedals once or twice a year.

Sealed-bearing Components

A final dirt-fighting strategy is to use commercial sealed-bearing components—hubs, bottom brackets, and pedals with rubber or plastic wiper seals designed to keep dirt out.

Some high-grade bikes have these as original equipment, but most sealed-bearing components are purchased as upgrades. Rebuilding is simple, using standard ball-bearing cartridges, or else the component is discarded when worn out. This book includes instructions for installing and rebuilding sealed-bearing hubs, crankbearings, and pedals.

Sealed-bearing components use *radial-contact* bearing cartridges. Their construction is different from that of conventional angular-contact bearings, and so special procedures are necessary in adjusting them. These procedures are covered in the instructions on rebuilding sealed-bearing components in Chapter 8 and Chapter 15.

6 • BASIC REPAIR PROCEDURES

This chapter covers procedures most often needed to get moving again after an on-road breakdown—procedures every bicyclist should know: removing and replacing wheels, tube and tire repair, and cable and lever maintenance.

Because of lack of knowledge, beginning bicyclists are afraid of flat tires and other minor on-road problems. After you have fixed a couple of flat tires, you will regard them as only a small inconvenience, taking just a few minutes of your time.

REMOVING WHEELS

You must remove a wheel to replace a tire and for other mechanical work on the wheel assembly. You may also need to remove the wheels to transport a bicycle by car, airplane, train or bus.

CAUTION: When shipping a bicycle as baggage, install "dummy" axles in place of the wheels. Without the support of wheel axles, the front and rear forks of the bicycle frame are easily bent.

A repair stand is convenient when removing a wheel, but not needed; for on-road repairs, correct positioning of your body lets you remove the wheel gracefully. When removing the front wheel, stand in front of the bicycle with the wheel clamped between your knees, and lift on the handlebars. When removing a rear wheel, stand to the left of the bicycle and lift the bicycle off the wheel with your *left* hand on the *right* seatstay and the saddle braced against your side.

CAUTION: Do not turn a bicycle with dropped handlebars upside down. You will damage the brake cables.

If you are working on a bicycle with caliper brakes, sight down over the tire to see if there is enough room for the tire to clear the brake shoes. If there is not

sufficient clearance, it will be necessary to release the brake shoes farther than normal in order for the tire to clear. This is accomplished by loosening a quick-release assembly at the brake lever or at a centerpull brake-cable hanger. On some centerpull brakes, you may slip the transverse cable loose from one brake arm (see page 352).

If none of these convenient ways of spreading the brake shoes is possible, remove the mounting nut from one of the brake-shoe holders, and then remove the complete brake shoe from the brake. Still another method, provided you have a pump or air supply handy, is to deflate the tire, which will then usually clear the shoes, and you need not disturb the brake shoes or the brake adjustment.

Removing a Front Wheel

After loosening a rim brake as described above, remove a front wheel with a nutted hub by loosening

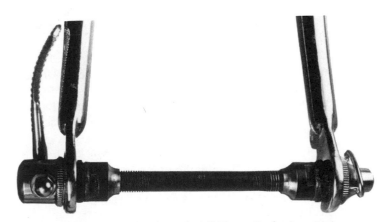

When shipping a bicycle, always install "dummy" axles to protect the forks from being crushed together.

This tourist has just had a flat tire, but he is smiling because he is prepared. Standing at the left side of the bicycle, he lifts it by the right seatstay to remove the rear wheel. Besides his tube-repair kit, he is carrying a spare tire rolled into three loops on the rear rack.

like a wingnut. Flip the lever completely over, then lift the bicycle off the wheel. The quick-release assembly is a pressure clamp, not a nut and bolt.

Removing a Rear Wheel—Derailleur Type

Many people believe that removing the rear wheel of a derailleur-geared bicycle must be more difficult than removing a single-sprocket rear wheel. In fact, the opposite is true, because the shifting mechanism of the derailleur-geared bicycle is attached to the frame, not the wheel.

To remove the rear wheel from a derailleur-geared bicycle, loosen the rim brake as discussed at the beginning of this section. If the wheel has a hub brake, disconnect the cable at the brake and undo the brake-arm clamp from the left chainstay. Many hub brakes have quick-release cables which can simply be slipped off the brake.

Shift the chain onto the smallest rear sprocket, to get it out of the way of the wheel as much as possible. Next, loosen the axle nuts or quick-release lever, just as for a front wheel.

Then stand at the left side of the bicycle and lift up on the right seatstay with your left hand, stabilizing the bicycle by bracing the saddle against your left side. With your right hand, pivot the derailleur toward the rear of the bicycle. The wheel will now be free to slip down and forward, out of the forkend slots and off the chain. If necessary, help the wheel along with your right knee.

Once the wheel is free of the slots, tilt the bicycle toward you and lift it, so the wheel clears the lower part of the chain. Set the bicycle down on its *left* side so you don't damage the rear derailleur.

the two axle nuts, one on each side. Hold the bicycle upright with one hand while turning the wrench with the other. Then stand in front of the bicycle and lift it off the wheel. If basket or fender supports are attached to the axle, remove the axle nuts, and then slide the supports off the axle prior to removing the wheel. If you remove the axle nuts, note the positions of all of the parts, so you can put them back in the correct order. Unless basket or fender supports are attached to the axle, it is *not* necessary to remove the axle nuts; only loosen them. Then all axle hardware will stay in its correct position.

If the wheel has a hub brake, disconnect the cable at the brake and undo the brake-arm clamp from the fork blade before loosening the axle nuts. Many hub brakes have quick-release cables which can simply be slipped off the brake.

Remove a quick-release wheel by pulling the lever outward, away from the wheel, *not by trying to turn it*

Removing a Rear Wheel—Non-derailleur Type

To remove a single-sprocket rear wheel, loosen the rim brake as discussed at the beginning of this section. Remove the cable from a cable-operated drum brake. Many hub brakes have quick-release cables which can simply be slipped off the brake.

Loosen a three-speed cable adjusting barrel locknut, and then remove the barrel from the indicator spindle. Remove the mounting screw from the brake-arm strap of a coaster brake or drum brake, and then slide the brake arm free of the strap. If a plastic protector is used on the right-hand axle nut, remove the protector. Loosen both axle nuts by turning them in a counterclockwise direction.

Usually there is no need to remove the axle nuts. If fender or rack support brackets are clamped under the axle nuts, you must remove them. If you do, take note of the washer and support arrangement on the axle.

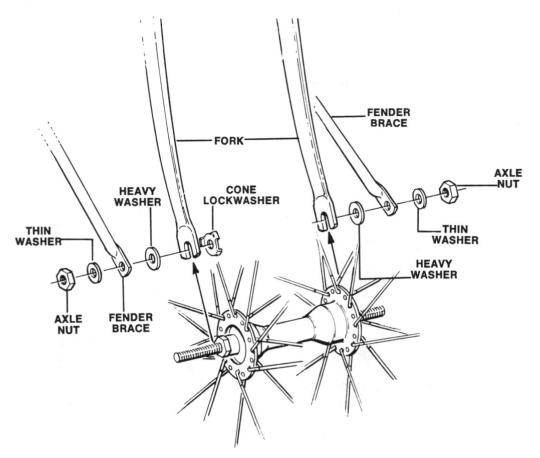

Exploded view of a nutted front-wheel hub, showing the arrangement of parts mounted on the axle. The cone lockwasher is used only on some Schwinn hubs; see the text for explanation.

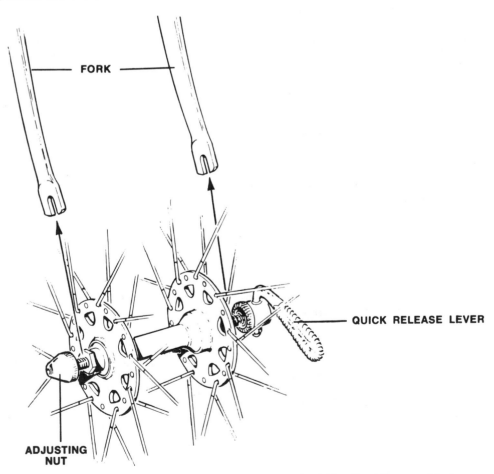

Pulling the quick-release lever away from the hub allows you to remove the wheel quickly without the use of tools.

Some bicycles have serrated washers installed against the frame to prevent the wheel from moving forward under tension of the chain. Washers are usually installed between the fender and accessory supports to keep them from twisting when the axle nuts are tightened.

INSTALLING WHEELS

The following remarks apply to all types of wheels. Read them, then turn to the instructions which follow for the different types of wheels.

If the wheel which you are installing is not the original one, also read the section on exchanging wheels, below. There are several fine points which you must check to be sure that the new wheel will fit the bicycle.

Before installing a wheel, spin the axle and note whether either end is off-center, indicating that it is bent. A bent axle will not center the wheel properly. Check that the hub bearings turn freely but without excessive sideplay. As described in the chapters on hubs, sealed-bearing and quick-release hubs should be adjusted looser than conventional nutted hubs.

Use a hub-cone wrench and adjustable wrench to check that the hub-cone locknuts are securely tightened against the cones. A loose right cone will tighten into the hub, damaging the bearings. Some Raleigh and Schwinn front hubs do not have locknuts. If there is only *one* set of wrench flats on each side of the hub, don't put one wrench on either side, tighten the two cones toward each other, and smash the bearings!

Make sure that the tire will clear the shoes of a rim brake; if necessary, open the brake quick release, remove one brake shoe, or deflate the tire.

After installing the wheel, check that it centers correctly in the frame and between the brake shoes. If the brake is off-center so it drags, adjust it as described in Chapter 16. If the wheel is off-center in the frame, either the wheel or the frame is out of alignment; instructions for correcting this problem are in Chapter 17 (wheel) and Chapter 18 (frame).

Installing a Front Wheel

Guide the axle into the front-fork dropout slots, with the cone lockwasher on the right side (sprocket side) of the fork, until the axle is seated against the ends of the slots.

If heavy washers are used against the fork, make sure these are at the *outside,* under the axle nuts. If the bicycle has fender braces or accessory supports to be clamped under the axle nuts, then you will have to replace axle washers and nuts after installing the wheel. Slide all parts onto the axle, making sure there is a washer on the outside of the fork blade and directly

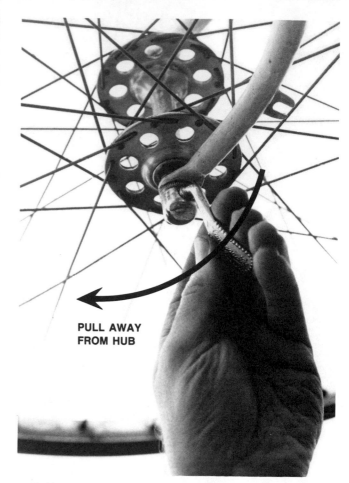

PULL AWAY FROM HUB

To loosen a quick-release wheel, pull the lever away from the hub as shown. It is *not* a wingnut.

under the nut. *Oil the axle threads so the nuts will not strip.*

Lower the bicycle onto the wheel, making sure that the axle washers are at the outside of the fork blades. Then tighten the axle nuts or quick-release assembly. If the wheel has a drum brake, follow the further instructions in the non-derailleur rear wheel part of this section.

Tighten a quick-release by rotating the cam lever through 180 degrees *at right angles to the wheel* until it is parallel with the fork blade. Reach your hand around the fork blade so you can push the quick-release lever harder. It should take most of the strength of your hand to push it down. If it will not go down all the way or if it goes down too easily, advance or back off the adjusting nut on the opposite side of the wheel.

CAUTION: The quick-release assembly is a pressure clamp, not a wingnut. If you try to screw it down like a wingnut, you will never get it tight enough, and the wheel is likely to come off.

The clamping action of the quick-release assembly compresses the axle and tightens the bearing adjustment. Unless you have checked the bearing adjust-

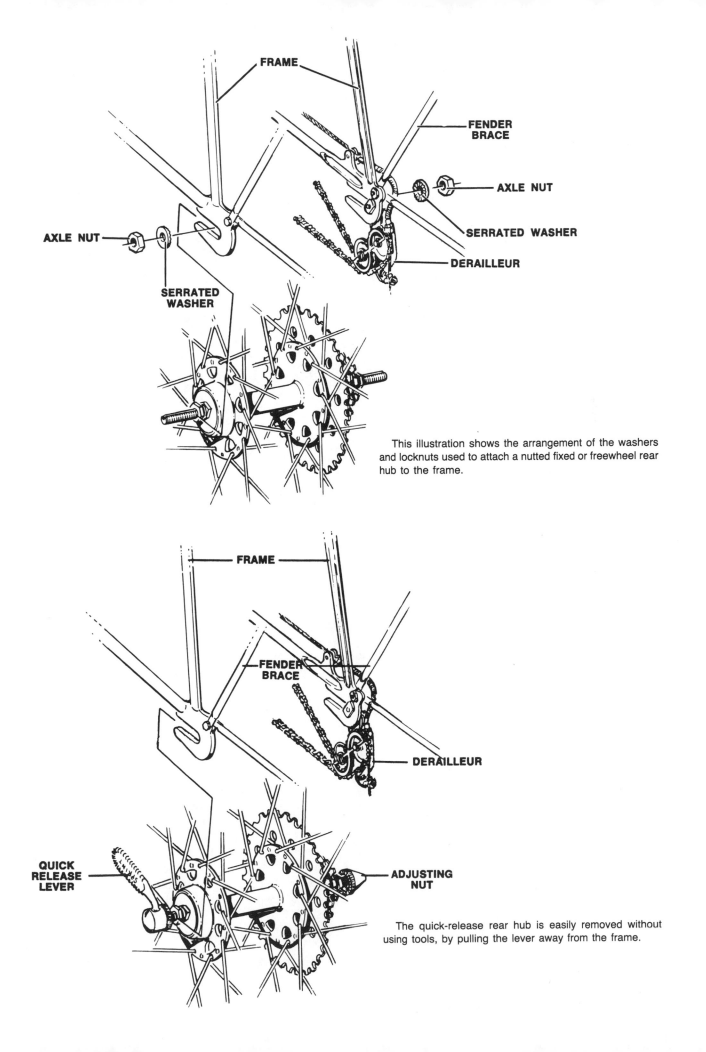

FRAME

FENDER BRACE

AXLE NUT

SERRATED WASHER

DERAILLEUR

AXLE NUT

SERRATED WASHER

This illustration shows the arrangement of the washers and locknuts used to attach a nutted fixed or freewheel rear hub to the frame.

FRAME

FENDER BRACE

DERAILLEUR

QUICK RELEASE LEVER

ADJUSTING NUT

The quick-release rear hub is easily removed without using tools, by pulling the lever away from the frame.

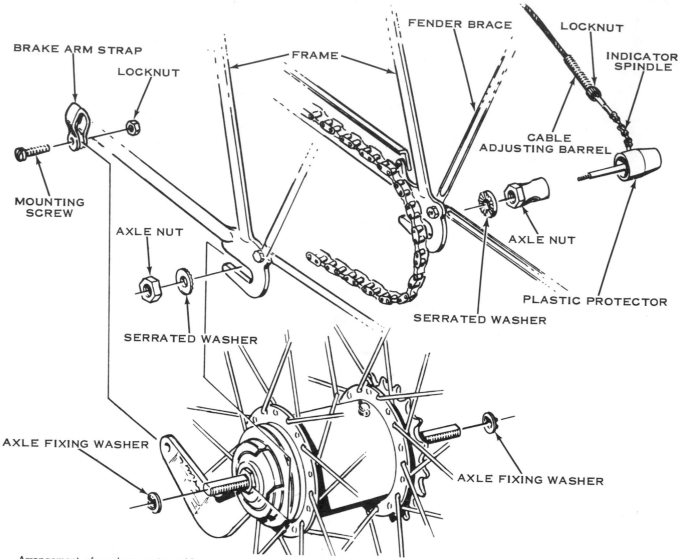

Arrangement of washers, nuts, cable, and brake-arm strap of a Sturmey-Archer S3C hub, typical of non-derailleur rear hubs. All coaster-brake and drum-brake hubs use a brake arm, and all multispeed hubs use a shift-control cable or cables.

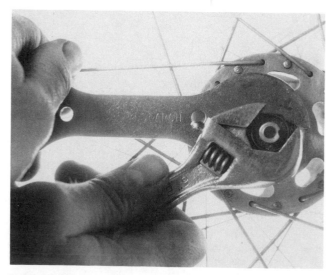

Check the tightness of the locknuts before installing a wheel.

ment before, test it now as described on page 123.

A conventional nutted hub with cone locknuts will not need bearing adjustment after installation. Some British and Schwinn front hubs do not have cone locknuts. Only one bearing cone of these hubs is adjustable. It must be on the *left,* so it cannot tighten into the bearing.

Loosen the left (flatted) cone of the British hub and tighten the right cone until it runs up against its shoulder on the axle and will turn no more. Then install the wheel, with the flatted cone on the left. Tighten the right axle nut, then adjust the left cone and tighten the left axle nut. Tightening the axle nut changes the bearing adjustment slightly, so recheck and readjust as necessary. General instructions on adjusting bearings are in Chapter 8.

The Schwinn hub has a cone lockwasher, shown in the exploded drawing in this section. This lockwasher

To tighten a quick-release front hub, press the lever down toward the frame. You may hook your fingers over the fork blade for extra force. If it is too easy or too hard to press home, loosen the lever, then turn the adjusting nut on the opposite side a fraction of a turn while holding the lever.

The flanged Raleigh front-hub cones must be used with a recessed Raleigh fork.

goes on the *right,* locking the right cone to the fork. Adjust the left cone as with the British hub.

Finish by tightening a rim-brake quick release, replacing a brake shoe, or inflating the tire. Make sure that the wheel turns smoothly and the brake works properly before riding the bicycle.

Installing a Rear Wheel—Derailleur Type

Unless fender or rack braces are mounted under the axle nuts, replace all axle hardware loosely before reinstalling the wheel. Refer to the exploded drawings in this section. *Oil axle threads to keep axle nuts from stripping.*

Adjust the rear derailleur to its outermost (high-gear) position. Stand at the left side of the rear of the bicycle as you did to remove the wheel. Hold the wheel in your right hand, by the rim, with the sprockets facing away from you.

Lift the bicycle and place the upper part of the wheel between the rear forks. Transfer your right hand to the rear derailleur and pull it toward the back of the bicycle. Lower the bicycle and tilt it toward you so the upper chain engages the top of the smallest rear sprocket. Lower the bicycle onto the wheel, guiding the hub axle to the front of the forkend slots. If the wheel has a nutted axle, make sure that the axle washer on each side is *outside* the slot. If it is not, lift the bicycle slightly and adjust the washer's position.

If the derailleur is mounted to the forkend with a separate hanger as shown, or if the forkend slots are vertical, push the axle all the way into the right slot. If the hanger is a built-in part of the right forkend, place the axle about halfway back in the slot; the best position depends on the type of rear derailleur and the size of the sprockets. Many bicycles with built-in hangers have threaded adjusting screws to position the rear wheel.

At this time, tighten the right axle nut of a nutted hub, but do not tighten a quick release yet.

If the wheel is equipped with a drum brake, now attach the brake-arm assembly *loosely* to the left chainstay, as described in more detail in the later part of this section on non-derailleur rear wheels.

Next, kneel at the left side of the bicycle. Hold it upright with your left shoulder. Unless the bicycle has wheel-position adjusting screws or vertical forkend

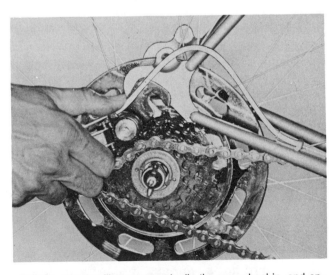

Pull the rear derailleur rearward, slip the rear wheel in, and engage the *upper* chain on the smallest rear sprocket to position the wheel for reinstallation.

Hold the rear wheel centered between the chainstays while tightening the quick-release lever or rear axle nut.

Rear-wheel axle-adjustment screws let you center the wheel once; it will automatically settle in the correct position from then on.

slots, hold the front of the wheel centered by wedging your left thumb and index finger between the wheel and the chainstay on either side. Then tighten the quick release or the left axle nut.

Tighten a quick release by rotating the cam lever through 180 degrees *at right angles to the wheel* until it faces the rear of the bicycle. Reach your hands around the spokes so you can push the quick-release lever harder. It should take most of the strength of your hand to push it down. If it will not go down all the way or if it slips into place too easily, advance or back off the adjusting nut on the opposite side of the wheel.

CAUTION: The quick-release assembly is a pressure clamp, not a wingnut. If you try to screw it down like a wingnut, you will never get it tight enough, and the wheel is likely to come off.

The clamping action of the quick-release assembly compresses the axle and tightens the bearing adjustment. Unless you have checked the bearing adjustment before, test it now as described on page 123. A conventional nutted hub with cone locknuts will not need a bearing adjustment after installation.

If the wheel is equipped with a drum brake, now tighten the bolt that holds the brake-arm strap to the left chainstay and reattach the cable according to the instructions in the part of this section on non-derailleur rear wheels.

Finish by tightening a rim-brake quick release, replacing a brake shoe, or inflating the tire. Before the bicycle is ridden, check that the wheel turns freely, the brake works properly, and the bicycle shifts properly through all the gears.

Replacing a Rear Wheel—Non-derailleur Type

Unless fender or rack braces are mounted over the ends of the axle, mount all axle washers and nuts loosely before installing the wheel. The exact hardware used will vary with the make and type of hub. If you have lost track of the position of the nuts and washers, check the exploded drawings in the chapters on rebuilding each type of hub. *Oil the axle threads to prevent the nuts from stripping.*

Coaster-brake or geared rear hubs use special hardware to resist forces which try to turn them in the frame.

The axle gear of a geared hub tries to turn the axle. Special non-turn washers *inside* the forkend slots prevent the axle from turning, while still leaving room for the normal washers under the nuts at the outside. Sturmey-Archer hubs use a non-turn washer at either end of the axle, as shown in the exploded drawing in this section. Shimano hubs use only one such washer; see the exploded drawings in the hub chapter for details.

When a coaster or drum brake is applied, a brake arm, strapped to the frame, resists the powerful braking force. A hub with gears *and* a brake needs non-turn washers *and* a brake arm. Since the angle of the brake arm is adjustable, the brake arm does not prevent the axle from turning.

When installing the wheel, engage the chain over the sprocket teeth, then slide the axle back into the forkend slots, with the non-turn washer tabs indexing with the slots at the *inside.* The chain should tighten, stopping the wheel from moving farther back. If the non-turn washers are not completely inside the front of the slots, or if the axle is all the way back and the chain is still loose, you must add or remove chain links. This may be necessary if you have installed a larger or smaller sprocket.

If the wheel is equipped with a drum brake or coaster

To adjust the slack of a non-derailleur chain, tighten the right axle nut *lightly,* turn the crank, and tap on the lower chain with the wrench.

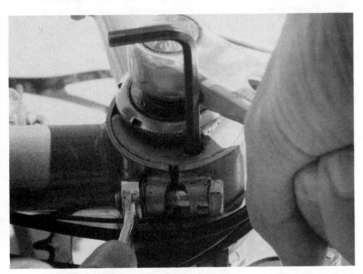

Adjustment of the synchronizing chain of a tandem is similar to adjustment of a non-derailleur drive chain. Loosen the eccentric bottom bracket with a wrench and change its position by levering it with an Allen wrench or similar tool, pushed by the crank.

brake, now attach the brake-arm assembly *loosely* to the left chainstay. If the brake-arm strap has several mounting holes, bend the strap around the chainstay so as to bring the brake arm as close to the frame as possible.

Tighten the right axle nut partway with the wrench, so it can still slip in the slot. Then turn the crank. With a coaster-brake or fixed-gear hub, lift the rear wheel and turn the crank forward. You can freewheel other hubs backward. Since no chainwheels or sprockets are perfectly round, their high spots will tighten the chain and pull the rear axle slightly forward in the forkend slots.

Turn the crank until the chain is at its tightest, then tap on the middle of the lower chain with the wrench

handle to pull the axle forward slightly. Turn the crank again to see that the chain never becomes completely tight. It should never bind, or vibrate like the string of a musical instrument. At its tightest, it should have about ¾ inch of total vertical play. When you are satisfied with the chain adjustment, tighten the right axle nut.

CAUTION: If the chain is too tight, it will pull on the hub and crank assemblies and damage the bearings. If the chain is too loose, it could fall off, disabling a coaster brake and the drive.

Next, kneel at the left side of the bicycle. Hold the front of the wheel centered by wedging your left thumb and index finger between the wheel and the chainstay on either side. Then, holding the wrench in your right hand, tighten the left axle nut.

Recheck the chain adjustment. If centering the wheel has affected it, loosen the right axle nut, readjust the chain, retighten the nut, then loosen the left axle nut, recenter the wheel, and retighten.

Now, if the wheel is equipped with a drum brake or coaster brake, tighten the bolt which clamps the brake arm to the frame.

CAUTION: The brake arm must already be in its final position. The clamp bolt must not force it into position, or it could bend the rear axle and cause the hub bearings to bind.

Reattach any cables. Instructions for adjusting shifter cables begin on page 241 in Chapter 14. After reconnecting a drum-brake cable, check the brake adjustment. The brake lever should have as little wasted motion as possible without making the brake drag. Test that the brake cable will not slip by grasping the brake lever tightly with both hands.

Finish by tightening a rim-brake quick release,

After adjusting the chain slack and tightening the right axle nut, center the rear wheel with your left hand and tighten the axle nut with your right hand.

replacing a brake shoe, or inflating the tire. Test that the wheel turns smoothly, the brake works properly, and the hub shifts properly through all gears before riding the bicycle.

Exchanging Wheels

It is simplest to reinstall a wheel on the bicycle for which it was originally intended. Hub width and other dimensions differ from one wheel to another. Problems in exchanging wheels are most common with lower-priced equipment. High-quality equipment is fairly well standardized, except for tire dimensions and rear-hub widths.

CAUTION: Never force a frame to accept a hub of the wrong width. To adapt hub width, axle spacers must be added or removed, or else the frame must be carefully rebent so the forkends are parallel. Instructions are in the chapters on hubs and on the frame.

To compare tires and rims, refer to the ISO (International Standards Organization) system of rim and tire measurement. This uses numbers like 37-622; the first number is the tire or rim width and the second is the inside diameter of the tire in millimeters. The common 27-inch (630mm) size, of British origin, is slightly larger than the French 700C (622mm) size. Either will fit most adult bicycles. A slightly larger rim often improves the performance of caliper brakes by increasing their leverage.

It may be necessary to file the forkend slots to accept a thicker axle. To avoid wheel-centering problems, do not file the upper surfaces of the slots, where the weight of the bicycle and rider rest on the axle.

Chainline may vary from one rear hub or freewheel to another. On a single-sprocket system, check that the chain runs straight. On a derailleur-geared system, readjust the rear derailleur as necessary so that it reaches the inner and outer sprockets without jumping beyond them. A different rear derailleur may be needed if the sprockets on the new wheel are much larger or smaller.

CAUTION: Always check rear derailleur travel when installing a different rear wheel. Failure to do this may result in damage or an accident the first time the bicycle is ridden.

Many hubs have one type or another of *retention device* to keep a loose wheel from falling off. Flanged Raleigh front-hub cones or nuts can be used only with a recessed Raleigh forkend, unless a ⅜-inch washer is used to cover the flange. Other retention devices can usually be removed if the matching part is not on the frame. Just be sure that you, and the rider of the bicycle, know how to tighten the axle nuts or quick release securely.

TIRE MAINTENANCE

Modern bicycle tires are divided into two broad groups: conventional clincher "wired-on" tires and tubular tires.

The *clincher tires* are similar to automobile tires which use inner tubes. The tire, or casing, is made of cloth for strength, coated with rubber for traction and tread wear. The inner tube is made of airtight rubber and filled with pressurized air. Without the cloth of the casing holding it in place, the inner tube would blow up like a balloon.

Clincher tires—more properly called *wired-on* tires—are used on children's and adult bicycles for almost all purposes except track and road racing. Clincher tires are easy to repair, because the inner tube is exposed as soon as the casing is removed from the rim. Many diameters, widths, weights, and tread patterns are available for heavy-duty or sport use.

Tubular tires, also called sew-ups, are sewn together on the inside next to the rim, completely encasing the inner tube within the tire. The tire is mounted to the wheel with a special cement to prevent it from "creeping" over the edge of the rim under the pressure of a high-speed turn. Tubulars are available only in light weights and in a few sizes. Their use is limited to racing and to training for racing.

Tubulars are not practical for average riding on city streets, because the tire and tube are almost paper-thin, which means they are vulnerable to punctures and other road-hazard damages.

In addition to its light weight, another advantage of

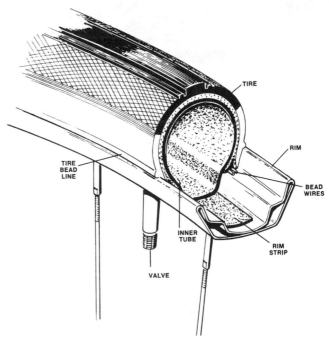

Cutaway view of a typical clincher tire, showing the principal parts of the tire and rim.

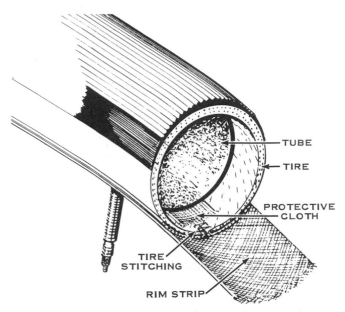

Cutaway view of a typical tubular (sew-up) tire, showing the principal parts of the tube and tire.

the tubular tire is that it can be folded and carried under the seat as a spare. Because it is difficult to repair but can be quickly changed, the spare is usually mounted and the patching work performed at a later, more convenient time. The repaired tire is then carried as a spare.

Clincher-type and tubular tires cannot be interchanged on the same rim. Each must be used only on a wheel designed for its specific use. For this reason, many serious cyclists have two sets of wheels and tires, one set for the clincher tires used for normal riding and the other with tubular tires mounted for racing.

The type and design of tire treads for bicycles is as varied as those for the automobile. A wide range of patterns is available to meet the preference of the individual rider and the purpose for which he intends to use his bike.

Thorn-resistant tubes are available for riding through areas that abound in cactus vegetation. Thorns shed from these plants are blown onto the roadway, where they lie in wait for the cyclist, ready to do their dirty work. One defense against such an attack is to install a device commonly called a "thorn puller" in the Southwestern United States or a "tire saver" in other areas. This is a very lightweight device (approximately ½ ounce) attached to the pivot bolt of the caliper-brake

Maximum strain is placed on a tire and wheel when cornering hard. Seconds after this picture was taken during a criterium race, a rear tubular tire rolled off the rim as a rider crossed the railroad tracks, resulting in nasty skin burns on his arms and legs. Proper inflation and careful attention to maintenance, especially cementing of tubulars to the rim, cannot be overemphasized.

assembly on the side opposite the brakes. The puller actually rides on the tire, and if a thorn or piece of glass is picked up, it will scrape it off during the next revolution of the wheel to prevent puncture of the tire.

Tire Size Markings

There are several national systems of tire size markings. Sometimes the same markings are used for different sizes. The most common confusions are:

BRITISH 27-inch (630mm) is slightly larger than FRENCH 700C (622mm). If you will be using tubulars and clincher tires on the same bicycle, use the 700C size, whose rim diameter is exactly the same as for tubulars. Using 27-inch wheels would require repositioning the brake shoes.
SCHWINN 26 × 1⅜ S-5, S-6 (597mm) = BRITISH 26 × 1¼, slightly *larger* than BRITISH 26 × 1⅜ (590mm).
SCHWINN 24 × 1⅜ S-5, S-6 (546mm) = BRITISH 24 × 1¼, slightly *larger* then BRITISH 24 × 1⅜ (540mm).
20 × 1¾ (419mm) and all fractional sizes ending in ¾ are slightly *larger* than corresponding decimal sizes: 20 × 1.75 (405mm), etc.

The markings in millimeters are the only ones which can be trusted. Fortunately, they now appear on almost all new tires, like this: 28-622. The 28 refers to the width of the tire and the 622 to its inside (bead seat) diameter, both in millimeters.

A rim can accommodate a range of tire widths, but the tire inside diameter must be exact. Never force a tire. For a full chart of tire sizes, refer to *Sutherland's Handbook for Bicycle Mechanics.* The bike shop where you buy tires should have a copy.

Inflation

One of the most common causes of tire failure, and the one that the rider can control, is failure to maintain the correct pressure. **CAUTION: A bicycle inner tube is thin and has a small inner volume, so air seepage is rapid. Pressure should be checked every week. Many tubulars have gum-rubber (latex) inner tubes, which improve rolling performance but require reinflation every day.** A soft tire makes the bicycle hard to pedal, and leads to rim and tire damage. As the bicycle goes over a bump, the soft tire is crushed against the rim. The rim is dented, the inner tube punctured, and the tire bruised. Often all three need replacement. The hub axle may also be bent.

Overinflation is one of the most common causes of blowouts and usually occurs at the neighborhood service station. If the tire pressure is low and the rider

feels he can make it to the station, he may then attach an air hose with 200 psi (pounds per square inch) pressure. Since a bicycle tire is so much smaller than a car tire, it can fill and blow off the rim in a second or less.

Never use a service station air hose which is not equipped with a built-in gauge. A wall-mounted air dispenser with a crank and dial is relatively safe, though it may overinflate a tire by 10 or 20 pounds. A hose with a squeeze lever and pressure gauge on the end is safe if you use it carefully. The gauge works only when the lever is released. Squeeze the lever for a fraction of a second to let air into the tire, then release it to read the gauge. Repeat until the tire reaches its correct pressure. If you hold the lever down too long, the tire will blow out.

After using a service station air hose, check the pressure with your own pressure gauge.

Using a Hand Pump

Every bicycle should be equipped with a frame-mounted hand pump to inflate the tire after an on-road repair.

Correct use of this type of pump is necessary to inflate the tire to full pressure. With each stroke, pull the pump handle out all the way and push it down all the way. Because air is compressible, a bicycle pump does not work quite the same as a water pump. The first part of the downstroke only compresses the air in the pump; at high pressures the pump puts air into the tire only with the last few inches of the stroke.

If you hear a hissing sound, check the tightness of the connections. The tire is losing air, and you will never inflate it fully.

If your arms are not strong, brace your pumping arm against your side and the pump against your knee. If this doesn't do the trick, rest the end of the pump on the ground or against a wall. Then you can push the pump with your weight, not just your arm muscles.

CAUTION: Make sure that you do not pull on the tire valve with the pump; you could tear off the valve or pull a pump hose apart. Hold one hand around the rim and pump head, or if you are resting the pump head against a wall or the ground, place a tool handle under it so it transfers its force to the ground.

A pump with a hose lets you carry hoses for each type of valve, to help another bicyclist in distress. The trouble is in removing the hose from a Schraeder valve. As you unscrew the hose, air escapes from the tire. It can easily lose 20 or 30 pounds of pressure.

One remedy for this is to clip the spring from the valve core and pry the pusher from the pump hose. Metal valve caps include the tiny wrench which will unscrew the valve core. A high-pressure bicycle tire

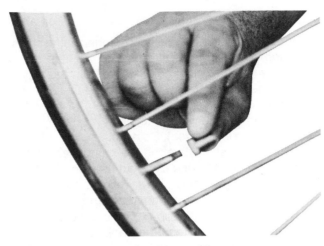

An adapter is required to fit a Schraeder pump to a tube with a Presta valve. Open the valve stem of the tube, thread the adapter onto the stem, inflate the tire, remove the adapter, and then close the valve stem.

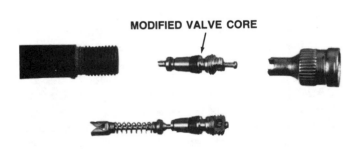

MODIFIED VALVE CORE

Clipping the spring assembly from a Schraeder valve and removing the pusher from the pump hose avoids air loss when unscrewing the pump. Many metal valve caps, as shown, include the small wrench to remove the valve core. Always use a valve cap, to prevent dirt from entering and making the valve leak.

will hold its valve closed without a spring (but use a valve cap). Any pump or service station hose can inflate a modified valve, but a modified pump hose will not inflate a standard valve.

Tubular tires and some clincher-type tires are equipped with a Presta or Woods Continental-type valve. In order to use a service station air supply, an adapter is required that screws onto the valve stem. The Presta valve is not spring-loaded, but must be rotated counterclockwise to open it prior to inflating, and then rotated clockwise to close it after the desired pressure is reached. If you use a press-on-type bicycle pump, you do not need an adapter, but you must push

it on quickly and remove it fast, using a quick rap with your fist to prevent leakage.

Most tires have the recommended inflation pressure embossed on the side wall. If the tire is not so marked or the marking is illegible, the following chart can be used as a guide for minimum pressures to be used for the tire sizes indicated. If the tire bulges noticeably, because of an above-average load, its life can be extended by adding approximately 5 psi to the amount listed.

Inflation Chart

Tire Width (inches)	(mm)	Pressure (psi)
1	25	100–110
1⅛	28	90–100
1¼	32	70–85
1¾	47	40–45
2.125		35–45

Tubular tires	
Track—smooth surface	
Front tire	80–110
Rear tire	90–120
Road—uneven to rough surface	
Front tire	70–90
Rear tire	75–100
Touring	
Front tire	85–100
Rear tire	75–90

Always carry a spare tube or tube repair materials with you. For bicycles equipped with clincher-type tires, a repair kit or a spare tube can be carried with very little additional weight. A spare tubular tire can be folded and carried under the seat for quick and easy access. If you carry a spare tubular tire, be sure to refold it every few days to prevent a set from developing at the fold. Fold the tire with the tread on the outside and the valve stem positioned at one end of a fold so it does not chafe against the tire, and so the cemented surfaces all face each other. Then fold it twice more to fit in your tire bag.

Types of Tire Damage

Blowouts are most often caused by overinflation at a service station when attempting to bring the tire up to pressure. Blowouts can also be caused by the tire's not being evenly seated on the rim. As the tire is inflated the bead is forced over the rim, causing part of the tube to escape. Overloading a bicycle with underinflated tires may also result in a blowout.

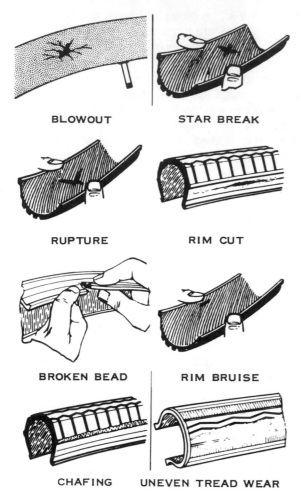

BLOWOUT   STAR BREAK

RUPTURE   RIM CUT

BROKEN BEAD   RIM BRUISE

CHAFING   UNEVEN TREAD WEAR

Types of tire damage discussed in the text. The best protection against tire injury is careful riding, with a sharp eye for road hazards.

Ruptures are usually caused by running over sharp objects, jumping curbs, or riding over a rough hole in pavement or concrete.

Star breaks result from running over pointed objects, such as rocks or pieces of metal, and are difficult to detect from the outside of the tire. Therefore, if the cause of the flat is not readily determined, inspect the inside carefully for this type of damage.

Broken beads can almost always be traced to the use of improper tools when mounting the tire. To prevent breaking a bead, use only your hands or a smooth, rounded tool when working the tire onto the rim. Never use a screwdriver or other pointed tool.

Rim bruises and *rim cuts* may be the result of running into a curb, jumping over a curb, or running into rocks, holes, or other objects with the tire underinflated.

Chafing on the side of the tire may be caused by a crooked wheel, misalignment of the wheel in the frame, or a generator roller that is not properly positioned.

Uneven tread wear may be the result of brakes that grab or lock when applied, or of making skidding stops.

Clincher Tire Repair

If the cause of the flat is easily recognized, such as a nail, thorn, or piece of broken glass, the tube can be repaired without removing the wheel from the bicycle. Mark the damaged area of the tire with a piece of chalk or crayon, and then work one side of the tire off the wheel using a pair of tire levers (as shown in the accompanying illustration). Do not use a screwdriver or pointed tool. First, deflate the tire completely, holding the valve open and squeezing out as much air as you can. Then push one side of the tire inward so it can fall into the well along the centerline of the rim. This will allow part of the tire to slip over the edge of the rim. One lever can be hooked on an adjacent spoke while the other lever is being used to pry the bead off the rim. Pull the tube from the tire in the area of your chalk mark on the tire, and the puncture can usually be located. Mark the spot and you are ready to make a repair.

If the cause of the flat cannot be determined from an inspection of the exterior of the tire, or if the tire or tube must be replaced, the wheel will have to be removed from the bicycle and then the tube completely removed from the tire.

As described above, deflate the tire, push one side into the well of the rim, and then work that side loose from the rim using tire levers. With a narrow rim, start near the valve, since the part of the tire opposite the valve will go into the well more easily. After one side of the tire is off the rim, pull the tube out of the tire. **CAUTION: Be careful when removing the tire from the rim not to break the bead or to pinch the tube, causing further damage.** Remove the other side of the tire from the rim, and then pull off the rim strip.

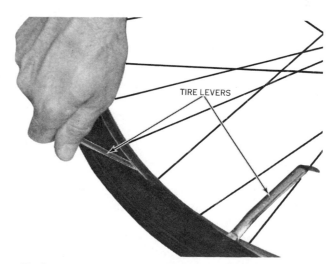

TIRE LEVERS

Tire levers ease the job of removing a clincher tire. With a narrow rim, start near the valve, so the opposite side can easily fall into the well of the rim. Some tires with nonmetallic, flexible bead wires require a special plastic tire lever. Never use a sharp tool such as a screwdriver, which can make a new hole in the tube.

Check the spoke heads and file smooth any protrusion that might damage the tube.

Inflate the tube slightly, and then immerse it in a container of water. Move the tube slowly through the water and watch for bubbles, indicating the leak. When the source of the escaping air is discovered, dry the tube and mark the hole with a piece of chalk or crayon.

Always remove the cause of a puncture, or it will flat the tire again. If necessary, spread the sidewalls of the tire and look for the puncturing object from the inside. A tiny wire or shard of glass may not be visible from the outside.

If a tire has a hole more than ⅛ inch long, it must be covered with a "boot"—a piece of heavy cloth slipped into place to keep the inner tube from ballooning out. It's wise to carry a boot about 2 inches square in your tire-repair kit. You can cut a temporary boot from a discarded lightweight tire; glue it in place with contact cement when you get home. If a hole in the tire is more than ½ inch long, your best hope is to carry a spare tire, though a "bandage" of duct tape wrapped around tire and rim can get you to the next bike shop. Don't use the rim brake on that wheel!

Making a Cold-patch Repair

① Roughen the area around the puncture, using a piece of medium-grit sandpaper, or by rubbing it on clean pavement until the rubber looks dull. Do *not* use the grater supplied with auto patch kits; bicycle inner tubes are too thin for this. Work on an area slightly larger than the patch you intend to use. The patch should overlap the puncture by ½ inch on all sides.

② Apply an even coating of cement onto the tube and allow it to dry until it is tacky. Do *not* install the patch while the cement is still wet! The cemented area must overlap the patch on all sides.

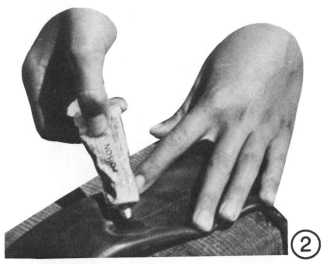

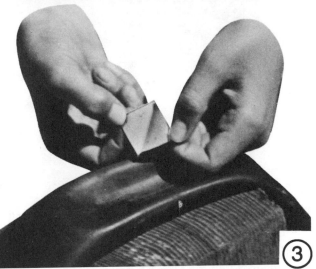

③ Separate the backing from the patch and place the center over the hole, with the adhesive side facing down. Hold the patch firmly in place for a short time to allow the cement to set, and then sprinkle some talcum powder over the patch to prevent it from sticking to the tire.

Installing a Clincher Tire and Tube

④ Stretch the rim tape around the rim, starting at the valve-stem hole. Be sure the strip is the correct width. It must not be wide enough to cover any portion of the bead part of the rim.

The purpose of the rim tape is to shield the inner tube from the spoke heads. An adhesive-backed cloth rim tape works better than a rubber one with a narrow rim, because a rubber rim tape is likely to break around the valve hole. If a rim has large, recessed spoke holes, a cloth rim tape *must* be used. A rubber rim tape would allow the inner tube to bulge into the spoke holes and blow out.

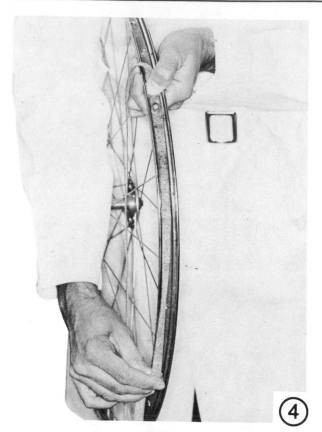

A rim strip which is too wide for the well of the rim will ride up on the shoulder, causing a lump in the tire.

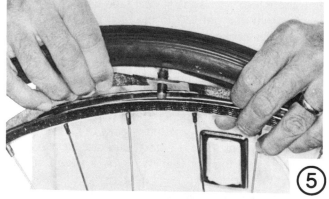

A good rim tape can be made of ½-inch-wide glass fiber filament tape or of duct tape ripped lengthwise. Use two or three layers. Cut out the valve hole with a utility knife after pressing the tape into place.

⑤ Inflate the tube just enough to hold its shape, and then insert it into the tire. A tube with a flexible rubber valve-stem base *must* be used with a narrow rim; a valve stem with a metal washer or nut will hold the valve out of position, stretch the inner tube around the valve stem, and lead to a blowout. If this happens even with a rubber valve stem, install a leather washer

around the valve stem or build up a ramp of plastic rubber material on both sides of the valve hole in the rim.

Feed the valve through the hole in the rim strip and

wheel rim. Position both sides of the tire bead into the wheel rim except in the area of the valve.

⑥ Now deflate the tube. Use your thumbs to work both beads of the tire onto the rim in both directions, starting opposite the valve. If you have difficulty working both sides of the tire onto the wheel at the same time, do one side and then work the other into position, using the tire levers for installing the final portion. **CAUTION: Be careful not to pinch the tube.** Inflate the tire partly and check to be sure the bead is properly positioned in the rim and the valve stem is straight. Press the valve into the tire to make sure that its base is *inside* the tire, not wedged between the tire and the rim. Spin the wheel to make sure that the tire is evenly seated, then inflate it to the specified pressure and install it on the bicycle.

Tubular Tire Repair

Special materials are needed to repair a tubular tire. They can be purchased in kit form. The kit includes very thin patches, plus a large piece to enable you to cut one to your own size, waxed linen thread, a needle, a thimble, some fine sandpaper, a tube of rubber cement, and a small colored marking pencil. The quantity of items is enough to make about a dozen repairs. In addition to the kit, you will need a sharp knife or single-edged razor blade and some talcum powder. **CAUTION: Do not attempt to repair a tubular tire with a thick patch; it will cause a lump inside the tire, which will thump each time the tire rotates.**

A repair kit for tubular tires contains all of the items needed to make about a dozen repairs, as described in the text.

Remove the wheel and damaged tire from the bicycle. If the tire is not mounted, install it on an old rim if you have one handy. If not, you will have to work with just the tire. Inflate the tire to approximately 60 psi, and then slowly rotate it in a container of water; watch for air bubbles. You may notice air seeping from around the valve stem for a short time. This is normal, because the tire has a rubber strip cemented over the sewing in the area of the valve and this is the only place trapped air can escape except from an injury. When you locate

the puncture, mark the spot with the colored pencil from the kit or a piece of chalk. Remove the valve nut and deflate the tire. Remove the tire from the rim by working it off with your hands and thumbs, starting on the side of the wheel opposite the valve. **CAUTION: Do not use any type of tool or you may damage the tire or the tube.**

If tape is used on the rim, be careful not to wrinkle it or pull it loose from the rim unless you intend to remove it for inspection or work on the spoke heads.

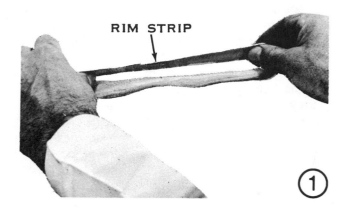

RIM STRIP

① Carefully peel back 5 inches of the rim strip from the tire on both sides of the puncture. Make a couple of marks across the stitching with the pencil. This will ensure that the original holes are used during the restitching so the tire will retain its proper shape. Fold the tire at the stitching, and then carefully cut about 2 inches of the stitching on both sides of the injury, using a single-edged razor blade or sharp knife. Work cautiously to prevent cutting the tire cords or the tube. Remove the old thread.

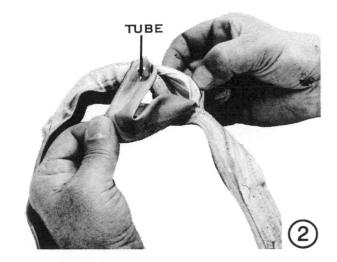

TUBE

② Push back the protective cloth and pull out about 6 to 8 inches of the tube. Inflate the tube slightly with a hand pump and locate the puncture by holding the tube close to your face and feeling for escaping air. Or wet the area with soapy water, and then watch for bubbles. Dry the tube thoroughly and mark the hole plainly with a colored pencil or piece of chalk.

③ Deflate the tube and stretch it out on a flat surface until it is free of wrinkles. Roughen the area around the injury with a piece of sandpaper. Be careful not to let any dust or dirt enter the tire casing. Work an area slightly larger than the size of the patch you intend to use. Cover the buffed area with a smooth coating of cement and allow it to dry until it has a hard glaze. Remove the backing from the patch, and then place the center of the patch over the hole, with the adhesive side facing down. Hold the patch firmly in place for a short time to allow the cement to set. Sprinkle some talcum powder over the patch to prevent it from sticking to the tire. *NOTE: If the tire casing has a small fracture, apply a canvas or regular patch on the inside of the tire following the same procedure used for patching the tube. Use hardware-store contact cement. However, if you do patch the casing, the tire should be used only for a spare, because it has lost considerable strength.*

④ Place the protective cloth over the tube and smooth it free of wrinkles. Fold the tire at the stitching and align the pencil marks you made before cutting the tire open. This will ensure that the old holes are aligned and that the tire will retain its proper shape. Thread the needle with the waxed linen thread from the kit and begin stitching the tire, starting a few stitches back from the cut. Make the first few stitches over the end of the thread to prevent having to make a knot for the thread to hold. **CAUTION: Be extremely careful during the sewing operation to ensure that the holes on both sides of the tire are aligned, and that the tube is not punctured with the needle. Pull the thread up snug, but not so tight that the thread cuts into the casing.** Place the end of the thread under the last few stitches, and then pull the stitches taut. This is a sailmaker's method and eliminates the necessity of knotting the thread at the end of the job.

⑤ Apply a thin coating of rubber cement to the rim strip and to the tire over the repaired area, and let it dry for a few minutes. Position the rim strip on the tire evenly and without wrinkles.

Installing a Tubular Tire

New tubulars often are hard to install until they have been prestretched. Before installing a brand-new tire, stretch it over a rim without using rim cement or tape, inflate it to full pressure, and leave it overnight. Old, dry cement on the tire-stretching rim is all right, but don't add any new cement. It is helpful to keep a couple of old, dented rims to use for stretching tires.

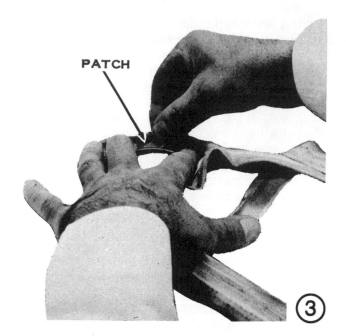

PATCH

③

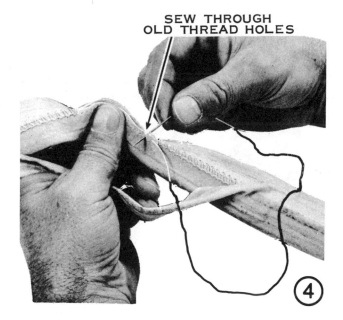

SEW THROUGH
OLD THREAD HOLES

④

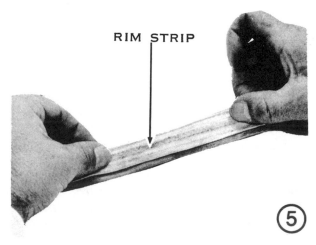

RIM STRIP

⑤

For a quick on-road tubular tire replacement, both the tire and rim must have a layer of tire cement. Do not use a brand-new tire as your spare. If necessary, mount and remove a tire so that it will have cement.

⑥ On the wheel on which you will finally install the tire, check all the spoke heads to be sure they do not protrude to cause tire damage. If any of the heads do extend above the rim, file them smooth. Remove any old tape that is wrinkled or dirty, or if you suspect it will not hold the tire properly. If cement is used instead of tape and it is dirty or flaky or does not appear to be in good condition, clean the rim thoroughly with solvent. It is not good practice to apply new cement over the old because a buildup will result in bulged areas on the rim. If the tire is old and overstretched, use rim tape to build up the rim. Apply new rim tape by starting about 8 inches from the valve hole and setting it evenly in the rim channel. The tape is a double-coated type, with adhesive material on both sides. Pull the tape firmly around the rim and overlap the starting end by approximately 2 inches. Press the tape firmly into the rim channel with the handle of a wrench or other rounded object.

If cement is used, apply two or three light coats to the tire and the rim, allowing each to dry until tacky before applying the next. Use *road-type* tire cement from a bike shop or trim cement from an auto-parts store. (Track-type tire cement is not made for easy tire replacement.)

For an on-road repair, use a tire which has been on a rim previously, as described above. Unless it was cemented recently, use care in cornering. If you might need the spare tire in a race, apply fresh cement to it before the race.

⑦ Cut a valve-stem hole in the tape with a sharp knife or single-edged razor blade. Deflate the tire completely or until there is just enough air to give it a little shape. Place the valve stem through the hole in the rim, with the wheel in an upright position, as shown. Position the tire in place on the rim by working it on with your hands and moving it in both directions from the valve.

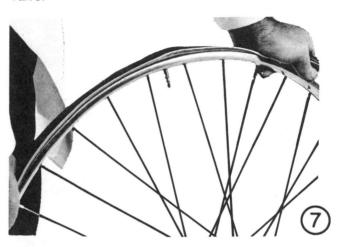

⑧ As you reach the opposite side of the rim from the valve, lift the wheel clear of the ground and work the last section on with your thumbs. Use a roll-on motion, but do not use a tool when mounting tubular tires. Inflate the tire slightly and work it around to lie properly on the rim. Inflate the tire to the recommended pressure and tighten the valve nut. Spin the wheel and check to be sure the tire is aligned properly on the rim and running true. If it is not running true, deflate the tire, smooth out the twisted parts with your hands, inflate the tire, and then recheck it for running true. Clean any excess cement from the rim and tire with alcohol. If cement was used instead of the rim tape, allow the wheel to set for several hours, preferably overnight, before riding on it.

RIM TAPE

8"

VALVE HOLE

⑥

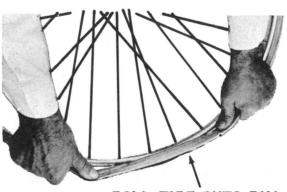

**ROLL TIRE ONTO RIM
USE HANDS—NO TOOLS**

⑧

CABLE AND LEVER MAINTENANCE

Brake and shifting cable lubrication and replacement should be given careful attention in order to maintain your bicycle in a safe and operable condition. As soon as a cable shows evidence of damage or fraying, it should be replaced, to ensure your ability to stop in an emergency.

How a Cable Works

To understand how a bicycle cable works, examine a cable in its housing. The cable is made of multistrand steel wire, twisted together like rope. The plastic-coated housing is a spiral of steel wire like a coil spring, but with each turn tight against the next. To pull the cable out of one end of the housing, you must also push the housing back. At the far end, the cable pulls and the housing pushes. This is clear if you attach an anchor bolt (cable clamp bolt) to the far end of the cable. When the anchor bolt hits the end of the housing, you can't pull the cable any farther out of the housing.

Now let's look at the cable in a sidepull brake system. Just like your hands, the brake lever pulls the cable *and pushes against the housing.* At the brake, the cable pulls one brake arm and the housing pushes the other. If you haven't thought about cables, you probably think that a sidepull brake applies unequal force to the two sides of the rim. In fact, the cable and housing each squeeze their brake arm against the rim with equal force.

The cable is a clever idea not only because it applies two forces, but also because it can carry forces around curves and change their direction. A cable is much simpler than any system of rods or levers that might operate a brake or shift mechanism. Imagine the Rube Goldberg lever contraption that would be needed to get from the handlebar to a rear-wheel brake!

Cable Maintenance

A cable can fail suddenly. A loose anchor bolt can slip, or the cable can fray and snap. These are good reasons to have two independent brakes, and to service the cables regularly.

A cable going around a curve rubs against the inside of the housing like a rope wrapped around a tree. This creates friction. The cable must be lubricated with

How a cable works. As you pull the cable-end button and the housing apart, the other end of the cable and the housing are pulled together.

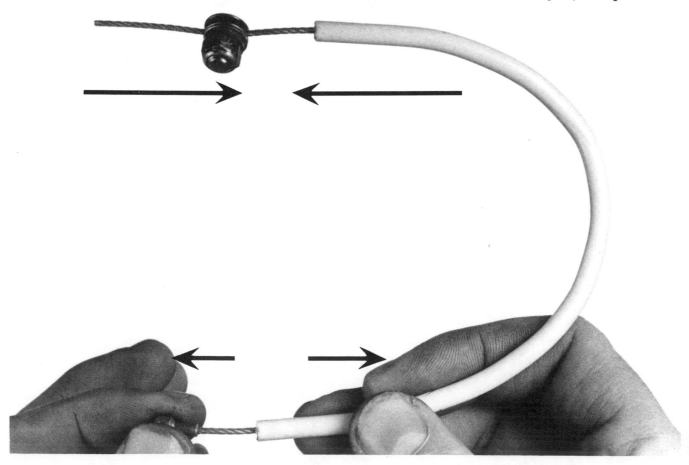

grease or oil to keep the friction down and to prevent rust. It is also important to avoid sharp kinks or bends, which snag the cable.

An unlubricated, rusty, or kinked cable works stiffly. The cable jumps along in little steps, making the brake hard to modulate. The brake may fail to release when you let go of the lever.

A drop of oil where the cable emerges from the housing is helpful between overhauls, but for a full lubrication and inspection, the cable must be removed from the housing.

The procedures that follow are essentially the same for cables of all types of tourist and hooded lever-type brakes.

Removing Brake Cables

To remove a brake cable on either sidepull or center-pull caliper brakes, front or rear, first loosen the cable anchor bolt nut, and then pull the cable out of the anchor bolt and the lower housing. Next, squeeze the brake lever, pull the housing and ferrule back on the cable, push the cable-end button free of the retainer slot, and then pull the cable out of the upper housing-and-lever assembly.

Take your old cable along when purchasing a new one, to assure that it will be long enough. It is best to replace the housing, not just the cable, especially if the old housing is kinked or bent. If the only new cable or housing you can get is too long, you can cut off the excess when you install it.

The two brakes are used differently. Most people in North America learn to operate the front brake with the left hand, but there are exceptions. Install the brake cables to suit the rider. **CAUTION: Reversed cables can cause a loss of control.**

Installing Brake Cables

Before installing the new cable, lay the housing along the frame in the position it will finally take. Mark the housing to cut it to length. The housing should be as short as possible while still meeting its attachment points straight-on. The shorter and straighter the cable, the more smoothly it will work. Precut cables and housings are almost always too long, because they are made for the biggest bicycles.

Cut a cable housing with a wire cutter, after removing the inner cable. Then smooth and flatten the cut end with a file. Often you can rescue a kinked cable housing by cutting off an inch or so of the damaged end—usually the end at the lever. Do not cut the inner cable to length until you have installed it.

Apply a thick coating of multipurpose grease in the areas of the cable where it is enclosed in the housing.

To remove the cable from either sidepull or centerpull/cantilever caliper brakes, first loosen the anchor bolt nut and then pull the cable free of the anchor bolt.

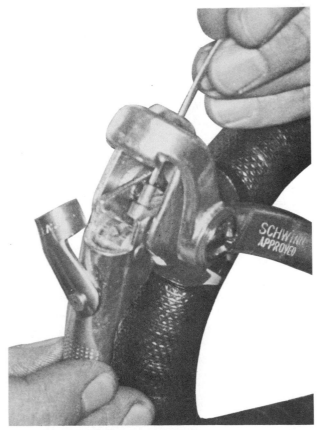

At the brake lever, insert the cable-end button through the ferrule hole in the lever hood, then place the button in the slot at the inner side of the brake lever.

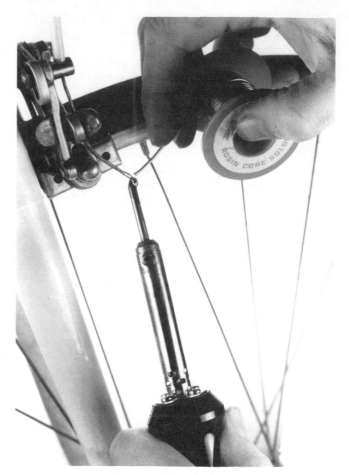

After feeding the cable through the housings and anchor bolt, clamp the brake shoes with a "third-hand" tool or a length of string or old toestrap, pull the cable taut with a pair of pliers, and tighten the anchor bolt nut.

THIRD HAND TOOL

Prevent the end of the cable from fraying by soldering together the strands at the cut end, or else use "super glue."

Place a drop or two of high-quality cycle oil on the cable-end button.

Push the lubricated inner cable through the ferrule and the upper housing. Leave approximately 6 inches of the cable, with the button on it, exposed from the end of the housing. Insert the cable-end button through the ferrule hole in the bracket, and then place the button in the retainer slot at the inner side of the brake lever. Pull the cable taut, and then seat the ferrule in the bracket. Slide the cable housing up against the ferrule.

Feed the free end of the cable through the lower housing and cable anchor bolt. Squeeze the brake shoes against the wheel rim, using a "third hand" tool, or tighten a piece of cord around both arms and through the wheel. Pull the cable taut with a pair of pliers and simultaneously tighten the anchor nut. Remove the "third hand" tool or piece of cord. The brake shoes should release to about ⅛ inch from the rim.

Tighten the anchor bolt securely, but do not over-tighten it. You could strip the threads, or break the bolt at the hole where the cable goes through. Expect to break a few bolts before you get a feel for the correct adjustment. Oil the threads before tightening. Test that the anchor bolt is tight enough by squeezing the brake lever as hard as you can with *both* hands.

If the brake shoes release more than ⅛ inch or do not move clear of the rim, make a final adjustment by turning the adjusting barrel. *NOTE: Brake shoes will wear in use; therefore be sure to check the distance of the shoes from the rim periodically and make an adjustment if necessary.*

Once the cable is installed, cut it off about 1 inch past the anchor bolt.

New bikes usually come with a plastic or metal cap over the end of the cable. This has to be removed to overhaul the cable. A more effective tactic is to apply rosin-core solder to the end of the cable, or use a drop of liquid "super glue" to cement the strands of the cable together. If the cable is of the extra-flexible braided stainless-steel type, solder will not stick; you must use glue. If there is any grease or oil on the cable end, clean it with solvent before soldering or glueing it.

Servicing Brake Levers

A brake lever is held to the handlebar by a clamp band. On drop-bar levers, the bolt which tightens the band is inside the lever hood. You must remove the

If a brake lever is secured to the handlebar by a partial clamp band, as shown, the tabs of the nut inside the lever must face inward, away from the handlebar.

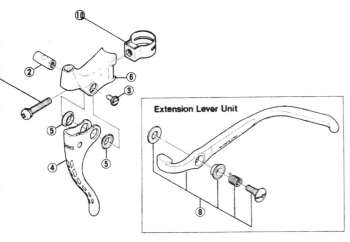

Exploded view of the Shimano model BL-Z304, a typical dropped-handlebar brake lever.

ITEM	DESCRIPTION
2	Pull-up stud
3	LD cap
4	Main lever assembly
5	Bushing A
6	Lever bracket
8	Extension lever unit
9	Clamp screw
10	Clamp band

cable to get at the clamp band. By loosening a brake quick release, or by removing one brake shoe and squeezing the brake arms together, you can slip the cable out of the slot in most levers without disturbing its length adjustment.

Most steel handlebars are 22mm in diameter and most aluminum handlebars are 23.5mm in diameter. Different-sized clamp bands are required. The size usually is marked on the clamp band.

Some clamp bands are loop-shaped, but with most levers the clamp band is U-shaped, with a hole at either end which clips to a special tabbed nut on the tightening bolt. The tabs must face away from the handlebar.

It is very important to tighten the brake levers securely. Especially when out of the saddle, the rider may pull very hard on them. Test them by trying to twist them around the handlebars.

Rubber brake-lever hoods make the levers more comfortable and give a better grip. Slip them over the lever hoods before installing the cables. It is easiest to install hoods from the handlebar side, before installing the brake levers.

Rubber hoods and brake extension levers get in each other's way. Unless the handlebars are too far from the rider—a serious problem in itself—rubber hoods are preferable to extension levers. After unscrewing an extension lever, you can hacksaw off the extra-long brake lever pin that holds it in place, and then install a rubber hood. This is simpler than disassembling the entire lever mechanism to install a shorter pin.

Shift-control Cables

Instructions for shift-control cables are very similar to those for brake cables. Refer to the brake-cable instructions for a description of basic maintenance procedures. This section deals with derailleur control cables; for multispeed hubs, refer to Chapter 14.

The most common problem with a derailleur-control cable is loosening of the adjusting wingnut on the control lever. This wingnut sets the friction to keep the lever from slipping. When the wingnut loosens, the cable slips and the derailleur shifts by itself. Some people struggle all the time in high gear because nobody showed them how to adjust the wingnut while riding.

Frame and stem-mounted shift-control assemblies are almost identical, as can be seen in the two accompanying exploded views. The main difference is that the lever assembly does not have to be disassembled on the stem-mounted unit in order to replace the cable. Instead, the adjusting wingnut can be loosened.

Separate procedures are included for the fingertip controls installed in the end of the handlebars.

On bicycles equipped with front and rear derailleurs, the right-side lever must always control the rear derailleur and the left-side lever the front derailleur.

Several methods are used to mount the control cables on the frame. A solid cable housing may be used, extending from the control to the derailleur unit, held in place by one or more cable clips. Another

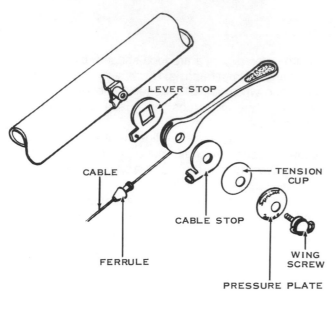

CABLE

FERRULE

LEVER STOP

CABLE STOP

PRESSURE PLATE

TENSION CUP

WING SCREW

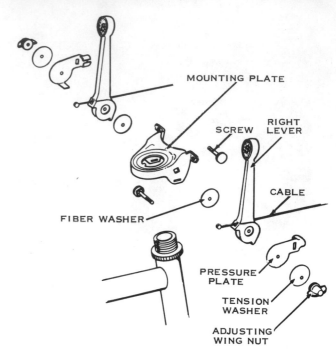

MOUNTING PLATE

SCREW

RIGHT LEVER

CABLE

FIBER WASHER

PRESSURE PLATE

TENSION WASHER

ADJUSTING WING NUT

Exploded view of a typical stem-mounted shift-control lever assembly. The hole in the lever for the control cable must always face to the rear.

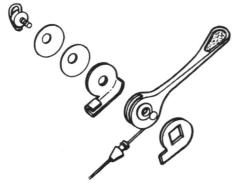

Exploded view of a typical frame-mounted shift-control lever assembly. Mountings differ from brand to brand—important if they are brazed to the frame. The control levers often differ left from right. With the straight side of the lever facing toward the frame, the buttonhole should be at the bottom.

method is to have a split housing and the fittings either welded to the frame or clamped with mounting screws.

Be sure to take your old cable with you when purchasing a new one to ensure that the new cable will be long enough.

Removing a Frame- or Stem-mounted Lever Control Cable

For a rear derailleur control cable, turn the pedals and shift the chain onto the smallest sprocket of the rear cluster and the smallest chainwheel. Move the control lever to the full-forward position. Next, loosen the cable anchor bolt nut at the rear derailleur and pull the cable and housing out of the anchor bolt and adjusting barrel. Slide the cable housing off the cable and the cable out of the fulcrum on the frame. Pull the cable out of the housing and the clips at the hanger set.

For frame-mounted control units, remove the adjusting screw at the control lever, and then remove the pressure plate, dished tension cup, cable stop, and lever from the lever stud, as shown in the accompany-

ing exploded drawing. Remove the cable-end button from the lever.

For stem-mounted control units, loosen the adjusting screw and then pull the cable out through the back side of the lever.

For a front derailleur control cable, loosen the cable anchor bolt nut, and then pull the cable out of the bolt and cable guide. Slide the cable housing off the cable and the cable out of the frame clip.

Remove the adjusting screw at the control lever, and then remove the pressure plate, dished tension cup, cable stop, and lever from the lever stud. Remove the cable-end button from the lever.

Installing a Frame- or Stem-mounted Lever Control Cable

Before installing a new cable, apply a thick coating of multipurpose lubricant in the areas where it is enclosed in the cable housing. Place a drop or two of high-quality cycle oil on the cable-end button.

For frame-mounted control levers, guide the cable-end button into the button hole in the control lever. Assemble the cable stop, tension cup, pressure plate, and wing screw in the order shown in the accompanying exploded drawing.

For stem-mounted control levers, feed the lubricated cable through the back side of the lever and through the mounting bracket hole. Seat the cable-end button in the lever hole. Slide the cable through the housing and clips to the derailleur.

At the rear derailleur, position the chain onto the smallest sprocket at the rear cluster with the control lever in the full-forward position. Turn the cable-

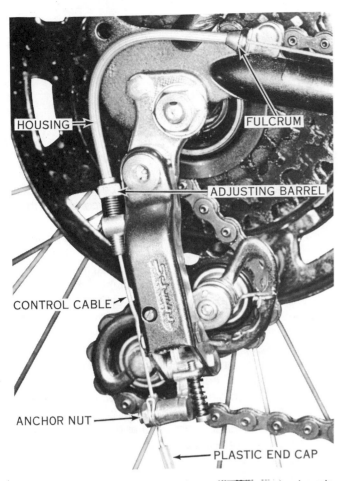

HOUSING

FULCRUM

ADJUSTING BARREL

CONTROL CABLE

ANCHOR NUT

PLASTIC END CAP

Typical control-cable hookup to the rear derailleur, showing principal attachment points, as discussed in the text.

Typical front derailleur control-cable routing.

At the rear derailleur, slide the cable into the cable guide and anchor bolt. Draw the cable taut and be sure that the cable housing is seated properly. Tighten the anchor bolt nut securely and cut off excess cable, leaving about 1 inch beyond the anchor bolt.

adjusting barrel down as far as it will go. Slide the cable through the barrel and the cable anchor bolt. Pull the cable taut with a pair of pliers. Check to be sure the housing is properly seated in the fulcrum and adjusting barrel. Tighten the anchor bolt nut. Cut off any excess cable, leaving approximately 1 inch beyond the anchor

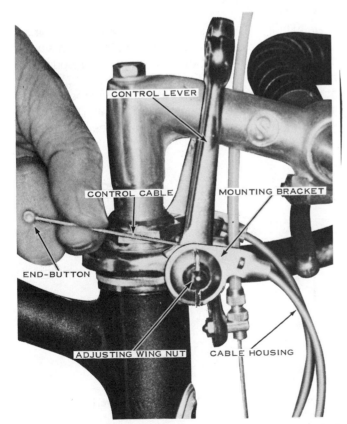

CONTROL LEVER

CONTROL CABLE

MOUNTING BRACKET

END-BUTTON

ADJUSTING WING NUT

CABLE HOUSING

After lubricating the control cable with multipurpose grease and dripping oil into the housing, feed the cable through the back of the lever and through the mounting-bracket hole. Seat the cable-end button in the lever hole.

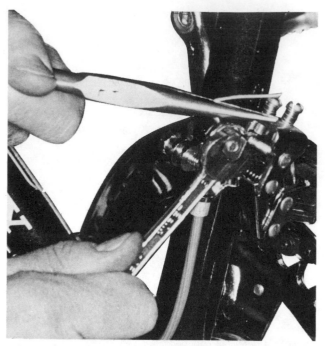

At the front derailleur, guide the cable into the cable guide and anchor bolt. Draw the cable taut and be sure that the cable housing is seated properly. Tighten the anchor bolt nut securely and cut the cable, leaving about 1 inch beyond the anchor bolt.

bolt. Solder or glue the end of the cable to keep it from fraying.

At the front derailleur, position the chain onto the smallest chainwheel with the control lever as far forward as possible. Guide the cable into the cable guide and anchor bolt. Draw the cable taut and be sure the cable housing is seated properly. Tighten the anchor bolt nut securely. Cut off any excess cable, leaving approximately 1 inch beyond the anchor bolt, and then solder or glue the end of the cable to keep it from fraying.

Check the tension adjustment on the control lever; tighten the wingnut just enough to prevent the chain from shifting by itself. *NOTE: A new cable may stretch after it has been in use. Take out the slack by turning the derailleur's adjusting barrel.*

Removing Fingertip Control Cables

Procedures for replacing a control cable for the front or rear derailleur are essentially the same, except for the work at the derailleur unit and the adjustment. The rear derailleur control must always be connected to the right-hand lever and the front derailleur control to the left-hand lever.

For the rear derailleur control cable, place the control lever in the full-forward position and then turn the pedals to allow the chain to shift onto the smallest sprocket of the cluster. Remove the cable from the cable anchor bolt and adjusting barrel. Slide the cable housing off the cable, and then remove the cable from the fulcrums or clips.

For the front derailleur control cable, loosen the cable anchor bolt and then pull the cable out of the bolt and cable guide or housing.

NOTE: The remainder of the procedures apply to both front and rear derailleur control cables.

Remove the locknut from the handlebar control lever, using the correct-size metric wrench, and then take out the lever screw. Push the lever bushing out of the mounting body, and then remove the lever and washers (on both sides of the lever) from the mounting body. Pull the cable out of the cable housing and the lever holes.

Details of other brands of fingertip levers may differ from the ones shown. On some, you remove a screw first, rather than a locknut. Many have a spring or ratchet inside the lever to pull against the cable and make shifting easier. In this case, the lever mechanism fits into a slot in the mounting body, which keeps the spring or ratchet from rotating out of position.

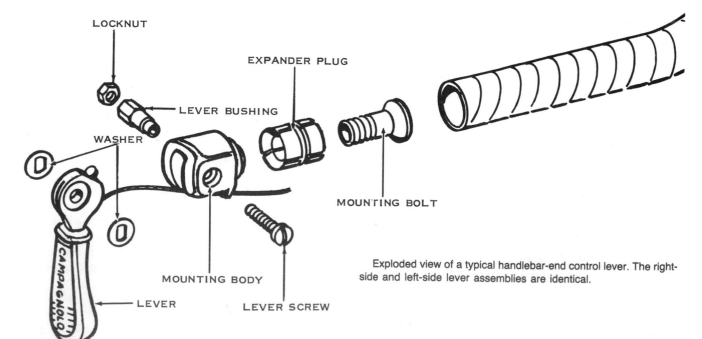

Exploded view of a typical handlebar-end control lever. The right-side and left-side lever assemblies are identical.

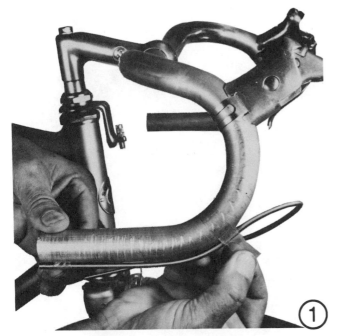

1

third the width of the tape. Leave about 2 inches of tape beyond the end of the handlebar, cut off the excess, and then tuck the end of the tape inside the handlebar.

③ Insert the control body into the handlebar, with the slotted portion of the body facing down and the cable hole aligned with the cable housing. Secure the body in the handlebar by turning the mounting screw inside the body counterclockwise with the correct-size Allen wrench.

④ Place a washer on each side of the lever, and then guide the lever into the mounting body, with the lever key indexed with the keyway in the body. Install the mounting bushing into the mounting body, with the flats of the bushing aligned with the flats of the washers and the head fully seated in the hexagon hole in the body.

⑤ Thread the mounting screw into the body until the lever is snug, and then install and tighten the locknut.

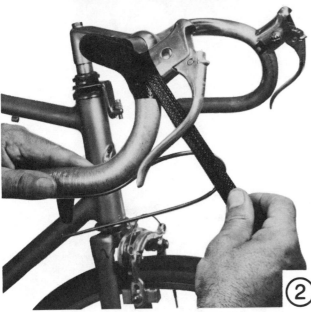

2

If the mounting body is to be removed in order to install new tape on the handlebars, insert the correct-size Allen wrench in the hexagonal hole of the mounting body. Turn it clockwise until the body is loose, and then pull the body out of the handlebar, as indicated in the accompanying exploded view. Remove the handlebar tape and cable housing, if it needs to be replaced.

Installing Fingertip Control Cables

① Position the end of the cable housing at the bottom of the handlebar and let it extend approximately ⅛ inch past the end of the bar. Temporarily install the mounting body in the end of the handlebar to align the end of the housing with the mounting body's housing stop. Secure the housing in place with a piece of tape.

② Tape the handlebar, beginning about 2 inches from the stem and overlapping each turn about one-

3

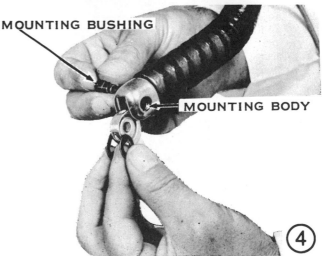

MOUNTING BUSHING

MOUNTING BODY

4

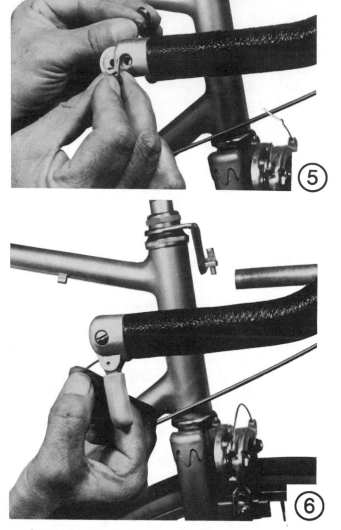

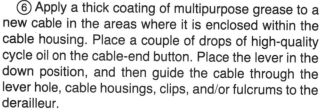

⑥ Apply a thick coating of multipurpose grease to a new cable in the areas where it is enclosed within the cable housing. Place a couple of drops of high-quality cycle oil on the cable-end button. Place the lever in the down position, and then guide the cable through the lever hole, cable housings, clips, and/or fulcrums to the derailleur.

⑦ At the rear derailleur, position the chain onto the smallest sprocket of the cluster with the control lever in the full-down position. If the lever has a return spring, you will have to tighten the lever's adjusting screw to hold it in the down position.

Turn the derailleur's cable-adjusting barrel down as far as it will go. Slide the cable through the barrel and the cable anchor bolt. Pull the cable taut with a pair of pliers. Check to be sure the housing is properly seated in the fulcrum and the adjusting barrel. Tighten the anchor bolt nut. Cut off any excess cable, leaving about 1 inch beyond the anchor bolt. Solder or glue the end of the cable to keep it from fraying.

⑧ Check the tension on the control lever as follows. Shift the chain onto the largest sprocket at the rear cluster, and then release the lever while continuing to pedal. If the chain shifts onto one of the smaller sprockets, loosen the locknut, tighten the pivot screw until the lever action is stiff enough to prevent the chain from moving off the largest sprocket, and then retighten the locknut.

⑨ At the front derailleur, rotate the cranks forward to position the chain, and place the control lever in the down position. Draw the cable taut with the housing properly seated. Tighten the anchor nut securely. Cut off excess cable, leaving approximately 1 inch beyond the anchor bolt. Solder or glue the end of the cable to keep it from fraying.

Check the adjustment of the control lever by pulling the lever back to shift the chain while you spin the crank. If the chain shifts back to the other chainwheel after the lever is released, tighten the lever wingnut or adjusting screw until the lever has just enough friction to prevent this.

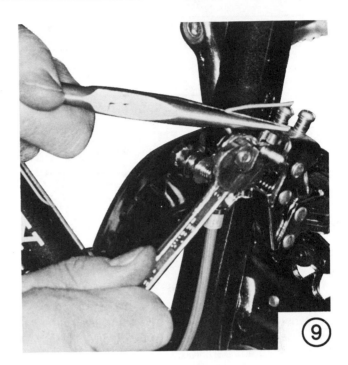

7 • THE MULTI-SPROCKET DRIVETRAIN

Transferring power from the rider's feet to the rear wheel is the job of the bicycle's drivetrain: pedals, crankset, chain, derailleurs, freewheel body, and rear sprockets.

The chain is the first part that must be removed in many drivetrain maintenance procedures, and it frequently requires service. Instructions for maintenance of the chain begin on page 105.

Trace drivetrain problems as fully as possible *before* disassembling the drivetrain for service. Many problems result from mismatched or misaligned parts. Other problems are caused by one part but show up in another. For example, when the chain jumps off the sprockets, the problem may be in a derailleur.

For these reasons, this chapter gives a unified problem chart for all of the parts of a drivetrain, and instructions for inspection before disassembly and after reassembly.

DRIVETRAIN PROBLEMS

The troubleshooting chart below applies primarily to derailleur-equipped bicycles. See Chapter 13 for information on single-sprocket drivetrains, Chapter 14 for information on internally geared and coaster-brake hubs, and Chapter 8 for information on simple hubs.

Front Derailleur and Crank-related Problems

Chain does not shift to outer chainwheel.

Possible cause:	Corrective action:
High-gear limit screw is advanced too far.	Readjust.
Derailleur is bent.	Straighten or replace.
Derailleur is dirty or rusted; pivots stiff.	Rebuild or replace.
Cable is dirty, rusted, or kinked.	Rebuild cable.
Cable is misadjusted.	Adjust cable length.
Derailleur travel is insufficient.	Replace derailleur.
Derailleur is too high above chainwheels.	Reposition derailleur.
Bottom-bracket axle is too long.	Replace axle.

Chain falls off outer chainwheel.

Possible cause:	Corrective action:
High-gear limit screw is backed out too far.	Readjust.
Outer chainwheel or crank assembly is bent.	Straighten or replace.
Chainwheel tooth is bent.	Straighten.
Derailleur is bent.	Straighten or replace.
Derailleur is too high above chainwheels.	Reposition derailleur.
Chain link is stiff or bent.	Replace chain or adjust link.

Chain does not shift to inner chainwheel.

Possible cause:	Corrective action:
Low-gear limit screw is advanced too far.	Readjust.
Front derailleur is bent.	Straighten or replace.
Cable is dirty, rusted, or kinked.	Rebuild cable.
Cable is misadjusted.	Adjust cable length.
Derailleur is dirty or rusted; pivots stiff.	Rebuild or replace.
Derailleur travel is insufficient.	Replace derailleur.

Chain falls off inner chainwheel.

Possible cause:	Corrective action:
Front derailleur is bent.	Rebuild or replace.
Low-gear limit screw is backed out too far.	Readjust.
Chainwheel or crank assembly is bent.	Straighten or replace.
Chainwheel tooth is bent.	Straighten tooth.
Chain link is stiff or bent.	Replace chain or adjust link.

Chain drags on bottom of front chain cage.

Possible cause:	Corrective action:
Derailleur is too high above chainwheels.	Reposition derailleur.
Short-cage derailleur is used with wide-range chainwheels.	Use long-cage derailleur.

Chain jumps over middle chainwheel of triple chainwheel set.

Possible cause:	Corrective action:
Half-step derailleur is used with crossover gearing.	Use crossover derailleur.
Chainwheel spacing is too narrow.	Adjust spacing.

Chain drops between chainwheels.

Possible cause:	Corrective action:
Chainwheel spacing is too wide.	Adjust spacing.
Narrow chain is used when not necessary.	Replace chain.
Chainwheel is reversed.	Install chainwheel with smoother side in toward bike.

Rear Derailleur and Freewheel-related Problems

Chain does not shift to smallest rear sprocket.

Possible cause:	Corrective action:
High-gear limit screw is advanced too far.	Readjust.
Rear derailleur is bent.	Straighten or replace.
Derailleur is dirty or rusted.	Rebuild or replace.
Cable is dirty, rusted, or kinked.	Rebuild cable.
Cable is too tight.	Adjust cable.
Derailleur travel is insufficient.	Replace derailleur.
Derailleur pulley is too far below sprockets.	Adjust or replace derailleur.
Chain is too long.	Shorten chain.

With the super-low gear obtainable with modern equipment, even this steep hill is easy to climb.

Chain shifts beyond smallest rear sprocket.

Possible cause:	Corrective action:
High-gear limit screw is backed out too far.	Readjust.
Rear derailleur is bent.	Straighten or replace.
Small-sprocket tooth is bent.	Straighten tooth.
Chain is too long and loose.	Shorten chain.
Chain link is stiff or bent.	Replace chain or free link.

Chain does not shift to largest rear sprocket.

Possible cause:	Corrective action:
Low-gear limit screw is advanced too far.	Readjust.
Rear derailleur is bent.	Straighten or replace.
Derailleur is dirty or rusted.	Rebuild or replace.
Cable is dirty, rusted, or kinked.	Rebuild cable.
Short-cage derailleur is used with large sprockets.	Replace derailleur.
Derailleur travel is insufficient.	Replace derailleur.
Cable is too loose.	Adjust cable.
Chain is too short.	Replace entire chain.

Chain shifts beyond largest rear sprocket.

Possible cause:	Corrective action:
Low-gear limit screw is backed out too far.	Readjust.
Rear derailleur is bent.	Straighten or replace.
Large-sprocket tooth is bent.	Straighten tooth.
Chain link is stiff or bent.	Replace chain or adjust link.
Freewheel bearings are loose.	Adjust bearings.

Chain shifts across two rear sprockets at once.

Possible cause:	Corrective action:
Rear derailleur pivots are worn.	Replace derailleur.
Rear derailleur pivots are loose.	Rebuild derailleur.
Jockey pulley is too far below sprockets.	Adjust or replace derailleur.
Wide chain is used with narrow cog spacing.	Use narrow chain.
Rear sprocket bevel faces outside.	Reverse sprocket(s).
Cable is dirty, rusted, or kinked.	Rebuild cable.
Toothless jockey pulley is used with Sedisport chain.	Replace jockey pulley.
Jockey pulley is worn.	Replace jockey pulley.

Rear derailleur strikes spokes.

Possible cause:	Corrective action:
Rear derailleur is bent.	Straighten or replace.
Rear derailleur pivots are loose.	Rebuild or replace.
Rear wheel is improperly spoked.	Rebuild; see Chapter 17.

Chain hangs loose in some gears.

Possible cause:	Corrective action:
Ultra-wide-range touring gearing.	Normal condition.
Chain is too long.	Shorten chain.
Rear derailleur pivots are stiff.	Rebuild or replace.
Rear derailleur is bent.	Rebuild or replace.
Short-cage rear derailleur is used with large sprockets.	Replace derailleur.

Chain binds when backpedaling.

Possible cause:	Corrective action:
Rear shift lever is in another gear.	Instruct rider.
Chain angle is excessive.	Correct chainline.
Chain is dirty or rusted.	Clean or replace chain.
Chain link is stiff or bent.	Replace chain or adjust link.

Shifting-related Problems

Bike shifts gears by itself.

Possible cause:	Corrective action:
Shift lever friction screw is too loose.	Tighten friction screw.
Cable is dirty, kinked, or misadjusted.	Rebuild cable.

Shifting is difficult.

Possible cause:	Corrective action:
Derailleur is dirty or rusted.	Rebuild or replace.
Derailleur pivots are stiff.	Rebuild or replace.
Cable is dirty, rusted, or kinked.	Rebuild cable.
Cable is too tight or loose.	Adjust cable.
Derailleur is bent.	Straighten or replace.
Shift lever friction screw is too tight.	Adjust friction screw.

Freewheel Assembly Problems

Threading freewheel to hub is difficult.

Possible cause:	Corrective action:
Attempt to mate French and English threads.	Use another freewheel.
Failure to grease threads.	Grease and reinstall.
Crossthreading.	Align and reinstall.

Hub threads are stripped.

Possible cause:	Corrective action:
Attempt to mate French and English threads.	Replace hub.
Crossthreading.	Replace hub.

Sprockets are loose on freewheel.

Possible cause:	Corrective action:
Too few or incorrect sprockets.	Reassemble.
Incorrect sprocket spacers are installed.	Exchange spacers.
Lugged sprocket is caught on edge of flange.	Reassemble to freewheel.

Noises and Surprises

Chain jumps forward while coasting.

Possible cause:	Corrective action:
Freewheel bearings are adjusted too tight.	Add a shim.
Freewheel pawls are dirty or rusted.	Lubricate freewheel.
Freewheel pawls are damaged.	Replace freewheel.

Chain jumps forward while pedaling.

Possible cause:	Corrective action:
Old chain is used with new sprockets.	Replace chain.

Possible cause:	Corrective action:
Chain link is stiff.	Loosen link.
Chain or sprockets are severely worn.	Replace chain or sprockets.
Chainwheel or sprocket tooth is bent.	Straighten tooth.
Chain is dirty or rusted.	Clean or replace chain.
Freewheel pawls are sticking.	Replace freewheel.

Wheel creaks and pings when riding but not on work stand.

Possible cause:	Corrective action:
Spokes are loose.	See Chapter 17.
Rear derailleur is striking spokes.	See that category in problem chart.

Wheel makes clunking noise each time around when pedaling.

Possible cause:	Corrective action:
Outer freewheel bearing race is loose.	Tighten.
Freewheel bearings are adjusted too loose.	Remove a shim.
Sprocket tooth is bent.	Straighten or replace.

Chain squeaks.

Possible cause:	Corrective action:
Chain is unlubricated.	Lubricate chain.

Chain makes grinding noise at front.

Possible cause:	Corrective action:
Lever is misadjusted.	Instruct rider.
Derailleur is bent.	Rebuild or replace.
Derailleur travel is insufficient.	Replace derailleur.
Derailleur is dirty or rusted; pivots are tight.	Rebuild or replace.
Limit screw is misadjusted.	Adjust limit screw.
Bottom-bracket axle is too long.	Replace axle.
Cable is dirty, rusted, or kinked.	Rebuild cable.
Cable is misadjusted.	Adjust cable.
Bent chainwheel strikes derailleur or frame.	Straighten or replace.

Each turn of crank causes click, clunk, or squeak.

Possible cause:	Corrective action:
Pedal is loose on crank.	Tighten pedal.
Pedal parts are loose.	Repair or replace pedal.
Chainwheel is loose on crank.	Tighten chainwheel bolts.
Chainwheel tooth is bent.	Straighten tooth.

Crank is loose on spindle.	Tighten crank.
Crank is striking front derailleur.	Adjust derailleur.
Bottom-bracket bearings are worn.	Rebuild bottom bracket.
Bottom-bracket cup is loose.	Rebuild bottom bracket.
Saddle or seatpost creaks.	Grease seatpost.

Every three or four turns of crank produce clunk, click, or squeak.

Possible cause:	Corrective action:
Chain is dry.	Lubricate.
Chain link is bent.	Straighten or replace.
Chain has been assembled from different pieces.	Replace chain.

Chain runs noisily at rear.

Possible cause:	Corrective action:
Chain angle is excessive.	Correct chainline.
Derailleur is bent.	Rebuild or replace.
Limit screw is misadjusted.	Adjust limit screw.
Derailleur is dirty or rusted; pivots are stiff.	Rebuild or replace.
Cable is dirty, rusted, or kinked.	Rebuild cable.
Cable is misadjusted.	Adjust cable.
Pulley bearing is stiff.	Rebuild pulley.
Forkend or fender bolt rubs chain.	Adjust hub spacing.
Derailleur is between gears.	Instruct rider.

INSPECTING THE DRIVETRAIN

Evaluate a drivetrain before disassembling it for rebuilding. There's no point in rebuilding worn-out or damaged components. You may avoid a second disassembly if you make a note of needed adjustments before rebuilding.

Test the drivetrain with the bicycle on the work stand. Listen for unusual noises and look for improper operation. If the drivetrain doesn't shift smoothly to all gears, try to find out why. Look especially for mismatched and worn-out parts. Points to check follow in the rest of this chapter.

Inspect the drivetrain again after reassembling it. There are several important adjustments to make after you have overhauled components or installed new ones.

CAUTION: If you fail to check derailleur limit-screw settings and chain length after rebuilding a drivetrain, there is risk of serious damage or even a crash the first time the bicycle is ridden.

The Right Gears for the Rider

All too likely, the gears originally installed on a bicycle will not serve the rider's needs well. Differences in terrain and riding style are too great.

Also, gearing systems are often designed not for best performance, but rather to calm the bike purchaser and the manufacturer's lawyers. The bicycle can be shifted into every possible combination, but at a cost: The shifting pattern is too complicated to remember, there is no gear low enough to climb a steep hill in comfort, and some gears duplicate others.

If you are rebuilding a drivetrain, read Chapter 9 on gearing patterns and decide whether there is room for improvement. Often you can make a big improvement while replacing sprockets which are worn out anyway.

Chainline and Chain Angle

Chainline is the distance between the chain and the centerline of the bicycle. A *chain angle* develops when the chainline is not the same at the front chainwheel and rear sprocket.

In the single-sprocket drivetrain of a coaster-brake or internally geared bike, the chain runs in a straight line for highest efficiency and lowest wear.

In a drivetrain with derailleurs, the chain often must run at an angle, since not all of the sprockets can be in line with each other. The smaller the angle, the better the drivetrain works. If chain angles are extreme, the chain may bind on a rear sprocket during backpedaling, bending the rear derailleur.

Each (front) chainwheel should be centered on the sprockets used with it. Each chainwheel should ideally be used with no more than four rear sprockets, or five on a special narrow-spaced freewheel.

This means that a "ten-speed" bike really has only eight gears, and a "twelve-speed" only ten. Actually, the gears in the midrange overlap, so nothing much is lost.

Inspect chain angles before disassembling a drivetrain. If a bicycle has been crashed, a chainline problem may be due to a bent frame, so check for this first. The most common problem, however, is de-

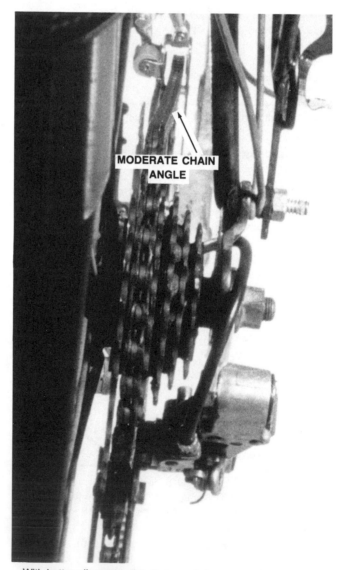

EXCESSIVE CHAIN ANGLE

EXCESS SPACE

Too long a crank axle or excess space to the right of the freewheel leads to an excessive chain angle, inefficiency, noise, and wear.

MODERATE CHAIN ANGLE

With better alignment, the chain angle is more moderate and the drivetrain runs more smoothly.

liberate installation of the (front) chainwheels too far to the right.

A triple chainwheel set displaced to the right allows use of the small, inner chainwheel with the small, outer sprocket; the chain won't rub the side of the larger chainwheel. This way, the uninformed new-bike customer will be satisfied that every gear works.

When assembling a drivetrain, make the chain angle as small as possible for the *useful* chainwheel-sprocket combinations. A very small inner chainwheel should be used only with the two or three largest, inner rear sprockets, so don't disturb the chainline of a larger chainwheel on its account.

Chainline can be corrected at the rear wheel if there is extra space between the smallest sprocket and the right rear forkend. Move the freewheel and hub to the right; use a narrower spacer at the right end of the rear axle and extra washers at the left end under the locknut (see Chapter 8 on hubs). The spokes must be readjusted slightly to recenter the rim (see Chapter 17 on wheelbuilding). This is advantageous, because the shallower dishing of the wheel makes it stronger. Remember to readjust the derailleur's limit screws!

It is also possible to alter the chainline by using a bottom-bracket spindle of a different length. Check with a bike shop or *Sutherland's Handbook for Bicycle Mechanics* to find a spindle which moves the chainwheels by the needed amount. The chainline of some replacement sealed-bearing bottom-bracket assemblies can be adjusted after installation.

In the rare case that the chainwheels are too far to the left, use a longer bottom-bracket spindle. Installing a wider spacer on the right end of the rear wheel's axle would weaken the wheel.

Parts Compatibility

Especially on a bicycle which has been serviced by an inexperienced mechanic, check that the parts of the drivetrain are made to work with one another.

Every year, more and more new types of derailleurs, chains, and sprockets are sold. Not all work well with each other. Wide-range gearing requires long-cage derailleurs with the necessary chain-takeup capacity; narrow-range racing gearing works best with short-cage derailleurs.

The sideways shifting range of derailleurs also varies. Generally, expensive derailleurs sweep farther than inexpensive ones, but no hard-and-fast rules apply. You may have to use a different derailleur if you're switching to a triple chainwheel set or a wider freewheel. But check that the insufficient range isn't just due to an overadvanced limit screw or misadjusted cable.

To check freedom of rotation of the crank bearings, disengage the chain from the chainwheels as shown.

Friction

To test for drivetrain friction, spin the crank backward. In a well-oiled, clean drivetrain, the crank will turn three or four times before coming to rest. In a gritty, rusty drivetrain, it will stop after one turn or less. This drivetrain wastes the rider's energy.

After removing the rear wheel and disengaging the chain from the chainwheels, you can spin each part by itself to locate the source of the excess friction. If it isn't in the freewheel or crank assembly, it is in the chain.

Listen to the freewheel as you spin it backward. A well-lubricated freewheel ticks fairly quietly but evenly; a dry freewheel's pawls click loudly as metal hits metal. Damaged pawls which don't engage fully will miss a beat now and then.

Derailleur Damage and Wear

Sometimes it is obvious that a derailleur is bent; but often it is not obvious. When a bicycle falls on its right side, the rear derailleur may bend inward. Even a slight bend can shift the chain or pulley cage into the spokes. Look at the rear derailleur from behind to see whether its pulley cage is in line with the sprockets. If it's badly bent, the bicycle must not be ridden until the derailleur is replaced or straightened.

A front derailleur is protected by the crank, and so is most usually bent when the chain jams in it. It can also work poorly if its mounting clamp is incorrectly positioned on the frame's seat tube. Shifting often improves if you reshape the chain cage slightly with an adjustable wrench; see Chapter 12.

Derailleur pivots loosen up with wear. To check for looseness, hold each derailleur by the part which guides the chain and rock it toward and away from the centerline of the bicycle. A little play is normal, but if the chain moves a substantial fraction of the distance between sprockets, shifting will be sloppy. Sometimes excess play can be adjusted out, but more often the derailleur must be replaced.

A bent rear derailleur. The chain cage is not parallel to the freewheel sprockets.

Derailleur Adjustments

Derailleur limit screws must be adjusted so that the derailleur sweeps the full range of sprockets or chainwheels, but no farther. If a limit screw is advanced too far, the chain will not reach one or more sprockets. If a limit screw is backed out too far, the chain will fall off. This can cause serious damage, especially if a rear derailleur shifts the chain into the spokes of the rear wheel.

Check limit-screw adjustments after replacing a derailleur, rear wheel, sprocket cluster, or crankset. The new part may not position sprockets or chainwheels as they were before.

The derailleurs should be close to the sprockets so they don't waste motion dragging chain sideways. The front derailleur's chain cage should clear the front chainwheels by no more than ¼ inch. The rear derailleur's upper (jockey) pulley should ride close under the sprockets. Details on correcting these adjustments are given in Chapters 11 and 12.

Chain Wrap

Inspect the rear derailleur for good chain wrap. The farther the chain wraps around a sprocket, the lower the stress and wear. Shifting becomes easier, and the chain is less likely to jump off. Chain wrap is especially important on small rear sprockets, which have few teeth to work with. Good chain wrap is achieved by modern rear derailleurs whose body places the pulleys ahead of the sprockets. Adjusting the derailleur body to place the jockey pulley close to the sprockets, as described in Chapter 11, also improves chain wrap.

Chain Length

The chain must always be long enough so that it can climb onto the large-rear-sprocket-large-front-chainwheel combination without jamming. Always check this after adjusting the derailleurs, replacing a chain, or changing sprocket or chainwheel size.

CAUTION: If the chain is too short, the rear derailleur and possibly other parts will be seriously damaged. After reassembling a drivetrain, test chain length on the work stand before riding the bicycle, shifting to the large-large combination in all three possible ways—with the front derailleur, with the rear derailleur, and with both at once.

Aside from this caution, the optimum chain length depends on the design of the rear derailleur and on the gear range. As described in Chapter 11, different types of rear derailleurs work best with different chain lengths.

A wide gear range may require a chain nearly as short as possible so that it will not hang slack when the small chainwheel is used. Don't worry if the chain hangs loose in unused small-small combinations. If such a combination is selected unintentionally, no harm results.

Crank, Chainwheel, and Pedal Problems

Yank in and out on one arm of the crank to check for looseness. This may be in the bearings or where the crank arm attaches to its spindle. After removing the chain, give the crank a spin to check for binding.

Check the pedal bearings by spinning them, or if they are unbalanced by toeclips, let them rock like pendulums. They should coast smoothly to a stop, but there should be no excess play in the bearings.

Either the crankarm, the pedal spindle, or the frame is bent, since the pedal is not at a right angle to the frame tubes.

Check for bent chainwheels; these will weave in and out as you turn the crank.

Check for a bent crank or pedal by placing a square against the seat tube and down tube to see that the pedal spindle is at right angles to the central plane of the frame. Check once with the pedal high and again with the pedal forward. To tell whether the bend is in the pedal, hold the cage from turning while you unscrew the pedal. If the pedal is bent, the outer end of the pedal will "orbit" in a little circle.

The pedals and cranks are not, strictly speaking, part of the shifting system, but it is easiest to work on all of these parts at once.

Freewheel Problems

Look for worn, hooked sprocket teeth and for reversed sprockets with the bevel on the outside. Wiggle the freewheel to check for excess play in the bearings. Spin it backward to see whether its bearings bind. If the freewheel has internal problems, it's usually simplest to use an entirely new freewheel.

Precleaning

Drivetrain parts pick up a lot of dirt from the road and the chain. Hold the chain with rags or wear rubber gloves when removing it. After removing the derailleurs and freewheel from the bicycle, first clean the outside dirt off them. Clean them again more thoroughly after disassembly.

CHAIN MAINTENANCE AND REPAIR

Bicycle chains are classified as wide (⅛ inch) for use in single-sprocket systems, and narrow (³⁄₃₂ inch) for use on derailleur-equipped bicycles. The widths are measured between the side plates. Narrow (derailleur) chains come in three types:

1. Conventional, with flat side plates and protruding rivets;

2. Shimano Uniglide, with bulged-out side plates and protruding rivets;

3. Extra-narrow "Ultra" or Sedisport, with rivets flush with the side plates, for use with extra-narrow-spaced freewheels.

Narrow chain seems to work on most systems, and shifts better in some cases. With a special narrow-spaced freewheel, narrow chain *must* be used. Uniglide chain works best with Shimano "twist-tooth" sprockets, not always so well with other sprockets. A special rivet tool is required for Uniglide chain.

Links can be added or removed to obtain the desired

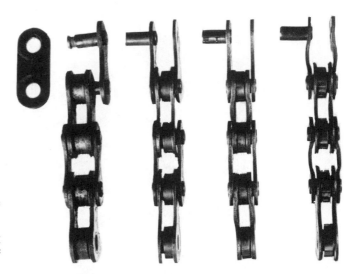

Samples of four types of chain. From left to right: wide single-sprocket chain with its master link; conventional derailleur chain; narrow derailleur chain, the same width inside but with shorter rivets; Shimano Uniglide chain, with bowed side plates.

length. The wide-type chain with the master link cannot be used on a derailleur bicycle, because the extra width plus the master link will not pass through the cage of the derailleur, and the distance between the sprockets of the cluster is not sufficient to permit the chain to make a complete rotation without binding.

Chain Removal and Installation—Derailleur Bicycles

To remove the chain from a derailleur-equipped bicycle, a rivet extractor is required. This handy little tool can be purchased at any bike shop complete with an extra punch.

Back out the punch by turning the tool handle counterclockwise, and then lay any one of the links of the chain over the flanges, with the rivet aligned with the punch. Push the rivet almost all the way out by turning the handle clockwise, but leave approximately ¹⁄₃₂ inch of the rivet holding the chain roller. One method of gauging how far to push the rivet out is to count six complete turns of the handle once the punch is firmly against the rivet. Back out the punch, and then remove the tool.

Hold the chain on both sides of the extended rivet, and then bend the chain slightly to unhook it from the

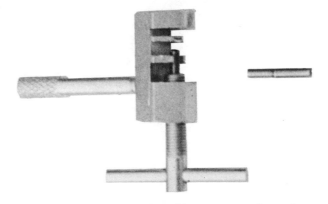

A rivet-extractor tool, complete with an extra punch, can be purchased at any bike shop. Uniglide chain requires a special rivet tool.

A rivet-extractor tool is used to disconnect the chain on derailleur-equipped bicycles. Count six turns of the handle to push the rivet free of the inner link plates.

rivet, as shown in the accompanying illustration. Remove the chain from the chainwheel and rear derailleur unit.

To install the chain, feed the end with the extended rivet around the chainwheel, with the rivet facing out (away from the bicycle) to make the extractor tool easier to use. Feed the other end of the chain around the rear sprocket cluster and through the derailleur cage. Bring the two ends together in the tool, and then push the rivet through by turning the handle clockwise.

If the rivet was accidentally pushed out of the side plate during removal, place the roller link of the chain between the side plates, with the chain lying on its side

on a flat surface. Hold the rivet in position with a pair of needle-nosed pliers and, at the same time, tap the rivet into the side plate until it extends approximately $1/32$ inch past the inside of the plate. Continue to install the chain in the normal manner as described above.

Cleaning and Lubricating

A dirty and/or slightly rusted chain can be restored by first removing it from the bicycle, soaking it in solvent, and then working on the rusted area with a stiff wire brush. An inexpensive tool with rotary brushes and a solvent bath is now available to clean a derailleur chain without removing it from the bicycle. Let the chain dry thoroughly, and then check each link for free movement. In a derailleur chain, it is easy to see a stiff link; it won't straighten as it comes off the sprocket. You may have to loosen a non-derailleur chain slightly to look for the stiff links. If a link is stiff because of bent

This tool allows a chain on a derailleur-type bicycle to be cleaned without removing it from the bicycle.

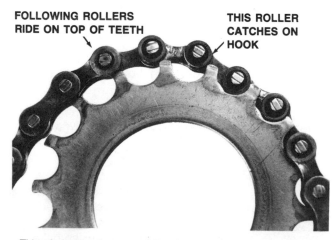

This chain has been partially disassembled to show how the shorter links of a new chain catch and jump forward on the teeth of a worn sprocket.

To disconnect the chain after the rivet has been almost pushed out, bend the chain slightly and unhook it from the rivet.

side plates, discard the link, and if the chain is now too short, replace it.

If the side plates are not bent but the link is too stiff, bending the chain *sideways* (at right angles to the way it normally pivots over the sprockets) will usually free it. Another method to free up a stiff link is to place it on the inner plate of the extractor tool and then rotate the handle about a third of a turn to push the side plates apart. Shift the extractor to the other side and move the rivet back until it is equidistant from the plates on both sides. The chain should be replaced if the links are rusted so badly that they cannot be made to flex properly as the chain moves around the sprocket and chainwheel, or if it has lengthened excessively because of wear.

Measure a used chain against an accurate stamped or etched metal ruler or against a new chain. Twelve double links of new chain are exactly 1 foot. If they are more than ⅛ inch over, the chain is due for replacement. If you are using a metric ruler, 15 double links are exactly 381mm when new, and the chain should be replaced if the measurement exceeds 385mm. When you replace a chain, you must also replace or regrind the outer (smaller) rear freewheel sprockets; a new chain on worn sprockets will work on the test bench, but it will jump forward as you apply force to the pedals.

A chain for a one-speed or internally geared bike may be lubricated with cycle oil by soaking it and then wiping off the excess.

A chain used with derailleurs needs to be clean and well lubricated to shift smoothly. Many people prefer to use lightweight spray oil, though it must be applied every week or so to keep the chain from squeaking. Several brands of lube are available in spray-can form. Each contains a liquid that carries the lubricating agent to the inner bearing surfaces of the chain and then evaporates, leaving only the dry lubricant.

When using a spray lubricant, shift the chain to the smallest freewheel sprocket. Tilt the bicycle slightly to the right and turn the crank backward while squirting the lubricant from the rear, along the top run of chain at the freewheel. If any lubricant gets on the rim or tire, wipe it off promptly.

Lubricant is needed around the rollers, and also between the inner and outer side plates, to reach the rivets inside. An exception is the Sedisport chain.

To lubricate the chain, tilt the bicycle slightly to the right, spin the crank, and spray lightweight lubricant as shown. Clean any excess lubricant from the wheel rim.

Lubricating its rollers will also lubricate the pivots, since its unusual construction allows lubricant to run clear through. You may take advantage of this by using heavier oil and applying it only to the rollers of a Sedisport chain.

New chains are lubricated at the time of manufacture with an antirust grease. This is generally too heavy and sticky for good service. Clean it off and relubricate before installing the chain.

Following a trip in the rain or through water, wipe the chain dry and lubricate it.

Do Not Mix Chains

New chains of different models may have rivets of different sizes and will wear at different rates. Old chains have worn differently; the jump between chain sections will make a clunking noise and put extra stress on sprocket teeth. If you need to build up a long chain, use new chains of the same brand and model.

On a derailleur-equipped bike, generally use the same length as before if you are not changing chainwheels, sprockets, or the rear derailleur. Changes in chain length may be needed if you are switching rear derailleurs or sprockets. Instructions vary for different types of rear derailleurs; see Chapter 11.

8 • SERVICING SIMPLE FRONT AND REAR HUBS

A front hub is clearly simple. A rear hub with a multiple freewheel looks much more complicated—but it isn't as bad as it looks. The basic mechanism of both hubs is the same. The freewheel is external to the hub bearing mechanism. A cable-operated disk or drum brake, or a hub generator, is also external to the bearing mechanism.

For these reasons, this chapter covers most front and rear hubs. Sealed-bearing hubs are covered at the end of the chapter. Hubs with internal gears or coaster brakes are a different story, and are covered in Chapter 14.

Step-by-step fully illustrated instructions are given here, along with a detailed exploded drawing showing every part of the hub. The keyed photographs, coupled with the exploded view, support the text to tell you verbally and visually exactly what to do and why.

TYPES OF HUBS

The front and rear hubs covered here may be attached to the bicycle frame with nuts or with a quick-release mechanism. Hubs may have conventional cup-and-cone bearings or cartridge-type sealed bearings. An expander-type drum brake, disk brake, or generator may be fitted to the hub or built into the hub shell.

Nutted Hubs

All types of hubs with cup-and-cone bearings and without an expander brake or quick-release mechanism can be considered in this category. They have the least number of parts and have been commonly used for many years. Differences between various makes of conventional hubs include the weight and strength of

This is a typical nutted front-wheel hub. Overhaul procedures begin on page 113.

materials used in manufacture, the size and shape of the hub flanges, and the type of bearings and bearing cups.

Conventional nutted cup-and-cone bearing hubs may be made of aluminum or steel, and may have small-diameter or large-diameter spoking flanges, and large or small weight-carrying capacity depending on their application.

The conventional hub consists of an axle passing through the hub shell (to which the spokes are attached), a ball-bearing assembly at each end of the hub shell, and axle nuts to hold it all in place. The cones of the bearings act as the inner ball-bearing races and, as they are shifted together on the threaded axle, become the means of adjusting the bearing play. On most American-manufactured hubs, the bearing balls are held in place with a retainer; on most imported hubs, the balls are loose in a bearing cup formed in the end of the hub shell. Some lightweight hubs have removable bearing cups.

Instructions for overhaul of nutted hubs begin on page 113.

Quick-release Hubs

The quick-release hub can be considered a light-weight conventional hub fitted with a mechanism that allows it to be removed quickly from the bicycle without the use of tools. The axle of the quick-release hub is hollow, allowing a full-length stud called a *skewer* to hold it to the fork. This is accomplished by one end of the skewer's having a cam-action body and spring secured to it with a cam lever and nut. The other end of the stud is fitted with an adjusting nut and centering spring. To remove the wheel, it is a simple matter to flip the cam lever through 180 degrees, at right angles to the axle. When installing a quick-release wheel, hold the cam lever with one hand and turn the adjusting nut with the other hand until you can just press the cam lever down with all the strength of the palm of your hand. Then the wheel will be held securely. **CAUTION: The cam lever of a quick-release hub is not a wingnut. It tightens by flipping over, not by screwing tight. If you use it like a wingnut it will not be tight enough and the wheel could fall out.** Instructions for overhaul of quick-release hubs begin on page 120.

This is an Atom internal-expanding brake hub. Overhaul of the bearing parts for drum-brake hubs are covered in this chapter. Overhaul instructions for the brake parts are in Chapter 16, beginning on page 360.

This is a typical quick-release front-wheel hub. Overhaul procedures begin on page 120.

Disk-brake and Drum-brake Hubs

This type of hub includes a cable-actuated disk brake or internal-expanding, double-shoe drum brake which may be either integral or threaded to the hub shell. The principle of the axle, ball bearings, adjustable cones, and attachment to the fork is the same as with other hubs. Instructions for rebuilding the brake parts are in Chapter 16.

Generator Hubs

These are very similar to the internal-drum-brake hub, except that the drum encloses an electrical generator used to power a lighting system for the bicycle. After removing the generator, overhauling is the same

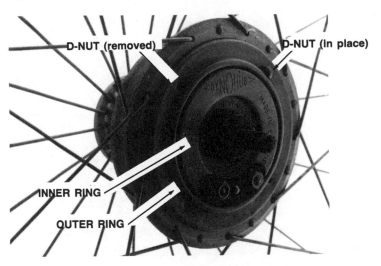

The Sturmey-Archer Dynohub generator is similar to a drum brake. Remove the generator parts after removing the D-nuts; then the bearings may be overhauled.

as for a conventional hub. **CAUTION: Do not separate the inner and outer ring of the generator at any time during overhauling, or you will seriously weaken the magnet.**

Fixed and Freewheel Rear Hubs

A rear hub may be of any of the types just described—nutted, quick-release, disk-brake or drum-brake, or generator. A rear hub differs from a front hub in having a longer rear axle, and threads at the right side of the hub shell to accept a freewheel or fixed sprocket for the drive chain. The sprocket of the fixed hub is attached directly to the hub shell, which results in the hub turning at the same rate as the sprocket.

The freewheel rear hub can be used with a single sprocket or with a series of varying-size sprockets. The

A typical fixed rear-wheel hub, with the sprocket attached directly to the hub. Instructions for overhauling this type of hub begin on page 124.

A freewheel rear hub, with the sprocket cluster attached to the hub through a freewheel body. Instructions for overhauling this type of hub begin on page 124.

This freewheel hub has a quick-release mechanism which allows it to be removed and installed without using tools. Overhauling instructions for this type of hub begin on page 124.

sprocket or sprockets are threaded onto a freewheel body, and this body is attached to the hub shell. With this type of arrangement, the hub shell turns at the same rate as the sprocket, just as with a fixed hub, when it is being driven by the chain. But when the sprocket is slowed or ceases to turn, the hub shell continues to rotate—thus the term "freewheel." The combination of a freewheel body with various-size sprockets and a derailleur to move the chain from one sprocket to another, provides the rider with several gearing ratios for varying conditions.

The freewheel rear hub with quick-release combines the advantages of the freewheel hub with the ability to remove and install the wheel without the use of tools.

After you have removed the wheel (page 70) and the freewheel (page 151) or fixed sprocket (page 207), rebuilding a rear hub is very nearly the same as rebuilding a front hub. A rear hub usually has extra spacers on the right end of the axle to make room for the freewheel. Thread them onto a wire or lay them on a table in order, so you can put them back on the axle as they were before.

Instructions for overhaul of rear hubs begin on page 124.

Cartridge-type Sealed-bearing Hubs

In this type of hub, the bearing mechanism at either side of the hub is a preassembled, sealed radial-contact cartridge unit. Servicing procedures are very different from those for a hub with conventional bearings; they are described beginning on page 126.

SERVICE NOTE

If you are just learning how to rebuild hubs, start with the front hub, which is simpler.

Unless force-lubricated with oil or grease (page 67), conventional cup-and-cone-bearing hubs should be rebuilt every year, or more often if ridden frequently in foul weather. As grit from the road begins to contaminate the lubricant in a hub, the bearing races begin to wear.

Frequent rebuilding will keep the bearings clean and prolong their life. Replacing the bearing balls and bearing cones as they begin to wear will prevent them from releasing metal chips into the lubricant and damaging the bearing cups. The cups may be difficult or impossible to replace.

Hubs may need bearing adjustment between rebuilds, generally because they have been misadjusted. Before you put a hub into service, check bearing adjustment unless you rebuilt the hub yourself. Correct bearing adjustment requires more care than is usually given, and can result in greatly extended bearing life.

Before adjusting bearings, it is very important to determine whether you are working on a sealed-bearing or cup-and-cone-bearing hub. Hubs with an unthreaded axle have sealed bearings and are not adjustable, but some sealed-bearing hubs have threads and look the same as cup-and-cone-bearing hubs until you remove the bearing dustcaps. Also, some hubs labeled "sealed" have conventional bearings with an added rubber seal in the dustcap.

CAUTION: The adjustment procedures for a cartridge-bearing hub are very different. Adjusting it the same way as a cup-and-cone-bearing hub can lead to rapid wear. Look for identification on the hub shell; if you are still not sure which type of hub you are adjusting, remove one locknut and cone to check.

Parts Interchangeability

Bearing balls are the same for all brands. Just be sure to use ones of the same size as those you removed from the hub. Bearing retainers for some hubs may be hard to find, but it is best anyway to replace them with loose balls.

Even if only one cone is worn, replace both. Always use exact replacement cones if at all possible. Slight differences in the shape of the bearing cone can make it incompatible with the cup and dustcap of a hub for which it was not intended. Threading of cones and axles also varies, even within the same make and model.

With careful selection, it is usually possible to find usable cones when exact replacements are not available. This way you can save the trouble of rebuilding a wheel on a new hub. Sometimes you can even upgrade the smoothness and wearing qualities of a hub by installing higher-quality cones.

First, check that the substitute cones will fit through

If you find a sleeve nut and bearing cartridge as shown, instead of a cone and bearing balls, turn to page 126 for overhaul instructions.

the hub's dustcaps. Then test the fit in the bearing cups by applying a light film of grease to a bearing cone and installing it. Remove it and examine the track left by the bearing balls in the grease. The ball track should be in the *middle* of the curved bearing surface. If the ball track is at the inner or outer margin, the bearing parts will wear quickly.

A replacement axle assembly is generally sold as a unit. Even if only the bearing cones need replacement, it is good to buy the assembly. This will assure that threading of all parts is compatible and will eliminate any possibility of stripped threads or a bent axle.

BEARING TRACK

When substituting hub cones, the bearing track must fall in the center of the cone's bearing surface.

Axle Lengths

The most important dimension affecting the fit of a hub to a bicycle is the length between the hub's locknuts. This must closely match the spacing between the inside surfaces of the frame's forkends, which hold the wheel. **CAUTION: If the forkends must be sprung apart or forced together to install a hub, they will be out of parallel and will bend the axle, resulting in hub problems.**

The axle of most lightweight front hubs is about 100mm (3¹⁵⁄₁₆ inches) between the locknuts. Children's bicycles and English three-speed bicycles typically have a shorter front axle, approximately 91mm (3⁹⁄₁₆ inches).

Axles of single-sprocket rear hubs are typically 110mm or 117mm between the locknuts; hubs with a multi-sprocket freewheel are typically 122mm or 126mm. A 126mm spacing is required for a wide-spaced six-speed freewheel or a seven-speed freewheel. With a narrower freewheel, 126mm spacing has the advantage of reduced wheel dishing. All-terrain bikes and tandems often have an even wider spacing, between 130mm and 140mm, to make room for a wide tire or a hub brake.

If the hub is too narrow for the fork, it is easiest to modify the hub. Adjusting the width of a nutted axle is easy: Just add or remove spacer washers under the locknuts. A quick-release axle must be replaced if too short, or hacksawed and filed to length if too long. If more spacers are added or removed on one side than on the other, the wheel must be redished to recenter the rim.

If the hub is too wide and there are no extra axle spacers to remove, the frame must be bent to increase the width between the forkends. After altering the spacing, you must also adjust the forkends so they are parallel. Instructions are on page 395. If you are not confident of your ability to do this, take the job to a mechanic who has the needed tools and experience.

Problems with Simple Hubs

The following problem chart is for hubs with cup-and-cone bearings. Cartridge-bearing hubs are discussed later in this chapter.

Hub turns roughly or binds.

Possible cause:	Corrective action:
Lubricant is contaminated.	Rebuild hub.
Cone, cup, or bearing balls are worn.	Rebuild hub.
Cones are overtightened.	Adjust bearings.
Cones are wider than holes in dustcaps.	Use correct cones.
Cups do not match cones.	Use correct cones.
Too many loose balls are installed.	Remove one ball.
Bearing balls are of wrong size.	Use right size.
Bearing retainer is installed backward.	Rebuild hub.
Bearing retainer is of wrong size.	Rebuild hub.
Bearing retainer is bent.	Replace retainer.
Dustcap is bent.	Rebuild hub.
Axle is bent.	Rebuild hub.
Forkends are bent.	Align fork.

Wheel has excessive sideplay (looseness).

Possible cause:	Corrective action:
Cones are adjusted too loose.	Adjust bearings.
Cones, cups, or bearing balls are worn.	Rebuild hub.
Cone locknut is loose.	Tighten and adjust.
Axle has been bent.	Rebuild hub.
Axle is broken.	Rebuild hub.
Cup is loose in hub shell.	Use correct cup.

Hub wears quickly.

Possible cause:	Corrective action:
Cup and cone are mismatched.	Use correct cone.
Bearing balls are wrong size.	Use correct size.
Lubricant is contaminated or insufficient.	Rebuild hub.

Axle nuts will not hold wheel tightly.

Possible cause:	Corrective action:
Axle nut threads are stripped.	Replace nut.
Axle threads are stripped.	Replace axle.
Axle washer has been omitted.	Install washer.
Forkends are bent.	Align fork.

Quick-release clamp will not hold wheel tightly.

Possible cause:	Corrective action:
Quick-release clamp is used as a wingnut.	Use as clamp.
Adjusting nut is not set correctly.	Adjust.
Adjusting nut or skewer threads are stripped.	Replace.
Axle is off-center or wrong length.	Adjust or replace.
Forkends are bent.	Align fork.

Cones or locknuts are hard to thread to axle.

Possible cause:	Corrective action:
Threads are mismatched.	Use correct parts.
Axle threads are burred.	Replace axle.

Cones or locknuts are loose on axle.

Possible cause:	Corrective action:
Threads are mismatched.	Use correct parts.
Threads are stripped.	Replace damaged parts.

Tools and Supplies You Will Need

Wrench to fit axle end nuts

Thin (bearing-cone) wrenches

Tweezers

Bearing balls or retainer to fit your hub:

Most front hubs use 10 to 12 $\frac{3}{16}$-inch balls per side.

Campagnolo Record, Maillard, and Zeus front hubs use 9 $\frac{7}{32}$-inch balls per side.

Most rear hubs and some heavy-duty front hubs use 9 ¼-inch balls per side.

(Note: if your hub uses balls in a retainer, you can replace the retainer with loose balls.)

Grease

Tools and Supplies You May Need

Bearing cones to fit your hub
Replacement axle to fit your hub
Dustcaps to fit your hub
Locknuts and keyed lockwashers to fit your hub
Bearing cups to fit your hub
Quick-release parts (quick-release hub only)
Drift punch
Hammer
Hacksaw
File
Vise or large wrench (to remove a freewheel from a rear hub)
Freewheel remover (to remove a freewheel from a rear hub)

OVERHAULING A NUTTED FRONT CUP-AND-CONE HUB

The following step-by-step illustrated procedures provide complete instructions for disassembling, assembling, and adjusting a conventional nutted front hub. Many of these procedures also apply to quick-release hubs and rear hubs, and the sections on these hubs therefore refer to this section rather than repeat the information.

Detailed exploded drawings show all internal parts of typical steel and aluminum hubs. For photographic clarity, the illustrations were made of hubs without the tire, rim, or spokes.

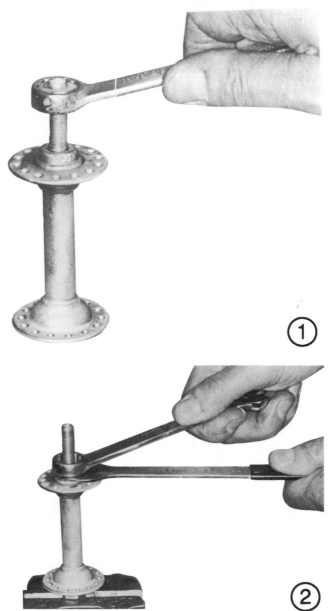

Disassembling

① After the wheel has been removed (see page 69), remove the two axle nuts.

Remove the axle nuts of a conventional hub by unscrewing each one while holding the cone. Sometimes you can remove the axle nuts by hand, but if the axle threads are damaged, you may have to use wrenches.

② Place a thin cone wrench on the cone flats, and an open-end or adjustable wrench on the locknut of one side of the hub. Loosen the locknut by turning it counterclockwise, and then remove the cone. Some hubs have only one locknut, or none. In this case, remove whichever cone is easiest.

③ Remove the bearing retainer assembly from the bearing cup of the hub, and then lift off the hub shell. If you are working on a lightweight hub with a dustcap and loose bearing balls, remove the dustcap by prying it up with a screwdriver. Work around the cap edge and it will pop out. Be careful not to crimp or distort the cap. Remove and count the bearing balls.

If the two bearing cones or the two ends of the axle are different, note this as you slide the axle out. Some axle assemblies are not the same at both ends, and it is important to reassemble them the same way as before.

④ Lift off the other bearing retainer assembly. Remove the dustcap and loose bearing balls from the other end of the lightweight hub. It is easiest to leave

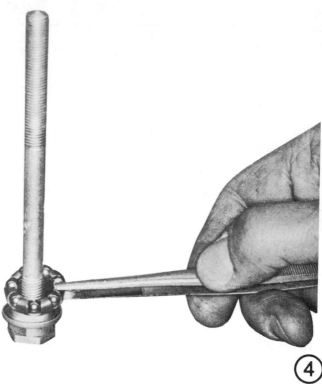

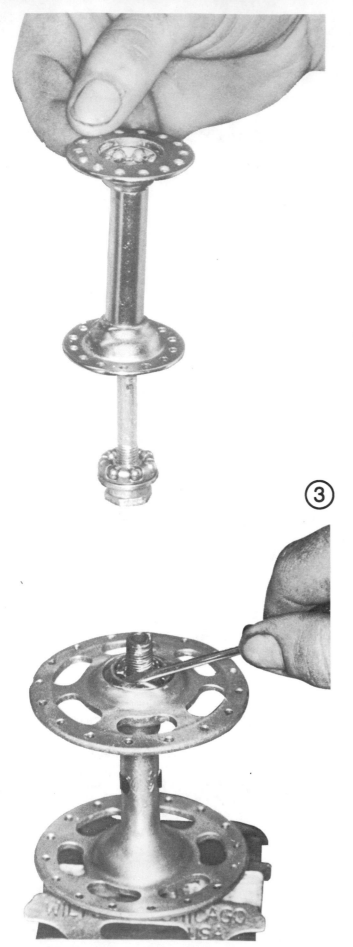

one locknut and bearing cone on the axle at this point, saving you the trouble of adjusting its position later.

Cleaning and Inspecting

Clean all parts in solvent and rinse them, or wipe them dry with a lintless cloth. Keep all cleaned parts on paper towels to avoid contamination. Cover them with a clean towel to keep grit from entering the internal parts and bearings. A tiny piece of grit can do a tremendous amount of damage if allowed to work on a part over an extended period of time.

The bearing cones are the first part of the bearing assembly to wear. Inspect the bearing surface of the *cones* for scoring (scratchlike marks), pitting (pencil-point dots), and excessive wear (dull spots). A shiny appearance of the ball track is normal. Inspect the threads of the cones for stripping.

Don't bother to inspect the bearing balls or retainer. Simply replace them with new ones. The hub's load capacity can be increased by replacing a retainer with loose bearing balls; there will be more balls than the retainer can hold.

Inspect the bearing cups of the hub shell for scoring, pitting, or excessive wear. Check the hub flanges for cracks between the spoke holes.

If you are working on a hub with removable bearing cups and a cup needs to be replaced, remove it from the hub by tapping it out with an off-center drift punch and hammer from the other end of the hub. **CAUTION: Do not remove the cup unless it has to be replaced because it is very difficult to remove without damaging it.**

Removing the dustcap of a lightweight hub.

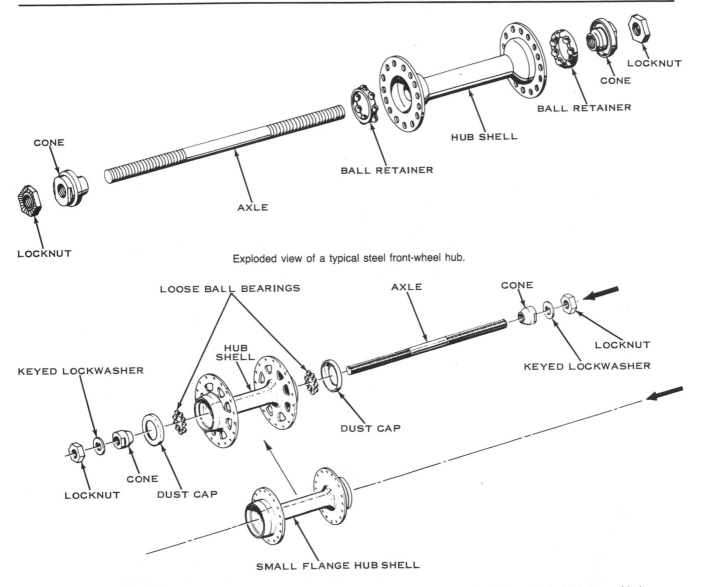

Exploded view of a typical steel front-wheel hub.

Exploded view of a Schwinn-Approved, Sprint, Normandy, or Atom lightweight front-wheel hub, typical of this type of hub.

In many hubs with aluminum shells, the hole through the back of each bearing cup is larger than the hole through the axle barrel, so there is no exposed surface to hit with the drift punch.

You can often replace cups in such a hub, though it will not look like new afterward. If you drill two small holes 180 degrees apart through the back of each hub flange, you can insert a punch and push the cups out. Better bike shops will carry replacement cups to fit most hubs, but cup dimensions may vary slightly between brands. Take the old cups with you, and measure carefully with a caliper (the shop should have one). After reassembling the hub, seal the holes in the flanges with epoxy glue.

In some steel hubs, the bearing cups are one piece with the hub shell. The only possible repair if the cups are worn out is to rebuild the wheel on a new hub, or replace the entire wheel.

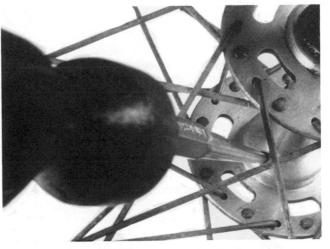

If worn-out bearing cups do not overlap the axle opening, they may still be driven out by drilling through the back of the flanges and pounding them out with a hammer and punch.

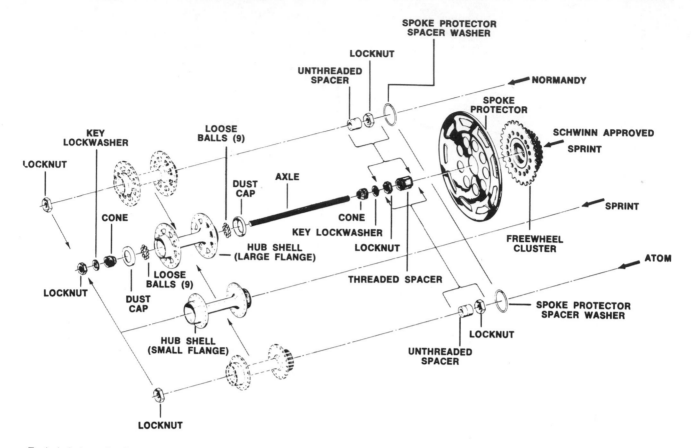

Exploded view of a Schwinn-Approved, Sprint, Normandy, or Atom freewheel rear-wheel hub, typical of this type of hub. The spoke-protector plate and its spacer washer are sometimes omitted.

Check the *axle* and locknuts for signs of damage or stripped threads. Roll the axle slowly across a smooth, flat surface such as a pane of glass. If the cone and locknut are still installed on one end, roll the long end of the axle, with the cone and locknut hanging over the edge of the surface. Check both ends and the center to see whether they wobble or rise off the surface.

If the axle is bent, do not discard it until you have measured its length and threading against the new one to make sure they are the same. If necessary, shorten a new axle with a hacksaw and file the end clean before installing it in the hub. **CAUTION: Correct length is essential in a replacement axle for a quick-release hub.**

Check the *dustcaps,* if they are of the removable type, to be sure they are not crimped or distorted, which could have happened during disassembly.

Assembling

⑤ Unless one cone and locknut are still installed on the axle, thread one of the cones on. With a nutted

front axle, it should be about 1 inch from the end; with a nutted rear axle, about 1⅛ inches; with a quick-release, hollow axle, about ⅜ inch. For a hub with an integral drum brake or generator, thread the cone to the same position as before disassembly. Some hubs have a shoulder on the axle at one end; if so, thread the same cone against it as before disassembly (in this case, the two cones are often different). Install the cones as you noted before disassembly.

⑥ Pack both bearing retainers with a generous amount of multipurpose grease. Work it throughout the bearings and the retainers with your fingers. If you are working on a hub with loose bearing balls, apply a generous amount of lubricant to both bearing cups of the hub. If you replaced a removable bearing cup, install it by using a socket the same size as the bottom of the cup, and then tapping the cup into place with a hammer. **CAUTION: Be sure the socket is the correct size; that it sits squarely on the cup; and that you tap the socket squarely to ensure that the cup goes into place evenly and without damage.**

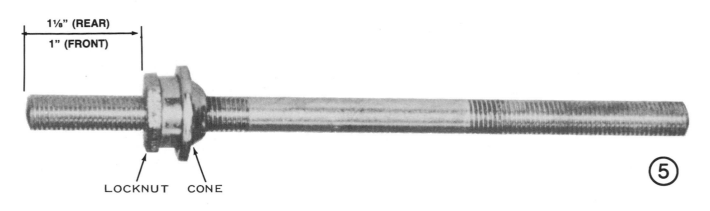

1⅛" (REAR)
1" (FRONT)

LOCKNUT   CONE

⑤

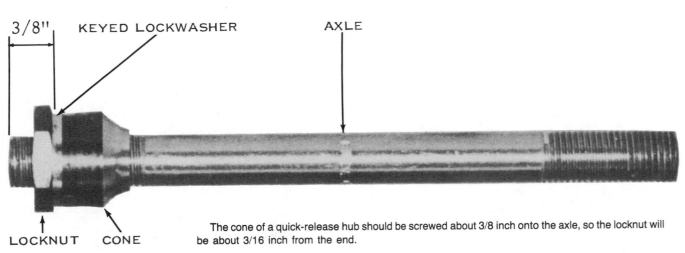

3/8"   KEYED LOCKWASHER   AXLE

LOCKNUT   CONE

The cone of a quick-release hub should be screwed about 3/8 inch onto the axle, so the locknut will be about 3/16 inch from the end.

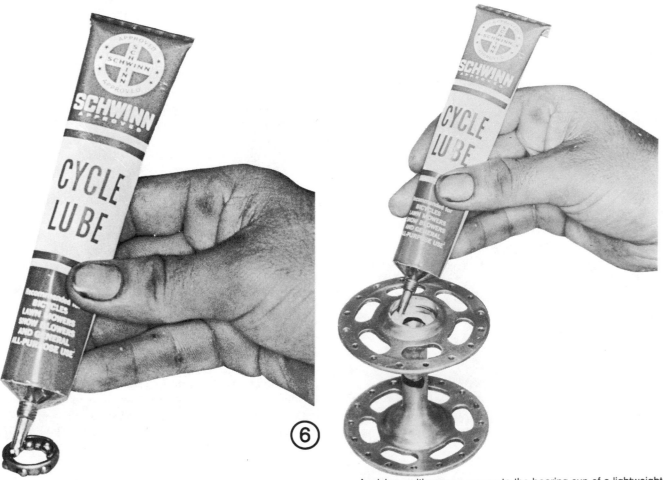

⑥

Applying multipurpose grease to the bearing cup of a lightweight hub. The lubricant must be applied first to hold the loose bearing balls in place during assembly. Use plenty.

⑦ Slip one of the bearing retainers onto the cone, with the bearing balls facing toward the center of the axle. This will allow them to roll on the inside of the bearing cup in the hub and on the tapered part of the cone.

⑦

If you are installing loose bearing balls, place each bearing ball in the lubricated bearing cup at the end of the hub with a pair of tweezers. Install balls until a full circle of them fills the cup, but make sure you have not installed too many. There should be some clearance. If you push one ball around the cup with the tweezers, it should push all the others ahead of it, leaving a small gap behind the tweezers.

If there is no gap and a ball pops out of line instead

Push the balls around in a circle with the tweezers to check that you have installed the right number. There must be a small gap behind the tweezers.

(like a mouth with crooked teeth because there isn't enough room for them), remove one ball.

Tap the dustcap into place over the bearing cup with a mallet. Install the bearing balls and dustcap in the other end of the hub shell in a similar manner.

⑧ Slide the hub over the axle and into place on the bearings. The lubricant will hold the bearings in place while you slide the hub over the axle.

The right end of a rear hub's axle will be longer than the left, to allow room for the freewheel. Install the axle from the left end. Install the axle from the side opposite a front hub brake. With a front brakeless hub, both ends are usually the same.

⑧

⑨ If the hub uses bearing retainers and does not have a separate dustcap, push the second lubricated bearing retainer into the other bearing cup of the hub.

⑩ Thread the other cone and locknut onto the axle, with the bearing race facing the bearing assembly and the knurled side of the locknut facing up.

Check that the length of the axle is correct on both ends. With a nutted hub, the axle need not be perfectly centered to engage the nuts. With a quick-release hub, centering is very important: The axle should stick out slightly less than the thickness of the forkends after installing all cones, lockwashers, locknuts, and spacers. On a rear hub, install them now to check spacing. If an end of a quick-release axle is too short, it will not

Installing a lightweight hub on the axle. Note how the grease and the dustcap keep the bearing balls from falling out.

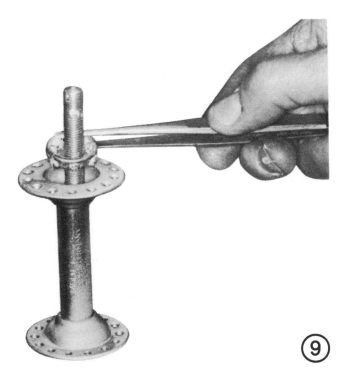

⑨

engage the forkend slot; if it is too long, its end will push against the quick-release cam lever body or adjusting nut, keeping the cam from clamping against the forkend.

⑩

The end of the quick-release hub's axle must fall level with or just short of the outer face of the forkend.

If the axle is off-center, loosen both locknuts and thread the cones along to center it. Then retighten one cone. Tighten the remaining loose cone finger-tight against the bearing retainer, and then back it off approximately a fifth of a turn for a rough adjustment.

⑪ Hold the cone with a thin wrench or cone pliers, and then tighten the locknut against the cone.

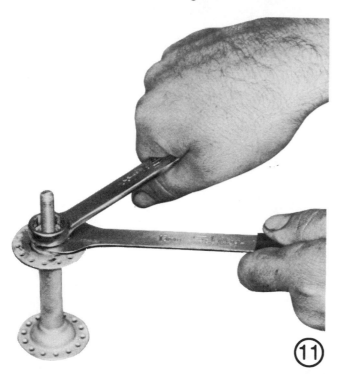

⑫ Now check the bearing adjustment. Twirl the axle slowly between your fingers, like a safecracker trying to feel the combination on a lock. The axle should turn smoothly and easily; you should feel only the slight, smooth resistance of the grease. If the axle grinds or catches, the cones are too tight.

Loosen one of the locknuts, back off the cone approximately an eighth of a turn, and then retighten the locknut.

To see whether the cones are too loose, push one end of the axle lightly from side to side with your fingers, like checking for a loose tooth. If it wiggles much at all, the cones are too loose. **CAUTION: If the cones are adjusted too tight, it will cause binding and scoring of the hub. If the cones are adjusted too loose, it will cause fatigue, which can result in a damaged hub or broken axle.**

If you are working on a front quick-release hub, now refer to step ④ on page 122. If working on a rear hub, refer to step ② on page 125. If you are working on an internal-expanding brake hub, refer to step ⑥ on page 363. If you are working on a nutted front hub, reinstall the axle nuts, then the wheel as described on page 72.

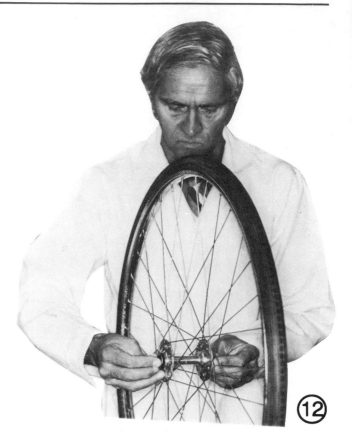

OVERHAULING A QUICK-RELEASE FRONT HUB

A quick-release hub is very similar to the nutted hub just described, except for the way the axle is held to the bicycle frame. Instead of nuts to hold the axle in place, there is a quick-release clamp assembly. This allows the wheel to be installed and removed without tools.

Typical quick-release front-wheel hub.

Disassembling

① After you have removed the wheel (see page 69), grasp the quick-release lever with one hand, then unscrew the quick-release adjusting nut and remove the centering spring from the other end of the axle.

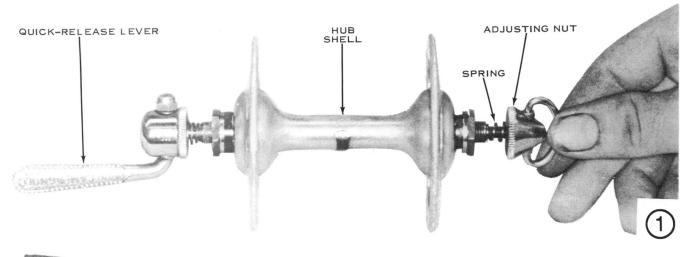

QUICK-RELEASE LEVER

HUB SHELL

ADJUSTING NUT

SPRING

①

CAM LEVER BODY

SKEWER

TENSION SPRING

QUICK-RELEASE LEVER

②

② Remove the skewer by pulling it out of the axle. Remove the centering spring.

③ If you are going to overhaul the quick-release assembly, remove the acorn nut, lockwasher, quick-release lever, and cam lever body from the skewer. Some hubs have a snapring instead of an acorn nut.

Cleaning and Inspecting the Quick-release Assembly

Clean all parts of the quick-release assembly.
Check the quick-release skewer for cracks, bends, and stripped threads. Also check the adjusting nut, cam lever, and acorn nut for stripped threads.
Check both centering springs for cracks, breaks, or bends. When you press on the ends of each spring

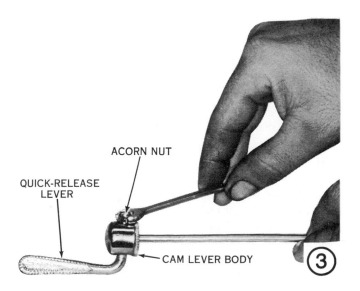

ACORN NUT

QUICK-RELEASE LEVER

CAM LEVER BODY

③

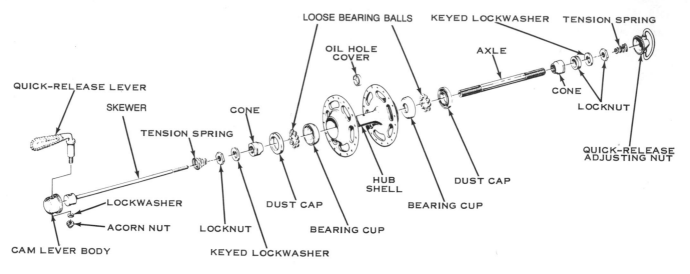

Exploded view of a Schwinn-Approved, Sprint, Normandy, and Atom quick-release front-wheel hub, typical of this type of hub.

with your thumb and index finger, it should squeeze down smoothly into flat coil.

Next, disassemble, clean, and reassemble the bearing assemblies. If working on a rear wheel, turn to step ① on page 125; if working on a front wheel, go to step ② on page 113.

Reassembling the Quick-release Assembly

④ Place the cam lever body on the skewer and then align the holes in the body and the skewer. *NOTE: The body can go on either way.*

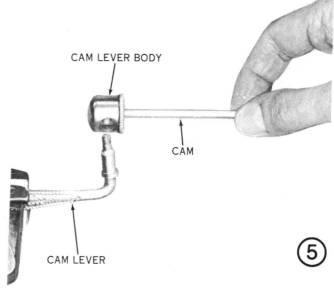

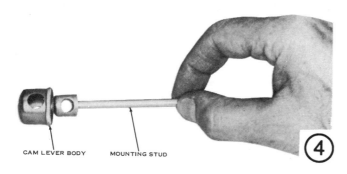

⑤ Install the quick-release lever through the large hole in the cam lever body until it is fully seated. Rotate the quick-release lever. You should be able to move it from a forward position (90 degrees to the mounting stud) through a full 180 degrees, where the lever will be pointing 90 degrees to the skewer in the opposite direction. If the lever cannot be rotated a full 180 degrees, remove the lever, rotate it 180 degrees, and then reinstall the lever in the cam lever body.

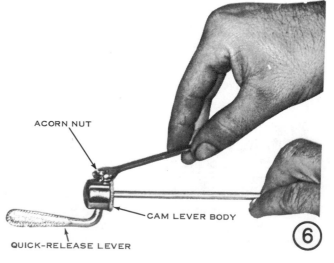

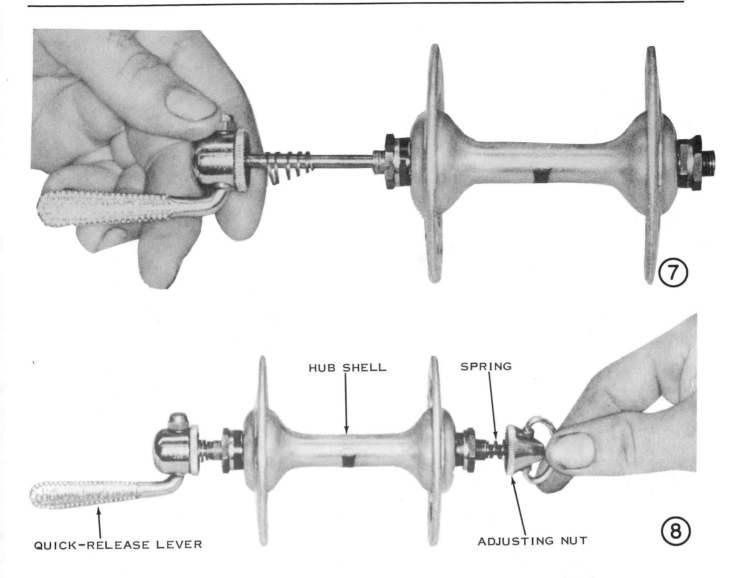

QUICK-RELEASE LEVER   HUB SHELL   SPRING   ADJUSTING NUT

⑥ Place the lockwasher onto the lever shaft, then thread the acorn nut on and tighten it firmly.

⑦ After reassembling the hub bearings, slide one of the centering springs onto the skewer, with the small end of the spring facing the hub, as shown. Insert the skewer through the axle. On a rear wheel, the lever should be on the left side, so the rear derailleur doesn't get in its way. On a front hub, it can go either way, since the wheel can go in either way.

⑧ Slide the other centering spring onto the skewer, with the small end of the spring facing toward the hub. Start the adjusting nut onto the skewer by rotating it several turns.

Finishing Up

Install the wheel on the bicycle (page 72).

Perform a final bearing adjustment, as follows here.

CAUTION: The bearing-cone adjustment of a quick-release hub must be tested while the wheel is installed on the bicycle. It is impossible to perform an accurate adjustment if the quick-release lever is not clamped in place.

Final Bearing Adjustment, Quick-release Hub

When you tighten a quick-release lever, the cam lever body and adjusting nut press the forkends against the cone locknuts, compressing the axle slightly and tightening the bearing adjustment. If you adjust a quick-release hub with the quick-release assembly loose, the bearings will bind after it is tightened. After installing the wheel on the bicycle, you must perform a final bearing check.

If you are testing a rear wheel, do not place the chain over the freewheel but leave the chain hanging underneath. You will be unable to test the bearing adjustment if the chain keeps the wheel from turning freely.

Now, if you lift the wheel slightly off the ground, or

For a final test that bearings of a quick-release hub have not been overtightened, let the wheel coast to a stop like a pendulum. It should stop smoothly, not abruptly.

with the bike on a repair stand, the wheel will probably start to turn; if it doesn't, give it a little push. Watch how it comes to a stop. It should rock slowly and evenly like a pendulum, around its heaviest point—usually where there is a spoke-mounted reflector or at the tire valve. If it jerks to a stop, the cones are too tight.

Next, try to wiggle the rim sideways. If it moves more than the tiniest amount (with a light "clunking" feeling), the cones are too loose.

Loosen the quick-release lever and adjust the bearings if necessary. Then tighten the skewer and test again; repeat until the adjustment is correct.

If you rebuild many quick-release hubs, you may wish to saw a pair of forkends off a trashed frame, so you can clamp the quick-release assembly in them and test the bearing adjustment by twirling the axle, the same as with a nutted hub.

OVERHAULING A FREEWHEEL OR FIXED REAR-WHEEL HUB

The following step-by-step illustrated instructions cover disassembling, assembling, and adjusting a typical *freewheel rear hub.* The sprocket cluster is attached to the hub through the freewheel body.

The illustrations in this section were made of a Schwinn-Approved freewheel hub that is identical to the following hubs: Normandy, Sprint, and Atom. They are typical of this type of unit.

The freewheel is threaded to the rear hub.

The *fixed hub* is similar in construction to the freewheel hub, except for the method of mounting the single-drive sprocket, which is threaded directly onto the hub in this case. Because the overhaul procedures for both types of hubs are almost identical, four related illustrations of the fixed rear-wheel hub are included alongside the sequential steps. The illustrations are of an Atom fixed rear-wheel hub, typical of this type of unit.

This freewheel hub has a quick-release mechanism which allows it to be removed and replaced without using tools.

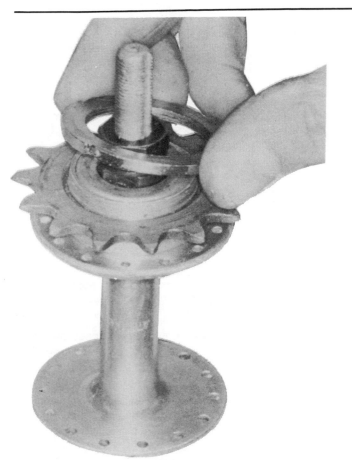

The sprocket is attached to the fixed rear-wheel hub by a right-hand thread, and secured by a lockring with a left-hand thread.

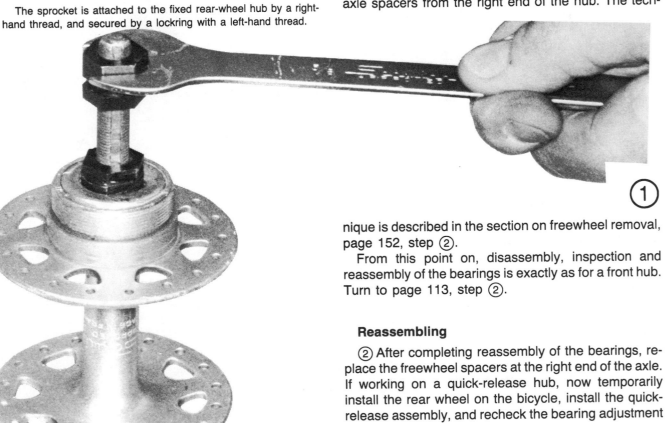

①

An exploded view earlier in this chapter shows all parts of a Normandy, Schwinn-Approved, Sprint, and Atom freewheel rear hub. Freewheel rear hubs of other manufacturers may vary slightly, because of the number of loose bearing balls; threaded or unthreaded spacer on the sprocket end of the axle; and/or removable or fixed bearing cups in the ends of the hub shell.

An exploded view of a typical fixed rear hub shows its unique features.

For photographic clarity, the illustrations were made of a hub without the tire, rim, and spokes.

Preliminary Steps

Remove the wheel (page 69).

If working on a quick-release hub, remove and inspect the quick-release assembly (page 120). If working on a nutted hub, remove the axle nuts and washers (page 113).

Remove the freewheel (page 151). If overhauling a fixed-sprocket hub, removing the sprocket is not necessary to rebuild the bearings. You may wish to remove it if it is worn or is of the wrong size; instructions are on page 207.

Disassembling

① Unless you have already done so, remove the axle spacers from the right end of the hub. The technique is described in the section on freewheel removal, page 152, step ②.

From this point on, disassembly, inspection and reassembly of the bearings is exactly as for a front hub. Turn to page 113, step ②.

Reassembling

② After completing reassembly of the bearings, replace the freewheel spacers at the right end of the axle. If working on a quick-release hub, now temporarily install the rear wheel on the bicycle, install the quick-release assembly, and recheck the bearing adjustment with the quick-release assembly clamped, as described beginning on page 123. **CAUTION: Bearings of a quick-release hub will be too tight, leading to rapid wear, if the adjustment is checked without the quick-release assembly clamped.**

②

Finishing Up

Replace the freewheel (page 154).
Replace the wheel (page 72).

SEALED-CARTRIDGE-BEARING HUBS

In recent years, hubs using preassembled, radial-contact, lifetime-lubricated sealed-bearing cartridges have become popular as an alternative to conventional angular-contact cup-and-cone bearings.

Cartridge-bearing hubs offer unusually smooth operation and freedom from rebuilding. However, like all moving parts, they do eventually wear out, and they can also be damaged by abuse.

The best way to service most cartridge-bearing components such as pedals and crankbearings is to replace them. Hubs are an important exception, because of the time and expense involved in respoking a wheel on a new hub.

The Phil Wood hub is an example of a cartridge-type sealed-bearing hub. The axle assembly with its cartridge bearings is shown below the complete hub. Overhaul procedures begin on page 130.

Slight roughness and noise are acceptable in a cartridge-bearing hub as in any other ball-bearing assembly. Slight endplay in the axle is also normal; in fact, there must be endplay for the bearing cartridges to function properly. Do not take apart a cartridge-bearing hub unless it is truly necessary to do so. However, if the bearings are very loose, tight, noisy, or rough, the hub should be serviced.

Some cartridge-bearing hubs cannot be rebuilt without removing them from the wheel, because the spoke flanges overlap the bearing cartridges.

Note that details of rebuilding procedures vary between models of hubs. Special tools and parts may be needed. If you are rebuilding a hub other than the specific model described here, read the manufacturer's instructions before proceeding. If you are not sure that you can solve the problem, take the entire wheel to a

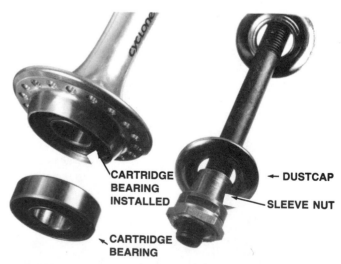

The SunTour sealed-bearing hub uses cartridges, like the Phil Wood hub, but its axle construction is different. Overhaul procedures begin on page 127.

bike shop equipped with the proper knowledge and tools.

Replacement bearing cartridges can be obtained from industrial bearing supply houses as well as from bike shops. Take the old cartridge with you or make a note of its identifying markings to make sure you get the correct replacement. Cartridges are sold with or without seals. Make sure that the ones you buy have a seal on at least one side.

There are two fundamentally different types of rebuildable cartridge-bearing hubs: those with and those without sleeve nuts threaded to the axle. The sleeve nuts support the bearing cartridges and look much like the bearing cones of a conventional hub. In hubs without sleeve nuts, the bearing cartridges rest directly on the axle.

Cartridge-bearing Hubs with Sleeve Nuts

Identify a cartridge-bearing hub with sleeve nuts by its markings, or by the presence of bearing cartridges. **CAUTION: A cartridge-bearing hub with sleeve nuts may look very similar to a conventional hub, especially if dustcaps hide the bearing cartridges. The bearing-adjustment procedures differ. Do not adjust bearings until you know what type of hub you are working on. Remove one sleeve nut (or cone) and dustcap if necessary, to check.**

Repair procedures for cartridge-type hubs with sleeve nuts begin after this section.

The sealed-bearing hub with sleeve nuts looks very much like a conventional cup-and-cone-bearing hub until you have removed the parts from one end of the axle. A different bearing-adjustment procedure is necessary.

Cartridge-bearing Hubs Without Sleeve Nuts

Cartridge-bearing hubs without sleeve nuts are easily identified. The bearing cartridges are usually visible, and the absence of sleeve nuts or cones is easily

seen—though the axle may be threaded and have locknuts and spacers.

In these hubs, there is no bearing adjustment. The axle is prevented from slipping sideways by a raised shoulder or snapring between the bearing cartridges.

The Sturmey-Archer Elite ST drum-brake hub has a threaded axle but no sleeve nuts. Overhaul procedures for this type of hub with or without brake begin on page 130.

OVERHAULING A CARTRIDGE-BEARING HUB WITH SLEEVE NUTS

The following instructions explain how to inspect, disassemble, and overhaul a cartridge-bearing hub with sleeve nuts. The instructions are for a SunTour or Specialized hub, typical of this design. Illustrations include exploded drawings of front and rear hubs of this type.

SunTour Cyclone sealed-bearing hub.

Tools and Supplies You Will Need

Manufacturer's instruction sheet
Cone wrench to fit sleeve nuts

Open-end, box-end, or adjustable wrench for lock-nuts

Bearing-removal tool (for bearings held by interference fit or threadlock compound)

Mallet (for bearings held by interference fit or threadlock compound)

Old axle, for use as a punch

Bearing-insertion washers (for bearings held by interference fit)

Threadlock compound, if specified by manufacturer

Small utility knife (for bearings held by threadlock compound)

New bearing cartridges to fit your hub

Tools and Supplies You May Need

Axle
Sleeve nuts
Locknuts
Dustcaps
Axle nuts or quick-release parts

Preliminary Steps

Remove the wheel from the bicycle (page 69).

Remove the freewheel from a rear wheel (page 151). If the bearings were binding, check now to see whether removing the freewheel frees them. If so, improper freewheel threading was probably distorting the bearing seats.

Remove the axle nuts (page 113) or quick-release assembly (page 120).

Disassembling

① Remove the locknut, sleeve nut, and, if present, the dustcap from one end of the hub. Keep track of the order and orientation of the parts.

② Push the axle out the other end of the hub. You may have to tap it lightly with a mallet to release it. Remove the remaining dustcap, if any, from the axle. To avoid having to recenter the axle when reassembling the hub, leave the remaining sleeve nut and locknut in place.

Now check the bearing cartridges to see whether they turn smoothly and freely. If they do, replace the axle; the cartridges probably do not need to be replaced.

③ Place the bearing-remover tool in each bearing cartridge to be removed. With a mallet, using an axle as a punch, tap out the bearing cartridge. Since this may damage the axle, it is best to use an old axle.

CAUTION: Unless the bearing cartridge comes out very easily, removing it will damage it. Do not remove it unless you are sure that it must be replaced.

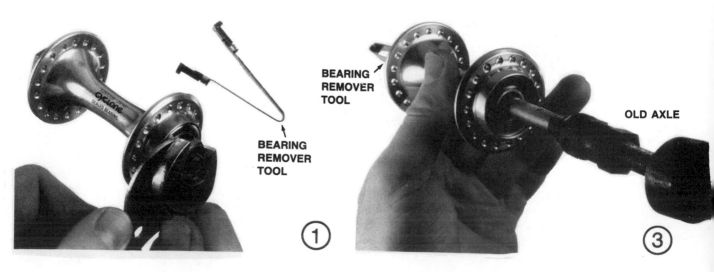

BEARING REMOVER TOOL

BEARING REMOVER TOOL

OLD AXLE

Cleaning and Inspecting

Discard removed bearing cartridges, unless they came out of the shell very easily.

If the bearings were glued into the hub shell bearing seats with threadlock compound, there will be plastic residue visible on bearing cartridges and in bearing seats. Scrape it out with a small utility knife.

Clean the hub shell, axle, locknuts, and sleeve nuts with solvent. In a hub with bearing cartridges secured by threadlock compound, wash the inside of the hub shell with detergent and rinse with water to make sure no traces of solvent, oil, or grease remain. **CAUTION: Do not clean the inside of the hub shell if you have left the old bearing cartridges in. You may contaminate the lubricant.**

Inspect the axle, locknuts, and sleeve nuts for stripped threads. Check the sleeve nut and locknut you have left in place by trying to tighten them toward one another on the axle.

Roll the axle on a flat surface (protruding over the edge if you have left one sleeve nut in place) to make sure it is not bent.

Check the bearing seats of the hub shell for distortion which may have occurred because of incorrectly installed bearings.

Check the freewheel threads of a rear hub and the brake disk threads of a brake hub for stripping or distortion. A French-threaded freewheel on an English-threaded cartridge-bearing hub will damage the threads and also distort the bearing seat, causing binding; the hub must be discarded.

Check the dustcaps, if any, for distortion.

Check the spoke flanges for cracks between the spoke holes.

Reassembling

④ Position a *new* bearing cartridge at each end of the hub shell, as shown here. Make sure it is square with the end of the shell. If there is a plastic or rubber sealing ring on only one side of each cartridge, it must face toward the outside of the hub. Position a special dished bearing-insertion washer over each bearing cartridge, as shown.

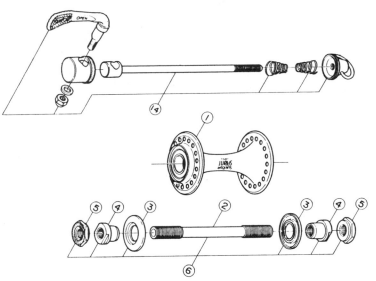

Exploded drawing of a SunTour sealed-bearing front hub.

ITEM	DESCRIPTION
1	Hub shell
2	Axle
3	Shield
4	Sleeve nut
5	Lock nut
6	Axle set
14	Quick release

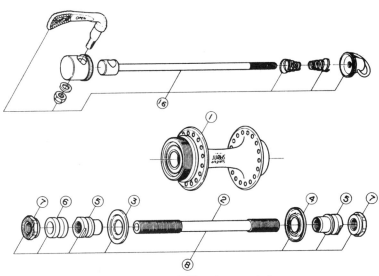

Exploded drawing of a SunTour sealed-bearing rear hub.

ITEM	DESCRIPTION
1	Hub shell
2	Rear axle
3	Right shield
4	Left shield
5	Sleeve nut
6	Spacer
7	Lock nut
8	Axle set
16	Quick release

NEW BEARING CARTRIDGE   BEARING INSERTION WASHER

④

Note: In the SunTour hub illustrated here, the outside diameter of the bearing cartridges is very slightly larger than that of the shell bore, securing them by an interference fit. Other hubs may have bearing cartridges secured to the shell with a slip fit (looser fit) and threadlock compound rather than with an interference fit. In this case, bearing-insertion washers are not needed; however, be very careful not to apply excessive force when seating the bearing cartridges.

⑤ By turning the sleeve nuts toward each other, press the bearing cartridges into the hub shell.

CAUTION: The bearing cartridges must be installed in the shell by force on the outer ring. Force applied to the inner ring (for example, by leaving out the bearing-insertion washers) will damage the cartridges.

⑥ Remove the axle and bearing-insertion washers, then reassemble the axle, cones, spacers, and locknuts on the hub. Adjust the cones until the axle is barely tight, then back one of them off a quarter of a turn and tighten the locknut. Twirl the axle to make sure that the bearings do not bind. If threadlock compound was used to secure the bearing cartridges, roll the hub along on the tire, rim, or hub flanges while pressing down on the axle ends. This will align the bearing cartridges.

Do not attempt to eliminate all endplay. For a detailed explanation of cartridge-bearing adjustment, see the introduction to cartridge bearings, page 126.

CAUTION: If the sleeve nuts are adjusted to elim-

inate all endplay, the bearings will be too tight. This is true even in a cartridge-bearing hub with a nutted axle—but leave a bit of extra play in a hub with a quick-release axle.

Finishing Up

Replace the quick-release assembly (page 122) or axle washers and nuts (page 72).

For quick-release hubs, check the bearing adjustment with the wheel installed in the bicycle and readjust as necessary (page 123). Leave a very slight amount of endplay in the final adjustment, even with the quick-release assembly tightened.

Replace the freewheel on a rear hub (page 154).

Replace the wheel on the bicycle (page 72).

OVERHAULING A CARTRIDGE-BEARING HUB WITHOUT SLEEVE NUTS

The following instructions explain how to inspect, disassemble, and overhaul a cartridge-bearing hub without sleeve nuts. The instructions are for a Sturmey-Archer Elite ST drum-brake hub. Illustrations include exploded drawings of front and rear hubs of this type. Differences between this hub and other hubs of similar construction are explained in the individual steps.

Sturmey-Archer sealed-bearing drum-brake rear hub.

Tools and Supplies You Will Need

Manufacturer's instruction sheet

Open-end, box-end, or adjustable wrench for locknuts, if any

Bearing removal tool (for bearings held by interference fit or threadlock compound)

Mallet (for bearings held by interference fit or threadlock compound)

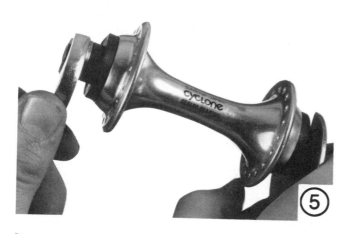

⑤

⑥

Bearing-insertion washers (for bearings held by interference fit)
Threadlock compound, if specified
Small utility knife (for bearings held by threadlock compound)
New bearing cartridges or axle assembly

Tools and Supplies You May Need

Axle
Locknuts
Dustcaps
Axle nuts or quick-release parts

Preliminary Steps

Remove the wheel from the bicycle (page 69).
Remove the freewheel from a rear wheel (page 151).
Remove drum-brake parts, if any (page 360). A threaded-on brake disk may be removed, though this is not necessary (page 361).
Remove the axle nuts (page 113) or quick-release assembly (page 120).

Disassembling

① Hardware may be different for the two ends of the hub. Make a note of this, or string parts on a wire to avoid confusion. Remove the locknut and dustcap, if any, from one end of the hub. If this is a rear hub with a larger-diameter bearing cartridge at the right side, remove the *left* locknut. Check whether threads extend inside the bearing cartridge at one end of the hub and make a note of which way the axle faces.

①

② Push the axle out of the hub, using the quick-release skewer and cup tool, a mallet, or a bearing-

removal tool as described on page 128. Push on the end from which you have removed the locknut, or the left end of a rear hub if there is a larger bearing cartridge in the right end. One or both bearing cartridges will come off with the axle. One bearing cartridge may remain in place or may be trapped in the shell between the two bearing seats of a large-barrel hub.

CAUTION: Unless the bearing cartridge comes out very easily, removing it will damage it. Hammering will always damage it. Do not remove it unless you are sure that it must be replaced.

②

③ Remove the second bearing cartridge, if it is not yet free of the hub shell.

If the axle assembly is now loose but one end of it is trapped inside the shell (Phil Wood front hubs), scrape threadlock compound off the exposed bearing race of the hub shell so you can reverse the extractor and push the axle out in the opposite direction.

If one bearing cartridge is still seated in the hub, reverse the axle or removal tool and push this cartridge out.

The axle assembly can be extracted from the Phil Wood hub using this tool, which fits through the hub axle like a quick-release skewer. The tool presses on the axle at one end and on the hub barrel at the other end.

③

Cleaning and Inspecting

Phil Wood instructions state that bearing cartridges are still usable, though noisier, after disassembly; for optimum performance and service life, it is best to replace the axle assembly. Bearing cartridges removed by hammering are damaged seriously and *must* be replaced.

If the bearings were secured in the hub shell with threadlock compound, scrape it out with a small utility knife.

Clean the hub shell, axle (unless discarding it), and locknuts (if any) with solvent. In a hub with bearing cartridges secured by threadlock compound, wash the inside of the hub shell with detergent and rinse with water to make sure no traces of solvent, oil, or grease remain.

Inspect the axle and locknuts for stripped threads.

Roll the axle on a flat surface to make sure it is not bent.

Check the bearing seats of the hub shell for distortion which may have occurred because of incorrectly installed bearings.

Check the freewheel threads of a rear hub and the brake-disk threads of a brake hub for stripping or distortion. Installing a French-threaded freewheel on an English-threaded cartridge-bearing hub will damage the threads and also distort the bearing seat, causing binding; the hub must be discarded.

Check the dustcaps, if any, for distortion.

Check the spoke flanges for cracks between the spoke holes.

Reassembling

④ Position *new* bearing cartridges or a new axle assembly for insertion of bearings into the bearing seats. Make sure they are square with the end of the hub shell. If there is a plastic or rubber sealing ring on only one side of each cartridge, it must face toward the outside of the hub. Position a bearing-insertion washer over each bearing cartridge, as shown. The bearing-insertion washers used must be a loose fit in the hub shell and on the axle. Use extra washers if necessary. If one end of the axle is different from the other, it must be inserted in the same orientation as before.

Note: In the Sturmey-Archer hub illustrated here, the outside diameter of the bearing cartridges is very slightly larger than that of the shell bore, securing them by an interference fit.

Some hubs, such as Phil Wood hubs, have bearing cartridges secured to the shell with a slip fit (looser fit) and threadlock compound rather than with an interference fit. In this case, bearing-insertion washers

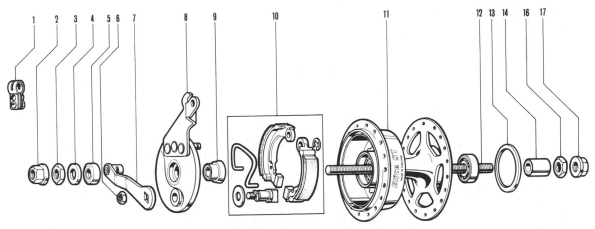

Exploded drawing of the Sturmey-Archer Elite ST sealed-bearing drum-brake rear hub.

Rear Alloy Hub Brake

ITEM	DESCRIPTION
1	Brake Arm Clip
2	Axle Nut
3	Locknut
4	Washer 1.6mm (¹⁄₁₆")
5	Brake Plate Spacer
6	Brake Lever Nut
7	Brake Lever Assembly
8	Brake Plate and Arm Assembly
9	Brake Plate Bush

ITEM	DESCRIPTION
10	Brake Shoe Service Kit
11	Hub Shell 36 hole
12	Replacement Axle Unit 162mm (6³⁄₈")
	NB This assembly includes hub bearings and 1 of items 2, 3, 4, 5, 9, 13, 14, 16, 17
13	Sprocket Spacing Washer 1.6mm (¹⁄₁₆")
14	Spacer
16	Locknut
17	Axle Nut

④

are not needed; however, be careful not to apply excessive force when seating the bearing cartridges.
In a Phil Wood hub, both bearing cartridges are

preassembled to the axle assembly, which is slipped through from one end of the shell.

⑤ If the hub uses an interference fit, carefully press the bearing cartridges into the hub shell by threading the axle nuts down on the bearing-insertion washers. With a Phil Wood or similar large-barrel hub in which the complete axle assembly is replaced, slip the axle assembly, with both bearing cartridges, into its final position *after* applying the prescribed amount and type of threadlock compound.

CAUTION: Unless an easy, slip fit, the bearing cartridges must be installed in the shell by force on the outer ring. Force applied to the inner ring (for example, by leaving out bearing-insertion washers) will damage the cartridges.

⑥ If bearing-insertion washers were used in assembly, remove the bearing-insertion washers, then reassemble the axle, cones, spacers, and locknuts on the hub. If threadlock compound was used to secure the bearing cartridges, roll the hub along on the tire, rim, or hub flanges while pressing down on the axle ends. This will align the bearing cartridges.

Finishing Up

Replace drum or disk-brake parts, if any (page 363).

Replace the freewheel on a rear hub (page 154).

Replace the quick-release assembly (page 122) or axle washers and nuts (page 72).

Replace the wheel on the bicycle (page 72).

9 • GEARING IMPROVEMENTS

Let's start this chapter on gearing improvements with a nice picture. Here's Clarence Coles, one of the authors of this book, in authentic costume on an 1878 high-wheeler which he restored. On this bicycle, the cranks are attached directly to the big front wheel—just as on a child's tricycle of today.

In high-wheeler days, a bicyclist with longer legs could straddle a bigger wheel and ride faster. Bicyclists would say that they had a "54-inch wheel" or a "60-inch wheel"—the distance across the front, driving wheel of the bicycle. Children on their tricycles have a 16- or 20-inch wheel. They pedal very fast but they don't get anywhere.

The modern chain-driven bicycle, introduced in the 1890s, solves this problem. The drive ratio depends on the size of the sprockets, not only on the size of the wheel.

Let's have an example. Let's say that the rear sprocket has 21 teeth, the front chainwheel has 42 teeth, twice as many, and the bike has 27-inch wheels, half as big as the high wheeler's.

Then, one turn of the crank pulls 42 links of chain. Since the sprocket on the rear wheel has only 21 teeth, the rear wheel turns around twice while the cranks turn once.

Thanks to the chain drive, this bike with 27-inch wheels goes just as far for one turn of the cranks as a 54-inch high-wheeler. Your great-grandfather with his new chain-driven bicycle would say that it was like a 54-inch wheel. Today, we say "54-inch gear," probably because "54-inch wheel" sounds odd when the wheels are actually much smaller.

With chain drive, you can choose any gear you want, not just the two-to-one ratio in our example. You can have a higher gear without longer legs. You can shift

High-wheeled "ordinaries" preceded the chain-drive bicycle. One of the authors, Clarence Coles, wearing an authentic outfit of the era, rides an 1878 machine he restored. Notice the straight handlebars, the spokes radiating directly out from the hub (no crossed spokes), and the step above the rear wheel used for mounting. Drive was to the front wheel, just as on the child's tricycle of today.

gears too, with internally geared hubs, or with multiple sprockets and cable-operated derailleurs (duh-rye-YERS)—French for "derailers"—which derail the chain.

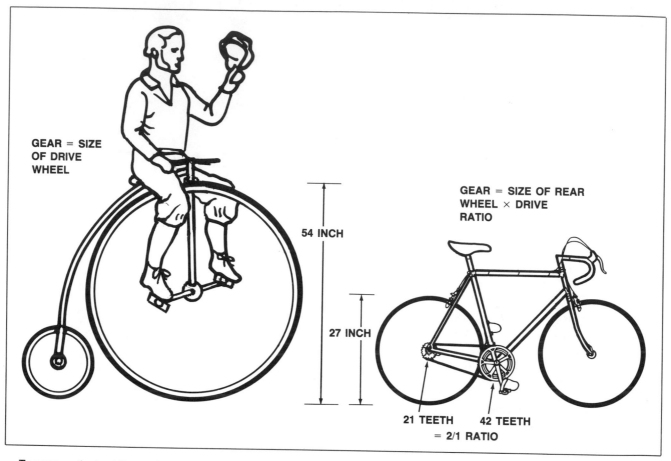

GEAR = SIZE OF DRIVE WHEEL

54 INCH

27 INCH

GEAR = SIZE OF REAR WHEEL × DRIVE RATIO

21 TEETH   42 TEETH
= 2/1 RATIO

To compare the two bikes and calculate the "gear" of the chain-drive bike, we take the number of teeth on the front chainwheel, divide it by the number on the rear sprocket, and multiply it by the size of the rear wheel.

PLANNING THE DERAILLEUR GEARING SYSTEM

Given the choice of five, ten, or more gears, what do we want from them?

Experience has shown three requirements for a derailleur gearing system:

• A high gear of 85 to 100 inches and a low gear of 20 to 50 inches, depending on style of riding and terrain.

• Small steps between gear ratios—5 to 10 inches.

• A simple, easy-to-remember sequence of shift-lever movements.

To keep track of these requirements, we draw a little chart.

This particular chart is for a twelve-speed bicycle, with two chainwheels, six sprockets, and 27-inch wheels. The number of teeth on the two chainwheels is shown at the top. The number of teeth on the six rear sprockets is shown on the left side. We calculate the gear for each combination: number of front chainwheel teeth, divided by number of rear sprocket teeth, times the wheel diameter.

FRONT CHAINWHEEL TEETH

27" WHEEL		52	42	
	14	100.3	xxxx	
	15	93.6	75.6	
REAR	17	82.6	66.7	EQUIVALENT
SPROCKET				WHEEL
TEETH	19	73.9	59.7	DIAMETER
	21	66.9	*54.0*	("GEAR")
	24	xxxx	47.3	

For example, this chart includes (in italics) the same 54-inch gear mentioned before, with a 42-tooth front chainwheel, 21-tooth rear sprocket, and 27-inch wheel: 42 divided by 21 and multiplied by 27 is 54.

Each gear number is written at the row and column of its chainwheel and sprocket, except that we xxxx out gears that shouldn't be used because of bad chain angles (page 102). Notice that you get a higher gear with a *bigger* front chainwheel or with a *smaller* rear sprocket.

Crossover Gearing

Looking at the chart, we see that the big and small chainwheels give two gear ranges with some overlap. The system shown in our chart is called "crossover," since you cross over from one chainwheel to the other to switch gear ranges. It is possible to cross over at different places besides the one shown. The crossover system is very popular with bicycle racers, because it is simple to shift. That's important, when one fumbled shift can lose a race.

The lines connecting the numbers show one possible shift pattern. Most of the lines are vertical, showing shifts between rear sprockets. The diagonal line represents what's called a "double shift": you shift both the front and the rear.

The modern derailleur gearing system allows a wide range and narrow steps. The gear pattern shown here is crossover, with small jumps between the rear sprockets and a big jump between the front chainwheels.

Why the double shift? Say you were speeding up. If you shift from the small front chainwheel to the big one, you'll go all the way from the 67-inch gear to the 83-inch—a big, uncomfortable jump. So you shift the rear derailleur back one step to get your 74-inch gear. When you're riding, you don't have to think about this: You simply adjust the rear derailleur according to what gear feels right.

The system shown here doesn't have any very low gears. Racers have to struggle and suffer up hills or be left behind, so racers don't use low gears.

For the rest of us, let's look at another twelve-speed crossover system:

FRONT CHAINWHEEL TEETH

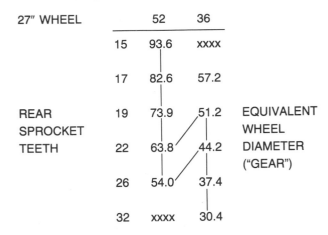

27" WHEEL		52	36	
	15	93.6	xxxx	
	17	82.6	57.2	
REAR	19	73.9	51.2	EQUIVALENT
SPROCKET				WHEEL
TEETH	22	63.8	44.2	DIAMETER
				("GEAR")
	26	54.0	37.4	
	32	xxxx	30.4	

This shifts just the same as the racing crossover, except that the gear range is a bit lower. The jumps are very even, and there's a choice of two good places to make the crossover shift.

Half-step Gearing

Besides crossover, there's another practical gearing pattern. Here's an example:

FRONT CHAINWHEEL TEETH

27" WHEEL		52	47	36	
	14	100.3	90.6	xxxx	
	17	82.6	74.6	xxxx	
REAR	21	66.9	60.4	46.3	EQUIVALENT
SPROCKET					WHEEL
TEETH	26	54.0	48.8	37.4	DIAMETER
					("GEAR")
	32	xxxx	39.7	30.4	

The shift pattern is easy to remember and the gear progression is smooth. The small jump between the 52-tooth and 47-tooth chainwheels is used for "fine tuning." The jump between chainwheels is half as big as between the sprockets, so this is called the "half-step" system. The 36-tooth chainwheel extends the range at the low end. Tourists like the half-step system because it provides a wide range and narrow steps.

Only one problem: The half-step progression uses combinations with excessive chain angles. You can do without the x'ed-out 52/32 combination, since small jumps aren't important at the lower end of the range; but you need the 47/14 combination, shown in italics. By changing the smallest rear sprocket to a 15-tooth, you can skip over the problem combination and still have a 93.6-inch top gear, plenty high for touring:

FRONT CHAINWHEEL TEETH

27" WHEEL		52	47	36	
	15	93.6	xxxx	xxxx	
	17	82.6—74.6		xxxx	
REAR	21	66.9—60.4		46.3	EQUIVALENT
SPROCKET					WHEEL
TEETH	26	54.0—48.8—37.4			DIAMETER
					("GEAR")
	32	xxxx	39.7—30.4		

The half-step system uses a small jump between the large chainwheels to "fine-tune" the rear shifts. The small inner chainwheel is for extra-low gears.

Improving Stock Gearing

Here's an "eighteen-speed" gearing setup found on many new bikes:

FRONT CHAINWHEEL TEETH

27" WHEEL		52	44	36	
	14	100.3	xxxx	xxxx	
	17	82.6	69.9	xxxx	
REAR	20	70.2—59.4		48.6	EQUIVALENT
SPROCKET					WHEEL
TEETH	24	58.5	49.5	40.5	DIAMETER
	28	50.1	42.4	34.7	("GEAR")
	32	43.9	37.1—30.4		

The jump at the high-gear end is nearly 20 inches—much too big. Notice that the duplicate gears make this into only an *eight*-speed crossover system. We could make it into a crossover system, but with the few changes shown in the next chart in italics, this becomes a very workable modified half-step system:

FRONT CHAINWHEEL TEETH

27" WHEEL		52	*48*	36	
	15	93.6	xxxx	xxxx	
	17	82.6—76.2		xxxx	
REAR	20	70.2—64.8		48.6	EQUIVALENT
SPROCKET					WHEEL
TEETH	24	58.5—54.0		40.5	DIAMETER
	28	50.1—46.3		34.7	("GEAR")
	32	43.9	40.5	30.4	

You will rarely find a suitable gearing progression on a new bicycle or an off-the-shelf freewheel. Fortunately, improvements can be very easy. Usually you will need to replace only a couple of rear sprockets, and maybe one front chainwheel.

Options for Gearing Improvement

Choices for gearing improvements depend on the rider's needs and budget and on the equipment already on the bicycle.

Some models of cranksets are more adaptable than others. On inexpensive cranksets, one or both chainwheels are often riveted in place and cannot be replaced.

On higher-grade cranksets, all chainwheels are replaceable, but the available size varies. Road-racing cranksets go as low as 38 to 42 teeth; general-purpose cranksets go to 34 or 36; true touring cranksets may have under 30.

The largest available rear sprocket may be 28 to 34 teeth, and the smallest 11 to 14. Not all intermediate sizes may be available.

Parts are widely available for some brands and models, and unavailable for others. Here's a strategy to get the best gearing improvement with the least expense and trouble:

1. Decide the highest and lowest gear you need. Racers and tandem riders use high gears of 100 to 110; the rest of us will find 90 to 95 high enough. The lowest road-racing gear is in the high 40s. For general-use pleasure riding, a 30-inch gear is low enough; for an all-terrain bike or for hilly touring with baggage, a gear in the 20s is none too low. Temper these recommendations according to your strength as a rider.

2. After deciding what high and low gear you need, go to a couple of bike shops and find out whether parts for your freewheel and crankset are available. If so, write down their chainwheel and sprocket size limits. If not, get information on replacement freewheels and cranksets. Examine your crankset and freewheel. Count the teeth and draw up a gear chart like the ones in this chapter.

3. Check the gear chart for your bicycle against the available replacement parts. If possible, plan a suitable system by replacing a couple of sprockets, using your present crankset and/or freewheel.

Think about replacing the freewheel before you think about replacing the crankset. Replacing the freewheel is simple and inexpensive. A modern six-sprocket freewheel will fit in the space of a five-sprocket freewheel while allowing a wider range and/or smaller jumps. The narrow freewheel must be used with a special chain; see page 105. A good crossover system can be built with almost any crankset, as long as you do not need an extremely low gear. You may need to install a

wide-range rear derailleur if you are installing a larger rear sprocket.

A half-step system allows a wider range, but is usually more complicated and expensive to install than a crossover system. You will probably have to rebuild the crank hanger to install a longer spindle, unless your bicycle already has triple chainwheels. With the very small inner chainwheel used in many half-step systems, a replacement, wide-range front derailleur may be necessary.

4. Once you have settled on the changes you are going to make, replace the necessary parts, following the disassembly and assembly instructions in the chapters on freewheels, cranksets, and derailleurs.

RECOMMENDED GEARING PROGRESSIONS

The following list of gearing recommendations will cover most requirements. All are calculated with a 27-inch rear wheel. A smaller rear wheel requires a *larger* front chainwheel or *smaller* rear sprocket to make the top gear high enough. A freewheel with an 11- or 12-tooth small sprocket is especially useful in this application.

Crossover Progressions

Crossover gearing is more or less free-form, as long as jumps between sprockets increase evenly from the high-gear (small-sprocket) end to the low-gear (large-sprocket) end. Two-tooth jumps are the maximum at the high-gear end.

The exact chainwheels used with a crossover system are not very important, as long as they give the needed high gear. The smaller the inner chainwheel, the lower the bottom gear, though big jumps between adjacent chainwheels can make the crossover shift clumsy. Here are a few examples of good crossover progressions:

A narrow-spaced freewheel fits six sprockets into the space taken by the normal freewheel's five. A special narrow chain must be used.

Rear Sprocket Teeth	Front Chainwheel Teeth	High Gear	Low Gear
13-14-15-16-17-18	52-42	108.0	63.0
	"Corncob" racing crossover for flat roads		
14-15-17-19-21-24	52-42	100.3	47.3
	Racing crossover for hilly roads		
15-17-19-22-26-32	52-36	93.6	30.3
	Wide-range crossover		
15-17-19-22-26-32	52-44-36	93.6	30.3
	Wide-range single-step crossover		
15-17-20-24-30	52-36	93.6	32.4
	Wide-range crossover; easily adapted from common 14-17-20-24-28 freewheel		
14-16-18-20-23-28	46-36-26	88.7	25.0
	With only the 46- and 36-tooth chainwheels, medium-range; add the 28 and it's wide-range—mountain-bike gearing.		

Half-step Progressions

Half-step progressions require careful coordination of the jumps between front chainwheels and rear sprockets. For this reason, the number of good half-step progressions is limited.

It is possible to raise or lower the number of chainwheel teeth in any of the progressions here as long as this is done proportionally for all chainwheels. Check out any such changes carefully with a gear chart to make sure that the jumps between gears remain even.

Like the example given earlier in this chapter, the following half-step systems are modified to avoid excessive chain angles. After choosing a system, plot out a gear chart to see the shift pattern. A rider must be aware of the gear pattern when using a modified half-step progression; these progressions are not for casual riders. The progressions here are grouped into categories according to limitations of available chainwheel and sprocket sizes.

Five-speed freewheel with 14-tooth minimum, 52-tooth outer chainwheel, 34–36-tooth minimum chainwheel.

Rear Sprocket Teeth	Front Chainwheel Teeth	High Gear	Low Gear
14-16-20-25-30	52-47-34	100.3	30.5
15-17-21-26-32	52-47-36	93.6	30.4
15-17-22-27-34	52-46-36	93.6	28.6
15-17-22-27-34	52-46-34	93.6	27.0

Six-speed freewheel with 14-tooth minimum, 52-tooth outer chainwheel, 34–36-tooth minimum chainwheel. Note that a special adapter is needed to use the 23–25 tooth sprockets in these progressions on Sun-Tour New Winner freewheels. There is a less expensive Pro-Compe model which allows these progressions.

Rear Sprocket Teeth	Front Chainwheel Teeth	High Gear	Low Gear
14-16-20-24-28-32	52-47-36	100.3	30.4

An easy adaptation from the common 14-17-20-24-28-32 freewheel, as are the next two progressions

Rear Sprocket Teeth	Front Chainwheel Teeth	High Gear	Low Gear
15-17-20-24-28-34	52-48-36	93.6	28.6

Has only one gear using the small chainwheel; the following progressions have two

Rear Sprocket Teeth	Front Chainwheel Teeth	High Gear	Low Gear
15-17-20-24-28-34	52-48-34	93.6	27.0
14-16-19-23-28-34	52-48-34	100.3	27.0

Rear Sprocket Teeth	Front Chainwheel Teeth	High Gear	Low Gear
13-14-17-21-25-32	50-45-28	103.8	23.6
13-15-18-22-27-34	48-44-28	99.7	22.2 Can be built with available Shimano Biopace chainwheels
13-14-17-21-25-32	48-43-26	99.7	21.9
12-14-18-23-27-34	46-41-26	103.4	20.6
12-14-18-23-27-34	45-40-26	101.3	20.6
12-14-17-21-26-34	46-41-24	103.5	19.1
13-15-19-24-28-34	46-41-24	95.5	19.1

Fully interchangeable chainwheels and sprockets, wide-range crankset, and five-speed freewheel. With the wider lateral spacing between sprockets and the smaller range of sprocket sizes, the five-sprocket freewheels will shift more crisply than narrow-spaced six-speed freewheels.

Rear Sprocket Teeth	Front Chainwheel Teeth	High Gear	Low Gear
14-16-20-25-30	50-45-32	96.4	28.8
14-16-20-25-30	48-43-30	92.6	27.0
14-16-21-27-34	50-44-28	96.4	22.2
14-16-21-27-34	47-41-26	88.7	20.6
14-16-20-26-34	47-41-24	90.6	19.1
13-14-18-23-28	47-42-28	97.6	27.0
13-14-18-23-28	45-40-26	93.5	25.1
13-15-19-24-30	45-40-26	93.5	23.4

Fully interchangeable chainwheels, wide-range six-sprocket freewheel. The SunTour New Winner freewheel requires an adapter for many of these and does not allow others, but the SunTour PS-6000 and other freewheels allow some or all; a high-performance rear derailleur is needed to shift these consistently.

For long-chain recumbent bicycles and front-drive tandems. Half-step progressions do not need to be modified, since the long chain reduces chain-angle problems. The following progressions are recommended. Progressions with the high gear in the 110-inch range are for tandems, which have an aerodynamic advantage.

A 13-tooth rear sprocket is recommended only for occasional downhill use on a tandem, because of the doubled loading of the drivetrain. A normal-spaced (not narrow) six-speed freewheel with wide (130-mm or greater) dropout spacing is recommended on a tandem for increased wheel strength, reduced wheel dishing, and positive shifting through the long cable.

Rear Sprocket Teeth	Front Chainwheel Teeth	High Gear	Low Gear
14-17-21-26-32	50-45-30	96.4	25.3
14-17-21-26-32	58-52-34	111.9	28.7
13-16-20-25-31	47-42-28	97.6	24.4
13-16-19-23-28-34	46-42-28	95.5	22.2
13-16-19-23-28-34	53-48-32	110.1	25.4

10 • SERVICING FREEWHEELS

The hub shell with a freewheel body attached, including single or multiple sprockets, is driven forward at the same speed as the sprocket. If more than one sprocket is used, it is referred to as a "cluster." When the sprocket speed is reduced or stopped, the freewheel body allows the hub to continue turning, thus the term "freewheel." This freewheel action is accomplished through a pair of pawls and an internal-ratchet arrangement within the freewheel body. Turning the exterior portion of the body forward causes the pawls to catch in the ratchets and rotate the hub. When the sprocket or cluster rotation is reversed (turned rearward), the pawls ride over the ratchets, enabling the rider to hold the pedals stationary or reverse their rotation while the bicycle is moving forward. In the early days of the freewheel body and sprocket cluster, it was quite mystifying to see a rider come to a stop using the handbrakes while simultaneously pedaling backward.

Splined or notched freewheel bodies are used on virtually all bicycles equipped with a freewheel mechanism, regardless of the manufacturer. The only difference between the two types is the method of removing the complete cluster assembly from the hub and the method of attaching the individual sprockets to the freewheel body.

SERVICE PROCEDURES

The sprockets of most single- and multiple-sprocket freewheels are removable, and are available in a range of sizes. Remove sprockets to replace worn ones or to change the gear range. Instructions for sprocket removal and installation begin on this page. Suggestions for gear progressions begin on page 135.

Freewheel removal and installation is necessary to exchange freewheels, and sometimes to replace a broken spoke or rebuild the rear hub. Instructions begin on page 151.

It is sometimes necessary to overhaul the freewheel's bearings and ratchet mechanism. Instructions begin on page 155.

Freewheel Problems

Freewheel problems are easily confused with problems in other parts of the drivetrain. See the unified list of drivetrain problems and possible causes, page 98.

Tools and Supplies You Will Need

Freewheel-remover tool to fit your freewheel
Two chain whips (freewheel vise also helpful)
120 ⅛-inch bearing balls
Pin spanner
Cup spacer (for sealed-bearing hubs)
Vise, or large adjustable wrench
Small flat-bladed screwdriver
Tweezers
SunTour New Winner bearing-adjusting tool (for New Winner only)
Threadlock compound

SPROCKET REMOVAL AND INSTALLATION

You may exchange sprockets to improve the gear range on your bicycle, or to replace worn sprockets.

Single-sprocket Freewheels

The sprocket of some single-speed freewheels is integral with the outer body and cannot be removed.

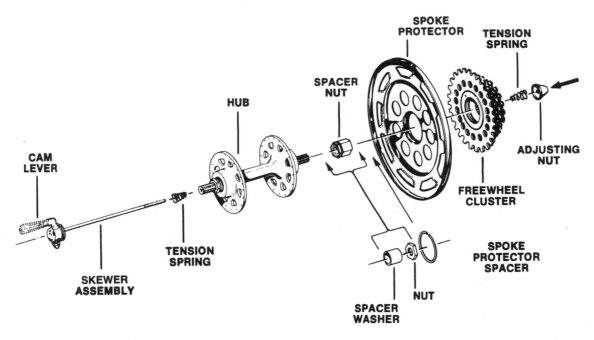

Exploded drawing of a rear hub with a freewheel cluster, showing how the freewheel is threaded to the right side of the hub. The spoke-protector plate is optional, and there is more than one type of spacer arrangement at the right side of the hub, as shown.

On other single-speed freewheels, the sprocket is held in place with a snapring, like the sprocket of a three-speed hub (page 206).

Atom and Regina Freewheels with Left-threaded Sprockets

Older-model Atom and Regina multiple freewheels have sprockets threaded to the left side. Identify these by the brand markings on the cover plate, and by the largest sprocket, which is level with the back of the freewheel body.

It is necessary to remove these Atom and Regina freewheels from the hub to remove the two largest sprockets or to get at the right rear spokes. Instructions begin on page 148.

Modern Lugged Multiple Freewheels

On newer-model *lugged* freewheels, all sprockets are removable from the right side. One or more outer sprockets are threaded and the remaining ones are secured by lugs. Identify these freewheels by looking at their left (wheel) side. You will see a flange behind the largest sprocket, with cutouts for the lugs. Instructions for removing sprockets from these freewheels begin immediately following this section.

SERVICING SPROCKETS ON A LUGGED FREEWHEEL

Disassembling

First remove the wheel (page 69).

Unless you have a freewheel vise, it is easiest to remove the sprockets with the freewheel still on the wheel.

① Place the wheel on the bench with the freewheel facing up. Remove the high-gear chain protector, if any, using a pin spanner. Rotate it counterclockwise while holding one of the sprockets with a chain whip. The protector can also be removed by using a hammer and a drift punch in one of the protector's holes. If you use this method, keep the punch in the same plane as the surface of the protector and use quick, sharp blows of the hammer to jar the protector loose. If the chain protector does not have two holes on its surface, then it is held in place with a snapring. Pry the ring out of its recess with a screwdriver.

② Wrap one chain whip around the smallest sprocket, to turn it counterclockwise. Wrap the other chain tool around the second-smallest sprocket, to turn it clockwise. If the two chains interfere, wrap the second chain whip around the third sprocket. Place the handles of the two chain whips nearly in line; pull them together with both hands.

FLANGE   LUGS

The modern freewheel *(left)* has its larger sprockets secured by lugs and a flange. All sprockets can be removed from the right side. The older Regina/Atom design *(right)* requires that the freewheel be removed from the rear wheel to remove the larger sprockets.

①

Some freewheels have a chain protector held in place by a snapring. The snapring can be pried out with a screwdriver.

CAUTION: Sprockets may let go suddenly. The hand position shown lets you pull with both hands for maximum force, and without risk. Another position may send a hand into the spokes or the sprocket teeth.

Only the smallest sprocket may come off, or the two smallest sprockets may come off together. (If so, you will need a freewheel vise to separate them.) There may be spacer washers behind the sprockets. Save them, keeping track of their position by threading them onto a wire in order with the sprockets.

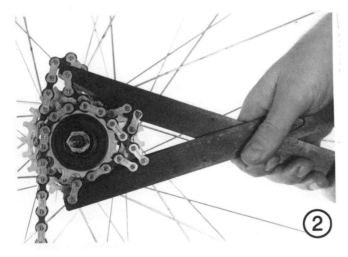

③ If you are removing all sprockets, repeat step ② for all threaded sprockets. If you are removing only enough sprockets to use a freewheel remover, stop as soon as the freewheel face is clear.

Check the interior perimeter of each sprocket as you come to it. If it has lugs as shown, the sprocket can be pulled straight out and off the body. If the sprocket does not have the lugs, it must be removed with a chain whip. The outermost sprocket is always threaded, but some freewheels have alternating positions with threaded and lugged sprockets.

④ There is an elegant trick for on-the-road spoke replacement. You use the bicycle's drive chain instead of sprocket tools.

Pull the chain out of the rear derailleur. Leave it engaged on a front chainwheel, with the right pedal behind top position. Depending on the length of the

UPPER CHAIN
ON INNER
SPROCKET

LOWER CHAIN
ON OUTER
SPROCKET

④

chain, you may be able to proceed without disconnecting a link. If disconnecting a link is necessary, push from the left side with the chain rivet extractor tool, so you push the rivet to the right (see page 105).

Now loop the lower run of chain around the bottom of the smallest sprocket. Loop the upper run of chain over the top of the next sprocket if it will fit, otherwise the third sprocket. Get as much slack out of the chain as you can.

CAUTION: Keep your hand away from the chain and sprockets. They could jam your fingers when they let go.

Step on the pedal and turn it backward, or turn the rear wheel backward. The difference in sprocket sizes will pull the chain tight and unscrew the small sprocket.

Just as with sprocket tools, repeat this procedure as many times as necessary to loosen all of the threaded sprockets. If you are careful not to jam one sprocket into the next, you won't need to remove the wheel and take off the sprockets until all are loosened.

Cleaning and Inspection

Soak the sprockets and spacer rings in solvent and brush off accumulated dirt. Rinse and wipe clean.

Clean the outside of the freewheel body with a toothbrush and a small amount of solvent. Wipe clean with a rag. Avoid letting dirty solvent run into the hub bearings.

Check the sprockets for wear, visible as "hooking" of the back edge of each sprocket tooth. Worn sprockets must be replaced or reground whenever a new chain is installed. Also check for bent teeth.

Check the spokes at the right side of the hub for damage which may have resulted from the chain's jamming between them and the freewheel.

Check that the freewheel body turns smoothly and without binding. Try to rock the inner body inside the outer one, to check for excessive play in the bearings. If there is binding or too much play, the number of shims in the freewheel body should be adjusted (see page 155).

Check the freewheel body and sprocket threads and lugs for wear or stripping.

Check the outside of the freewheel body for cracks.

Assembling

⑤ Lightly grease the outside of the freewheel body where the sprockets attach, especially the threaded portion. Install the largest lugged sprocket over the freewheel body so that it indexes with the slots in the body.

CAUTION: The tops of the teeth of many freewheel sprockets are beveled. The low side of the bevel must face toward the left (large-sprocket) side of the freewheel. If the bevels face the outside, shifting will be very poor.

If the sprockets of a multiple freewheel are beveled, the bevels must face the larger sprockets, for smooth shifting.

⑥ Slide the appropriate spacer ring or rings into place flush against the largest sprocket. Repeat steps ⑤ and ⑥ for each smaller sprocket until you reach a threaded sprocket position.

⑦ Install the threaded sprocket. Make sure that the lugged sprockets behind it are properly centered and secured on the freewheel body. Look at the sprockets edge-on to make sure they are properly installed in order of size and the lateral spacing between all of them is even.

Repeat steps ⑤, ⑥, and ⑦ until all sprockets and spacers are installed. When you have finished, they should be snug in place, but there is no need to tighten them. They will tighten during pedaling.

Finally, install the wheel (page 72).

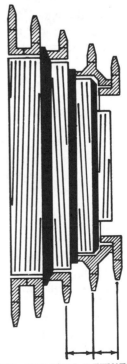

EQUAL SPACING BETWEEN FIRST, SECOND, AND THIRD SPROCKETS

This freewheel vise is available for clamping the freewheel body and sprocket cluster in a bench vise.

SERVICING SPROCKETS ON A FULLY THREADED FREEWHEEL

All sprockets on older-type Atom and Regina freewheels are threaded. The inner two sprockets are left-hand-threaded and remove from the inside. Loosening the inside ones tightens the outside ones, and vice versa. It takes a trick to remove all at the same time.

Unless you have a freewheel vise, it is easiest to work with the freewheel installed on the wheel. However, you will have to remove the freewheel from the wheel before unscrewing the two inner sprockets.

The left-handed threading can be confusing unless you recall a simple rule: All sprockets unscrew *opposite the direction of pedaling*.

Disassembling

First remove the wheel (page 69), then remove the freewheel (page 151).

① It is easy to use chain whips if a freewheel is threaded onto the hub of a wheel. After removing the freewheel, grease the hub threads and thread it back on loosely. Or if you have a freewheel vise, chuck the largest sprocket in it.

Working with the right (small sprocket) side of the freewheel facing up, wrap one chain whip around the smallest sprocket so as to turn it counterclockwise. Wrap a second chain whip around the second-smallest sprocket so as to turn it clockwise. If the two chains interfere, wrap the second tool around the third sprocket. Place the handles of the two chain whips nearly in line; pull them together with both hands.

CAUTION: Sprockets may let go suddenly. The hand position shown lets you pull with both hands for maximum force, and without risk. Another position may send a hand flying into the spokes or the sprocket teeth.

Only the smallest sprocket may come off, or the two smallest sprockets may come off together. In this case, you will need a freewheel vise to separate them.

If you are removing all sprockets, repeat this step until three or four sprockets are left. If you are removing only enough sprockets to use a freewheel remover, stop when the freewheel face is clear.

② Wrap one chain whip around the largest sprocket, to turn it counterclockwise. Wrap the other chain whip around the third-largest sprocket, to turn it clockwise. Loosen the largest sprocket.

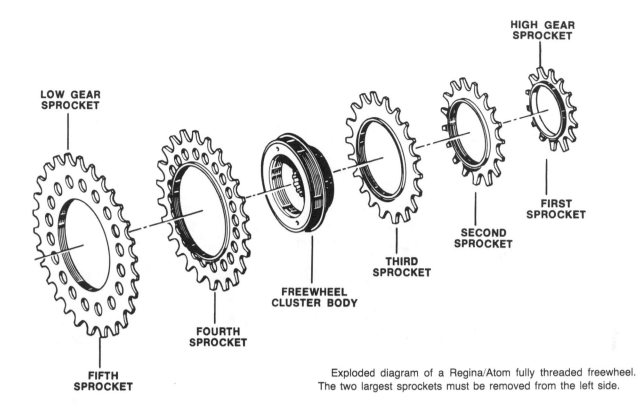

LOW GEAR SPROCKET

FOURTH SPROCKET

FIFTH SPROCKET

FREEWHEEL CLUSTER BODY

THIRD SPROCKET

SECOND SPROCKET

FIRST SPROCKET

HIGH GEAR SPROCKET

Exploded diagram of a Regina/Atom fully threaded freewheel. The two largest sprockets must be removed from the left side.

③ If the fourth- and fifth-largest sprockets came off together, lightly grease the sprocket threads of the freewheel and replace these sprockets. Repeat step ② with the chain whips on the second- and fourth-largest sprockets, to loosen the second-largest sprocket.

④ Tighten the two largest sprockets against *each other,* like a bearing cone and locknut. Do *not* tighten them against the freewheel body shoulder. If these sprockets are not too close together in size, you can use chain whips for this step. Otherwise, you will need to remove the freewheel from the rear wheel and chuck the largest sprocket in a freewheel vise.

①

②

③

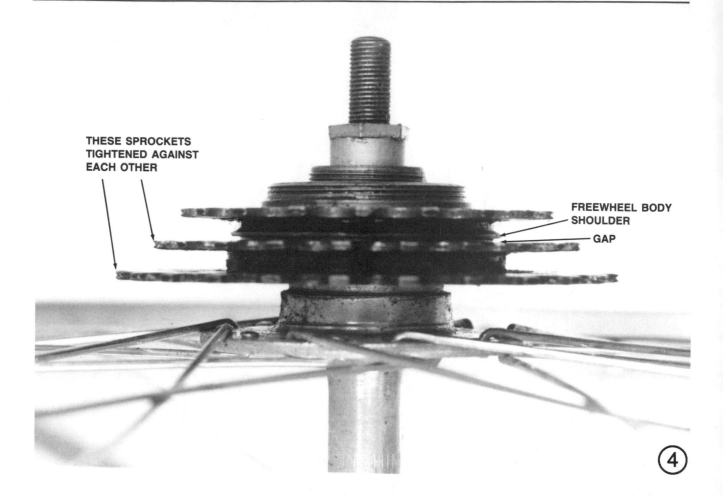

THESE SPROCKETS
TIGHTENED AGAINST
EACH OTHER

FREEWHEEL BODY
SHOULDER

GAP

④

⑤ Now hold the freewheel by the largest sprocket and remove sprockets from the small side until only two are left.

⑤

⑥

⑥ Loosen the two largest sprockets from each other, turning the larger one opposite the direction of pedaling. If the freewheel is installed on a wheel, remove it (page 151). Then unscrew the two largest sprockets and remove them.

Cleaning and Inspection

Soak the sprockets in solvent and brush off accumulated dirt. Rinse again and wipe clean.

Check the sprockets for wear, visible as "hooking" of the back edge of each sprocket tooth. Worn sprockets must be replaced or reground whenever a new chain is installed. Also check for bent teeth.

Check the spokes at the right side of the hub for

damage which may have resulted from the chain's jamming between them and the freewheel.

Check that the freewheel body turns smoothly and without binding. Try to rock the inner body inside the outer one, to see that there is not excessive play in the bearings. If there is binding or too much play, the number of shims in the freewheel body should be adjusted (see page 155).

Check the threads of the sprockets and freewheel body for wear or stripping.

Check the outside of the freewheel body for cracks.

Assembling

⑦ Turn the fourth (next-to-the-largest) sprocket counterclockwise onto the freewheel body, with the shoulder of the sprocket facing up. **CAUTION: The fourth and fifth sprockets have left-hand threads.** Use care when starting the sprockets onto the body to prevent cross-threading. Turn the fifth sprocket onto the body, with the shoulder facing down. *NOTE: The shoulders of the fourth and fifth sprockets must face each other for the proper chain clearance.*

⑧ Carefully thread the third, second, and first sprockets clockwise onto the freewheel body, with the shoulder of each facing the fourth sprocket. *NOTE: The sprockets must be installed with one shoulder between each sprocket for the proper chain clearance.* Tighten each sprocket in turn using a chain whip.

Finally, replace the freewheel on the wheel (page 154) and install the wheel (page 72).

FREEWHEEL REMOVAL AND INSTALLATION

You remove a freewheel to install a replacement freewheel, to get at the right-side rear wheel bearings for rebuilding, or to get at the spokes of the rear wheel.

It is not always necessary to remove the freewheel to get at the spokes.

With most freewheels and a large-flange rear hub, you can get at the spokes after removing the sprockets, easier for on-the-road repair; see page 142.

The Maillard Helicomatic freewheel may be removed using only the small lockring tool supplied. It is easier to remove this freewheel to get at the spokes, rather than to remove its sprockets.

Removing the sprockets from the Shimano Freehub lets you get at the spokes even with a small-flange hub. Remove the freewheel body only if it is damaged and must be replaced. Special instructions for this begin on page 154.

Preliminary Steps

Remove the wheel (page 69).

Remove the quick-release skewer (page 120) or the axle nuts and washers (page 113).

Remove the outer spoke protector and outer sprockets as necessary to gain access to the freewheel body (page 142).

Disassembling

① Look into the center of the freewheel body. If there are splines around the sides of the opening, you are working on a splined-body freewheel cluster. If the sides of the interior of the freewheel body are smooth and there are two notches in the bottom of the opening, you are working on a notched-body freewheel cluster.

This cup tool must be used when removing a notched freewheel from a sealed-bearing hub, in order to prevent excess sideways force to the bearing cartridges.

② Try the fit of the freewheel remover on the splines or notches. Remove the axle spacer only if the freewheel-remover tool cannot be fully inserted over it to engage the splines or notches of the freewheel body.

If removal of the spacer is necessary, hold the left cone with a cone wrench, to keep the axle from turning. **CAUTION: If you hold the left locknut instead, it may unscrew.** Remove the axle spacer from the right end of the axle by turning it counterclockwise. Some hubs may have a thin locknut and then a thick, un-threaded spacer; in this case, remove both. To avoid disturbing the bearing adjustment, do not remove the inner, cone locknut.

③ For the notched-body freewheel, place the tool over the axle, with the ears of the tool fully indexed in the slots of the freewheel body. **CAUTION: To avoid stripping the notches in the freewheel body, use the correct tool for the model of freewheel you are working on, and check carefully that the tool is fully seated to provide a secure grip.**

With a quick-release hub, install the quick-release unit as shown. With a nutted hub, install an axle nut. Screw the quick-release adjusting nut or axle nut finger-tight against the freewheel remover, then back it off one-half turn.

Note: For the splined-body freewheel, install the tool, but it is usually not necessary to clamp the tool with the axle nut or quick-release skewer.

④ Position the wheel over a vise, freewheel side

down. Tighten the vise against the flats of the freewheel remover. Grasp the rim of the wheel, holding it steady and level, and turn it counterclockwise *no more than half a turn* until you feel the freewheel body loosen.

CAUTION: Be very careful not to turn the wheel any farther than is necessary to loosen the freewheel. If you turn it farther, the freewheel remover will jam against the axle nut or quick-release nut. Then it can damage axle bearings or break the quick-release skewer. The problem is especially serious with sealed-bearing hubs. Some sealed-bearing hubs are sold with a special cup tool to support the left end of the quick-release skewer and prevent bearing damage during freewheel removal.

When the freewheel body has loosened, remove the wheel from the vise, remove the quick-release or axle nut, and unscrew the freewheel body the rest of the way. Remove it, and the spoke protector if there is one.

If you do not have a vise, use a 12- or 15-inch adjustable wrench. *NOTE: Secure even a splined freewheel remover with the axle nut or quick-release nut if you use a wrench, because of the unbalanced force from the wrench.*

For an on-the-road repair, a handy tool called the Pocket Vise lets you turn a SunTour freewheel remover with a fencepost or even your bicycle's handlebar stem.

If the notches of a freewheel break, you can often chip them off square with a hammer and cold chisel and try again. If this doesn't work, disassemble the freewheel (page 155) so that you can clamp a vise on the inner body, or else tack-weld the body together and turn the freewheel by a sprocket.

Cleaning and Inspection

Soak the freewheel in solvent, then scrape and wipe off dirt. Narrow strips of cloth are useful to clean between the sprockets. Finally, rinse off the traces of dirt.

Clean the hub threads with a little solvent on a toothbrush. Wipe the threads dry with a rag. Avoid letting dirty solvent run into the hub bearings unless you are going to rebuild them.

Check the threads of the hub and freewheel body for wear or stripping.

Check the spokes at the right side of the hub for damage which may have resulted from the chain's jamming between them and the freewheel.

④

Check that the freewheel body turns smoothly and without binding. Also try to rock the inner body inside the outer one, to see that there is not excessive play in the bearings. If there is binding or too much play, the number of shims in the freewheel body should be adjusted (see page 155).

Check the sprockets for wear, visible as "hooking" of the back edge of each sprocket tooth. Worn sprockets must be replaced or reground whenever a new chain is installed. Also check for bent teeth.

Assembling

⑤ If you are installing a freewheel different from the one you removed, check that the threading is compatible. There are four standards for freewheel threads:

	Diameter	Thread pitch		
English	1.370 inches	24	TPI	(threads per inch)
ISO	1.375 inches	24	TPI	
Italian	1.378 inches	24	TPI	
French	1.366 inches	25.4	TPI	

French-standard freewheels are sometimes marked "metric."

Threading does not correspond to the country in which parts were made, but, more or less, to the country in which a bicycle or rear wheel was assembled. Some French bikes have English freewheel threads!

CAUTION: A French-threaded freewheel will thread onto a 24 TPI hub—or vice versa—though with difficulty. Use only hand force to install a freewheel. If the freewheel becomes progressively harder to turn as you thread it on, stop and remove it. It will permanently damage the threads and is likely to strip in use.

English, ISO, and Italian threads are more or less compatible with each other. An Italian-threaded freewheel will fit somewhat loosely on an English hub; the freewheel body will rock noticeably even when threaded on most of the way. This combination is usable if the rider isn't too heavy or strong.

The normal way to check threading is with a thread-pitch gauge and vernier caliper. If you do not have these tools, check the fit of freewheels on a hub shell which you know to have English threading.

⑥ Lightly grease the hub threads and the inside of the freewheel body. Carefully align the freewheel over the end of the hub threads and thread it onto the hub by hand. If it becomes hard to turn before it is threaded on all the way, stop and remove it to check for crossthreading or mismatched threads. Otherwise, thread it all the way down. There is no need to tighten it; it will tighten with pedaling.

Finishing Up

Replace sprockets (page 144).

Replace the quick-release skewer (page 120) or axle nuts (page 113).

Install the wheel (page 72).

Adjust the rear derailleur limit screws (page 166).

CAUTION: A new freewheel may be wider or narrower than the one it replaces. Check the adjustment of the rear derailleur limit screws to avoid the risk of jamming the chain.

SHIMANO FREEHUB BODY REMOVAL AND INSTALLATION

The freewheel body of the Shimano Dura-Ace EX Freehub is removable by unscrewing like a conventional freewheel, but *after* removing the axle assembly (see Chapter 8). Use Shimano tool T1-FH10. **CAUTION: The threads of the Shimano Freehub's freewheel body and hub shell must be free of oil when reassembling them. The freewheel body**

must be securely tightened in place, as its position affects the axle bearing adjustment.

The freewheel body of most other Shimano aluminum-shell Freehubs is pressed into place. Remove it *after* the hub axle. Use Shimano tool TL-FH30, which works like a gear puller, or substitute for this tool by leaving the small sprocket on the hub, hanging it between vise jaws, and tapping the hub shell out with a large punch. Press the assembly back together in a vise after removing the dustcaps, or use the Shimano tool.

The freewheel body of Shimano Freehubs with multisection hub barrel is not removable.

OVERHAULING A FREEWHEEL BODY

You will not often have to overhaul a freewheel body. Its bearings are almost immune from wear. When you coast, the bearings are turning, but they are under almost no load. When you pedal, the bearings are under load, but the inner and outer freewheel body do not move relative to each other.

Pawls and pawl springs can break, but usually then the ratchet is damaged too and the freewheel body should be replaced, not overhauled. Often the bearing race is tightened harder at the factory than you can hope to do at home. *Do not overhaul a freewheel body unless there is a good reason to do so.*

It is, however, important to know how to take apart a freewheel body in the following situations:

1. If the notches for the freewheel remover are stripped. You can remove a freewheel by disassembling the body and clamping its inner part in a vise. (Exception: SunTour old Winner, which must be welded together.)

2. If the bearings are too tight or too loose. You take the freewheel body apart to add or remove shims. (Exception: SunTour Winner series use a double-nut bearing adjustment requiring a special tool for adjustment.)

3. If the outer freewheel bearing race unscrews during a ride. Temporary repairs have been made by replacing lost bearing balls with the little metal beads of a key chain or even with strips of leather shoelace. The freewheel may not coast properly after a repair like this; to avoid damaging the rear derailleur, you may have to keep pedaling all the time.

Except in these cases, it is enough to wash a freewheel in solvent at every major overhaul and then drip oil through the body to lubricate it.

NOTE: The Shimano Freehub body may be disassembled after *the axle has been removed (see Chapter 8). Use Shimano tool TL-FH40 except for the FH-MX15 freewheel, which requires tool TL-FW40.*

Disassembling

Most freewheels use 100 to 150 ⅛-inch bearing balls. Have them on hand before you start the job. First remove the wheel (page 69).

STANDARD FREEWHEEL TOOL

①

① A splined-body freewheel can be overhauled while held by the freewheel remover, inserted from the back; a notched-body freewheel must be threaded to the bicycle wheel and tightened by pedaling in low gear, or else it will be impossible to retighten the bearing race. If you decide to discard the freewheel after taking it apart, the inner part of the body can easily be clamped in a vise and removed from the hub.

CAUTION: If you are disassembling the entire wheel, remove the freewheel before removing the spokes.

If a chain protector or outer sprockets overhang the freewheel cover plate, remove them; see page 142. Also remove any other sprockets you will be reusing; sprocket removal is harder once the freewheel body has been disassembled.

Check the bearing adjustment so you will know whether you might need to add or remove shims before reassembly. If the inner body binds in the outer body, bearings are too tight; if it rocks, they are too loose.

② Rotate the bearing race in a clockwise direction with a pin spanner wrench, or drift punch and hammer. **CAUTION: The bearing race has left-hand threads and must be turned clockwise to remove it.**

If the bearing race is very tight, secure the pin tool with a large washer and the axle nut; or else remove the quick release and place the wheel on the floor, freewheel up, and have someone stand on the pin tool while you break the bearing race loose with light hammer blows.

②

Hold the outside of the freewheel and turn it over; catch the loose bearing balls and spacers. If you are only doing a bearing adjustment, there is no need to take the freewheel apart any further. Proceed to step ⑬. Otherwise, lift the wheel off the sprocket cluster. Be prepared to catch loose bearing balls from the left race, which will fall down through the body.

NOTE: On the SunTour New Winner, the bearing race is adjusted by a cone-and-locknut assembly with right-hand threads. Use the larger end of the SunTour New Winner tool to turn the bearing race slightly clockwise. Then use the smaller end of the tool to unscrew the locknut counterclockwise. If you are only adjusting the bearings, do not take the freewheel body apart; proceed to step ⑬. **CAUTION: The tool must be secured by the quick release or axle nut to prevent stripping.**

③ Pry the pawl spring out of its recess with a screwdriver, and then remove the pawls.

Cleaning and Inspecting

Clean all parts in solvent and rinse them, or wipe them dry with a lintless cloth. Keep all cleaned parts on paper towels to avoid contamination.

Inspect the bearing balls for a dulling of the surface, indicating wear or corrosion. Replacing the entire set will ensure even distribution of the bearing load.

Thoroughly inspect the main cluster body. Check the internal and external parts for stripped threads; bearing surfaces for scratchlike scores or pits; and the internal ratchet teeth for cracks, chips, or broken edges.

Check the pawls for broken edges, cracks, or signs of excessive wear.

Inspect the pawl spring for a crack or loss of tension.

Check the bearing race for stripped threads. Bear in mind that it has left-hand threads. Check the bearing surface for scores, pits, or corrosion.

Check the shims for cracks, distortion, or signs of excessive wear from damaged bearings.

Assembling

④ Place the pawls into the recesses of the main cluster body, with the contour of the pawl following that of the body, as shown.

⑤ Secure the pawls in place with the pawl spring. Check to be sure the spring is fully seated in the slots of the pawls, with one end of the spring on each side of the projection, as shown in the illustration.

⑥ Lay the cluster on the bench with the largest sprocket facing up. Apply a generous amount of multi-purpose grease to the bearing race.

⑦ Imbed loose bearing balls into the lubricant. *NOTE: The number of bearings may vary with different models of freewheel bodies.*

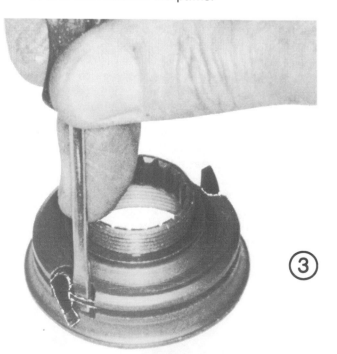

③

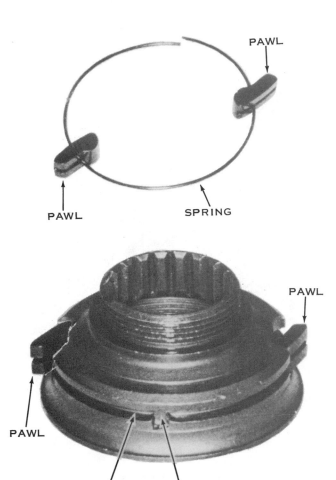

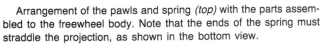

Arrangement of the pawls and spring *(top)* with the parts assembled to the freewheel body. Note that the ends of the spring must straddle the projection, as shown in the bottom view.

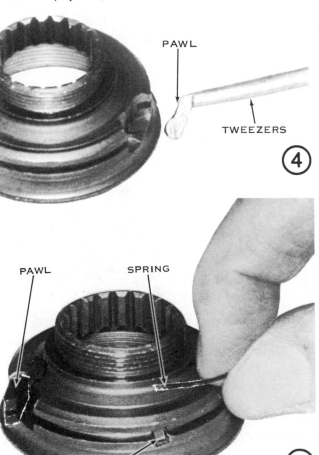

⑧ Insert enough ball bearings to fill the perimeter of the bearing race snugly, and then take one out for clearance.

⑨ Place the main freewheel body in position on top of the bearings, with the external threads facing down.

⑩ Depress each of the pawls to their retracted position, and then push the main freewheel body down until its upper surface is below the surface of the outer body by approximately the thickness of the dust ring.

⑪ Place the dust ring, if any, on top of the main freewheel body, and then tap it into position with a mallet. The ring must seat flush with the surface of the outer body flange to hold the main body and the bearings.

⑫ Turn the cluster over. Run oil into the body to lubricate the pawls. Then apply a light coating of multipurpose grease to the bearing cup of the outer body. Carefully avoid getting any oil or grease on the threads of the inner body.

bearing balls into the lubricant as you counted during disassembly. *NOTE: The number of bearing balls on this side may also vary with different models of freewheel bodies.* If the count was lost, insert enough ball bearings to fill the cup snugly, and then remove one bearing for clearance.

⑬ Insert shims, which provide the bearing adjustment. Add one of the thinnest kind if the bearing adjustment was too tight before disassembly; remove one if the adjustment was too loose.

NOTE: On the SunTour New Winner, there are no shims.

⑭ Spread a thin coating of multipurpose grease on top of the shims. Imbed the same number of loose

⑮ Thread the bearing race into the main body by turning it counterclockwise. **CAUTION: The bearing race has left-hand threads.** Securely tighten the bearing race with a pin-spanner wrench or a drift punch and hammer.

With some freewheels, especially SunTour Pro-Compe and Perfect models, it is difficult to tighten the bearing race enough with a pin spanner to prevent unscrewing. It is a good idea to use threadlock compound on the threads between the inner body and the bearing race.

Check the assembly and bearing adjustment as follows: Hold the freewheel body in your left hand and rotate the sprocket cluster in both directions. The sprocket cluster should rotate freely and without sideplay when it is turned counterclockwise. You should be able to hear the pawls riding over the internal ratchets. The pawls should catch when you attempt to turn the cluster clockwise, also causing the body to rotate in your left hand. If the body is too tight, remove the

bearing race and add a shim. If the body has sideplay, remove the bearing race, take out a shim, and then reinstall the race. Recheck the adjustment again. Remove or install shims until the cluster rotates freely, but without sideplay.

NOTE: On the SunTour New Winner, thread on the bearing race clockwise, then the lockwasher and locknut. Adjust the bearing race and tighten the locknut moderately. **CAUTION: The tool must be secured by the axle nut or quick release.** *At this point, the bearing adjustment should be slightly too tight. Then turn the bearing race slightly counterclockwise to tighten it firmly against the locknut and make the final bearing adjustment. This procedure applies the heaviest load on the larger end of the tool, which is less likely to strip.*

To finish up, reinstall sprockets (page 142) and install wheel on bicycle (page 72).

11 • SERVICING REAR DERAILLEURS

The rear derailleur has two important functions to perform. First, it must move the chain back and forth from one sprocket to another, and second, it must keep the chain under constant tension. The length of the chain required when it is engaged on the smallest sprocket at the rear wheel and on the smallest chainwheel at the hanger set is much less than the opposite combination, when the chain is engaged on the largest sprocket and the largest chainwheel.

All rear derailleurs, regardless of make, style, or the precision of parts used in their construction, operate on the same basic principle. Two small pulleys, housed in a cage assembly, move by means of two traversing arms under spring tension and are actuated through a cable connecting to a shift lever, mounted at the front of the bicycle. The traversing arms, together with the cage holding the pulleys, form and maintain a perfect parallelogram. It is this principle that allows the upper or "jockey" pulley to stay in vertical alignment with each sprocket of the cluster and thus shift the chain from one sprocket to another. The pulley cage is under spring tension to keep the lower pulley forced toward the rear of the bicycle and the chain tight when it is engaged on any normally used combination of front and rear sprockets.

Limit screws are installed to restrict the amount of jockey pulley travel for the largest (low-gear) sprocket and the smallest (high-gear) sprocket.

SERVICE PROCEDURES

To the owner of a bicycle equipped with a multi-sprocket freewheel attached to the rear hub, the rear derailleur is one of the most critical pieces of equipment on the bike.

Because the derailleur is exposed, it is easily damaged if the bicycle falls on its right side. Sand, dirt, and other abrasive materials thrown onto it by the rear wheel and chain cause the mechanism to require periodic cleaning, lubricating, adjustment, or overhaul.

The next section of this chapter provides complete procedures for removing, installing, and adjusting a rear derailleur. The location of adjustment screws, method of attachment to the bicycle, and control-cable hookup may vary among manufacturers, but the principles are basically alike and the following instructions cover typical units.

The remaining sections give detailed procedures for complete overhaul of all major types of rear derailleurs.

All of the parts of a drivetrain must be in good condition and correctly adjusted for it to work well. A problem in one part may seem to be in another: for example, poor rear-derailleur shifting may result from incorrect chain length. Inspect a drivetrain before disassembling it; see page 98.

What Service Do Rear Derailleurs Need?

Rear derailleur pulleys wear, and the pantograph—the variable parallelogram formed by the arms and cage—can seize up from accumulated dirt. Both of these problems can easily be solved by rebuilding.

The pulleys require most frequent service—cleaning and relubrication. Unless the parallelogram pivots have worn out, cleaning and relubricating them usually restores like-new performance. If you are only disassembling the pulleys, clean the parts with a toothbrush, taking care not to get solvent into the upper pivot and pulley-cage pivot.

Rebuild the upper pivot and pulley-cage pivot only if they clearly need relubrication or adjustment. Some can be difficult to reassemble, for you must hold parts in position against spring force.

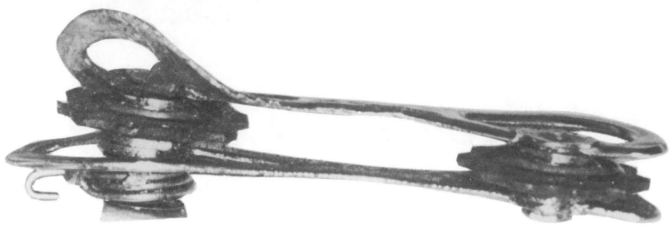

Damage to the chain cage of a rear derailleur caused by backpedaling when between gears.

Check for these problems before disassembly: worn pivots, resulting in excess play and sloppy shifting; or a badly bent derailleur, the result of the bicycle's falling on it or the chain's jamming in it. With these problems, it often makes sense to replace the entire derailleur. Sometimes it is possible to build up a good, working unit by combining used parts.

Rear Derailleur Capacity

Some rear derailleurs are designed to work with narrow-range racing gearing, others with intermediate or wide-range gearing. A racing derailleur can be readily identified by its short pulley cage, and a touring derailleur by its long pulley cage, to take up chain with large differences in sprocket and chainwheel size.

A racing derailleur has a relatively simple job. Since the small racing sprockets are very nearly the same size, the racing derailleur only has to move the chain sideways to position it under the desired sprocket.

A touring derailleur has a harder job. To clear the large-diameter inner sprocket, the upper, *jockey* pulley has to be much lower than a racing derailleur's. A touring derailleur which only moved the pulleys sideways would hang far below the smaller, outer sprockets. Shifting would be sloppy—two-sprocket jumps or no shift at all.

Many derailleurs have design refinements to overcome this problem. Careful adjustment, and sometimes minor modifications, are necessary to make the most of a derailleur's shifting performance.

Adjusting Rear Derailleurs for Positive Shifting

The less chain between the rear derailleur's upper (*jockey*) pulley and the sprockets, the less wasted motion, and the more positively the derailleur will shift. No derailleur will position the pulley equally close to

sprockets of widely different sizes, but any derailleur should be adjusted as close as possible without interference. If a derailleur hangs far below the sprockets in all gears, either it is wrong for the application, it is mounted on the wrong hanger, or it is out of adjustment.

The three major types of rear derailleurs are *fixed-jockey-pulley*, *raised-jockey-pulley*, and *tracking*. They allow adjustment of the pulley-sprocket distance in different ways and to different degrees.

In *fixed-jockey-pulley* derailleurs, the derailleur body does not move forward or back during use, and the upper pulley is directly in line with the pulley-cage pivot. Most Huret and many SunTour long-cage derailleurs are of this design.

Some fixed-jockey-pulley derailleurs have no adjustment for pulley-sprocket spacing. SunTour derailleurs have an "angle adjusting screw." As you back this screw out, the pulley rises closer to the sprockets. If this adjustment is not sufficient or is unavailable, it may help to file back the derailleur or hanger stop tab. Fixed-jockey-pulley derailleurs work best with a relatively short chain, to maximize chain tension.

In *raised-jockey-pulley* derailleurs, the jockey pulley is above and behind the chain-cage pivot. When you shift to smaller sprockets, the jockey rises. The pulley also rises when a smaller chainwheel is selected, making the raised-upper-pulley feature most effective if the chainwheels are of nearly the same size.

Adjust a raised-jockey-pulley derailleur by choosing the chain length to place the pulley highest when the chain is on the smallest sprocket. If possible, also adjust the position of the derailleur body to bring the pulley close to the sprockets.

In *tracking* derailleurs, the pulley cage "floats": A spring governs the spacing between the jockey pulley and the sprockets. The spring may be in a *guide cage* in between the body and the pulley cage, as in the SunTour Le Tech derailleur shown in the accompany-

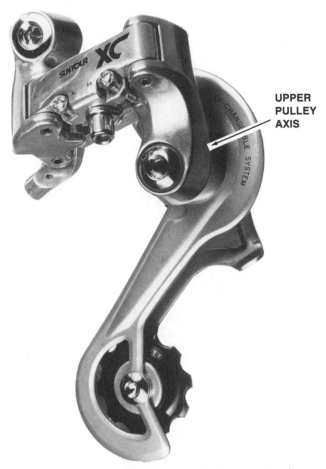

The SunTour XC is a concentric-jockey-pulley long-cage touring rear derailleur. The forward-angled pantograph and the large chain-pushing guide at the jockey pulley help achieve positive shifting.

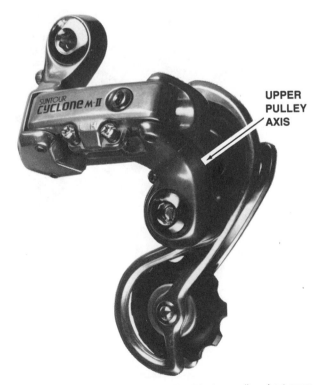

The SunTour Cyclone Mark II is a raised-jockey-pulley short-cage racing rear derailleur. The position of the upper, jockey pulley changes as different sprockets are selected.

The Shimano Super Plate is a tracking derailleur with an intermediate guide cage between the pantograph and the pulley cage.

ing photograph; with most Simplex and Shimano derailleurs, the spring is in the upper pivot. Tracking derailleurs are especially well suited to wide-range touring gearing, with extreme differences in sprocket sizes.

Adjust a tracking derailleur by changing the relative force generated by its two springs. Weakening the guide-cage or upper pivot spring will pull the derailleur closer to the sprockets. More details are given in the rebuilding instructions later in this chapter.

Tracking derailleurs usually work best with a relatively long chain, placing the pulleys nearly in a vertical line when the small sprockets are selected. This increases the leverage, raising the pulleys toward the sprockets.

Instructions furnished with many derailleurs do not stress pulley position enough. For example, SunTour instructions say to place the body level with the floor; in many cases, it could be raised, achieving a significant improvement in shifting performance. Sometimes, filing back the angle stop or changing derailleur hangers is necessary for best performance, especially when using a touring derailleur with a small sprocket cluster and chainwheels of widely different sizes.

Rear Derailleur Mounting

The *derailleur hanger* fastens the rear derailleur to the frame at the right rear forkend. The derailleur hanger may be integral with the forkend or it may be a bolt-on piece. It has a mounting hole, which may be threaded or unthreaded. Some brands of hangers have an angle stop tab or notch to position the derailleur body, while others use a locknut.

A nonstandard hanger may not position the derailleur correctly. Replacing a bolt-on hanger is easy, but if a frame has an integral hanger and you must change derailleur brands, try to find one that is a close match. An unthreaded mounting hole in a hanger can be threaded (10 × 1mm), or sometimes an angle stop can be filed to fit.

Five rear derailleur hangers show different mounting-hole positions and angle stops. Left to right: SunTour touring, SunTour racing, Shimano/Italian, Huret, Simplex.

REMOVING, INSTALLING, AND ADJUSTING THE DERAILLEUR

The following step-by-step illustrated instructions cover removal of a typical derailleur unit. Though the method of attachment to the bicycle and the control-cable hookup may vary, the principle is similar for all derailleurs and the following procedures can be easily used for all such units.

It is usually easiest to remove the rear wheel before the rear derailleur; see page 69. The wheel must be removed if the derailleur has a bolt-on hanger or a locknut behind the hanger.

① Look at the inside arm of the pulley-cage assembly. If the inside of the cage is relieved, as on many SunTour units, simply lift the chain free and remove it from the derailleur. If the inside arm is continuous between the pulleys, remove the tension pulley spindle and the pulley from the cage. This simple step eliminates the need for unlinking the chain in order to remove the derailleur.

② Loosen the cable anchor nut, pull the cable free of the anchor bolt, and then draw it out of the cable adjusting barrel. Loosen the mounting bolt securing the

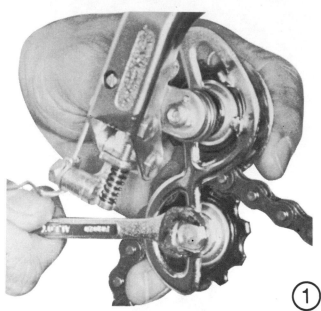

derailleur hanger to the frame. Slide the hanger free of the rear-frame dropout. If the derailleur is attached directly to the frame, hold the pivot bolt with the correct-size Allen wrench, and then remove the locknut. Turn the pivot bolt counterclockwise until it is free of the frame, and then remove the derailleur, shim washer, stop plate, and spacer, as shown in the illustration.

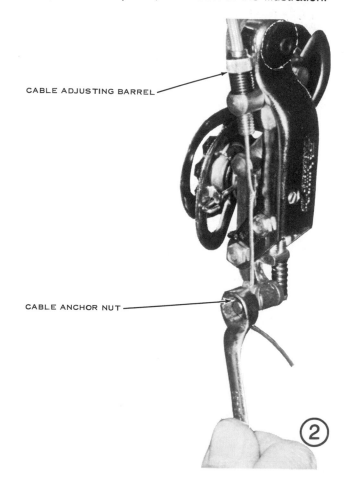

CABLE ADJUSTING BARREL

CABLE ANCHOR NUT

Installing the Derailleur

The following illustrated procedures provide step-by-step instructions for installing a derailleur on the bicycle.

③ Guide the derailleur hanger into the rear-frame dropout, with the nut on one side of the dropout and the hanger on the other side, until the shoulder of the nut seats against the end of the dropout slot. Align the slot in the hanger with the slot of the dropout, and then tighten the nut securely. To install a derailleur unit to a frame with an integral hanger, insert the pivot bolt into the outer arm. Slide a thick spacer onto the pivot bolt with the rounded side facing the derailleur, as shown in the illustration. Install the stop plate on the pivot bolt, with the small pin facing outward, and then install the shim washer. Thread the pivot bolt into the mounting hole on the forkend of the bicycle frame securely, and then back it off about one quarter of a turn, or until the derailleur unit pivots freely without sideplay. Hold the pivot bolt adjustment and thread the locknut on tightly. Check the pivot bolt adjustment and tighten or loosen it as required by first backing off the locknut slightly, tightening or loosening the pivot bolt, and then retightening the locknut.

With a 14mm end wrench and a 5mm Allen wrench, it is possible to adjust the tension of the Simplex upper pivot spring to make this derailleur track close to the sprockets.

spacer or stop plate to assemble. Often there is no locknut. If there is no locknut, tighten the pivot bolt securely; do not back it off.

On Shimano derailleurs, pull the pulley cage forward while tightening the pivot bolt. This will assure that the stop tab seats against the angle stop on the derailleur hanger. Check that it has seated properly.

The pivot bolt and locknut control the tracking of Simplex derailleurs. By rotating the pivot bolt clockwise, a Simplex derailleur may be made to track closer to the sprockets.

④ Check the pivot-bolt adjustment. The derailleur unit should pivot freely without sideplay. If an adjustment is required after it is mounted on the bicycle, hold the pivot bolt with an Allen wrench and loosen the locknut. Tighten or loosen the pivot bolt, and then retighten the locknut.

③

NOTE: Many derailleurs are simpler to mount to an integral hanger than the one shown. Usually there is no

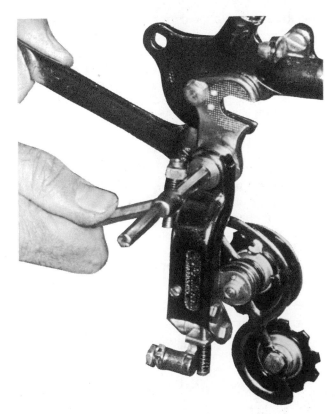

④

⑤ Feed the control cable through the guide, adjusting barrel, and anchor bolt. Secure the anchor bolt finger-tight to hold the cable in place.

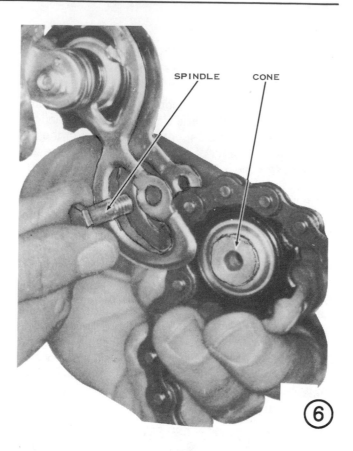

SPINDLE   CONE

⑥

⑤

⑥ Engage the chain on the tension pulley, and then install the pulley into the cage with the spindle. Tighten the spindle, and then lift the chain clear of the pulley. Check a Huret ball-bearing pulley for free rotation without sideplay. If an adjustment is required, loosen the spindle slightly, tighten or loosen the cone of the pulley, and then retighten the spindle. If the inner arm of the cage assembly is relieved, simply engage the chain on the pulley.

If you have removed the wheel, now replace it; see page 72.

⑦ Place the rear shift lever in the full-forward position, and then check to see that the chain is still engaged on the smallest sprocket. Pull the control cable taut, and then secure it by tightening the anchor nut.
CAUTION: Check the adjustment of the derailleur's limit screws after replacing it.

Adjusting the Derailleur Limit Screws

⑧ Place the chain on the smallest sprocket and the shift lever in the high-gear (full-forward) position. Ro-

⑦

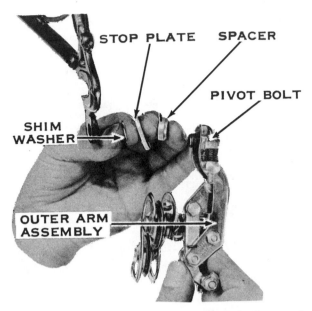

STOP PLATE   SPACER

PIVOT BOLT

SHIM WASHER

OUTER ARM ASSEMBLY

Arrangement of the parts on the pivot bolt of a derailleur attached directly to the bicycle frame.

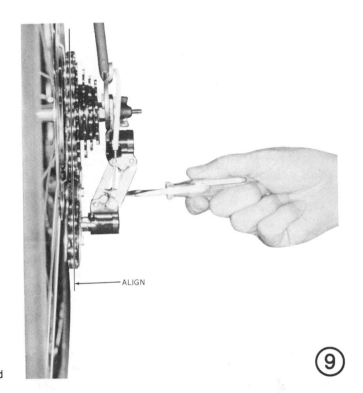

ALIGN

⑨

tate the high-gear adjusting screw clockwise or counterclockwise until the centerline of the jockey pulley is aligned with the centerline of the smallest sprocket.

⑨ Move the chain to the largest (low-gear) sprocket either by hand or by using the shift lever. Set the shift lever to the low-gear (full-rearward) position. Adjust the low-gear screw until the centerline of the jockey pulley is aligned with the centerline of the largest sprocket.

⑩ To make an alternate adjustment for the high-gear sprocket, proceed as follows: Position the chain onto the second-smallest sprocket by hand. Turn in the high-gear limit screw until it contacts the main traversing arm and holds the chain on the second-smallest sprocket. Place the control lever in the high-gear position, and then loosen the cable anchor bolt slightly. Rotate the cranks in the driving direction and, at the same time, turn out the high-gear limit screw until the chain drops down onto the smallest sprocket. Pull the cable through the anchor bolt until it is taut, and then tighten the bolt firmly. Force the shift lever down several times to prestress the cable.

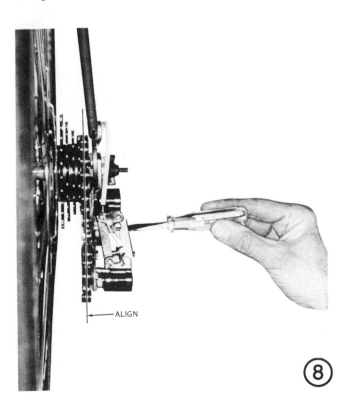

ALIGN

⑧

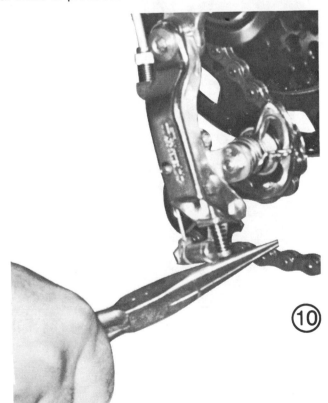

⑩

Straightening a Bent Derailleur

NOTE: The following steps should be performed only if necessary and with caution to avoid damage to the derailleur.

The techniques described here will correct simple bends of the derailleur or hanger which result from the bicycle's falling on its right side. Whenever a derailleur has been bent, check also for loosened or seized pivots. If damage cannot be corrected, the derailleur must be replaced entirely or in part.

If the following inspection procedures reveal that the pulleys are not in line *with each other,* the pulley cage is bent. In this case, do not try to straighten the derailleur yet. Disassemble the derailleur to straighten the pulley cage before trying to straighten the hanger.

① Check the *vertical* alignment of the derailleur by sighting along the plane of the pulleys while the pulleys are in the *vertical* position. The vertical centerline of the pulleys should be parallel with the plane of the sprockets. If the derailleur is out of line, bend the derailleur into position by hand, or use an Allen wrench fitted in the pivot bolt as a lever to bend the unit.

② Check the *horizontal* alignment of the derailleur by sighting along the plane of the pulleys while the pulleys are in the *horizontal* position. The centerline of the pulleys should be parallel with the plane of the sprockets. If the derailleur is out of line, bend the derailleur by hand or by using the correct-size Allen wrench in the pivot bolt for leverage.

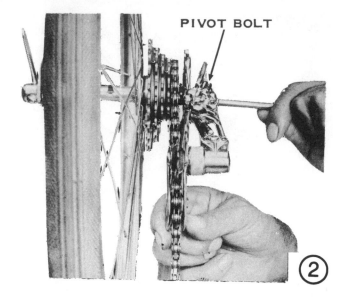

PIVOT BOLT

①

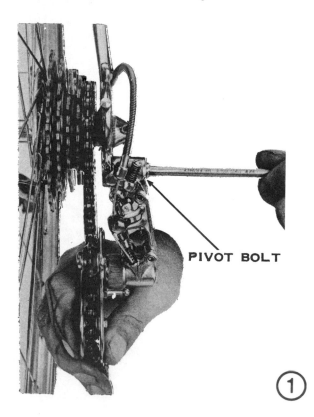

PIVOT BOLT

②

Shimano sells a special tool for precise alignment of integral derailleur hangers. This tool's precision is required when using a derailleur incorporating the Shimano Index System.

CAUTION: Always readjust derailleur limit screws after straightening the derailleur.

Cleaning and Inspecting

The following procedure applies to all rear derailleurs described in this section.

Check all structural, supporting parts for bending, distortion, or damage. After the derailleur has been disassembled, bent pulley-cage side plates can often be straightened by pounding them with a hammer on a flat surface.

Check pivot spindles and the bearing surfaces on which they turn for wear. Check the parallelogram-cage (pantograph) pivots for looseness. On most rear derailleurs, these are riveted and the entire body assembly must be replaced if they are worn.

Pulleys with sealed ball bearings are available as replacement items. Check these for rough running. It is possible to pry off one of the seals with a large pin for cleaning and relubrication. Minor roughness is normal, but if the pulley still runs very roughly, it should be replaced.

Some Huret derailleurs use loose ball bearings. Replace the bearing balls; check the pulleys and bearing cones for wear and pencil-point pits.

SERVICING SHIMANO DERAILLEURS

Shimano rear derailleurs are tracking derailleurs (see page 162) with the tracking spring in the upper pivot. The Shimano Super Plate derailleur, described in the following overhaul procedure, adds an intermediate guide cage between the body and the pulley cage. Other Shimano derailleurs differ, causing differences in assembly; these are explained in the individual steps.

NOTE: Names for the parts of the derailleur are not the same as in the Shimano parts catalog. Shimano uses unusual and confusing names. Refer to the catalog when ordering replacement parts.

Exploded diagrams of the Shimano Super Plate rear derailleur and Shimano 600 rear derailleur appear later in this section.

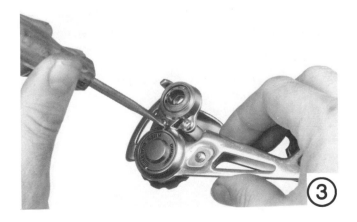

Tools and Supplies You Will Need

15mm socket wrench or crankbolt wrench (Super Plate)
10mm box or open-end wrench
8mm socket or end wrench
6mm Allen wrench
3mm Allen wrench (Super Plate, some others)
Small box or open-end wrenches, or adjustable wrench
Medium flat-blade screwdriver
Medium Phillips screwdriver
Pliers
Cycle oil
Grease
Replacement parts as necessary

Preliminary Steps

Inspect the drivetrain (page 98).
Remove the wheel from the bicycle (page 69).
Remove the derailleur (page 164).

NOTE: The upper pulley of the Super Plate derailleur can be removed without disassembling the derailleur completely. Turn the large nut at the inside of the pulley to remove it. Do not *turn the screw inside the nut.*

Disassembly

① Rotate the pulley cage slightly counterclockwise to release pressure on the stop pin. Unscrew the stop pin. Release spring force on the cage by allowing it to rotate clockwise.

Many Shimano derailleurs have no stop pin, but only a tab on the cage to limit its rotation. In this case, proceed to the next step. Some inexpensive Shimano derailleurs have the pulley cage assembled to the body with a snapring. Remove the decorative cap, then pry up the snapring.

② With a 6mm Allen wrench, unscrew the spindle, releasing the cage. Remove the spindle, the cupped

plastic washer under the spindle's head, the spring, and the large plastic washer.

Derailleurs without stop pin: Unscrew the spindle two or three turns, push the spindle's head in, and rotate the cage past the stop. Then remove parts as above. The large plastic washer will be absent from some derailleurs.

③ Remove the small screw in the middle of the cover plate. Remove the cover plate, the cable pulley, and the small bushing under the cable pulley.

All except Super Plate: Remove the thick washer before the spring. This washer looks like the cable pulley, but there is no cable or bushing. Then jump ahead to step ⑥.

④ With a 10mm wrench, remove the locknut; remove the cable.

⑤ Unscrew the pulley-cage spindle and remove the pulley cage, small washer, and cable guide. Remove the plastic bushing inside the spindle hole in the guide cage.

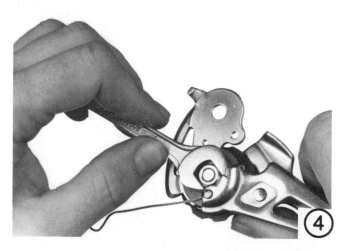

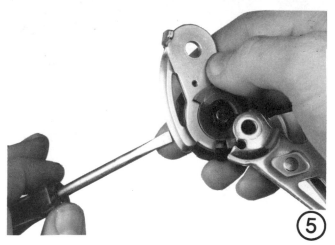

⑥ With a 3mm Allen wrench, unscrew the idler pulley bolt. Remove the idler pulley with its bushing and cover plates.

All except Super Plate: remove both pulleys. Many Shimano derailleurs use bolts with 8mm hex heads to secure the pulleys.

⑦ This step and the next are easiest with the derailleur body chucked in a vise, between wooden blocks to protect the finish.

With a screwdriver, pry the snapring loose from the back of the upper pivot.

CAUTION: Don't undertake this step and the next unless you have a good reason to take the upper pivot apart. Wear safety glasses. Don't be surprised if parts fly around the room.

⑧ Release the stop plate from the stop tab on the body by turning it slightly counterclockwise, then pull the stop plate out. Turn it clockwise to release spring tension. Remove the stop plate, spring, and plastic bushing.

On many Shimano derailleurs, the outer (right) end of the spring is bent radially outward rather than lengthwise. With these derailleurs, remove the spring through the right (outer) end of the upper pivot recess after removing the spindle and plastic bushing.

⑨ With the guide cage chucked in a vise, or alternatively levering a screwdriver against the lower pivot spindle and a 7mm Allen wrench as shown, remove the jockey pulley, bushing, and two flat washers, using a 14mm crankbolt wrench or a socket wrench.

CAUTION: Be sure that you have removed the plastic bushing from the inside of the pulley cage spindle hole. If you do not, you may damage it.

All except Super Plate: Omit this step.

⑩ Remove the nut and washer and the cable anchor bolt.

Cable attachment may vary among Shimano derailleurs. Some have a non-removable bolt, but all use a nut and washer.

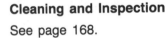

Cleaning and Inspection

See page 168.

Assembly

⑪ Replace the cable anchor bolt in its recess in the body. Replace the washer and nut.

Cable attachment may vary among Shimano derailleurs. Some have a non-removable bolt, but all use a nut and washer.

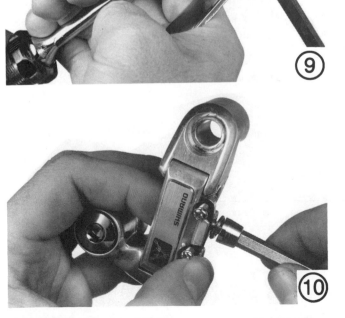

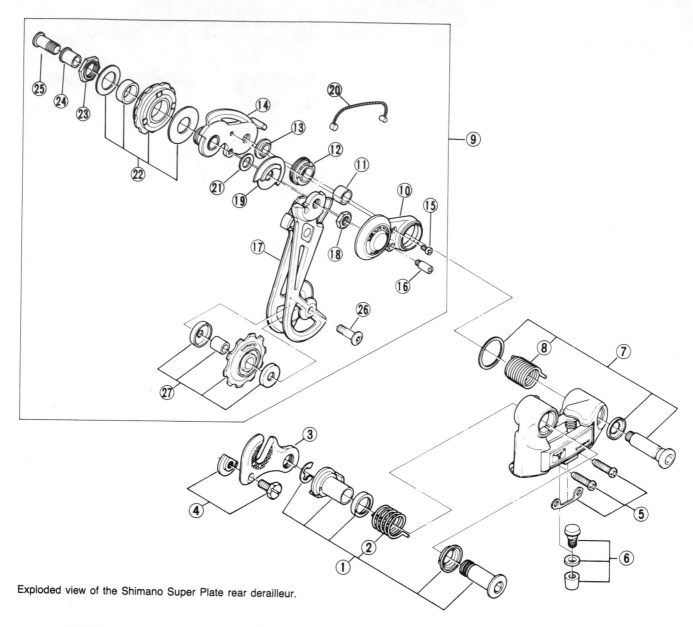

Exploded view of the Shimano Super Plate rear derailleur.

ITEM	DESCRIPTION	ITEM	DESCRIPTION
1	Bracket axle assembly	15	S.P. cap fixing screw
2	B-tension spring	16	Plate stopper screw
3	Adapter	17	Pulley plate unit
4	Adapter screw and nut	18	Locknut
5	Stroke-adjusting screw and plate	19	Wire lead
6	Cable fixing bolt unit	20	Wire
7	Plate axle assembly	21	Spacer
8	P-tension spring	22	Guide pulley unit
9	Pulley plate assembly	23	Guide pulley fixing nut
10	S.P. cap	24	Sleeve for guide pulley axle
11	Sleeve for plate mounting bush	25	Guide pulley axle
12	Plate mounting bush	26	Tension pulley fixing bolt
13	Plate mounting plate	27	Tension pulley unit
14	S.P. plate		

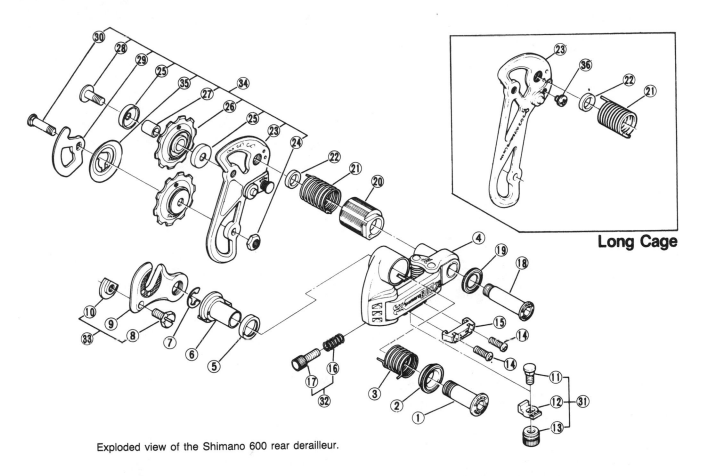

Long Cage

Exploded view of the Shimano 600 rear derailleur.

ITEM	DESCRIPTION	ITEM	DESCRIPTION
1	Adapter mounting bolt	20	Spring cover
2	Adapter mounting collar	21	P-tension spring for short cage
3	B-tension spring		P-tension spring for long cage
4	Mechanism assembly	22	Plate mounting bushing
5	Sleeve	23	Inner cage plate for short cage
6	Adapter bushing		Inner cage plate for long cage
7	Stop ring (Ø7mm)	24	Pulley nut
8	Adapter screw	25	Pulley cap
9	Adapter	26	Pulley
10	Adapter nut	27	Pulley bushing
11	Cable fixing bolt	28	Pulley bolt A
12	Cable fixing washer	29	Outer cage plate
13	Cable fixing nut	30	Pulley bolt E
14	Stroke adjusting screw	31	Cable fixing bolt unit
15	Stroke adjusting plate	32	Cable adjusting barrel and spring
16	Cable adjusting spring	33	Adapter screw and nut
17	Cable adjusting barrel	34	Pulley plate assembly
18	Plate mounting bolt	35	S.B. cap
19	Plate mounting collar	36	Hatch plate fixing screw

⑫ Grease the hole in the upper pulley. Replace the large flat washer, bushing, upper pulley, smaller flat washer, and nut on the guide cage in the order shown. As shown in step ⑨, tighten the nut to secure the pulley assembly. Then replace the plastic sleeve in the upper pulley assembly.

All except Super Plate: Omit this step.

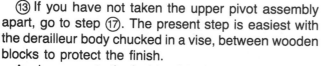

⑫

⑬ If you have not taken the upper pivot assembly apart, go to step ⑰. The present step is easiest with the derailleur body chucked in a vise, between wooden blocks to protect the finish.

Apply grease to the inside of the derailleur body, the inside of the outer bushing, and the outside of the inner bushing. Install the spring, seating the spring leg in the hole in the pivot recess. Install the outer bushing *cupped side out,* the spring, and the stop plate. Center the cylindrical sleeve of the stop plate in the outer bushing.

If the spring leg is bent outward instead of length-wise, install the spring through the outer (bolt-head) end of the upper pivot recess, and then install the plastic outer bushing over it.

⑬

⑭ Wear safety glasses for this step. Grasp the larger tab of the stop plate with pliers. Rotate it counter-clockwise until it passes the stop tab on the derailleur body. Then push it in and release it clockwise so that it comes to rest against the stop tab.

⑮ Install the pivot bolt and snapring.

⑭

⑮

⑯ Grease the smooth bearing surface of the pulley-cage spindle. Install the plastic bushing and spindle in the guide cage as shown.

All except Super Plate: Omit this step and go to step ㉒.

⑰ Lightly grease the flat side of the cable guide. Place the thin washer and then the cable guide on top of the guide cage as shown. The thin washer goes on *first.* Lay the pulley cage's outer plate over the cable guide. Thread in the pulley-cage spindle from underneath.

CAUTION: Be sure that the plastic bushing has been reinstalled in the pulley-cage spindle hole. If it is not, the assembly will not fit together properly.

⑱ Install the locknut. Adjust the pulley-cage spindle and tighten the locknut so that the guide cage rotates freely but without play. Install the large end of the cable in its recess in the pulley cage.

⑲ Grease the small bushing. Place the small bushing on the guide cage, flat side down. Place the cable pulley over it with the holes for the spring facing up. Install the cable end in its recess.

⑳ Slide the cable pulley assembly and cover plate onto the guide plate. Test that the cable is engaged on the pulley by trying to turn it clockwise with a screwdriver. Install the small screw to hold the cover plate in place.

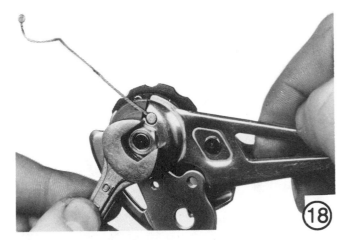

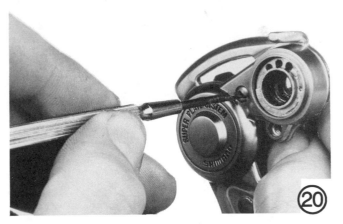

㉑ Grease the threads and smooth outer diameter of the spindle, and the cupped face of the outer bushing. Install the outer bushing cupped side out, and the spindle and the spring small end out. Make sure the end of the spring indexes in its hole in the body assembly. Install the large plastic washer over the cover plate.

All except Super Plate: Also install the thick metal washer on the inner end of the spring. If one end of the spring is bent outward, install the spring from the outer

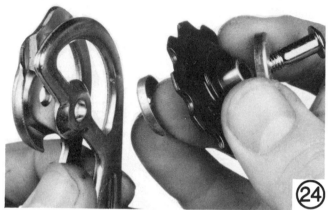

end of the recess, before the plastic bushing. There may be no large plastic washer.

㉒ Install the spring leg in one of the holes in the pulley. Counterclockwise holes make the derailleur track closer to the freewheel sprockets, best with a smaller cluster. Thread the spindle partway onto the guide plate, then rotate the guide plate one full turn counterclockwise past the stop tab until the tension cage is below the body. Tighten the bolt the rest of the way.

All except Super Plate: The spindle threads directly to the pulley cage. There may be only one hole for the spring.

㉓ Hold the cage below the body and thread in the stop screw. Release the cage.

Some Shimano derailleurs have no stop screw, but only a stop tab. If so, omit this step.

㉔ Grease the hole in the lower pulley. Install the bushing, lower pulley, pulley covers, and bolt. Tighten the bolt with a 3mm Allen wrench.

All except Super Plate: Both pulleys install this way. Many use a bolt with a 10mm hex head.

Finishing Up

Replace the derailleur on the bicycle (page 165).
Replace the wheel (page 72).
Adjust the drivetrain (page 102).

SERVICING SUNTOUR DERAILLEURS

Most SunTour derailleurs with "Tech" in their name are tracking derailleurs with an intermediate sprung cage. The others are fixed-jockey-pulley or raised-jockey-pulley derailleurs.

Many parts are interchangeable among SunTour rear derailleur models *of similar construction*. The most important differences are in the tension spring and associated parts.

Instructions here are for the Le Tech, the most complicated SunTour derailleur. Differences are explained in the individual steps. Exploded drawings of the Le Tech and Road VX GT derailleurs appear later in this section.

Preliminary Steps

Inspect the drivetrain (page 98).
Remove the wheel from the bicycle (page 69).
Remove the derailleur (page 164).

Tools and Supplies You Will Need

4mm Allen key (some models)

6mm Allen key

SunTour upper pulley tool (a few models)

Needlenose pliers (some models)

Medium Phillips screwdriver

Small flat-blade screwdriver

Small box or open-end wrenches, or adjustable wrench

Cycle oil

Grease

Replacement parts as necessary

Look at the derailleur to see what tools you need. Only a few models require the special SunTour tool to disassemble the upper pulley. Most require only a box-end, open-end, or adjustable wrench.

Disassembly

① Rotate the pulley cage slightly counterclockwise. With a medium Phillips screwdriver, remove the stop screw. Rotate the cage clockwise to release spring force.

Mountech type (includes Superbe Tech GTL, AG Tech): The screw is on the back of the pulley cage. All others: There is a stop pin instead of a stop screw.

② With a 4mm Allen wrench, remove the spring cover bolt. Make a note of which slot the spring is assembled to at both ends; there may be as many as six possible positions at the spring's smaller diameter. Then remove the spring cover and spring. The spring may have two layers or a single layer.

CAUTION: The position of the spring at each end affects the performance of the derailleur. Do not fail to note this before removing the spring.

All except Le Tech: This step sometimes uses a Phillips screwdriver and sometimes a 6mm Allen

wrench. If you see a narrow slot inside an Allen fitting, omit this step and go to step ④.

③ Rotate the guide-cage stop away from the guide-cage stop pin. Unscrew the stop pin and rotate the guide cage clockwise, releasing spring force.

Derailleurs without intermediate cage: The part you are removing is the pulley cage, since there is no guide cage.

④ Remove the cage tension nut using a 6mm Allen wrench. Pry out the shim (thin metal washer) and plastic bushing. Gently rock the body assembly up off the cage. Be sure to catch the very small rectangular metal bushing which will push up out of the slotted end of the stud inside the opening. Only if necessary for replacement, pry the flat, coiled tension spring out of the body assembly by grasping it with the slotted stud of the cage and twisting it clockwise while gently pulling them apart.

Mountech, Superbe Tech GTL, AG Tech: Using a 10mm wrench to loosen the nut at the back, do this step for the spring inside the upper pulley; keep track of the several bushings around the pulley by threading them onto a wire in order. Then do steps ③ *and* ④ *again for the guide-cage pivot.*

⑤ With the SunTour upper pulley tool, remove the upper pulley nut. Remove the shield plates, upper pulley, bushing, and guide cage. A substitute tool can be made by filing notches in one end of a short piece of 11mm- or 7/16-inch-outside-diameter metal tubing, and drilling a hole through the other end to turn it with a screwdriver blade or Allen wrench.

Fixed-upper-pulley derailleurs: Many do not require the special tool. Some use a hex nut, and some have wrench flats on the pivot stud. On some, the cage plates unscrew from one another after removing a small bolt. Raised-upper-pulley derailleurs and Mountech type: Skip this step.

⑥ With a 9mm end wrench or socket wrench, remove the lower pulley bolt. Remove the lockwasher, outer cage plate, pulley, bushing, and pulley covers.

The bolt may remove with another type of wrench. Many SunTour derailleurs have inner and outer cage plates riveted together, and there may be no lockwasher or nut. On a raised-jockey-pulley derailleur, remove both pulleys as in this step.

⑦ Don't do this step unless there's a reason; getting these parts back together is a bit tricky. With a 4mm

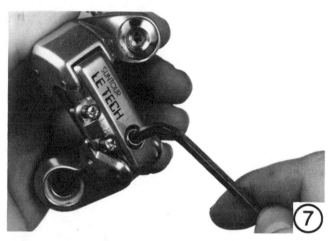

socket wrench, unscrew the cable anchor nut and remove the bolt.

⑧ If there's a reason, remove the upper pivot bolt and nut with a 6mm Allen wrench and the ends of needlenose pliers.

Many SunTour derailleurs do not have a nut; once the derailleur is removed from the hanger, the pivot bolt falls out. Others use a locknut behind the hanger. Keep track of any washers that are part of this assembly.

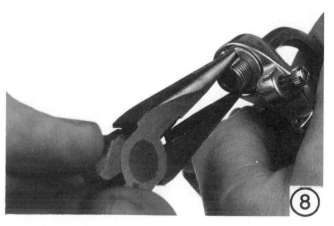

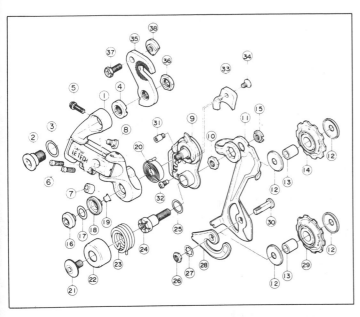

Exploded view of the SunTour Le Tech rear derailleur.

ITEM	DESCRIPTION
1	Body assembly
2	Mounting bolt
3	Adjusting shim
4	Mounting nut
5	Angle-adjusting screw
6	Stroke-adjusting screw
7	Cable anchor nut
8	Cable anchor bolt
9	Guide pulley cage
10	Guide pulley axle hex nut
11	Inner cage plate
12	Pulley dust shield
13	Pulley bushing
14	Guide pulley
15	Guide pulley axle slotted nut
16	Tension nut
17	Adjusting shim
18	Bushing
19	Spring retainer
20	Tension spring
21	Spring cover bolt
22	Tension cage spring cover
23	Tension cage spring
24	Tension cage axle
25	Adjusting shim
26	Tension cage nut

ITEM	DESCRIPTION
27	Star washer
28	Tension pulley cage
29	Tension pulley
30	Tension pulley bolt
31	Upper cage stop pin
32	Lower cage stop pin
33	Plastic guard plate
34	Guard plate screw
35	Mounting bracket
36	Mounting locknut
37	Mounting bracket fixing bolt
38	Mounting bracket fixing nut

Cleaning and Inspecting

See page 168.

⑨ Replace the upper pivot bolt. With needlenose pliers, reinstall the nut.

Many SunTour derailleurs do not have a nut. The upper pivot bolt will be loose until the derailleur is assembled to the hanger. Keep the parts together with a wire or tape. Reinstall any washers that are part of this assembly.

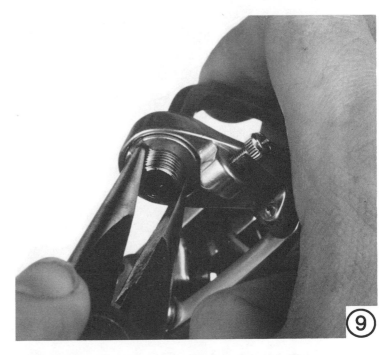

⑩ Wedge the body assembly open by placing an object between the high-gear limit screw and the forward end of the body. A large (8mm) threaded chain-

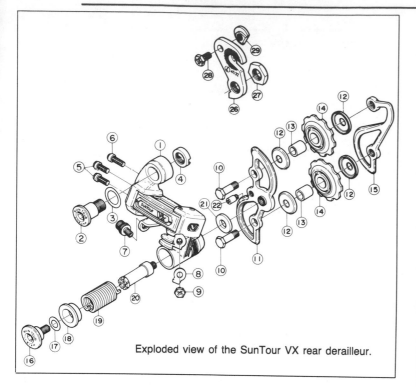

Exploded view of the SunTour VX rear derailleur.

ITEM	DESCRIPTION
1	Body assembly
2	Mounting bolt
3	Shim
4	Mounting nut
5	Stroke-adjusting screw
6	Angle-adjusting screw
7	Cable tension adjuster
8	Cable anchor clamp
9	Cable anchor bolt
10	Pulley axle bolt
11	Outer cage
12	Pulley cover
13	Pulley bushing
14	Pulley
15	Inner cage
16	Cage tension bolt
17	Shim
18	Bushing
19	Spring
20	Cage tension axle
21	Washer
22	Cage stop pin
26	Bracket
27	Mounting locknut
28	Bracket retainer bolt
29	Bracket retainer nut

wheel bolt fits well. With tweezers or a small screwdriver, maneuver the cable anchor bolt into its recess in the body, with the tapered end of the hole facing the direction from which the cable enters the body. With a 4mm Allen wrench, thread on the anchor bolt nut.

Many SunTour derailleurs have the cable attachment in different places. Most are easier to assemble.

⑪ Grease the hole in the lower pulley. Replace the lower pulley assembly—pulley covers, pulley axle bolt, bushing, pulley, outer cage plate, lockwasher, and nut, using tools as in step ⑥.

Many derailleurs lack a lockwasher, and sometimes the pulley axle bolt is threaded into the cage plate. Raised-jockey-pulley derailleurs: Install the upper pulley the same way as the lower one.

⑫ Grease bearing surfaces, then assemble the guide cage, pulley cage, jockey pulley, bushing, pulley covers, and nut, using the SunTour jockey pulley tool as in step ⑦.

Fixed-upper-pulley derailleurs: Many do not require the special tool. Some use a hex nut, and some have wrench flats on the pivot stud. Raised-jockey-pulley derailleurs: Skip this step.

⑬ If you have removed the flat, coiled tension spring from the body, replace it by grasping it with the slotted stud of the cage, twisting it clockwise while pushing gently. Index the spring in the slot with the cage *hanging below the body as shown.* **CAUTION: If the cage is half a turn out of position, the derailleur will function poorly.**

Grease the bearing surfaces of the pivot. Press the body assembly into place with its spring notch indexed over the plastic cap on the cage. Then install the small rectangular bushing *flared side down,* the plastic bushing, the thin metal washer, and the nut.

If the spring is made of round wire, not a coiled, flat strip of metal, omit this step and go to step ⑮. Moun-

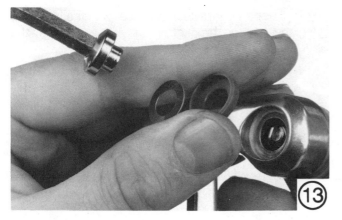

tech, Superbe Tech GTL, AG Tech: Using a 10mm end wrench, do this step and step ⑭ once for the guide-cage pivot, then once more for the spring inside the upper pulley. Grease the hole in the pulley. Install the several bushings around the pulley in order.

⑭ Rotate the guide cage one full turn counterclockwise. Hold the cage out of the way while you screw in the stop pin. This is easiest if you glue the pin to the screwdriver with a dab of grease, or chuck the body assembly in a vise. Use soft jaws to avoid scratching the finish.

Derailleurs without intermediate cage: The part you are installing is the pulley cage, since there is no guide cage. Mountech type: The second stop pin you install is on the back of the jockey pulley assembly.

⑮ Replace the coiled wire spring in its original position, unless you want to change sprocket-to-pulley spacing. Loosening the spring at either its inner or outer attachment will bring the jockey pulley closer to the sprockets. Replace the spring cover; then, using a 4mm Allen wrench, replace the bolt.

All except Le Tech: Spring adjustment controls chain tension, not pulley position. More tension gives crisper shifting at some expense in wear and pedaling efficiency. The spring may have two layers or a single layer. This step sometimes requires a Phillips screwdriver and sometimes a 6mm Allen wrench. If you have already replaced all springs, skip this and the next step.

⑯ Rotate the pulley cage one full turn counterclockwise. With a medium Phillips screwdriver, install the stop screw. Release the cage against the stop screw.

All except Le Tech: There is a stop pin instead of a stop screw.

Finishing Up

Replace the derailleur on the bicycle (page 165).
Replace the wheel (page 72).
Adjust the derailleur (page 102).

SERVICING CAMPAGNOLO OR SIMPLEX REAR DERAILLEURS

The following step-by-step illustrated instructions cover disassembling, cleaning and inspecting, and assembling a Campagnolo or Simplex rear derailleur.

The illustrations were made of a Campagnolo Nuovo Record rear derailleur, which is almost identical to the others. The instructions begin with the derailleur removed from the bicycle.

Complete procedures for removing, installing, and adjusting the derailleur are explained earlier in this chapter.

Each derailleur assembly can be identified by the manufacturer's name embossed on the exposed surface of the outer arm. A detailed exploded drawing of this derailleur, showing all internal parts, appears later in this section.

Tools and Supplies You Will Need

Small, flat-blade screwdriver
5mm or 6mm Allen wrench
Needlenose pliers
Small open-end or box-end wrenches or adjustable wrench
14mm cone wrench (Simplex)
Replacement parts as necessary

Preliminary Steps

Inspect the drivetrain (page 98).
Remove the wheel from the bicycle (page 69).
Remove the derailleur (page 164).

Disassembling

① Take out the low-gear adjusting screw by turning it counterclockwise, and then remove the spring. Back out the high-gear adjusting screw completely, and then remove the spring.

② Clamp the derailleur in a vise, with the jaws gripping the forkend bracket. Remove the cable anchor bolt and the cable guide washer.

③ Rotate the derailleur cage assembly slightly to relieve pressure on the stop stud, and then remove the stud. Allow the cage to rotate until the tension on the pulley-cage spring is released.

④ Remove the pulley-cage spindle using a correct-size Allen wrench.

Simplex: Hold the nut next to the pulley cage with a 14mm cone wrench and unscrew the pulley cage clockwise.

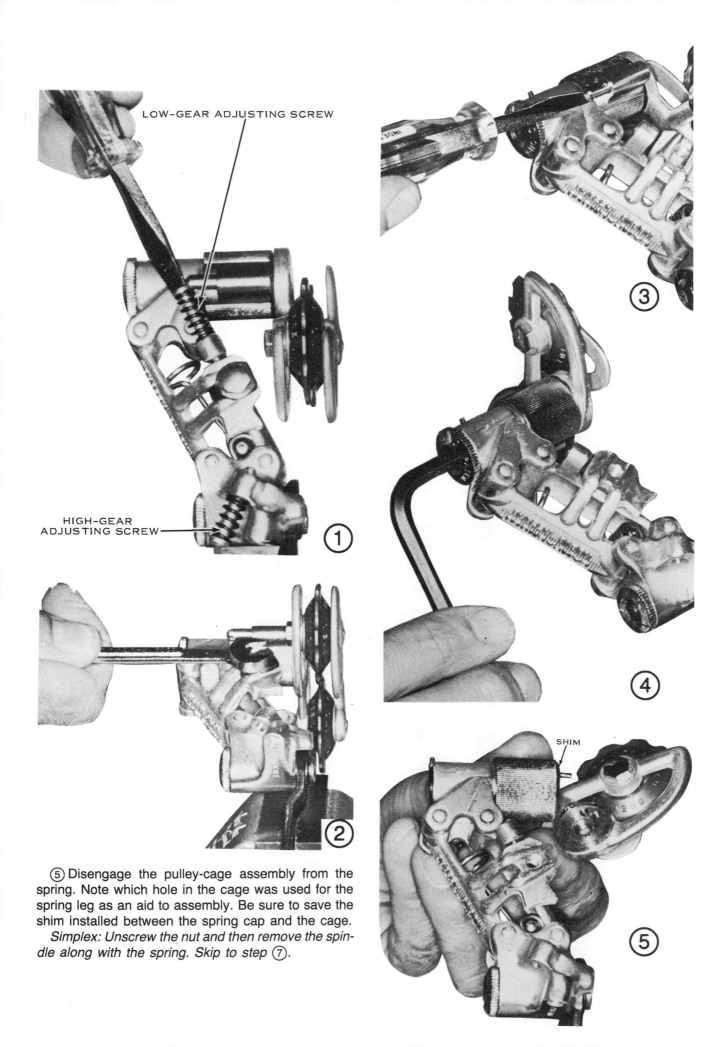

LOW-GEAR ADJUSTING SCREW

HIGH-GEAR
ADJUSTING SCREW

① ② ③ ④ ⑤

SHIM

⑤ Disengage the pulley-cage assembly from the spring. Note which hole in the cage was used for the spring leg as an aid to assembly. Be sure to save the shim installed between the spring cap and the cage.

Simplex: Unscrew the nut and then remove the spindle along with the spring. Skip to step ⑦.

⑥ Withdraw the spring cap from the end of the traversing-arm assembly, and then slide the spring out of the other end.

⑦ Grasp the traversing spring firmly with a pair of needlenose pliers; pull it out of the arm and relieve the tension.

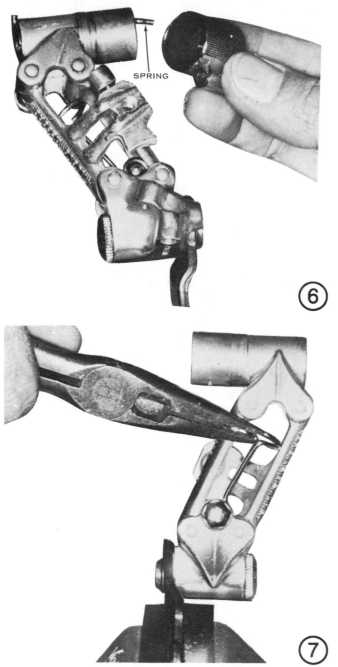

SPRING

⑥

⑦

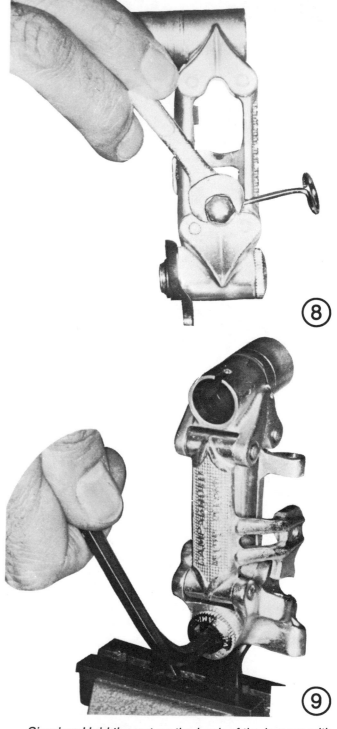

⑧

⑨

⑧ Remove the spring pivot bolt and the traversing spring.

⑨ Remove the pivot bolt, using an Allen wrench, and then separate the forkend bracket from the traversing-arm assembly.

Simplex: Hold the nut on the back of the hanger with a 14mm wrench, and the pivot bolt with a 5mm Allen wrench. Unscrew the nut. Then unscrew the pivot bolt and remove it with the spring inside the upper pivot.

Some Campagnolo models, such as the 1985 Record and Rally, have a sprung upper pivot. Disassembly is similar to that for Shimano derailleurs.

⑩ Disassemble the cages by removing the spindles.

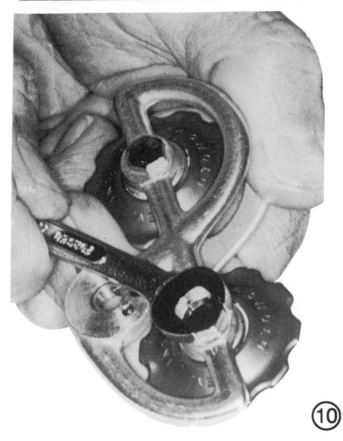

⑪ Pry out the dustcaps with a screwdriver, and then push the bushing out of the center of each pulley.

Cleaning and Inspecting

See page 168.

Assembling

CAUTION: The derailleur assembly has many threaded aluminum parts. Use care when installing bolts and spindles to prevent stripping the threads by overtightening.

⑫ Coat both bushings with a small amount of multi-purpose grease, and then insert them into the center of the pulleys.

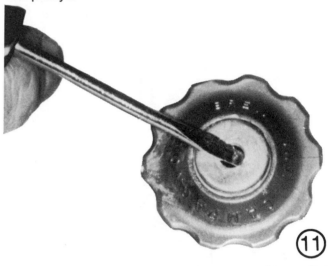

Exploded view of the Campagnolo Record rear derailleur.

HIGH GEAR
LIMIT SCREW

DERAILLEUR
HANGER

BOLT

LOCKNUT

CABLE
ANCHOR
BOLT

SPRING

INNER
CAGE
SIDE

OUTER
CAGE
SIDE

PULLEY

CAP

CAP

STOP
STUD

SPINDLE

PIVOT
BOLT

SPRING
PIVOT
BOLT

BUSHING

CAP

TRAVERSING
ARM
ASSEMBLY

PULLEY
CAGE
SPRING

SPRING
CAP

CAP

SPINDLE

PULLEY

SPRING

SPINDLE

TRAVERSING
SPRING

PULLEY
CAGE
SPINDLE

LOW GEAR
LIMIT SCREW

⑬ Place the dustcaps in position on both sides of each pulley.

⑭ Arrange the cage parts in the pattern shown for ease in assembly.

⑮ Combine the cage assembly parts and secure them with the spindles. *NOTE: If the tension pulley was removed to avoid unlinking the chain when you took the derailleur unit off the bicycle, do not install it at this time; it will be installed later.*

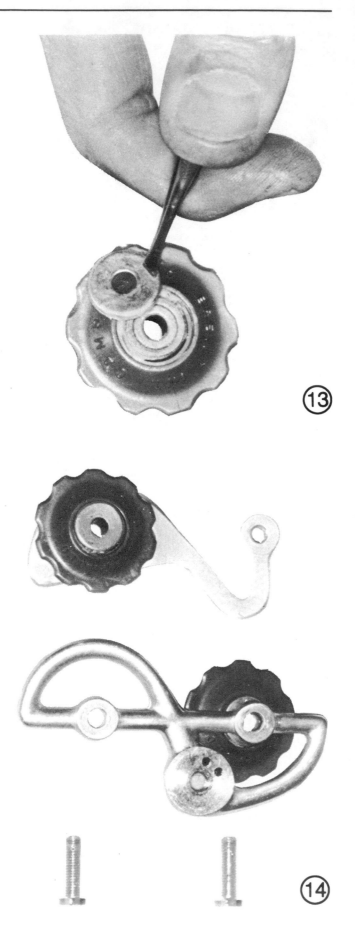

⑬

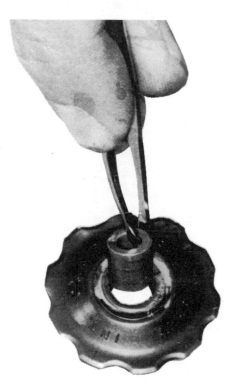

⑫

⑭

⑯ Clamp the forkend bracket in a vise, with the jaws gripping the hooked end. Attach the traversing-arm assembly to the bracket, with the pivot bolt and the hook of the bracket facing away from the side with the adjusting screws, as shown. The bolt has a shoulder that will "bottom out" when fully tightened.

Simplex: Grease the bearing surfaces of the upper pivot bolt. Install the spring on the bolt and insert them together into the body assembly. If the derailleur is mounted on a removable hanger, install the hanger and the locknut behind it. Otherwise, just thread on the locknut to keep the parts from falling out.

Some Campagnolo derailleurs have a sprung upper pivot. Reassembly is similar to that for Shimano derailleurs.

⑰ Apply a thin coating of multipurpose grease to the traversing spring, and then lay it in position behind the flange of the traversing-arm assembly, with the loop of the spring facing toward the arm assembly body. Slide

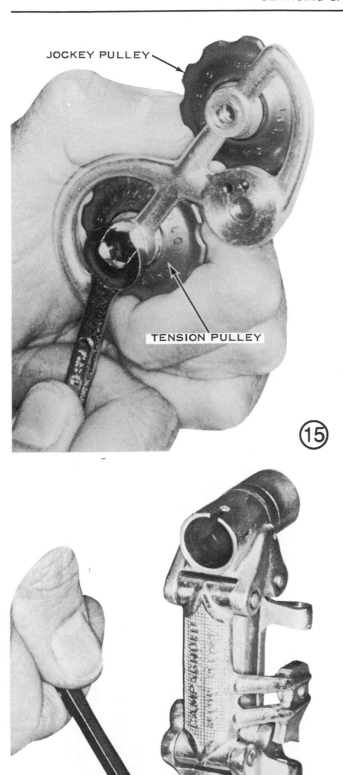

JOCKEY PULLEY

TENSION PULLEY

⑮

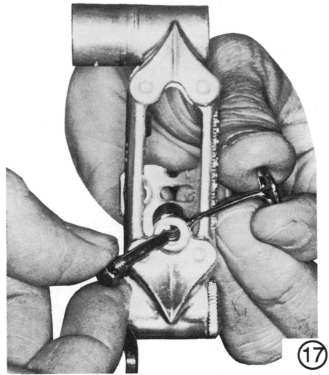

⑰

⑯

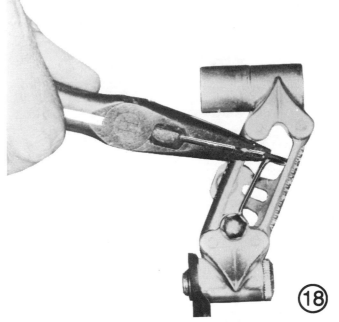

⑱

the spring pivot bolt through the flange and spring. Tighten it securely.

⑱ Grasp the loop end of the spring firmly with a pair of needlenose pliers, and then force it into the traversing-arm assembly body.

⑲ Coat the pulley-cage spring with a thin layer of multipurpose grease, and then insert it through the traversing-arm body so the small hook-end of the spring indexes in the slot, as shown.

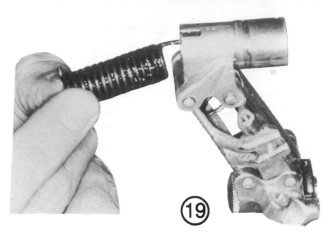

(19)

Simplex: Grease the spring and the bearing surfaces of the spindle. Insert the spindle with the spring into the body.

20 Slide the spring cap over the assembly body, with the spring leg through the same hole as you noted during disassembly. If you are unable to recall which hole was used, insert the spring leg through the hole that will give the least spring tension. If more tension is desired later on, the cage assembly can be removed and the other hole used.

Simplex: Install the nut on the pulley-cage spindle and tighten it finger-tight against the body assembly.

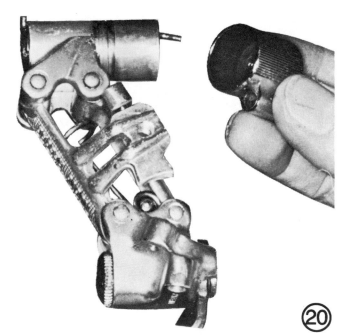

20

21 Place the thin shim in position, with the spring leg through the matching hole used for the cap. Mate the cage assembly to the traversing-arm assembly using the same matching hole for the spring leg as you used for the cap and shim.

Simplex: Thread the pulley cage onto the spindle.

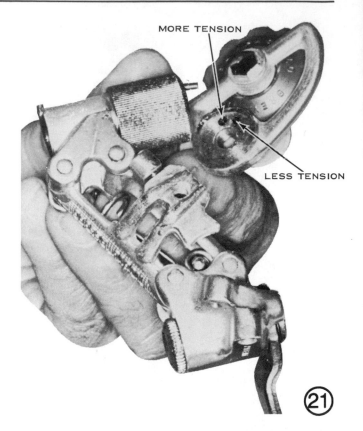

MORE TENSION

LESS TENSION

21

Using a 14mm cone wrench and 5mm Allen wrench, tighten the nut against the cage while adjusting the pivot for minimal play without binding. Skip to step 23.

22 Insert the pulley spindle through the traversing-arm body, and then thread it into the cage assembly. Tighten the spindle securely, using an Allen wrench. The shoulder on the spindle will "bottom out" to prevent you from tightening it too much or stripping the threads.

23 Rotate the pulley-cage assembly one full turn in the direction shown to put tension on the spring.

24 Hold the pulley cage with tension on the spring and the hole for the stop stud clear of the traversing-

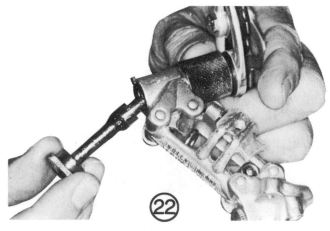

22

arm body. Thread the stop stud into place securely, and then let the cage spring back until the stop stud bears against the body.

㉕ Place the cable anchor guide in position, with the ear of the guide indexed between the two frame members of the traversing-arm assembly, as shown. Thread the cable anchor bolt finger-tight into the flange of the traversing body.

㉖ Slide one of the springs onto one of the adjusting screws, and then thread the screw approximately five turns into the high-gear adjusting hole for a preliminary setting. Slide the other spring onto the remaining adjusting screw, and then thread the screw about five turns into the low-gear adjusting hole for a preliminary setting.

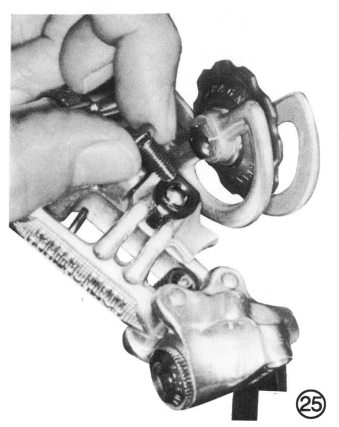

㉕

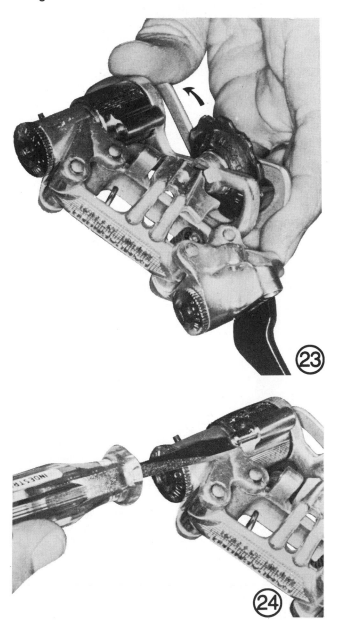

㉓

㉔

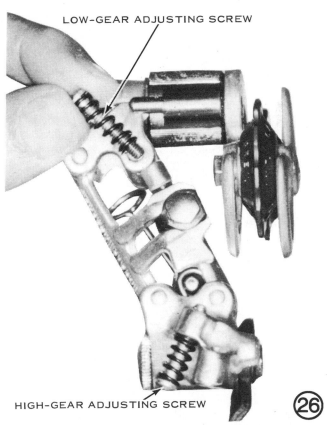

LOW-GEAR ADJUSTING SCREW

HIGH-GEAR ADJUSTING SCREW

㉖

Finishing Up

Replace the derailleur on the bicycle (page 165).
Replace the wheel (page 72).
Adjust the derailleur (page 102).

SERVICING SACHS-HURET DERAILLEURS

Sachs-Huret makes several models of rear derailleurs. Most are of simple construction with a fixed jockey pulley and fixed upper pivot. The very old Allvit series, seen in the illustrations for cable adjustment in this chapter, has a pantograph with threaded, adjustable pivots. The Duopar, a tracking derailleur with an intermediate cage, appears complicated, but no parts of this cage can be disassembled, so servicing is no more difficult than for the others. The Rival, described here, is a recent model, more complicated in that it is a tracking derailleur with a sprung upper pivot.

To help with servicing of older Huret derailleurs, an exploded drawing of the Huret Allvit derailleur appears later in this section.

Preliminary Steps

Inspect the drivetrain (page 98).
Remove the wheel from the bicycle (page 69).
Remove the derailleur (page 164).

Tools You Will Need

Small flat-blade screwdriver
Small open-end or box-end wrenches
6mm Allen wrench
Tweezers (ball-bearing-pulley models)
Cone wrenches (ball-bearing-pulley models)

Disassembling

① With a small screwdriver, pry up the plastic cover. Pry off the snapring.
Many Huret derailleurs lack this part.

② Rotate the pulley cage slightly counterclockwise to disengage it from the stop tab, then slide the pulley-cage spindle out of the body assembly. Remove the spring and plastic collar.

Many other Huret derailleurs have the pulley-cage spindle threaded to the body assembly and secured by a locknut. Unscrew the locknut and then remove the spindle using a screwdriver. Recover all parts: The spring between the body and the cage is sandwiched between two thin washers and coiled around a cylindrical bushing.

Allvit series with bolt-and-locknut adjustable parallelogram pivots: Dismantle these, removing the locknuts and threaded pivot bolts. Keep track of the order of the parts.

③ Remove the pulley bolts, pulleys, pulley covers, and bushings.

Many Huret derailleurs use adjustable ball-bearing pulleys. The pulley bearing cones are threaded to each other, and the upper one is threaded to the outer pulley cage. Identify these pulleys by the wrench flats on the pulley cones. Unscrew the pulley cones and remove the bearing balls.

④ Do this step only if there is a good reason. Pry off the upper-pivot snapring. Push out the pivot bolt with the outer pushing. Keep your fingers away from the

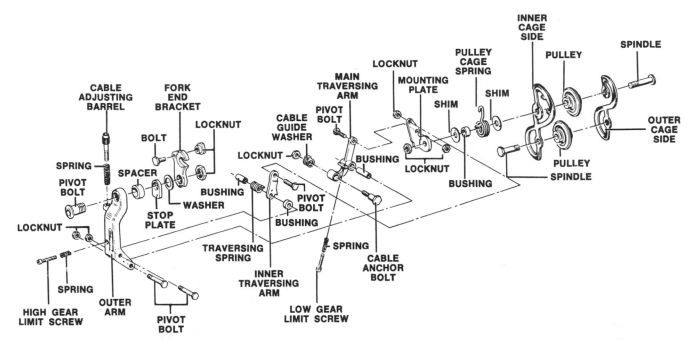

Exploded view of the Huret Allvit (Schwinn-Approved) rear derailleur.

outer end of the spring, which will snap out of its slot in the body assembly. Remove the spring and inner bushing.

Many Huret derailleurs do not have a spring in the upper pivot. The assembly is held to the derailleur hanger by a locknut. Unscrew the locknut and remove the upper pivot parts. Keep them in order.

Cleaning and Inspecting

See page 168.

Reassembling

⑤ Grease the bearing surfaces of the upper pivot. Reinsert the upper pivot spring and inner bushing into

the body assembly, with the spring indexed into the hole in the bushing. Insert the upper pivot bolt and outer bushing. With pliers, rotate the leg at the outer end of the spring counterclockwise into its slot in the body.

Huret derailleurs without spring in upper pivot: Reassemble the upper pivot parts in the order you dismantled them. If there is a D-shaped plate, its raised tab faces the derailleur hanger.

⑥ Press the assembly together with pliers to seat the spring, and reinstall the snapring.

Huret derailleurs without spring in upper pivot: If the derailleur will be mounted on a bolt-on derailleur hanger, install this now and screw on the locknut, removing excess play but allowing free rotation. If an integral derailleur hanger will be used, screw the locknut on to keep the upper pivot from coming apart.

⑦ Grease the pulley bushings and the holes in the pulleys. Reassemble the bushings, pulleys, and cover plates to the pulley cage. Tighten the pulley-cage bolts.

Huret derailleurs with ball-bearing pulleys: Place a thin coat of grease in the bearing race of each pulley. Place loose ball bearings in the bearing race of each pulley until they fit with a small amount of clearance between each bearing, but not enough so you could insert another one. Apply a thin coating of multipurpose grease over the bearings.

For pulleys with loose bearing balls, grease the cup inside the pulley and insert the bearing balls.

Thread a cone bushing finger-tight into each pulley. Hold each side of the cone bushing with your thumb and forefinger and spin the pulley to be sure it rotates freely. It must not have any sideplay when you attempt to wiggle the pulley on the cone bushing. If the pulley drags or has sideplay, loosen or tighten the cone bushing as required.

Arrange the inner and outer cage sides and the two pulleys in the pattern shown, with the extended threaded area of the jockey pulley facing up, and the spring hooks on the inner cage side facing away from the pulleys. Turn the jockey pulley tightly into the inner

Then install the bearing cones.

cage. Check the pulley for freedom of rotation, with just a discernible amount of sideplay. Back the pulley out of the cage and adjust the cone bushing, if necessary. Insert the short spindle through the inner cage, through the tension pulley, and into the threaded hole in the closed loop of the outer cage. NOTE: If the tension pulley was removed to keep from breaking (separating) the chain for removal of the derailleur from the bicycle, do not install it at this time. It will be installed later. Tighten the spindle securely, and set the assembly to one side.

Reassemble the four body cage pivots, if they have threaded pivots. Adjust the locknuts for minimum play without binding.

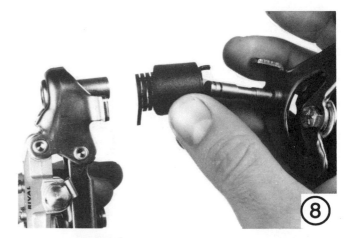

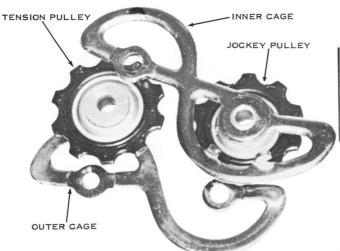

Assemble the chain cage as shown, securing the cones.

(8) Install the plastic collar over the pulley-cage spring, with the flat end of the sleeve facing the lengthwise spring leg. Grease the pulley-cage spindle. Insert the spring leg into the pulley cage. Insert the pulley-cage spindle into the body assembly. Rotate the pulley cage one turn counterclockwise to tension the spring.

Huret derailleurs with pulley cage threaded into body assembly: Insert the pulley-cage spindle through the hole in the upper pulley. Place one thin washer, then the bushing, spring—hooked end down—and other thin washer over the spindle. Thread the spindle into

the body assembly, indexing the spring leg in the hole in the body assembly.

(9) Replace the snapring over the *second* slot in the spindle and replace the snapring. Snap the plastic cover over the end of the spindle.

Huret derailleurs with threaded pulley-cage spindle: Install the locknut on the end of the spindle, and tighten it, adjusting the spindle for minimum play without binding.

Finishing Up

Replace the derailleur on the bicycle (page 98).
Replace the wheel (page 69).
Adjust the derailleur (page 164).

12 • SERVICING FRONT DERAILLEURS

The purpose of the front derailleur is to shift the drive chain from one chainwheel to another in order to change the gearing ratio. There are two such chainwheels mounted at the hanger set on a ten-, twelve-, or fourteen-speed bike, and three on a fifteen- or eighteen-speed bike.

SERVICE PROCEDURES

The *parallelogram-type front derailleur* contains two pivot arms, which form and maintain a parallelogram. The sides of the chain guide can, therefore, be kept in alignment with the edges of the chainwheels as the guide shifts the chain from one chainwheel to the other. On most front derailleurs, pulling on the control lever moves the derailleur away from the bicycle frame and shifts the chain from the smaller chainwheel to the larger. Spring tension returns the chain guide toward the bike frame, and this shifts the chain onto the smaller wheel when the control lever is pushed back. The pivot arms on many parallelogram-type front derailleurs are riveted together and, therefore, cannot be disassembled for overhauling.

Modern front derailleurs use the parallelogram principle, similar to the rear derailleur. Some older derailleurs use a spring-loaded push-rod mechanism. If you have a push-rod derailleur that isn't working well, replace it with a modern parallelogram type.

Capacity

The most important difference between front-derailleur models is in their *capacity*—the difference between chainwheel sizes which they will handle. Bicycle racers tend to use chainwheels with a 10-tooth or smaller difference. A racing derailleur is made to work best with this small difference between chainwheel sizes. Bicycle campers, who carry heavy baggage, tend to use wide-range chainwheel sets like 26 and 52 teeth. A touring derailleur has a *long cage* to handle the large difference in chain takeup between the two chainwheels of very different sizes.

A touring derailleur will work with racing chainwheels, though a racing derailleur will work better. A racing derailleur will not work with wide-range touring chainwheels; the chain will drag on the bottom of the cage when you shift to the small chainwheel.

Different models of touring derailleurs work better with *half-step* and *crossover* gearing systems: See Chapter 9 for an explanation of these terms.

Low-normal and High-normal

Most front derailleurs shift to the outer (large, high-gear) chainwheel when the cable is tensioned. These

CHAIN RUBS BOTTOM OF CHAIN CAGE

If a racing front derailleur is used with a wide-range touring chainwheel set, the chain will drag on the bottom of the chain cage.

The crossover touring derailleur *(left)* has a wide inner cage plate for use when steps between all chainwheels are large. The half-step touring derailleur *(center)* is for triple chainwheel sets in which the middle chainwheel is almost as big as the outer one. The short-cage racing derailleur *(right)* works only with small differences between chainwheel sizes.

are called *low-normal* derailleurs. Some SunTour *high-normal* models shift to the inner (smaller, low-gear) chainwheel when the cable is tensioned. Either type works well; high-normal derailleurs are better for quick downshifts, but may be slow on upshifts. To avoid confusion when shifting, it is best to use the same type on all of your bicycles.

Front Derailleur Problems

All parts of the drivetrain must be in good condition and correctly adjusted for it to work well. A problem in one part may seem to be in another. For example, poor front-derailleur shifting may result from a bent chainwheel. Before beginning overhaul of a front derailleur, read the list of drivetrain problems and their possible causes in Chapter 7.

What Service Do Front Derailleurs Need?

A front derailleur's mechanism can freeze up from rust or dirt, and the chain cage can wear or bend. The main reasons to overhaul a front derailleur are to clean, relubricate, and readjust it and to straighten minor bends. If it is badly bent, it must be replaced.

OVERHAULING A PARALLELOGRAM-TYPE FRONT DERAILLEUR

The following step-by-step illustrated instructions cover disassembling, assembling, and adjusting a typical front derailleur. The illustrations were made of a Schwinn-Approved unit made by Huret—a typical example of the "house branding" of components made by outside suppliers. An exploded drawing of this type of derailleur appears later in this chapter. An exploded view of a Campagnolo Record front derailleur is also included.

Each derailleur unit can be identified by the manufacturer's name embossed on the exposed surface of the chain guide and on the face of the mounting clamp.

Tools and Supplies You Will Need

Screwdrivers
Adjustable wrench
Small box-end and open-end wrenches
Allen wrenches (some models)
Pliers
Cable cutters
Cycle oil
Multipurpose grease
Replacement parts as necessary

Disassembling

Read the introductory material on drivetrains (page 98) unless you are already familiar with it.

① Loosen the acorn nut on the cable anchor bolt, and then free the control cable from the derailleur. Remove the clamp bolt, acorn nut, washer, and clamp. Remove the locknut, lockwasher, bushing, and bolt from the rear of the derailleur guide, and then remove the derailleur from the bicycle.

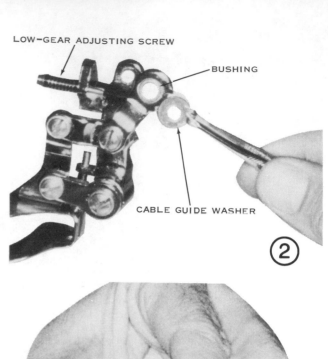

LOW-GEAR ADJUSTING SCREW

BUSHING

CABLE GUIDE WASHER

②

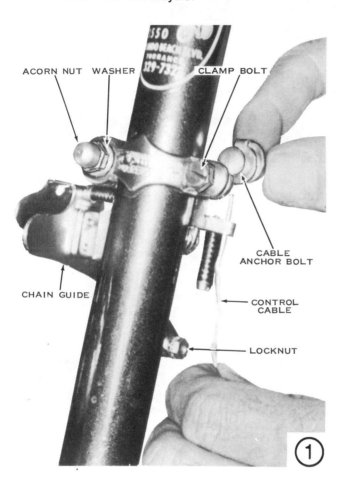

ACORN NUT WASHER CLAMP BOLT

CABLE ANCHOR BOLT

CHAIN GUIDE

CONTROL CABLE

LOCKNUT

①

② Turn the low-gear adjusting screw into the main body as far as possible. Remove the acorn nut, and then the cable anchor bolt. Pull the cable-guide washer free, and then remove the bushing. *NOTE: Some models of derailleurs use two washers instead of the single guide washer shown.*

③ Remove the two bolts from the chain-guide bracket, and then remove the chain guide. Be careful not to lose the small bushing on the bolt that passes through the bracket and the end of the pivot arm. *NOTE: The pivot arm cannot be removed because the end of the bolt securing it is flared during manufacture.*

④ Hold the main pivot bolt with a screwdriver, and then remove the locknut.

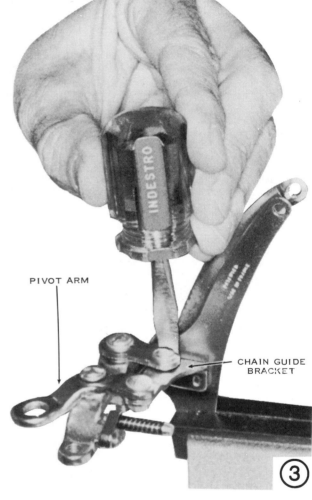

PIVOT ARM

CHAIN GUIDE BRACKET

③

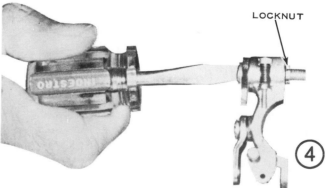

LOCKNUT

④

⑤ Back out the main pivot bolt. Remove the link and the traversing spring. Take out the low-gear and high-gear limit screws and their springs.

Cleaning and Inspecting

Inspect all parts for stripped threads.

Check the springs for a crack or loss of tension.

Inspect the inside surfaces of the chain guide for damage caused by the chain.

Inspect the linkage for being bent, twisted, or damaged.

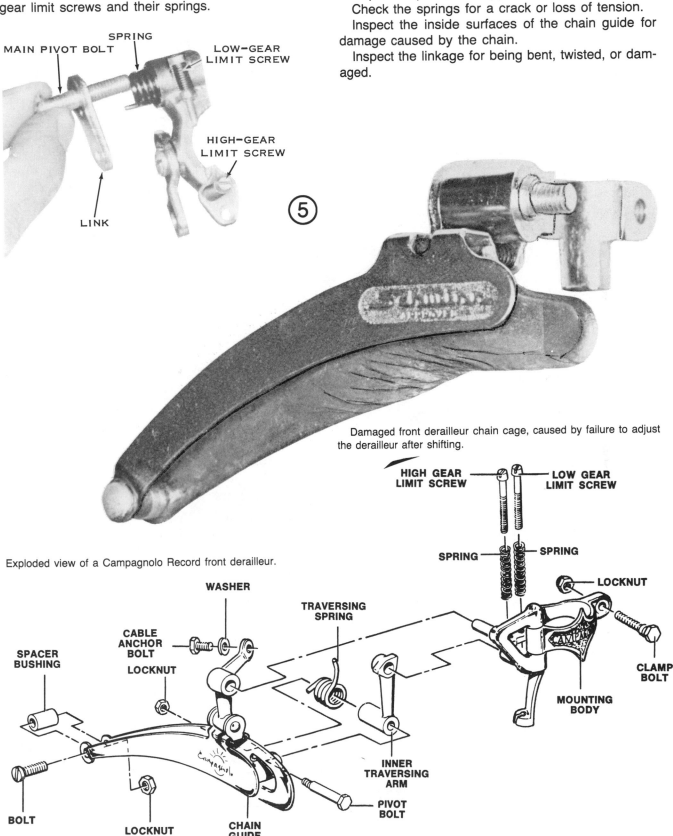

MAIN PIVOT BOLT — SPRING — LOW-GEAR LIMIT SCREW — HIGH-GEAR LIMIT SCREW — LINK — ⑤

Damaged front derailleur chain cage, caused by failure to adjust the derailleur after shifting.

Exploded view of a Campagnolo Record front derailleur.

HIGH GEAR LIMIT SCREW — LOW GEAR LIMIT SCREW — SPRING — SPRING — LOCKNUT — CLAMP BOLT — MOUNTING BODY — WASHER — TRAVERSING SPRING — CABLE ANCHOR BOLT — LOCKNUT — SPACER BUSHING — BOLT — LOCKNUT — CHAIN GUIDE — PIVOT BOLT — INNER TRAVERSING ARM

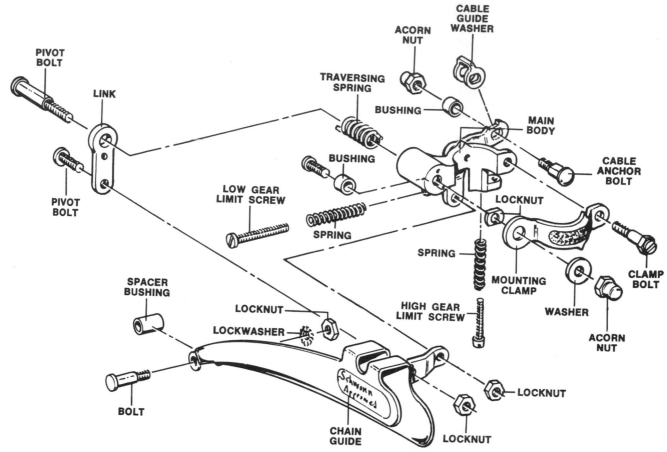

Exploded view of a Huret front derailleur.

Assembling

⑥ Lightly grease all pivot bearing parts. Slide the shorter limit screw spring onto the low-gear limit screw (the screw with the larger head), and then thread it into the body as far as it will go. Insert the high-gear limit screw through the other limit spring, and then thread it into the body about five turns. Apply a thin coating of multipurpose grease to the traversing spring.

⑦ Insert the traversing spring into the main body, with one leg of the spring indexed through the hole in the body. *NOTE: The spring may be installed either way.* Slide the link onto the main pivot bolt, with the flat side facing the threaded end of the bolt. Thread the pivot bolt into the body, with the exposed leg of the spring indexed in the hole of the link. Check to be sure the other spring leg is still indexed in the hole of the body. Tighten the bolt securely, and then back it off approximately a quarter turn as a preliminary adjustment.

⑧ Hold the adjustment of the pivot bolt with a screwdriver; thread the locknut onto the bolt and tighten it securely. Check the link adjustment; it should rotate freely (under tension of the spring) with no end-

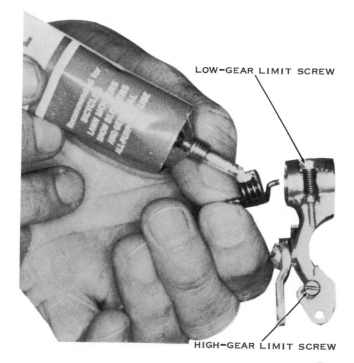

LOW-GEAR LIMIT SCREW

HIGH-GEAR LIMIT SCREW

⑥

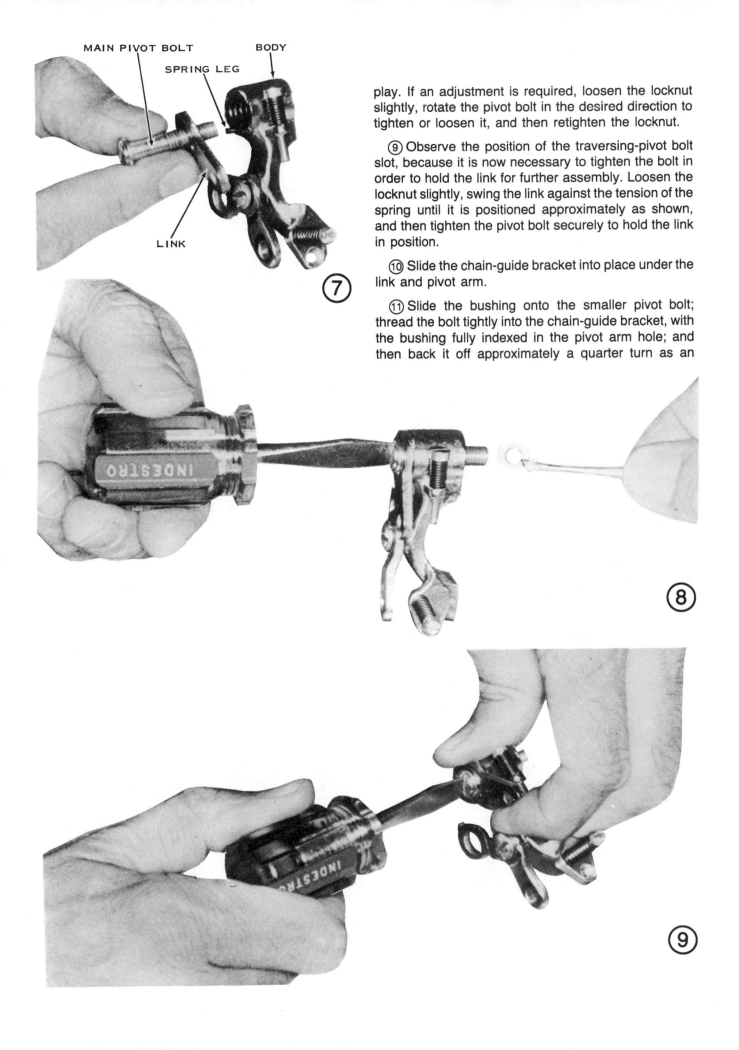

MAIN PIVOT BOLT   BODY

SPRING LEG

LINK

⑦

play. If an adjustment is required, loosen the locknut slightly, rotate the pivot bolt in the desired direction to tighten or loosen it, and then retighten the locknut.

⑨ Observe the position of the traversing-pivot bolt slot, because it is now necessary to tighten the bolt in order to hold the link for further assembly. Loosen the locknut slightly, swing the link against the tension of the spring until it is positioned approximately as shown, and then tighten the pivot bolt securely to hold the link in position.

⑩ Slide the chain-guide bracket into place under the link and pivot arm.

⑪ Slide the bushing onto the smaller pivot bolt; thread the bolt tightly into the chain-guide bracket, with the bushing fully indexed in the pivot arm hole; and then back it off approximately a quarter turn as an

⑧

⑨

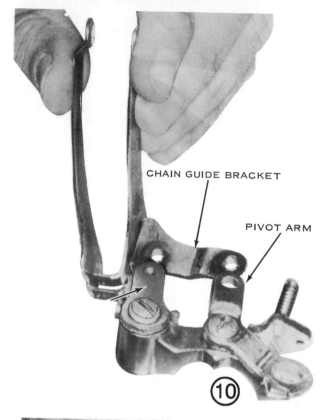

CHAIN GUIDE BRACKET

PIVOT ARM

⑩

⑪

adjustment. Hold this adjustment with a screwdriver while you install and then fully tighten the locknut.

⑫ Thread the larger pivot bolt through the link and into the chain guide. Tighten it firmly, and then back it off approximately a quarter turn as an adjustment. Hold this adjustment with a screwdriver, and then install and securely tighten the locknut.

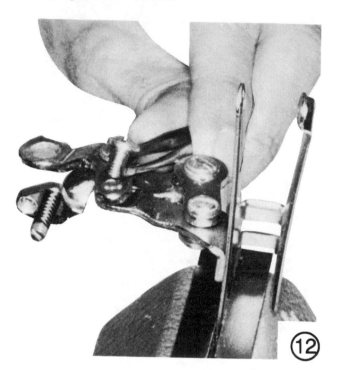

⑫

⑬ Loosen the traversing-pivot bolt to the same position you noted in step ⑨ before you tightened it to hold the link in position. Hold this adjustment with a screwdriver while you firmly tighten the locknut.

⑭ Insert the bushing in the hole of the traversing arm. Slide the cable-guide washer onto the arm, as shown, with the hole having the flats facing the rear of the derailleur. If the derailleur you are working on uses two washers instead of the cable-guide washer shown, proceed as follows: Slide the cable anchor bolt through the arm, with the head of the bolt facing away from the body. Install a thin washer, a thick washer, and then the acorn nut. Some derailleurs have a stud riveted to the arm with the same arrangement of washers. Back out the low-gear adjusting screw approximately halfway, for a preliminary setting.

⑮ Install the anchor bolt from the back side of the pivot arm, with the flats on the bolt indexed with the flats of the washer. Thread the acorn nut onto the anchor bolt.

⑯ Place the derailleur in position on the bicycle, with the chain between the sides of the chain guide. Insert the bolt from the outer side of the guide, as shown. Slide the bolt through the spacer bushing. Ro-

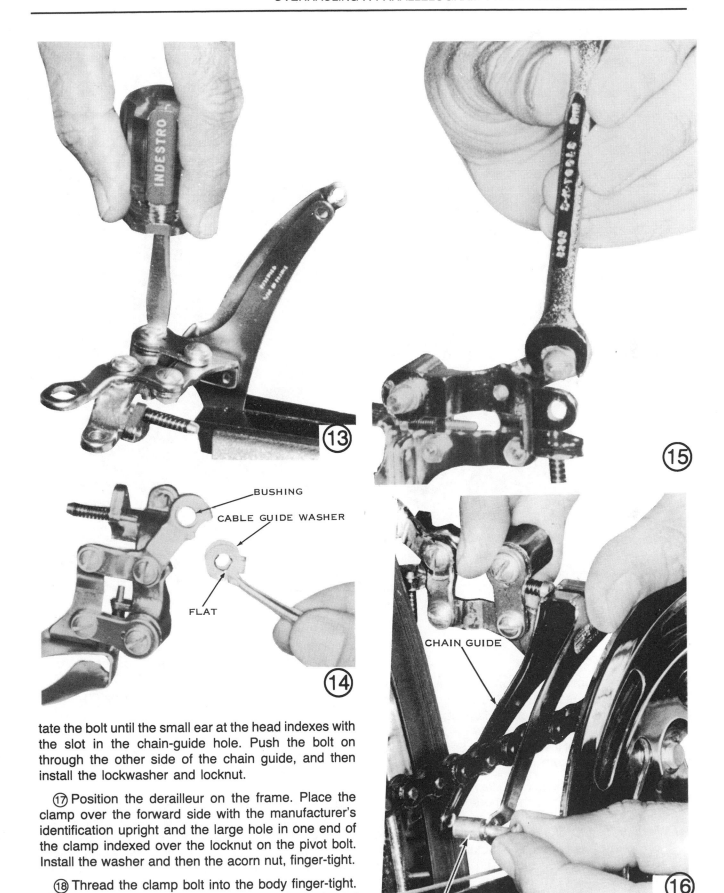

BUSHING

CABLE GUIDE WASHER

FLAT

CHAIN GUIDE

SPACER BUSHING

tate the bolt until the small ear at the head indexes with the slot in the chain-guide hole. Push the bolt on through the other side of the chain guide, and then install the lockwasher and locknut.

⑰ Position the derailleur on the frame. Place the clamp over the forward side with the manufacturer's identification upright and the large hole in one end of the clamp indexed over the locknut on the pivot bolt. Install the washer and then the acorn nut, finger-tight.

⑱ Thread the clamp bolt into the body finger-tight. Feed the control cable through the hole in the body and

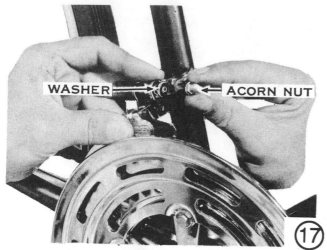

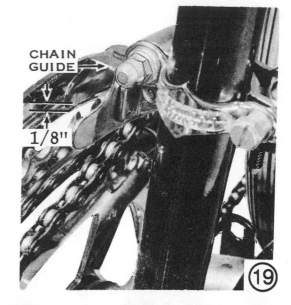

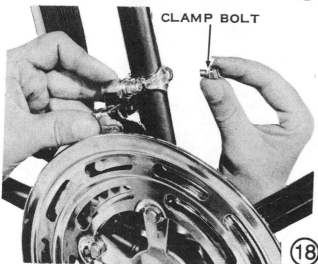

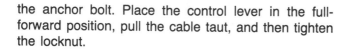

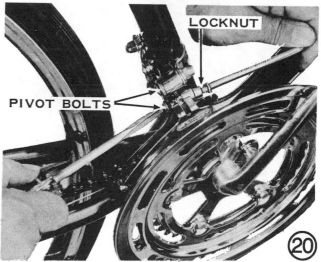

the anchor bolt. Place the control lever in the full-forward position, pull the cable taut, and then tighten the locknut.

Making a Major Adjustment

⑲ Shift the derailleur unit on the frame until the lower edge of the outer chain guide is not over ⅛ inch above the tip of the teeth of the largest chainwheel. Rotate the derailleur until the chain guide is parallel with the flat surface of the chainwheel. Securely tighten the mounting-plate acorn nut and bolt.

⑳ Check the movement of the traversing arms to be sure they pivot freely and that the spring returns the derailleur to the nonextended position. If the pivot arms seem to bind or the derailleur remains in the extended position, loosen the pivot-bolt locknut. Turn the pivot bolt clockwise until it is snug, and then back it off approximately a quarter turn. Hold this adjustment with a screwdriver while you securely tighten the locknut.

Repeat this procedure for the other pivot bolts by first loosening the locknut, firmly tightening the pivot bolt, holding the adjustment with a screwdriver, and then firmly tightening the locknut. *NOTE: On some front derailleurs, the traversing-arm linkages are riveted and cannot be adjusted.*

Setting the Low-gear Limit Screw

㉑ Shift to the low-gear (largest) rear sprocket and the low-gear (smaller) chainwheel. If the shift lever moves all the way to one end of its travel before it can bring the front derailleur to the correct position, loosen the cable anchor locknut and readjust the cable. In the lever's forward (slack-cable) position, which selects low gear (the small chainwheel) on most derailleurs, leave the cable anchor locknut loose until you have adjusted the limit screw.

LOW-GEAR CHAIN WHEEL

CABLE

CABLE ANCHOR BOLT LOCKNUT

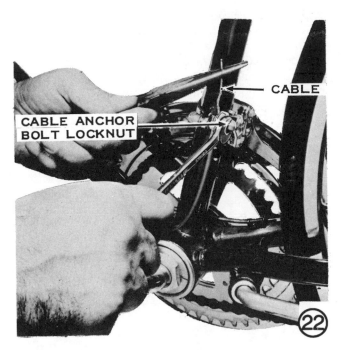

CHAIN

CHAIN GUIDE

1/32"

㉑

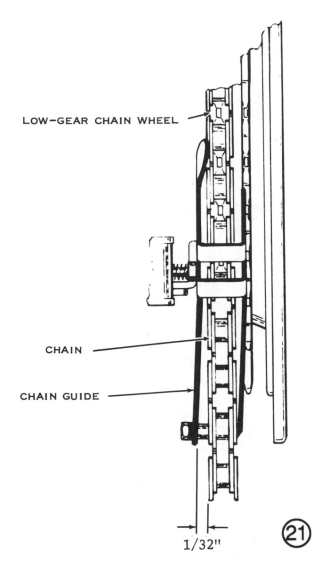

㉒

Turn the low-gear limit screw until the inner side of the chain guide just clears the inner side of the chain (by approximately ⅟₃₂ inch), as shown. *NOTE: The illustration exaggerates the clearance for clarity.* If the front derailleur does not have a low-gear limit screw, loosen the chain-guide mounting bolt and position the chain guide until the inner side of the chain guide just clears the inner side of the chain and the guide follows the contour of the chainwheel. Tighten the mounting bolt.

㉒ Pull the cable taut with a pair of pliers, and then tighten the locknut. Force the control lever down several times to prestress the cable and casing.

If the low-gear limit screw cannot be adjusted far enough, then you will need to use a different front derailleur or a longer bottom-bracket axle. Triple-chainwheel sets often need a front derailleur with extra reach to the inside.

Setting the High-gear Limit Screw

㉓ Place the chain onto the high-gear (smallest) rear

HIGH-GEAR CHAIN WHEEL

CHAIN GUIDE

CHAIN

1/32"

㉓

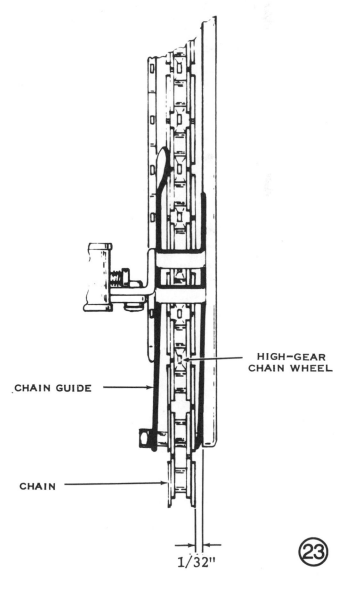

sprocket. *NOTE: The crank must be rotated in the forward direction while making this adjustment.* Turn out the high-gear limit screw until the derailleur shifts the chain onto the high-gear (larger) chainwheel. Move the front control lever very slightly until the outer side of the chain guide just clears the outer side of the chain (by approximately 1/32 inch). Leave the front derailleur in this position, and then turn in the high-gear limit screw until it just contacts the traversing arm.

If the shift lever is all the way at one end of its travel, again loosen the cable anchor locknut and readjust the cable.

If the high-gear limit screw cannot be adjusted far enough, then you will need to use a different front derailleur or a shorter bottom-bracket axle. Triple-chainwheel sets need a front derailleur with extra reach to the outside.

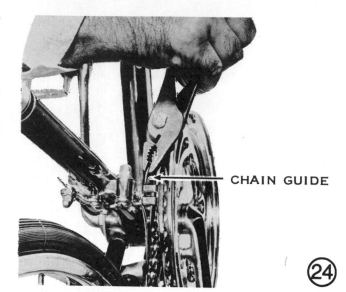

CHAIN GUIDE

24

Adjusting the Chain Guide

24 Rotate the crank in the forward direction and, at the same time, shift the chain back and forth from one chainwheel to the other. If movement of the chain onto the large chainwheel is sluggish, use a pair of pliers to bend the front end of the inner side of the chain guide toward the chain. If the chain rubs or makes noise when it is positioned on the largest rear sprocket and the largest chainwheel, or vice versa, adjust the position of the control lever until the chain runs clear of the guide. **CAUTION: Do not turn the limit screws, which have already been adjusted.**

The Non-derailleur Drivetrain

13 • THE SINGLE-SPROCKET DRIVETRAIN

A single-sprocket drivetrain without derailleurs is used when the bicycle has a fixed-gear, coaster-brake, or multispeed geared hub, or a conventional rear hub with a single-speed freewheel. The chain is held in place, with a slight amount of slack, by adjustment of rear-wheel position in the dropouts.

The chain and rear sprocket of a single-sprocket drivetrain require special service procedures and are covered here. Correct gearing with a single-speed or geared hub is also covered.

Chain adjustment is usually performed when the wheel is replaced on the bicycle, and is covered in the section on replacing the wheel (page 72).

The crankset and pedals of a single-sprocket drivetrain are the same as those of a multi-sprocket drivetrain. These parts are covered in Chapter 15.

A single-sprocket freewheel is similar to a multi-sprocket freewheel, and is covered in Chapter 10.

It is not necessary to remove the sprocket to rebuild most single-sprocket hubs, but it is convenient to replace a worn sprocket when rebuilding a hub. Instructions for sprocket replacement are therefore included in the overhaul sequence for each hub in Chapter 14.

PROBLEMS WITH SINGLE-SPROCKET DRIVETRAINS

The following problem chart lists only problems with the chain and sprockets. Crank and pedal problems are the same as for a multi-sprocket drivetrain, and are covered in the problem chart in Chapter 7. Problems unique to different models of hubs are covered in Chapter 8 and Chapter 14.

General Problems

Chain falls off.

Possible cause:	Corrective action:
Chain is elongated due to wear.	Replace chain and sprocket.
Chain is loose.	Readjust rear-wheel position.
Chainwheel is bent.	Straighten or replace.

Chain runs roughly.

Possible cause:	Corrective action:
Chain is new and sprocket is old.	Replace sprocket.
Chain is too tight.	Reposition rear wheel.
A chain link is stiff.	Free link.
Chain is dirty.	Clean chain.
Sprocket or chainwheel is bent.	Straighten.
Chainline is incorrect	Align sprockets.
Hub is defective.	See Chapter 8 or Chapter 14.
Crankset is defective.	See Chapter 15.

Lugged-sprocket Problems

Sprocket will not stay in place.

Possible cause:	Corrective action:
Snapring is bent or distorted.	Replace snapring.
Too few spacers are used with sprocket.	Use correct spacers.
Dustcap under sprocket is missing.	Install dustcap.
Sprocket hole is oversize.	Use correct sprocket.

Sprocket cannot be installed.

Possible cause:	Corrective action:
Sprocket hole is undersize.	Use correct sprocket.

Chain or sprocket strikes spokes.

Possible cause:	Corrective action:
Spacers are improperly installed.	Reinstall.
Dish of sprocket faces wrong way.	Reverse sprocket.

Threaded-sprocket Problems

Sprocket unscrews.

Possible cause:	Corrective action:
Sprocket or lockring is loose.	Tighten.

Threading is difficult.

Possible cause:	Corrective action:
Threads are mismatched.	Use correct parts.
Threads have not been greased.	Grease and reinstall.
Parts have been cross-threaded.	Align parts.

Hub threads are stripped.

Possible cause:	Corrective action:
Threads are mismatched.	Replace hub.
Parts have been cross-threaded.	Replace hub.

LUGGED SPROCKETS

Modern coaster-brake and multispeed hubs use a three-lug sprocket held in place by a snapring. It is very easy to remove the sprocket, by prying off the snapring. Spacers and a dustcap may be installed along with the sprocket. **CAUTION: Reinstall all spacers and the dustcap when you replace the sprocket. Otherwise the sprocket will be loose.**

Most lugged sprockets are dished, allowing a chainline adjustment by reversing the sprocket. Chainline may also be adjusted by replacing spacers inside or outside the sprocket.

To secure the sprocket, the snapring should be tapped lightly into its groove with a hammer and punch. Do not pound hard, or you could damage the hub's bearings.

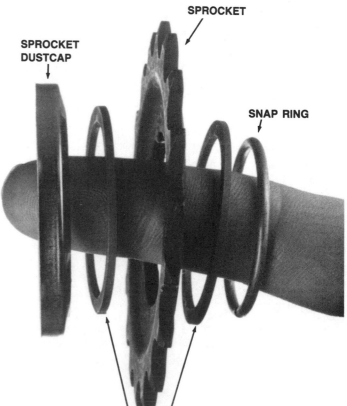

A three-lug sprocket is secured by a snap ring and may be positioned by one or two spacer washers. The dish of the sprocket and position of the spacer washers determine the chainline.

Interchangeability of Lugged Sprockets

Three-lug sprockets of the following brands are interchangeable:

Sturmey-Archer (and copies of the AW three-speed)
Karat
Shimano
SunTour
Fichtel und Sachs/Komet/Torpedo
NK (three-speed hub only)

NK, Bendix, and some other brands of coaster brakes have three-lug sprockets which look similar, but the central hole is not of the same size.

THREADED SPROCKETS

Sprockets of fixed-gear hubs are threaded on *clockwise* and are secured with a lockring threaded on *counterclockwise*. The lockring prevents the sprocket from unscrewing during backpedaling. Some early-model coaster brakes use the same arrangement of right-threaded sprocket and left-threaded lockring.

CAUTION: It is possible to thread a fixed sprocket onto a hub made for a freewheel, but without a left-threaded lockring, it will unscrew. This can be dangerous if it happens during riding. For a fixed gear, always use a hub with the special dual threading for sprocket and lockring.

It is not possible to tighten a threaded sprocket with the usual tools, which are made for narrow derailleur chain. It is easy to tighten the sprocket after installing the wheel on the bicycle, by stepping down on a pedal. Then tighten the lockring by turning it *counterclockwise* with a spanner wrench or a drift punch and hammer.

Some older three-speed hubs have a threaded sprocket. This can be removed by unscrewing it counterclockwise, but only after disassembling the hub. When overhauling the hub, it is best, if possible, to install a modern three-lug driver. If you must remove the threaded sprocket, chuck it in a vise and turn the arms of the driver with a bar of metal. Pedaling will tighten the new sprocket after installation.

Interchangeability of Threaded Sprockets and Lockrings

Most fixed sprockets and hubs have 24 threads per inch. Some hubs and sprockets have 1mm threading (25.4 threads per inch). These threadings are the same as English and French multiple-freewheel threadings.

Left-threaded lockrings are sold in at least three different threadings. An English-threaded lockring will go very loosely onto a French-threaded hub, and will strip if tightened. Lockring threadings tend to be con-

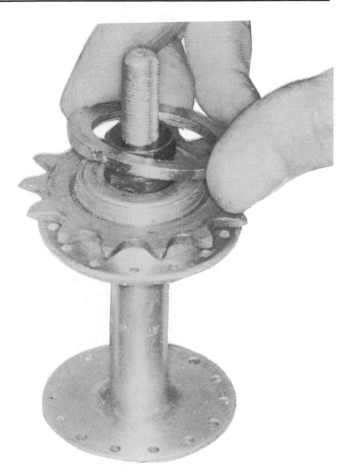

The sprocket of the fixed rear-wheel hub is attached by means of a right-hand thread. The lockring that holds it in place has a left-hand thread.

stant with each manufacturer, regardless of the sprocket threading used on a particular hub.

CAUTION: Never force a sprocket or lockring, or use one which threads on loosely and wobbles. The hub threads will almost certainly be ruined, and the sprocket or lockring may unscrew or strip during a ride.

GEAR RATIOS

In high gear, a multispeed hub turns the hub shell faster than the sprocket; in low gear, slower. The gear ratios of Sturmey-Archer and Shimano three-speed hubs are .75, 1.00, and 1.33 (¾, 1, and ⁴⁄₃). The gear ratios of the Sturmey-Archer five-speed hub are .67, .79, 1.00, 1.26, and 1.50 (⅔, ¹⁵⁄₁₉, 1, ¹⁹⁄₁₅, and ³⁄₂). The middle gear is direct drive, calculated as in Chapter 9, page 135; multiply by the ratios given here for the other gears.

Three-speed bikes as sold usually try to match the top gear of a ten-speed, and the second gear is labeled as the "normal" gear. Then the middle and top gears lie to either side of the best range for level-ground riding.

Fortunately, replacement sprockets are sold in sizes from 12 to 22 teeth. When you overhaul the hub, use the opportunity to make the *top* gear the "normal" gear. The best three-speed gearing makes top gear about 76 inches, second gear about 57 inches, and low gear about 43 inches (see Chapter 9, page 135). On a common three-speed bike with a 46-tooth front sprocket and 26-inch wheels, you'll need a 21-tooth rear sprocket. Count chainwheel teeth—a different chainwheel requires a different sprocket.

The best gearing for the five-speed hub uses the same sprocket as the three-speed. The five-speed's gears will then be 38, 45, 57, 72, and 85 inches. The fourth gear is ideal for level-ground riding, the fifth for downhill sprints.

Three- and five-speed hubs' quick shifting and the lower gearing will give you acceleration to beat derailleur-equipped bicyclists and many cars across intersections when the traffic light turns green.

A single-speed bike should have a gear of about 65 inches (see Chapter 9, page 135) for average adult use; it should be lower for a child or for hilly country. Many single-speed bikes are geared too high. Change the sprocket or chainwheel as needed to improve gearing.

SINGLE-SPROCKET CHAIN

Coaster brakes and multispeed hubs use a wide chain with a master link (separable link) which allows its easy removal from the bicycle. For details about different types of chain, see page 105.

Install a new chain with a new sprocket, even if a longer chain isn't needed. An old chain will run very roughly on a new sprocket. Check that the chain runs straight, not at an angle, between the front chainwheel and rear sprocket; reposition sprocket spacers or reverse a dished sprocket if necessary. If you can achieve the correct chainline, you can renew a worn sprocket by turning it over so that it drives on the unused side of the teeth.

Chain Length

If the chain is too long, it may jump off the chainwheel or sprocket. Loss of drive is bad enough, but a dropped chain also disables a coaster brake, and can cause the wheel or pedals to jam.

If the chain is too short, the rear wheel will sit too far forward in the dropout slots, and is at risk of pulling out.

Before removing the rear wheel to rebuild a hub, check that the chain length places its axle in the middle of the dropout slot. When installing a new chain on a non-derailleur bike, line the new chain up against the old one to compare their lengths. If you are changing sprocket or chainwheel sizes, add 1 full link (wide and narrow half-links) for every 4 teeth. *NOTE: Be sure to cut the chain so that a roller link is on each end of the chain. The* master link *will bridge them.*

Chain Removal and Installation—Non-derailleur-type Bicycles

To remove the chain from a single-speed or internally geared bicycle, first loosen the axle nuts at the rear wheel and then move the wheel forward slightly to obtain slack in the chain.

Locate the master link of the chain. This link can be identified by a wide link plate or by a U-shaped plate that fits between the rollers. Bend the link to one side or pry the U-shaped plate off using a screwdriver. Remove the chain from the chainwheel and rear sprocket.

A chain for a one-speed or internally geared bike may be lubricated with cycle oil by soaking it and then wiping off the excess.

To install the chain, place it over the chainwheel and then turn the crank to allow the chain to drop between the sprocket and the chain guard. Feed the other end of the chain around the rear sprocket.

Fit the master link into the chain rollers on each end of the chain. Position the side plate on the master link rivet. Hold the chain on each side of the master link, and then bend the chain toward the side plate until the side plate snaps onto the other rivet. Some master links have an additional U-shaped snap-on plate that must be installed to hold the link together.

If you have removed the wheel or installed a new sprocket, the chain must be adjusted; see page 76.

Bend the master link toward the large link plate as shown to release it and disassemble the chain. Some master links have a U-shaped clip which must be pried loose with a screwdriver.

14 • GEARED AND COASTER-BRAKE HUBS

Bicycles equipped with a derailleur unit and track racing bicycles with fixed rear hubs have a very simple hub. On other types of bicycles, however, the rear hub contains the most individual parts and is the most intricate assembly. This is due in part to the several functions it must perform and the fact that almost all the parts are encased in the hub shell—completely hidden from view.

This chapter covers hubs in the following three categories: single-speed rear hubs with coaster brake, multispeed rear hubs, and three-speed rear hubs with coaster brake.

The *single-speed rear hub with coaster brake* consists of a hub that can freewheel and a sprocket-activated internal brake arrangement. The hub shell turns forward and at the same speed as the sprocket. If the speed of the rear-wheel sprocket is reduced or stopped, the hub shell can continue to turn independently of the sprocket; therefore the term "coasting." When the direction of the sprocket is reversed (turned rearward), the internal brake unit forces disks or brake shoes to bear against the interior surface of the shell, slowing or stopping the hub. Instructions for overhaul of coaster-brake hubs begin on page 214.

The *multispeed rear hub* usually has three gearing ratios available between the sprocket and the hub shell and can freewheel or coast when the sprocket speed is reduced or stopped. The gearing ratios are "low," when the hub shell turns slower than the sprocket; "middle," when the shell turns at the same speed as the sprocket; and "high," when the shell turns faster than the sprocket. The gearing ratios are changed by moving a control cable connected to the hub. The Sturmey-Archer five-speed hub is a special case, with its two control cables. It has two high gears, two low gears, and a middle gear.

All manufacturers stamp their names on the brake arm or the hub shell, and this is an excellent method of identifying the hub you are servicing.

The service instructions for shoe-type single-speed rear hubs with coaster brake, such as this Bendix, begin on page 217.

Manufacturers of multispeed rear hubs and the pages on which the overhaul procedures begin are as follows: Shimano, page 256; Sturmey-Archer AW, Styre, Schwinn-Approved Styre, Brampton, Hercules,

The Nankai disk-type single-speed rear hub with coaster brake is similar to the Mattatuck, Hawthorne, and New Departure hubs. Service instructions for these hubs begin on page 229.

The Sturmey-Archer AW three-speed hub without coaster brake is widely used; the SunTour, Hercules, Styre, Brampton, and Nankai hubs are identical in construction. Models with built-in cable-operated drum brakes and generators have also been sold. Overhaul procedures for these hubs begin on page 240.

Service instructions for Shimano three-speed rear hubs without coaster brake begin on page 256.

SunTour, and Nankai, page 240; Sturmey-Archer five-speed, page 275.

The *three-speed rear hub with coaster brake* combines all the features of the three-speed rear hub, described above, with a sprocket-activated internal brake mechanism. When the sprocket is rotated rearward, the hub shell is slowed until it stops.

Manufacturers of three-speed coaster hubs and the pages on which the overhaul procedures begin are as follows: Sturmey-Archer, page 286; Shimano, page 302.

SERVICE NOTES

Replacement parts are no longer made for many older coaster-brake and three-speed hubs. It's a shame to throw away an entire wheel because of a minor problem with the hub, but check parts availability before disassembly. Keep a spare of an old hub if you can find one. Some models are common on discarded bicycles. Often they are "garage bikes" in nearly new condition.

Internal parts of many hubs can be replaced with parts from newer models. When this is possible, it is indicated before the rebuilding instructions.

Axle Rotation

All multispeed hubs and coaster brakes try to turn the axle in the forkend slots. The twist from a coaster brake is very strong, and a *brake arm* strapped to the left chainstay is necessary to resist this.

The twist from the sun gear of a multispeed hub is weaker, but *non-turn* or tab washers must be installed to resist it.

The Sturmey-Archer five-speed hub is available with this lightweight aluminum shell, as is the three-speed hub. The five-speed hub is similar to the earlier four-speed version, and most parts are interchangeable. A drum-brake version is also sold. Rebuilding instructions begin on page 275.

CAUTION: Proper installation of antirotation parts is essential if the hub is to remain securely fastened in the frame. For details, see Chapter 6, page 76.

Service procedures for the Sturmey-Archer S3C and TCW Mark III three-speed rear hubs with coaster brake begin on page 286.

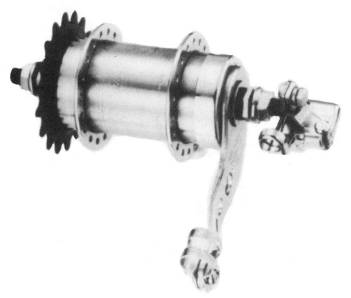

Service procedures for the Shimano 3SC and 3CC three-speed rear hubs with coaster brake begin on page 302.

Bearing Retainers

It is best to rebuild most of a bicycle's bearings with loose bearing balls. Load capacity is increased, and though installation goes somewhat slower, you save time in not having to buy special retainers.

Multispeed hubs and coaster brakes are an important exception to this rule. These hubs have an internal cavity into which the bearing balls can fall, to wedge in the mechanism. Except where loose balls are specified, use the retainers supplied by the manufacturer.

Fortunately, retainers are available wherever you can buy the other parts necessary to rebuild a hub. If you cannot obtain new parts, it is usually possible with care to remove old balls from a retainer and install new ones.

Lubrication

Correct lubrication is essential to good performance of multispeed and coaster hubs.

Single-speed coaster brakes, and the shoes of multi-speed coaster brakes, should be lubricated with a *high-temperature* grease, as they can become very hot in operation. It may seem strange to lubricate the braking surfaces; however, braking force squeezes the grease out of the brake contact area.

Multispeed hub bearings should be lubricated with grease to hold bearing balls in place during assembly and to help keep oil from flowing out of the hub too fast. *Do not get grease on the pawls; it can make them stick.*

Multispeed hubs must be lubricated with a *good cycle oil* to control wear and friction in the gears.

After rebuilding, add a couple of teaspoons of oil at the oil cup on the shell. Also remove the shifter chain or pushrod and drip oil into the hollow end of the axle—both ends if possible. Spin the axle and turn the hub over a few times to spread oil from the middle of the hub.

The metal oil cup of older Sturmey-Archer hubs is not oiltight. Unscrew it and replace it with the newer plastic oil cup.

Some recent Shimano hubs do not have an oil cup. This does not mean that they are permanently lubricated. It means that they must be oiled through the end of the axle.

Internally geared hubs should be reoiled lightly every couple of weeks, to flush out dirt and metal particles.

CAUTION: *Never* use "household" oil, such as 3-in-1, advertised to "clean metal surfaces." This oil smells sour and feels watery when rubbed between the fingers. It contains acid which dissolves protective coatings and fills the hub with a brown paste. Also do not use lightweight spray oil; it is too thin.

Multispeed Hub Cables and Control Levers

NOTE: Most problems with geared hubs have to do with the cable. If the hub does not shift properly, look first for a kinked, sticking, or wrongly adjusted cable. Try to fix the cable before you decide that you have to disassemble the hub.

Multispeed hub control levers work only with the same brand of hub, because of the different length of cable pull for shifts. Cable end fittings are different with each brand of lever.

A multispeed hub must have a click stop for each gear. Do not use a derailleur control lever. Operating "between gears" will soon damage the hub.

A trigger control works much better than a twist-grip or lever control. The trigger has positive, locking stops for each gear position; the other controls have click stops which easily slip.

STURMEY-ARCHER HUBS—RIGHT-SIDE CABLE

① To install a cable in a Sturmey-Archer trigger control, push the control lever past low-gear position. The cover plate will lift, allowing you to thread the cable through.

Caution: When threading the cable along the frame, make sure that it is not kinked and that clamps are tight and will not slide out of position. See page 88.

③ Thread the indicator spindle to the adjusting barrel. For a coarse adjustment, pull the cable through the clamp on the adjusting barrel or move one of the frame clamps along a frame tube. For a fine adjustment, thread the adjusting barrel looser or tighter on the indicator chain.

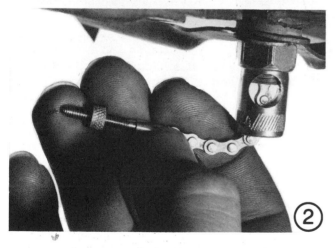

④ Check that the "neutral" gear falls partway between middle- and high-gear positions; test by trying to freewheel the pedals forward. Shift to low gear and try to pull the cable out to the side; there should be no free play, but the cable should not be tight. Shift to high gear; the cable should hang slightly slack.

⑤ With the control lever in the middle position, lock the adjusting barrel in position with the locknut. **CAUTION: The locknut must be tightened, or the adjusting barrel will unscrew.** In the middle gear, the shoulder on the *correct* indicator spindle will be level with the end of the axle. A shorter indicator spindle will work, though then this check on cable adjustment cannot be made.

STURMEY-ARCHER FIVE-SPEED HUB SHIFTERS

The best shifting devices for a five-speed hub are a pair of Sturmey-Archer three-speed trigger controls.

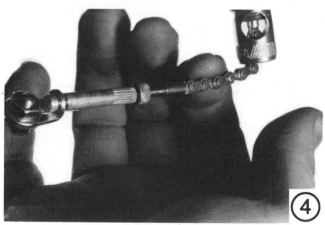

② Thread the indicator spindle clockwise into the right end of the axle until it is finger-tight, then unscrew it *less than five-eighths of a turn* until the adjusting barrel aims toward the cable.

CAUTION: The indicator spindle is sold in four lengths. If too long, it will hang up and the hub will not go into low gear. If you see only axle threads through the window in the side of the axle nut, install an additional washer under the nut. You should then see chain links. If you see only the shaft of the indicator spindle, replace it with a shorter one.

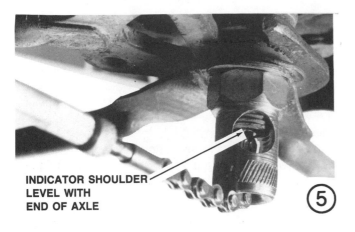

INDICATOR SHOULDER
LEVEL WITH
END OF AXLE

(5)

To install cables in the Sturmey-Archer single-lever control for the five-speed hub, slide them in from the underside. Do not disassemble this control unit; reassembly may be very difficult!

To install the cable in the Shimano trigger control, remove the cover and guide plate.

The right-side cable works just like the cable of a Sturmey-Archer three-speed hub.

The left-side cable has two positions. Use a trigger control's middle- and high-gear positions. In the middle-gear position, the cable should be tight; this will ensure the correct cable adjustment and keep the trigger from slipping into its unused low-gear position.

The five-speed hub can also be shifted using a Sturmey-Archer single-lever trigger control. *Avoid the dual-lever controls which have been sold with earlier versions of the five-speed hub. They slip out of gear too easily.*

SHIMANO THREE-SPEED HUB CABLES AND CONTROL LEVERS

Shimano three-speed hubs shift by means of a pushrod inside the hollow axle. In coaster-brake hubs the pushrod is at the *left* end of the axle, and in the brakeless hubs it is at the *right* end. A bellcrank (right-angled lever assembly) converts cable pull into pushrod push.

There are three types of bellcrank: threaded, lock-bolt, and Positron. Any Shimano three-speed shifter system will work with any Shimano three-speed hub.

CAUTION: The Positron system's click stops are in the bellcrank, not in the trigger. Use the Positron bellcrank only with the Positron single-strand cable and clickless shift control. Do not mix Positron shifter parts with others.

Assembly instructions below are for the threaded bellcrank. Variations in instructions for the other bellcranks are given in italics.

① Install the pushrod in the *right* end of a brakeless three-speed hub or the *left* end of a coaster-brake three-speed hub. Check the pushrod length. More than one length is sold. When lightly held in place, it should extend $7/16$ inch (11mm) from the end of the axle.

(1)

②

② Threaded: Thread on the thin bellcrank locknut. Thread the bellcrank onto the axle as far as it will go, then back it off until it lines up with the cable. Tighten the locknut against it.

Lockbolt and Positron: Loosen the lockbolt. Install the bellcrank, aligning it with the cable. Push it onto the axle as far as it will go, then tighten the lockbolt.

③ Lockbolt and threaded: Place the shift control in the N or 2 gear position. Install the cable as with the Sturmey-Archer cable, and adjust until the N on the bellcrank paddle is in the middle of the bellcrank window. Tighten the adjusting barrel locknut.

Positron: Move the shift control to the 3 position. Loosen the cable clamp on the bellcrank. Shift the bellcrank to the position marked "SET" and tighten the cable clamp.

③

SERVICING COASTER BRAKES

The coaster brake dates from the 1890s. Before it was invented, most bicycles had a fixed gear and a spoon brake—a simple handbrake which pressed against the tire—or no brake at all. Pedals could outrun the rider's feet on a downhill ride. Combining freewheeling with braking, the coaster brake was a tremendous improvement.

A coaster brake is reliable, and unaffected by weather. These are significant advantages, but the gay nineties are long gone. Even when skidding the rear wheel, a coaster brake is only half as powerful as a pair of modern handbrakes used with skill. A coaster brake will overheat on long downhill runs. Since it prevents backpedaling, it is inconvenient with toeclips and straps.

A coaster-brake hub *and separate handbrake* are a good choice for a child who cannot yet modulate handbrakes, or on a bicycle used for utility trips in changeable weather. Dual handbrakes are preferable for more usual adult use.

CAUTION: If the chain comes off the sprocket, a coaster brake is disabled. Make sure the hub axle nuts and brake-arm strap are securely tightened, and check chain adjustment frequently. Every vehicle needs at least two independent braking systems, in case one fails. An adult bike with a coaster brake should also have a front handbrake. For a small child, place the handbrake on the rear wheel.

How Coaster Brakes Work

Power input from the rear sprocket is through a *drive screw* which has a threaded extension inside the hub, like a bolt. The threads engage a *drive clutch* which is internally threaded, like a nut.

When the rider pedals forward, the threads pull the drive clutch to the right, and its outer surface jams into a cone-shaped part of the inside of the hub shell to drive the bicycle forward.

When the rider pedals backward, the threads push the drive clutch to the left, where it jams into the brake assembly. A small *retarder spring* lightly holds the drive clutch from turning when it is between its end positions; this lets the drive screw's threads get it started one way or the other.

In an *internal-expanding shoe-type brake,* brake shoes wedge outward against the inside of the hub shell. The shoes are prevented from turning with the hub shell by a *brake arm* strapped to the bicycle frame. In the *multiple-disk-type brake,* a stack of metal disks press against each other. Even-numbered disks are keyed to the rotating hub shell and odd-numbered disks are keyed to the stationary axle and brake-arm assembly.

Overhaul instructions are given here for the Bendix, a representative internal-expanding shoe-type coaster brake, and the Mattatuck, a representative disk-type brake.

Repair Procedures

As you disassemble an unfamiliar coaster brake, lay all parts out in order and in their proper orientation on a sheet of paper. Remove one or a few at a time for cleaning.

Before you go to a bike shop to buy replacement parts, make a note of the make and model of the hub. Lay out the parts on a sheet of paper in their correct order. Mark the position of worn parts on the sheet of paper. Take worn parts with you to the bike shop to compare with their replacements.

As you reassemble the hub, the ball retainers always go in *flat side outward.*

The retarder spring is the "brain" of the coaster-brake hub. It must be installed correctly for the hub to work. There are many types: snap-on bands, wire rings, even coil springs. There may be other, "helper" springs inside the hub, but the retarder spring can always be identified by its function: to exert a light drag on the clutch cone. Only one coaster-brake design lacks a retarder spring: the Sturmey-Archer SC and copies, which use dual roller clutches.

Many types of retarder spring are attached at one end so they drag more stiffly in one direction than in the other. The spring should produce a *light* drag when the clutch cone is rotating forward and a heavier drag when braking. A reversed spring will cause excess wear or prevent the brake from engaging. Test for correct operation after installing the retarder spring, and again after installing the driver.

The fixed bearing cone is at the right end of some coaster-brake hubs and at the left end of others. Tighten the fixed cone down securely with its locknut unless it is already permanently attached to the axle; perform the bearing adjustment at the other end of the axle. The chart with this section indicates which is the fixed cone.

Parts Availability and Interchangeability

The following chart summarizes the family relationships of common coaster-brake models. Hubs listed together will fit in the same hub shell; many, but not all, internal parts are interchangeable. Parts availability for each model is also indicated.

Hubs bearing the name of a bicycle manufacturer are usually "house-branded" versions of hubs listed below. For details on interchangeability or help in identifying a "house-branded" hub, ask the bike shop salesperson to consult the tables in *Sutherland's Handbook for Bicycle Mechanics.*

BRAND AND MODEL	PARTS AVAILABLE?	FIXED CONE SIDE	DISTINCTIVE FEATURES
Bendix Original	No	Left	Threaded sprocket
Bendix Red Band (RB)	No	Left	Splined sprocket
Bendix RB-2	No	Left	3-lug sprocket
Bendix Junior	No	Left	Like RB-2; 1 brake shoe
Bendix 70	Yes	Left	3-lug sprocket, 2 shoes
Bendix 70J	No	Left	Like 70, 1 shoe
Bendix 76 short lead	Yes	Left	3-lug sprocket, 4 shoes
Bendix 76 long lead	Yes	Left	Zinc-plated driver, retarder
F & S Torpedo Boy	Yes	Right	"Junior" model
F & S Boy	Yes	Right	Same as Torpedo Boy
F & S Pixie	Yes	Right	Same as Torpedo Boy
F & S Komet Super	Yes	Right	Loose balls in driver
Schwinn-Approved	Yes	Right	24 TPI axle threads
F & S Komet Super 161	Yes	Right	Short clutch cone
F & S Sachs Jet	Yes	Right	Long clutch cone
Centrix	Yes	Right	Similar to Sachs Jet
Karat	Yes	Right	Similar to Sachs Jet

BRAND AND MODEL	PARTS AVAILABLE?	FIXED CONE SIDE	DISTINCTIVE FEATURES
New Departure	Yes	Left	Threaded sprocket
Mattatuck	No	Left	Lugged Sprocket
Hawthorne	No	Left	Threaded sprocket
Nankai (NK)	Yes	Left	9-thread driver
Shimano 333	No	Left	Older, disk-type
Shimano A-type 42	No	Left	42mm chainline, shoe type
Shimano A-type 45	No	Left	45mm; on Ross bicycles
Shimano B-type	No	Left	Coiled retarder, shoe type
Shimano D-type	Yes	Left	Nearly same as B-type
Shimano Mity Mite	No	Left	"Junior" model
Sturmey-Archer SC	No	Right	Roller drive
Schwinn-approved Mark IV	No	Right	Same as Sturmey-Archer SC
Perry B-100	No	Right	Roller drive, threaded sprocket
Torpedo	No	Right	Roller drive
Sturmey-Archer SC1	No	Right	Cone drive
SunTour Type I	No	Left	4 shoes, 2-piece spring
SunTour Type II	No	Left	4 shoes, 1-piece spring
SunTour Type III	Yes	Left	3 shoes, 1-piece spring

Problems with Coaster Brakes

Hub freewheels backward, no brake.

Possible cause:	*Corrective action:*
Cone or shoe (disk) tabs are worn.	Rebuild hub.
Drive screw or drive clutch threads are damaged.	Rebuild hub.

Hub freewheels forward, no drive.

Possible cause:	*Corrective action:*
Sprocket splines or threads are stripped.	Replace sprocket.
Drive screw or drive clutch threads are stripped.	Rebuild hub.
Retarder is damaged or backward.	Rebuild hub.

Hub sings while coasting.

Possible cause:	*Corrective action:*
Hub shell conical surface is worn.	Replace hub shell.
Axle is bent.	Rebuild hub.

Grinding noises.

Possible cause:	*Corrective action:*
Chain is too tight.	Adjust chain.

Bearing cones are too tight.	Adjust cones.
Ball retainer is damaged or reversed.	Rebuild hub.
Retarder spring is backward.	Rebuild hub.
Axle is bent.	Rebuild hub.
Dustcap is bent.	Replace dustcap.
Lubrication is poor.	Rebuild hub.
Brake arm is pulling left cone.	Realign arm.

Brake is weak or grabby.

Possible cause:	*Corrective action:*
Brake parts are worn.	Rebuild hub.
Brake arm is loose from frame.	Tighten brake arm.
Lubrication is incorrect.	Rebuild hub.

Backpedals too far.

Possible cause:	*Corrective action:*
Brake assembly is worn.	Rebuild hub.
Some disks are missing (disk-type).	Rebuild hub.
Cone adjustment is too loose.	Adjust cone.

OVERHAULING A SHOE-TYPE SINGLE-SPEED COASTER HUB

The following step-by-step illustrated instructions cover disassembling, cleaning, inspecting, and assembling a Bendix (1946–1961), Bendix RB (1961–1963), Bendix RB2 (since 1963), and Bendix 70J rear-wheel hub with coaster brake. The hubs are identified by the name stamped on the brake arm and/or on the hub shell. Differences between these hubs are illustrated in detailed exploded drawings and are pointed out in the text. Exploded drawings of several other shoe-type brakes are also shown. The following procedures apply basically to the Bendix 70J hub. Deviations from this hub that might cause problems during assembly, including specific parts that are not interchangeable, are called to your attention in the individual steps.

For photographic clarity, the illustrations were made of a hub without the tire, rim, and spokes.

Bendix single-speed rear hub with internal-expanding shoe-type coaster brake. Most coaster brakes are of the shoe type, except for New Departure, Mattatuck, Hawthorne, Nankai, and early Shimano 3.3.3.

Tools and Supplies You Will Need

Adjustable wrench
Hook spanner (some models)
Hammer and punch (some models)
Cone wrenches
Tweezers
Small flat-blade screwdriver
High-temperature grease
Ball retainers to fit your hub
Replacement parts as needed

Preliminary Steps

Read introductory material on single-sprocket systems (page 205).
Read introductory material on coaster brakes (page 214).
Remove the wheel (page 69).

Disassembling

① Remove the axle nut, washer, and serrated spacer from the right end of the axle.

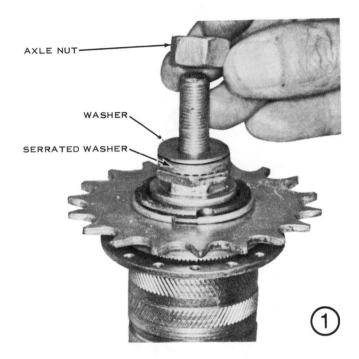

AXLE NUT

WASHER

SERRATED WASHER

① Remove the snapring from under the drive-screw flange by prying it out and up with a screwdriver. Lift the sprocket off the drive screw. *NOTE: The early-model Bendix hub has a lockring instead of a snapring.* Remove the lockring by turning it clockwise with a spanner wrench or hammer and drift punch. Rotate the sprocket counterclockwise and remove it from the drive screw.

③ Remove the dustcap by prying up with a screwdriver, as shown. Work around the cap edge and it will pop out. Be careful not to crimp or distort the cap.

④ Hold the adjusting cone with a thin wrench or cone pliers, and then remove the locknut and cone.

⑤ Reach in with a pair of needlenose pliers, and remove the ball-bearing-retainer assembly. Turn the drive screw in a counterclockwise direction to remove it from the axle. Remove the second ball-bearing retainer with a pair of needlenose pliers.

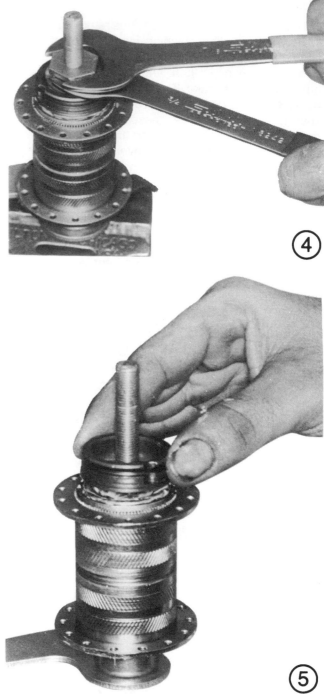

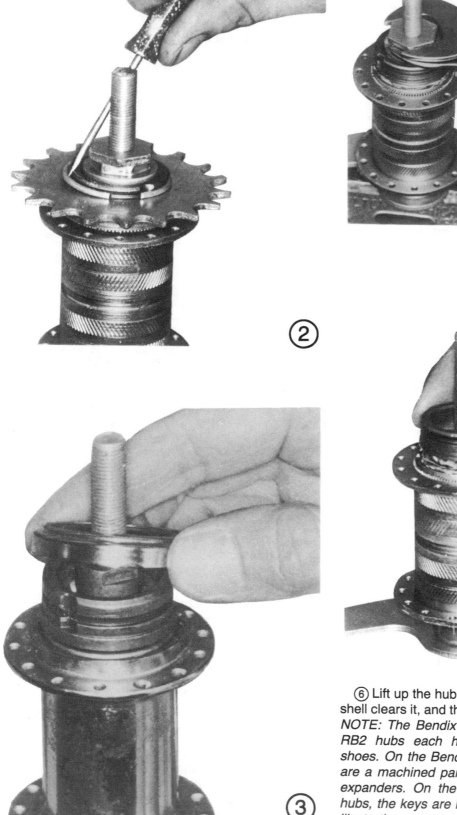

⑥ Lift up the hub shell, catch the brake shoe as the shell clears it, and then remove the shell from the axle. *NOTE: The Bendix Original, Bendix RB, and Bendix RB2 hubs each have two crescent-shaped brake shoes. On the Bendix RB2 hub, the brake-shoe keys are a machined part of the brake-arm and drive-side expanders. On the Bendix Original and Bendix RB hubs, the keys are loose as indicated in the exploded illustration on page 220.*

(6)

(7) Remove the complete drive-side expander unit, with the clutch, by lifting it off the axle.

(7)

(8) Separate the drive clutch, retarder spring, and drive-side expander.

(9) Remove the locknut, dustcap, and brake-arm side expander. Remove the ball-bearing retainer from the brake-arm side expander.

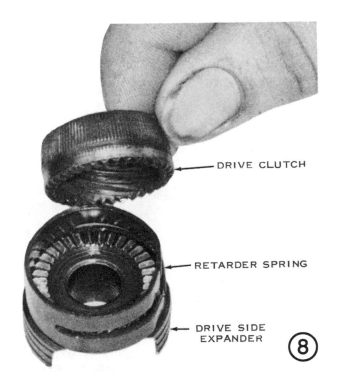

— DRIVE CLUTCH

— RETARDER SPRING

← DRIVE SIDE EXPANDER

(8)

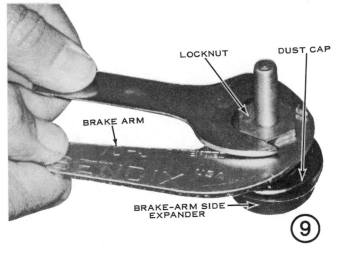

LOCKNUT   DUST CAP

BRAKE ARM

BRAKE-ARM SIDE EXPANDER ←

(9)

Cleaning and Inspecting

Clean all parts in solvent and rinse them, or wipe them dry with a lintless cloth. Keep all cleaned parts on paper towels to avoid contamination. Cover them with a clean towel to keep grit from entering the internal parts and bearings. A tiny piece of grit can do a tremen-

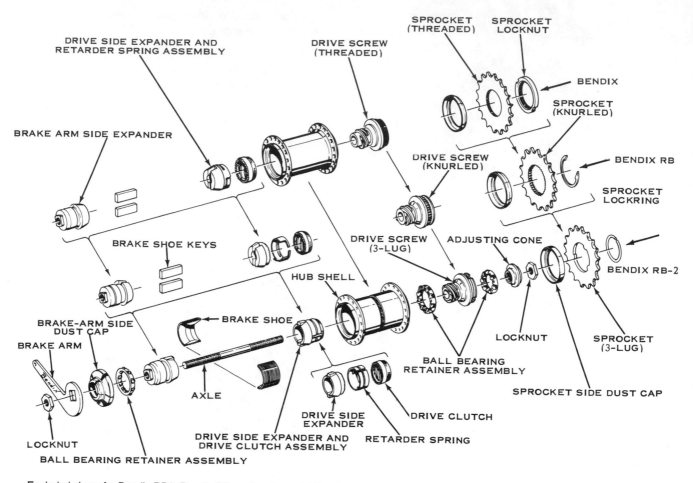

Exploded view of a Bendix RB2, Bendix RB, and early-model Bendix single-speed rear hub with coaster brake. Parts separated from the main line are not interchangeable.

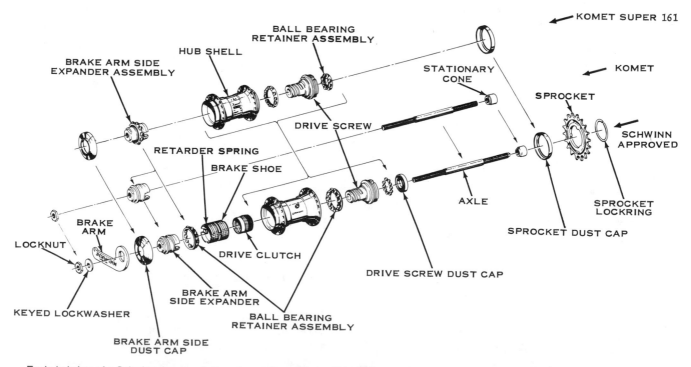

Exploded view of a Schwinn-Approved, Komet, and Komet Super 161 single-speed rear hub with coaster brake. Parts separated from the main line of the figure are not interchangeable with the Schwinn-Approved; all others are.

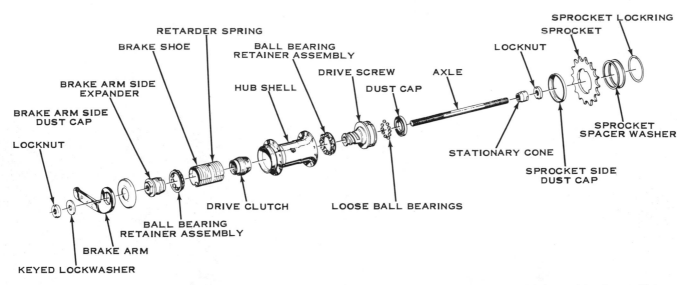

Exploded view of a Pixie and F&S Torpedo Boy single-speed rear hub with coaster brake. All parts of these two hubs are interchangeable.

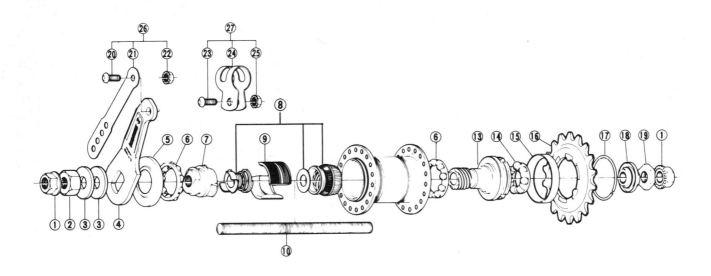

Exploded view of a Shimano D-type single-speed rear hub with coaster brake. This hub is almost identical with the earlier-model B-type, and all parts are interchangeable.

ITEM	DESCRIPTION	ITEM	DESCRIPTION	ITEM	DESCRIPTION
1	Flange nut	13	Driver	23	Clip screw M6×14mm (⁹⁄₁₆″)
2	Arm nut	14	Ball retainer A	24	Brake-arm clip (band type)
3	Arm washer	15	Right-hand dustcap	25	Clip nut (M6)
4	Brake arm	16	Sprocket wheel	26	Brake-arm clip assembly (flat type)
5	Left-hand dustcap	17	Snapring	27	Brake-arm clip assembly (band type)
6	Ball retainer C	18	Cone with dustcap		
7	Brake cone	19	Locknut		
8	Clutch cone unit	20	Clip screw M5×14mm (⁹⁄₁₆″)		
9	Brake shoe (pair)	21	Brake-arm clip (flat type)		
10	Hub axle	22	Clip nut (M5)		

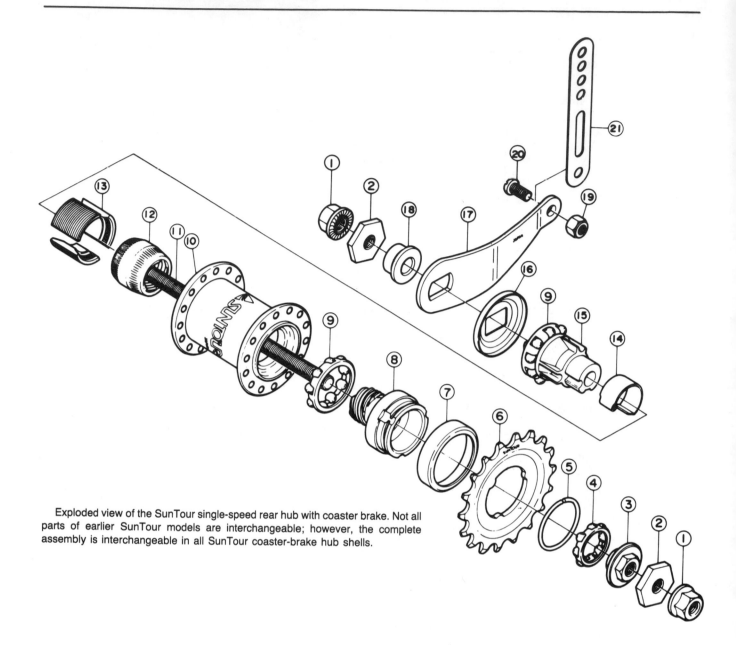

Exploded view of the SunTour single-speed rear hub with coaster brake. Not all parts of earlier SunTour models are interchangeable; however, the complete assembly is interchangeable in all SunTour coaster-brake hub shells.

ITEM	DESCRIPTION	ITEM	DESCRIPTION
1	Axle nut	12	Clutch cone
2	Locknut	13	Brake shoe
3	Cone screw	14	Clutch spring
4	Ball retainer	15	Brake cone
5	Snapring	16	Dust cover
6	Sprocket	17	Brake arm
7	Dust cover	18	Arm bushing
8	Driver	19	Brake-arm clip nut
9	Ball retainer	20	Brake-arm clip bolt
10	Hub shell	21	Brake-arm clip
11	Axle		

dous amount of damage if allowed to work on a part over an extended period of time.

It is best to replace the three ball-retainer assemblies rather than to inspect them. Check the adjusting-cone bearing surface for scores (scratchlike marks), pits, or other damage. Check the cone for stripped threads.

Inspect the bearing surface of the brake-arm side expander for scores, pits, or other damage. Check the expander for stripped threads.

Inspect the drive-side expander and drive clutch for worn, chipped, or damaged teeth.

Check the splines of the drive screw for cracks, chips, or worn edges.

Replace the retarder spring with a new one to ensure proper service following assembly.

Check the axle and locknuts for signs of damage or stripped threads. Roll the axle slowly across a smooth flat surface and check both ends for being out-of-round or watch the center of the axle to see if it rises off the surface. Either of these indications means the axle is bent and must be replaced.

Check both dustcaps to be sure they are not crimped or distorted, which could have happened during disassembly.

Inspect the bearing surfaces of the hub shell for scores, pits, or excessive wear. Check the flanges of the hub shell for cracks, and to be sure they are not loose.

Inspect the brake shoe or shoes for damage, burrs, or glazed lining surfaces.

Inspect the sprocket for wear to the driving faces of the teeth. Consider replacing the sprocket with one of another size to improve the gearing (see page 207).

Check the brake arm to be sure it is not bent or damaged. *NOTE: All parts of the Bendix 70 and Bendix 70J hubs are interchangeable except for the brake arm, brake-side expander, drive-side expander, and the brake shoes, one of which is used on the 70J and two on the 70. Parts that are not interchangeable between the Bendix Original, Bendix RB, and Bendix RB2 are noted in the exploded illustration on page 220.*

Assembling

⑩ Pack one of the outside ball-bearing-retainer assemblies with a generous amount of multipurpose lubricant. Work the lubricant throughout the bearings and retainer with your fingers.

⑪ Place the lubricated ball-bearing assembly on the brake-arm side expander, with the bearing balls facing the bearing race of the brake-arm side expander, as shown.

⑫ Thread the brake-arm side expander onto the axle until the outside edge of the expander is 1⅛ inches from the end of the axle.

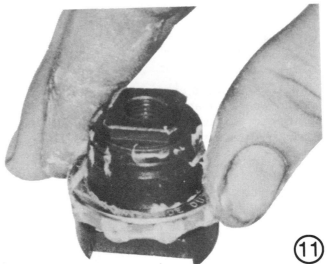

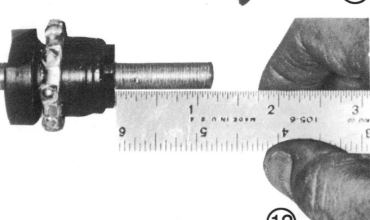

⑬ Position the axle in a vise, with the installed items facing up. **CAUTION: Use soft vise jaws to protect the axle threads.** Place the dustcap over the brake-arm side expander and bearing assembly. Push the cap down firmly to seat the bearing assembly on the brake expander.

⑬

⑭ Install the brake arm on the brake-arm side expander, with the manufacturer's identification facing up. Thread the axle nut onto the axle finger-tight against the brake arm.

⑮ Position a cone locknut gauge over the axle and on the locknut. Hold the brake arm and tighten the locknut until the end of the gauge is even with the end of the axle. If a cone gauge is not available, use a measurement of 1 inch from the surface of the locknut to the end of the axle.

⑭

⑯ Snap a new retarder spring on the drive-side expander, and then install the drive clutch in the retarder spring, with the teeth of the expander engaging the teeth of the clutch, as shown. **CAUTION: Always replace the retarder spring with a new one to ensure proper service after assembly.**

CAUTION: Many models of coaster brake have a retarder spring attached at one end. If the spring is installed backward, it will cause excess wear, and the brake may not engage. Check that the spring exerts a light drag when the drive clutch is turned in the direction of forward rotation. The drag may be the same or greater when the drive clutch is turned backward.

⑰ Shift the axle in the vise so the jaws grip the locknut. Apply a liberal amount of multipurpose grease to the outside surface of the retarder spring, and then slip the complete unit onto the axle.

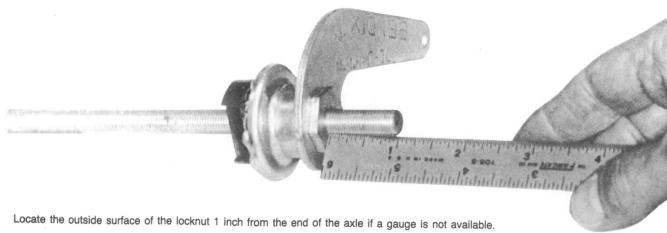

Locate the outside surface of the locknut 1 inch from the end of the axle if a gauge is not available.

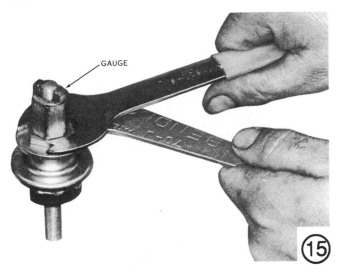

GAUGE

⑮

DRIVE CLUTCH

RETARDER SPRING

DRIVE SIDE EXPANDER

⑯

TAPERED RAMP

⑰

⑱ Coat the inside surface of the brake shoe with multipurpose grease. Position the brake shoe against the tapered ramps of the brake side of the expander unit and the drive side of the expander unit. The grease will hold the shoe in place. *NOTE: The Bendix Original, Bendix RB, and Bendix RB2 hubs each have two crescent-shaped brake shoes. On the Bendix RB2 hub, the brake-shoe keys are a machined part of the brake-side and drive-side expanders. On the Bendix Original and Bendix RB hubs, the keys are loose, as indicated in the exploded illustration on page 220. If you are working on one of these three hubs, coat the inside surface of both brake shoes with multipurpose grease, and then position them against the tapered ramps of the brake-side and drive-side expanders. If you are working on the Bendix Original or Bendix RB hub, place the two brake-shoe keys in the slots of the brake-side and drive-side expanders.*

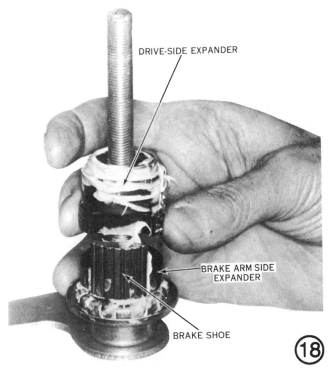

DRIVE-SIDE EXPANDER

BRAKE ARM SIDE EXPANDER

BRAKE SHOE

⑱

⑲ Apply a moderate amount of premium-quality cycle oil to the inside surface of the hub shell.

⑳ Remove the assembly from the vise. Slide the oiled hub shell over the axle, with the large opening facing the brake, and simultaneously push in on the brake shoe, as shown. The hub shell should slide into place against the dustcap.

㉑ Apply a generous coating of multipurpose grease to the sprocket-side ball-bearing-retainer assembly. Work the lubricant throughout the ball bearings and the retainer. Install the bearing assembly over the axle,

SPROCKET-SIDE
BALL BEARING
RETAINER ASSEMBLY

DUST COVER   BRAKE SHOE

with the flat side of the retainer facing up. Push the retainer into place onto the bearing race of the drive-side expander.

㉒ Apply a generous amount of multipurpose grease to the beveled splines of the drive screw. Twist the lubricated drive screw clockwise into place until it is seated against the ball-bearing retainer.

㉓ Pack the outside ball-bearing assembly with a generous amount of multipurpose grease. Work the lubricant throughout the bearings and the retainer with your fingers. Install the bearing assembly in the drive screw, with the flat side of the retainer facing up.

㉔ Thread the adjusting cone onto the axle. Bring the cone down snug, and then back it off approximately three-eighths of a turn, or until there is just a discernible amount of sideplay when you move the wheel rim up and down.

㉕ Install the locknut on the axle and tighten it against the adjusting cone. Hold the adjusting cone with a thin wrench or cone pliers, and then tighten the locknut securely.

㉖ Hold each end of the axle with your fingers. Slowly twist the axle with the thumb and forefinger of each hand—the wheel should not turn. If it does turn, the cones are too tight and must be loosened slightly. Back

DRIVE SCREW

BEVELED SPLINES

ADJUSTING CONE

(22)

(24)

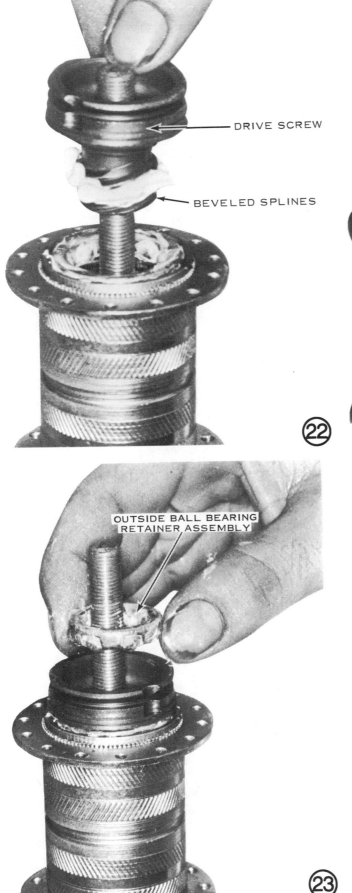

OUTSIDE BALL BEARING
RETAINER ASSEMBLY

(23)

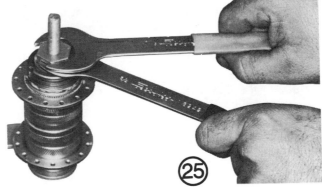

(25)

off the locknut on the axle end opposite the brake arm. Loosen the cone approximately an eighth of a turn, and then retighten the locknut. The cones are properly adjusted when the wheel rotates freely and comes to rest gradually with the valve stem or reflector at the lowest point of the wheel, and there is only the slightest trace of sideplay.

Another, very precise test for sideplay is to see whether the sprocket drags as you rotate the wheel forward. There should be a slight drag from the retarder spring, but not a heavy pull. Try to rock the sprocket from side to side. It should rock only slightly. Using these tests, you can adjust the bearings so that there is no noticeable sideplay at the rim.

(26)

(27)

CAUTION: If the cones are adjusted too tight, it will cause binding and scoring of the hub. If the cones are adjusted too loose, it will cause fatigue, which can result in a damaged hub or broken axle.

(27) Position the dustcap over the drive screw.

(28) Install the sprocket, with the lugs on the inner surface of the sprocket indexing with the recesses in the drive screw, and then slide the sprocket into place on top of the dustcap. If you are working on the Bendix Original hub, thread the sprocket onto the drive screw clockwise and tighten it securely with a sprocket vise or, after installing the wheel, by pedaling forward.

(29) Spread the snapring over the flange of the drive screw. Tap it lightly into place with a hammer and drift punch. If you are working on the Bendix Original hub, thread the lockring *counterclockwise* onto the drive screw, and then tighten it with a hammer and punch or a C-spanner wrench.

CAUTION: Tighten both the sprocket and the lockring securely, or else the sprocket could unscrew.

(30) Place the serrated spacer onto the axle, with the serrations facing down.

(31) Install the flat washer on the axle, and then thread on the axle nut.

Finally, replace the wheel (page 72).

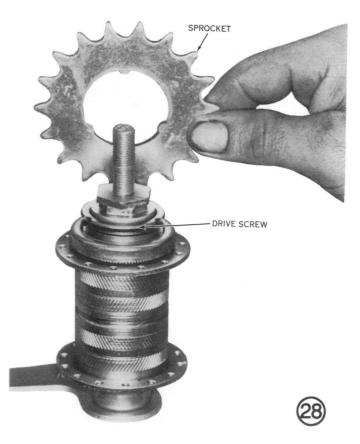

SPROCKET

DRIVE SCREW

(28)

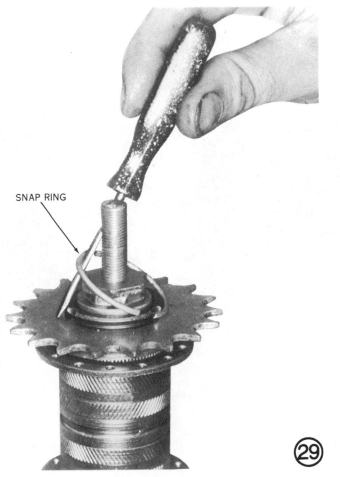

SNAP RING

(29)

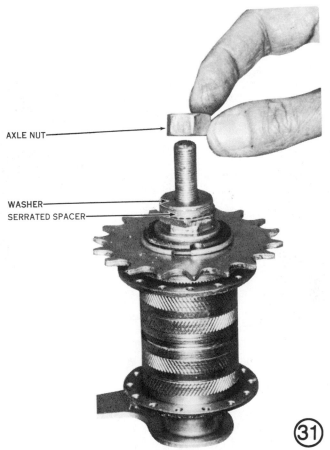

AXLE NUT

WASHER
SERRATED SPACER

(31)

SERRATED SPACER

(30)

OVERHAULING A DISK-TYPE SINGLE-SPEED COASTER HUB

The following step-by-step illustrated instructions cover disassembling, assembling, and adjusting the Mattatuck, Hawthorne, New Departure, Nankai, and Shimano 3.3.3 single-speed rear-wheel hubs with coaster brake. Each hub is identified by the manufacturer's name stamped on the brake arm and/or on the hub shell. These five hubs are basically alike, with many of the parts of the first four hubs being interchangeable. The Shimano 3.3.3 components cannot be interchanged with any other hub.

Differences between the hubs are illustrated in detailed exploded drawings and are pointed out in the text. The following procedures apply basically to the Mattatuck hub. Deviations from this hub that might cause problems during assembly, including specific parts that are not interchangeable, are called to your attention in the individual steps.

For photographic clarity, the illustrations were made of a hub without the tire, rim, and spokes.

The Nankai single-speed rear hub with disk-type coaster brake is similar to the Mattatuck, Hawthorne, and New Departure hubs. Most parts are interchangeable among them.

Tools and Supplies You Will Need

Adjustable wrench
Hook spanner (some models)
Hammer and punch (some models)
Cone wrenches
Tweezers
Small flat-blade screwdriver
High-temperature grease
Ball retainers to fit your hub
Replacement parts as needed

Preliminary Steps

Read introductory material on single-sprocket systems (page 205).
Read introduction to coaster brakes (page 214).
Remove the wheel (page 69).

Disassembling

① If you are working on a Mattatuck or Shimano 3.3.3 hub, remove the sprocket lockring by prying it up with a screwdriver and then lifting the sprocket up and off the drive screw. If you are working on a Hawthorne, New Departure, or Nankai hub, remove the lockring by turning it *clockwise* with a hammer and drift punch or C-spanner wrench, and then unscrew the sprocket by turning it counterclockwise.

② Remove the dustcap by prying up with a screwdriver, as shown. Work around the cap edge and it will pop out. Be careful not to crimp or distort the cap.

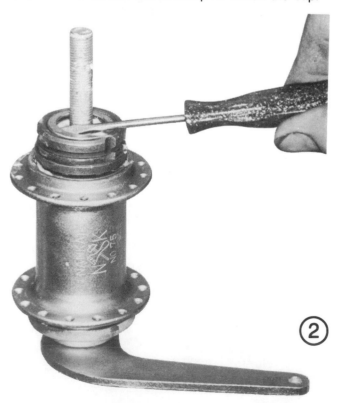

③ Remove the locknut and adjusting cone.

④ Pry the drive-screw dustcap out with a screwdriver. Work the screwdriver around the axle to keep from crimping or distorting the dustcap. *NOTE: The Shimano 3.3.3 hub does not have a drive-screw dustcap. On the New Departure hub this dustcap is a part of the sprocket locknut.*

⑤ Lift out the ball-bearing-retainer assembly from the drive screw.

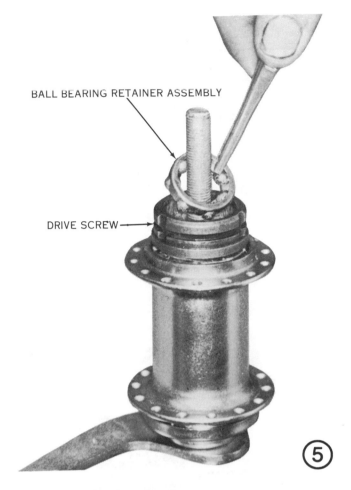

BALL BEARING RETAINER ASSEMBLY

DRIVE SCREW

⑤

ADJUSTING CONE

③

⑥ Remove the drive screw from the axle by turning it in a counterclockwise direction.

DUST CAP

④

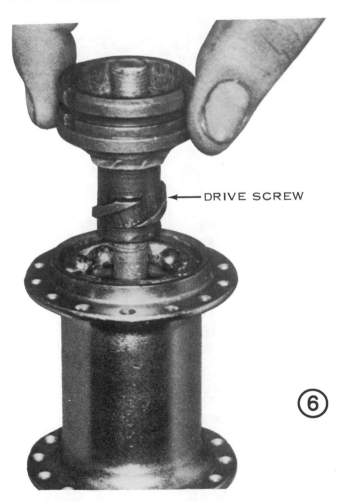

DRIVE SCREW

⑥

⑦ Lift the ball-bearing-retainer assembly out of the hub shell.

⑧ Lift the hub shell up and off the axle.

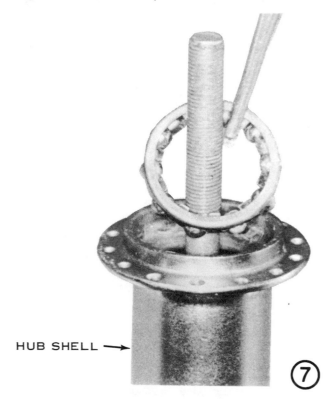

HUB SHELL ⟶

⑦

⑧

⑨ Remove the drive clutch.

⑩ Slide the brake clutch off the axle.

⑪ Remove the retarder spring from the brake clutch. If you are working on a Mattatuck hub, pry the spring off the brake clutch by inserting a narrow-bladed screwdriver through the spring slots, and then prying the spring off the brake clutch. If you are working on a Hawthorne, New Departure, Nankai, or Shimano 3.3.3 hub, insert a narrow-bladed screwdriver under the lower edge of the spring and pry it off the brake clutch.

⑫ Remove the steel and bronze brake disks, and then lift out the ball-bearing-retainer assembly. *NOTE: On the Shimano 3.3.3 hub, remove the spacer with the brake disks.*

⑬ Clamp the axle in a vise, with the jaws gripping the center (unthreaded portion) of the axle, or use a set of soft vise jaws to protect the axle threads. Remove the locknut by turning it in a counterclockwise direction. If you have trouble loosening the locknut, lower the axle in the vise until the jaws grip the flats of the disk-support sleeve for a better bite, and then loosen and remove the locknut. Shift the axle in the vise so the

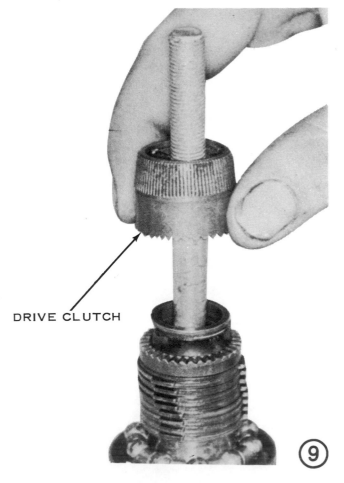

DRIVE CLUTCH

⑨

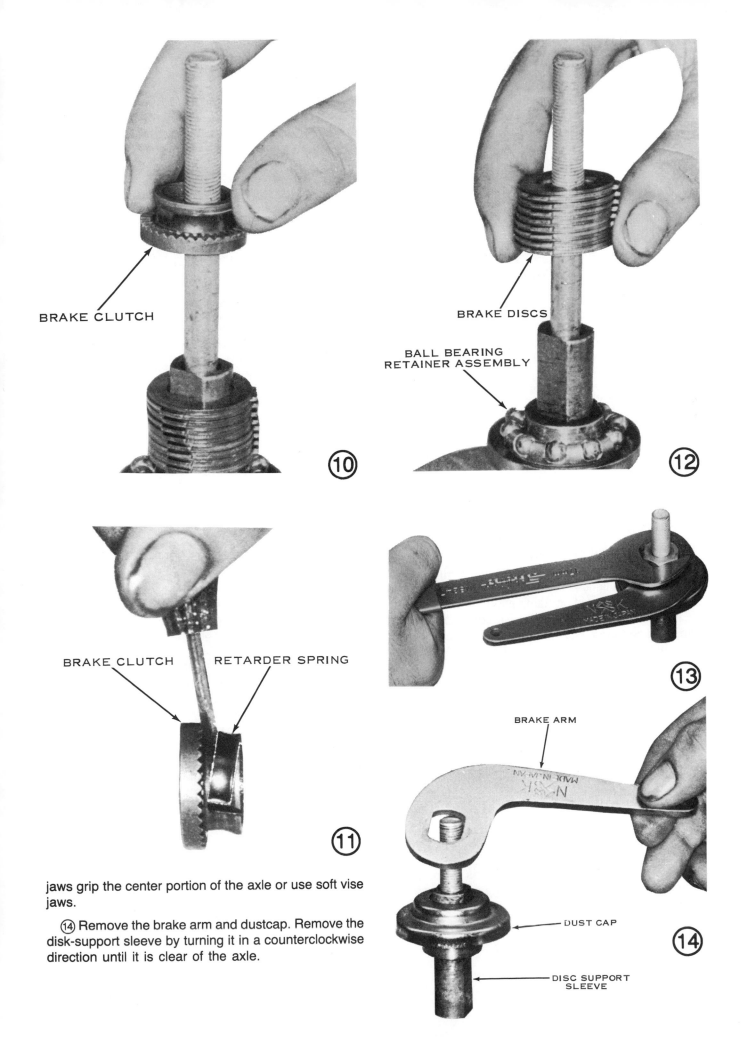

BRAKE CLUTCH

⑩

BRAKE DISCS

BALL BEARING
RETAINER ASSEMBLY

⑫

BRAKE CLUTCH RETARDER SPRING

⑪

⑬

BRAKE ARM

DUST CAP

DISC SUPPORT
SLEEVE

⑭

jaws grip the center portion of the axle or use soft vise jaws.

⑭ Remove the brake arm and dustcap. Remove the disk-support sleeve by turning it in a counterclockwise direction until it is clear of the axle.

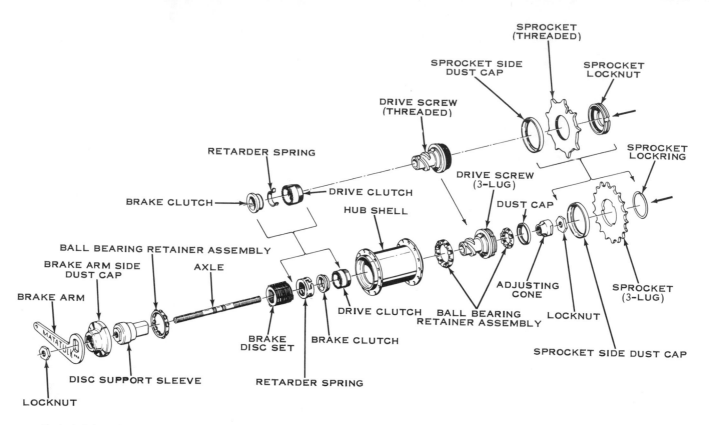

Exploded view of a Mattatuck single-speed rear hub with disk-type coaster brake. Parts separated from the main line of the figure apply to Hawthorne, New Departure, and Nankai hubs.

Cleaning and Inspecting

Clean all parts in solvent and rinse them, or wipe them dry with a lintless cloth. Keep all cleaned parts on paper towels to avoid contamination. Cover them with a clean towel to keep grit from entering the internal parts and bearings. A tiny piece of grit can do a tremendous amount of damage if allowed to work on a part over an extended period of time.

It is usually best to replace the bearing-retainer assemblies rather than to inspect them.

Check the adjusting-cone bearing surface for scoring (scratchlike marks), pits, or other damage. Check for stripped cone threads.

Inspect the bearing surface of the disk-support sleeve for scores, pits, or other damage. Check for stripped threads.

Inspect the drive clutch and the brake clutch for worn, chipped, or damaged teeth.

Check the splines of the drive screw for cracks, chips, or worn edges.

Check the axle and locknuts for signs of damage or stripped threads. Roll the axle slowly across a smooth flat surface and check both ends for being out-of-round, or watch the center of the axle to see if it rises off the surface. Either of these indications means the axle is bent and must be replaced.

Check the three dustcaps to be sure they are not crimped or distorted, which could have happened during disassembly.

Inspect the bearing surfaces of the hub shell for scores, pits, or excessive wear. Check the flanges of the hub shell for cracks and to be sure they are not loose.

Inspect the steel and bronze brake disks for worn surfaces or broken ears.

Check the brake arm to be sure it is not bent or damaged.

Inspect the sprocket for wear to the driving faces of the teeth. Consider replacing the sprocket with one of another size to improve the gear ratio (see page 207).

CAUTION: Use only Shimano 3.3.3 parts when replacing components on that hub. Do not attempt to use Shimano 3.3.3 parts on the Mattatuck, Hawthorne, New Departure, and Nankai hubs.

Assembling

⑮ Thread the disk-support sleeve onto either end of the axle until the outer edge of the sleeve shoulder is 1⅛ inches from the end of the axle. If you are working on the Shimano 3.3.3 hub, thread the disk-support

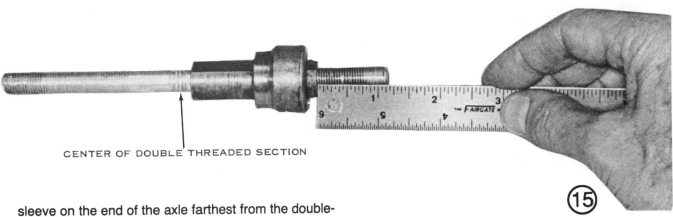

CENTER OF DOUBLE THREADED SECTION

sleeve on the end of the axle farthest from the double-threaded section.

⑯ Clamp the axle in a vise, with the disk-support sleeve facing up. **CAUTION: Use soft vise jaws to protect the axle threads from damage.** Slide the brake-side dustcap over the axle and down onto the disk-support sleeve. Place the brake arm on the dustcap, with the flats on the arm indexing with the flats on the disk-support sleeve and the manufacturer's identification facing up.

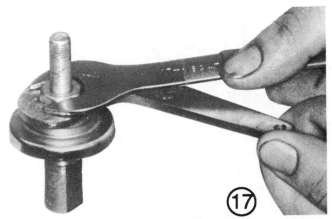

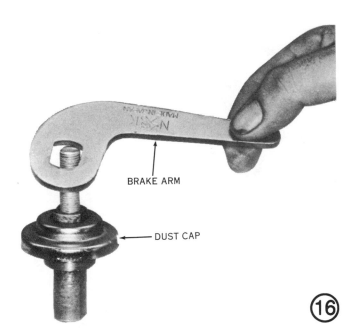

BRAKE ARM

DUST CAP

⑰ Thread the locknut onto the axle, and then tighten it against the brake arm securely by holding the arm and turning the locknut clockwise.

⑱ Pack one of the large bearing-retainer assemblies with a generous amount of multipurpose grease. Work the lubricant throughout the bearings and retainer with your fingers.

⑲ Remove the axle from the vise and turn it end for end, with the jaws gripping the locknut. Install the lubricated ball-bearing assembly on the disk-support sleeve, with the flat side of the retainer facing down, the ball bearings facing up.

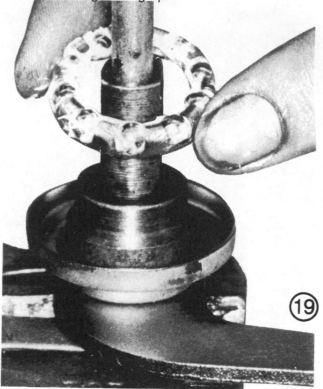

⑲

⑳ Slide one of the disks with a slotted hole onto the axle and disk-support sleeve, with the flats of the disk indexing with the flats on the sleeve. *NOTE: If you are working on a Shimano 3.3.3 hub, install the spacer onto the axle before the first steel disk.*

㉑ Install one of the disks with a round hole on top of the steel disk.

㉒ Continue to install the disks, alternating between the two kinds. Align the ears of the round-hole disks.

㉓ Snap a new retarder spring onto the brake clutch. **CAUTION: Always replace the retarder spring with a new one to ensure proper service after assembly.** The illustrated retarder spring and brake clutch are common to a Hawthorne, New Departure, Nankai, and Shimano 3.3.3 hub. The brake clutch on the Mattatuck hub is similar, but the retarder spring is quite different in shape, although it performs the same function. If you are working on a Mattatuck hub, install the retarder spring by snapping it onto the large end of the brake clutch. **CAUTION: The retarder spring, brake clutch, and drive clutch of the Mattatuck hub are not interchangeable with those on the Hawthorne, New Departure, and Nankai hubs.**

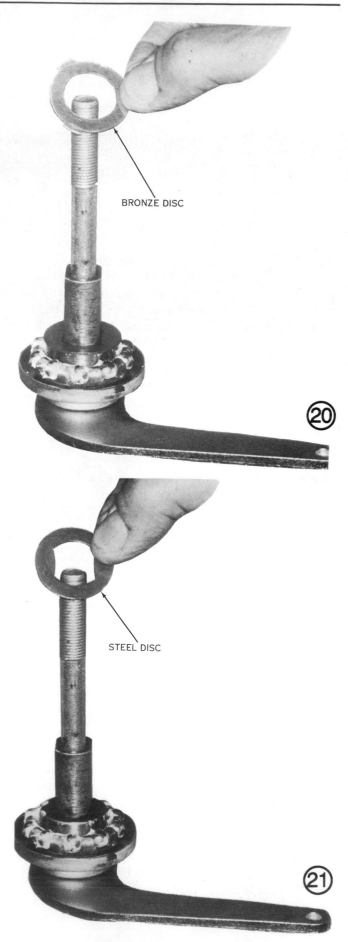

BRONZE DISC

⑳

STEEL DISC

㉑

STEEL DISC
BRONZE DISC

㉒

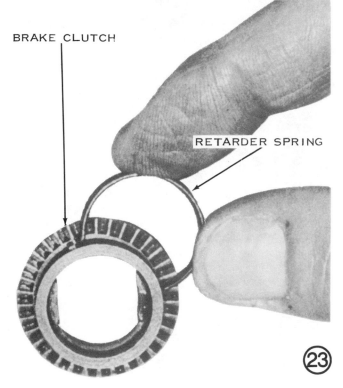

BRAKE CLUTCH

RETARDER SPRING

㉓

BRAKE CLUTCH

TOP STEEL DISC

㉔

㉕ Coat the brake disks and brake clutch with a generous amount of multipurpose grease.

㉕

㉔ Slide the brake clutch onto the axle, with the teeth facing up and the flats on the inside surface of the clutch indexing with the flats on the disk support sleeve. This will allow the clutch to sit on the top steel disk.

㉖ Slip the drive clutch over the axle, with the teeth facing down in order to index with the teeth of the brake clutch.

㉗ Remove the assembly from the vise. Install the hub shell over the assembled parts, with the largest opening facing down so the recesses on the inside surface of the shell index with the four rows of bronze disk ears. When properly installed, the lip on the lower flange of the hub shell will seat in the brake-arm dustcap.

㉘ Pack the other large bearing-retainer assembly with a generous amount of multipurpose grease. Work the lubricant throughout the bearings and retainer with your fingers. Insert the lubricated bearing assembly into the hub shell, with the flat side of the retainer facing up.

㉙ Apply a coating of multipurpose grease to the splines of the drive screw, and then thread the drive screw onto the axle in a clockwise direction as far as possible by hand. **CAUTION: If the drive screw has to be replaced, be sure to purchase the proper one for the hub you are working on. The drive screw of**

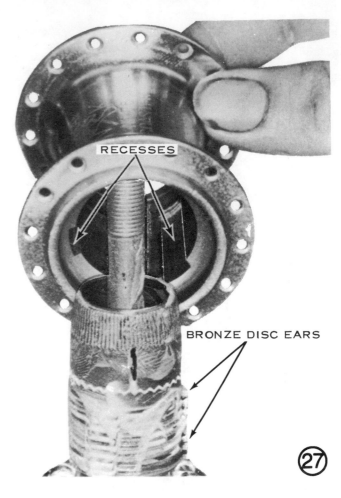

RECESSES

BRONZE DISC EARS

㉗

DRIVE CLUTCH

㉖

㉘

DUST CAP

BALL BEARING RETAINER ASSEMBLY

the Mattatuck hub is not interchangeable with the drive screw of the Hawthorne, New Departure, and Nankai hubs, although they appear similar.

㉚ Pack the remaining ball-bearing assembly with a generous amount of multipurpose grease. Work the lubricant throughout the bearings and retainer. Insert the lubricated bearing assembly into the bearing cup of the drive screw, with the flat side of the retainer facing up. Install the dustcap over the bearing assembly with the flat side facing up and then tap it into place with a hammer. **CAUTION: The dustcap of the Mattatuck hub is not interchangeable with that of the Hawthorne, New Departure, and Nankai hubs. If you have to buy a new cap, be sure to specify the hub you are working on.** *NOTE: The Shimano 3.3.3 hub does not have this dustcap. On the New Departure hub this cap is part of the sprocket locknut.*

㉛ Thread the cone and locknut onto the axle. Tighten the cone until it is snug, and then back it off approximately a quarter of a turn or until there is just a discernible amount of sideplay when you move the wheel rim up and down. Hold the cone with a thin wrench or cone pliers, and then tighten the locknut. Place the

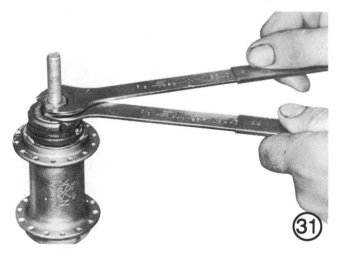

sprocket-side dustcap in position with the flat side facing up, and then tap it with a hammer until it is fully seated in the hub shell.

㉜ Remove the assembled hub and wheel from the vise. Hold each end of the axle with your fingers. Slowly twist the axle with the thumb and forefinger of each hand—the wheel should not turn. If it does turn, the cones are too tight and must be loosened slightly. Back off the locknut on the axle end opposite the brake arm. Loosen the cone approximately an eighth of a turn, and then retighten the locknut. The cones are properly adjusted when the wheel rotates freely and comes to rest gradually with the valve stem or spoke reflector at the lowest point of the wheel, and there is only the slightest trace of sideplay.

Another, very precise test for sideplay is to see whether the sprocket drags as you rotate the wheel forward. There should be a slight drag from the retarder spring, but not a heavy pull. Try to rock the sprocket from side to side. It should rock only slightly. Using these tests, you can adjust the bearings so that there is no noticeable sideplay at the rim.

CAUTION: If the cones are adjusted too tight, it will cause binding and scoring of the hub. If the cones are adjusted too loose, it will cause fatigue, which can result in a damaged hub or broken axle.

or a C-spanner. *This threads on counterclockwise.* **CAUTION: Tighten both the sprocket and the lockring securely, or else the sprocket could unscrew.** If you are working on a Mattatuck or Shimano 3.3.3 hub, install the sprocket onto the drive screw, with the lugs on the inside surface of the sprocket indexing with the recesses in the drive screw. Secure it by snapping the sprocket lockring over the lip on the drive screw. Tap the lockring lightly into its groove with a hammer and drift punch. Install the axle washer and axle nut.

Finally, replace the wheel (page 72).

③③ Install the sprocket. If you are working on a Hawthorne, New Departure, or Nankai hub, thread the sprocket onto the drive screw and tighten it securely by pedaling forward or with a sprocket vise. Then secure it with the sprocket lockring, using a hammer and punch

OVERHAULING A STURMEY-ARCHER AW OR SIMILAR THREE-SPEED HUB

The step-by-step illustrated instructions in this section cover disassembling, assembling, and adjusting a Sturmey-Archer AW or similar three-speed hub. Overhaul procedures are the same and parts are interchangeable for hubs made under the brand names Styre (Austria), Schwinn-Approved Styre, Brampton, Hercules, NK (Nankai), and SunTour. Sturmey-Archer also makes three-speed hubs with a generator or a cable-operated drum brake in the expanded left side of the hub shell; these hubs are the same as the AW except for the extra generator or brake parts. A detailed exploded drawing of the AW hub in this section shows internal parts.

For photographic clarity, the illustrations were made of a Sturmey-Archer AW hub without the tire, rim, and spokes.

How the Three-speed Hub Works

The Sturmey-Archer three-speed hub has an internal, *planetary* gearing system (named for its resemblance to a solar system with a sun and planets). The *sun pinion* (central gear) on the axle meshes with four *planet pinions* which surround it in a *planet cage;* the planet pinions in turn mesh with an outer *gear ring.* This arrangement makes the gear ring turn faster than the planet cage. Ratchet *pawls* at the outside of the gear ring and planet cage drive the hub shell forward and allow it to freewheel (coast) if you stop pedaling.

In low gear, power goes from the gear ring to the planet cage, which turns more slowly, and then to the outside of the hub. In high gear, power goes the opposite way, from the planet cage to the gear ring, which turns faster, and then to the outside of the hub. The second gear is direct drive through the gear ring, bypassing the planetary-gear system. A sliding cross-shaped *clutch* moved by the shift cable changes the place at which power is applied.

After you have taken out the internal mechanism as described in the following instructions for overhaul, you can turn the sprocket and see how the gear ring and planet cage turn at different speeds as you pull the indicator chain to different positions.

Especially notice how the clutch retracts the gear-ring pawls in low-gear position; then the gear ring can turn faster than the hub shell and let the planet-cage pawls drive. When riding, you'll notice that the planet-cage pawls tick like a clock in second and third gear, since they are turning more slowly than the hub shell.

Sturmey-Archer AW three-speed rear hub. A version with a lightweight aluminum shell is also available.

Problems with Sturmey-Archer Three-speed Hubs

Slips in first gear.

Possible cause:	Corrective action:
Planet cage pawls are sticking or worn.	Rebuild hub.
Control cable is kinked.	Replace cable.

Jumps from first gear to second; slips in second.

Possible cause:	Corrective action:
Cable is too loose.	Adjust cable.
Indicator chain or cable is sticking.	Service cable or chain.
Clutch is worn.	Rebuild hub.

No first or second gear.

Possible cause:	Corrective action:
Cable is very loose or broken.	Adjust or replace cable.

Slips in third gear.

Possible cause:	Corrective action:
Cable is too tight.	Adjust cable.
Clutch surfaces of pinion pins are worn.	Rebuild hub.
Clutch is worn.	Rebuild hub.
Clutch spring is weak.	Rebuild hub.

Jumps from third to second.

Possible cause:	Corrective action:
Gear ring pawls are sticking.	Rebuild hub.

Runs roughly.

Possible cause:	Corrective action:
Chain is too tight.	Adjust chain.
Lubrication is poor.	Add oil.
Bearing cones are too tight.	Adjust cones.
Axle is bent.	Rebuild hub.
Dustcap or bearing retainer is bent.	Rebuild hub.
There are too many balls in the ball ring.	Rebuild hub.
One pawl of a pair is sticking.	Rebuild hub.

Tools and Supplies You Will Need

Hammer
Drift punch
Adjustable wrench

Vise (or a second adjustable wrench)
15mm cone wrench
Thin-bladed screwdriver
Grease
Cycle oil *(not "household" oil!)*

Parts You Will Need

Two ball cages (bearing retainers), part HSA 284
24 ³⁄₁₆-inch bearing balls
Two low-gear pawls, part HSA 111
Four pawl springs, part HSA 120
Two pawls for gear ring, part HSA 119

Other Parts Likely Needing Replacement

Four planet pinions, part HSA 115
Clutch, part HSA 117
Sprocket (part number depends on size)

Preliminary Steps

Read chapter introduction (page 209).
Make sure you don't just have a cable problem (page 211).
Remove the wheel (page 69).

Disassembling

After removing the axle nuts, axle washers, and indicator spindle, proceed with the following steps.

① Make a note of the location of the two sprocket spacer washers; one or both may be on the outside. Also note whether the dish of the sprocket faces outward or inward. Then remove the sprocket lockring by prying it out of its recess in the driver with a narrow-bladed screwdriver.

② Lift off the sprocket, washers, and sprocket dustcap.

③ Remove the *left*-side locknut by turning it counterclockwise. Remove the axle spacer washer(s), cone lockwasher, and cone from the axle. Make a note of the number and thickness of spacer washers, or thread them on a wire so you can replace them as they were before.

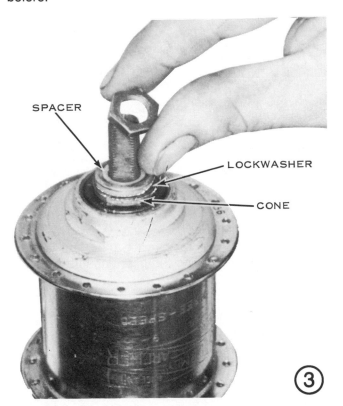

SPACER

LOCKWASHER

CONE

③

④

④ Loosen the ball ring by turning it counterclockwise with a hammer and drift punch or a special Sturmey-Archer spanner. To avoid damage if using a hammer and punch, cushion the rim or leave the inflated tire on the wheel. Continue to rotate the ball ring until it is free of the threads in the hub shell.

⑤ Lift the complete internal assembly straight up and out of the hub shell. **CAUTION: Be careful to keep the pawl pins, pawls, and springs from falling out and becoming lost.**

⑥ Clamp the assembly in a vise in a horizontal position, with the jaws gripping the axle flats at the left end. Remove the locknut, spacer washers if any, lockwasher, and cone from the axle. Thread them on a wire or make a note of the number and thickness of spacer washers.

⑦ Slide the driver off the axle.

⑧ Remove the clutch spring. Take off the spring cap, if so equipped.

⑨ Pull the right-hand ball ring free of the gear ring.

⑤

⑩ Disengage and remove the gear ring from the planet pinions by pulling the gear ring straight off.

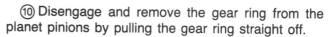

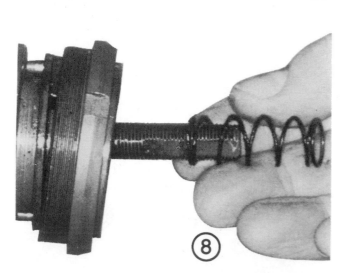

⑪ Remove the thrust washer and thrust ring, and then pull out the axle key.

⑫ Slide the clutch off the axle, then the clutch sleeve.

If you are working on a five-speed hub, turn now to step ① on page 278.

⑬ Disengage the internal teeth of the planet cage from the sun gear by pulling the cage straight off, and then withdraw it from the axle.

⑭ Hold the planet cage in your hand, with the gears

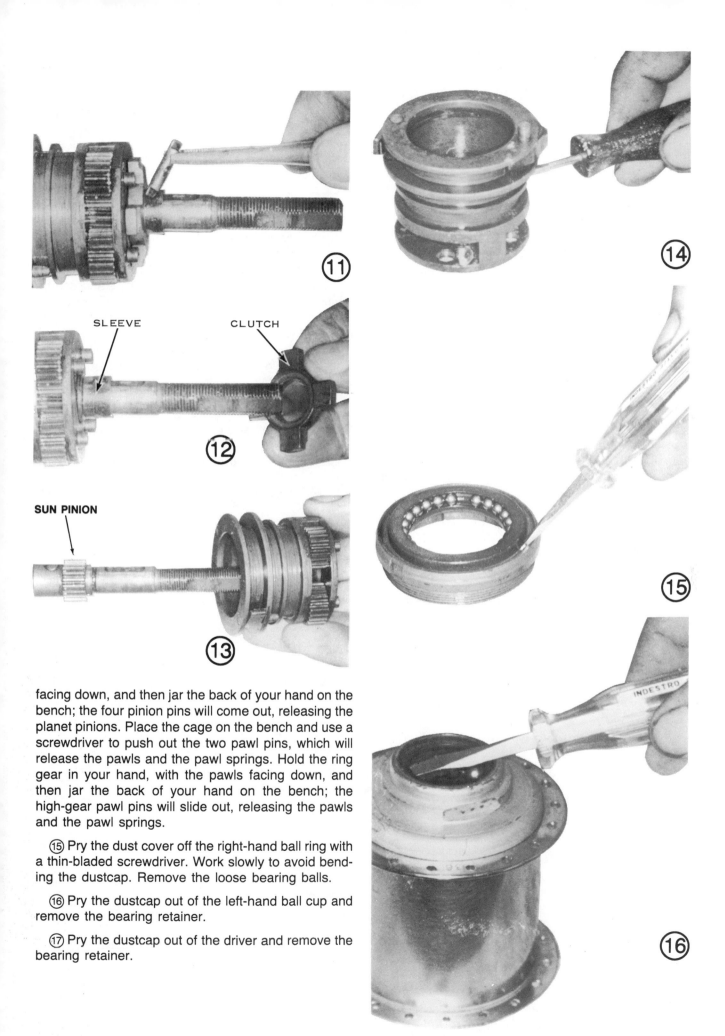

SLEEVE   CLUTCH

⑪

⑫

SUN PINION

⑬

⑭

⑮

⑯

facing down, and then jar the back of your hand on the bench; the four pinion pins will come out, releasing the planet pinions. Place the cage on the bench and use a screwdriver to push out the two pawl pins, which will release the pawls and the pawl springs. Hold the ring gear in your hand, with the pawls facing down, and then jar the back of your hand on the bench; the high-gear pawl pins will slide out, releasing the pawls and the pawl springs.

⑮ Pry the dust cover off the right-hand ball ring with a thin-bladed screwdriver. Work slowly to avoid bending the dustcap. Remove the loose bearing balls.

⑯ Pry the dustcap out of the left-hand ball cup and remove the bearing retainer.

⑰ Pry the dustcap out of the driver and remove the bearing retainer.

(17)

Cleaning and Inspecting

Clean all parts in solvent and rinse them, or wipe them dry with a lintless cloth. Keep all cleaned parts on paper towels to avoid contamination. Cover them with a clean towel to keep grit from entering the internal parts and bearings. A tiny piece of grit can do a tremendous amount of damage if allowed to work on a part over an extended period of time.

It is best to replace the two bearing retainers and the loose balls rather than to inspect them.

Inspect the bearing surface of the left-hand ball cup in the hub shell, both cones, the driver, and the ball ring for scores (scratchlike marks) and pits. Check both cones for stripped threads.

A worn or pitted left ball cup in a steel shell can be replaced; remove the ball cup only if necessary. Ball cups with wrench flats unscrew *clockwise*. A ball cup without wrench flats has a splined fitting and can be pounded out using a hammer and a block of wood. Support the left side of the hub shell on two other blocks of wood.

Inspect the axle for damaged or stripped threads. Check the sun gear on the axle for chipped or worn teeth. Check the axle slot to be sure the edges have not been rounded.

Inspect the planet pinions for chipped or worn teeth. Check the small end of the pinion pins for wear.

Inspect the clutch for worn driving arms.

Inspect the high- and low-gear pawls for worn driving edges.

Check the dustcaps to be sure they are not bent,

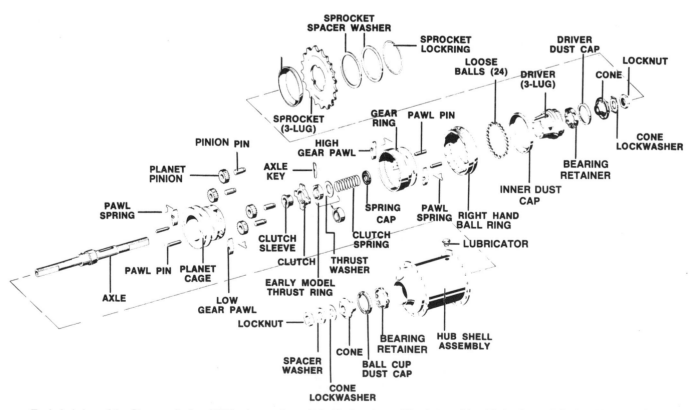

Exploded view of the Sturmey-Archer AW three-speed rear hub. Most parts are interchangeable with the Styre, Schwinn-Approved Styre, Brampton, Hercules, SunTour, and Nankai hubs.

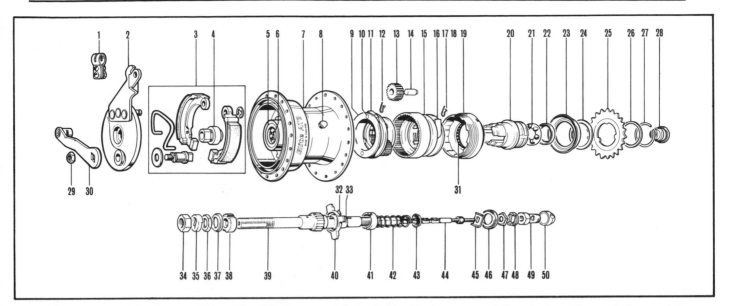

Exploded view of the Sturmey-Archer Elite AT3 three-speed hub with drum brake, representative of other Sturmey-Archer models incorporating a drum brake or generator in the left side. Except for the narrower planet cage, the gear mechanism is identical to that of the AW hub.

ITEM	DESCRIPTION	ITEM	DESCRIPTION
1	Brake-arm clip assembly	26	Sprocket spacing washer
2	Brake plate and arm assembly	27	Sprocket circlip
3	Brake shoes	28	Cone assembly right-hand
4	Left-hand cone	29	Brake lever nut
5	Cone dust cover	30	Brake lever assembly
6	Ball cage assembly left-hand	31	Inner dustcap
7	Hub shell assembly	32	Axle key
8	Lubricator	33	Clutch sleeve
9	Planet cage	34	Axle nut left-hand
10	Pawl pin	35	Serrated lockwasher
11	Left-hand low-gear pawl	36	Cone locknut
12	Pawl spring	37	Spacing washer
13	Planet pinion	38	Cone adjuster
14	Pinion pin	39	Axle with sun pinion
15	Gear ring	40	Clutch
16	Right-hand pawl for gear ring	41	Thrust ring
17	Pawl spring	42	Clutch spring
18	Pawl pin	43	Clutch spring cap
19	Right-hand ball ring	44	Gear indicator
20	Driver	45	Cone lockwasher
21	Ball cage assembly right-hand	46	Spacing washer
22	Outer dustcap	47	Cone locknut
23	Sprocket dustcap	48	Serrated lockwasher
24	Sprocket spacing washer	49	Axle nut right-hand
25	Sprocket	50	Indicator guard

crimped, or distorted, which could have happened during disassembly.

Inspect the high- and low-gear pawl-cage assemblies for cracks around the pawl-pin holes. Check the pawls for worn driving edges. Inspect the internal gear of the gear ring for worn or chipped teeth.

Check the axle key to be sure it is not bent, the edges are not rounded, and the threads in the key are not stripped.

Inspect the hub shell for chipped or worn ratchet teeth. Check the flanges of the shell for cracks.

Inspect the clutch spring for length and tension. The pawl springs should be replaced to ensure proper service.

Inspect the internal splines of the gear ring for wear.

Inspect the locknuts for stripped or damaged threads. Check the ears of the right-hand lockwasher to be sure they are not cracked or bent.

Inspect the sprocket for wear to the driving faces of the teeth. Consider replacing the sprocket with one of another size to improve the gear ratio (see page 207).

LONG LEG OF SPRING

(18)

Assembling

(18) Insert a low-gear (straight) pawl and new spring in the cage slot, with the long leg of the spring riding against the planet cage as shown, and the hook end pushing against the pawl. **CAUTION: New pawl springs must be installed to ensure proper service.** Push the pawl and spring into the slot until the hole in the pawl aligns with the hole in the cage flange, and then push the pawl pin into position, with the flat end of the pin facing up. When properly installed, the head of the pin will be flush with the surface of the cage flange, the pawl will be forced outward by spring tension, and the long end of the pawl will be facing out. Install the second pawl in a similar manner. Cover the ends of the pins with a light coating of multipurpose grease to hold them in place.

(19) Carefully turn the planet cage end for end on the bench to keep from jarring out the pawl pins. Slide one of the planet pinions into place, with the pin hole aligned with the hole in the cage flange. Insert one of the pinion pins into position, with the shoulder end of the pin facing up, as shown. Install the other three planet pinions in a similar manner.

(20) Position a new pawl spring on one of the high-gear (angled) pawls, with the loop of the spring aligned over the pawl hole. Face the long leg of the spring toward the gear-ring slot; the hook end must be under the pawl, as shown. **CAUTION: Always use new pawl springs to ensure proper service.**

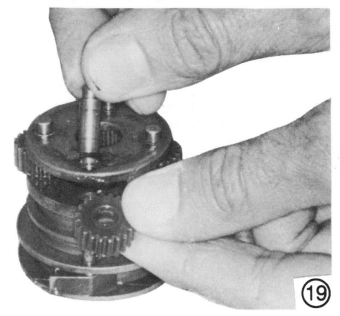

(19)

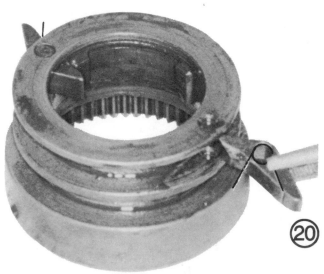

(20)

㉑ Push in on the pawl, against the tension of the spring, and then insert one of the pins, with the tapered end facing down. Install the other pawl, spring, and pin in a similar manner. Cover the ends of the pins with a light coating of multipurpose grease to hold them in place.

㉒ Apply a light coating of multipurpose grease to the bearing race inside the ball ring.

㉓ Place 24 ³⁄₁₆-inch bearing balls into the bearing race of the ball ring.

㉑

㉒

㉓

㉔ Position the dustcap on the ball ring, flat side up, and tap it lightly into place with a hammer until it is fully seated. Hold the hammer flat, and away from the hole through the center of the dustcap, to avoid denting the dustcap. Note the one-ball clearance, which is clearly shown in this illustration.

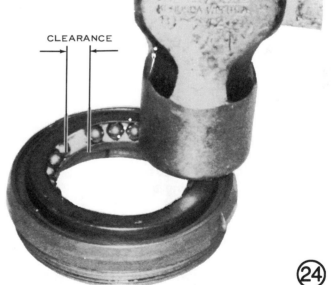

㉔

㉕ Pack one of the small bearing-retainer assemblies (ball cages) with a generous amount of multipurpose grease. Work the lubricant through the retainer with your fingers. Insert the lubricated retainer into the driver, with the flat side of the retainer facing up. Spread another light coating of lubricant over the bearing assembly.

㉖ Install the dustcap over the bearing assembly, with the flat side of the cap facing *down.* Tap the cap

lightly with a hammer until it is fully seated. **CAUTION: Any damage to the cap will cause the cone to drag and prevent a proper bearing adjustment.**

㉗ Pack one of the small ball-bearing-retainer assemblies (ball cages) with a generous amount of multipurpose grease. Work the lubricant through the retainer with your fingers. Insert the lubricated retainer into the ball cup in the left side of the hub shell, with the flat side of the retainer facing up. Spread another light coating of lubricant over the bearing assembly.

Install the dustcap over the bearing assembly, with the flat side of the cap facing *down.* Tap the cap lightly with a hammer until it is fully seated. **CAUTION: Any damage to the cap will cause the cone to drag and prevent a proper bearing adjustment.**

㉘ Clamp the axle in the vise in a horizontal position, with the slotted end facing out and the jaws gripping the axle flats. Slide the assembled planet-cage assembly onto the axle, with the planet pinions facing out, as shown. Work the cage back and forth until the pinions mesh with the teeth of the sun pinion on the axle, and then push the cage on as far as it will go.

㉙ Apply a small amount of premium-quality cycle oil to the pawls and to the planet pinions.

㉚ Slide the clutch sleeve onto the axle, with the flanged end toward the planet cage.

㉛ Install the clutch, with the notched ends of the ears facing away from the planet cage. Turn the clutch so the ears are flat against the surface of the planet cage between the pinion pins.

BEARING RETAINER   DUST CAP

LEFT-HAND BALL CUP

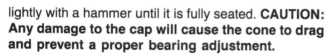

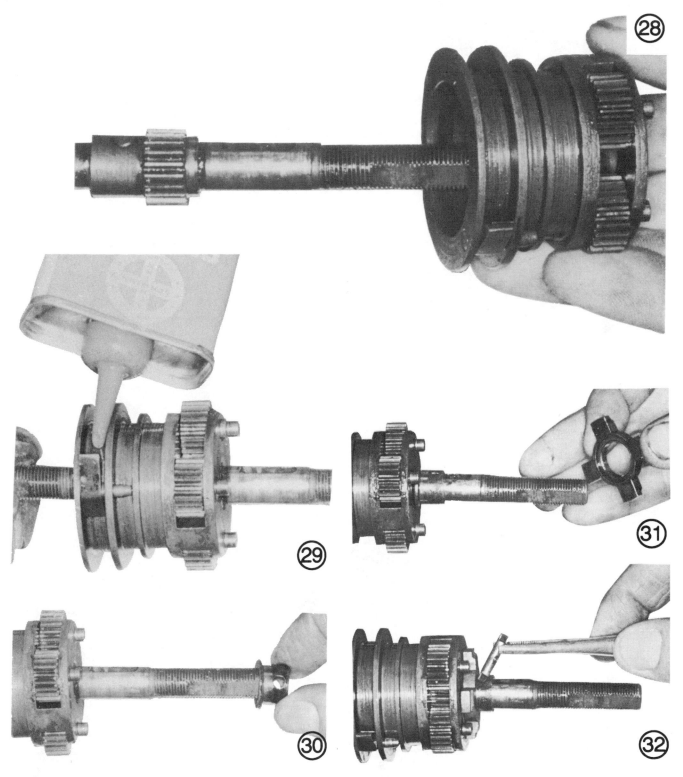

㉜ Insert the axle key through the hole in the clutch sleeve and through the slot in the axle, with the flat ends facing away from the clutch.

㉝ Slide the solid shaft end (with the short threads) of the indicator-spindle assembly through the hollow axle, and then thread it into the axle key by turning it clockwise. After you have tightened the indicator-spindle assembly finger-tight, check to be sure it is threaded properly into the axle key by pulling out on the spindle. It must not come out. This is necessary to assure that the axle key will remain in its correct position and will not be disturbed during installation of the remaining parts.

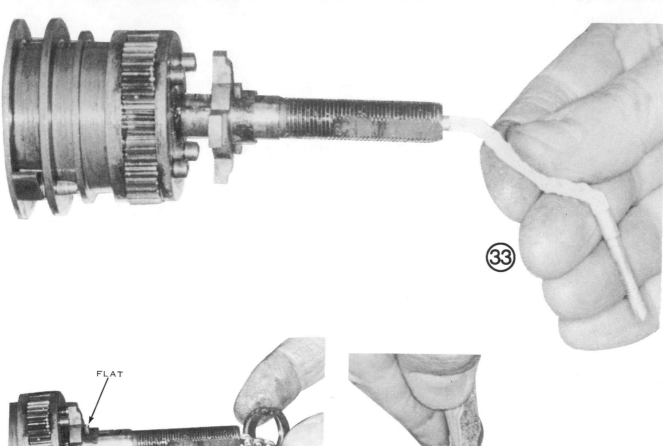

FLAT

㉞ Install the thrust ring, with the cutouts indexed over the flats of the axle key.

㉟ Hold the thrust ring firmly in place, and then check for 0.005–0.008-inch clearance between the thrust ring and the surface of the clutch. If the clearance is less than 0.005 inch, install a new axle key.

㊱ Slip the thrust washer onto the axle. *NOTE: Some Sturmey-Archer AW hubs do not have a thrust washer. If the thrust ring has a smaller opening at one end, a thrust washer is not required. If the thrust ring has the same size openings at both ends, a thrust washer must be installed.* Push the gear ring over the planet-cage assembly as far as it will go, with the internal teeth indexing with the teeth of the planet pinions.

㊲ Depress the two high-gear pawls, and then twist the right-hand ball ring clockwise into place over the

pawls. The ball ring should ratchet as it is turned clockwise and should engage the pawls when turned counterclockwise.

㊳ Slide the assembled driver unit onto the axle, and then turn it clockwise while pushing it into place. When

PLANET GEAR   THRUST WASHER

THRUST RING

36

38

37

39

40

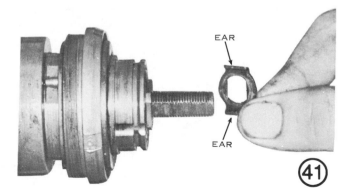

EAR

EAR

41

the slots in the driver index over the ears of the clutch, you will feel the driver engage and move slightly farther into the ball ring and ring-gear assembly.

㊴ Install a new clutch spring onto the axle and then the spring cap, if you removed a cap during disassembly. **CAUTION: A new clutch spring must be installed to ensure proper service.** Check that the spring cap will fit through the hole in the driver. If not, leave it off; it will only cause trouble.

㊵ Thread one of the cones onto the axle finger-tight, and then back it off a quarter of a turn. Remove the indicator-spindle assembly from the axle by twisting it counterclockwise until it is free of the axle key and then pulling it out.

㊶ Slide the cone lockwasher onto the axle, with the internal flats of the washer indexing with the axle flats. Twist the cone not more than a quarter of a turn counterclockwise to enable the ears of the lockwasher to engage the flats of the cone. **CAUTION: The purpose of this adjustment is to position the internals of the hub. If you treat this as a bearing adjustment, as tight as possible without binding, the hub will drag.**

㊷ Thread the locknut onto the axle, and then tighten it securely against the cone lockwasher.

㊸ Remove the assembly from the vise. Place the hub (wheel) in a horizontal position, with the tire against your chest and the left-hand ball cup of the hub facing up, as shown. *NOTE: For photographic clarity, the wheel and spokes are not shown.* Insert the assembled unit into the hub shell, with the low-gear pawls facing up. Turn the internal-drive assembly opposite

the direction of pedaling to allow the low-gear pawls to index with the ratchet inside the hub shell. When the pawls index, you will feel the assembly move farther into the hub, and the threads of the right-hand ball ring will engage the internal threads of the hub shell. When this occurs, turn the ball ring in the direction of pedaling until it is finger-tight.

㊹ Thread the cone onto the axle and back it off one turn.

㊺ Install the cone lockwasher, with the internal flats indexing with the flats of the axle. Slide the thick washer down the axle, with the flat side of the washer against the surface of the lockwasher.

㊻ Thread the locknut onto the axle against the cone.

㊼ Tighten the ball ring firmly by turning it in a clockwise direction with a drift punch and hammer, as shown.

Save the rim and floor or bench from damage by resting the wheel on the inflated tire.

㊽ Adjust the cone by tightening or loosening it with a cone wrench to obtain a trace of sideplay when the

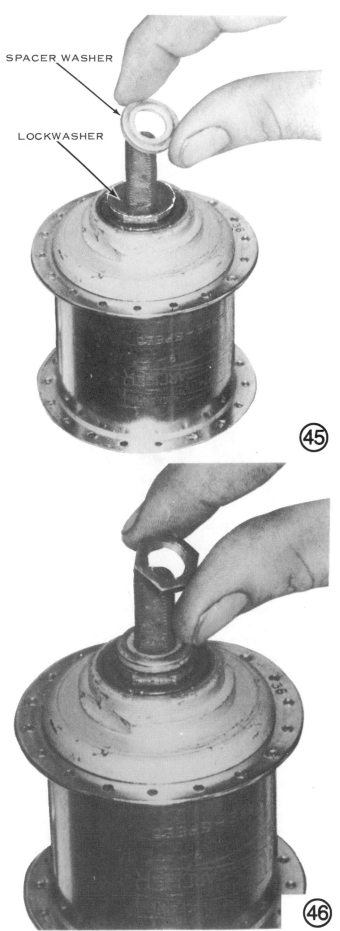

SPACER WASHER

LOCKWASHER

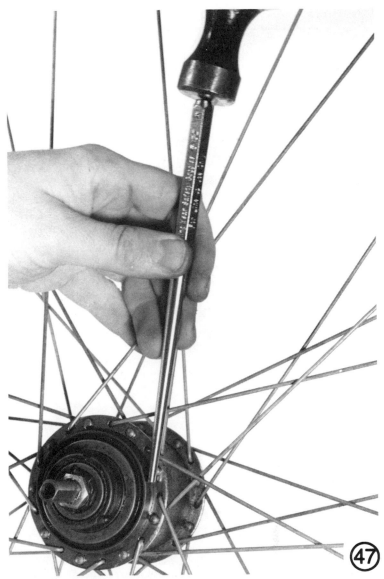

wheel rim is moved up and down, and then tighten the locknut. Hold each end of the axle with your fingers. Slowly twist the axle with the thumb and forefinger of each hand—the wheel should not turn. If it does, the adjusting cone is too tight and must be loosened slightly. Loosen the locknut, and then rotate the cone counterclockwise approximately an eighth of a turn. Retighten the locknut while holding the cone with a cone wrench. Recheck for sideplay and rotation as before. The cone is properly adjusted when the wheel rotates freely and comes to rest gradually, with the valve stem or spoke reflector at the lowest point of the wheel, and there is only the slightest trace of sideplay.

Another, very precise test for sideplay is to see whether the sprocket drags as you rotate the wheel forward. There should be a slight drag from the pawls, but if there is a heavy pull, the cones are too tight. Try to rock the sprocket from side to side. It should rock only slightly. Using these tests, you can adjust the bearings so that there is no noticeable sideplay at the rim.

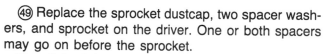

Replace the sprocket dustcap, two spacer washers, and sprocket on the driver. One or both spacers may go on before the sprocket.

The dish of the sprocket may face either inward or outward, depending on the desired chainline. Normally, replace the parts as they were before disassembling the hub.

Spread the snaring over the flange of the ball cup and tap it lightly into its groove with a hammer and drift punch.

Finishing Up

Add oil at the lubricator and the hollow axle end(s) (page 211.) **CAUTION: Failure to add oil will cause rapid hub wear.**

Install the wheel (page 72).

Adjust the cable (page 212).

OVERHAULING A SHIMANO THREE-SPEED HUB

The step-by-step illustrated instructions in this section cover disassembling, assembling, and adjusting Shimano three-speed hubs. The hub is identified by the stamping on the hub shell. Detailed exploded drawings showing all internal parts appear later in this section.

The Shimano three-speed hub works very much like the Sturmey-Archer (page 240), except that the entire planetary gear assembly is shifted left and right to select the different gears.

The hub has been sold in six models: FA type, F type, G type, and three versions of the newer cartridge type. All models are very similar. The cartridge type allows removal of the entire internal assembly from the hub shell as a unit. The cartridge type also has simplified pawls without pawl pins.

The many types of pawls make it easy to get the wrong ones, and the most recent model is the most durable. For this reason, many mechanics prefer to replace the entire internal assembly or driver, gearring, and planet-cage assemblies. They are available as preassembled units, and they are not expensive.

Cartridge-type internals can be installed in earlier hub shells; save the old hub's right ball cup to use with the cartridge internal assembly.

Shimano three-speed rear hub.

Problems with Shimano Three-speed Hubs

Gear is higher than selected gear.

Possible cause:	*Corrective action:*
Cable is too loose.	Adjust cable.

Hub slips forward.

Possible cause:	*Corrective action:*
Pawls are faulty.	Rebuild hub.

First gear instead of second.

Possible cause:	*Corrective action:*
Cable is too tight.	Adjust cable.
Return spring is faulty.	Rebuild hub.

Only runs in third gear.

Possible cause:	*Corrective action:*
Right-hand sliding key is out of position.	Rebuild hub.

Running is stiff or noisy.

Possible cause:	*Corrective action:*
Gear teeth are worn or chipped.	Rebuild hub.
Cones are too tight.	Adjust cones.
Axle is bent.	Rebuild hub.
Chain is too tight.	Adjust chain.
Broken parts are loose in hub.	Rebuild hub.

Tools and Supplies You Will Need

Adjustable wrench or 17mm wrench

15mm cone wrench

Shimano ball-cup tool XB-320 (except for cartridge hub)

Small flat-bladed screwdriver

Multipurpose grease

Good cycle oil (*not* "household" oil)

Parts You Will Need

CAUTION: Label parts when you buy them. Many look similar.

Hub Model	FA,F,G	Cartridge (older)	Cartridge G-3S23
Ball retainer A (2)	321 9022	321 9022	3-321 9022
Ball retainer B	321 9023	321 9081	3-321 9081
For ring gear:			
Pawl spring A (2)	321 1100		
Ring spring A		322 1100	322 1100
For driver:			
Pawl spring B (4)	321 1200		
Ring spring B (2)		322 1200	322 1200
For planet cage:			
Pawl spring C (2)	321 1300		
Ring spring C		322 1300	322 1300

Other Parts Likely Needing Replacement

NOTE: Pay special attention to the pawls. They differ from model to model. The RH cone for the newest cartridge model is black-plated. It is not interchangeable with earlier ones.

Hub Model	FA,F,G	Cartridge through 1981	Cartridge SG-3S21	Cartridge G-3S23
Ring-gear pawls:				
Pawl A (2)	321 0500	321 0500	321 0500	321 0500
Driver pawls:				
Pawl B (4)	321 0600			
Pawl F (2)		322 0600	322 0600	322 0600
Pawl A (2)		321 0500		
Pawl I (2)			322 0700	322 0700
Planet-cage pawls:				
Pawl C (2)	321 0700			
Pawl A (2)		321 0500		
Pawl I (2)			322 0700	322 0700
Driver	321 7100	322 9032	322 9032	322 9032
LH cone	321 9025	322 9025	322 9025	3-322 9025
RH cone	321 9024	321 9024	321 9024	3-321 9024
RH ball cup	321 5600			

Complete Internal Assembly and Modules

NOTE: Replace the complete internal assembly or modules to save time and to update the pawl design. The cartridge assembly will fit earlier hubs, as described above. Install the driver and ring gear listed here at the same time to avoid compatibility problems.

Internal assembly with 153mm axle, part 3-322-9902
Internal assembly with 173mm axle, part 3-322-9922
Complete ring gear, part 3-322 9014
Complete planet cage, part 3-322 9018
Complete driver, part 3-322-9009-2

Preliminary Steps

Read chapter introduction (page 209).
Make sure you don't just have a cable problem (page 211).
Remove the wheel (page 69).

Disassembly

① Make a note whether the dish of the sprocket faces inward or outward. Snap the sprocket lockring out of its recess with a narrow-bladed screwdriver. Lift off the sprocket and dustcap.
Cartridge: The latest (1983) model has a sealing ring behind the dustcap.

② Hold the right adjusting cone with a 15mm cone wrench; loosen the locknut with a 17mm cone wrench or adjustable wrench, then remove the nut and cone.
Cartridge: Wait to do this step later.

③ Remove the driver unit and ball-bearing-retainer assembly from the axle.
Cartridge: Wait to do this step later.

④ Install a Shimano ball cup tool over the end of the axle. Holding the tool with a vise or large wrench, remove the right ball cup.
Cartridge: Omit this step. The ball cup is not removable.

⑤ Turn the assembly end for end. Remove the left locknut, cone lockwasher, unthreaded cone, and then the spring.

Cartridge: The cone is threaded and there is no locknut; otherwise, instructions are the same.

⑥ Lift off the hub shell.

⑦ Turn the hub shell end for end and pop the dustcap out with a screwdriver. Work around the edge of the cap and be careful not to crimp or distort it.

⑧ Remove the bearing retainer.

⑨ Pull out the short and long axle keys.

Cartridge: Same except that there may be a washer instead of the first axle key. Remove only this washer or the first axle key. If there are two axle keys, they are of the same length.

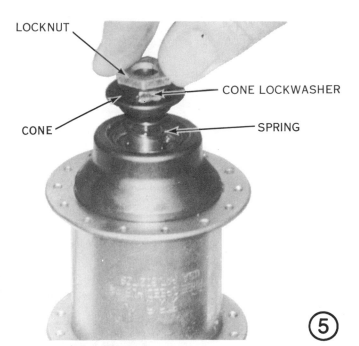

⑤

⑥

⑩ Withdraw the axle from the gear-ring ratchet and planet-cage ratchet assemblies.

Cartridge: Same, then remove the remaining axle key, the driver, and the large ball retainer, locknut, and cone.

⑪ Pry the cartridge retaining ring out of the slot in the gear-ring ratchet assembly, using a narrow-bladed screwdriver, and then remove it.

⑫ Remove the roller cover. Lightly tap and rotate the entire assembly on the bench at an angle to remove the four rollers.

⑦

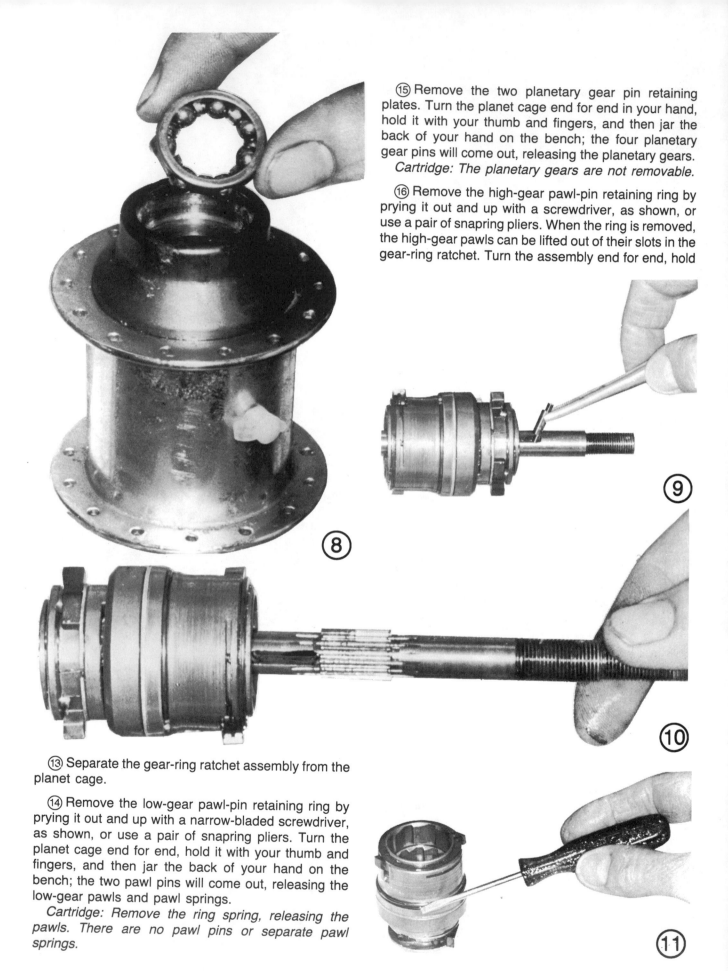

⑮ Remove the two planetary gear pin retaining plates. Turn the planet cage end for end in your hand, hold it with your thumb and fingers, and then jar the back of your hand on the bench; the four planetary gear pins will come out, releasing the planetary gears.

Cartridge: The planetary gears are not removable.

⑯ Remove the high-gear pawl-pin retaining ring by prying it out and up with a screwdriver, as shown, or use a pair of snapring pliers. When the ring is removed, the high-gear pawls can be lifted out of their slots in the gear-ring ratchet. Turn the assembly end for end, hold

⑬ Separate the gear-ring ratchet assembly from the planet cage.

⑭ Remove the low-gear pawl-pin retaining ring by prying it out and up with a narrow-bladed screwdriver, as shown, or use a pair of snapring pliers. Turn the planet cage end for end, hold it with your thumb and fingers, and then jar the back of your hand on the bench; the two pawl pins will come out, releasing the low-gear pawls and pawl springs.

Cartridge: Remove the ring spring, releasing the pawls. There are no pawl pins or separate pawl springs.

it with your thumb and fingers, and then jar the back of your hand on the bench; the two pawl spring pins will come out, releasing the springs.

Cartridge and F and G type: Remove the ring spring, releasing the pawls. There are no pawl pins or separate pawl springs.

⑰ Remove the pawl-pin retaining ring from the driver assembly by prying it up with a screwdriver, as shown. Turn the assembly end for end, hold it with your thumb and fingers, and then jar the back of your hand

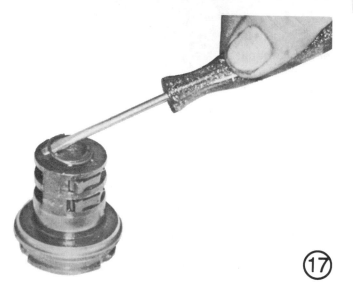

⑰

⑱

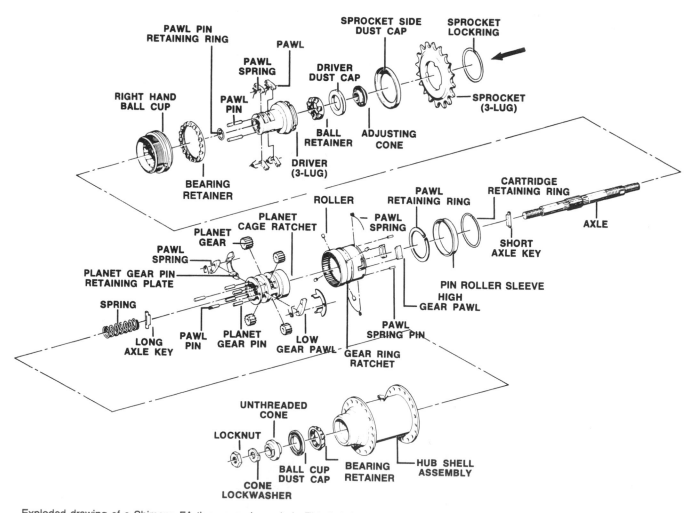

Exploded drawing of a Shimano FA three-speed rear hub. This hub is almost identical to models F and FG.

on the bench; the two long pawl pins will come out, releasing the four pawls and pawl springs.

Cartridge: Remove the ring springs over the end of the driver, releasing the four pawls. There are no pawl pins or separate pawl springs.

(18) With a thin-bladed screwdriver, pry the dustcap from the driver. Remove the bearing-retainer assembly.

Cleaning and Inspecting

Clean all parts in solvent and rinse them, or wipe them dry with a lintless cloth. Keep all cleaned parts on paper towels to avoid contamination. Cover them with a clean towel to keep grit from entering the internal parts and bearings. A tiny piece of grit can do a tremendous amount of damage if allowed to work on a part over an extended period of time.

It is simplest just to replace the three bearing retainers rather than to try to inspect them.

Inspect the bearing surface of both cones for scores (scratchlike marks), pits, or other damage. Check the cones for stripped threads.

Inspect the axle for stripped threads, and for worn or chipped teeth on the sun gear. Check the two axle slots for wear (rounded edges).

Check the dustcaps to be sure they are not bent, crimped, or distorted, which could have happened during disassembly.

Inspect the hub shell for damage, including chipped or worn ratchet teeth. Inspect the bearing cup for scores, pits, or excessive wear. Check the flanges of the hub shell for cracks.

Inspect all the pawls for worn or damaged driving edges.

NOTE: If the hub has been completely disassembled, all the pawl springs should be replaced to

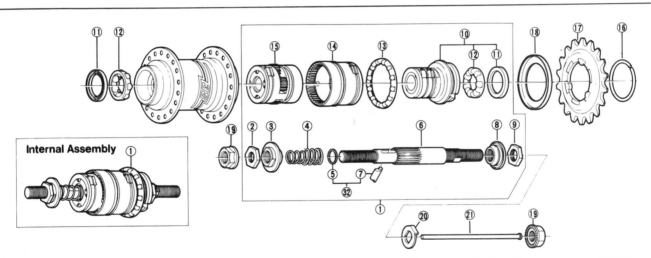

Exploded drawing of a Shimano cartridge-type three-speed hub. This hub can be removed from the shell without the use of a special tool.

ITEM	DESCRIPTION	ITEM	DESCRIPTION
1	Internal assembly	12	Ball retainer
2	Locknut	13	Ball retainer
3	Left-hand cone	14	Complete ratchet A
4	Clutch spring	15	Complete ratchet B
5	Washer for clutch spring	16	Snapring C
6	Hub axle	17	Sprocket
7	Sliding key BR	18	Dustcap
8	Right-hand cone	19	Flange nut
9	Locknut	20	Non-turn washer
10	Complete driver	21	Push rod
11	Dustcap A		

ensure proper service. The thrust spring should also be replaced.

Inspect the gear-ring ratchet, planet-cage ratchet, and planetary gears for chipped or worn teeth.

Inspect the right-hand ball cup for chipped or worn ratchet teeth. Check the bearing surface for scores or pits. Check for stripped threads.

Inspect the bearing surface of the driver for scores or pits.

Check both axle keys to be sure they are not bent or damaged.

Inspect the axle nuts for stripped or damaged threads.

Inspect the sprocket for wear to the driving faces of the teeth. Consider replacing the sprocket with one of another size to improve the gear ratio (see page 207).

Assembling

⑲ Lay the driver on the bench, resting on its side. Place a new pawl spring on the machined recess side of one of the pawls, with the hooked end of the spring catching over the edge of the pawl and the straight end of the spring perpendicular to the pawl. Align the spring coil over the hole in the pawl. **CAUTION: Be sure both ends of the spring are on the same side of the pawl and that the straight end of the spring faces in a counterclockwise direction.** Insert one of the pawl

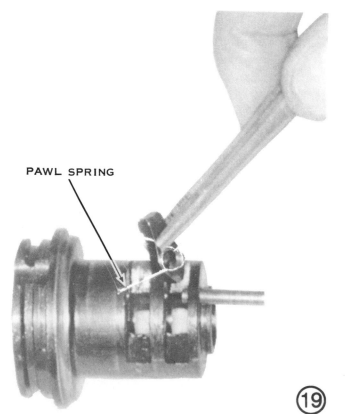

PAWL SPRING

⑲

pins partway into position until it is just barely through the first flange of the driver. Hold the spring and pawl with a pair of tweezers and insert them into one of the upper slots of the driver. When the hole in the pawl aligns with the pin, push the pin through just far enough to retain the pawl and the spring. When properly installed, the pawl can be depressed until it is almost flush with the outside surface of the driver.

Cartridge: Replace pawls A or I and the ring spring nearest the sprocket end of the driver.

⑳ Place another spring on the machined recess of the second pawl, and then insert it into the lower slot of the driver exactly as you did with the first pawl. When the hole in the pawl aligns with the pin, push the pin all the way in to retain the pawl and spring. Install the second set of pawls and springs in the driver in the same manner as for the first set. *NOTE: Late-model Shimano rear hubs use four right-hand-wound springs. Early model hubs used two right-hand- and two left-hand-wound springs. Whether right-hand or left-hand springs are used, be sure the spring is on the recessed surface of the pawl, both ends of the spring are on the same side of the pawl, and the straight end of the spring faces in a counterclockwise direction.*

Cartridge: Replace pawls F and the ring spring nearest the inner end of driver.

㉑ Snap the pawl-pin retaining ring into position, using a narrow-bladed screwdriver. Rotate the ring, if necessary, so the opening in the ring is not centered over one of the pins.

Cartridge: Omit this step. There is no pawl-pin retaining ring.

㉒ Pack the driver ball-bearing-retainer assembly with a generous amount of multipurpose grease. Work the lubricant throughout the bearings and retainer with your fingers. Insert the lubricated bearing assembly

⑳

Ⓜ️ Insert the two planetary-gear-pin retainer plates into position, with the holes in the plate aligned with the holes in the housing.

㉕ Place one of the pawl springs on the machined recess side of a low-gear pawl, with the hook end of the spring over the inside edge of the pawl, and the straight edge perpendicular to the pawl, as shown.

Cartridge: Install pawls A or I in the planet cage with their ring spring. Skip the next two steps.

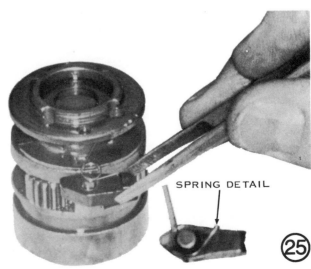

SPRING DETAIL

into the driver, with the flat surface of the retainer facing up. Place the dustcap in the driver, with the flat side facing down. Tap the dustcap lightly with a hammer until it is flush with the surface of the driver. Set the assembled driver aside.

㉓ Stand the planet cage on the bench, with the planetary-gear-pin holes facing up. Place the four planetary gears in position, and then insert the gear pins.

Cartridge: Skip this step and the next step. If planetary gears are worn, the entire ratchet must be replaced.

㉖ Push the pawl into place against the force of the spring until the hole in the pawl aligns with the hole in the housing flange, and then insert the pawl pin. Install the other pawl in the same manner.

㉗ Snap the pawl-pin retaining ring into place, using a thin-bladed screwdriver or snaping pliers. Rotate the ring, if necessary, so the opening in the ring is not over one of the pawl pins.

㉘ Place one of the high-gear pawl springs into position in the recess of the gear-ring ratchet housing, with the coil of the spring facing out and aligned with the spring-pin hole. Insert the spring pin. Position one of the pawls against the spring with the spring in the pawl slot. Push in on the pawl against the force of the spring, and then slide the knobbed end of the pawl into the retaining slot in the housing.

Cartridge: Install pawls A and their ring spring on the gear ring. Skip the next two steps.

㉙ Install the second pawl and spring in the same manner as you did the first one.

㉚ Snap the pawl retaining ring into place, using a thin-bladed screwdriver or snaping pliers. Rotate the ring, if necessary, so the opening in the ring is not directly over one of the pins.

㉛ Lower the assembled gear-ring ratchet unit down over the assembled planet-cage ratchet, as shown.

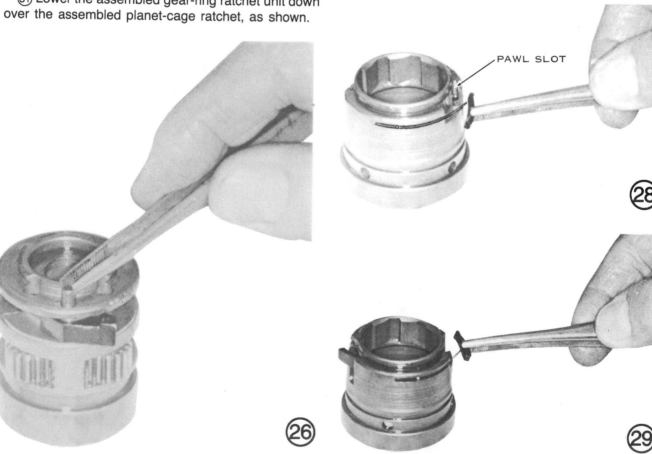

PAWL SLOT

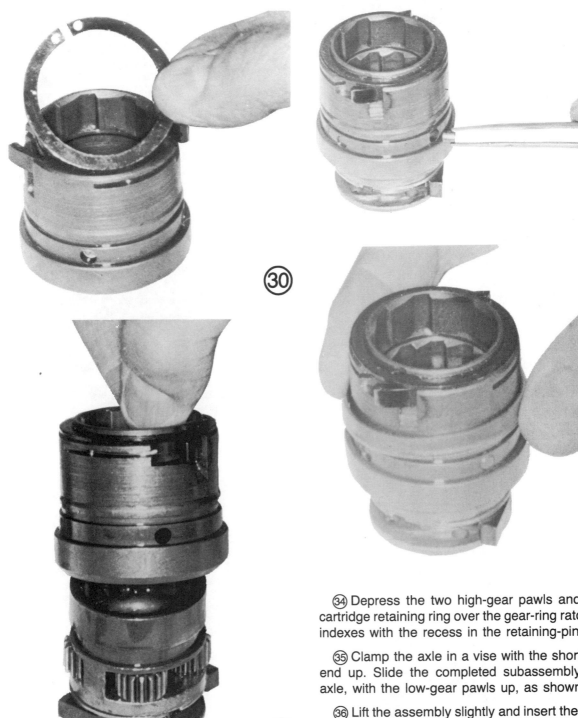

32 Insert the four cartridge retaining pins (rollers), using a small amount of multipurpose grease on the ends of the pins to hold them in place.

33 Slide the retaining-pin sleeve (roller cover) over the gear-ring ratchet, with the flange side down on the lip of the housing.

34 Depress the two high-gear pawls and slide the cartridge retaining ring over the gear-ring ratchet until it indexes with the recess in the retaining-pin sleeve.

35 Clamp the axle in a vise with the short threaded end up. Slide the completed subassembly onto the axle, with the low-gear pawls up, as shown.

36 Lift the assembly slightly and insert the short axle key into the axle slot with the flat side up. While you are holding the assembly, the key should fall to the bottom of the slot. Lower the assembly and you should be able to see the key flats fully indexed against the inner flanges of the planet-cage ratchet assembly. If the key has not dropped into position properly, raise the assembly just a little bit more until the key does drop into place.

37 Rotate the assembly on the axle and lubricate the internal mechanism with premium-quality cycle oil.

㉞

㉟

㊱

㊲

㊳ Install the long axle key in the keyway with the flat side down. The cutouts in the ends of the key should lie against the shoulder of the planet-cage ratchet assembly.

Cartridge: There may be a washer instead of the second axle key. If there are two axle keys, they are of the same length.

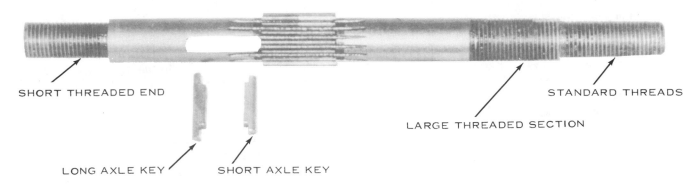

SHORT THREADED END

STANDARD THREADS

LARGE THREADED SECTION

LONG AXLE KEY   SHORT AXLE KEY

Details of the axle used in the Shimano FA three-speed hub. Note the long and short axle key placement as well as the positions of the notches. The cartridge-type hub may use two axle keys of the same length, or the long axle key may be replaced by a small washer.

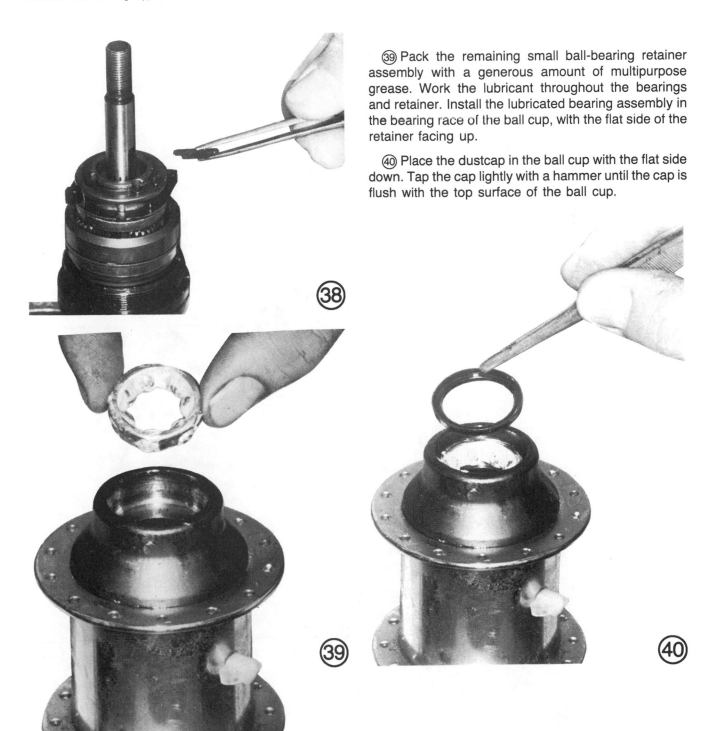

㊳ Pack the remaining small ball-bearing retainer assembly with a generous amount of multipurpose grease. Work the lubricant throughout the bearings and retainer. Install the lubricated bearing assembly in the bearing race of the ball cup, with the flat side of the retainer facing up.

㊵ Place the dustcap in the ball cup with the flat side down. Tap the cap lightly with a hammer until the cap is flush with the top surface of the ball cup.

㊶ Install a new thrust spring on the axle—either end down. Remove the assembly from the vise. Place the hub (wheel) in a horizontal position, with the tire against your chest and the left-hand ball cup of the hub facing up, as shown. *NOTE: For photographic clarity, the wheel and spokes are not shown.* Insert the assembled unit into the threaded end of the shell. Turn the internal-drive assembly counterclockwise to allow the low-gear pawls to index with the ratchet inside the hub shell. When the pawls index, you will feel the assembly move farther into the hub.

Cartridge: Install the thrust spring but do not insert the assembly into the hub shell.

㊷ Slide the unthreaded cone onto the axle against the force of the spring until the cone contacts the ball-bearing-retainer assembly. Hold the cone in place and slide the lockwasher onto the axle until the ears index over the shoulder of the axle. *NOTE: This cone is not adjustable.*

Cartridge: Postpone this step.

㊸ Thread the locknut onto the axle and tighten it firmly against the lockwasher.

Cartridge: Postpone this step.

㊹ Depress the pawls on the gear-ring ratchet assembly and slide the right ball cup over them.

㊶

Thread the ball cup into the hub shell and tighten it with the ball-cup tool.

Cartridge: If installing a cartridge unit in a cartridge shell, the ball cup is preinstalled. If installing a cartridge unit in an old-type shell, thread and tighten the ball cup into the shell, which is still empty. Do not install the cartridge unit yet.

LOCKWASHER

UNTHREADED CONE

SPRING

42

43

44

㊺ Pack the large ball-bearing-retainer assembly with a generous amount of multipurpose grease. Work the lubricant throughout the bearings and retainer with your fingers.

㊻ Push the lubricated ball-bearing assembly into the bearing race of the ball cup, with the flat side of the retainer facing out.

Cartridge: The instructions are the same, but the internal assembly is not yet installed in the hub shell.

㊼ Slide the driver assembly onto the axle.

㊽ Depress the driver pawls. Push and rotate the driver into the gear-ring assembly, allowing the pawls to index with the internal ratchets.

㊾ Slide the threaded cone onto the axle until it engages the large threaded portion, and then rotate it clockwise until it is finger-tight.

㊿ Thread the right locknut onto the axle but leave it loose.

(51) Making sure that the right cone is loose, tighten the left locknut.

Cartridge: Turn down the right cone as far as it will go, and tighten the right locknut against it. Run a teaspoon of oil into the hub shell, holding it tilted so the oil won't run out. Install the cartridge in the shell and thread on the left cone and locknut. The cartridge left cone is threaded, and there is a locknut but no lockwasher. **CAUTION: Failure to add oil will cause rapid wear.**

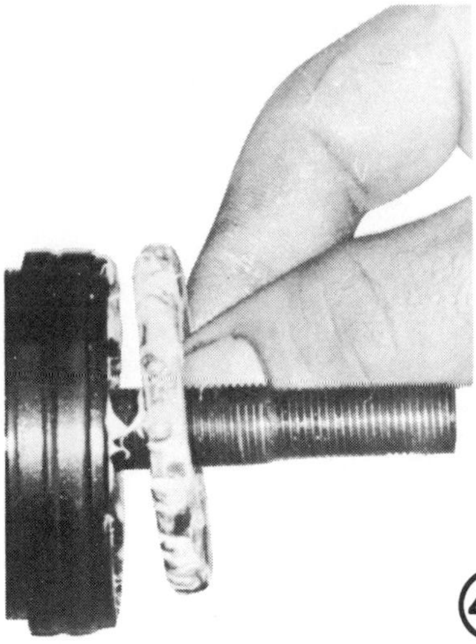

㊻

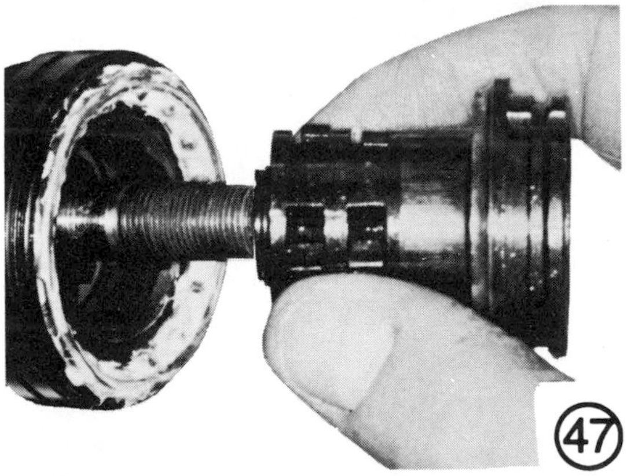

㊼

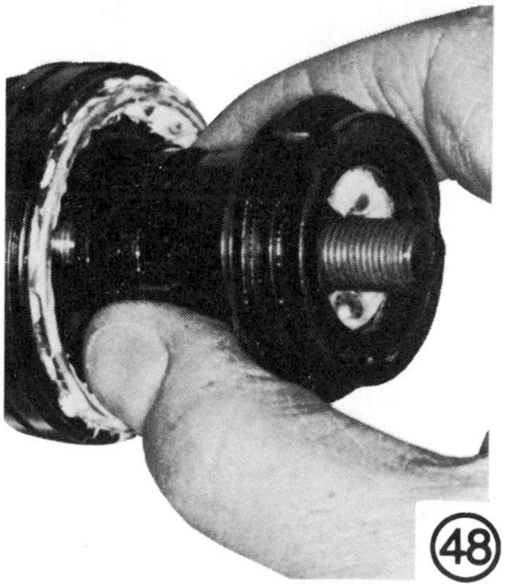

㊽

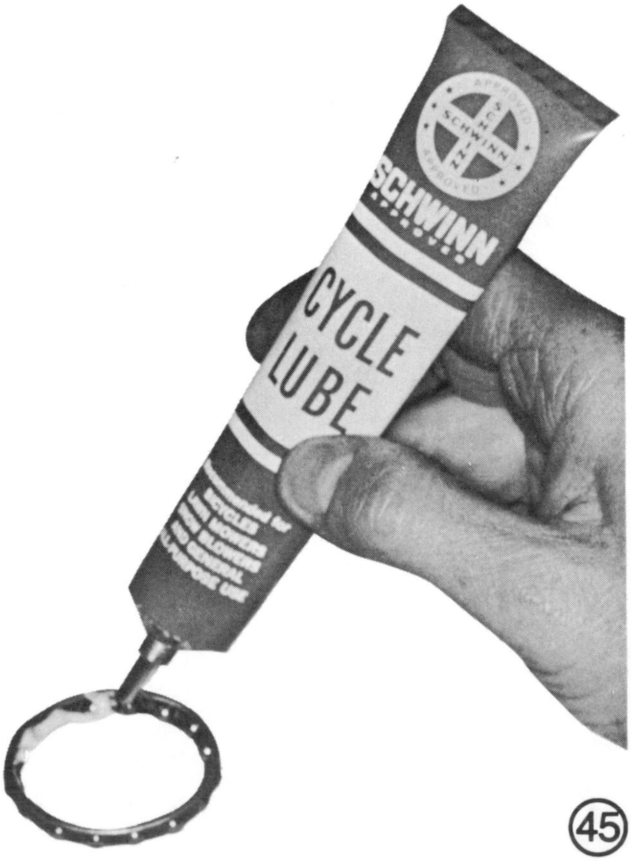

㊺

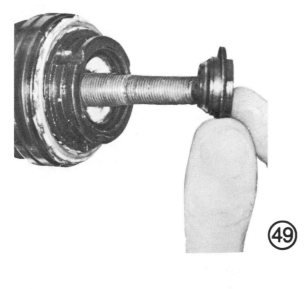

loosened slightly. Back off the locknut on the sprocket end of the axle. Loosen the cone approximately an eighth of a turn, and then retighten the locknut. The cones are properly adjusted when the wheel rotates freely and comes to rest gradually with the valve stem or spoke reflector at the lowest point of the wheel, and there is only the slightest trace of sideplay. **CAUTION: If the cone is adjusted too tight, it will cause binding and scoring of the hub. If the cone is adjusted too loose, it will cause fatigue, which can result in a damaged hub or broken axle.**

Another, very precise test for sideplay is to see whether the sprocket drags as you rotate the wheel forward. There should be a slight drag from the pawls, but not a heavy pull. Try to rock the sprocket from side to side. It should rock only slightly. Using these tests, you can adjust the bearings so that there is no noticeable sideplay at the rim.

Cartridge: Using the same procedure, adjust the left *cone, which is the adjustable cone on this model of hub.*

CAUTION: The adjusting cone of the older hub is on the right side, and that of the cartridge hub is on the left side.

㊾ Hold the locknut with a wrench and tighten the right cone with a thin wrench or cone tool until the cone is snug, and then back it off approximately a quarter of a turn, or until there is just a discernible amount of sideplay when you move the wheel rim up and down. Tighten the locknut securely. Hold each end of the axle with your fingers. Slowly twist the axle with the thumb and forefinger of each hand—the wheel should not turn. If it does turn, the cones are too tight and must be

㊾ Slide the frame lockwasher onto the axle with the ear facing up and the flats indexing with the flats on the axle.

㊼ Install the dustcap on the right-hand ball cup, with the flat side of the cap facing up.

㊽ Install the sprocket, with the lugs on the inner surface of the sprocket indexing with the recesses in the right-hand ball cup.

The dish of the sprocket may face either inward or outward, depending on the desired chainline. Normally, replace it as it was before disassembling the hub.

(53)

(55)

56 Spread the snapring over the flange of the ball cup and tap it lightly into its groove with a hammer and drift punch.

(54)

(56)

Finishing Up

If you haven't already oiled the hub, add oil at the lubricator if any, and the hollow axle end (page 211.) **CAUTION: Failure to add oil will cause rapid hub wear.**

Install the wheel (page 72).
Adjust the cable (page 212).

OVERHAULING A STURMEY-ARCHER FOUR- OR FIVE-SPEED HUB

The step-by-step illustrated instructions in this section cover disassembling, assembling, and adjusting a Sturmey-Archer Five-speed Alloy or S5/2 five-speed hub. The S5/2 and Five-speed Alloy are identical except for the hub shell; the S5.1, S5, and FW hubs are earlier models which are very similar. All differences between these hubs are in the axle assembly; the model is identified on the hub shell. Replacement axle assemblies and shifter parts for earlier-model hubs are no longer available; when rebuilding, you may use an S5/2 axle assembly to update the hub—and convert the four-speed FW hub to five speeds.

Sturmey-Archer also makes the AT5, a five-speed hub with a cable-operated drum brake at the left side. Except for the brake parts, this hub is substantially the same as the S5/2. Instructions for rebuilding the drum brake are in Chapter 16.

The S5/2 is most reliable when shifted with two Sturmey-Archer three-speed trigger controls or with the new five-speed single control. Discard the dual shift-lever assemblies sold with earlier five-speed hubs; they tend to slip out of gear.

Note that the S5/2 can be installed in an AW three-speed hub shell when rebuilding, so you can convert a rear wheel from three to five speeds without having to respoke it. In fact, the five-speed hub is identical to the three-speed except for the axle and planet-cage assemblies.

Exploded drawings of the S5/2 and AT5 hubs appear later in this section.

How the Five-speed Hub Works

Read the section on how the three-speed hub works (page 240), then this section.

The Sturmey-Archer five-speed hub is very much like the three-speed hub. The right shift cable moves the internal cross clutch; power travels through the planetary gears from outside to inside (first and second gears); directly from the sprocket to the wheel (middle gear); or through the planetary gears from inside to outside (fourth and fifth gears).

The difference is that the five-speed hub has *two* sets of sun and planet gears, shifted by the left cable.

Sturmey-Archer five-speed alloy hub. This hub is also available with a steel shell, and is similar to the earlier four-speed version.

So the five-speed hub has two different low gears and two different high gears, plus the direct-drive middle gear.

Problems with Sturmey-Archer Five-speed Hubs

Slips in first gear; jumps from fifth to third.

Possible cause:	*Corrective action:*
Left cable is sticking.	Service cable.
Primary sun pinion or axle dogs are worn.	Rebuild hub.
Pinion return spring is weak (S5.1) or wrong.	Rebuild as S5/2.
Bellcrank (S5) is damaged.	Rebuild as S5/2.

Slips in first and second gear.

Possible cause:	*Corrective action:*
Planet-cage (low-gear) pawls are sticking.	Rebuild hub.

Jumps from first or second gear to third.

Possible cause:	*Corrective action:*
Right cable is too loose.	Adjust cable.
Right indicator chain or cable is sticking.	Service cable or chain.

No first, second, or third gear.

Possible cause:	*Corrective action:*
Right cable is very loose or broken.	Service cable.

No second or fourth gear.

Possible cause:	*Corrective action:*
Left cable is very loose or broken.	Service cable.

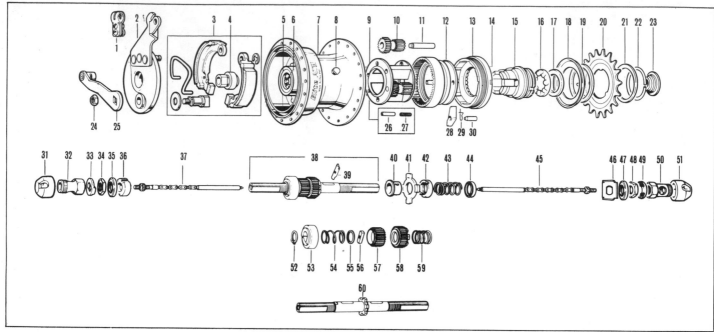

Exploded drawing of Sturmey-Archer AT5 five-speed hub with drum brake. The right ball cup is different from that of any other Sturmey-Archer hub.

ITEM	DESCRIPTION	ITEM	DESCRIPTION
1	Brake-arm clip assembly	22	Sprocket circlip
2	Brake plate and arm assembly	23	Cone with dustcap right-hand
3	Brake shoes service kit	24	Brake lever nut
4	Left-hand cone	25	Brake lever assembly
5	Cone dust cover	26	Left-hand pawl
6	Ball cage (with ball bearings 6.4mm [¼"])	27	Pawl spring
7	Hub shell assembly 36 hole (NB hub shell assembly includes items 5, 6 and 8.)	28	Pawl for gear ring
		29	Pawl spring
		30	Pawl pin for gear ring
8	Lubricator	31	Indicator guard
9	Planet cage with pawls and springs	32	Axle nut
10	Planet pinion	33	Serrated lockwasher
11	Pinion pin	34	Cone locknut
12	Gear ring	35	Spacing washer
13	Ball ring right-hand	36	Cone adjuster
14	Inner dustcap	37	Gear indicator left-hand
15	Driver	38	Axle assembly
16	Ball cage (with ball bearings 6.4mm [¼"])	39	Axle key
17	Outer dustcap	40	Clutch sleeve
18	Sprocket dustcap	41	Clutch
19	Sprocket spacing washer 1.6mm (1⁄16")	42	Thrust ring
20	Sprocket	43	Clutch spring
21	Sprocket spacing washer 1.6mm (1⁄16")	44	Cap for clutch spring
		45	Gear indicator right-hand

ITEM	DESCRIPTION
46	Cone lockwasher
47	Spacing washer
48	Cone locknut
49	Serrated lockwasher
50	Axle nut
51	Indicator guard
52	Circlip retainer
53	Dog ring
54	Pinion return spring
55	Washer for pinion return spring
56	Low-gear axle key
57	Secondary sun pinion
58	Primary sun pinion
59	Low-gear spring
60	Axle

Slips in second gear; jumps from fourth to third.

Possible cause:	Corrective action:
Left cable is too loose.	Adjust cable.
Dog ring is worn or loose.	Rebuild hub.
Dog-ring locknut is reversed (FW, S5, S5.1).	Reverse locknut.
Axle locknut has been used as dog-ring locknut (FW etc.).	Use dog-ring locknut.

Slips in third gear.

Possible cause:	Corrective action:
Right-side cable is too loose.	Adjust cable.
Clutch is worn.	Rebuild hub.

Slips in fourth and fifth gear.

Possible cause:	Corrective action:
Right-side cable is too tight.	Adjust cable.
Planet-cage dogs are worn.	Rebuild hub.
Clutch is worn.	Rebuild hub.

Jumps from fourth and fifth to third gear.

Possible cause:	Corrective action:
Gear-ring pawls are sticking.	Rebuild hub.

Runs roughly.

Possible cause:	Corrective action:
Planet pinions are incorrectly timed.	Rebuild hub.
Chain is too tight.	Adjust chain.
Lubrication is poor.	Relubricate.
Bearing cones are too tight.	Adjust cones.
Axle is bent.	Rebuild hub.
Dustcap or bearing retainer is bent.	Rebuild hub.
There are too many balls in the ball ring.	Rebuild hub.
One pawl of a pair is sticking.	Rebuild hub.

Tools and Supplies You Will Need

Hammer
Drift punch
Pointed punch (if installing riveted pawls)
Adjustable wrench
Vise (or a second adjustable wrench)
15mm cone wrench
Thin-bladed screwdriver
Grease
Cycle oil *(not "household" oil!)*
Circlip tool (optional)

Parts You Will Need

Two ball cages (bearing retainers), part HSA 284
24 3/16-inch bearing balls
Two low-gear pawls, part HSA 111
Four pawl springs, part HSA 120
Circlip retainer, part HSL 729
Two pawls for gear ring, part HSA 119
Two pawl pins for planet cage, part HSA 133
NOTE: Parts HSA 284, 111, 120, and 119 are the same as for the Sturmey-Archer AW three-speed hub. Instead of ordering parts HSA 111, 120, and 133 you can order a planet cage with pawls installed, part HSA 374. This saves a difficult step, as does the complete axle assembly HSA 329, 330, 331.

Other Parts Most Likely Needing Replacement

Three planet pinions, part HSA 134
Primary sun pinion, part HSA 345
Secondary sun pinion, part HSA 344
Clutch, part HSA 117
NOTE: The clutch, part HSA 117, is the same as for the Sturmey-Archer AW three-speed hub.

Parts Needed to Update FW, S5, or S5.1 to S5/2

PART	DESCRIP-TION	PART NO.
Axle	short	†HSA 339 (5⅞-inch)
	medium	†HSA 340 (6⅛-inch)
	long	†HSA 341 (6⅜-inch)
Gear indicator LH		HSA 126 (short, med. axles)
		HSA 316 (long axle)
Gear indicator RH		**HSA 125 (short axle)
		*HSA 126 (med., long axles)
RH axle nut		*HMN 129
LH axle nut		**HMN 129
Circlip retainer		†HSL 729
Dog ring		†HSA 343
Pinion return spring		†HSA 346
Pinion return spring washer		†HMW 488
Primary sun pinion		†HSA 345
Secondary sun pinion		†HSA 344
Low-gear axle key		†HSA 342
Low-gear spring		†HSA 347
Three planet pinions		***HSA 134

*Needed only for update from FW.
**Needed only for update from FW or S5.
***Same part as earlier models but should be replaced if worn, due to different wear pattern.
†Available as axle assembly HSA 329, 330, 331.

Preliminary Steps

Read chapter introduction (page 209).
Make sure you don't just have a cable problem (page 211).
Remove the wheel (page 69).

Disassembling

The five-speed hub is largely identical to the Sturmey-Archer three-speed hub. Start with step ① of the three-speed hub procedure, page 242. After step ⑫ of that procedure, return to this section to complete disassembly.

① Remove the assembly from the vise. Hold the assembly in your hand with two fingers on either side of the axle and jar it to remove the three pinion pins. The three pinions will fall out. Slip the planet cage off the right end of the axle.

② Clamp the axle assembly in the vise left end up, with the vise gripping the axle flats. Pry off the circlip

①

retainer, using circlip pliers or a thin-bladed screwdriver. Lift off the dog ring and pinion return spring.

Earlier models used a locknut instead of a circlip; flatten the lockwasher under the locknut and unscrew the locknut counterclockwise. This locknut is not the same as axle-end locknuts; if you are rebuilding with the old axle, save all axle assembly parts, as they are different from S5/2 parts. The FW and the S5 have no pinion return spring or washer, so don't look for them.

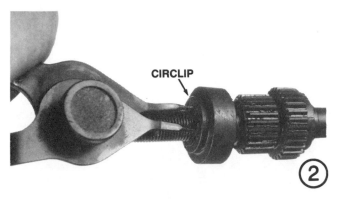

(2)

(3) Invert the axle and remove the pinion-return-spring washer.

(4) With the axle still inverted, push the two sun pinions up until the larger one meshes with the axle dogs. Slide the low-gear axle key out of its slot.

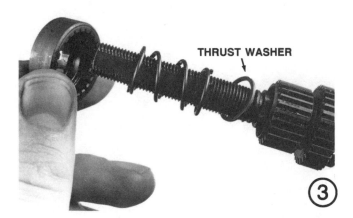

THRUST WASHER

(3)

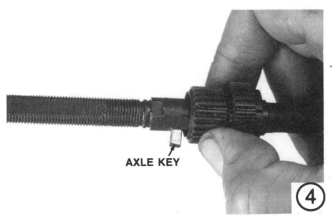

AXLE KEY

(4)

(5) Remove the two sun pinions and the low-gear spring.

(6) Pry the dustcap off the right-hand ball ring with a thin-bladed screwdriver. Work slowly to avoid bending the dustcap. Remove the loose bearing balls.

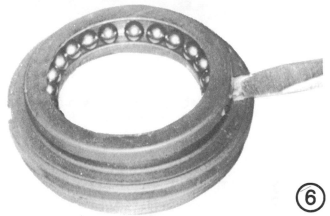

(5)

(6)

(7) Pry the dustcap out of the left-hand ball cup and remove the bearing retainer.

(7)

⑧ Pry the dustcap out of the driver and remove the bearing retainer.

⑨ Hold the gear ring in your hand, with the pawls facing down, and then jar the back of your hand on the bench; the high-gear pawls will slide out, releasing the pawls and pawl pins.

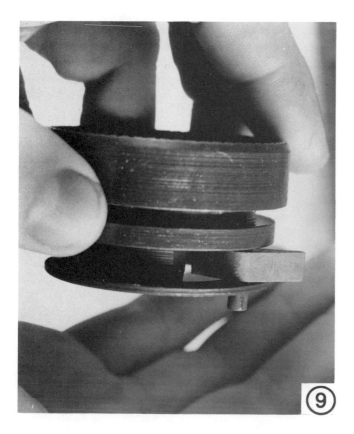

⑩ Planet-cage (left) pawl pins may be *hollow* or *riveted.* Unless you are installing a complete new planet-cage assembly or unless pawls are in good condition, drive out hollow pawl pins with the correct-size drift punch. Remove riveted pawl pins by filing or grinding the outside (left) end until you can push them through. Remove pawl springs and pawls.

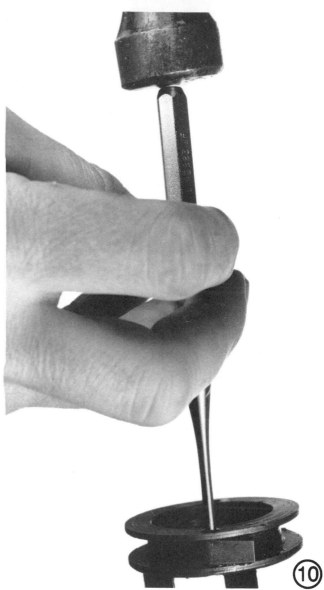

Cleaning and Inspecting

Clean all parts in solvent or compressed air; rinse them, or wipe them dry with a lintless cloth. Keep all cleaned parts on paper towels to avoid contamination. Cover them with a clean towel to keep grit from entering the internal parts and bearings. A tiny piece of grit can do a tremendous amount of damage if allowed to work on a part over an extended period of time.

It is best to replace the two bearing-retainer

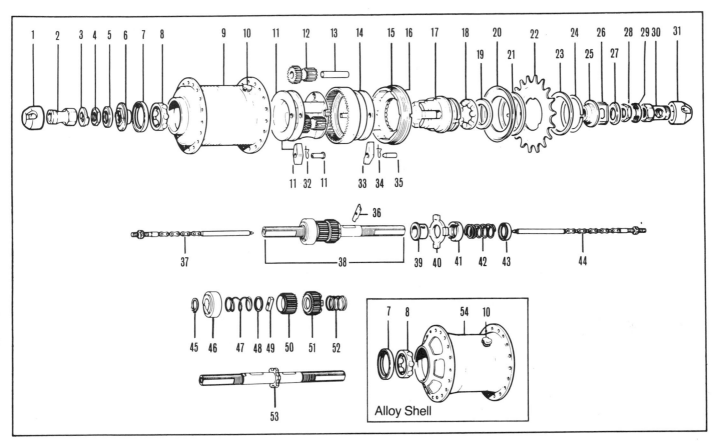

Exploded drawing of the Sturmey-Archer five-speed alloy and S5/2 five-speed hub. These are very similar to the AT5 hub, except for its drum-brake parts.

ITEM	DESCRIPTION	ITEM	DESCRIPTION	ITEM	DESCRIPTION
1	Indicator guard	19	Outer dustcap	38	Axle assembly
2	Axle nut	20	Sprocket dustcap	39	Clutch sleeve
3	Serrated lockwasher	21	Sprocket spacing washer	40	Clutch
4	Cone locknut	22	Sprocket	41	Thrust ring
5	Spacing washer	23	Sprocket spacing washer	42	Clutch spring
6	Cone with dustcap left-hand	24	Sprocket circlip	43	Cap for clutch spring
7	Outer dustcap	25	Cone with dustcap right-hand	44	Gear indicator right-hand
8	Ball cage	26	Cone lockwasher	45	Circlip retainer
9	Hub shell assembly	27	Spacing washer	46	Dog ring
10	Lubricator	28	Cone locknut	47	Pinion return spring
11	Planet cage with pawls, pawl pins, and springs	29	Serrated lockwasher	48	Washer for pinion return spring
12	Planet pinion	30	Axle nut	49	Low-gear axle key
13	Pinion pin	31	Indicator guard	50	Secondary sun pinion
14	Gear ring	32	Pawl spring	51	Primary sun pinion
15	Ball ring right-hand	33	Pawl for gear ring	52	Low-gear spring
16	Inner dustcap	34	Pawl spring	53	Axle
17	Driver	35	Pawl pin for gear ring	54	Hub shell assembly
18	Ball cage	36	Axle key		
		37	Gear indicator left-hand		

assemblies and the loose balls rather than to inspect them.

Inspect the bearing surface of the left-hand ball cup in the hub shell, both cones, the driver, and the right-hand ball cup for scores (scratchlike marks) and pits. Check both cones for stripped threads.

A worn or pitted left ball cup in a steel shell can be replaced; remove the ball cup only if necessary. Ball cups with wrench flats unscrew *clockwise*. A ball cup without wrench flats has a splined fitting and can be pounded out using a hammer and a block of wood. Support the left side of the hub shell on two other blocks of wood.

Inspect the axle for damaged or stripped threads. Inspect the axle dogs for worn or chipped driving edges. Check the axle slots to be sure the edges have not been rounded.

Inspect the sun and planet pinions for chipped or worn teeth. Check the dogs on the primary sun gear and on the right (flat) side of the planet cage for wear or chipping.

Inspect the high- and low-gear pawls for worn driving edges.

Check the dustcaps to be sure they are not bent, crimped, or distorted, which could have happened during disassembly.

Inspect the high- and low-gear pawl-cage assemblies for cracks around the rivets. Check both assemblies for worn driving edges. Inspect the internal gear of the ball ring for worn or chipped teeth.

Check the axle key to be sure it is not bent, the edges are not rounded, and the threads in the key are not stripped.

Inspect the hub shell for chipped or worn ratchet teeth. Check the flanges of the shell for cracks.

Inspect the clutch spring, low-gear spring, and pinion return spring for length and tension (compare with new springs).

The pawl springs must be replaced to ensure proper service.

Inspect the splines on the gear ring for a worn or glazed condition.

Inspect the locknuts for stripped or damaged threads. Check the ears of the right-hand lockwasher to be sure they are not cracked.

Inspect the sprocket for wear to the driving faces of the teeth. Consider replacing the sprocket with one of another size to improve the gearing (see page 207).

Assembling

⑪ Insert a low-gear (straight) pawl and new spring into the cage slot, with the long leg of the spring riding against the planet cage as shown, and the hook end pushing against the pawl. **CAUTION: New pawl**

springs must be installed to ensure proper service. Push the pawl and spring into the slot until the hole in the pawl aligns with the hole in the cage flange, and then push the pawl pin into position. If using riveted pawl pins, insert the pin from inside to outside, then hold the large (right) end of the pin against a hard surface. With a hammer and a pointed punch, flare the small (outer) end so the pin cannot slide out. Push on the pawl pins to make sure they are securely riveted and cannot slip out of their holes. If using hollow pawl pins, push the pin in with light taps of a hammer. Insert the second pawl spring and pin the same way as the first one.

⑫ Position a new pawl spring on one of the high-gear (angled) pawls, with the loop of the spring aligned over the pawl hole. Face the long leg of the spring toward the gear-ring slot; the hook end must be under the pawl, as shown. **CAUTION: Always use new pawl springs to ensure proper service.**

⑬ Push in on the pawl, against the tension of the spring, and then insert one of the pins, with the tapered end facing down. Install the other pawl, spring, and pin

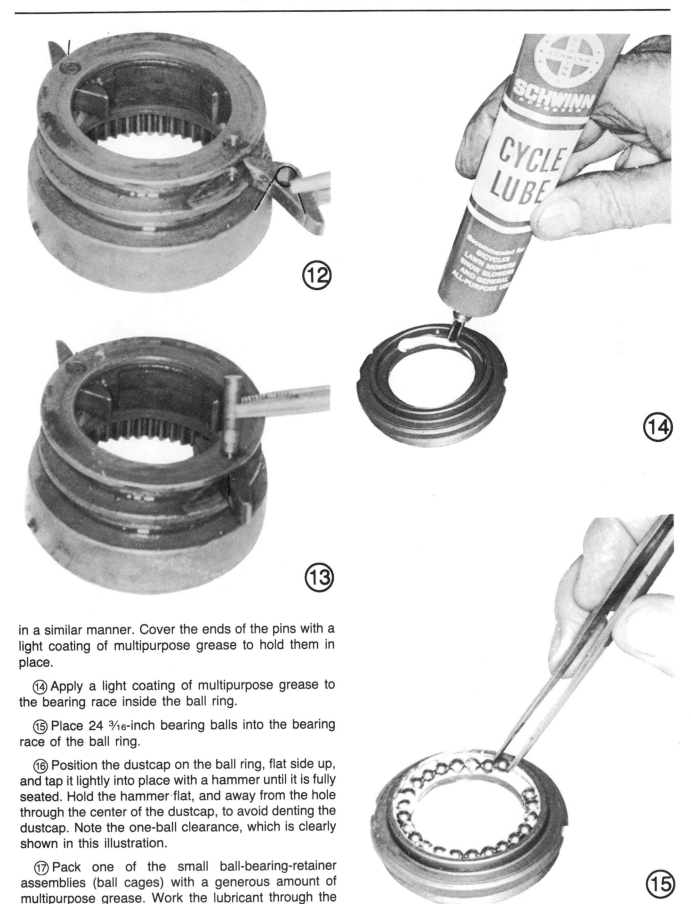

in a similar manner. Cover the ends of the pins with a light coating of multipurpose grease to hold them in place.

⑭ Apply a light coating of multipurpose grease to the bearing race inside the ball ring.

⑮ Place 24 3/16-inch bearing balls into the bearing race of the ball ring.

⑯ Position the dustcap on the ball ring, flat side up, and tap it lightly into place with a hammer until it is fully seated. Hold the hammer flat, and away from the hole through the center of the dustcap, to avoid denting the dustcap. Note the one-ball clearance, which is clearly shown in this illustration.

⑰ Pack one of the small ball-bearing-retainer assemblies (ball cages) with a generous amount of multipurpose grease. Work the lubricant through the

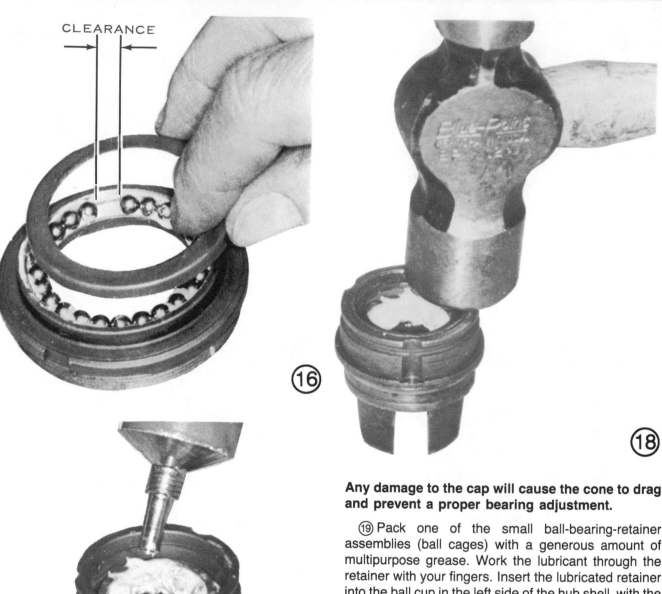

retainer with your fingers. Insert the lubricated retainer into the driver, with the flat side of the retainer facing up. Spread another light coating of lubricant over the bearing assembly.

⑱ Install the dustcap over the bearing assembly, with the flat side of the cap facing *down.* Tap the cap lightly with a hammer until it is fully seated. **CAUTION:**

Any damage to the cap will cause the cone to drag and prevent a proper bearing adjustment.

⑲ Pack one of the small ball-bearing-retainer assemblies (ball cages) with a generous amount of multipurpose grease. Work the lubricant through the retainer with your fingers. Insert the lubricated retainer into the ball cup in the left side of the hub shell, with the flat side of the retainer facing up. Spread another light coating of lubricant over the bearing assembly.

⑳ Install the dustcap over the bearing assembly, with the flat side of the cap facing *down.* Tap the cap lightly with a hammer until it is fully seated. **CAUTION: Any damage to the cap will cause the cone to drag and prevent a proper bearing adjustment.**

㉑ Slide the low-gear (light-gauge, short) spring over left end of the axle (end with flats for the dog ring). Insert the primary sun pinion, smooth face up, and the secondary sun pinion, smooth face down.

㉒ Push the pinions toward the center of the axle, so that the primary pinion engages the axle dogs. Turn the assembly over and insert the square, low-gear axle key. Let the pinions go. Look into the end of the axle. If you do not see the hole in the axle key, it is not correctly positioned; remove it and reinstall it.

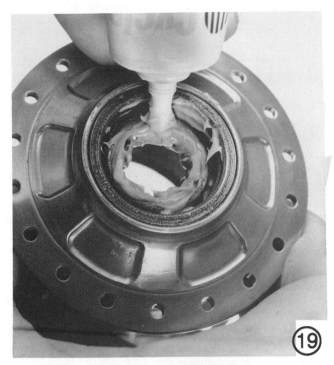

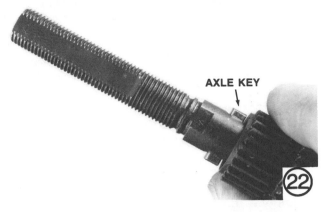

AXLE KEY

㉒

㉓ Install the washer, pinion return spring, and dog ring. Fasten the assembly in place with a *new* circlip retainer. Do *not* over expand the circlip. Carefully push the circlip into position with an axle nut, then a screwdriver, as shown. Make sure the circlip sits in its proper groove, not in the relieved area at the end of the axle threads. The dog ring should have no endplay. *(NOTE: The locknut of earlier models is relieved on one side. This side must face the dog ring. Pry up two sides of the thin washer under the locknut to secure it. If you use an axle-end locknut or install the dog ring locknut upside down, the dog ring will be loose.)*

㉑

DOG RING   **PINION RETURN SPRING**

CIRCLIP   **THRUST WASHER (HIDDEN)**

㉓

CIRCLIP   **DOG RING LOCKNUT**

New-model five-speed hubs use an axle assembly with a circlip *(left)*. If the hub has a locknut instead *(right)*, update it with a new axle assembly.

㉔ Clamp the flats of the left end of the axle in a vise. Slide the planet cage over the right end of the axle (end opposite the dog ring). Note that each planet pinion has one marked tooth—the mark is on the *inner* face of the *larger* gear on the pinion. Install the pinions and slide the pinion pins into place so the marked teeth all face outward (see diagram). This is called "timing" the pinions.

CAUTION: Do not let the planet cage turn on the axle during installation. The hub will run very roughly if the pinions are not properly timed.

From this point, reassembly is identical to reassembly of the Sturmey-Archer three-speed hub. Turn to step ㉚ on page 250 to complete reassembly.

㉔

OVERHAULING A STURMEY-ARCHER THREE-SPEED COASTER HUB

Sturmey-Archer has made three models of three-speed coaster brake hubs:

The early *TCW* has a left ball ring with 24 loose balls. This hub is rare, and spare parts are difficult to find.

The newer *TCW Mark III* can be identified by the markings on the hub shell, the large ball retainer in the left side, and the normal-width ball ring (same as on the AW three-speed) on the right side. Drive to the brake in this hub is through the gear train, so brake mechanical advantage depends on the gear chosen. This hub is quite common.

The *S3C,* the newest model, is very similar to the TCW Mark III except that the brake is driven separately from the gears, through a special set of reverse pawls. In the S3C, braking is equally powerful in every gear, and the brake still works if the hub is not properly in gear. The S3C has an extra-wide ball ring on the right—wider than that of most other Sturmey-Archer hubs.

Operation of these hubs is very similar to that of the Sturmey-Archer AW three-speed hub combined with a conventional internal-expanding shoe-type coaster brake.

Rebuilding instructions here are for the S3C. Deviations between it and the TCW Mark III which might cause problems during assembly, including specific parts that are not interchangeable, are called to your attention in the individual steps and the list below. Detailed exploded drawings of these hubs, showing all internal parts, appear later in this section. Where the overhaul procedure differs, usually the TCW Mark III procedure is the same as for the AW three-speed; reference is made to the appropriate step of the AW procedure.

CAUTION: Many TCW Mark III and S3C parts look similar but are not interchangeable. The S3C is a bit more complicated; many of its parts have been narrowed slightly, and the ball ring has been widened, to make more room in the hub shell.

TCW Mark III and S3C hub shells *are* interchangeable—you can substitute the complete internal assembly. If interchanged, you can identify the hubs by the ball-ring widths.

Sturmey-Archer TCW Mark III three-speed hub with coaster brake. The S3C hub is very similar.

Three Sturmey-Archer ball rings. The left one has an extra dust-sealing flange, but is interchangeable with the middle one. The thicker ball ring at the right is usable only with the S3C three-speed coaster-brake hub.

Problems with Sturmey-Archer S3C and TCW Mark III Hubs

Problems and solutions are the same as for the AW three-speed hub (page 241), with the following additions:

Second gear instead of first.

Possible cause:	Corrective action:
Ratchet ring is not seated on gear ring.	Rebuild hub.

Operation is noisy and rough.

Possible cause:	Corrective action:
AW/TCW Mark III ball ring has been installed in S3C.	Rebuild hub.
Wide TCW Mark III brake band has been installed in S3C.	Rebuild hub.
Brake actuating (retarder) spring is backward.	Rebuild hub.

Brake will not release.

Possible cause:	Corrective action:
Lubrication is poor.	Relubricate.
Tapered brake actuating surfaces are worn.	Rebuild hub.
Brake arm is misaligned at frame.	Loosen and reattach.

Cranks backpedal too far.

Possible cause:	Corrective action:
S3C ball ring has been installed in TCW Mark III.	Rebuild hub.

Brake is weak.

Possible cause:	Corrective action:
Wrong lubricant has been used.	Relubricate.
Brake band is worn.	Rebuild hub.
Thrust plate brake drive screw is chipped.	Rebuild hub.

No brake.

Possible cause:	Corrective action:
Brake actuating spring is faulty or missing.	Rebuild hub.
Driver pawls are stuck or missing (S3C).	Rebuild hub.

No brake in second gear or in third gear.

Possible cause:	Corrective action:
Cable is too tight or loose (TCW Mark III).	Adjust cable.

Easily Confused Parts

NAME	PART NUMBER		COMMENTS
	TCW Mark III	*S3C*	(How S3C part differs)
Brake arm	HSH 402	HSH 450	Larger diameter for cone
Left cone	HSH 405	HSH 447	Larger diameter for arm
Brake band	HSA 406	HSA 448	Narrower
Planet pinion	*HSA 115	HSA 292	Narrower
Pinion pin	HSA 170	HSA 293	Round end smaller
Planet cage	HSA 169	HSA 291	Narrower pinion slot
Gear ring	HSA 171	HSA 296	Tabs have clutch notch
Gear-ring pawl ring	HSA 172	HSA 307	Pawls narrower
Right-hand ball ring	*HSA 121	HSA 308	Wider
Axle			
5¾-inch	HSA 173		
6-inch		HSA 313	
6¼-inch	HSA 174	HSA 314	No flange next to gear
Axle key	*HSA 124	HSA 295	Square
Clutch	*HSA 117	HSA 294	Elongated

*Same as for AW three-speed

Tools and Supplies You Will Need

Hammer
Drift punch
Adjustable wrench
Vise (or a second adjustable wrench)
Cone wrench, 15mm
Thin-bladed screwdriver
Grease
Cycle oil *(not "household" oil!)*

Parts You Will Need

Driver pawl springs, part HSA 469 (S3C only)
Gear-ring pawl springs, part HSA 120 for TCW Mark III, HSA 253 for S3C
Planet-cage pawl springs, part HSA 120
Retainer, part HSA 164
Ball cage, part HSA 284
24 ³⁄₁₆-inch bearing balls
NOTE: Parts HSA 120 and 284 are the same as for the AW three-speed hub.

Other Parts Most Likely Needing Replacement

Clutch, part HSA 117 for TCW Mark III, HSA 294 for S3C
Brake band, part HSH 406 for TCW Mark III, HSH 448 for S3C
Gear ring, part HSA 171 for TCW Mark III, HSA 296 for S3C
Gear-ring pawl-ring assembly, part HSA 172 for TCW Mark III, HSA 307 for S3C
Planet-cage pawl-ring assembly, part HSA 168
Right-hand cone, part *HSA 101
Sprocket (part number depends on size)
NOTE: Parts HSA 117 and 101 are the same as for the AW three-speed hub.

Preliminary Steps

Read chapter introduction on geared hubs (page 241) and chapter introduction on coaster brakes (page 214).

Make sure you don't just have a cable problem (page 211).

Remove the wheel (page 69).

Disassembling

① Note how many of the two sprocket spacers under the snapring are on the outside of the sprocket, and whether the dish of the sprocket is facing toward the inside or the outside. The dish and spacers are used to align the sprocket with the chainwheel. Remove the snapring.

② Remove the spacers, the sprocket, and the sprocket dustcap.

③ Turn the hub over. Loosen but *do not remove* the left locknut, lockwasher, and adjusting cone by turning them counterclockwise. To turn the adjusting cone, use a hammer and drift punch or a hook-spanner wrench.

④ Rotate the ball ring counterclockwise as shown, using a drift punch and a hammer or a special Sturmey-Archer spanner. Do not unscrew it completely yet.

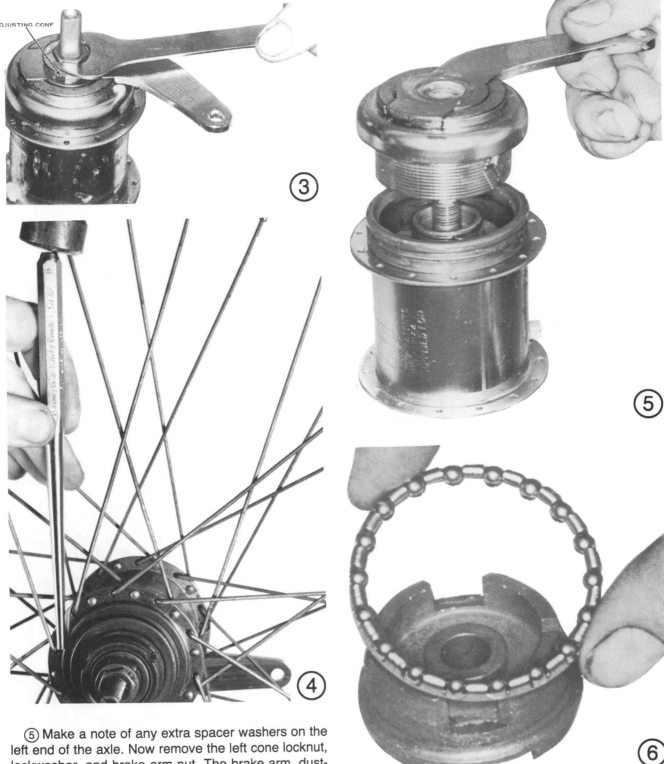

ADJUSTING CONE

③

④

⑤

⑥

⑤ Make a note of any extra spacer washers on the left end of the axle. Now remove the left cone locknut, lockwasher, and brake-arm nut. The brake arm, dust-cap, and left-hand cone may come off together or separately.

⑥ Remove the ball retainer from the left-hand cone.

⑦ *Do not turn the hub over.* Unscrew the ball ring from the underside of the hub shell and remove the complete assembly.

⑧ You may clamp the assembly in a vise to make this step and following steps easier. Remove the brake band, thrust plate, and planet-cage pawl ring. The thrust plate unscrews counterclockwise once it has engaged the axle threads.

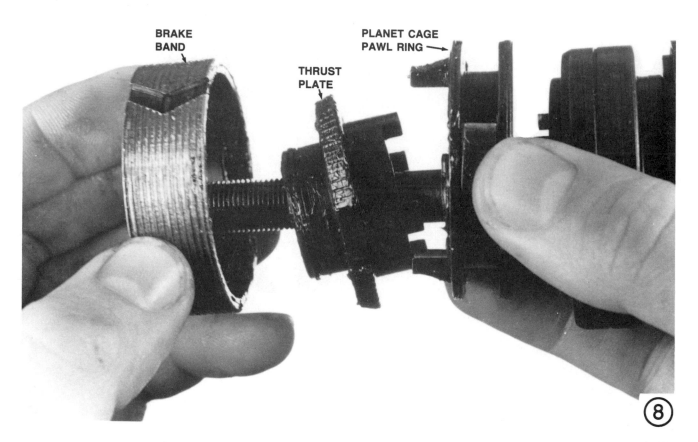

ring. **CAUTION: The S3C ball ring is wider than the ball ring for the TCW Mark III and other Sturmey-Archer hubs. Do not mix them up.**

TCW Mark III: Lift the ball ring off the gear-ring pawl ring. This hub has no ratchet ring.

⑫ Remove the gear-ring pawl ring.

⑬ Remove the gear ring.

⑭ Remove the clutch.

TCW Mark III: Slide the thrust ring off the axle. Pull the axle key out of the keyway in the axle (see step ⑪, page 244).

BRAKE
BAND

THRUST
PLATE

PLANET CAGE
PAWL RING →

⑨ Now turn the assembly over. Make a note of any extra spacer washers on the right end of the axle. Unscrew the right-hand locknut and remove the lock-washer. Hold down the ball ring while you unscrew the right-hand cone.

⑩ S3C: Keep holding the ball ring down and remove the spring cap, clutch spring, and driver. Turn the driver counterclockwise to disengage the pawls.

TCW Mark III: Remove the driver assembly, spring cap, and spring from the axle (see steps ⑦ and ⑧, page 243).

⑪ Lift off the ball ring. If the pawls will not dis-engage, remove it with the driver. Remove the ratchet

RATCHET RING

⑮ Remove the axle key. Lift out the pinion pins and remove the pinions.

TCW Mark III: Remove the clutch, and then slide the clutch sleeve off the axle (see step ⑫, page 244). Lift out the pinion pins and remove the pinions.

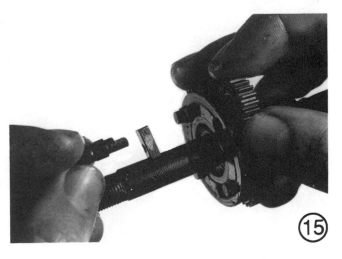

⑯ Turn the remaining assembly end for end in the vise, with the soft jaws gripping the flats of the axle. Pry the planet-cage circlip from the axle with a narrow-bladed screwdriver, and then remove the planet cage from the axle.

⑰ Pry the dustcap from the right-hand ball cup with a screwdriver. Work around the cap edge and be careful not to crimp or damage it. Remove the loose bearing balls.

⑱ If necessary, pry the brake arm off the dustcap, using a wide-bladed screwdriver, as shown.

⑲ Pry the dustcap from the driver with a screwdriver, as shown. Work around the cap edge and it will pop out. **CAUTION: Be careful not to crimp or damage the cap.** Remove the ball-bearing-retainer assembly.

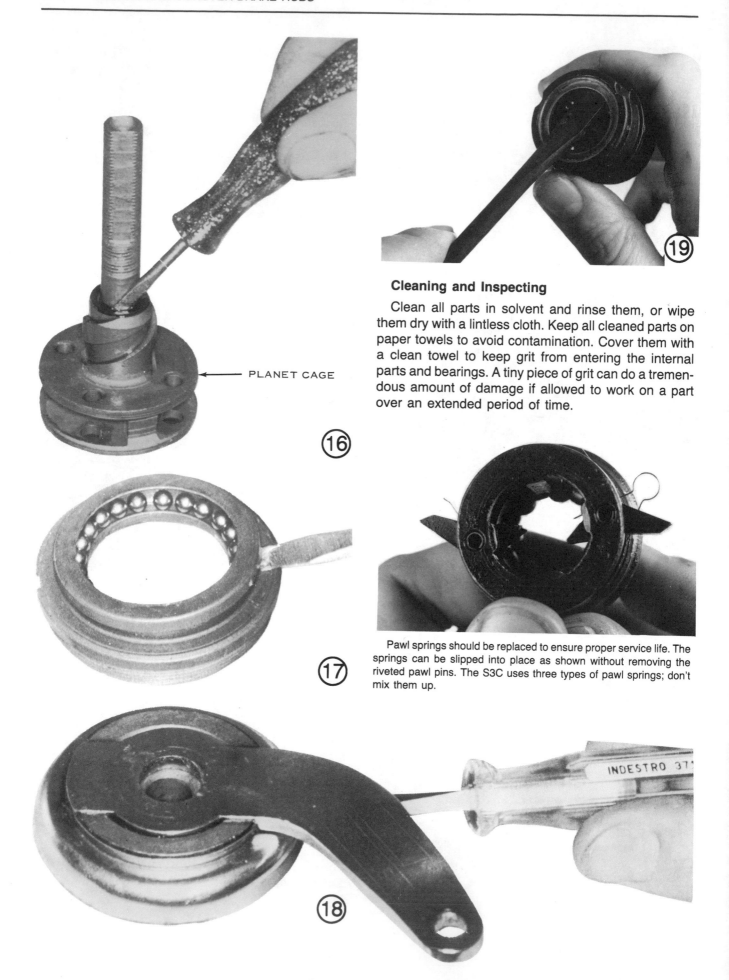

PLANET CAGE

(16)

(17)

(18)

(19)

Cleaning and Inspecting

Clean all parts in solvent and rinse them, or wipe them dry with a lintless cloth. Keep all cleaned parts on paper towels to avoid contamination. Cover them with a clean towel to keep grit from entering the internal parts and bearings. A tiny piece of grit can do a tremendous amount of damage if allowed to work on a part over an extended period of time.

Pawl springs should be replaced to ensure proper service life. The springs can be slipped into place as shown without removing the riveted pawl pins. The S3C uses three types of pawl springs; don't mix them up.

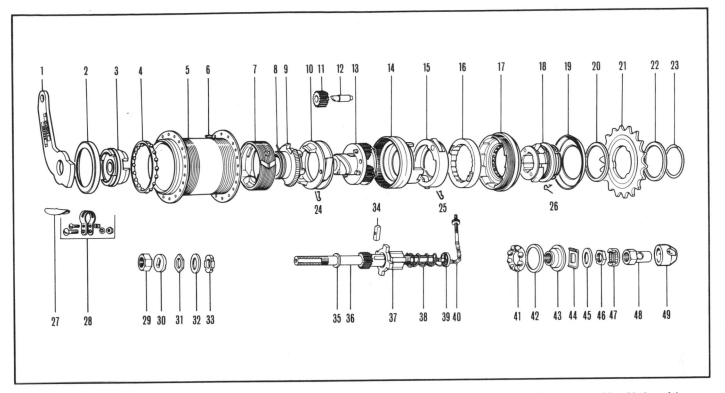

Exploded view of a Sturmey-Archer S3C three-speed rear hub with coaster brake. Though the hub shell is interchangeable with that of the TCW Mark III, many internal parts are not.

ITEM	DESCRIPTION	ITEM	DESCRIPTION
1	Brake arm	25	Pawl spring (gear ring) right-hand
2	Dustcap left-hand	26	Pawl spring (driver)
3	Cone left-hand	27	Strengthening pad
4	Ball cage assembly left-hand	28	Brake-arm clip assembly
5	Hub shell and ball cup assembly	29	Axle nut left-hand
6	Lubricator	30	Serrated lockwasher
7	Brake band assembly	31	Cone locknut
8	Brake actuating spring	32	Spacing washer
9	Brake thrust plate	33	Brake arm nut
10	Planet cage pawl ring	34	Axle key
11	Planet pinion	35	Planet cage circlip
12	Pinion pin	36	Axle
13	Planet cage	37	Clutch
14	Gear ring	38	Clutch spring
15	Gear ring pawl ring	39	Spring cap
16	Ratchet ring	40	Gear indicator
17	Ball ring assembly with dustcap	41	Ball cage right-hand
18	Driver assembly (including items 26, 41 and 42)	42	Outer dustcap
		43	Cone right-hand with dustcap
19	Sprocket dustcap	44	Cone lockwasher
20	Sprocket spacing washer 1.6mm (1/16")	45	Spacing washer
21	Sprocket	46	Cone locknut
22	Sprocket spacing washer 1.6mm (1/16")	47	Serrated lockwasher
23	Sprocket snapring	48	Axle nut right-hand
24	Pawl spring (planet cage)	49	Indicator guard

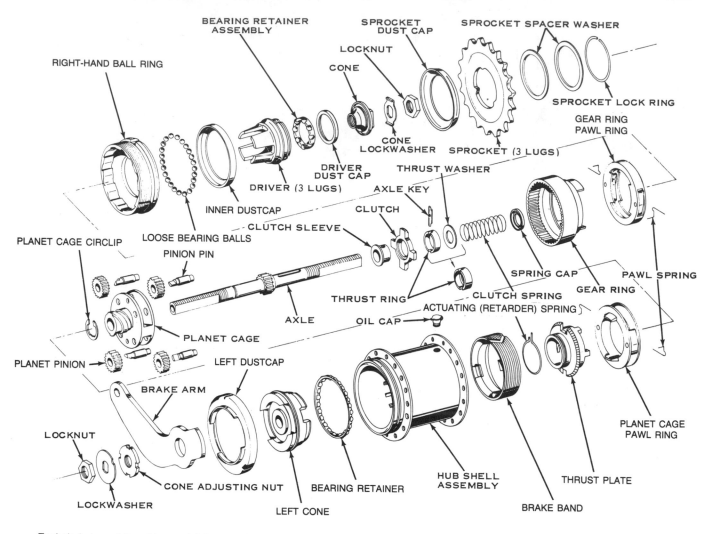

Exploded view of the older-model Sturmey-Archer TCW Mark III three-speed hub with coaster brake.

It is best to replace the two bearing retainers and the loose balls rather than to inspect them.

Inspect the bearing surface of the thrust plate, right cone, driver, and the right-hand ball ring for scores (scratchlike marks) and pits. Check the thrust plate and the cone for stripped threads.

Inspect the axle for damaged or stripped threads. Check the sun pinion on the axle for chipped or worn teeth.

Inspect the planet pinions for chipped or worn teeth. Check the small end of the pinion pins for wear.

Check the dustcaps to be sure they are not bent, crimped, or distorted, which could have happened during disassembly.

Inspect the gear ring for chipped or worn teeth and for damaged or worn splines.

Inspect the pawl-ring assemblies for cracks around the rivets. Check both assemblies for worn driving edges.

If pawls in either pawl ring are worn, replace the entire pawl-ring assembly, available as a unit. Pawl springs should always be replaced; old pawl springs can be slipped off with pawls in place. S3C driver pawls can be replaced without replacing the driver, as pawl pins are held in with a circlip.

CAUTION: Do not mix up pawl springs. The S3C uses three different types.

Inspect the actuator spring (retarder spring) on the thrust plate for wear and proper operation. If the spring needs replacement, be sure to install the new one with its long leg *ahead of* the gap, as shown in the exploded diagram. **CAUTION: Installing the spring backward will result in excessive drag and wear.**

Inspect the right-hand ball ring and the ratchet ring (S3C) for worn driving edges.

Inspect the locknuts and the cone adjusting nut for stripped or damaged threads.

Inspect the clutch for worn driving arms.

Check the clutch spring for length and stiffness (compare with a new spring).

Check the axle key to be sure it is not bent, the edges are not rounded, and the threads in the key are not stripped.

Inspect the brake band and the hub-shell braking surface for a worn or glazed condition.

Inspect the planet-cage circlip for worn ears.

Inspect the hub shell for chipped or worn ratchet teeth. Inspect the bearing cup for scores, pits, or excessive wear. Check the flanges of the shell for cracks.

Inspect the sprocket for wear to the driving faces of the teeth. Consider replacing the sprocket with one of another size to improve the gear ratio (see page 207).

Assembling

㉒ Clamp the axle in the vise, with the jaws gripping the flats of the axle and the slot facing down. Slide the planet cage onto the axle as far as it will go with the splines facing up and the internal teeth of the cage indexing with the sun gear on the axle. Press the planet-cage circlip into the axle groove to secure the planet cage.

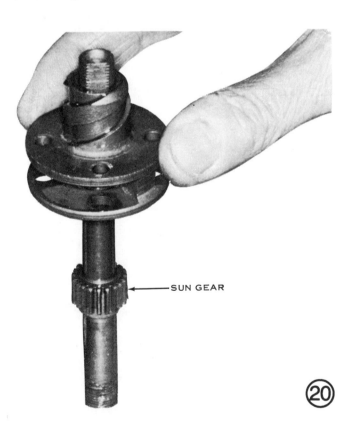

SUN GEAR

㉑

㉑ Turn the axle end for end in the vise, with the soft jaws gripping the axle flats. Slide one of the planet pinions into the planet cage, with the teeth of the pinion indexing with the teeth of the sun pinion. Insert the

pinion pin, with the flat-shaped end down and facing out, as shown. Install the other three planet pinions in a similar manner.

㉒ Place the axle key in the bottom of the axle slot, with the threaded hole in line with the axle.

TCW Mark III: Slide the clutch sleeve onto the axle, with the flanged end facing down. Install the clutch with the notched ends of the arms facing up. Insert the axle key through the hole in the clutch sleeve, with the flats at the ends of the key facing up (see steps ㉙ to ㉜, pages 250–251).

㉓ Slide the clutch onto the axle. It should cover the axle key and rest against the face of the planet cage. Install the gear ring with the internal teeth indexing with the teeth of the planet cage. Install the indicator spindle, threading it into the axle key.

TCW Mark III: Install the thrust ring, with the slots of the ring indexed over the flats of the axle key. Check

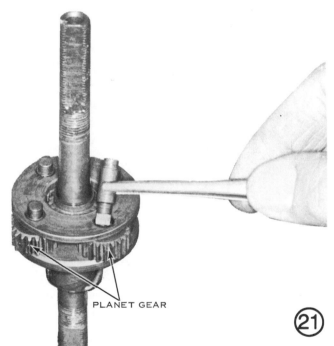

PLANET GEAR

㉑

AXLE KEY

㉒

for 0.005–0.008-inch clearance between the thrust ring and the surface of the clutch. If there is too little clearance, install a new clutch key. Install the indicator spindle (see steps ㉝ to ㉟, pages 251–252). Install the gear ring over the planet cage, with the internal teeth indexing with the teeth of the planet pinions.

㉔ Install the gear-ring pawl-ring assembly on the gear ring, with the smooth surface of the pawl rivets facing up and the internal shoulders indexing with the cutouts in the gear ring. You can tell that the gear-ring pawl-ring assembly is fully seated when the top of the gear ring is flush with the top surface of the pawl-ring assembly.

㉕ Install the ratchet ring, with its tabs (keys) engaged in the notches (keyways) of the gear-ring ears.
TCW Mark III: Omit this step. This hub does not have a ratchet ring.

㉖ Apply a light coating of multipurpose grease to the bearing race of the right-hand ball cup.

㉗ Place 24 ³⁄₁₆-inch bearing balls into the lubricated bearing race of the right-hand ball cup.

㉘ Place the ball-ring dustcap in position over the flange of the ball ring with the flat side facing up. Lightly tap the cap with a hammer until it is fully seated.

㉙ Install the ball ring. Push the pawls in and turn the ball ring until it engages the pawls.

㉚ Pack the driver bearing-retainer assembly with a generous amount of multipurpose grease. Work the lubricant throughout the bearings with your fingers. Install the lubricated bearing assembly into the driver with the flat side of the retainer facing up. Install the dustcap over the ball-bearing-retainer assembly with the flat side of the cap facing *down*. Tap the edge of the cap with a hammer until it is fully seated. Slide the driver down the axle over the spring until the slots engage over the lugs of the clutch assembly.

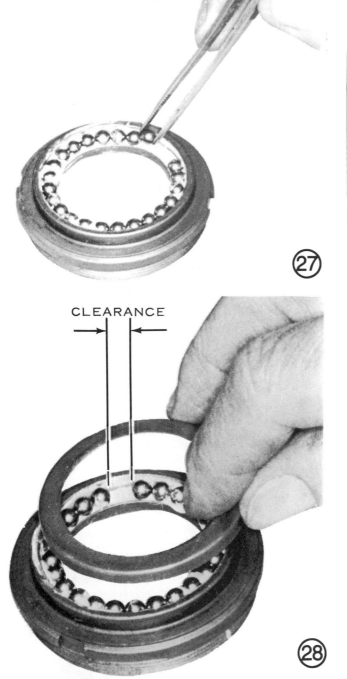

(27)

(29)

(28)

(30)

TCW Mark III: The appearance of the driver is different (no pawls) but the procedure is the same (see step ㉕, *page 249).*

㉛ Install the driver. Push its pawls in and turn it clockwise until it engages the ball ring.

TCW Mark III: Slide the driver down over the axle until the slots engage over the lugs of the clutch assembly (see step ㉚, *page 252).*

㉜ Install the clutch spring and spring cap. Check whether the spring cap is too big to fit through the driver; if so, leave it off.

㉝ Thread the cone onto the axle until it is finger-tight, and then back it off a quarter of a turn for a preliminary adjustment. Remove the indicator assem-

(31)

bly from the axle by twisting it in a counterclockwise direction until it is free of the axle key, and then pulling it out.

㉞ Guide the cone lockwasher over the axle, with the ears facing down and the flats indexing with the flats of the axle. If necessary, back off the cone no more than an additional quarter turn to align the flats of the cone with the tabs of the lockwasher. **CAUTION: This is not a bearing adjustment. It is to position the internal parts of the hub. If you adjust the right cone like a bearing, the hub will drag.**

㉟ Thread the locknut onto the axle, and then tighten it securely against the cone lockwasher.

㊱ Turn the axle end for end in the vise, with the soft jaws gripping the flats of the axle. Insert the thrust plate into the planet-cage pawl-ring assembly, with the shoulders of the pawl-ring indexing with the slots of the thrust plate. Turn each pinion pin until the flat sides of all the pins face out, as shown. Turn the assembled thrust plate and pawl-ring unit onto the planet-cage assembly clockwise until the pawl-ring seats flush on the surface of the planet cage. *NOTE: The flats of the pinion pins must face out to allow the pawl-ring assembly to seat squarely on the surface of the planet cage.*

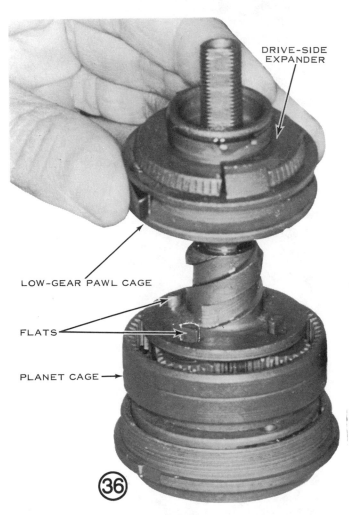

DRIVE-SIDE EXPANDER

LOW-GEAR PAWL CAGE

FLATS

PLANET CAGE

㊱

internal threads of the hub shell. When this occurs, turn the ball ring clockwise until it is finger-tight.

㊳ With the open end of the hub shell facing up, install the brake band into the hub shell with the keys facing up.

㊲

㊲ Remove the assembly from the vise. Place the hub (wheel) in an approximate horizontal position, with the tire against your chest and the brake side up. (For photographic clarity the wheel and spokes are not shown in the illustration.) Insert the assembled unit into the hub shell with the thrust plate up, as shown. Turn the assembly in a counterclockwise direction to allow the pawls on the planet-cage pawl-ring to index with the ratchet inside the hub shell. When the pawls index, you will be able to feel the assembly move farther into the hub, and the threads of the ball ring will engage the

KEYS

㊳

㊴ Pack the brake-side bearing-retainer assembly with a generous amount of multipurpose grease. Work the lubricant throughout the retainer with your fingers. Install the lubricated bearing assembly, with the flat side of the retainer facing up. Apply a second light coating of multipurpose grease to the inside surfaces of the ball bearings.

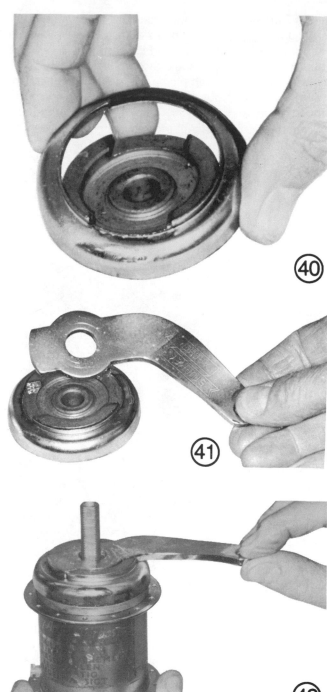

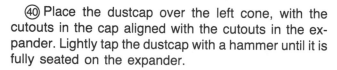

㊵ Place the dustcap over the left cone, with the cutouts in the cap aligned with the cutouts in the expander. Lightly tap the dustcap with a hammer until it is fully seated on the expander.

㊶ Position the brake arm in the cutouts of the dustcap and left cone, with the manufacturer's identification facing up, and then lightly tap it into place with a hammer.

㊷ Slide the brake-arm assembly onto the axle. Rotate the brake arm clockwise and counterclockwise until the lugs of the brake band engage the slots of the left cone.

There is an additional slot in the inner side of the left cone for the brake actuating spring. You may have to rotate the spring to engage this slot. When all parts are properly aligned, you will feel the assembly drop into place.

㊸ Thread the cone-adjusting nut onto the axle finger-tight.

㊹ Tighten the right-hand ball cup by turning it clockwise, using a drift punch and hammer, as shown.

Save the rim and the floor or bench from damage by resting the wheel on the inflated tire.

㊺ Hold one end of the axle with an adjustable wrench. Rotate the cone-adjusting nut with a hook-spanner wrench or hammer and punch to obtain just a trace of sideplay when the wheel rim is moved up and down.

㊻ Install the washer on the axle, then the locknut.
TCW Mark III: Install the lockwasher on the axle, with the internal flats of the washer indexing with the flats on the axle. Rotate the cone-adjusting nut slightly to allow the ear of the washer to index with the closest slot in the adjusting nut. Thread the locknut onto the axle tightly against the lockwasher.

㊼ Hold each end of the axle with your fingers. Slowly twist the axle with the thumb and forefinger of each hand—the wheel should not turn. If it does, the adjusting cone is too tight and must be loosened slightly. Loosen the locknut, and then rotate the cone counter-clockwise approximately an eighth of a turn. Retighten the locknut. The cone is properly adjusted when the wheel rotates freely, comes to rest gradually with the valve stem or a spoke reflector at the lowest point of the wheel, and there is only the slightest trace of sideplay.

Another, very precise test for sideplay is to see whether the sprocket drags as you rotate the wheel forward. There should be a slight drag from the

actuator spring and pawls, but not a heavy pull. Try to rock the sprocket from side to side. It should rock only slightly. Using these tests, you can adjust the bearings so that there is no noticeable sideplay at the rim.

TCW Mark III: The cone-adjusting nut can only be moved one notch at a time if the eared lockwasher is used.

CAUTION: If the cone is adjusted too tight, it will cause binding and scoring of the hub. If the cone is adjusted too loose, it will cause fatigue, which can result in a damaged hub or broken axle.

48 Install the sprocket dustcap, then the sprocket

spacers and sprocket the same way as before disassembly, unless you wish to change the chainline.

49 Snap the lockring into the recess of the driver and then tap it lightly into place with a hammer and drift punch.

Finishing Up

Add a total of 2 teaspoons of oil at the lubricator and the hollow axle end (page 211.) **CAUTION: Use without oil will cause rapid wear.**

Install the wheel (page 72).

Adjust the cable (page 211).

OVERHAULING A SHIMANO THREE-SPEED COASTER HUB

The Shimano three-speed coaster-brake hub works very much like the Sturmey-Archer version (page 241). The main difference is that the entire Shimano planet cage moves to the left to double as a right-side expander cone, wedging the brake shoes against the inside of the hub shell.

The hub has been sold in two major versions. The older version, the 3SC, required the right ball cup to be

Shimano three-speed hub with coaster brake.

removed from the hub shell for disassembly. The newer, cartridge version, the 3CC, does not require this step. Identify the version by the markings on the shell and brake arm.

The two versions are very similar. Many internal parts are interchangeable, including most that wear. Though more complicated than the three-speed hub without coaster brake, this hub is easier to overhaul.

The planet cage and ring gear of the cartridge version are available as complete assemblies. Cartridge-type internals can be installed in an older-type hub shell *if you use an old-type left dustcap.* The cartridge-type brake-arm assembly must be pried apart with a hammer and small screwdriver or chisel to replace the dustcap. Insert the screwdriver blade or chisel between the brake arm and dustcap; work carefully.

The instructions given here are for the older-type hub. The parts of the cartridge-type hub are very similar, but the order of disassembly is different. An exploded diagram of both types of hubs is included later in the section.

Problems with Shimano Three-speed Coaster-Brake Hubs

Gear is higher than selected gear.

Possible cause:	Corrective action:
Cable is too loose.	Adjust cable.

Hub slips forward.

Possible cause:	Corrective action:
Pawls are faulty.	Rebuild hub.

First gear instead of second.

Possible cause:	Corrective action:
Cable is too tight.	Adjust cable.
Return spring is faulty.	Rebuild hub.
Sliding clutch or planet cage is worn.	Rebuild hub.

Only runs in third gear.

Possible cause:	Corrective action:
Right-hand sliding key is out of position.	Rebuild hub.

Running is stiff or noisy.

Possible cause:	Corrective action:
Gear teeth are worn or chipped.	Rebuild hub.
Cones are too tight.	Adjust cones.
Axle is bent.	Rebuild hub.
Chain is too tight.	Adjust chain.
Broken parts are loose in hub.	Rebuild hub.
Brake arm is out of line.	Reattach brake arm.
There is too little brake-shoe play (3SC).	Adjust shoes.
Retarder (slide) spring is backward.	Reverse spring.
Clutch washer or thrust washer is absent.	Rebuild hub.
Ball retainer is backward.	Reinstall.

Weak or no brake.

Possible cause:	Corrective action:
Retarder spring is weak.	Rebuild hub.
Shoes are adjusted for too much play (3SC).	Adjust shoes.
Hub shell or brake shoes are worn.	Rebuild hub.
Shoe, cam, or planet-cage teeth are worn.	Rebuild hub.
Lubrication is poor.	Rebuild hub.

Tools and Supplies You Will Need

Adjustable wrench
Vise (or a second adjustable wrench)
Cone wrenches
Small open-end or box-end wrenches
Thin-bladed screwdriver
Shimano ball-cup tool XB-320 (for 3SC only)
Hammer (3SC, or if separating cartridge brake-arm assembly)

Chisel (if separating cartridge brake-arm assembly)
Grease
Cycle oil *(not "household" oil!)*

Parts You Will Need

Large bearing retainers (2), part 321 9023
Small bearing retainer (3SC only), part 333 3700
Driver with bearing retainer (3CC only), part
    334 9015
Ring gear pawl springs (2), part 333 3000
Planet cage pawl springs (2), part 333 2700

Other Parts Most Likely Needing Replacement

Brake shoe set, part 334 9008 for 3CC, 333 9031 for
    3SC
Spring guide and slide spring, part 333 9032

Complete Ring-gear and Planet-cage Assemblies

Ring gear, part 334 9010 for 3CC; not available for
    3SC
Planet cage, part 334 9009

Preliminary Steps

Read chapter introduction on geared hubs (page 241) and chapter introduction on coaster brakes (page 214).

Make sure you don't just have a cable problem (page 211).

Remove the wheel (page 69).

Disassembly

Note: Do the disassembly and assembly in the order given here for the older-model hub and in the different order indicated for the cartridge hub.

① Note whether the sprocket dishing faces in or out. With a small screwdriver, pry up the lockring; remove the sprocket and dustcap.

Cartridge: Do this step, then go to step ⑥, not to the next step.

② Loosen the right-hand locknut and bearing cone and remove them from the axle.

Cartridge: Do this step, then go to step ③.

③ Remove the driver, clutch spring, sliding clutch, cam, and ball retainer. Tap the sliding clutch on the bench top if necessary to remove the clutch washer from the sliding clutch. Remove the assembly from the left end of the hub shell.

Cartridge: Remove the clutch spring, driver, and lead

(new name for the cam). Remove the sliding clutch and tap it lightly on the benchtop to remove the clutch washer. Now remove the axle key and small spring. Go to step ⑧.

④ Install the Shimano ball-cup tool XB-320 in a vise. Place the wheel over the ball-cup tool and turn counterclockwise to loosen the ball cup. Alternatively, you can turn the tool with a large adjustable wrench. A workable substitute tool can be made by grinding the ends of the arms of a Sturmey-Archer cross clutch, and turning it with a driver on which you have ground wrench flats. If you don't mind destroying the ball cup, you can remove it by cutting a notch with a cold chisel and then turning it with a hammer and punch.

SLIDING CLUTCH

CLUTCH WASHER   CAM

③

④

⑤

Cartridge: Omit this step. The ball cup is not removable.

⑤ Unscrew the ball cup and remove it, then the ring gear. Remove the axle key and small spring from the axle.

Cartridge: The ball cup is not removable. Hold the ring-gear pawls in and lift it off over the sliding clutch. Then remove the ball retainer. Go to step ②.

⑥ Remove the left-hand locknut. Remove the brake arm, dustcap, left-side brake cone, brake shoes, and return spring.

Cartridge: Remove the two locknuts, washer, and sleeve. In the TC-100 (older cartridge model), the sleeve is part of the inner locknut. In the TC-200, the sleeve is inside the washer, under the inner locknut. Remove the brake-arm assembly, with the bearing retainer, coiled return spring, and retarder-spring assembly. If one of the springs needs replacing, you can unscrew the spring assembly counterclockwise. Pop the bearing retainer off over the left cone. The brake arm, dustcap, and left-side brake cone do not come apart. Go to step ⑦.

⑦ Loosen the stop nut, then remove it with the flatted washer and locknut. Remove the spring guide and planet cage.

Cartridge: You have already removed the spring guide with the brake arm. Remove the assembly from the right side of the hub shell, then remove the planet cage from the left end of the axle. Go to step ⑤.

⑧ With a punch or a nail, tap out the planet-cage pawl pins partway. Pull the pins out the rest of the way, catching the pawls and pawl springs. Repeat this operation for the ring-gear assembly.

Cartridge: Do this step, then go to step ⑨.

⑨ Remove the stop spring (snap band) from the planet cage, freeing the pinion pins. Remove the pinion pins and pinions. Remove the thrust washer from under the pinions. *Note: Some older planet cages like the one shown have the pinion pins riveted in place. If pinions or thrust washer are worn, the entire planet cage must be replaced.*

Cartridge: Do this step, then go to step ⑩.

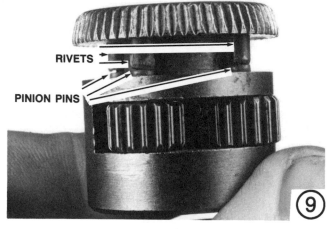

RIVETS

PINION PINS

⑩ Remove the dustcap from the driver by prying it up with a small screwdriver. Remove the bearing retainer.

Cartridge: The driver is sold as a complete unit, so omit this step unless installing a separate retainer. This completes the disassembly.

Cleaning and Inspecting

Clean all parts in solvent and rinse them, or wipe them dry with a lintless cloth. Keep all cleaned parts on paper towels to prevent contamination. Cover them with a clean towel to prevent grit from entering the internal parts and bearings.

It is best to replace the three bearing-retainer assemblies rather than to inspect them.

Inspect the bearing surfaces of both cones for scoring (scratchlike marks) and pitted surfaces. Check for stripped threads.

Inspect the axle for stripped threads and for worn or chipped sun-gear teeth.

Check the dustcaps to make sure they are not bent, crimped, or distorted.

Inspect the hub shell for damage, including chipped or worn ratchet teeth. Inspect the bearing cup for scores, pits, or excessive wear. Check the flanges of the hub shell for cracks and to be sure they are not loose.

Inspect all the pawls for worn or damaged driving edges.

NOTE: If the hub has been completely disassembled, all the pawl springs should be replaced to ensure proper service.

Inspect the gear-ring ratchet, planet-cage ratchet, and planetary gears for chipped or worn teeth.

Inspect the right-hand ball cup for chipped or worn ratchet teeth. Check the bearing surface for scores or pits. Check for stripped threads.

Inspect the bearing surface of the driver for scores or pits.

Check the return spring, slide (retarder) spring, pinion-pin stop spring, and clutch springs for correct shape.

Inspect the slide spring (retarder spring) for wear and proper operation. If the spring needs replacement, be sure to install the new one with its long leg *ahead* of the gap, as shown in the exploded diagram. **CAUTION: Installing the spring backward will result in excessive drag and wear.**

Check the mating threads of the driver and the cam (or lead) for wear.

Check the brake shoes and hub-shell braking surface for wear or glazing.

Check the teeth of the cam (or lead), ring gear, planet cage, and brake shoes for wear.

Check the axle key to be sure it is not worn or damaged.

Inspect the axle nuts for stripped or damaged threads.

Check the sliding clutch for rounded or chipped power-transmitting surfaces.

Inspect the sprocket for wear to the driving faces of the teeth. Consider replacing the sprocket with one of another size to improve the gear ratio (see page 207.)

Assembling

⑪ Coat the small bearing retainer with multipurpose grease, and work grease in between the bearing balls. Place grease in the driver's bearing cup. Install the retainer *flat side out* and then tap the dustcap in *flat side down* using a hammer.

Cartridge: The replacement driver assembly is sold as a unit with the dustcap and bearing retainer. Add grease if necessary. Go to step ⑫.

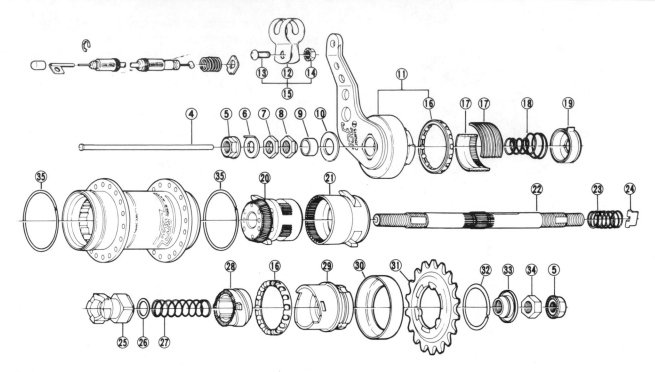

Exploded diagram of the Shimano 3CC three-speed hub with coaster brake. In most respects, this hub is the same as the earlier-model 3SC.

ITEM	DESCRIPTION	ITEM	DESCRIPTION
4	Push rod	20	Carrier assembly
5	Flange nut	21	Ring gear assembly
6	Non-turn washer	22	Hub axle 168mm (6⅝")
7	Locknut B	23	Clutch spring B
8	Stop nut	24	Axle key
9	Sleeve	25	Sliding clutch
10	Brake-arm washer	26	Clutch washer
11	Brake-arm assembly	27	Clutch spring A
12	Brake-arm clip (band type)	28	Lead
13	Clip screw M6×14mm (9/16")	29	Driver with ball retainer and dustcap
14	Clip nut (M6)	30	Seal cap
15	Brake-arm clip assembly (band type)	31	Sprocket
16	Ball retainer B	32	Snapring
17	Brake shoe assembly	33	Right-hand cone
18	Return spring	34	Right-hand locknut
19	Spring guide & slide spring	35	Seal spring

⑫ Place the thrust washer in its recess in the planet cage. Install the pinions, pinion pins, and stop spring. The flat section of the stop spring must go between two pinion pins *where there is not a pawl-spring hole.* *NOTE: Some early-model planet cages are riveted together.*

Cartridge: Do this step, then go to step ⑬.

⑬ Install pawls, pawl pins, and pawl springs in the gear ring and planet cage as shown. In the picture, one pawl and spring are shown outside the end of each assembly, for clarity. The angled pawls and long pawl springs are for the gear ring. Make sure that a pawl pin passes through the loop in each spring and that the pawls face in the direction of rotation. Test the pawls to see that they work properly.

Cartridge: The pawl pins for the gear ring are longer and are knurled at the outer end. When finished with this step, go to step ⑰.

⑭ Work is easiest if you chuck the right (flatted) end of the axle in a vise now. Install the planet cage over the hollow end of the axle. Install the spring guide, with its tabs indexed in the holes in the planet cage. The tab on the slide (retarder) spring must face as shown, so it exerts a *light* drag when the planet cage is rotating forward. Install the stop nut finger-tight, then back it off by one turn. Install the flatted washer and locknut. Tighten the locknut.

Cartridge: Install the planet cage, push down the planet cage pawls, and then slide the assembly into the right end of the hub shell. Go to the next step.

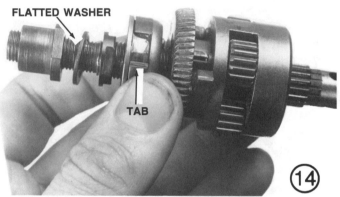
FLATTED WASHER
TAB
⑭

THRUST WASHER ⑫

⑮ Install the large return spring. Grease the large ball retainer and assemble it *flat side facing the outside of the hub* as shown. Grease the brake shoe (two-

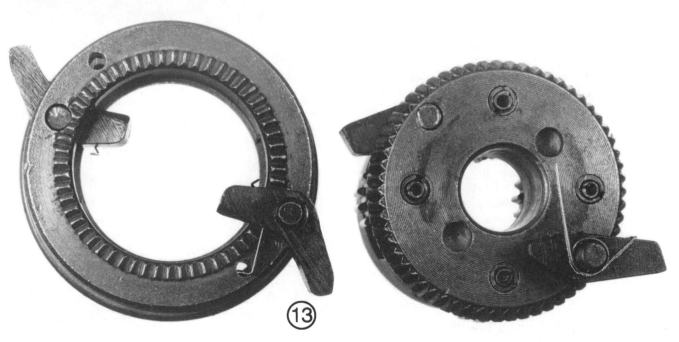
⑬

piece, held together by a circular spring) and install it *toothed inner edge down* with its lugs indexed in the cone slots, then slip the assembly into place so the narrow slot of the cone indexes on the retarder spring. **CAUTION: Failure to lubricate properly will lead to rapid wear.**

Cartridge: Add about a teaspoon of oil at the left end of the hub shell. Grease the brake shoes and place them in the hub shell toothed inner edges down. **CAUTION: Failure to lubricate properly will lead to rapid wear.** *If necessary, replace the return-spring and retarder-spring assemblies on the brake-arm assembly by turning the return spring clockwise. The slide spring must be as shown, with the tab to the left of the gap, aligned to enter the slot in the left brake cone. Grease the large bearing retainer and install it on the left cone flat side toward the outside of the hub. Install the brake-arm assembly, with the brake cone tabs indexed in the spaces between the brake shoes. Then turn it to seat the spring guide's small tabs in the planet cage. Go to the next step.*

⑯ Replace the dustcap, brake arm, and left locknut to hold the brake-shoe assembly in place. The brake shoe should have 0.5mm to 1mm (about ¹⁄₃₂ inch) of play left and right. If play is incorrect, remove the locknut and brake parts and readjust the stop nut and locknut in step ⑭. Turning the nuts toward the planet cage *decreases* play.

Cartridge: There is no brake-shoe adjustment. Install the flat washer, then push the sleeve in through the washer. Install the two locknuts. In the early cartridge model TC-100, the sleeve is part of the inner locknut. Adjust the bearing for minimal sideplay without binding. Go to step ㉑.

⑰ Remove the axle from the vise and turn it over. Install the short spring and the axle key *indented side down.*

Cartridge: With the hollow end of the axle down, install the smallest spring over the end of the axle.

Push the spring down and then install the axle key in the axle slot, indented side down. Go to step ⑲.

⑱ Turn the gear ring's pawls clockwise, then place it inside the right end of the hub shell *toothed end first.* Screw in the right ball cup and tighten it with the ball-cup tool.

Cartridge: Turn the axle over so the hollow end is up. Hold the gear ring with its gear teeth at its upper end, and turn the pawls counterclockwise; slide it down the axle into place. Go to step ⑭.

⑲ Slide the assembly into the left end of the hub shell. Add about a teaspoon of oil in the right end of the hub shell. **CAUTION: Failure to lubricate properly will lead to rapid wear.** Install the sliding clutch with the wavy end down, the cam with the toothed end down, the clutch washer, and the clutch spring. Grease the large ball retainer, and install it *flat side out,* then the driver.

(18)

Cartridge: The assembly is not yet in the hub shell. Install the sliding clutch wavy end down, the clutch washer, and the lead, toothed side down. Grease the large ball retainer and install it flat side out. Install the driver and the long clutch spring. Go to step ㉑.

㉑ Install the right-hand cone and locknut. Adjust the right-side bearing for minimal sideplay without binding.
Cartridge: The assembly is not yet in the hub shell. Install the right cone and tighten it against the shoulder

(20)

BEARING RETAINER (GREASED)

CLUTCH WASHER

CAM

(19)

on the axle. Then install the locknut and tighten it. This hub's bearing adjustment is on the other side. Go to step ⑱.

㉑ Reinstall the dustcap, then the sprocket, with the dish facing the same way as before, unless you wish to change the chainline. Spread the snapring over the flange of the driver with a small screwdriver, and tap it lightly into its groove with a hammer and punch.

Cartridge: This step completes the assembly.

Finishing Up

Add oil at the lubricator if any, and at the hollow end of the axle.

Replace the wheel (page 72).

Adjust the cable (page 213).

㉑

15 • CRANK HANGERS AND PEDALS

A complete hanger set consists of a spindle passing through the bottom bracket of the bicycle frame, chainwheels and cranks attached to the spindle, pedals threaded into the ends of the cranks, and the necessary bearings, bearing cups, washers, and locknuts or lockrings to hold it all together for efficient operation.

HANGER SETS

Three types of hanger sets are used on modern bicycles:

1. A *cottered crank assembly,* usually made of steel in three pieces with the cranks attached to the spindle by large cotters (tapered pins), is used on precision-built bicycles. Procedures for overhauling a cottered crank hanger set begin on page 316.

2. A *cotterless crank hanger set* is similar to the cottered crank type, except for materials used in its construction and the method of attaching the cranks to the spindle. This assembly is used on the best touring and racing machines. The spindle is made of steel and the cranks and chainwheels are made of lightweight, tough aluminum alloy. The cranks are secured to the spindle with crank bolts and a special tool set is required for each make and model in order to "pull" the cranks free of the axle. Procedures for overhaul of the cotterless crank begin on page 318.

3. A *one-piece unit* with the spindle and both cranks made from a single steel forging is commonly referred to as an American one-piece crank and is found on less expensive bicycles. Overhaul procedures for the one-piece hanger set begin on page 325.

Chainwheel Replacement

Bolt-on chainwheels are easily removed and replaced by unscrewing the bolts. The center opening in chainwheels is large enough that *it is not necessary to remove the right crank or pedal to remove most chainwheels.* Cleaning the teeth of chainwheels is much easier after removing them.

Straightening Chainwheels and Cranks

If you notice during your preliminary disassembly that a chainwheel wobbles from side to side, first remove the chainwheels from the crank, if they are bolted on (do not remove the crank from the spindle yet). Then straighten the arms of the crank assembly. Check their alignment by holding a wedge-shaped object such as a screwdriver blade against the chainstay so it just strikes the arms. Rotate the crank and note which arms are bent. Lever them toward or away from the chainstay as necessary.

Once the arms are straight, replace the chainwheel and straighten it by levering it carefully with an adjustable wrench, tightened to fit its width.

Cartridge-bearing Units

In recent years, several brands of hanger bearing units and pedals using sealed radial-contact cartridge bearings (see page 68) have appeared on the market. Service procedures for sealed units begin on page 335.

Hanger Problems

Problems in one part of the drivetrain may seem to be in another. Also, it is much easier to test for certain problems such as bent cranks before disassembly. Before disassembling a crank hanger or pedal, read the drivetrain problem chart and the section on inspecting the drivetrain in Chapter 7.

PEDALS

Pedals are classified as either the rubber-block or metal type. Several variations in style and construction of each are on the market.

Rubber-block pedals have two rubber pads secured

RATTRAP   RATTRAP

PROFESSIONAL TYPE

CAMPAGNOLO TRACK   CAMPAGNOLO ROAD

Examples of metal pedals.

to the pedal frame by bolts or studs; the frame rotates about a spindle which is attached to the crank. Bearings and cones are used at each end of the spindle. One of the cones is adjustable to provide minimum friction and efficient operation. Often, this type of pedal must be removed from the bicycle and partly disassembled in order to make an adjustment. It is used on almost all juvenile, coaster-brake, two-speed, and three-speed bicycles. Overhaul procedures for a rubber-block pedal begin on page 330.

Metal-type pedals are constructed quite differently from rubber-block pedals. A complete metal frame is used instead of the rubber pads. Such a surface provides an excellent grip and minimizes shoe slippage in wet weather or while pedaling under strained conditions. A wide variety of frame designs is available to suit the individual's preference for touring or racing. This type of pedal is used on almost all better five- and ten-speed bicycles. Overhaul procedures for metal pedals begin on page 331.

Toeclips and Straps

Toeclips and straps, attached to the pedals, increase pedaling efficiency and keep feet from slipping off pedals—a common cause of falls. Instructions for installing and adjusting toeclips and straps are in Chapter 2, page 24.

Locking shoe-pedal systems which replace toeclips and straps must also be adjusted similarly for efficient pedaling.

Rubber-block pedals are intended for use without toeclips and straps. Many, though not all, two-sided metal pedals are intended for all-terrain use where toeclips and straps are impractical. Most single-sided metal pedals *must* be used with toeclips and straps, because these pedals are top-heavy and will present their underside to the feet.

HEAVY DUTY   BOWED   DIAMOND TREAD

Examples of rubber-block pedals.

PARTS INTERCHANGEABILITY

Crank hangers are one of the areas of the bicycle where mismatch of parts is most likely to have serious consequences. Here are the potential problems and how to deal with them.

Pedals are sold in three threadings:

½ inch × 20 TPI (mostly for one-piece cranks)

14mm × 1.25mm (French, marked D and G)

9/16 inch × 20 TPI (English, Italian and ISO, marked L and R or D and S)

French and English pedal-to-crank threadings are just different enough to damage crank threads seriously. Many French bicycles today are sold with English threading. **CAUTION: Do not install a pedal if it begins to bind when partly threaded into the crank, or if it is loose and wobbly! Do not install a ½-inch pedal into an ISO-standard aluminum crank unless the pedal threads are at least ½ inch long.** Cranks with the increasingly rare French threading can easily be tapped out to the slightly larger English threading.

Cotterless crank extractor threads are not all of the same diameter. See the discussion of cotterless-crank removal, page 318.

Bottom-bracket cups of one brand may not hold the bearing balls in the correct-size circle for a spindle of another brand. Cottered-crank spindle ends are of two slightly different diameters, and cotter pins, three. The square ends of cotterless spindles are not standardized, and may damage cranks of another model, *even of the same brand.* Whenever possible, buy replacement parts of the same make and model, or buy a complete new set.

Frame and bottom-bracket threads have six different dimensional standards:

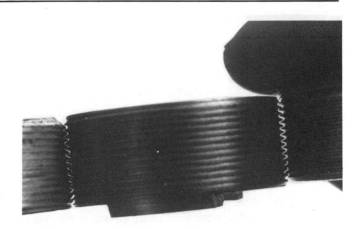

Two cups which have the same thread pitch will mesh tightly with each other *(left).* Two cups with different thread pitches will rock over each other *(right).*

The teeth of some chainwheels are flush with the inner face *(right).* The teeth of other chainwheels are centered between the faces *(left).* Except with innermost chainwheels of a few cranksets, the smoother face should face the inside, for positive shifting.

	Diameter	Thread pitch	Fixed-cup threading
English	34.8mm ×	24 TPI	Left
ISO	34.9mm ×	24 TPI	Left
Raleigh	34.9mm ×	26 TPI	Left
French	35mm ×	25.4 TPI (1mm)	Right
Swiss	35mm ×	25.4 TPI (1mm)	Left
Italian	36mm ×	24 TPI	Right

English and ISO bottom-bracket threadings are interchangeable. Attempts to interchange English/ISO, French/Swiss, and Raleigh cups will lead to stripped frame threads, so check before installing. Try to mesh the threads of the original and replacement bottom-bracket cups. If the thread pitch is different, they will rock over each other.

Chainwheels may be integral with the cranks, or may attach with bolts. The bolt circle diameter depends on the brand and model of crankset. There is interchangeability between some models and brands. Fortunately, chainwheels will either fit or obviously not fit.

Lateral spacing between chainwheels may vary even if the bolt circle diameter is the same. The teeth may be halfway between the faces or flush with the inner face. When one shoulder is tapered, it should face the bicycle's frame, for smooth shifting. On cranksets which use spacer washers, spacing can be adjusted by installing washers of a different thickness. Spacing should be such that the chain engages each chainwheel, neither skipping over it nor falling between chainwheels when shifted by the front derailleur.

Exact replacement parts are not always available, or you may need a shorter or longer spindle to move the chainwheels toward or away from the frame. If you have interchangeability problems, *take the original parts with you to the bike shop when you go to buy new parts,* and ask the salesperson to consult the bottom-bracket interchangeability tables in *Sutherland's Handbook for Bicycle Mechanics.*

Service Note

For optimum service, the hanger set should be overhauled, thoroughly lubricated, and adjusted every six months or once a year, depending on the extent of touring, type of terrain, or racing for which the bicycle is used.

OVERHAULING A COTTERED CRANKSET

The following step-by-step illustrated instructions cover disassembling, assembling, and adjusting a cottered crankset. *NOTE: A cotter is a tapered steel pin that holds the crank on the spindle.* A detailed exploded drawing of this type of crankset appears later in this section.

Tools and Supplies You Will Need

Hammer and drift punch and bottom-bracket support pipe; or cotter-pin press; or large Vise-Grip pliers
C-spanner wrench (optional)
File
Tweezers
Grease
Cycle oil
22 ¼-inch bearing balls
Replacement cotter pins and nuts

Tools and Supplies You May Need

Bottom-bracket tool set or 15-inch adjustable wrench
Replacement bottom-bracket bearing cups
Replacement bottom-bracket spindle

Removing and Disassembling

① Run penetrating oil into the gap between each cotter pin and crank. Loosen the acorn nut on the cotter of the right-side crank until it is approximately ⅛ inch above the end of the cotter. Support the underside of the crank with a length of pipe, with one end around the cotter and the other resting on a *hard* concrete or stone floor or block of metal. **CAUTION: The crank must be**

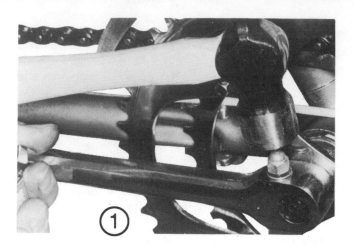

solidly supported to prevent damage to the bearings or the spindle while driving out the cotter. Strike the nut squarely with a single, sharp blow in order to loosen the cotter. **CAUTION: If the nut is not hit squarely and firmly, the cotter may bend and be very difficult to remove.** An alternate, and better, method is to remove the cotter nut and use a commercial *cotter-pin press.* It is also possible to press out

a cotter pin with large Vise-Grip pliers, squeezing between the threaded end of the cotter pin and the opposite side of the crank. These methods eliminate the risk of damage to the bearings and cotter pin.

②Remove the cotter nut, and then drive the cotter out with a drift punch. Place the punch in the center of the cotter and strike it a sharp blow. Slide the right-side crank-and-chainwheel off the spindle.

③Remove the left-side crank in a similar manner. From this point onward, disassembly of a cottered crank is identical to that of a cotterless crank. Read about parts interchangeability on page 315, then turn ahead to step ⑤ on page 319.

Assembling

From step ⑩, page 324.

④Oil the spindle and the cotter pin. Rotate the spindle so the flat on its right end faces forward. Slide

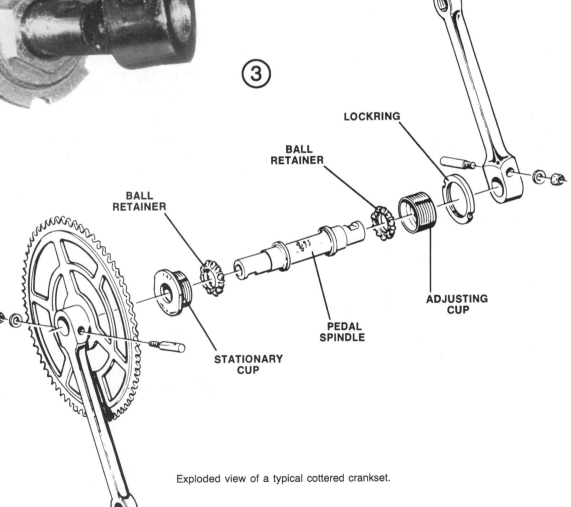

Exploded view of a typical cottered crankset.

the right crank into place, pedal end forward. Slide the cotter into place, with the flat in the cotter indexing with the flat in the spindle.

⑤ Slide the threaded end of the cotter over the pipe you used during disassembly. **CAUTION: The crank**

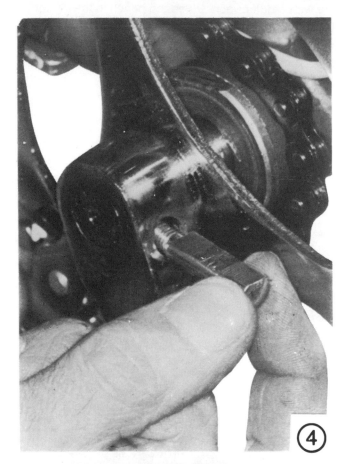

④

⑤

must be solidly supported to prevent damage to the bearings when you drive the cotter home. Strike the cotter a solid blow to seat it, and then check to be sure at least ¼ inch of thread is exposed. Install the washer, and tighten the nut to pull the cotter firmly into position. Strike the cotter once again, with the pipe under the crank, and then retighten the nut securely. Install the left-hand crank in a similar manner. Again, when the crank is held forward and horizontal, the flat of the spindle must face forward. Install the chain over the small chainwheel.

Alternately, use a commercial cotter-pin press or Vise-Grip pliers to install the cotter pin.

CAUTION: The cotter pin must be hammered or pressed in before tightening the nut. If you only slip in the cotter pin and tighten the nut, the crank will loosen.

OVERHAULING A COTTERLESS CRANKSET

The following procedures provide step-by-step illustrated instructions for disassembling, assembling, and adjusting a cotterless crank. A special tool is required for removing and installing a cotterless crank assembly; it consists of a socket for removing the crank bolt from the spindle and an extractor for pulling the crank free of the spindle. Most first-rate bicycle shops carry a complete line of cotterless-crank tool sets. Always specify the manufacturer of your crank when making a tool purchase and double-check to be sure you have the correct set before leaving the store. Attempting to work on a cotterless-crank assembly with the wrong tool can cause serious damage and result in a needless and expensive replacement of parts.

Tools and Supplies You Will Need

C-spanner wrench or hammer and punch
Crank extractor to fit your cranks
Allen wrench or screwdriver for dustcaps
Crankbolt wrench
Tweezers
Grease
Cycle oil
22 ¼-inch bearing balls (28 ³⁄₁₆-inch balls for Campagnolo Super Record)

Tools and Supplies You May Need

Bottom-bracket tool set or 15-inch adjustable wrench
Replacement bottom-bracket bearing cups
Replacement bottom-bracket spindle
Threadlock compound

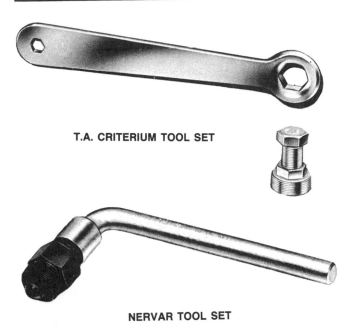

T.A. CRITERIUM TOOL SET

NERVAR TOOL SET

Examples of cotterless-crank tool sets. Be sure to use a set which fits correctly to prevent stripping the crank threads.

Removing and Disassembling

① Remove the dustcap from the right and left cranks using the correct-size Allen wrench. *NOTE: The dustcaps on many makes of cotterless cranks have a slot and must be removed with a wide-bladed screwdriver.*

② Remove the crank bolt or nut using a thin-walled socket or the socket from the cotterless-crank tool set.

Remove the washer. Disengage the chain from the chainwheel and let it rest on the frame. Mark the crank and axle so you can replace them in the same orientation (out of the four possible).

③ Thread the extractor part of the tool set into the crank, and then slowly rotate the extractor clockwise with the socket part of the tool to pull the crank free of the spindle.

The extractor has threads which mate with those inside the large end of the crank. Most cranks have 22mm-diameter threads, but older TA cranks have 23mm and older (pre-1982) Stronglight cranks have 23.35mm. A few early Lambert bicycles had 7/8 inch × 24 TPI threads.

The most common error is to use a TA extractor with older Stronglight cranks. It fits just tightly enough that it would seem to work and just loosely enough to strip out the threads. **CAUTION: Do not use an extractor which fits loosely.** The Park brand "Universal" extractor has threads for all *except* older Stronglight and Lambert cranks.

If the crank's threads are stripped, it can be removed with a gear puller.

The spindle may have a threaded stud or a threaded hole at its end. An extractor designed for a stud-end spindle may be used for a hollow-end spindle by inserting a small (undersized) bolt into the spindle to build up its end.

CAUTION: Exercise care when pulling the crank. The extractor works like a wheel puller for an automobile. As the extractor is moved in against the end of the spindle, the crank will be forced off. The crank is made of aluminum alloy and it is softer than the extractor or the spindle. Therefore, if you are having difficulty, remove the socket, tap the end of the extractor lightly with a hammer, and then rotate the extractor about an eighth of a turn. Repeat striking the extractor and turning it until the crank is loose. Remove the extractor from the crank.

④ Slide the crank free of the spindle. Remove the crank bolt, washer, and left-side crank in a similar manner.

⑤ Remove the lockring from the left-side adjustable bearing cup with a C-spanner or drift punch and hammer. The punch will do the job, but it will mar the lockring slightly.

⑥ Back out the left-side bearing cup until it is free of the frame. As the cup comes free, tilt the bicycle slightly to the right and pull on the spindle to hold it against the left-side bearing cup. This way you will keep loose bearing balls from falling out as you withdraw the spindle from the frame.

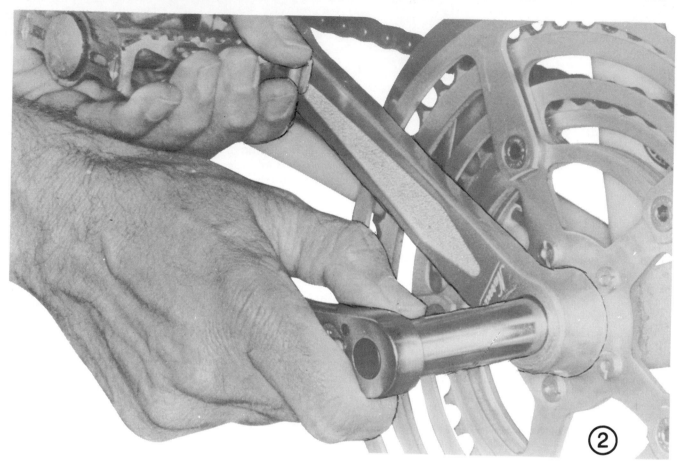

②

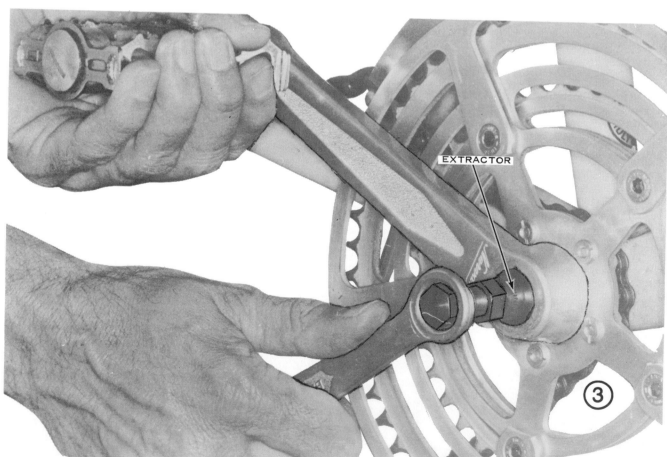

EXTRACTOR

③

⑦ Remove the right-side (*fixed* or *stationary*) cup only if necessary. *NOTE: Some fixed cups turn clockwise for removal, others counterclockwise. If in doubt, try both ways.*

A fixed cup's wrench flats may be narrow: Removal is positive with the special wrench for each brand of cup, but there are three substitute methods:

1. Use a 15-inch adjustable wrench. This is the technique shown in the illustration. If the flats on the bottom-bracket cup are narrow, clamp the wrench to the bottom-bracket cup with a large bolt inserted through the spindle hole. A variation: Lay the bicycle on its left side on the floor, resting the left end of the bottom bracket on a wooden block; turn the wrench while an assistant stands on its jaws to keep it from slipping.

2. Clamp the fixed cup's wrench flats in a vise and turn the entire frame.

3. Clamp a ½-inch or ⅝-inch-diameter bolt into the fixed cup using a stack of split-end lockwashers and a nut. Tighten the bolt and nut together with two large wrenches. Then turn them whichever way loosens the cup.

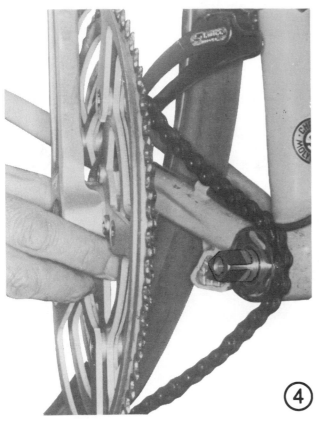

④

⑤

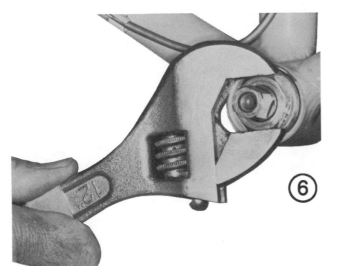

⑥

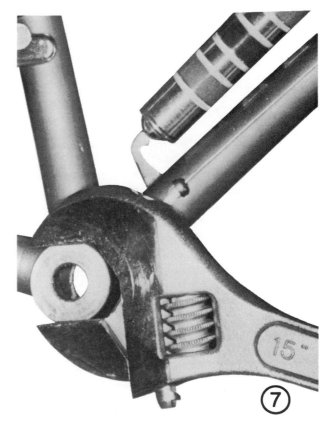

⑦

Cleaning and Inspecting

Clean all parts with solvent and blow them dry with compressed air or rinse them. Keep the cleaned parts on paper towels to avoid contamination. Cover them

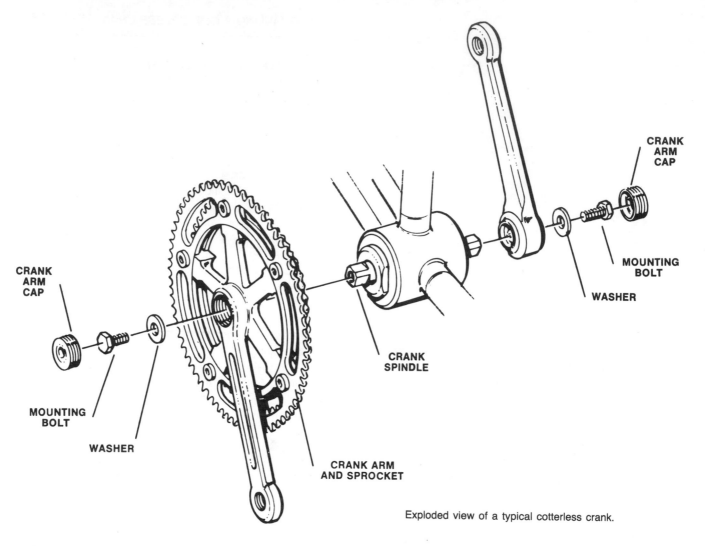

CRANK
ARM
CAP

CRANK
ARM
CAP

MOUNTING
BOLT

MOUNTING
BOLT

WASHER

WASHER

CRANK
SPINDLE

CRANK ARM
AND SPROCKET

Exploded view of a typical cotterless crank.

with a clean towel to keep grit from sticking to the internal parts and the bearings.

Remove bolt-on chainwheels from the crank, and clean them with solvent and a brush.

Check the bearing races of both bearing cups and the spindle for scores, pits, or corrosion. Inspect the threads of the cups, lockring, dustcaps, ends of the spindle, and the crank bolts for being stripped.

Check the chainwheels for bent teeth. If any of the teeth are out of line with the chainwheel, carefully bend them back using a wrench with steady, even pressure. Try not to bend them back and forth too much as this could cause metal fatigue and the teeth may snap off under strain while the bike is in use.

If working on a cottered crank, check the spindle for worn cotter keyways (rounded edges), pitted or scored bearing races, and other visible signs of damage. Check to be sure the spindle is not bent.

Inspect both cotters for stripped or damaged threads. Check them for rounded edges indicating the cotter has been loose in the crank. Check the cotter keyway of the cranks for excessive wear (rounded edges).

All other bottom brackets can be rethreaded to the

larger Italian size, and Campagnolo makes oversize Italian cups.

Check the lockring and locknut for stripped or damaged threads.

It is best to replace all of the bearing balls with new ones rather than to try to inspect them.

Almost all crank hangers use 11 ¼-inch bearing balls per side, except Campagnolo Super Record, which uses 14 ³⁄₁₆-inch balls per side. Most ball-bearing-retainer assemblies for crank spindles have only 7 or 8 balls. It is best to replace these retainers with 11 loose balls, increasing load capacity.

Assembling

⑧ Apply a generous coating of multipurpose grease to the inside race of the stationary bearing cup. Thread the lubricated cup into the frame and tighten it securely, using one of the techniques described in step ⑦.

Some stationary cups thread in clockwise, others counterclockwise. If the cup threads in clockwise, it will tend to unscrew while the bicycle is ridden, so it must be tightened especially hard. Use of threadlock compound here is not a bad idea.

Insert 11 ¼-inch bearing balls into the right cup after installing it in the frame, and into the left cup, shown here, before installing it with the crank spindle.

After securing the cup in the frame, turn the bicycle on its right side and insert the balls through the spindle opening in the cup. Look into the left end of the bottom bracket to make sure that there are 11 balls in a full circle. Also add grease and install 11 loose balls in the adjustable cup. If reinstalling bearing retainers, pack them with a generous amount of multipurpose grease. Work the lubricant throughout the bearings and retainer with your fingers, and then slide a retainer assembly onto each end of the spindle with the flat side of the retainer facing toward the center of the spindle. Coat the inside of the adjustable bearing cup with multipurpose grease.

It is a good idea to install a plastic bottom-bracket liner, available at bike shops, to prevent dirt from running down the frame tubes into the bearings. However, you will have to modify this liner to allow lubrication with an oil or grease fitting.

Notice that the distance from the bearing race to the end of the spindle is greater on one end. Hold the adjustable bearing cup in place on the short end of the spindle, and then slowly slide the spindle through the frame and stationary bearing cup on the right-side of the frame. The lubricant will hold the bearings in place provided you do not jar or bump the spindle during installation.

CAUTION: If the spindle is installed the wrong way, the inner chainwheel will be too close to the frame.

⑨ Thread the adjustable bearing cup into the frame, and then check the spindle rotation. It should turn freely, with only a discernible amount of endplay when you attempt to move the spindle in and out of the frame.

⑧

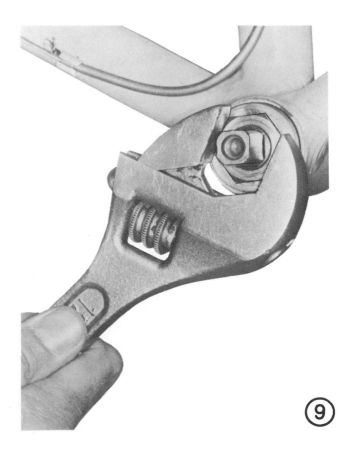

⑨

⑩ Turn the lockring onto the adjustable bearing cup and tighten it using a C-spanner wrench or a drift punch and hammer. Check the bearing adjustment by turning the spindle between your fingertips. The adjustment should be slightly tight: The spindle should turn freely most of the time, but it may bind lightly once every couple of turns. If the spindle is too loose, it will wear more quickly.

Loosen the lockring by turning it counterclockwise, and then rotate the adjustable bearing cup either clockwise to tighten and remove excessive endplay, or counterclockwise to allow the spindle to turn freely; tighten the lockring.

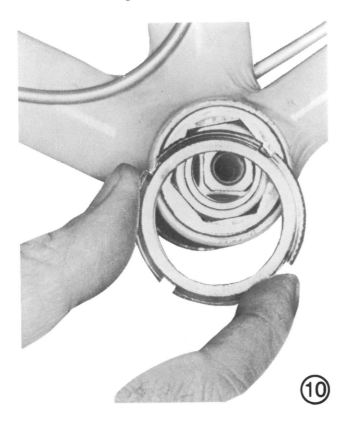

Tightening the lockring against the cup will *loosen* the bearing adjustment slightly. Usually, the cup will turn when you turn the lockring. It is easiest to make the final adjustment by tightening both at once. Be patient; you may have to make this adjustment several times before you get it just right.

Pipe cleaners wrapped around the spindle between it and each cup will partially seal the bearing and help prevent contamination of the lubricant.

If you are working on a cottered crank, return at this time to step ④ of the cottered-crank procedure on page 317.

⑪ Slide the chainwheels and right-side crank assembly onto the spindle with the flats inside the wheels indexed with the flats on the spindle; simul-

taneously engage the chain on the teeth of the small sprocket. If you are using the same crank and spindle as before, orient them the same way to minimize wear in the square fitting.

⑫ Slip the washer onto the crank bolt, and then thread it into the end of the spindle; tighten it using a thin-walled socket or the socket part of the cotterless tool set. Install the left-side crank in a similar manner, with the crank facing 180 degrees in the opposite direction from the right-side crank. **CAUTION: The crank bolt of each crank must be retightened every 50**

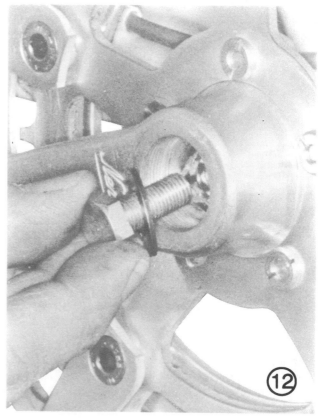

miles for the first 150 miles following an overhaul, but do not overtighten. Use only moderate force. The spindle Is made of steel and the crank of an aluminum alloy; therefore, if the crank is allowed to move on the spindle during pedaling, the machined fit of the crank will be ruined. If overtightened, it may crack. New bearing parts may also need readjustment after a break-in period.

⑬ Thread a dustcap into each crank. Tighten it securely, using a correct size Allen wrench, or a screwdriver if the cap has a slot.

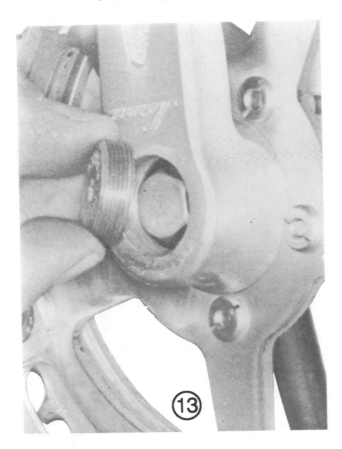

OVERHAULING A ONE-PIECE CRANK

The step-by-step illustrated instructions in this section cover disassembling, assembling, and adjusting American-type one-piece cranks. A detailed exploded drawing of this type of crank is included.

Tools and Supplies You Will Need

1 ⅛-inch open-end wrench or 12-inch adjustable wrench
Pedal wrench (½-inch opening)
Screwdriver
Drift punch

Hammer
Bearing retainers
Grease
Cycle oil

Supplies You May Need

Bearing cones
Hanger cups
Crank
NOTE: The threads of Schwinn one-piece cranks and bearing cones are different (28 TPI) from those of other brands (24 TPI). The bearing retainers also are different. The entire assembly is interchangeable.

Removing and Disassembling

① Remove the nuts and bolts securing the chain guard, and then slide off the guard.

② Remove the left-side pedal by turning its spindle clockwise. **CAUTION: The left-side pedal has left-hand threads.**

③ Remove the left-side locknut by turning it clockwise until it is clear of the ball cup and then sliding it off the crank. **CAUTION: The locknut has a left-hand thread.** Remove the keyed lockwasher.

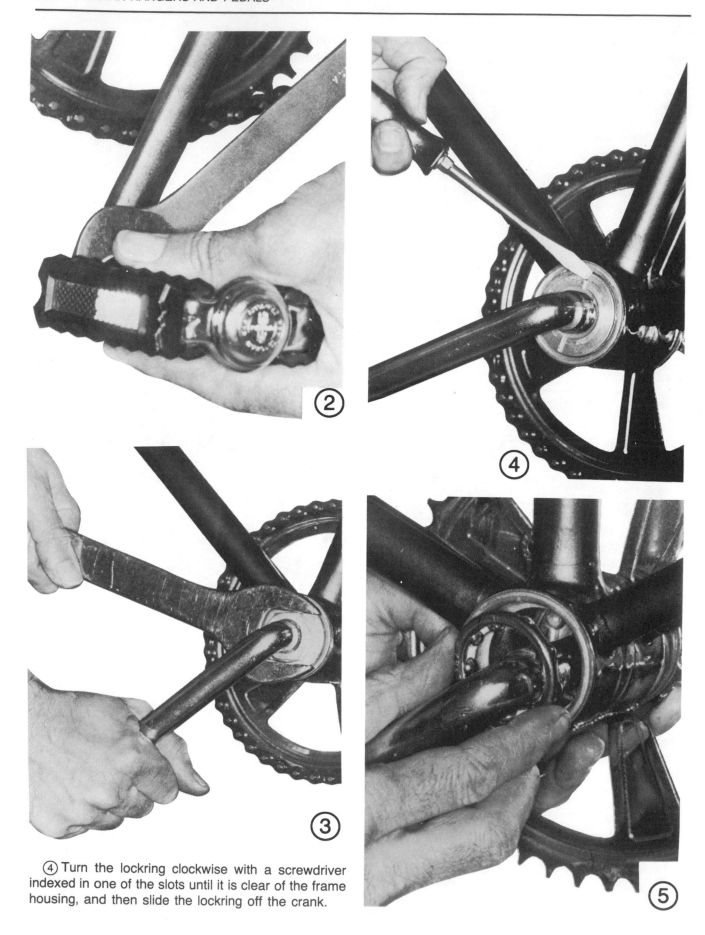

④ Turn the lockring clockwise with a screwdriver indexed in one of the slots until it is clear of the frame housing, and then slide the lockring off the crank.

BALL BEARING RETAINER ASSEMBLY

⑥ Remove the chain from the sprocket. Pull out the ball-bearing-retainer assembly from the housing.

⑥ Slide the crank assembly out of the frame housing from the sprocket side. Remove the sprocket-side ball-bearing-retainer assembly. Take off the right-side pedal by turning the spindle counterclockwise.

Cleaning and Inspecting

Clean all parts in solvent and wash them with detergent and water or wipe them dry with a lintless cloth. Clean out the inside of the frame housing with solvent and wipe it dry.

Check the threads on the crank arms to be sure they are not stripped or damaged. Check the teeth on the chainwheel. If any of them are not in line with the wheel, carefully bend them back using a wrench and a steady, even pressure. Try not to bend them back and forth too much as this causes metal fatigue and the teeth may snap off under strain while the bike is in use.

Check the frame housing for pits or scores (scratch-like marks) on the internal bearing races. If necessary, tap out the races with a hammer and punch and replace them. Check the bearing cores for wear or pitting of the bearing surfaces. Replace them if necessary.

It is best to replace the retainers and balls whether or not they show signs of wear. The retainers used in one-piece crank hangers are available at most bicycle shops.

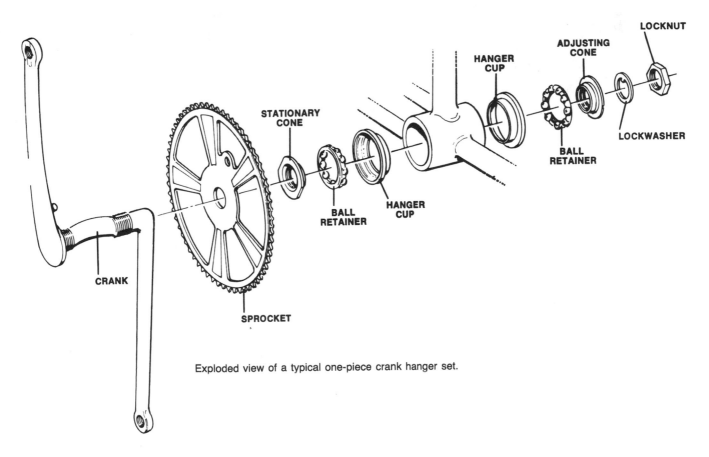

Exploded view of a typical one-piece crank hanger set.

Assembling

⑦ Pack both bearing-retainer assemblies with a generous amount of multipurpose grease. Work the lubricant throughout the bearings and retainer with your fingers. Slide one of the lubricated retainers over the crank and onto the chainwheel, with the flat side of the retainer against the chainwheel. Insert the crank through the frame housing, and then install the other lubricated retainer assembly, with the flat side facing out, as shown.

⑧ Engage the chain over the chainwheel with the links fitting properly onto the teeth. Thread the lockring counterclockwise into the frame housing.

⑨ Tighten the lockring counterclockwise with a screwdriver indexed in one of the slots. Adjust the lockring until the crank turns freely with just a discernible amount of endplay when you attempt to move the crank in and out of the frame housing.

⑩ Install the keyed lockwasher, with the key indexed to the keyway of the crank. *NOTE: This lockwasher keeps the lockring in place so that the bearing adjustment does not change during assembly.*

⑪ Thread the locknut onto the crank in a counter-clockwise direction. **CAUTION: The locknut has left-hand threads.** Tighten the locknut firmly against the lockwasher. There may be a dustcap between the locknut and lockwasher. It is a good idea.

It is easiest to feel the adjustment of the bearings before replacing the pedals, though it can be done after the pedals have been installed.

⑫ Grease the pedal threads. Turn the left-side pedal counterclockwise onto the crank. Turn the right-side pedal clockwise onto the crank. *NOTE: The pedals have an L or R stamped on the flat of the inside cone for identification.*

⑬ Tighten each pedal using a thin wrench on the flats of its spindle to turn it in the proper direction.

(14) Install the chain guard. Tighten the attaching bolts and nuts securely.

Adjusting

Check the adjustment of the crank by lifting the rear wheel clear of the floor and turning the crank, which should turn freely without drag and have only a discernible amount of endplay. If there is drag or excessive endplay, back off the locknut, and then tighten or loosen the lockring with a screwdriver. Retighten the locknut.

OVERHAULING RUBBER-BLOCK PEDALS

The following step-by-step illustrated instructions cover disassembling, assembling, and adjusting rubber-block pedals.

If a rubber-block pedal has a dustcap with wrench flats, the overhaul procedure is the same as for a metal pedal. Some rubber-block pedals disassemble as in the following steps, and some cannot be disassembled.

Tools and Supplies You Will Need

Pedal wrench, or 15mm open-end wrench, or adjustable wrench

Small open-end wrenches
Small screwdriver
Tweezers
Cycle oil
Grease
Bearing balls (usually about 50 $\frac{5}{32}$-inch)

Removing and Disassembling

(1) Remove the pedal from the crank, using a wrench to grip the flats of the spindle. *NOTE: The left-side pedal spindle has left-hand threads and must be turned clockwise to remove it. The right-side pedal spindle has conventional threads and must be turned counterclockwise to remove it.*

Hold the pedal cage so it doesn't turn. If the cage stays steady while you unscrew the pedal, the spindle is straight. If the outer end of the cage orbits in a little circle, the spindle is bent and must be replaced. If the spindle is bent, also check for a bent crank (page 104). Clamp the pedal in a vise with the jaws gripping the pads. Remove the nuts from the ends of each pad stud.

It is also convenient to work on the pedal without removing its spindle from the crank.

(2) Separate the spindle barrel from the dustcap and endplate, as shown.

From this point on, disassembly is the same as for a metal pedal. Turn to step (3) on page 331.

Assembling

From step (11), page 335.

(3) Slide the assembled spindle and barrel into position between the pedal pads, with the outer bearing

cup seated in the dustcap and the holes in the inner plate indexed over the pad studs. Thread both nuts onto the pad studs and tighten them securely. Grease the threads and thread the spindles onto the cranks. *NOTE: The left-side pedal has left-hand threads and must be turned on counterclockwise while the right-side pedal has conventional right-hand threads and must be turned on clockwise.* Each pedal can be identified by an L or R stamped on the flat of the spindle collar or on the threaded end of the spindle. Tighten the spindles securely.

CAUTION: Pedals stamped D and G have metric threading and should not be threaded into English-threaded cranks. Do not thread in a pedal which is difficult to turn or which wobbles loosely. See the section on parts interchangeability on page 315.

OVERHAULING METAL PEDALS

The following step-by-step illustrated instructions cover disassembling, assembling, and adjusting metal pedals. An exploded drawing of this type of pedal is included.

Tools and Supplies You Will Need

Pedal wrench, or 15mm open-end wrench, or adjustable wrench (6mm Allen wrench for some pedals)
Dustcap wrench (some brands)
Small open-end wrenches
Small screwdriver
Tweezers
Cycle oil
Grease
Bearing balls (usually about 50, $\frac{5}{32}$-inch)

Removing and Disassembling

① Remove the pedals from the cranks, using a wrench to grip the flats of the spindles. Turn the left pedal spindle clockwise and the right one counterclockwise.

Hold the pedal cage so it doesn't turn. If the cage stays steady while you unscrew the pedal, the spindle is straight. If the outer end of the cage orbits in a little circle, the spindle is bent and must be replaced. If the spindle is bent, also check for a bent crank (page 104).

It is also convenient to work on the pedal without removing its spindle from the crank.

② Clamp the pedal in a vise, with the closed end of the spindle facing up. Use a wrench to remove the dustcap. Some brands of metal pedals require a special dustcap wrench.

③ Remove the locknut and keyed washer.

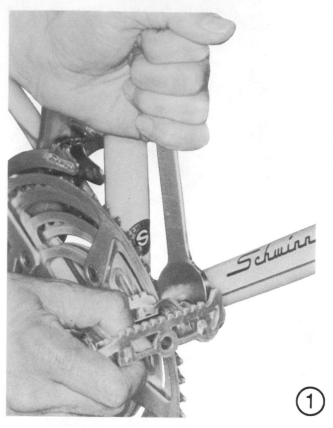

(1)

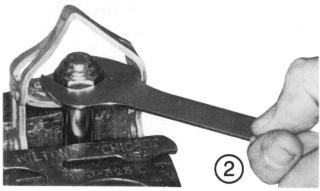

(2)

(3)

④ Remove the cone by turning it counterclockwise with a thin-bladed screwdriver, as shown. Remove and count the loose bearing balls.

⑤ Hold the pedal over a piece of cloth and withdraw the spindle. Catch the loose bearing balls.

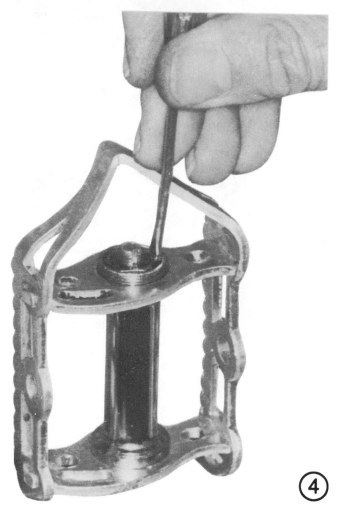

(4)

Cleaning and Inspecting

Clean all parts with solvent and rinse them or wipe them dry with a lintless cloth.

It is best to replace all of the bearing balls with new ones rather than to inspect them.

Check the spindle for stripped or damaged threads.

Check the bearing surface of the cone for scores (scratchlike marks) or pits.

Inspect the cone and locknut for stripped or damaged threads.

Inspect the bearing cups of the pedal for scores, pits, or corrosion.

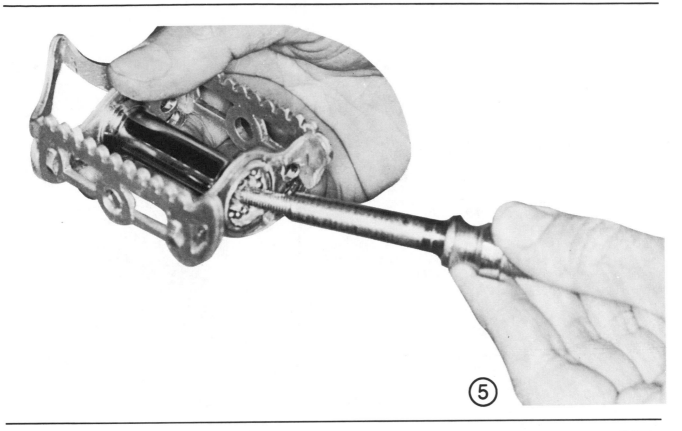

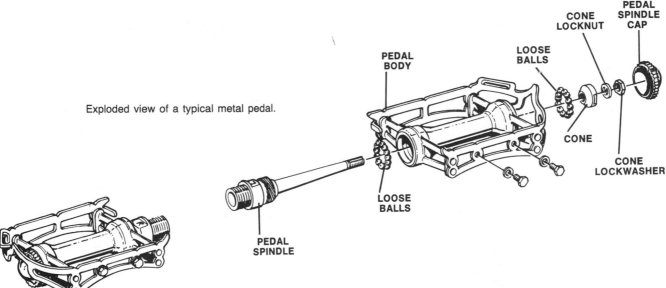

Exploded view of a typical metal pedal.

PEDAL BODY

CONE LOCKNUT

LOOSE BALLS

PEDAL SPINDLE CAP

CONE

CONE LOCKWASHER

LOOSE BALLS

PEDAL SPINDLE

Assembling

⑥ Apply a generous coating of multipurpose grease to the bearing cup at the open end of the pedal.

⑦ Imbed loose bearing balls in the lubricant. Cover the balls with lubricant. Carefully turn the pedal end for end, apply lubricant to the bearing cup on the other end, and then imbed loose bearing balls.

⑧ Clamp the spindle in the vise, with the jaws gripping the flats of the stationary cone. Carefully and slowly slide the pedal down the spindle into place with the closed end of the pedal facing up. **CAUTION: Don't bump the pedal or the bearings will be jarred out of place.**

⑨ Thread the adjustable cone onto the spindle finger-tight, then back it off approximately a quarter of a

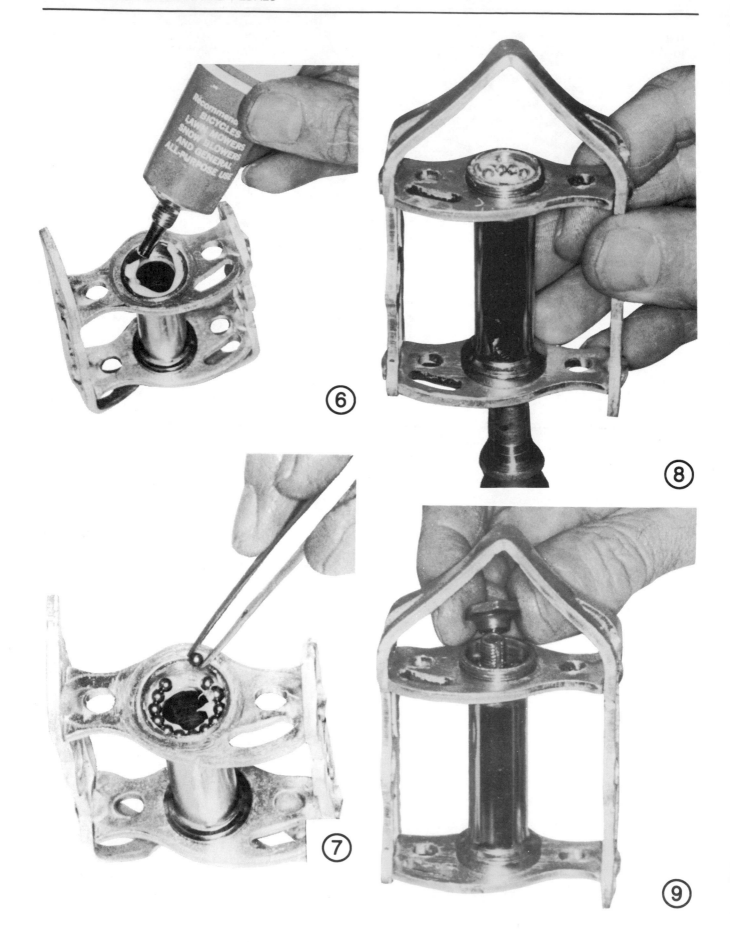

turn as a preliminary adjustment. Slide the lockwasher onto the spindle with the key indexing in the keyway of the spindle.

⑩ Thread the locknut onto the spindle. Hold the cone with the flat of a thin-bladed screwdriver, and then tighten the locknut. Rotate the pedal about the spindle and check to be sure it turns freely with just a discernible amount of endplay. If the pedal does not turn freely, loosen the locknut, and then back off the cone approximately an eighth of a turn. Hold the cone in place, and then retighten the locknut. If the pedal has too much endplay, loosen the locknut and tighten the cone about an eighth of a turn and then retighten the locknut while holding the cone with a screwdriver.

If you are working on a rubber-block pedal, return at this point to step ③ on page 330.

⑩

⑪ Turn the dustcap onto the pedal and tighten it securely with a wrench.

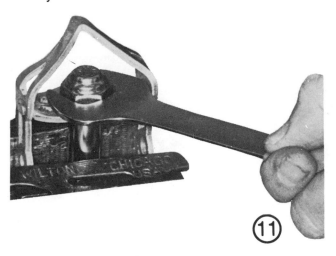

⑪

⑫ Grease the pedal threads and thread the pedal spindle onto the crank. The left-side pedal has left-hand threads and so must be threaded on counter-clockwise. The right-side pedal threads on clockwise. The spindles are stamped L and R on the inner end or on the wrench flat. Tighten the spindles in the crank securely.

CAUTION: Pedals stamped D and G have metric threading and should not be threaded into English-threaded cranks. Do not thread in a pedal which is difficult to turn or which wobbles loosely. See the section on parts interchangeability on page 315.

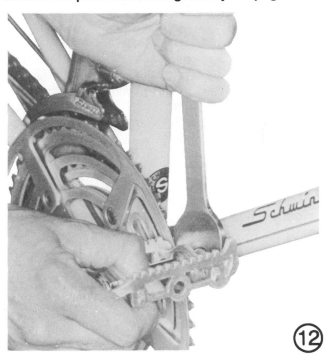

⑫

SEALED-BEARING BOTTOM-BRACKET UNITS

Several brands of sealed-bearing bottom-bracket units have been marketed, with the goals of reducing the need for maintenance and increasing ease of installation. Many are sold as replacement units, but they are appearing in increasing numbers on new bicycles as well. Two types of sealed-bearing bottom-bracket units are available:

1. Conventional angular-contact cup-and-cone assemblies as described above, with rubber sealing rings built into the bearing cups. These are often called "sealed mechanism" bottom brackets. Service these as described above, except that the cup seals may occasionally need replacing.

2. Assemblies using radial-contact cartridge bearing units (see page 68 for more information on this type of bearing unit). These assemblies are secured in the bottom-bracket shell by *mounting rings* which thread

into the shell like conventional cups. The mounting rings may be equipped with lockrings, like the adjustable cup of a conventional crank hanger assembly. Frequently, special tools are needed to install the mounting rings.

Cartridge-bearing Bottom-bracket Installation

Some brands of cartridge-bearing bottom-bracket assemblies, such as Phil Wood, have mounting rings without lockrings. The mounting rings fit over the ends of a single, elongated cartridge which contains the spindle and bearings. The assembly may be threaded right or left in the bottom-bracket shell to adjust the chainline. The two mounting rings are then tightened against the ends of the cartridge to secure it. Instructions for many of these units specify the use of threadlock compound, included with new units.

Some cartridge-bearing units, such as SunTour, have mounting rings with lockrings. These units may have a single, elongated cartridge, or they may have a separate bearing unit fitted into each mounting ring. The lockrings allow right-left adjustment *and also serve to adjust the bearings.* By adjusting the right mounting ring and tightening its lockring, position the spindle for correct chainline (see page 102). Then adjust the left

mounting ring and lockring for correct bearing clearance, following the manufacturer's instructions.

CAUTION: The bearing adjustment for a radial-contact cartridge-bearing unit is different from that for a conventional cup-and-cone bearing assembly. Do not attempt to remove endplay, or the bearing balls will ride up the side of the bearing races and cause premature wear. Read the manufacturer's instructions, and read the introduction to sealed bearings on page 68.

Some units have a cartridge with only one lockring or mounting ring. The cartridge is inserted into the right end of the bottom-bracket shell. Then the left end of the unit is secured by the mounting ring and/or lockring. Chainline is not adjustable with these units.

Servicing Cartridge-bearing Bottom-bracket Assemblies

For the most part, cartridge-bearing bottom-bracket assemblies are not meant to be serviced. If the spindle is bent or a bearing cartridge needs replacement, the usual procedure is to replace the entire unit or send it back to the factory for rebuilding.

CAUTION: In most cases, removing the bearings

Phil Wood crank-bearing assembly. The two mounting rings, at either end, secure the bearing cartridge in the bottom bracket; the procedure requires the special tool shown. Threadlock compound, supplied, prevents the mounting rings from slipping or unscrewing.

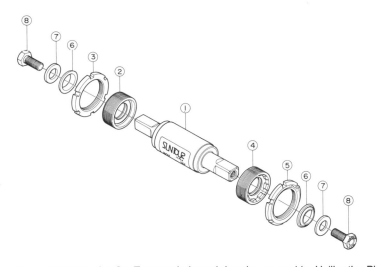

ITEM	DESCRIPTION
1	Cartridge
2	LH cup
3	LH lockring
4	RH cup
5	RH lockring
6	Dust seal
7	Washer
8	Bolt

Exploded view of a SunTour sealed crank-bearing assembly. Unlike the Phil Wood, this uses lockrings on its mounting rings.

from a cartridge-bearing unit will damage them. Do not attempt to take a cartridge-bearing unit apart unless you have the manufacturer's instructions on hand, as well as any special tools and replacement parts which may be necessary to reassemble the unit.

Cartridge-bearing bottom-bracket assemblies typically turn very smoothly when new. Some roughness is acceptable. Contamination of the lubricant is the main cause of bearing failure, manifested as severe roughness.

No bearing is immune to all-terrain bike abuse such as riding under water; a rebuildable "sealed mechanism" crank hanger and/or one with a grease fitting is best-suited to this type of abuse. Typically, a bearing will be serviceable for a long time after it becomes rough; there is little risk of becoming stranded because of bearing failure.

Besides wear, the other main problem requiring service to sealed-bearing bottom brackets is binding of the bearings. This is almost always due to misalignment. Radial-contact bearings are much less tolerant of misalignment than are cup-and-cone bearings.

As described above, assemblies using lockrings should not be adjusted to eliminate endplay, or binding will result. The remaining major cause of misalignment is a bent spindle; this requires replacement of the unit. Units with two separate bearing cartridges, one in each mounting ring, should be mounted only in a specially aligned bottom bracket. Conventional tolerances for thread alignment are not close enough.

CARTRIDGE-BEARING PEDALS

Like other cartridge-bearing units, these pedals are designed for long service without rebuilding. Typically, they carry a long warranty. Some bearing roughness is normal, but in the event of extreme roughness, indicating bearing failure, the preferred course is replacement under warranty.

As with all cartridge-bearing units, bearing seat alignment is critical. A bent shell or spindle must be replaced. Warranties do not cover damage from a crash, and until you have taken the pedal apart, you may not know which parts need replacement. Unless you want to risk an investment in the special tools and parts necessary for rebuilding, it makes good sense to replace the pedal or else take the repair to a bike shop equipped for the job.

With SunTour and Specialized cartridge-bearing pedals, which are typical, the bearing cartridges are secured in the shell with threadlock compound. They may be released by driving out the spindle with the special SunTour tool, according to the instructions furnished with the tool. *The bearing cartridges will be damaged by this procedure. Special, nonstandard replacement cartridges are required for some cartridge-bearing pedals.*

16 • BRAKES

Few things are more important to safe bicycling than are good brakes. Many serious accidents occur because of brake failure or poor brake performance. Also, many people ride their bikes slowly because they know that the brakes work poorly. Deteriorating performance creeps up, and it is easy to ignore.

Every bicycle, like any road vehicle, should be equipped with at least two brakes, for the most powerful braking and in case one fails. **CAUTION: Bicycles equipped with only a single brake have led to many serious accidents which could have very easily been avoided.** The brakes should pass the following tests:

1. Cables should withstand the full force of braking without slipping or jamming. To test this, grip each brake lever in turn with *both* hands, as hard as you can.

2. The front brake should lock the wheel and the rear brake should skid the wheel. While gripping each brake lever in turn with one hand, press your belly down on the saddle and try to roll the bicycle forward. Look down to see that the brake shoes are aligned squarely with the rim, and that there is not excessive play in the brake pivots. Note that a front caliper brake rotates upward and forward in use. Make sure brake shoes do not contact sidewalls. They can cause rapid wear, leading to a blowout.

3. Braking should be smooth, even, and easy to modulate. Once you have performed the preceding two tests, check this by riding the bicycle while applying the brakes lightly, then harder.

TYPES OF BRAKES

Four types of brakes are used on modern bicycles, and they are classified according to their method of operation as follows: (1) sidepull caliper brakes; (2) centerpull caliper and cantilever brakes; (3) cable-

Internal-expanding drum-type brake assembly.

operated hub brakes (disk and drum brakes); and (4) backpedaling (coaster) brakes used with single- or multiple-speed rear-wheel hubs.

This chapter contains overhaul procedures for sidepull and centerpull/cantilever rim brakes and cable-operated hub brakes.

The *coaster brake* mechanism is an integral part of the rear hub equipped with this type of braking arrangement. Therefore, complete instructions for most makes and types of coaster brakes are given in Chapter 14.

Rim brakes are mounted over the bicycle wheel and are activated by operating a hand lever that is connected to the braking mechanism by a cable. The wheel is slowed or stopped by the brake shoes being pressed against the wheel rim. These shoes are mounted on the ends of caliper-type arms. Regardless of manufacturer, all rim brakes are of either the sidepull, centerpull, or cantilever type.

Coaster brake and rear hub assembly.

Caliper brakes work like a pair of pliers, squeezing two brake shoes against the sides of the rim. The cable attachment points correspond to the handles of the pliers, and the brake shoes correspond to the jaws of the pliers. Just as the levering motion of the pliers transfers the force from the handles to the jaws, the brake's pivot or pivots transfer force to the shoes. The pivot or pivots also secure the brake to the bicycle's frame.

Side-pull Caliper Brakes

Both brake arms of sidepull caliper brakes have a common pivot point, which also serves as the mounting bolt for the assembly. Both arms extend to one side of the bicycle, as shown in the accompanying illustration. The actuating cable is attached to the arms to move one of them slightly upward and the other down-

ward when the brake lever on the handlebar is squeezed. This movement forces the two shoes against the wheel rim for the braking action. Overhaul procedures for sidepull caliper brakes begin on page 343.

Centerpull Caliper Brakes and Cantilever Brakes

The arms of centerpull-type caliper brakes have separate pivot points at the ends of a brake-arm bridge. A short cable connecting the ends of the arms passes through an anchor plate. The actuating cable is attached to this plate. When the brake lever on the handlebar is squeezed, the anchor plate rises slightly, both brake arms pivot, and the shoes are pressed against the wheel rim simultaneously, as indicated in the illustration.

Cantilever brakes are very similar to centerpull brakes, except that the two pivots are brazed or welded directly to the bicycle frame.

Overhaul procedures for centerpull and cantilever brakes begin on page 351.

Centerpull brake caliper assembly.

Cable-operated Hub Brakes

Disk and drum-type cable-operated hub brakes, shown in the accompanying illustrations, are similar to those used on automobiles. The assembly consists of a disk or drum attached to the rear-wheel hub, a shoe assembly, and the cable and lever assembly which presses the shoes against the drum or disk.

Disk and drum brakes may be either threaded to the hub or built into it. Overhaul procedures begin on page 360.

Sidepull caliper brake assembly.

Cantilever brake assembly. Except that it is mounted directly to the frame, it is very similar to a centerpull caliper brake assembly.

THE BRAKING SYSTEM

With so many types of brakes, it is important to know which type is best for any particular use, especially if you will be replacing the brakes on a bicycle.

Most bicycles for adult use are equipped with side-pull or centerpull rim brakes. It is easy to replace one type with the other, since they both attach to the bicycle the same way.

Centerpull brakes tend to have a "softer" feel than sidepull brakes, because they usually have a higher

mechanical advantage: Less force at the brake lever is required, but the brake lever must be pulled through a greater distance. Some bicyclists prefer centerpull brakes, some sidepulls, though either can perform well.

Caliper brakes don't work very well on a bicycle with fat tires, because the brake arms must be long to reach around the tires. This makes them less stiff and reduces the power of their grip. The direct frame mounting of cantilever brakes avoids this problem and keeps them from being fouled by mud. For these reasons, cantilever brakes are preferred for tandems, all-terrain bikes, and heavily loaded touring bikes. They also can provide powerful braking for a person with small or weak hands.

However, most models of cantilever brakes cannot be adjusted for use with slightly different rim sizes, as caliper brakes can. Also, cantilever brakes cannot easily be installed on a bicycle frame which does not already have the necessary *brake bosses;* the bicycle would have to be taken to a professional bicycle frame builder to install these. If you want cantilever brakes, it is by far easiest to buy a new bicycle or frame which is already equipped with them.

Wet-weather Braking

Performance of all rim brakes becomes poorer when the rim is wet. The problem can be managed, however.

With conventional rubber brake shoes, wet braking is much better with aluminum rims than with steel rims. Aluminum rims also tend to have a much more even braking surface, resulting in smoother (less "grabby") brake performance, and they are lighter. Replacing steel rims with aluminum ones is an inexpensive and effective way to upgrade the performance of any bicycle.

Special brake shoes with leather pads, made in foggy England, are available for use with steel rims. These improve wet braking dramatically.

A hub brake is largely or completely immune to wet weather. However, a coaster brake is available only for a single-sprocket hub, and is inconvenient with toe-clips. Cable-operated hub brakes don't have these limitations, but they are more expensive and heavier than caliper brakes, and they make the wheel more difficult to install and replace.

Still, a rear hub brake of one type or another is an excellent choice on a utility bicycle used often in wet weather. This should always be used with a front brake, in case it fails and because a rear brake alone provides only half as much power for a dry-pavement panic stop. A front rim brake may be used with a rear hub brake, though front hub brakes are also available.

A young child who cannot control a handbrake smoothly is best served by a coaster brake and a handbrake, both on the *rear* wheel.

Tandems must be equipped with especially powerful brakes. The most usual arrangement is a pair of cantilever brakes, front and rear, with a heavy-duty cable-operated rear disk or drum brake. The cantilever brakes are used for normal stops. The hub brake is used to slow the bicycle when traveling downhill. Using rim brakes for downhill speed control on a tandem can generate enough heat to melt the brake shoes or blow out a tire. **CAUTION: Controls for all three brakes**

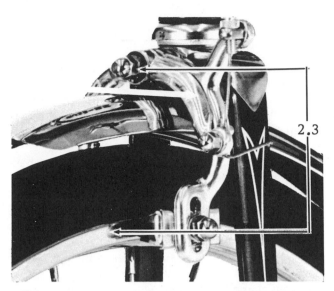

The reach of a caliper brake is the vertical distance between the mounting bolt and the centerline of the rim braking surface.

must be separate in order to use them properly. Avoid "double-cable" levers.

Parts Compatibility

Caliper brakes can be interchanged as mentioned above, but the *reach* a brake must have depends on the height of the brake mounting hole above the rim. This in turn depends on the tire size and on whether or not the bicycle is designed for use with fenders. Different models of brake have different reach.

Note: Generally, short-reach brakes work better, because they have more leverage. When there is a choice, use a larger rim diameter, allowing a shorter brake reach.

Parts of rim brake assemblies are different for each

A brake shoe with an unthreaded post. Often, as shown, the brake return spring is hooked over the locknut that holds the brake shoe in place.

model and should generally not be interchanged. Besides, if one part of a brake caliper assembly is bent or worn, other parts probably also need replacement; it is best in this case to buy an entirely new assembly.

Rim brake *shoes* can be interchanged, though there are two different types:

The *threaded type* has a threaded stud on the back of the brake shoe holder. An acorn nut and washer secure the stud to the brake arm. The slot in the brake arm is parallel to the braking surface of the rim. The brakes shown in the overhauling instructions in this chapter use threaded brake shoes.

The *unthreaded type* has an unthreaded post on the back of the brake shoe holder. This passes through a hole in a clamp bolt, which, with a spacer washer and nut, secures it to the brake arm. The slot in the brake arm is at a right angle to the braking surface of the rim. Brake shoes with unthreaded posts are most commonly found on French-made brakes and on cantilever brakes.

Both threaded-type and unthreaded-type brake shoes are available in light-duty and heavy-duty versions. Large, heavy-duty brake shoes provide more powerful braking even on a lightly loaded bicycle. **CAUTION: Heavy-duty brake shoes must be used on tandems and other bicycles requiring powerful brake performance.**

Parts for drum and disk brakes are interchangeable only with the same model or closely related models. Drum brakes which are built into a hub may require special axle and bearing parts. Consult the manufacturer's parts lists.

Many drum and disk brakes are not built into the hub; instead, the drum or disk is threaded to the left side of a special hub. The threads are the same as freewheel threads, but usually the space at the left side is not as wide. **CAUTION: Do not make the mistake of reversing the hub right for left. The freewheel will not fit, or may strip on the shorter threads for the brake.**

The brake-shoe assembly of drum and disk brakes is attached in one way or another to the bicycle frame. A special hub or special fittings on the frame may be required. In every case, correct alignment and secure mounting are very important, to avoid binding of brake or hub parts and to transfer the braking force to the frame.

SERVICING RIM BRAKES

Procedures for overhauling sidepull and centerpull/cantilever rim brakes are given separately because of their somewhat different construction. A single problem chart is given here, since most rim brake problems are similar for all of these types.

Problems with Rim Brakes

NOTE: *Many brake problems described here are actually cable or lever problems. Instructions for servicing cables and levers are in Chapter 6.*

Brake is weak, lever bottoms out, feels "spongy."

Possible cause:	*Corrective action:*
Cable is adjusted too loose.	Adjust cable.
Flimsy, long-arm caliper brake is installed.	Use stiffer brake or hub brake.
Brake shoes are small and soft.	Use heavy-duty shoes.
Brake is mismatched to lever.	Use long-pull lever.
Cable is excessively long or kinked.	Service cable.

Brake is weak, lever is hard to pull.

Possible cause:	*Corrective action:*
Cable is rusted or kinked.	Service cable.
Lever is mismatched to brake.	Use short-pull lever.

Brake chatters or buzzes.

Possible cause:	*Corrective action:*
Pivot(s) loose.	Adjust pivot(s).
Flimsy, long-arm caliper brake is installed.	Use stiffer brake or hub brake.
There is oil on rim and shoes.	Clean rim and shoes.

Brake squeals.

Possible cause:	*Corrective action:*
Caliper pivot(s) loose.	Adjust pivot(s).
Shoes are not fitted to rim.	Toe in or sand shoes.
Flimsy, long-arm caliper brake is installed.	Use stiffer brake or hub brake.

Brake shoes leave rubber on rim.

Possible cause:	*Corrective action:*
There is oil on rim and shoes.	Clean rim and shoes.
Shoes are of poor quality.	Replace shoes.

Brake rubs tire when applied.

Possible cause:	*Corrective action:*
Caliper pivot(s) loose.	Adjust pivot(s).
Shoes are misaligned or loose.	Align and tighten shoes.
Rim is out of true.	True wheel.

Brake grabs; braking is uneven.

Possible cause:	Corrective action:
Rim width is uneven; "blip" on rim.	Replace or repair rim.
Wheel is out of true.	True wheel.
There is oil on rim and shoes.	Clean rim and shoes.
Caliper pivot(s) loose.	Adjust pivot(s).
Rim is corroded.	Clean or replace rim.

One brake shoe drags after lever is released.

Possible cause:	Corrective action:
Rim is out of true.	True wheel.
There is impact damage to rim.	Repair rim.
Brake is off center.	Center brake.
Rim is off center.	Center rim.
Frame is misaligned.	Straighten frame.
Brake is adjusted too tight.	Loosen cable slightly.
There is no slack in cable housing.	Rearrange cable.

Brake will not release.

Possible cause:	Corrective action:
Cable is kinked or rusted.	Service cable.
Caliper pivot(s) over-tightened.	Adjust pivot(s).
Lever pivots are bent or corroded.	Service or replace lever.

OVERHAULING SIDEPULL CALIPER BRAKES

This section provides step-by-step illustrated instructions for disassembling, assembling, and adjusting a typical set of sidepull caliper brakes. Procedures for front and rear brakes are essentially the same, except as noted in the specific step.

The illustrations in this section were made of a Schwinn-Approved set of sidepull caliper brakes, typical for this type of assembly. An exploded view showing all parts is provided.

Sidepull caliper brakes of other manufacturers may vary slightly because of the shape of the spring, the type of pivot bolt, the arrangement of bushings and washers, and the knob design on the brake shoes. An exploded view showing all parts of the Phillips and Raleigh sidepull caliper brakes also is provided.

Note: Many brake problems can be tested only before disassembly. Perform the three tests listed on page 338; then use the problem chart on page 342 to help locate the source of the problem. Only a partial disassembly may be necessary.

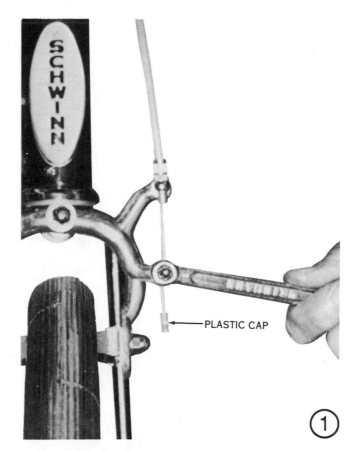

PLASTIC CAP

①

Usually, the cable and lever should be overhauled at the same time as the brake.

Tools and Supplies You Will Need

Small wrenches
Thin wrench to fit inner nut on pivot bolt
Needlenose pliers
Screwdriver
"Third-hand" tool, old toestrap or length of cord
Brake shoes as required
Grease

Removing the Caliper Assembly

① Loosen the cable-adjusting nut. Remove the plastic cap from the end of the cable.

② Back off the knurled collar on the cable guide until the cable and guide can be pulled free of the brake-arm eyebolt.

③ Remove the locknut, lockwasher, and washer from the pivot bolt on the back side of the forks for the front caliper brakes or from the front side of the frame for the rear brakes.

Note: A brake can be overhauled with the pivot bolt in place. This approach is especially helpful if you do not have a vise handy. Remove the pivot bolt during the cleaning and inspection step, to check that it is not bent and that its threads are not stripped.

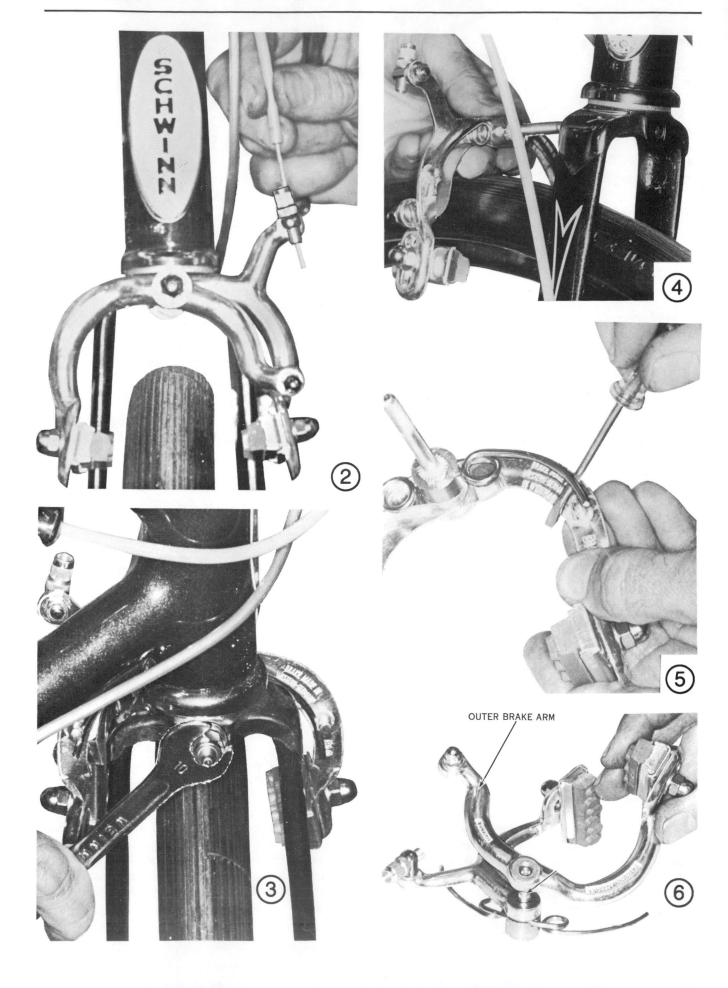

OUTER BRAKE ARM

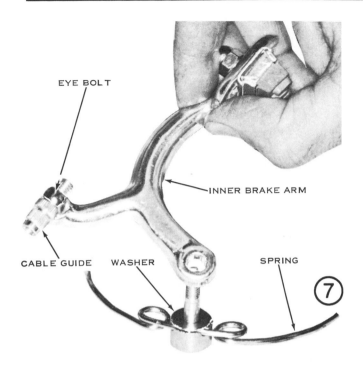

EYE BOLT

INNER BRAKE ARM

CABLE GUIDE WASHER SPRING

⑦

Note: If brake shoes do not need replacement, there is no need to remove them from the brake arms. Leaving them in place will assure that they seat on the rims as they did before, reducing break-in problems.

Cleaning and Inspecting

Clean all parts, except the brake shoes, with solvent and then rinse them, or wipe them dry with a lintless cloth.

Inspect the pivot bolt, anchor bolt, and adjusting-barrel assembly for stripped threads. Check the threads of all nuts to be sure they are not stripped or damaged.

Check the brake arms to be sure they are not bent or twisted.

Check the spring for a crack or lost tension.

Check the brake shoes for wear. If brake shoes are more than three or four years old, it is best to replace them even if not worn; rubber deteriorates with age.

④ Withdraw the pivot bolt and complete brake assembly from the front fork or rear frame.

⑤ Pry the spring ends up over the spring posts on each brake arm.

⑥ Clamp the long end of the pivot bolt in a vise, using soft jaws to protect the threads. Remove the locknut, adjusting nut, and washers. Lift off the outer brake arm and washer from the pivot bolt. Remove the anchor nut and bolt.

⑦ Lift off the inner brake arm, washer, and spring. Remove the cable guide and eyebolt from the inner brake arm.

⑧ Remove each brake-shoe nut and washer; you may then force the shoe out of the open end of the holder with a screwdriver. Many brake shoe holders are closed on both ends. If yours are, it is easiest to leave the shoe in the holder and replace the entire assembly if necessary.

Assembling

⑨ Clamp the long end of the mounting bolt in a vise with soft jaws to protect the threads. Lay the center of the spring in the mounting-bolt groove, with the ends of the spring arched back toward the opposite side of the bolt from the groove and on the lower side of the coil, as shown.

Note: If you do not have a vise, it is easiest to reassemble the mounting bolt to the frame now (steps ⑮ to ⑰).

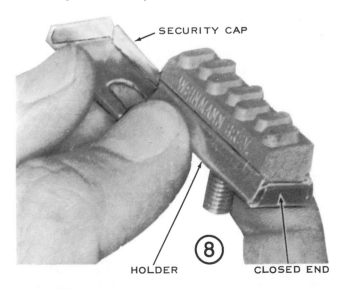

SECURITY CAP

⑧

HOLDER   CLOSED END

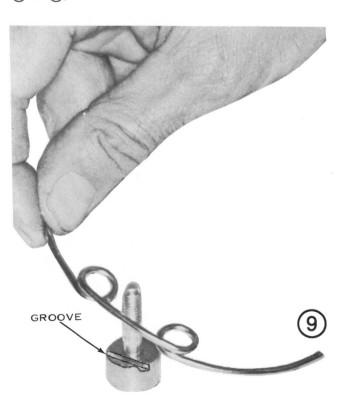

GROOVE

⑨

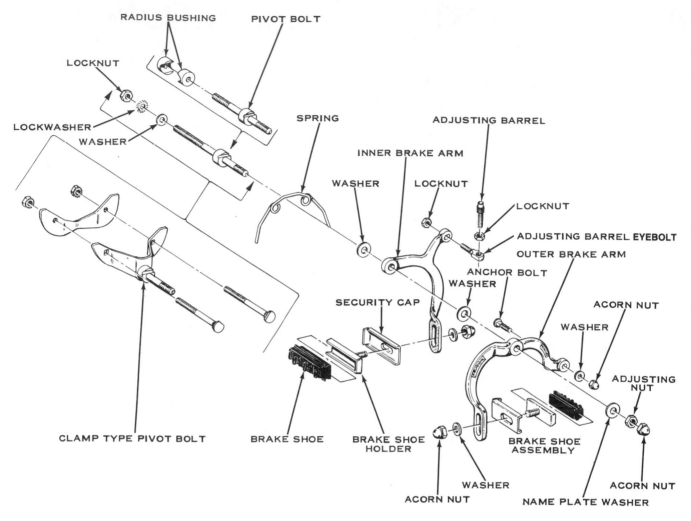

Exploded view of a Schwinn-Approved, Weinmann, or Dia-Compe sidepull brake caliper assembly.

⑩ Slide a new brake shoe into each of the brake shoe holders. Install the assembled brake shoe units on each brake arm so the closed end of the holder faces forward and the beveled surface of the shoe matches the angle of the wheel rim when installed on the bicycle. **CAUTION: The brake shoe assembly must be installed with the closed end of the holder facing forward to prevent the shoe from working out when the brakes are applied.**

Note: Many brake shoe holders are closed at both ends, and are replaced as a unit.

⑪ Thread the adjusting-barrel eyebolt onto the forward side of the brake arm, and then thread the adjusting barrel all the way into the eyebolt, with the locking collar on the same side as the knurled end, as shown. Insert the anchor bolt through the front side of the outer brake arm, and then install the nut finger-tight. Position the washer over the spring on the pivot bolt. Lubricate the bearing surfaces of the pivot bolt and brake arms lightly with grease. Place the inner brake arm on the pivot bolt, with the spring knob facing down and the arm arched in the same direction as the spring on that side.

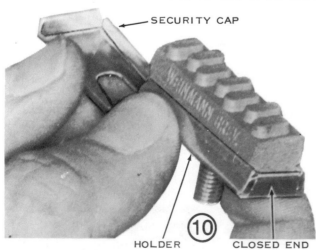

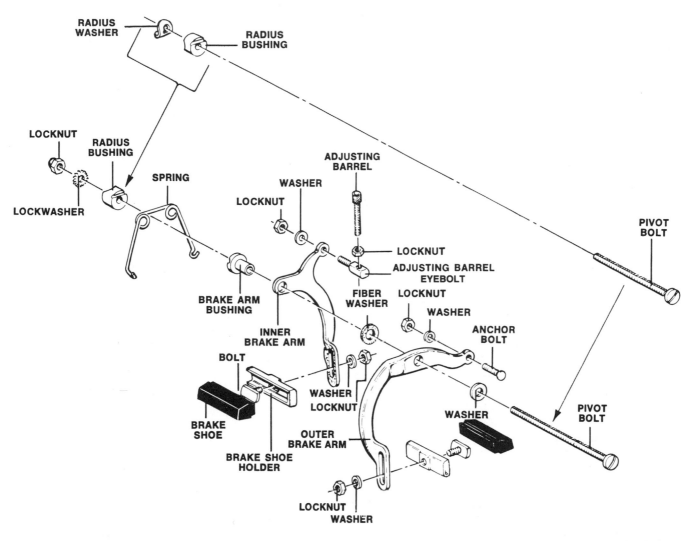

Exploded view of a Raleigh or Phillips sidepull brake caliper assembly. This has no acorn nut or locknut at the head of the pivot bolt. Rather, the entire pivot bolt is turned to adjust the pivot clearance.

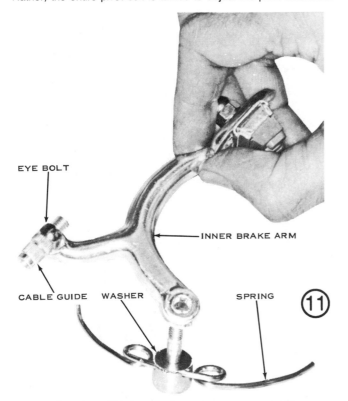

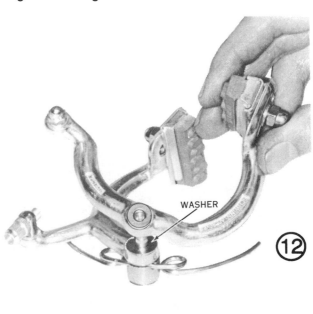

⑫ Position the washer on top of the inner brake arm, and then install the outer brake arm, with the spring knob facing down.

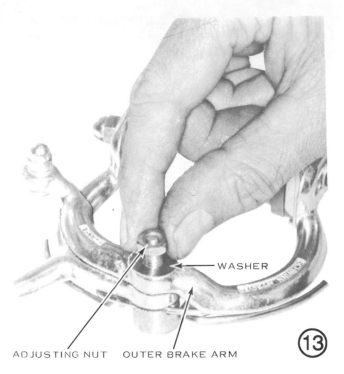

WASHER

ADJUSTING NUT   OUTER BRAKE ARM

⑬

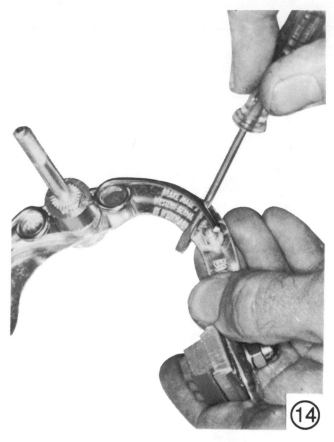

⑭

⑬ Place the nameplate washer or plain washer on top of the outer brake arm. Thread the adjusting nut onto the pivot bolt finger-tight, and then back it off approximately a quarter turn for operating clearance. Check movement of the brake arms, which should rotate freely without any endplay (movement back and forth on the pivot bolt). Hold the adjusting nut in position, and then turn the locknut tight against the adjusting nut.

⑭ Remove the assembly from the vise, turn it over, and then snap the ends of the spring over the spring knobs with a screwdriver.

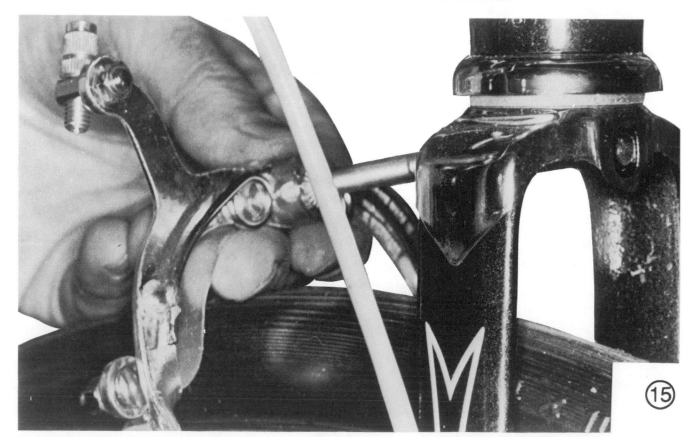

⑮

⑮ Install a radius bushing onto the pivot bolt, with the flat side of the bushing against the brake arm. Slide the pivot bolt through the mounting hole in the front fork or rear frame.

⑯ At the front-wheel position, slide a radius bushing onto the pivot bolt, with the flat side facing out. Slide a washer and then a lockwasher onto the mounting bolt. Slide on the lamp or fender bracket, if any. Tighten the locknut securely.

Note: Newer brakes use a locknut with a nylon friction insert. This is highly recommended for replacement use, as it eliminates any possibility of the locknut's unscrewing. **CAUTION: Many accidents have been caused by a brake's falling into the wheel, hanging from the brake cable.**

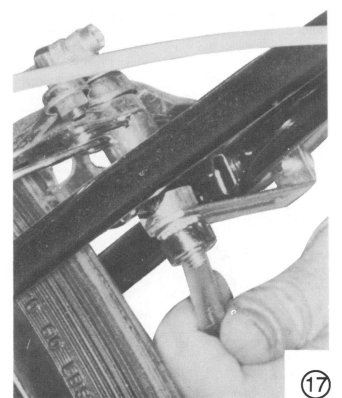

⑰

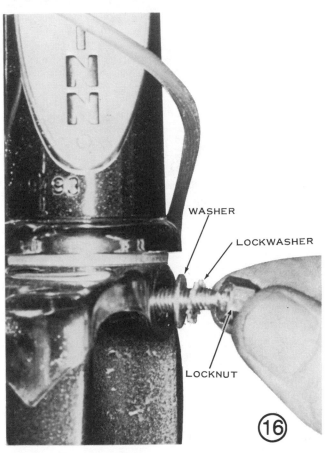

WASHER

LOCKWASHER

LOCKNUT

⑯

⑰ Position the reflector bracket on top of the radius bushing at the rear-wheel position, and then install the washer, lockwasher, and locknut.

The brake pivot bolt may be used as a mounting point for a fender, reflector, or baggage rack. If so, install this under the locknut or radius washer.

⑱ Check the brake arms for free movement. If they do not rotate easily, loosen the locknut slightly, and then turn the adjusting nut approximately a quarter turn. Hold the adjusting nut, and then retighten the

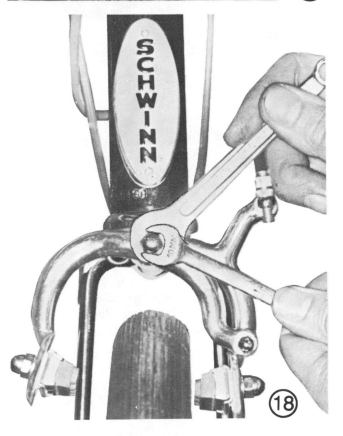

⑱

locknut. The arms should move freely but must have no endplay when you push a brake shoe forward and backward in line with the rim.

⑲ Squeeze the brake shoes against the rim, using a "third-hand" tool, or tighten a piece of cord around both arms and through the wheel. Feed the cable through the adjusting barrel and anchor bolt. Pull the cable taut with a pair of pliers and simultaneously tighten the anchor nut. Remove the "third-hand" tool or piece of cord. The brake shoes should release to about ⅛ inch from the rim. If they release more than ⅛ inch or do not move clear of the rim, loosen the anchor bolt nut, tighten or loosen the cable as required, and then re-tighten the nut. For fine adjustments, use the adjusting barrel. When the adjustment is complete, tighten the adjusting-barrel locknut securely against the adjusting-barrel eyebolt.

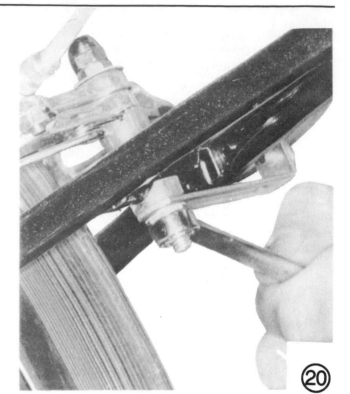

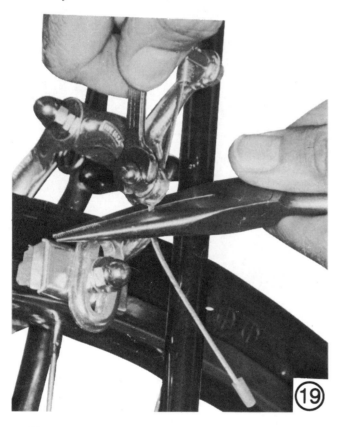

⑳ Center the assembled brake unit over the wheel rim, by loosening the mounting locknut slightly and then turning the brake arms and pivot bolt until the brake shoes are approximately equally distant from the wheel rim. Tighten the pivot bolt locknut securely.

㉑ Loosen the acorn nut of each brake shoe slightly, and then move the shoe assembly in the brake-arm slot until the top edge of the shoe is approximately ¹⁄₃₂ inch below the top of the wheel rim. Tilt the shoe to the approximate angle of the wheel rim, and then tighten the acorn nut securely. **CAUTION: Misalignment of brake shoes can lead to rapid wear of the tire sidewalls, and a blowout.**

Note that the front brake rotates upward and forward

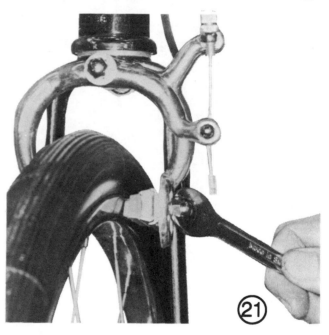

as the wheel pulls on it during use, so lower the front end of the front brake shoes slightly.

㉒ Check to be sure the front end of the brake shoe is approximately ¹⁄₃₂ inch closer to the wheel rim than the rear end. If it is not, grip the brake arm with a wrench directly below the brake-shoe assembly, and then twist the arm slightly until the front end of the shoe contacts the wheel rim first when the brake lever is actuated. This position will keep the brake from squeaking. Pulling a piece of sandpaper between the

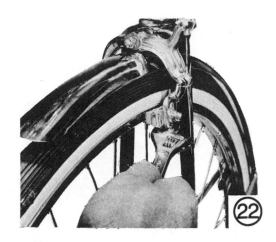

Adjust the brake shoe so that its upper edge is 1/32 inch below the top of the wheel rim, as shown.

shoe and rim will also help break in a new shoe.

Test the brake, using the three steps described on page 338. Do not ride the bicycle or allow it to be ridden until you are sure that the brakes work correctly.

OVERHAULING CENTERPULL AND CANTILEVER BRAKES

The following step-by-step illustrated procedures cover disassembling, assembling, and adjusting a typical set of centerpull or cantilever brakes. Procedures for front and rear caliper brakes are essentially the same, except as noted in the specific step.

The illustrations in this section were made of a Schwinn-Approved set of centerpull caliper brakes, typical of this type of assembly. An exploded view showing all parts of these brakes is provided.

Brakes of other manufacturers may vary slightly because of the springs used, the arrangement of bushings and washers, the type of pivot stud or bolt for securing the brake arms to the bridge, and the knob design on the brake shoes.

Note: Many brake problems can be checked only before disassembly. Perform the three tests listed on page 338; then use the problem chart on page 342 to help locate the source of the problem. Only a partial disassembly may be necessary.

Usually, the cable and lever should be overhauled at the same time as the brake.

Tools and Supplies You Will Need

Small wrenches
Needlenose pliers
Screwdriver
"Third-hand" tool, old toestrap or length of cord
Brake shoes as required
Grease

Removing the Caliper Assembly

① Remove the acorn nut and washer from one of the brake arms. Pull the brake arm away from the tire enough to slide the stud of the brake shoe assembly out of the slot in the brake arm.

Unthreaded type: Loosen the nut on the eyebolt that holds the brake shoe stud. Rotate the brake shoe down and slide the stud out of the eyebolt. Remove the eyebolt. This may require unhooking the return spring from the eyebolt.

② Remove the brake shoe and holder from the security cap, if any. A brake shoe may be removed from an open-ended holder, but many holders are closed at both ends. In this case, replace the holder and shoe assembly if the shoe is worn.

If the brake shoes do not need replacement, do not remove them from the brake arms. They will fit the rims better if their position is not changed.

③ Compress the brake arms against the wheel rim and, simultaneously, turn the cable end of the opposite arm from which the brake shoe was removed, until the cable is aligned with the slot in the brake arm. Slide the cable free of the arm. Remove the cable from the other brake arm in a similar manner.

④ Remove the nut, lockwasher, and radius bushing from the mounting bolt at the rear-wheel position. Remove the nut, lockwasher, and spacers from the front-wheel position.

The brake bolt may serve to hold a fender bracket, lamp, reflector, or baggage rack. If so, remove them.

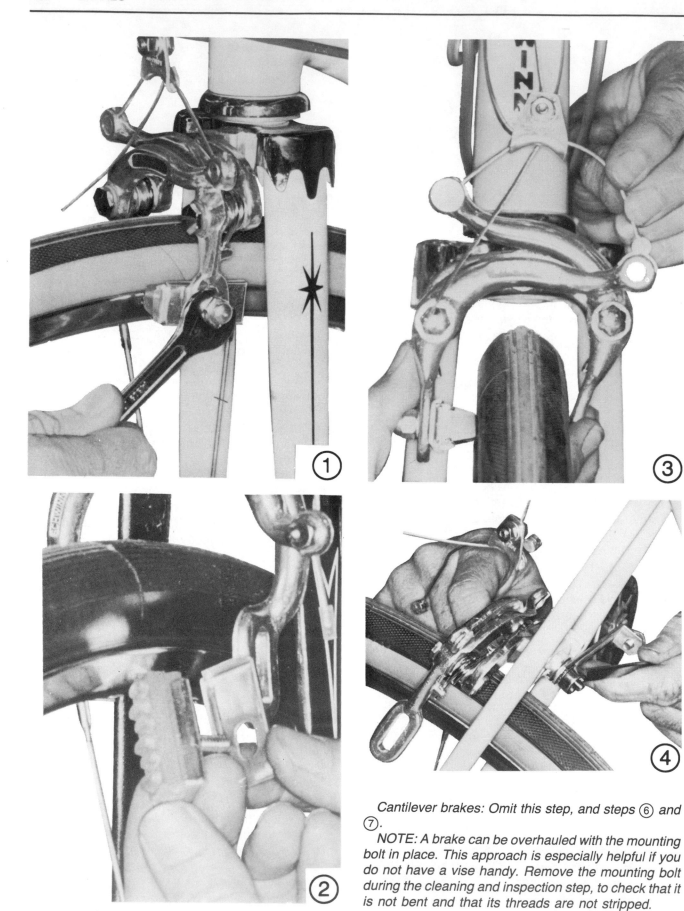

Cantilever brakes: Omit this step, and steps ⑥ and ⑦.

NOTE: A brake can be overhauled with the mounting bolt in place. This approach is especially helpful if you do not have a vise handy. Remove the mounting bolt during the cleaning and inspection step, to check that it is not bent and that its threads are not stripped.

⑤ Withdraw the complete brake unit, including the mounting bolt and the other radius bushing, from the frame. Slide the radius bushing off the mounting bolt.

⑥ Lay the brake unit on the bench, with the mounting bolt facing up. Pry the spring end from each of the brake-arm anchor posts with a screwdriver. Remove the nuts from the pivot bolts.

⑦ Turn the complete assembly over. Remove the outer brake arm and pivot bolt from the bridge. Lift off the spring. Withdraw the pivot bolt and note the arrangement of the steel bushing in the center of the brake arm and the nylon bushing on each side. Remove the inner brake arm from the bridge, and then lift the bolt and bushings from the arm. Withdraw the mounting bolt from the bridge.

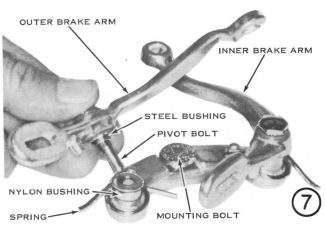

⑦

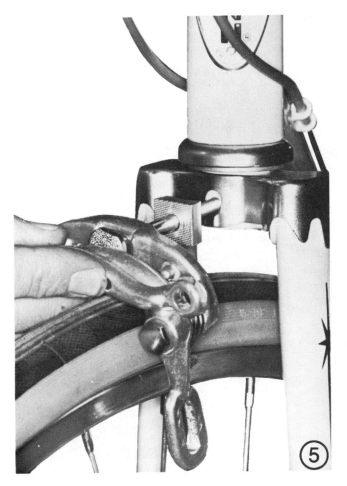

⑤

Cleaning and Inspecting

Clean all parts except the brake shoes with solvent and rinse them, or wipe them dry with a lintless cloth.

Inspect the mounting bolt, pivot bolts, anchor bolt, and adjusting-barrel assembly for stripped threads. Check the threads of all the nuts to be sure they are not stripped or damaged.

Check the brake arms to be sure they are not bent or twisted.

Check the springs for cracks or lost tension.

Check the brake shoes for wear. If brake shoes are more than three or four years old, it is best to replace them even if not worn; rubber deteriorates with age.

Assembling

⑧ Insert the mounting bolt through the bridge, with the flats of the bolt head indexing with the recesses in the bridge.

NOTE: If you do not have a vise, it is easiest to reassemble the mounting bolt to the frame now (steps ⑫ and ⑬).

⑨ Slide one of the nylon bushings onto a pivot bolt, with the flat side of the bushing against the bolt head. Slide the steel bushing onto the bolt, and then insert the assembled bolt through the inner brake arm from the side opposite the spring anchor post.

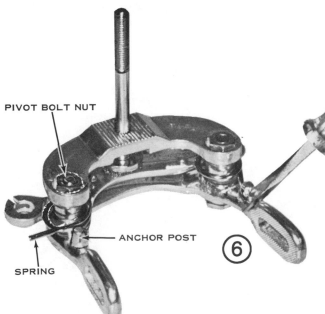

⑥

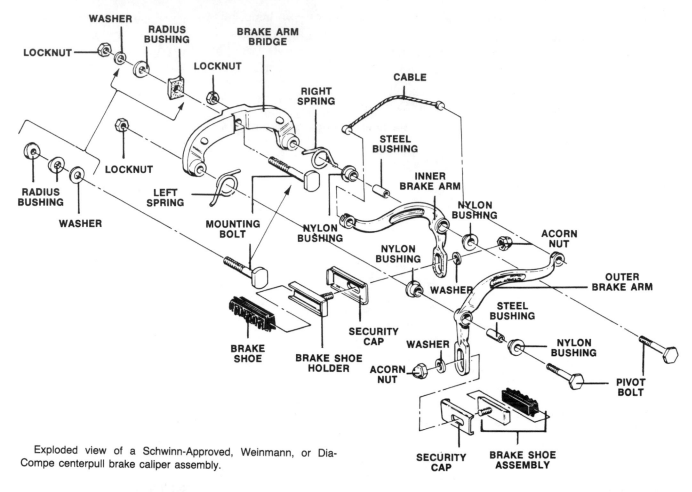

Exploded view of a Schwinn-Approved, Weinmann, or Dia-Compe centerpull brake caliper assembly.

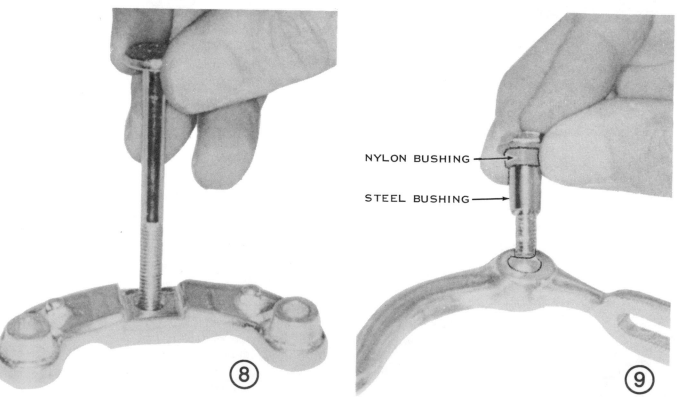

⑩ Grease the bushings and the openings in the brake arms lightly. Place the right-side sleeve on the bridge, with the hooked end of the spring on top of the coil facing away from the bridge; and then place the straight end of the spring on the lower side of the post, as shown. *NOTE: The right and left springs are identified by the hook end being on top of the coil and facing outward when placed on the spring post.* Hold the inner brake arm and assembled pivot bolt in place, and then

point for a lamp, reflector, fender, or baggage rack. If so, install this under the locknut. Install the lockwasher on the bolt, thread the locknut on, and then tighten it securely.

NOTE: Newer brakes use a locknut with a nylon friction insert. This is highly recommended for replacement use, as it eliminates any possibility of the locknut's unscrewing. **CAUTION: Many accidents have been caused by a brake's falling into the wheel.**

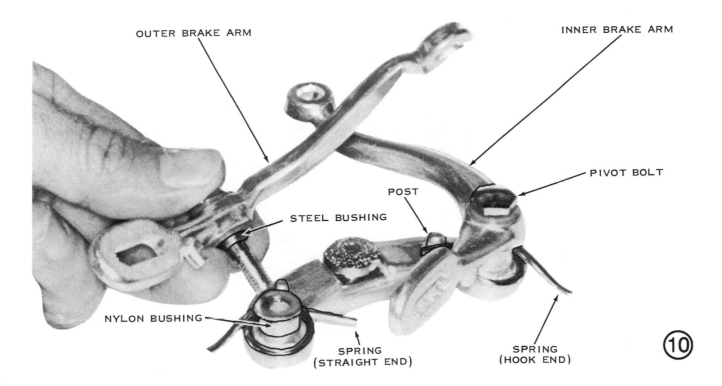

OUTER BRAKE ARM — INNER BRAKE ARM — PIVOT BOLT — POST — STEEL BUSHING — NYLON BUSHING — SPRING (STRAIGHT END) — SPRING (HOOK END) ⑩

insert the bolt through the bridge. Slide another nylon bushing onto the bolt, with the flat side facing out, and then thread the locknut onto the bolt and into the slot in the bridge. Hold the nut in place, and then tighten the pivot bolt. Install the outside brake arm in a similar manner.

⑪ Turn the assembled unit over, and then snap the hook end of the springs over the anchor posts on the brake arms.

Unthreaded-type shoes: Install the spring over the pivot; but you will snap it into place only after installing the brake shoes.

⑫ Slide the spacer and radius bushing onto the mounting bolt, with the concave side of the bushing facing up, and then install the bolt through the hole in the front forks or rear frame.

⑬ Install the radius bushing on the mounting bolt, with the concave side against the frame.

The brake mounting bolt may be used as a mounting

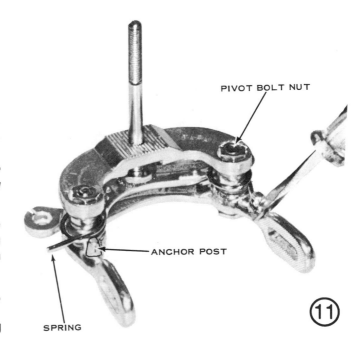

PIVOT BOLT NUT — ANCHOR POST — SPRING ⑪

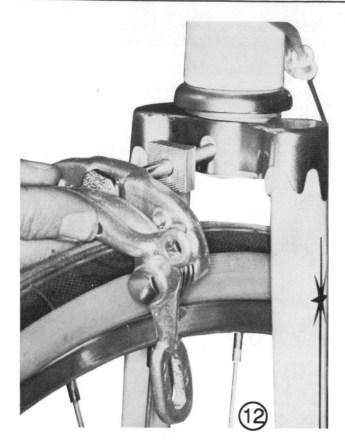

⑫

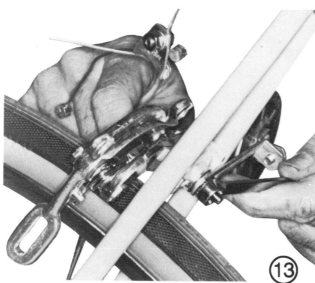

⑬

cap will then be facing toward the rear of the bicycle. **CAUTION: The brake shoe assembly must be installed with the closed end of the holder facing forward to prevent the shoe from working out when the brakes are applied and subsequent complete loss of braking ability at that wheel.** Install a washer, and then thread an acorn nut onto the brake shoe bolt finger-tight.

NOTE: Many brake shoe holders are closed at both ends, and are replaced as a unit.

Unthreaded-type brake shoes: Install the eyebolt through the brake arm on the side opposite the brake's frame mounting. Install the thin washer, then the locknut, rounded end in, on the threads of the eyebolt.

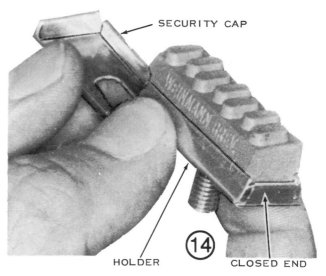

SECURITY CAP

HOLDER   ⑭   CLOSED END

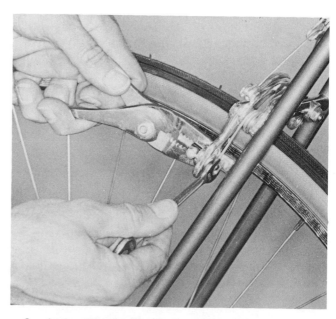

⑭ Push a new brake shoe into each of the brake shoe holders until the shoe contacts the closed end of the holder. Insert the brake-shoe-holder bolt through the slot of the security cap, if any, with the open end of the holder toward the closed end of the cap, as shown. Install an assembled brake shoe into one of the brake arms, with the closed end of the holder facing forward and the beveled surface of the shoe matching the angle of the wheel rim. The closed end of the security

On a brake with unthreaded posts, hold the brake shoe in position while tightening the nut behind the brake arm.

Install the large spacer washer. Slide the brake shoe post through the hole in the eyebolt and tighten the locknut. Snap the return spring over the locknut.

⑮ Insert one end of the brake cable loop into the hole and slot of the brake arm without the brake shoe assembly being installed. Squeeze the brake arms together against the wheel rim, and then insert the other end of the brake cable loop into its hole and slot.

With a centerpull brake, there is usually an adjusting barrel at the brake lever or at the brake cable hanger above the brake. Loosen the knurled locknut, if any, on the adjusting barrel and thread the adjusting barrel all the way down, so the large end of the adjusting barrel is as close as possible to the eyebolt or brake lever. Then retighten the locknut.

⑯ Install the other brake shoe assembly on the brake arm, with the closed end of the brake shoe holder facing forward. Install a washer, and then thread an acorn nut onto the brake shoe bolt; tighten it securely.

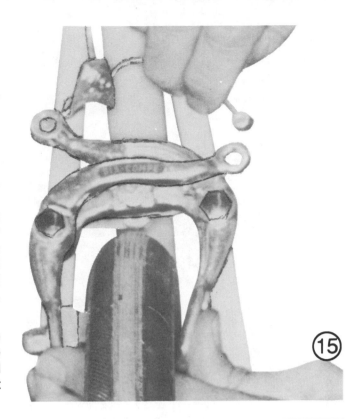

⑮

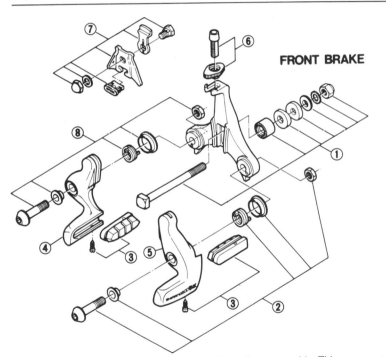

FRONT BRAKE

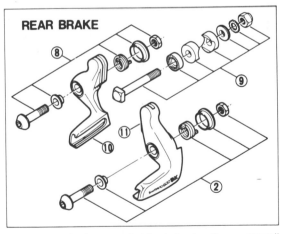

REAR BRAKE

Exploded view of a Shimano Parapul brake caliper assembly. This uses a cam to move the brake arms, but is similar to other centerpull brake assemblies.

ITEM	DESCRIPTION	ITEM	DESCRIPTION	ITEM	DESCRIPTION
1	Center bolt assembly for front	5	Arm B	9	Center bolt assembly for rear
2	Pivot bolt assembly–M (left side for front brake or right side for rear brake)	6	Cable adjusting bolt and nut	10	Arm C
		7	Carrier assembly	11	Arm D
3	Brake shoe and shoe fixing screw	8	Pivot bolt assembly–N (right side for front brake or left side rear brake)		
4	Arm A				

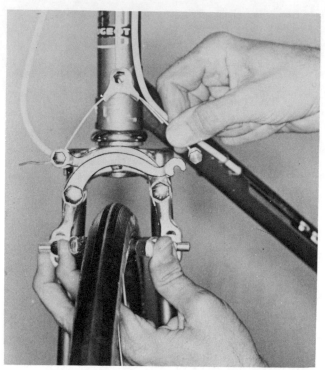

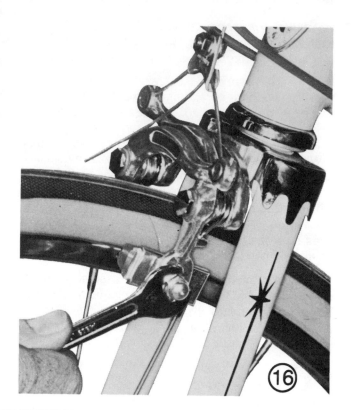

On some centerpull brakes such as this Mafac, the transverse cable may simply be hooked under the brake arm.

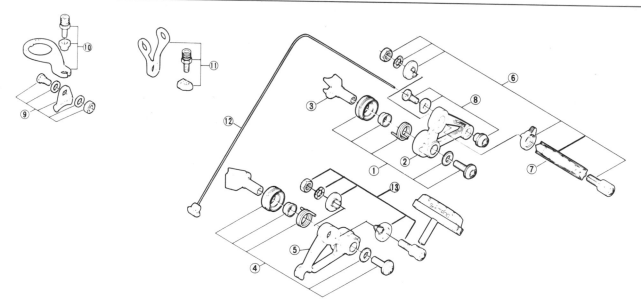

Exploded view of a Shimano DeOre cantilever brake, which uses tapered washers to adjust brake-shoe angle.

ITEM	DESCRIPTION	ITEM	DESCRIPTION	ITEM	DESCRIPTION
1	Anchor link fixing bolt unit	5	Hooking link with bush	9	Cable carrier assembly
2	Anchor link with bush	6	Brake shoe fixing bolt unit	10	Front cable hanger assembly
3	Front mounting shaft / Rear mounting shaft	7	Brake shoe / Brake shoe assembly 4 pieces	11	Rear cable hanger assembly
4	Hooking link fixing bolt unit	8	Wire fixing bolt unit	12	Center wire 380mm
				13	Brake shoe fixing bolt unit

Adjusting

⑰ Center the assembled brake unit over the wheel rim, by loosening the mounting locknut slightly and then turning the brake-arm bridge and mounting bolt until the two pivots are equally high. Tighten the lock-nut securely.

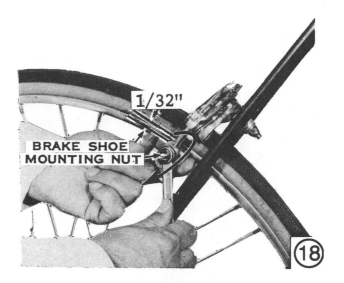

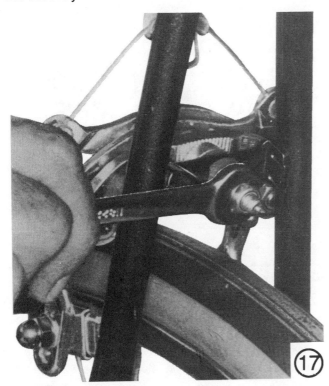

⑱ Loosen the acorn nut of each brake shoe slightly, and then slide the shoe assembly in the brake-arm slot until the top edge of the shoe is approximately 1/32 inch below the top of the wheel rim. Tilt the shoe to the approximate angle of the wheel rim, and then tighten the acorn nut securely. **CAUTION: Misalignment of brake shoes can lead to rapid wear of the tire side-walls, and a blowout.**

Note that the front brake rotates forward and upward as the wheel pulls it during braking, so lower the front end of the front brake shoes slightly.

An unthreaded brake shoe should be slid as far as possible into the mounting bolt, so the brake arm rests against the shoe. This makes the shoe much less likely to slip.

CAUTION: Cantilever brake shoes should always angle up toward the tire. Then, if they slip, they will collapse away from the spokes. Before installing the transverse cable on a cantilever brake, rotate each brake arm to make sure that no part of it could go into the spokes if the cable broke.

⑲ Check to be sure the front end of the brake shoe is approximately 1/32 inch closer to the wheel rim than the rear end. If it is not, grip the brake arm with a

wrench directly below the brake shoe assembly, and then twist the arm slightly until the front end of the shoe contacts the wheel rim first when the brake lever is actuated. This will keep the brake from squeaking. Some brakes with unthreaded posts have washers to adjust this angle. Pulling a piece of sandpaper between the shoe and rim will also help break in a new shoe.

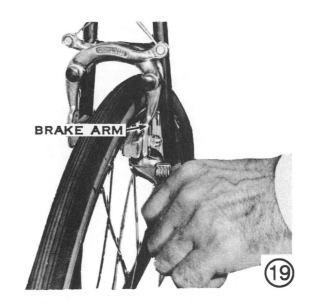

⑳ The brake shoes should be approximately 1/8 inch from the rim. If the brake shoes rub the rim or if they are too far from it, slide the cable through the anchor bolt on the stirrup which joins the main cable to the transverse cable. For fine adjustments, use the adjusting barrel at the stirrup or brake lever. Some brakes are adjustable at the transverse cable also, as shown.

Test the brake, using the three steps described on page 338. Do not ride the bicycle or allow it to be ridden until you are sure that the brakes work correctly.

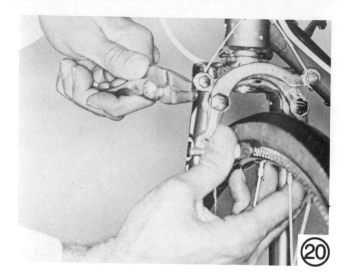

OVERHAULING A HUB WITH EXPANDER-TYPE BRAKE OR DISK BRAKE

Drum brakes differ in detail, though basic construction is similar. Keep track of parts during disassembly by threading them onto wires or laying them out on a table in order.

Hub brakes may be built into the hub or threaded to it. To remove a threaded-on brake drum or disk, grasp the brake lever tightly, then turn the wheel backward or roll the bicycle backward until the disk or drum loosens. Removing the drum or disk may be necessary to replace a broken spoke. With a Phil Wood disk brake, you must reposition the rubber bumper at the top of the chainstay as shown, to take the reversed force.

The overhaul instructions for disassembling and assembling the bearings of a brake hub are the same as for a conventional hub or sealed-bearing hub. If the reason for working on the hub is to improve brake performance, it is not necessary to take apart the bearings. However, a hub that needs new brake shoes probably is due for a bearing overhaul too. Follow the instructions in Chapter 8.

Problems with Drum Brakes

NOTE: Many brake problems described here are actually cable problems. Instructions for servicing cables are in Chapter 6.

Many brake problems can be tested only before disassembly. Perform the three tests listed on page 338; then use the problem chart below to help locate the source of the problem. Only a partial disassembly may be necessary.

On a tandem with rim brakes in addition to the hub brake, the hub brake's main purpose is to control downhill speed. It need not be able to lock the wheel, though it must be resistant to fading. Test it on a long, steep hill.

Atom hub with internal-expanding two-shoe-type cable-operated brake.

Brake is weak, lever bottoms out, feels "spongy."

Possible cause:	Corrective action:
Cable is adjusted too loose.	Adjust cable.
Brake is mismatched to lever.	Use long-pull lever.
Cable is excessively long or kinked.	Service cable.
Shoes are worn.	Replace shoes.

Brake is weak, lever is hard to pull.

Possible cause:	Corrective action:
Cable is rusted or kinked.	Service cable.
Lever is mismatched to brake.	Use short-pull lever.
There is oil on drum or disk.	Clean, replace shoes.

Brake grabs; braking is uneven.

Possible cause:	Corrective action:
Wheel is out of true.	True wheel.
There is oil on drum or disk.	Clean, replace shoes.
Drum or disk is warped.	Replace drum or disk.

Brake drags after lever is released.

Possible cause:	Corrective action:
Brake is adjusted too tight.	Loosen cable slightly.
There is no slack in cable housing.	Rearrange cable.
Axle is bent.	Replace axle.

Brake will not release.

Possible cause:	Corrective action:
Cable is kinked or rusted.	Service cable.
Lever pivots are bent or corroded.	Service or replace lever.

Tools and Supplies You Will Need

Small wrenches
Needlenose pliers
Screwdriver
Brake shoes as required
Grease

Removing a Built-in Drum Brake Mechanism

First disconnect the cable (page 88) and remove the wheel (page 69).

① Remove the locknut and keyed lockwasher or spacer washer under it.

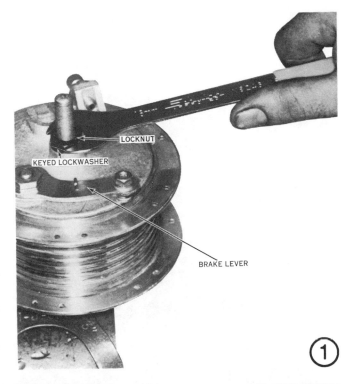

To remove a brake drum or disk which is threaded to the hub, clamp the brake lever and rotate the wheel backward. With the Phil Wood brake shown, the brake arm bumper must be repositioned under the chainstay, as shown, for removal.

② Lift the complete brake shoe assembly off the end of the axle.

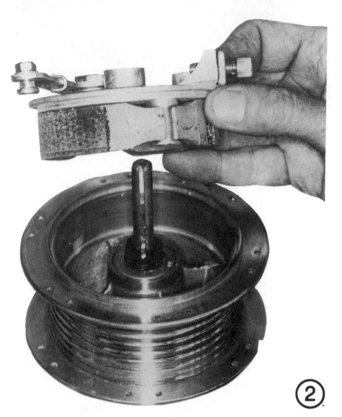

Disassembling the Brake Mechanism

③ Put the brake assembly back onto the axle upside down to hold it steady. Remove the spring on the stationary post side by grasping the spring firmly with needlenose pliers and unhooking it from one of the knobs, as shown.

④ Hold one brake shoe in each hand, and then slide both shoes toward the center of the plate and off the brake cam. Remove the remaining spring from the brake shoes.

⑤ Some Sturmey-Archer brake cams are asymmetric. Note which way the longer end faces. Loosen the locknut on the brake cam, swing the brake lever away from the center of the brake plate, and then unhook the brake-lever spring. Remove the locknut, brake lever, and spring. Remove the cable-adjusting sleeve and locknut. Remove the cable anchor nut and bolt from the brake lever.

Cleaning and Inspecting

When you clean the hub parts, *do not clean the brake shoes,* because solvent will make them slippery.

Check the brake shoes for breaks or cracks and the linings for glaze and for excessive or uneven wear.

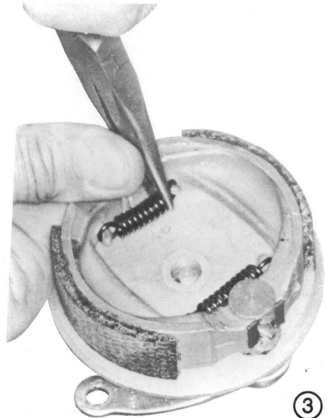

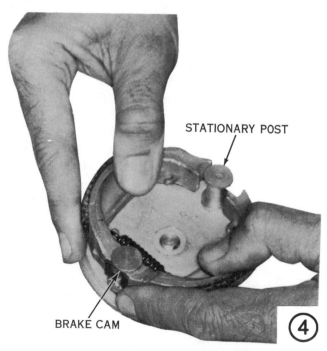

STATIONARY POST

BRAKE CAM

Check the brake shoe springs for damage, cracks, breaks, or weak tension. You should have had considerable difficulty unhooking the springs from the knobs, which shows that the spring tension is satisfactory.

Inspect the brake-lever spring for cracks or breaks.

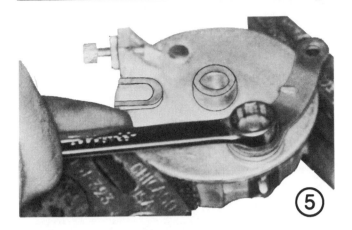

(5)

Installing a Built-in Drum-brake Mechanism

Perform the following steps after reassembling the hub's bearings (see Chapter 14).

Some hubs may have a spacer washer or bushing which must be installed before the brake shoe assembly. Reinstall this as it was before disassembly.

Assembling the Brake Mechanism

(6) Place the brake plate in a vise, with the stationary post and brake cam facing up. Set the two brake shoes on the brake plate so the brake shoe cam ends will ride on the flats of the brake cam. If the brake-lever assembly was removed, install the brake cam through the brake plate so the brake cam and stationary post are on the same side of the plate. Some Sturmey-Archer brake cams are asymmetric. Align with the long end facing outward for the front brake and inward for the rear brake. If the brake-lever assembly was not removed, reach under the plate and unhook the brake-lever spring to assist in assembly. Turn the brake cam so the flats line up toward the center of the brake plate, allowing the brake shoes to come together as closely as possible. Hook one end of either spring over a hook on one side of the cam post. Grasp the spring firmly with needlenose pliers, and then stretch it enough to hook it over the other brake shoe hook. Install the other spring in a like manner. Remove the assembly from the vise. Hook the brake-lever spring over the inside edge of the lever.

(7) If the brake lever and spring were removed, place the spring over the brake-cam threaded end, with the small ear of the spring through the small hole in the plate.

(8) Install the brake lever on the brake cam so the lever is approximately at a right angle to the flats on the

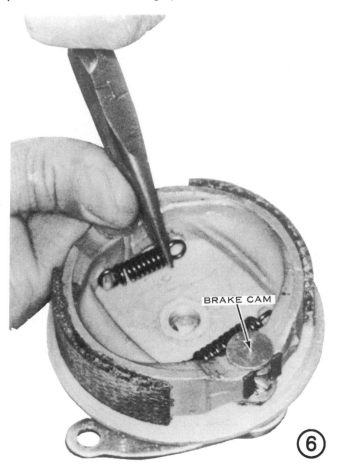

BRAKE CAM

(6)

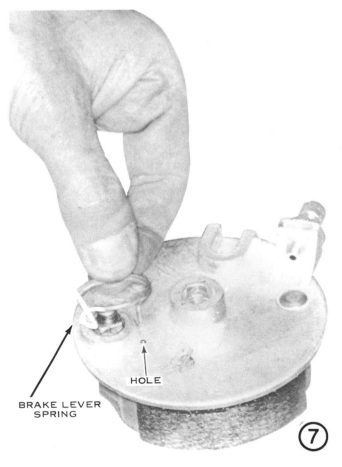

BRAKE LEVER
SPRING

HOLE

(7)

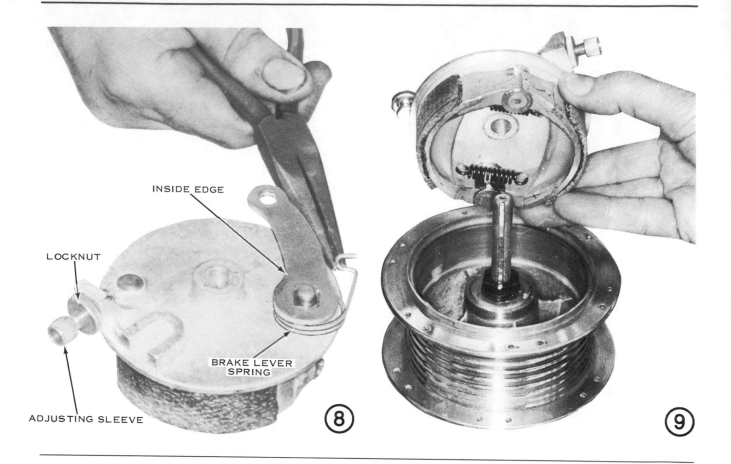

INSIDE EDGE

LOCKNUT

ADJUSTING SLEEVE

BRAKE LEVER
SPRING

⑧

⑨

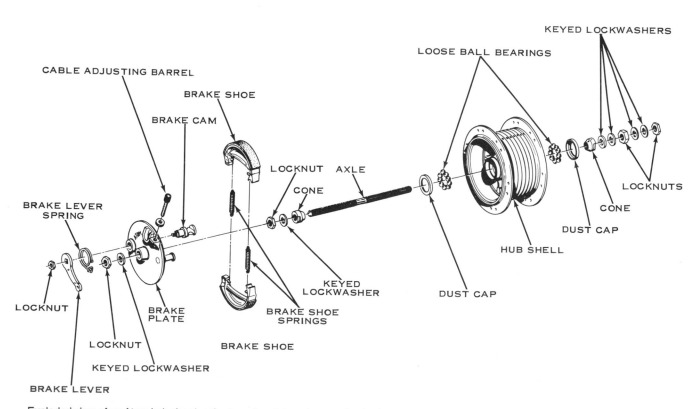

CABLE ADJUSTING BARREL

BRAKE SHOE

BRAKE CAM

BRAKE LEVER
SPRING

LOCKNUT   AXLE

LOCKNUT

CONE

KEYED LOCKWASHERS

LOOSE BALL BEARINGS

LOCKNUTS

CONE

DUST CAP

HUB SHELL

KEYED
LOCKWASHER

DUST CAP

LOCKNUT

BRAKE
PLATE

LOCKNUT

KEYED LOCKWASHER

BRAKE LEVER

BRAKE SHOE
SPRINGS

BRAKE SHOE

Exploded view of an Atom hub showing the two-shoe internal-expanding brake mechanism. A similar hub is the Sturmey-Archer shown on page 130 in Chapter 8.

cam and the lever offset is up away from the surface of the brake plate. Thread the locknut onto the brake cam and tighten it against the brake lever. Hook the brake-lever spring over the inside edge of the brake lever. Install the adjusting sleeve and locknut with approximately the same number of sleeve threads visible on either side of the flange. Install the cable anchor bolt and nut on the brake lever.

Installing the Brake Mechanism

⑨ Install the assembled brake shoe mechanism. The springs will hold the brake shoes in the retracted position, and this should allow the assembly to slide easily into the hub shell.

⑩ Install a keyed lockwasher, with the key indexed with the keyway in the axle. Thread a locknut onto the axle, and tighten it against the lockwasher and brake plate.

For other models of hub brakes, the particular washers, spacers, and locknuts may vary. Reinstall them in the positions they were in before you disassembled the hub.

Finally, replace the wheel (page 72) and reconnect the cable (page 89).

Test the brake, using the three steps described on page 338. Do not ride the bicycle or allow it to be ridden until you are sure that the brakes work correctly.

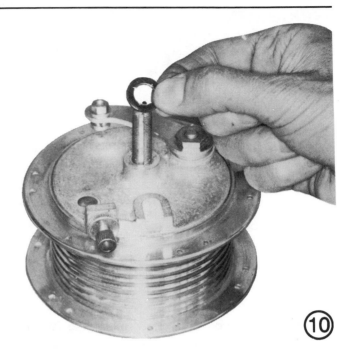

⑩

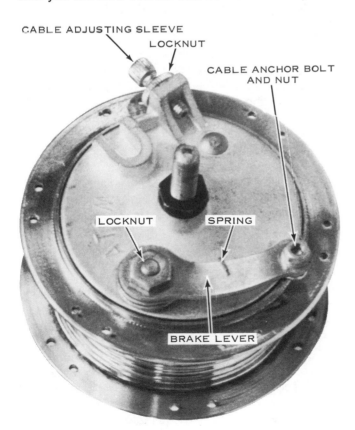

Details of the Atom brake support plate.

17 • WHEELBUILDING AND WHEEL REPAIR

With patience, you can learn to make stronger and rounder wheels than are sold on most new bikes—or you can improve the wheels you have. Since the rim, hub, and spokes are separate parts, you can assemble a wheel using whichever parts suit your needs. Wheelbuilding skills also can help you out of trouble on the road, if a wheel needs repair.

Wheelbuilding and wheel repair are demanding tasks. The instructions here are as clear as possible. However, the final steps of tensioning and trueing the wheel require skilled hands and eyes. It is a good idea to have the help of a practiced wheelbuilder for your first wheel; expect to spend several hours with it. When you gain more experience, you might finish a wheel in an hour.

You will probably need to repair a wheel before you have a reason to build a new one. However, building a wheel with a new rim is much easier than repairing a wheel with an old, bent rim. There are two ways around this problem:

1. Make a wheelbuilding project for yourself. Build a wheel just for practice, or for a spare.

2. If one of your bike's wheels needs repair, either build a new wheel or replace the rim (see page 388).

HOW SPOKED WHEELS WORK

A tension-spoked bicycle wheel is a remarkable structure capable of supporting over 100 times its own weight. Because of its open construction, it also lets sidewinds blow through, important to the bicycle's stability. Developed between 1870 and 1890, it is one of the main advances which made the bicycle practical.

Let's look at the wheel to see how it supports its load.

The *hub,* at the center, transfers loads from the frame of the bicycle; the hub contains the axle and bearings which allow the wheel to turn. At the left and right ends of the hub are the *flanges* with *spoke holes* into which the spokes are inserted.

The *spokes* are lengths of steel wire. At the hub end, each spoke has a head like a nail and is bent over at a right angle. The head fastens the spoke into a spoke hole.

At the rim end, the spoke has threads like a bolt. A *spoke nipple*—a lengthened nut—threads onto the spoke and secures it to the rim.

The *rim* is a round hoop of metal, U-shaped in cross-section. The spoke nipples fit through the spoke holes at the base of the U, and the tire fits between the *rim flanges* at the top of the U.

If you pluck the spokes of a completed wheel like guitar strings, you'll hear them ring and feel that they're strongly tensioned. The tension of the spokes is the key to how the wheel supports its load.

All of the spokes pull inward on the rim, with a force of 100 to 250 pounds each. The spoke tension generates nearly a ton of compression at any point along the rim. All of the spokes work against each other around the rim to hold it steady. For example, spokes at twelve o'clock and six o'clock in the rim might be able to collapse it down by bulging out the sections at three o'clock and nine o'clock—but the spokes at three o'clock and nine o'clock hold those parts of the rim in.

When you sit on the bicycle, your weight tries to flatten the rim where the wheel rests on the ground. You can see the flat spot in the tire. The rim flattens a little too—not enough for you to see, but enough partly to loosen the three or four spokes closest to the bottom.

Let's say that each spoke is under 100 pounds of tension and you put a 150-pound load on the wheel. Three spokes at the bottom with their tension reduced to 50 pounds will support the load.

In reality, the math isn't quite so neat—the middle

spoke would probably slacken more than the others—but the tension reduction does in fact support the load. You can prove it to yourself by plucking the spokes like harp strings as someone sits on the bike. Only the tension of three or four bottom spokes changes very much. Their musical pitch will fall as the load increases.

Compare bicycle spokes with the untensioned, heavy spokes of a wooden wagon wheel. The bottom spoke of the wagon wheel goes into *compression* as the load pushes up from the rim—the wheel stands on the spoke. But a reduction in tension in a wire spoke works just the same as an increase in compression in a wooden spoke. As the spokes at the bottom of the bicycle wheel loosen, they *reduce their upward pull* on the bottom of the rim—the result is exactly the same as *increasing a downward push:* The rim is supported against the weight load.

The *tension preload* in bicycle spokes makes this possible, because tension holds the spoke straight. That's why lightweight wire spokes work in the bicycle wheel.

Compression would try to bend and crumple a spoke sideways. That's why the wagon wheel has thick, heavy spokes. If you push on the two ends of a bicycle spoke, you'll see that they would support only a few ounces in compression.

Besides weight, a bicycle has two other loads to support: sideways loads and turning loads.

Sideways (lateral) loads are easy to understand. The spokes going from the rim to the two sides of the hub, left and right, brace the rim against moving sideways. To resist a sideways load at the rim, spokes on one side tighten while spokes on the other side loosen. Sideways loads are relatively small on a bicycle, because it leans into turns. On an adult tricycle or a wheelchair, sideways loads are greater, and spoke breakage is much more frequent.

Look at a rear wheel from the right side to understand how it supports *torsional (turning) loads.* Some spokes point counterclockwise from the hub flanges and others point clockwise. The driving force from the hub sprocket is clockwise, so it loosens the clockwise spokes and tightens the counterclockwise spokes.

BUILDING A WHEEL

The instructions here will result in a wheel with the counterclockwise spokes at the inside of the flanges. These spokes are laced (woven) over the outside of the clockwise spokes. As the sprocket applies power to a rear wheel, the change in tension on the spokes pulls the lacing points toward the centerline of the bicycle. A wheel laced the other way will sometimes rub the rear derailleur during hard pedaling when using the innermost sprocket.

The spoking pattern is relatively unimportant on a front wheel or on a non-derailleur rear wheel, but the pattern given here is as good as any.

Professional wheelbuilders install all of the spokes in the hub first, and then assemble them to the rim. The wheel assembly procedure here is not quite as fast, but it is more foolproof for a beginner. The resulting spoke pattern is the same.

Supplies You Will Need

Hub, complete with axle nuts or quick-release assembly
Rim
Spokes with spoke nipples
Spoke wrench to fit spoke nipples
Small flat-bladed screwdriver
Grease
Work gloves
Trueing stand, or bicycle adapted to use as trueing stand
Spare spoke or small metal ruler, and rubber band (if using bicycle)

Supplies You May Need

Rim washers
Spoke head washers
Flat file
Rim jack
Hammer
Pliers
Electrical tape

Preliminary Steps

Choose a rim. Use a good-quality, *new* rim; there's little point in taking the trouble to build a wheel with an inferior or bent rim. Aluminum-alloy rims have important advantages over steel rims. They are easier to true and to repair; also, rim brakes work much better on aluminum rims in wet weather.

Choose a hub. It is preferable to use a hub with thick aluminum flanges. Thin steel flanges are much more likely to break spokes, though there is a way around this problem; see "Wheelbuilding Refinements," page 381. A large-flange hub is preferable for heavy driving or hub-brake loads, as in the rear wheel of a tandem, and can make it easier to replace broken spokes next to a freewheel; otherwise, flange size is of little importance. If reusing an old hub, make sure the bearings are in good condition before taking the trouble to build it into a wheel.

CAUTION: Remove a freewheel or brake disk before clipping the spokes out of a wheel. If you can't use the rim to unscrew the freewheel or brake disk, you cannot remove them and may not be able to install new spokes. Also, a multispeed or coaster-brake hub may need to be in a fully spoked wheel for the first steps of disassembly.

Count the spoke holes; the rim and the hub must have the same number of holes.

Decide what gauge of spokes to use; 14-gauge (2mm) plain-gauge spokes are best for medium and heavy-weight rims. A very lightweight, narrow rim will not withstand the tension of these heavy spokes, and should be spoked with light-gauge spokes (15- or 16-gauge, 1.8mm or 1.5mm shaft). Light-gauge spokes are most durable if the ends are *butted*—thicker than the center section, to give extra strength where stress is greatest.

Spokes are available in zinc-plated carbon steel (dull appearance) and in stainless steel (shiny appearance). Carbon-steel spokes are cheaper and somewhat stronger. Stainless-steel spokes are best for prolonged use in wet conditions or salt air. Whichever you choose, use high-quality, name-brand spokes. Cheap spokes made of inferior steel will break prematurely.

Determine the length of spokes you need, and buy *new* spokes and nipples. It is easiest if you bring the rim and hub with you to the bike shop, or if you buy all wheel parts at once. A bike shop should be able to select the correct spoke length, given the model and size of rim, the flange size of the hub, and the spoke cross pattern. Common spoke cross patterns are *cross-three* and *cross-four*. Spoke length is different for these two patterns. There is no important difference in wheel strength.

When you buy spokes, make a note which pattern they will build.

Be sure that your spoke wrench fits the flats of the spoke nipples; not all are the same. If necessary, buy a new spoke wrench.

The following assembly instructions are for cross-three spoking. Where instructions differ for cross-four spoking, they are given in italics.

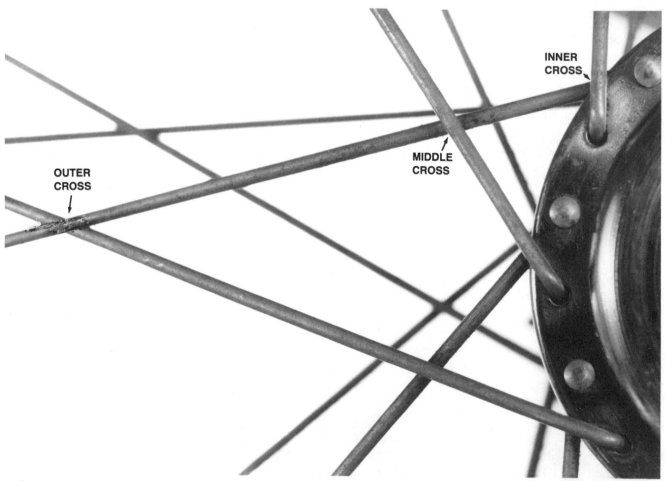

In a cross-three wheel, shown here, each spoke crosses three others from the same hub flange of the wheel. The outermost cross *(arrow)* is *laced*, with the inside spoke passing over the outside one so they help support each other.

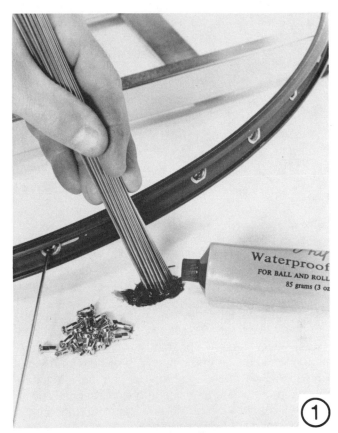

A butted spoke *(right)* has ends thicker than the shaft for extra strength where threading and the bend weaken the spoke. A plain-gauge spoke *(left)* is the same thickness over its entire length. To see why both have been used here in the same wheel, see the note on balanced spoking, page 381.

Spoking the Wheel

① With a clean tool, place a gob of grease on a scrap of paper, and dip the spoke threads in it. **CAU-TION: Do not dip spokes directly into the grease container—you could contaminate the grease.** Make sure that grease fills the spoke threads. Also scoop grease into the small end of each spoke nipple; with the end of a spoke, grease the nipple seat of each spoke hole in the rim. If you do not lubricate the threads and spoke holes, the spokes will be difficult to tighten.

② Looking at the rim from the outside (tire side), the two spoke holes on either side of the valve hole will be *clockwise* or *counterclockwise* compared to the line of the rim. Determine which your rim is. The rim shown here is *counterclockwise.*

The countersinking of the spoke hole is intended, as shown, to support the bend of the spoke, not the head. If spoke holes are countersunk on one side, insert spokes so the countersinking cradles the bend.

③ Determine which is the right side of the hub. Most have a right and left side—see hub section, page 108, if in doubt. Insert the first right spoke, from outside to inside. If every second spoke hole is countersunk (beveled) on the outside of the flange, insert the spoke into a hole which is *not* countersunk on the outside. Insert spokes from outside to inside into every second spoke hole in the right side of the hub, beginning the count with your original right-side spoke.

④ Clamp the rim between your knees; hold the hub in your left hand; hold the spoke with your right hand. Position them as in the assembled wheel, with the right (spoke) side of the hub on your right, and the valve hole at the top of the rim.

Counterclockwise rim: Insert your first spoke into the *second* rim spoke hole past the valve hole.

Clockwise rim: Insert the spoke into the first *rim spoke hole past the valve hole.*

In either case, this spoke hole is on the same side of the rim as the hub flange with the spoke. Fasten the spoke by threading a nipple on four or five turns.

FIRST RIGHT-SIDE SPOKE HOLE AHEAD OF VALVE HOLE.

④

⑤ Lay the wheel on its left side. Bring the right-side spokes up to the rim in order and insert them into every fourth hole, beginning the count with your original right-side spoke. Fasten each spoke by threading on a nipple four or five turns.

⑥ Insert the first left spoke into the hub from outside to inside. Spoke holes in the two flanges are staggered, with the holes in one flange halfway between those in the other flange. Lay the spoke across the hub, parallel with the hub barrel, to see how the holes in the two flanges are aligned with each other.

③

⑤

Counterclockwise rim, as shown here: Insert the first left spoke into the hub spoke hole *behind* the first right spoke.

Clockwise rim: Insert the first left spoke into the hub spoke hole just ahead of the first right spoke.

⑦ Insert the first left spoke into the first or second rim spoke hole past the valve hole, whichever is empty. Fasten the spoke by threading a nipple on four or five turns. The screwdriver in the photograph indicates the

⑥

position of the valve hole. Note the two spokes in two holes past the valve hole.

Check your work. Make sure that your two spokes next to the valve hole are in spoke holes in the hub as nearly in line with each other as possible. They should not cross.

⑦

⑧ Lift the wheel off the bench. Insert spokes from outside to inside into every second spoke hole in the left side of the hub, beginning the count with your original left-side spoke. Lay the wheel on its right side. Bring the left-side spokes up to the rim in order, inserting them into every fourth spoke hole, beginning the count with your original left-side spoke. Fasten each spoke by threading on a nipple four or five turns.

Looking at the right side of the wheel, spokes should lie in pairs as shown. No spokes should cross. Spoke holes in the rim should be in groups of four—two occupied, then two empty—all the way around.

⑨ Lift the wheel up. Insert spokes into all of the empty holes in the right hub flange from inside to outside. Lay the wheel down on its left side. Twist the hub clockwise (looking from the right). Make sure that all of the spoke nipples in the rim are seated full-depth in the rim holes.

⑩ Now rotate one of your new spokes counterclockwise.

Cross-three spoking: Pass the new spoke over two and then *under* one of the previously installed right-flange spokes.

⑧

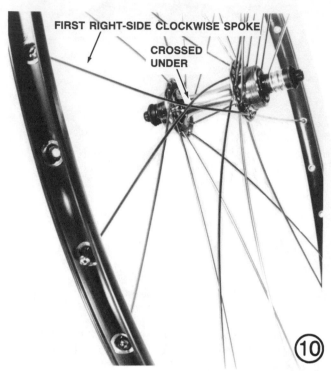

FIRST RIGHT-SIDE CLOCKWISE SPOKE

CROSSED UNDER

⑩

⑨

Cross-four spoking: Pass the new spoke over three and then under *one of the previously installed right-flange spokes.*

You will have to bend the spoke slightly to get it under. Putting the spoke under at the final cross is called *lacing.* It strengthens the wheel somewhat, and keeps the spokes of a rear wheel away from the derailleur.

Bring the threaded end of the new spoke up to the second rim spoke hole past the end of the spoke it crossed under. There will be a left-flange spoke in the hole next to your new spoke's. The new spoke will be just about long enough to reach the correct hole. Fasten the spoke by threading a nipple on four or five turns. If the nipple won't reach, check again that previously installed nipples are seated.

CAUTION: It is a common error to install the first counterclockwise right-flange spoke next to another right-flange spoke. As shown in the photograph, it must be next to a left-flange spoke. It must be in the second hole from the right-flange spoke it crossed under.

⑪ Install the remaining right-flange spokes the same way, in every fourth spoke hole. Check your work. On the left side of the hub, every second spoke hole should be occupied, with spoke heads facing outward. On the right side of the hub, every spoke hole should be occupied, with spoke heads alternating facing inward and outward.

Looking from the right (fully spoked) side of the

wheel, either the first or second rim spoke hole coun-terclockwise of the valve hole should be empty. Spokes in the rim should alternate right-left-right-empty, all the way around. All spoke nipples should seat well in the rim now. If any spokes seem much too long or short, either the spokes are the wrong length or you have laced the wheel incorrectly.

⑫ Lift the wheel up and install spokes from inside to outside into the remaining empty spoke holes in the left hub flange. Lay the wheel on its right side, new spokes up. Rotate one of the new spokes clockwise.

Cross-three spoking: Pass the spoke over two left-flange spokes and then *under* one.

Cross-four spoking: Pass the spoke over three left-flange spokes and then under *one.*

Bring the threaded end of the new spoke up to the rim and install it in the second spoke hole past the spoke it crossed under. It should be nearly parallel to a spoke from the other flange in the next rim hole. Fasten the spoke by threading a spoke nipple on four or five turns.

⑪

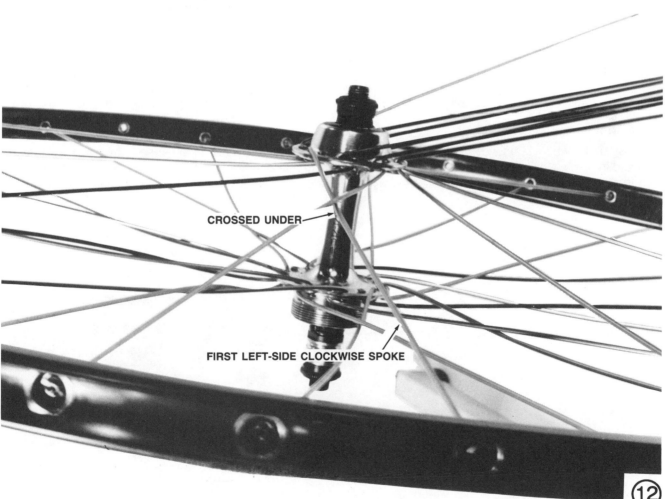

CROSSED UNDER

FIRST LEFT-SIDE CLOCKWISE SPOKE

⑫

⑬ Install the remaining spokes in the remaining empty rim spoke holes. Check your work. The wheel should look like the one in the photograph. The spokes next to the valve hole should angle away from it, to make room for the pump. Every second spoke should be a right-side spoke. All of the spoke crossings closest to the rim should be laced.

Tensioning and Trueing

Lacing of the wheel is now complete; all spokes are fastened in place. Next, you tighten and true the wheel on a trueing stand, or on a bicycle adapted to serve as one.

A trueing stand is constructed much like the front or rear fork of your bicycle, except that it is made for quick mounting and removal of wheels. It also has *feelers* to indicate the rim alignment.

You adapt a bicycle to use as a trueing stand by improvising feelers. Turn the brake shoes around, with the rubber brake blocks on the outside and the studs on the inside. The studs are your feelers for true (sideways wobble). Your feeler for hop (in-out wobble) is a small metal ruler or spare spoke fastened just above the rim with a rubber band looped around the back of the fork.

It is possible to true a wheel just as accurately on the bicycle as on a trueing stand; it just takes a little longer. You may have no choice when making an emergency repair.

Whether you are using a trueing stand or a bicycle, the feelers scrape against the high spots of the rim. The sound accurately points out the high spots without your even having to look.

When adjusting the rim's true (sideways position), you push the feelers to one side to find the high spots on that side; push the feelers the other way to find the high spots on the other side.

When removing hop (in-out wobble), you place a feeler so that it rubs on the top of one of the rim flanges.

The procedure described here has only a few steps, but each step is made up of many adjustments to spoke tension. As you approach the end of the procedure, you will alternate many times between sideways trueing, in-out trueing, and centering the wheel. With practice, as you gain speed, the steps will merge into one another as you achieve more than one adjustment at a time.

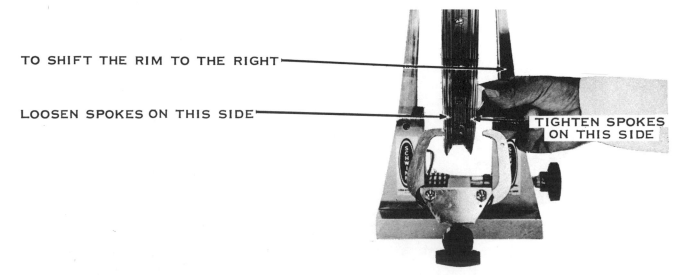

TO SHIFT THE RIM TO THE RIGHT

LOOSEN SPOKES ON THIS SIDE

TIGHTEN SPOKES ON THIS SIDE

To check the lateral alignment of the rim, the trueing stand's feelers are placed at the sides of the rim.

TIGHTEN SPOKES IN CENTER OF HIGH SPOT

LOOSEN SPOKES ON OUTSIDE OF HIGH SPOTS

To check the radial alignment ("hop") of the rim, the trueing stand's feelers are placed under the flanges of the rim.

The bicycle adapted for use as a trueing stand has the brake blocks reversed with the posts on the inside, and a small metal ruler held over the rim with a rubber band.

⑭ Install the wheel in your trueing stand or bicycle. If installing a rear wheel, do not engage the chain; leave it hanging under the wheel. Thread down all of the spoke nipples with the screwdriver, as nearly the same amount as you can. Gauge them by how many spoke threads stick out past the small end of the nipple. The nipples should still be loose. Next, starting at the valve hole, go around the rim as many times as necessary, tightening each nipple one turn at a time until the nipples just engage the rim.

Do not expect the wheel to be very true after this first spoke adjustment. It could easily weave from side to side by ½ inch or more.

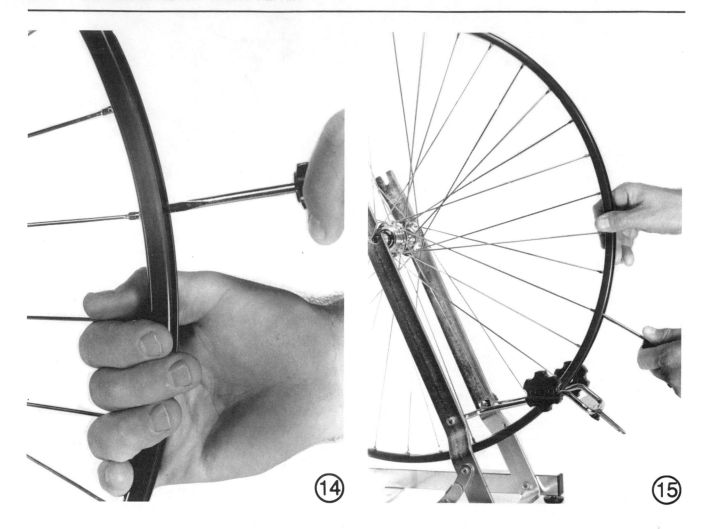

⑭   ⑮

⑮ Turn the wheel with your weaker hand and hold the screwdriver in your better hand. Look for wobbles where the rim passes through the feelers. When you find a section of the rim with a wobble, hold the near end of this section with your hand and bring it to the feelers. Then, keeping your grip on the same point in the rim, draw it toward you until the other end of the wobble is at the feelers. In this way, you mark off the section of the rim you will work on. Then hold the wheel steady while you adjust all of the spokes between the feelers and your hand.

Wobbles will probably be so coarse at first that you can see them easily without using the feelers. Direct your attention to the worst wobble you can find, in-out or side to side. Correct it and move on to the worst remaining wobble.

In-out trueing: If part of the rim is too far to the outside, tighten the spokes there, or if too far to the inside, loosen the spokes there. Turn each nipple a couple of turns at a time, then go to the next nipple. Taper off the correction at the ends of the affected section. Check the correction and repeat as necessary.

Side-to-side trueing: If a length of rim is too far to the left, loosen the spokes on the left and tighten the spokes on the right in that part of the rim; you tighten the spokes opposite the side with the bulge because you are trying to pull the rim away from the bulge. By using equal amounts of loosening and tightening, you avoid affecting the in-out adjustment. Turn each nipple no more than one turn during each adjustment. Taper off the correction at the ends of the part of the rim you are adjusting.

If any spokes are getting so tight the screwdriver doesn't turn them easily, loosen them. If any nipples are so loose that they turn freely, tighten them until they just engage the rim. *At the end of this step, every spoke should be just tight enough to keep the nipple from turning freely—no tighter.*

With a good, new, round rim, no severe wobbles should remain even though the spokes are slack. Side-to-side wobbles should be less than ½ inch total, and in-out wobbles less than ³⁄₁₆ inch. There should be no sharp kinks. If the rim doesn't pass this test, first check to see whether any spokes are much tighter than the others. If so, loosen them and go back to step ⑭.

If all of the spokes are just barely tight but severe

wobbles remain, the rim is bent. In this case, go to page 389 for rim-repair techniques. If you are new to wheelbuilding, get an experienced wheelbuilder to help you. If you try to unbend a rim without much experience, you will almost certainly make it worse.

⑯ Adjust the centering of the rim. First, make sure that all washers and locknuts are installed on the axle as they will be when the wheel is mounted on the bicycle. On a rear wheel for use with a multi-sprocket freewheel, this includes a long spacer on the right side. The right flange of the rear hub is moved inboard to make room for the freewheel. The rim needs to lie midway between the outer locknuts, not midway between the spoking flanges.

For this reason, the right-side spokes of the rear wheel approach the hub at a steeper angle than the left-side spokes. Tighten the spokes on the right side an extra three turns before checking the centering. Then check, and if necessary, adjust again.

The spokes on both sides of a front wheel approach the hub at the same angle. When you check the centering of a front wheel, you will be correcting only for errors that occurred as you made your first spoke adjustments.

The traditional tool to check the centering is a *dishing gauge.* You can buy one of these at a bicycle shop or make one out of a sheet of plywood, a bolt and wingnut, and, as a feeler for the hub, a strip of metal with a hole drilled in one end. You could also stack blocks on your workbench under two opposite points on the rim and measure the distance from the bench top to the hub locknut. Then turn the wheel over and compare measurements.

An equally good but slower way to check wheel centering is to reverse the wheel in the bicycle fork or trueing stand and compare the sideways position of the rim. For example, if you reverse the wheel and the rim is farther to the left, then loosen the left spokes and/or tighten the right spokes.

⑰ Once the rim is reasonably round, true, and centered, begin tightening spokes with the spoke wrench. Start at the valve hole and go all around the wheel tightening each spoke nipple one and a half turns. As long as the spokes are still easy to turn with the spoke wrench, keep tightening them, giving them another half turn each time around. If you get partway around the wheel and the spokes begin to feel very tight, go back the way you came, loosening every spoke back to the valve hole by half a turn.

CAUTION: The spoke wrench appears to tighten the spokes counterclockwise, because the part of the spoke nipple that engages the wrench is at the

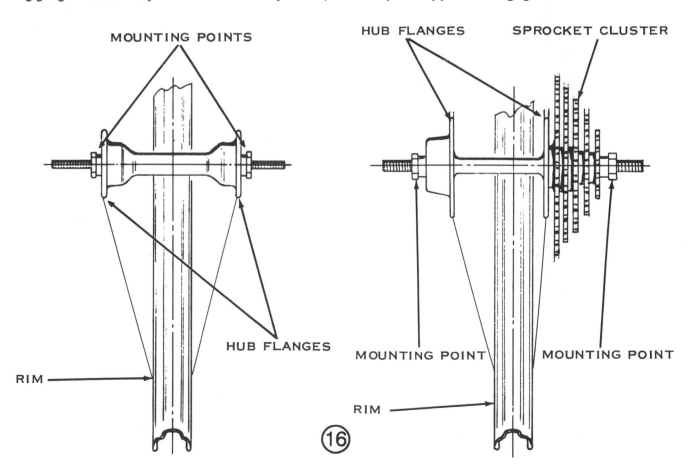

MOUNTING POINTS

HUB FLANGES

HUB FLANGES   SPROCKET CLUSTER

RIM

⑯

MOUNTING POINT   MOUNTING POINT

RIM

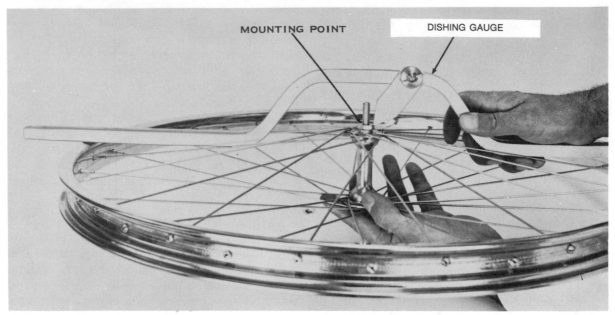

The traditional tool for measuring the centering of the rim is the *dishing gauge*. Centering may also be checked on the bicycle or trueing stand by reversing the wheel left for right.

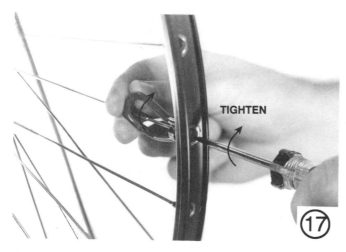

inside of the rim. **To avoid confusion, position your face outside the rim, so you are looking at the outside end of the spoke and at the spoke nipple's screwdriver slot. This turns normally, clockwise, to tighten. However, do not place your eyes directly in the line of the rim. If a spoke breaks during trueing, it can shoot out of the rim like an arrow.**

⑱ If necessary, *set the spokes* at their ends—in other words, straighten out curved sections next to the hub and spoke nipples. Setting the spokes reduces their flexing and increases their life.

If the hub flanges are so thick that outside spokes do not lie flat, bend the spokes down with pliers. Line the jaws with several layers of tape so you do not scratch the spokes or hub. Or use a screwdriver to lever the spokes near the hub, two at a time. On a small-flange

hub, you may tap the spokes flat with a wooden or plastic mallet. Do not use the mallet on a large-flange hub, or you could bend the flanges.

If the spokes curve as they approach the rim—most likely with a large-flange hub—bend them where they exit the nipples. You can use pliers or else pull crossed pairs of spokes toward each other with your hands.

⑲ Adjust the round and true of the rim, using the spoke wrench. As before, mark off the work area of the rim between your hand and the feelers, as in step ⑭. At first, long sections of the rim may need correction, but after you've worked on the wheel a little while, most corrections will be on three to six spokes. When you've finished each correction, run the corrected area back through the feeler to see how much of a change you have made. Spoke-wrench adjustments are similar to the one you used earlier with the screwdriver.

To correct a sideways bend, loosen the spokes on the side toward the bend, and tighten the spokes on the other side by an equal amount. Turn the spokes only half a turn or less at this stage. As the wheel becomes more and more true, reduce this to a quarter turn or an eighth turn.

CAUTION: The low angle of the cone of spokes at the rim magnifies sideways corrections. Do not overcorrect, or you will make the lateral wobbles in the rim worse, rather than better.

To correct a high spot, tighten the spokes at the high spot. Tighten them no more than one turn for each correction. As the wheel becomes more true, reduce this to half a turn. Use the same total number of turns

CURVED SPOKE IN NEED OF SETTING

⑱

⑲

on spokes on both sides of the wheel, so you don't disturb sideways adjustments. Unless the spokes become very tight or there is a severe low spot, don't loosen the spokes in low spots. This way, you will slowly be increasing the tension of the spokes as you work.

⑳ Rims are made from a straight bar of metal bent around into a hoop. Somewhere—often exactly opposite the valve hole—there is a joint.

The joint in some rims is *pinned*—fastened together with pegs, or pins, force-fitted into hollow channels in the rim sidewalls. A pinned rim will have a visible line where the two ends of the hoop meet. Usually, the label will be pasted over the joint to hide it.

Often the rim will twist or dip slightly at a pinned joint. If the error was severe, you will have corrected it already at step ⑮. You may still have to make a slight compromise, leaving a bit of extra wobble at the joint.

Some rims have a *welded* joint. The rough, welded surface is sanded and polished to blend in with the rest of the rim. Find the weld by looking for sanding marks between the flanges. Since this area is not visible once the tire is installed, rim makers sand it but don't bother to polish it.

Often, too much metal is removed in sanding, leaving a hollow spot in the top of each rim flange. You may find yourself loosening spokes at the joint to try to

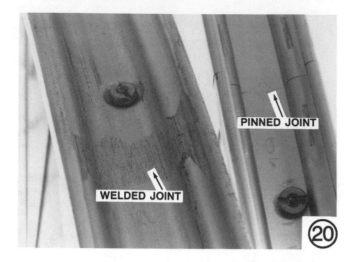

make it match the rest of the rim. Avoid this: Rock the area of the joint back and forth past the feeler to get an idea how the two ends of the rim approach the joint. At this one place, you will have to imagine where the top of the flange would normally be, and adjust the spokes accordingly.

Every correction you make will disturb other, earlier corrections, but as you keep working, the errors should become smaller and smaller. As the wheel improves, check the centering every once in a while as in step ⑯.

㉑ Check spoke tension. As the wheel approaches correct alignment, all spokes should feel about the same and ring at nearly the same musical pitch, except for the spokes on the left side of a rear wheel, which are looser because of dishing. These spokes should be at nearly the same lower tension and lower musical pitch.

In a wheel with a new, good rim, no spoke should feel unusually loose or tight. Pitch variations are usually less than three musical semitones. If you cannot get the rim true without a wide variation in tension between spokes, the rim is bent and the spokes are forcing it

into line. If this is the case, go to step ⑦ on page 386 for procedures to correct rim misalignment.

Because the spokes support their weight load by reduction of tension, the wheel is strongest if the spokes are tight. You can check the tension of your new wheel against a well-built wheel by comparing the feel of the spokes; a very accurate test is possible by musical pitch, according to the following chart. If you don't happen to have a piano in your workshop, a pitch pipe is helpful. For spokes of lengths between those on the chart, use in-between pitches.

Spoke length	Butted spokes	Plain-gauge spokes
300mm	G#	F#
285mm	A	G
260mm	B	A
200mm	E	D
150mm	A#	G#

The pitches begin in the octave above middle C and are higher for smaller wheels. Pluck the spokes where they cross. Use musical pitch only as a guide to whether the general range of tension in the wheel is correct. Do *not* attempt to equalize the pitch of the spokes. Since no rim is perfect, different spokes will have to be at slightly different tensions to hold the rim true and round.

The pitches given here are for both sides of a front wheel, and for the right side of a rear wheel. The spokes in the left side of a dished rear wheel will be at a lower pitch.

㉒ During the final stages of trueing, *stress* the wheel two or three times by pulling groups of four spokes toward each other with your hands, as hard as you can. Wear heavy work gloves so you don't hurt your fingers. You will hear the spokes creak as they indent the metal of the hub and rim. The wheel will be slightly out of true after you have stressed it. Retrue it afterward.

If you don't stress the spokes, the wheel will go out of true and the spokes will loosen when it is first ridden.

With a good rim, it is possible to make the wheel so true that no error is visible except perhaps at the joint. This gives not only the satisfaction of doing a good job, but also the smoothest rim-brake performance and steadiest ride.

As you make your final adjustments for hop (in-out wobble), place the feeler on top of one flange, then the other, while undercorrecting for each flange. Most rims twist slightly at one place or another, so the best adjustment for hop is an average between the two

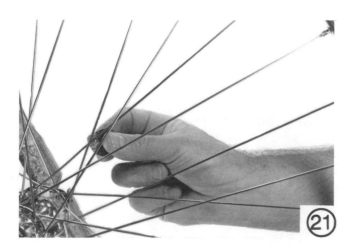

FILED SPOKE END

㉓

㉒

flanges. To check your averaging, spin the wheel and sight across the underside of the rim where the spokes are. If you have averaged the hop well, the underside of the rim will not twitch visibly except perhaps at the joint.

The final corrections are for small errors in sideways position of the rim. As you finish up the wheel, turn the spokes about an eighth of a turn *past* the position you want, and then back. This way, you will correct for twisting of the spokes as the nipples drag them along.

㉓ Unless the rim has deeply recessed spoke-hole sockets, protruding spoke ends will puncture the inner tube. If spokes are a little too long, level them down with the edge of a flat file.

You are now ready to install the rim tape, inner tube, and tire; instructions begin on page 83.

Wheelbuilding Refinements

The above instructions are all you need for most wheels. Here are a few additional pointers for special cases.

THIN HUB FLANGES

Use #2 (or 2mm) brass washers, available at camera repair shops, model train shops, and better

hardware stores. Slide one or two washers onto each spoke before inserting it in the hub flange, to pull the bend against the flange. Sometimes you may need to use one more washer on a head-out spoke than on a head-in spoke.

THIN, UNREINFORCED RIMS

Rim washers, sold at better bike shops, will help prevent the rim from dimpling around the spoke holes and loosening the spokes. It's better to use a reinforced rim in the first place.

BALANCED REAR SPOKING

As mentioned above, the left rear spokes are looser than the others because of the dishing of the wheel. Overdished wheels, common with seven-speed and

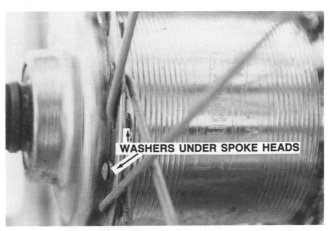

WASHERS UNDER SPOKE HEADS

Small washers slipped over the spokes before inserting them in the rim will reduce stress on spokes from a thin hub flange.

wide six-speed freewheels, collapse and/or break spokes at an alarming rate.

It is best to reduce the dishing as much as possible. Many bicycles have extra space between the freewheel and the right rear forkend. In this case, use a smaller spacer on the right end of the rear hub axle and add a few spare washers on the left. Then redish the wheel, and don't forget to readjust the rear derailleur limit screws.

When building a new rear wheel, a nice trick is to use heavier spokes on the right side. Then all spokes can be brought up to their best working tension: Left spokes will slacken less severely under weight load. A good combination is 2mm plain gauge on the right and 2mm/1.5mm butted on the left.

SMALL-DIAMETER RIMS

These generally use smaller numbers of spokes than large rims. With fewer spokes, the maximum cross number is smaller; cross-three is maximum for a 32- or 28-spoke wheel, cross-two for a 24-spoke wheel. Spokes tighten more quickly, since they stretch less.

EXTRA-LARGE HUB FLANGES

Some brake hubs are very large. For each doubling of hub flange diameter size over 70mm, halve the cross number, or spokes could overlap at the hub flanges and nipples could jam in the rim spoke holes.

HEAVY-DUTY WHEELS FOR TANDEMS, LOADED TOURING, AND BIG PEOPLE

Heavy-gauge spokes (bigger than 2mm/14 gauge) are not recommended; they can overstress the area around each spoke in the rim, and require drilling out the spoke holes. The most practical approach to heavy-duty wheels is to use 48 spokes. Rims drilled with 48 holes are readily available, and hubs may be ordered from several manufacturers. Five-cross is the maximum with 48 spokes.

RACING WHEELS

It is common to use 32 or 28 spokes. The advantage is not in the very slightly reduced weight, but in lower air drag from the spokes. Don't attempt a 28-spoke full-size wheel unless you're an expert wheelbuilder. Use a strong rim. These wheels need frequent inspection.

SPOKE-LENGTH FORMULA

Spokes are measured by hanging them over the end of the ruler, so the measured part is from the threaded end to the inside of the bend. Your bike shop counter person will probably look up spoke lengths in a table, but if you like math, you can use this formula:

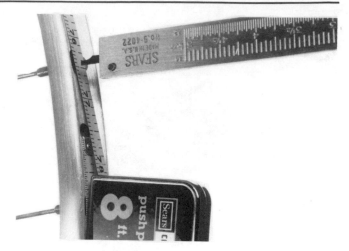

Measure rim circumference with a narrow tape measure, as shown. Then divide by pi (3.14) to find the diameter of the measured circle. If the spoke holes are recessed, then subtract twice their depth (as measured with the depth gauge shown, or the end of a spoke and a ruler) to arrive at the effective diameter for spoking.

$$L = \frac{y}{2} + .998 \sqrt{\frac{D^2}{4} + \frac{d^2}{4} - \frac{Dd}{2} \cos \frac{720\,n}{N} + w^2}$$

.998 = multiplying factor to account for spoke stretch

L = spoke length

D = diameter of rim at spoke holes. Measure the largest diameter of the rim at several places and take the average in case it isn't perfectly round; or—more accurately—measure the circumference in the well of the rim with a ¼-inch-wide flat metal tape measure, hooking the tab at its end in the valve hole, and divide by pi (3.14). With either method of measurement, subtract 2x depth to nipple seating surface if the spoke holes are recessed.

d = diameter of hub spoke hole circle

N = number of spokes

n = number of crosses

w = width of hub from centerline to flange

y = diameter of hub spoke holes

WHEEL REPAIR

The following steps show how to evaluate a damaged wheel and repair it.

Wheel repair is challenging. Practice building new wheels before attempting to repair damaged wheels. If you find a wheel becoming worse as you work on it, turn the job over to an experienced wheelbuilder or else rebuild with new parts.

Problems with Rims and Spokes

Spoke nipples will not turn easily.

Possible cause:	Corrective action:
Spoke nipples are un-lubricated.	Use penetrating oil.
Spoke nipples are cor-roded.	Rebuild wheel.

Spoke is broken.

Possible cause:	Corrective action:
Spoke(s) loose.	Retension wheel.
Spoke reflector has caused strain.	Replace spoke.
Spokes have been dam-aged by chain.	Replace damaged spokes.
Wheel is overdished for wide freewheel.	Redish.
Spoke ends were not set during building.	Rebuild wheel.
Accident damage.	Rebuild or repair.

Wheel creaks and pings only when riding, not on work stand.

Possible cause:	Corrective action:
Spokes are loose.	Tension wheel.

Spoke tension is uneven.

Possible cause:	Corrective action:
Rim is damaged by impact.	Rebuild or repair.
Trueing job was poor.	Retrue.

Rim has in-out irregularity.

Possible cause:	Corrective action:
Rim is damaged by impact.	Rebuild or unbend.
Trueing job was poor.	Retrue.

Wheel is collapsed, potato-chip-shaped.

Possible cause:	Corrective action:
Wheel is overdished for wide freewheel.	Unbend and redish.
Spokes are loose.	Unbend and retension.
Accident damage.	Rebuild or repair.

Rim is out of true to side.

Possible cause:	Corrective action:
Accident damage.	Rebuild or repair.
Spokes are too heavy for rim.	Rebuild.
Spokes were not stressed during building.	Stress and retrue.

Wheel Evaluation and Repair Procedure

Proceed through each of the steps below until you have diagnosed and repaired the wheel's problems. First, a few words of caution:

CAUTION: Do not bring a spoke wrench any-where near a damaged wheel until you have evalu-ated the problem.

When a wheel is damaged by impact, the *rim* be-comes bent, loosening some spokes. If you tighten the loose spokes, you will bend the rim farther. If you readjust spoke tension to force the rim back into align-ment, spoke tension will be very uneven and the wheel will be weak.

In most cases, wheel damage does not break spokes or even stretch them. If you leave the spokes alone, they will guide you in unbending the rim. If you go to work with the spoke wrench first, you will end up making a much bigger job for yourself.

If the wheel can still turn, leave it on the bicycle. This may help with the diagnosis. *Do not* remove the tire from the wheel either, until you have evaluated the problem. Many repair procedures require that you leave the tire in place.

① Check the rim sidewalls for brake shoe wear. An aluminum rim can collapse if deeply worn. A steel rim is safe unless deeply rusted. If the rim fails inspection, replace the rim and spokes. Remember to remove a freewheel or brake disk before cutting old spokes.

Check the hub for cracks around the spoke holes. Check the rim for cracks and sharp kinks. A rim with smooth bends, even large ones, can usually be re-paired; discard a cracked or folded rim. Note that pinned-joint rims have a normal crack across the joint, perfectly straight and smooth, unlike one produced by damage.

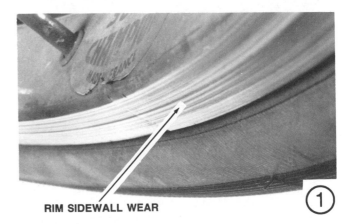

RIM SIDEWALL WEAR ①

② Most commercial wheels are built without greas-ing the spokes or nipples. The nipples become difficult to turn as they corrode to the rim and spokes. If you try to adjust the spokes, you may round off the wrench flats of the nipples instead.

Unless the spoke nipples have been recently, properly lubricated, drip penetrating oil into the rim spoke holes and the spoke threads. Let the wheel stand for a few minutes so the oil can soak in. Before turning spokes, deflate the tire.

When you turn a spoke, start by loosening it, since it will turn more easily to loosen. If a spoke is hard to turn, don't force it. Give it another dose of penetrating oil. Then tighten the four neighboring spokes half a turn to release tension from the difficult spoke. When you succeed in turning it, loosen the neighboring spokes back to where they were. Remember, the spoke wrench appears to turn clockwise to loosen spokes, since it attaches to the inner end of the spoke nipple (see further explanation at step ⑰, page 377).

③ Remove the tire, tube, and rim tape if this step is necessary.

If a spoke nipple is rounded so the spoke wrench slips, lubricate it, then loosen it with small Vise-Grip pliers and replace it. Or else cut *one spoke at a time* with a wirecutters and install a new spoke and nipple. If many nipples are rounded, cut out all of the old spokes and rebuild the wheel.

CAUTION: Removing more than one spoke at a time may cause the rim to distort.

④ In a rear wheel, the chain can jam between the sprocket and the right-side spokes. Damaged spokes should be replaced. Usually, the wheel is pulled slightly out of true but the rim is undamaged. The hub flange may be bent, especially if it is of large diameter. A bent steel flange is serviceable unless cracked; a bent aluminum flange is likely to break, so the hub should be replaced.

⑤ If a spoke is broken, try to figure out why. Spokes most commonly break at the bend where they exit the hub flange. Is the flange thin, so it supports the bend poorly? Are the spokes curved near the hub, from failure to set them when the wheel was built? If a wheel has already broken several spokes, others will break soon, and all should be replaced.

Loose spokes are usually first to break, since they flex more. Often, a rock, curb, or pothole impact leaves a flat spot in the rim and loosens spokes. These spokes often break at the rim end. If the average spoke tension of the wheel is low, expect spokes to break frequently.

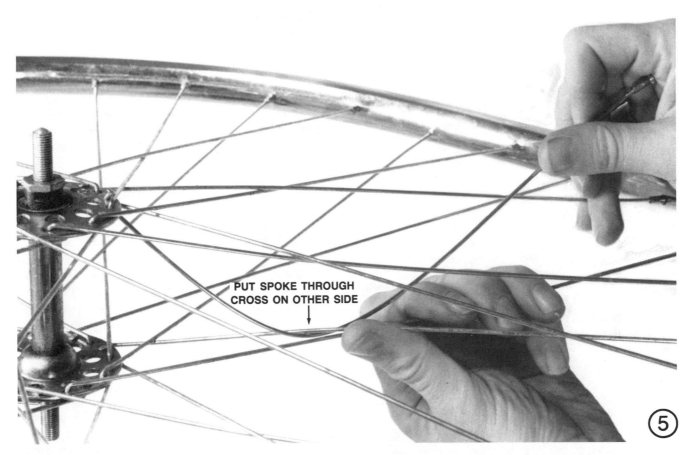

PUT SPOKE THROUGH
CROSS ON OTHER SIDE
↓

⑤

Rear-wheel spokes are likely to break if the wheel is overdished to make room for a wide six- or seven-speed freewheel. For solutions, see the note on "Balanced Spoking," page 381.

A wheel reflector may break a spoke, since spokes were never meant to support a load in their middle. Do not use wheel reflectors with light spokes. Use only wheel reflectors which attach to two or more spokes with soft plastic clamp pieces held in place by metal screws. Avoid wheel reflectors which pry the spokes apart, which can flutter in the wind, or which use metal setscrews that cut into the spokes.

To sum up: A broken spoke is usually a warning sign of another problem. Until you solve that problem, more spokes will break. Keep reading ahead until you understand the problem and learn its solution.

If a spoke is broken and nothing else seems wrong, simply replace it. Install the new spoke so it lies the same way as the spoke four holes away in the rim. If it inserts from outside to inside, you will have to bend it slightly and thread it between laced spokes on the opposite side of the wheel. As you pull the replacement spoke up to normal tension, the wheel should come almost back into true. Small adjustments to neighboring spokes may then restore the wheel completely. If this succeeds, you can raise your hopes.

If the broken spoke is next to a freewheel or brake disk, you may have to remove this to install a new spoke. On the road, the usual approach is to carry a freewheel-remover tool (see page 151) and go to the nearest farm or service station that will let you use a vise. There are a couple of tricks:

• You may prepare and carry temporary spokes with the head partially filed away so that you can insert them without removing the freewheel.

• The Maillard Helicomatic freewheel, on its special hub, is easily removable with the small portable tool supplied. The Pocket Vise, a lightweight tool, lets you use a fencepost or handlebar stem to remove some brands of freewheels.

• With a Shimano Freehub, or with a conventional freewheel and large-flange hub, it is possible to get at the spokes by removing only the sprockets from the freewheel. There is a trick for removing sprockets without tools; see page 145.

⑥ If you hear a creaking and pinging in a wheel as you ride, but not when you get off your bike and spin the wheel, suspect a loose spoke. Your weight slackens the spoke and lets it scrape against the spoke over which it is laced. When you spin the wheel, it is not under load, so it is quiet.

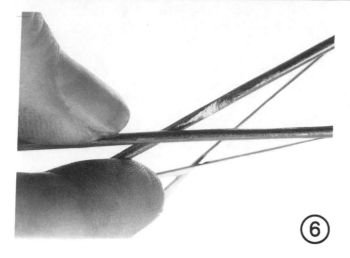

⑥

Looking where a loose spoke is laced over another, you may see that they have worn hollows in each other. This happens only with loose spokes.

Music often goes with a dance: The creaking and pinging often mark time for a sideways lurch or wobble at low riding speeds. This is due to rim motion as loose spokes slacken completely under weight load.

⑦ Check the average spoke tension of the wheel. For a test of normal tension, see step ㉑ of the wheelbuilding section, page 380.

If the rim loosened and went slightly out of true in the first few miles of riding, the spokes probably were not stressed when the wheel was built. They loosened as they seated in the hub flanges and rim holes. Remove the tire, inner tube, and rim tape. Set the spokes if necessary, as in step ⑱ on page 378. Stress the spokes as described in step ㉒ of the wheelbuilding section, page 380, then tension and retrue the wheel.

If the spokes loosened and the wheel went badly out of true, but there is no accident damage, the spokes are probably too heavy for the rim. Look for stretching or cracking of the inner face of the rim around the

spoke holes. If the rim is cracked, replace it. Rebuild the wheel with a stronger rim, or add rim-reinforcing washers.

If all spokes are loose and there are no other visible problems, it was probably built loose. Check carefully for bends and flat spots in the rim. If it is in good condition, remove the tire, inner tube, and rim tape. Lubricate the spokes and nipples with penetrating oil— or even better, remove nipples one at a time and apply grease as in step ① of the wheelbuilding section, page 369. If you are careful to retighten each nipple the same amount you loosened it, you won't disturb the alignment of the wheel by much. Then, bring the wheel up to correct tension, beginning with step ⑰ of the wheelbuilding section, page 377.

Many people believe that spokes loosen because the nipples unscrew. Not so, unless spokes are already very loose. Glueing spoke threads with threadlock compound, or crimping the nipples with pliers, only makes the wheel difficult or impossible to repair.

Check for evenness of spoke tension. Uneven tension can make a wheel break spokes or collapse.

If the *loose* spokes are in the low spots of the rim, then the rim has been damaged by rock, curb, or pothole impacts. The next steps deal with this problem.

If spoke tension is very uneven but the wheel is relatively true, then someone has readjusted spokes to force a bent rim back into alignment. You must loosen all of the spokes so you can see the actual shape of the rim; then unbend the rim (see below) and retrue the wheel. It may be simpler to install a new rim.

If the *tight* spokes are in the low spots of the rim, then in-out wobble ("hop") is probably due to a bad trueing job: The spokes are pulling the rim out of line. Readjusting the spokes will probably solve the problem. Remember to lubricate the spoke nipples first.

⑧ Hold the wheel opposite a light source so that you can see bright light all around the rim. This will make irregularities in the sidewall easy to see. Check both sides. Also, hold the rim sidewalls lightly between your thumb and index finger, running them lengthwise to feel for irregularities.

There may be one slight dip in the sidewalls at the joint of a welded rim. This is normal. Sidewall bulges in one or more spots are almost certainly due to rock, curb, or pothole impacts. These are common when tires are underinflated.

A bulge in the sidewall—a "blip"—makes a rim brake grab, a dangerous condition. One or more spokes will also probably be loose near the blip.

A mild blip can be repaired so that the rim can give good service. If the rim has more than two or three blips, replace it. If the rim is cracked or crumpled at the blip, repair it only to ride slowly to the next bike shop.

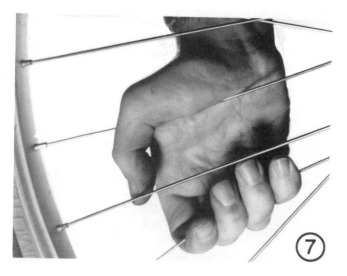

⑦

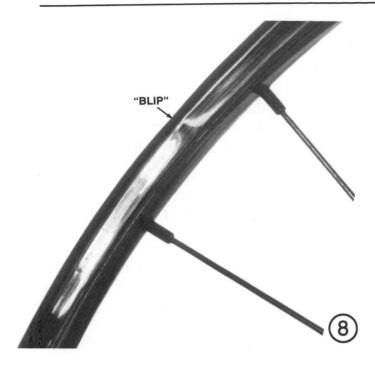

"BLIP"

⑧

To fix a blip, leave the tire on the rim and inflated. Loosen the five or six spokes centered on the blip. Loosen the closest spokes by five turns, tapering off away from the blip.

⑨ Rest the wheel on a benchtop or on the ground, with the blip facing up. With the flat face of a hammer, carefully flatten the blip. Keep the face of the hammer level with the way you want the rim surface to end up. Turn the wheel over and work on the other rim flange; blips usually occur on both sides at once. Do not re-tighten the spokes yet.

Special tools are also available for removing blips, and are advantageous if you do this work often.

CAUTION: Steel rims have hollow sidewalls. Use light blows and hold the hammer face level. If you

indent the rim sidewall, you cannot push it back out.

Aluminum rims have single-thickness sidewalls. If you hammer too hard, you can push them back out by levering with an adjustable wrench, though it's best to avoid bending them more than necessary.

A blip often occurs along with a bent or broken hub axle. Check for this; see page 115.

⑩ Along with a blip, there is usually a flat spot in the rim. A flat spot may also occur without a blip, especially in an aluminum rim with parallel sidewalls. If the rim is kinked or cracked, attempt repair only in an emergency.

Spinning the wheel in a trueing stand or on the bicycle, look across the inner surface of the rim from one side to the other, at the brake shoes or feelers. The rim may hop slightly at one place—the joint of the rim. A welded rim may have been sanded to eliminate the welding bead. Otherwise, the rim should not hop more than $1/16$ inch. A well-trued rim will be much better than this.

If the rim has serious hop, try to determine its cause. If the hop is in the form of flat spots where spokes are loose, it was caused by curb, rock, or pothole impacts. The rim must be unbent to repair this damage.

Fortunately, this type of impact rarely damages the spokes. It pushes the rim inward, loosening spokes rather than overstressing them. You can repair or re-place the rim without replacing the spokes—see steps ⑪ and ⑫ below.

⑨

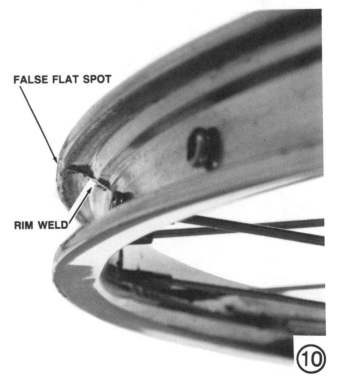

FALSE FLAT SPOT

RIM WELD

⑩

⑪ If you choose to repair the rim, then loosen the spokes around the flat spot as described in step ⑨ unless you have already done it to repair sidewall blips.

Pull the flat spot out. Two types of rim jacks are available for this job. The jack illustrated rests against the inflated tire and hooks under the rim. Another type of jack is a stick which expands between the hub barrel and the rim.

Pull until the spokes you have loosened take up tension. The spokes keep you from pulling the rim too far. Remove the jack and retighten the spokes the same amount you loosened them. If the flat spot is substantially gone, minor spoke tension adjustments will complete the job. If there is still a flat spot after you've retightened the spokes, loosen them by seven turns and pull out the flat spot again.

CAUTION: Use a rim jack which rests on the hub barrel only on a hub with a barrel made of thick metal. This jack can dent the thin hub barrels of some three-speed hubs and sealed-bearing hubs.

It is also possible to remove a flat spot with a rubber mallet, if you remove the four or five adjacent spokes. Put the tire back on the rim and inflate it. Rest the wheel on the tire to one side, then the other, of the flat spot as you work. Be careful, since there are no spokes protecting you from pushing the rim too far.

For an on-the-road repair, tie the flat spot of the rim to a fencepost with a pair of toestraps or a length of rope. *With the inflated tire on the wheel to protect the rim,* roll the wheel up and down the fencepost to pull out the flat spot.

A fencepost and length of rope may be used as an on-the-road substitute for a rim jack.

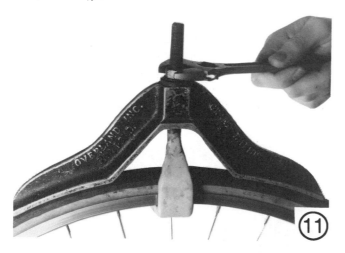

⑪

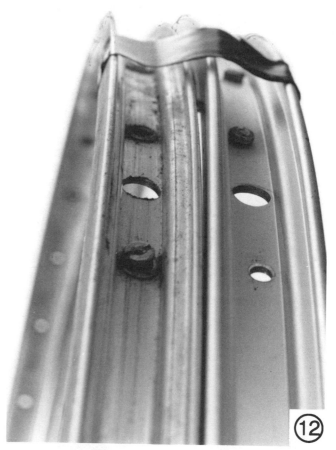

⑫

⑫ If the rim has flat spots but no severe sideways bends, and if the spokes appear to be in good condition, you can transfer the spokes to a new rim, and avoid the chore of relacing the wheel. Your new rim must use the same length of spokes as the old one; also, the spoke drilling must be counterclockwise or clockwise, the same as the old rim (see step ② of the wheelbuilding section, page 369).

Remove the tire, inner tube, and rim tape. Lubricate the nipples with penetrating oil, and tape the old rim to the new one, with the valve holes side by side. Remove the nipple from each spoke, grease it and the spoke threads, and thread the spoke to the new rim.

When you have transferred all spokes to the new rim, go to step ⑭ of the wheelbuilding section, page 375, for tensioning and trueing.

⑬ If the wheel has collapsed into a potato-chip shape, you may be able to pop it back nearly into correct alignment. This succeeds frequently with a lightweight aluminum rim but rarely with a steel rim.

Since you will apply considerable force to the end of the axle, remove a quick-release skewer and centering springs (page 120) or a three-speed shifting chain (page 211). Do not remove the tire and inner tube; you may need them to complete the repair.

Lay the wheel on its side. Rest a foot on one of the high areas of the rim. Rest the toe of your other foot on the ground and lever down on the opposite high spot with the heel of this foot, using increasing force until the wheel pops into shape. It is usually easiest to work with the right side of a dished rear wheel facing up.

If you don't succeed the first time, turn the wheel over and try again. Push the wheel *past* center until it stays straight.

In some cases, only minor retrueing and tensioning will restore the wheel to service. Check carefully for uneven spoke tension and for other types of damage

described above before giving the wheel your stamp of approval.

CAUTION: If the wheel still has a total sideways wobble of more than ½ inch after popping it into shape, do not attempt to align it by adjusting the spokes. Go on to the next step to unbend the rim.

⑭ If the wheel has a sideways bend but is not (or is no longer) collapsed into a potato-chip shape:

If the rim is crumpled or cracked, or has sharp kinks, replace rim and spokes. If the bend is smooth, leave the tire on the rim, fully inflated. Locate the worst bend accurately. Sight over the rim while the wheel turns slowly. Stop the wheel against the floor.

⑮ Hold the wheel horizontally in front of you, with the bend facing away from you and down. "Chop" down with the wheel like an ax, so it lands at a 45-degree angle on the edge of the tire tread. Start with gentle blows, then increase their force until you remove the bend.

Then go back to step ⑭ and check the wheel for smaller bends remaining in other places, and correct them in the same way.

Once the wheel has no more than ½ inch total sideways wobble and no sharp kinks, finish the alignment by adjusting spoke tension. If the ax-chop technique will not unbend the rim, replace the rim and spokes.

Then check the wheel for other problems according to the steps above, before returning it to service. Be sure to check that the average tension is high enough; sideways bending can stretch spokes.

18•FRAME AND STEERING

The conventional, steel bicycle frame consists of steel tubes joined by the process of *brazing,* similar to the soldering of electrical wiring. The bicycle frame's joints are heated with a gas torch, and molten brass is flowed into them. The brass melts at a lower temperature than the steel, which glows red-hot but remains solid. The brass solidifies and sticks to the steel tubes, effectively gluing them together.

The joints may be reinforced by sleevelike *lugs,* or by building up layers of brass to form rounded *fillets.* Some steel frames are not brazed, but *welded*—the steel at the joints is itself melted together.

A small but increasing percentage of frames are made of lightweight aluminum, titanium, or graphite-epoxy composite material. Most all-aluminum or titanium frames are welded, but composite frames must be "screwed and glued" together.

Steel frames of good quality very rarely break apart, though they may bend if abused. The frame should be inspected after an accident, whenever the bicycle is overhauled, or if the bicycle steers poorly. This chapter will help you check a frame and decide how to repair damage. Procedures for rebuilding the headset (steering bearings) are given beginning on page 397.

CHECKING FOR DAMAGE

When checking a frame for damage, first look for the obvious: bent or crumpled tubes. A frame tube which has simply been bent by impact can generally be straightened. A deeply dented or crumpled tube should be replaced, and usually it is simpler to replace the entire frame.

Head-on impact damage is common. It bends back the front fork, and may crumple the top tube and down tube at their front ends. A fork can be replaced. The frame can be more or less straightened, but rippling of the top tube or down tube cannot be corrected. If someone else caused the accident which led to this damage, this person owes you a new frame.

In a step-through (lady's type) frame, a front-end impact may also bend the seat tube at its junction with the top tube. Impact to seatstays bends them easily, since they are thin.

Look for damaged fittings, such as the seatpost clamp and forkends. Look also for cracks, especially at joints between tubes. Remove the wheels and check that the forkends are of the right width. Installing a hub of the wrong width for a fork can bend both the fork and the hub's axle.

Check that the forkends are parallel. You can make a measuring tool from a *straight* hub axle by sawing it in half.

Run a string tightly from one rear forkend and around the head tube to the other forkend. Measure the distance from the string to the seat tube on each side. If the two measurements are not equal, the rear end of the bicycle is bent to one side.

Other damage includes rust, chipped paint, and stripped threads on the fork or at the bottom bracket.

THE BICYCLE STEERING MECHANISM

The steering mechanism of the bicycle includes the handlebars, front fork, and front wheel. The *headset bearings* permit this assembly to pivot within the *head tube* of the frame.

The handlebars are secured at their center by the *handlebar stem.* A clamp and tightening bolt keep the handlebars from rotating in the stem. Usually, tape and control levers must be removed from one side of the handlebars to exchange the stem.

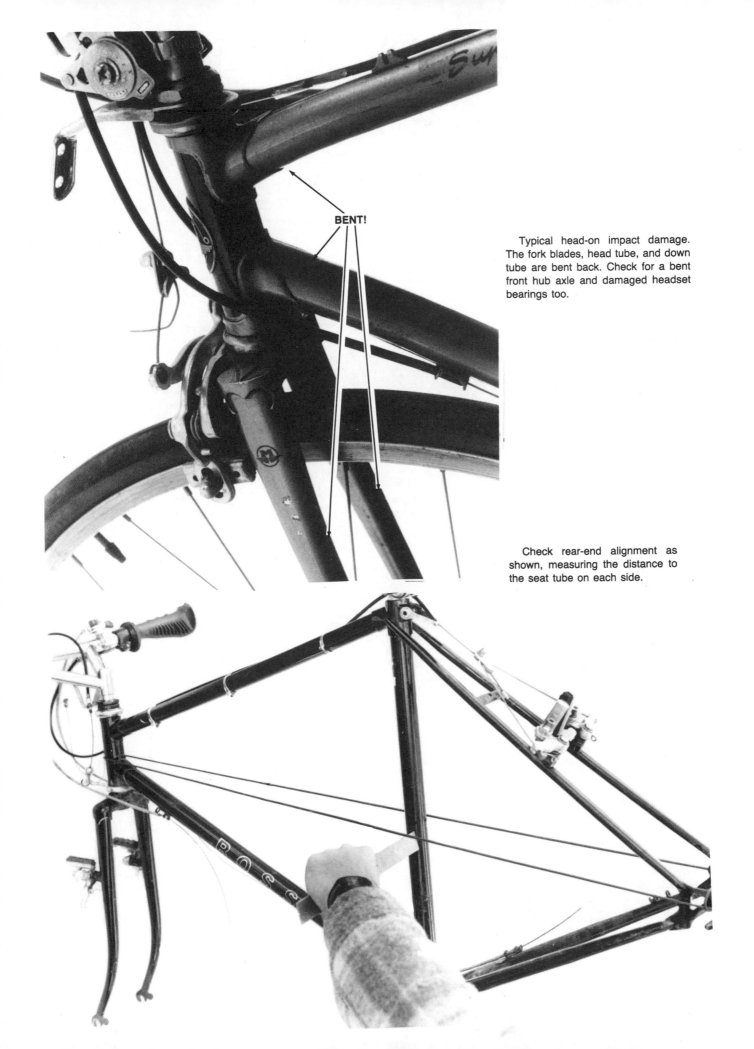

BENT!

Typical head-on impact damage. The fork blades, head tube, and down tube are bent back. Check for a bent front hub axle and damaged headset bearings too.

Check rear-end alignment as shown, measuring the distance to the seat tube on each side.

TRACK RACING TYPE

ENGLISH STYLE

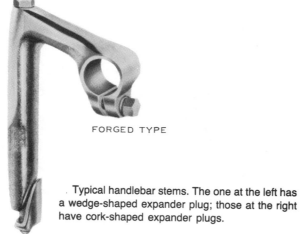

FORGED TYPE

Typical handlebar stems. The one at the left has a wedge-shaped expander plug; those at the right have cork-shaped expander plugs.

Modern handlebar stems use a recessed Allen-head expander bolt.

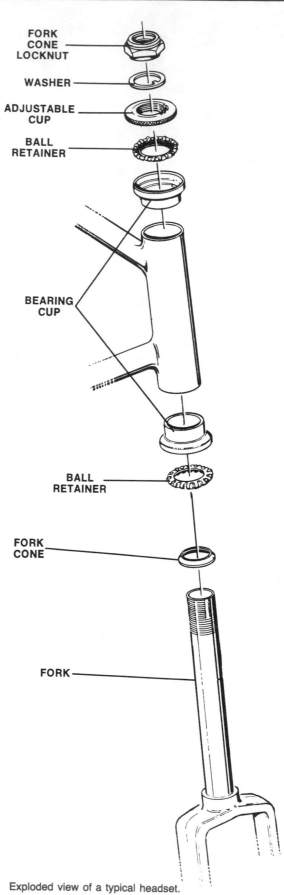

FORK CONE LOCKNUT

WASHER

ADJUSTABLE CUP

BALL RETAINER

BEARING CUP

BALL RETAINER

FORK CONE

FORK

Exploded view of a typical headset.

The stem is secured to the fork by an *expander plug* at its lower end, tightened by the *expander bolt* which runs to the top of the stem. The expander plug may be shaped like a cork or like a wedge. A wedge-shaped plug grips tighter and must be used on an all-terrain bike with extra-wide handlebars.

The headset (steering) bearings of a bicycle are conventional cup-and-cone bearings, like those of a hub, only larger.

The top race of the headset is threaded onto the fork *steerer tube* (upper part of the fork) and is secured with a tabbed lockwasher and a locknut, the same way as a bearing cone of a conventional wheel hub. The threading allows adjustment of bearing play, just as it does on a hub.

Each of the remaining three races—the upper and lower head tube race and the fork crown race—is secured by a *press fit (interference fit):* a tight fit between smooth, cylindrical surfaces of parts which must be forced into place to assemble or disassemble them. The interference fit holds the parts together securely without the need for threads or a locknut.

Steering Alignment

A bicycle's steering mechanism is simple, but needs precise alignment to track properly. A correctly aligned bicycle steers itself—an important safety feature. For example, when the front wheel meets the road again after bouncing over a bump, steering instantly corrects itself to balance the bicycle. Self-steering also makes no-hands riding possible.

CAUTION: A bicycle which steers poorly is hazardous. It does not self-correct balance, or send the normal signals about balance to your hands.

The front fork of the bicycle is angled forward, and also *raked* (bent forward) at its lower end. Still, a line through the steering bearings hits the road *ahead* of the front tire. Like a furniture caster, the front wheel follows behind its steering pivot. The *trail* or *caster* pulls the wheel into line with the direction the bicycle is traveling.

A shallower steering angle or shorter rake gives more trail, which makes the bicycle maneuver faster but increases sensitivity to road irregularities. Racing bikes usually have more trail than touring bikes or utility bikes.

Testing Steering

No-hands riding is an excellent test for most steering problems. You should be able to ride no-hands while sitting straight up. If you cannot ride no-hands or if you

Despite the forward tilt and rake of the fork, the tire contact patch trails the steering axis, making the bicycle self-steer like a furniture caster.

must lean to one side, examine the bicycle for the cause of the problem.

First, check for overtightened headset bearings by tilting the rear wheel up so that the front fork is vertical. With the front wheel lifted slightly off the ground, the fork should turn freely and smoothly as you wave the bicycle slightly from side to side. This test is even more sensitive if you remove the front wheel.

The bearings may bind at all positions or only at some. Bearings which bind evenly may only need adjustment. Bearings which bind unevenly indicate poor alignment, resulting from carelessly machined bearing seats or a bent fork.

To test for excess play in the headset, bounce the front wheel off the floor from a height of 2 or 3 inches. The front wheel assembly should vibrate with a low, musical hum. If the bearings clunk back and forth, the headset is loose.

To find the loose parts, squeeze the front brake lever with one hand and place a finger of the other hand across the headset bearing; try to rock the bicycle forward and backward. The bearing adjustment may

To check freedom of movement of the headset, swing the bicycle gently from side to side with the head tube vertical.

Check for excess headset play by holding a finger across the bearings. Hold the front brake and rock the bicycle back and forth.

bent fork steerer tube. The tire should sit accurately along the centerline of the frame.

FRAME REPAIR

Some frame work is simple, but many repairs should be left to a professional mechanic.

CAUTION: Moderate bending of a steel frame or fork is safe. Aluminum, graphite, and other frame

be too loose, or press-fit parts of the headset may be loose.

If these tests do not reveal why the bearings do not work smoothly, overhaul the headset; the bearings are likely worn.

If you have to lean to one side to ride no-hands, the bicycle is out of alignment. If you must lean to the *right,* the wheels are tracking too far to the *left.* The problem may be in a wheel, the front fork, or the frame—or in more than one of these.

A gross error is easy to spot, but even a small error can cause problems. To trace the problem, loosen and retighten the front wheel so you are sure that it is seated all the way into the forkend slots. Look at the top of the front wheel between the fork blades. It should be evenly centered. If it is not, reverse the wheel. If the wheel is off-center in the opposite direction, the rim needs to be centered. If the wheel is off-center in the same direction, the fork blades are bent.

Repeat this test with the rear wheel, checking for wheel centering between the seatstays.

Sight from front to back against one side of the head tube to check for a twisted frame. The head tube should be perfectly parallel to the seat tube. Sight from above, over each side of the front tire, to check for a

Check for frame twist by sighting along the side of the head tube. This head tube is twisted slightly counterclockwise.

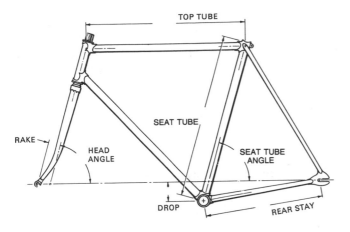

Names for frame measurements. Note that the seat tube is measured from the center of the crank spindle to the top of the top tube.

materials develop microscopic cracks when bent, and will eventually break. The damaged part or the entire frame must be replaced. Follow the manufacturer's instructions.

This caution aside, almost anything goes in an emergency. An automobile jack or hefty arm-foot push between the front forkends and bottom bracket will correct head-on impact damage so you can complete a day's tour. A bent seatstay may be straightened by standing on it. But emergency measures like these will not restore the frame to good working condition, and may cause additional damage.

What professional-quality frame work can the home mechanic confidently do?

It is simple and inexpensive to replace a damaged front fork. Repairing a fork, on the other hand, requires special tools and knowledge, and is best reserved for an unusual or expensive fork. The *steerer tube*—the part of the fork which is inside the frame—is hard to straighten, and it must be straight for the bearings to work smoothly.

Get an exact replacement fork if you can, or else check the threading of the steerer tube and the interference fit on the fork crown bearing race: Milling (reducing the diameter of the bearing seat) may be needed to achieve the correct interference fit (see the section on headset bearings, page 390). Milling, like fork realignment, requires special tools and is a job for a professional mechanic. You can shorten the steerer tube of your replacement fork with a hacksaw, if necessary. Do it with the upper bearing race threaded onto the fork; removing it will clean up the threads.

When replacing a damaged fork, check the headset and frame for damage, too.

Moving forkends toward or away from one another to fit a hub of a different width can easily be accomplished with hand force and a rubber mallet, once the wheel has been removed. Pushing one fork blade forward or back relative to the other will correct centering at the top of the wheel, and moving the blades sideways in

the same direction will correct centering where the tire meets the road.

Using the techniques described in the section on inspecting frames, page 390, measure carefully to be sure that the forkends are centered. The ultimate test for front-fork centering is to be able to ride no-hands without leaning. After recentering, the forkends must be readjusted to be parallel.

CAUTION: Nonparallel forkends will bend the hub axle. Parallelism can be tested with a split hub axle and corrected with a large adjustable wrench. A professional tool is available which adjusts and measures forkend parallelism at the same time.

Realigning the rear triangle is easier than realigning a front fork; use a string around the head tube to check centering of the rear forkends.

As long as it is not crumpled or rippled, a bent frame tube can be straightened by careful work with a rubber mallet. To avoid denting a thin-walled tube, make a cushion from a block of hardwood. Drill a hole through the block the same diameter as the frame tube, then saw the block in half lengthwise through the hole. After straightening the tube, check frame alignment and correct it if necessary.

Touching up chipped paint is easy, but be sure to sand away rust. A complete paint job should be left to a professional framebuilder or auto body shop. The frame must be sandblasted or chemically cleaned and then rustproofed before the final coats of paint are applied. A poor paint job will not last, and will not protect the frame.

Temperature changes can cause water to condense inside the frame. When a frame is ready for reassembly, coating the inside of the tubes with oil will help prevent rust. A small drain hole drilled in the underside

A *straight* hub axle sawed in half will reveal when forkends are out of parallel.

of the bottom bracket shell is a good idea, in conjunction with a plastic sleeve to keep dirt out of the crank-bearings.

More complicated repairs such as a twisted front end should generally be taken to a professional bicycle framebuilder. The cost of tools and the time to learn these repairs are not justified unless you take in work from other people. Unless the frame is unusual or expensive, a complicated repair may cost more than replacing it.

PARTS COMPATIBILITY

The frame and steering mechanism present more difficulties with parts compatibility than any other part of the bicycle. Use exact replacement parts if at all possible.

CAUTION: Never force a handlebar, stem, head-set, or other part if it does not fit correctly. A part which does not fit properly will not be properly secured. Many good frames have been ruined by stretching them out of shape.

Seatposts are available in .2mm increments from 25mm to 27.4mm. A good bike shop will have all sizes, at least in the higher-quality product lines.

Handlebars are sold in varying center diameters; generally, Italian handlebars are slightly thicker than others. If a handlebar will not fit through the opening in a stem, or fits loosely before clamping, do not force the fit.

Where the stem fits into the fork, three diameters are common:

Inches	mm	Nationality
.833	21.15	USA, Japan
.866	22.0	France
.875 (⅞")	22.2	England, Italy, Japan

There are three common fork threadings:
24 TPI; English, Italian, Japanese
25.4 TPI (1mm); French
26 TPI; Raleigh Industries

Press-fit dimensions and stack heights of headsets vary widely. If at all possible, use an exact replacement. With the aid of the headset tables in *Sutherland's Handbook for Bicycle Mechanics,* a bike shop may be able to help you find an acceptable substitute. If none can be found, the head tube and fork crown can be milled to fit a common headset. Shims of beer-can aluminum also may afford a quick-and-dirty solution to your problem.

Hub and fork widths vary; fortunately, forks can easily be bent to fit different hubs. See Chapter 8 and Chapter 14 on hubs and the section of this chapter on frame repairs.

Bottom-bracket threadings of frames vary. See Chapter 15 for details.

Problems with Frames and Steering

This chart covers most frame and steering problems. Look in the chapters on hubs, brakes, and other components for problems relating to their attachment to the frame.

Difficult or loose threading of headset upper race to fork.

Possible cause:	Corrective action:
Mismatched threading standards.	Use matched parts.
Threads of fork are damaged.	Clean up threads.

Steering binds, cannot ride no-hands.

Possible cause:	Corrective action:
Front fork is bent.	Replace fork.
Headset bearings are too tight.	Adjust bearings.
Headset bearings are misaligned.	Have frame milled.
Headset bearings are worn or damaged.	Replace.

Front end clunks when braking or riding over bumps.

Possible cause:	Corrective action:
Headset locknut has loosened.	Tighten.
Headset bearings are too loose.	Tighten.
Fork crown race is loose on fork.	Replace fork, or mill fork and replace headset.
Head tube has expanded, loosening pressed race.	Take to framebuilder.

Sore shoulder, must lean to one side to ride no-hands.

Possible cause:	Corrective action:
Front fork is bent.	Replace fork.
Frame is twisted.	Have frame straightened.
Front-wheel spokes are misadjusted.	Retrue wheel.
Wheel is not fully into fork-end.	Reinsert wheel.

Front wheel rubs side of fork.

Possible cause:	Corrective action:
Front fork is bent.	Replace fork.
Wheel is not fully into fork-end.	Reinsert wheel.

Rear wheel rubs chainstay, chain jumps off sprockets.

Possible cause:	Corrective action:
Wheel is improperly inserted.	Reinsert wheel.
Frame is bent.	Straighten.

Fork and hub width do not match.

Possible cause:	Corrective action:
Nonstandard replacement parts have been used.	Replace, or rebend fork.
Fork is bent.	Straighten or replace.

Seatpost or stem is frozen in place.

Possible cause:	Corrective action:
Part was not greased before inserting.	Use penetrating oil; heat.
Oversize seatpost or stem was hammered in.	Replace frame or fork.

Seatpost will not clamp tightly to frame.

Possible cause:	Corrective action:
Seatpost diameter is too small.	Replace.
Frame is stretched from overtightening.	Shim; take to framebuilder.
Seatpost clamp bolt is stripped.	Replace.

Stem will not clamp tightly into fork.

Possible cause:	Corrective action:
Stem diameter is too small.	Replace.
Stem expander bolt is stripped.	Replace.
Fork steerer is bulged from overtightened stem.	Replace fork.

Handlebars will not clamp tightly to stem.

Possible cause:	Corrective action:
Handlebar diameter is too small.	Replace handlebars or stem.
Handlebar clamp bolt is stripped.	Replace.

Seatpost, stem, or handlebars cannot be installed.

Possible cause:	Corrective action:
Diameter is too large.	Replace.
Frame, fork, or stem is dented or burred.	Replace, or remove burr.

OVERHAULING A HEADSET

This section provides step-by-step illustrated instructions for disassembling, assembling, and adjusting a typical headset. The illustrations were made of a headset on a Peugeot bicycle, but they apply to all makes of bicycles.

To obtain maximum service, the headset should be overhauled, thoroughly lubricated, and adjusted at least once a year.

Tools and Supplies You Will Need

Mallet, or hammer and wood block, for stem expander bolt
End wrench or Allen wrench for stem expander bolt
Large wrench or pin spanner for top locknut
Hammer and punch, if removing bearing races
Wood blocks to reinstall head tube bearing races
Pipe hammer to replace fork crown race
Tweezers
Replacement bearing balls
Multipurpose grease

Disassembling

First remove the wheel (page 69).

① Loosen the stem bolt on top of the handlebar stem approximately two turns. **CAUTION: The wedge will fall down into the head of the frame if you back the bolt out too far.** Strike the head of the bolt squarely with a single, sharp blow of a mallet to jar loose the wedge at the bottom of the stem.

On a bicycle with centerpull or cantilever brakes, there will be a cable hanger for the front brake. The most common type is as shown in the photographs for steps ③ and ④, but on many all-terrain bikes it is part of the handlebar. If so, unhook the brake's transverse cable now (see step ③ on page 351) so you can lift the handlebar off.

② Lift up on the handlebars to remove the stem from the frame head. If the stem is rusted in place, apply some penetrating oil or Liquid Wrench around the stem and the bolt, let it set for a few minutes, and then tap the stem from side to side with a mallet while attempting to pull it out. If the wedge has fallen into the

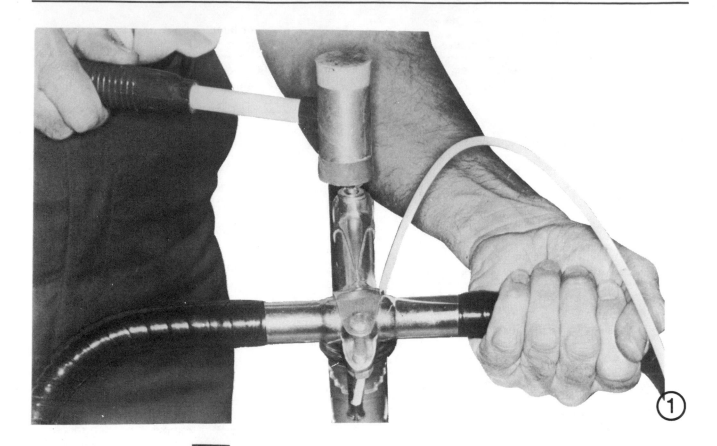

head of the frame, turn the bicycle upside down and shake the wedge out after you have removed the handlebar stem.

③ Remove the headset locknut by turning it counterclockwise. If you do not have a wrench designed to fit, a large adjustable wrench (12-inch or larger) will usually do the job. Some locknuts have holes for a pin tool instead of wrench flats.

④ If a centerpull or cantilever brake cable hanger is clamped like a washer under the headset locknut as shown, remove it. You will have to loosen the brake cable. The easiest way is to unhook the cable at the brake, as shown; see step ③ on page 351.

If the bicycle has sidepull brakes, the simplest way to get the front caliper out of the way is to remove it from the front fork. Leave it attached to the handlebar by the cable.

⑤ Lift the lockring off the adjustable cup.

⑥ Grasp the adjustable cup firmly between your fingers and unscrew it. If it does not come off easily, turn it, as shown, with a large wrench, a pair of locknut pliers, or a pair of expandable water-pump-type pliers. **CAUTION: Be sure the teeth of the pliers are covered with plastic, rubber, or tape to prevent damage to the knurled surface of the cup.**

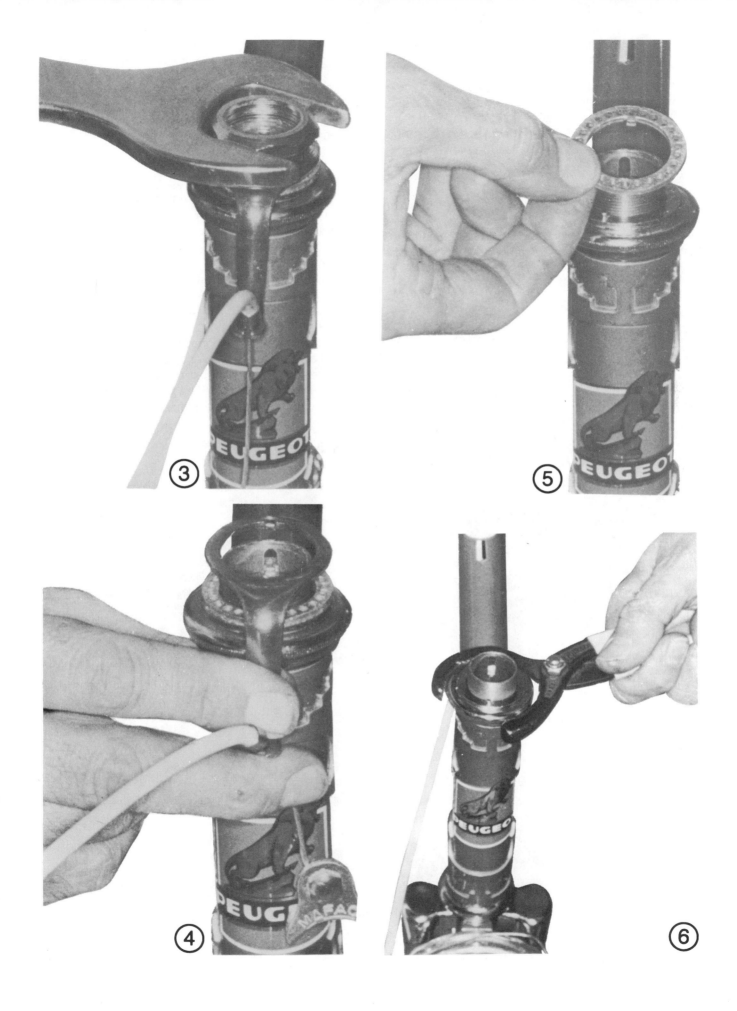

③

④

⑤

⑥

⑦ Remove the loose bearing balls from the upper bearing cup. Hold the fork tightly against the head of the frame and, at the same time, carefully turn the bicycle upside down. Pull the fork out of the head tube, and then remove the loose balls in the lower bearing cup. *NOTE: On some headsets the balls may be held in a retainer.*

⑧ Wipe off the grease in the bearing races which are still attached to the fork crown and frame. Inspect the races for wear, pitting, and *brinelling* (indentations from the bearing balls). If the bearing races need to be

replaced, remove them by working around them carefully with a hammer and punch. Avoid getting them tilted inside the head tube, as you could damage the bearing seats.

Cleaning and Inspecting

Clean all parts in solvent and rinse them, or wipe them dry with a lintless cloth. Keep all cleaned parts on paper towels to avoid contamination, especially the bearings.

Do not bother to inspect the bearing balls. It is best just to replace them. Most bearing retainers do not have as many bearing balls as you could install loose; using loose bearing balls will reduce wear, and can salvage brinelled bearing races.

Check all parts for stripped threads.

Hold a straightedge or ruler up against the fork steerer to make sure that it is straight. Also, check it for bulges from an overtightened handlebar-stem expander plug. If the fork is damaged, replace it.

Assembling

⑨ If you are replacing the fork or headset, check all new parts against the old ones to make sure that they

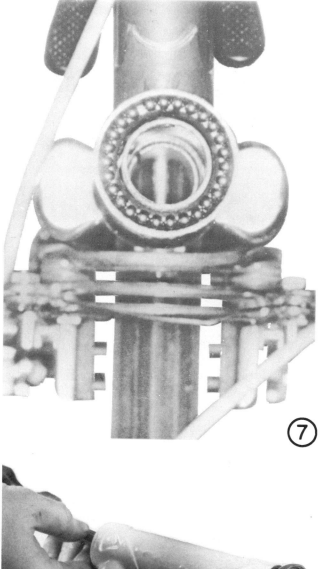

⑦

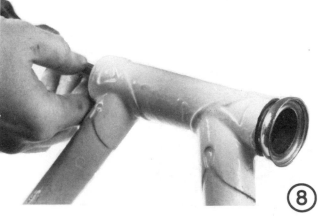

⑧

⑨

will fit. Check threading and press-fit dimensions, and fork steerer tube length.

If you have removed worn bearing races from the head tube and fork crown, install new races now. Install the races in the head tube by pounding them into place with a hammer cushioned by a block of wood. Support the opposite end of the head tube on another block of wood to avoid damaging it, and be careful to push the races in straight so you do not stretch the head tube.

The best way to install a new fork crown race is by hammering it into place with a length of pipe that just fits over the fork steerer, but you may use a hammer and punch if you work very carefully, on the flat, top surface.

⑩ Turn the bicycle upside down and coat the inside of the lower bearing cup with a liberal amount of multipurpose grease. Imbed the same number of loose bearing balls that you counted during disassembly. If the count was lost, insert enough balls until they fit snugly around the edge of the cup, and then remove one for the proper clearance. If the bearings are held in a retainer, pack both assemblies with a generous amount of multipurpose grease. Work the lubricant throughout the bearings and retainer with your fingers. Insert one of the retainers in the lower ball cup, with the flat side facing down (with the bicycle upside down) into the cup. Cover the bearings with lubricant, and

then slide the fork stem through the frame head. Hold the fork tight against the frame to hold the bearings in place, and then turn the bicycle right side up. Apply a generous amount of multipurpose grease to the upper bearing cup. Imbed the same number of balls you counted during disassembly, or fill the cup and then remove one ball for the proper clearance. If retainers are used, insert the other assembly into the bearing cup, with the flat side facing down (with the bicycle right side up).

⑪ Check to be sure the bearing balls fit snugly and evenly, with just enough room for one more (for proper running clearance), as indicated in the illustration.

⑫ Cover the bearings with a thin layer of lubricant.

⑬ Thread the adjustable cup onto the fork stem flat side up. Turn the cup until it is finger-tight, and then check that the bearings turn smoothly and evenly, without binding. If they do not turn smoothly, the bearing races may be misaligned, or you may have too many or the wrong size of bearing balls in one of the bearing races. After testing it, back it off by a sixth of a turn.

⑭ Install the lockring, with the ear indexed in the slot of the fork stem. Most lockrings are plain, flat washers with only an ear for the fork slot. Some lockrings, as

⑫

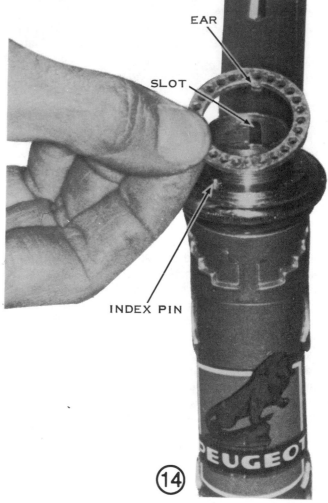

EAR

SLOT

INDEX PIN

⑭

⑬

shown, index a pin or a knurled surface on the bearing race. Use these lockrings only with a matching bearing race. You may have to rotate the bearing race slightly in order for the holes or knurling to index.

⑮ Place the centerpull or cantilever cable housing stop, if any, on top of the lockring, with the long projection that holds the cable facing forward.

⑯ Thread the locknut onto the fork steerer tube threads and tighten it moderately. **CAUTION: It must go on at least three turns before tightening up, or else it is in danger of stripping.**

⑰ Lubricate the stem bolt and wedge threads with high-quality cycle oil to prevent thread seizure and to ensure proper tightening. Grease the outside of the stem. Slide the stem into the fork steerer tube until it is at the desired height, and then hand-tighten the stem expander bolt. On newer bicycles, the handlebar stem has a mark to indicate the maximum height the stem can be raised. **CAUTION: Do not raise the stem above this mark, because the contact surfaces of**

the stem would be insufficient for safe cycling. If the handlebar stem does not have a maximum height mark, measure 2½ inches from the lower end of the stem, make your own mark, and then raise the stem to the desired height but not so high that the mark shows above the locknut. Swing the handlebars right or left until the upper portion of the handlebar stem is aligned with the wheel. Hold the wheel between your legs for a firm grip, and then tighten the stem bolt. **CAUTION: A cork-shaped expander plug can bulge out the fork steerer tube. Do not overtighten it. With this type of plug, it should be possible, though not easy, to turn the handlebars while holding the wheel between your legs.**

Now readjust the headset bearings. Both the headset locknut and the handlebar stem affect bearing adjustment, so the final adjustment should be made *after* these parts have been installed.

Adjust the bearings so they are as tight as possible without binding when the fork points forward. Some slight binding or looseness at other positions is relatively less important.

CAUTION: Failure to adjust the headset bearings carefully will result in a loose or binding headset, and in reduced steering control.

⑱ Replace the wheel (page 72). Return the caliper brakes to the operating position. If you removed the cable from the bridge of a centerpull or cantilever brake, replace the cable. If you removed a sidepull brake from the front fork, reinstall the locknut and washer.

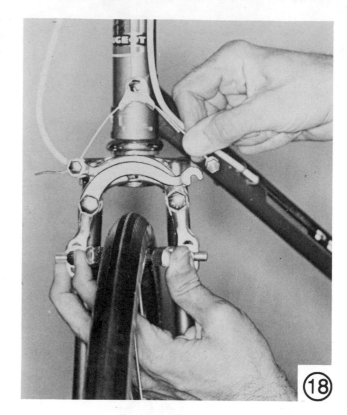